W9-BZH-136

# First Language Acquisition

Babies are not born talking. They *learn* language, starting right after birth. How does this process take place? When do children master the skills needed to use language successfully? What stages do they go through as they learn to understand others and to talk themselves? This new edition of Eve Clark's best-selling, comprehensive textbook focuses on children's acquisition of a first language, the stages of development they go through, and how they use language as they learn. It follows children from their first sounds and words to the acquisition of adultlike skills in persuading, instructing, and storytelling, whether children are acquiring just one language or two at once. Skilfully integrating extensive data with coverage of current theories and debates, it is an essential guide to studying first language acquisition for courses in linguistics, developmental psychology, and cognitive science.

EVE V. CLARK is the Richard W. Lyman Professor in the Humanities and Professor of Linguistics at Stanford University. Her books include *Psychology and Language* (with H. H. Clark), *The Ontogenesis of Meaning*, *The Acquisition of Romance*, *The Lexicon in Acquisition*, and *Constructions in Acquisition* (with B. F. Kelly). She is an active researcher in the field who works on all aspects of meaning acquisition.

# First Language Acquisition

## SECOND EDITION

EVE V. CLARK

*Stanford University*

CAMBRIDGE UNIVERSITY PRESS
Cambridge, New York, Melbourne, Madrid, Cape Town, Singapore, São Paulo, Delhi

Cambridge University Press
The Edinburgh Building, Cambridge CB2 8RU, UK

Published in the United States of America by Cambridge University Press, New York

www.cambridge.org
Information on this title: www.cambridge.org/9780521732932

© Eve V. Clark 2009

This publication is in copyright. Subject to statutory exception
and to the provisions of relevant collective licensing agreements,
no reproduction of any part may take place without
the written permission of Cambridge University Press.

First published 2003
Sixth printing 2007
Second edition 2009

Printed in the United Kingdom at the University Press, Cambridge

*A catalogue record for this publication is available from the British Library*

ISBN 978-0-521-51413-2 hardback
ISBN 978-0-521-73293-2 paperback

Cambridge University Press has no responsibility for the persistence or
accuracy of URLs for external or third-party internet websites referred to
in this book, and does not guarantee that any content on such
websites is, or will remain, accurate or appropriate.

To Damon Alistair
for all his talk

# Contents

# Tables, boxes, and figures

## Boxes

## Figures

# Acknowledgements

This book has grown out of my research and teaching on first language acquisition, where, over the years, I have expanded the range of topics to cover something approaching what small children have to tackle as they take on the learning of a first language, together with the many steps they then take on the way to becoming skilled speakers. This book has also evolved over the years in light of repeated discussions with colleagues and students on what we can – and can't – assume about the process of acquisition, and what each assumption buys – or fails to buy us – theoretically.

Funding for my own research has come from the National Science Foundation, the National Institutes of Child Health and Human Development, the Spencer Foundation, and the United States–Israel Bi-National Science Foundation. I also received invaluable support from the Max-Planck-Institute for Psycholinguistics, Nijmegen, The Netherlands (Anne Cutler, Wolfgang Klein, Willem J. M. Levelt, and Stephen C. Levinson, Directors) in 1997–1998 when I first began this project. I am immensely grateful to my colleagues there for providing a stimulating atmosphere, and I am especially indebted to Melissa Bowerman for many discussions, then and over the years, about the course of acquisition.

I also wish to thank those who gave me critical readings and invaluable comments on the first edition. They include Paul Bloom, Nancy Budwig, William (Bill) Croft, Katherine Demuth, Susan A. Gelman, and Adele E. Goldberg. I have also benefited from the many comments and suggestions from colleagues who have used the first edition in their classes, as well as from graduate students who raised questions, pointed out inconsistencies, and brought new findings to my attention. I owe thanks to Michelle M. Chouinard, Barbara F. Kelly, Jean-Philippe Marcotte, David A. McKercher, and Andrew D.-W. Wong, and I am particularly grateful to Inbal Arnon, Bruno Estigarribia, Casey Lew-Williams, Marie-Catherine de Marneffe, and Nola Stephens, whose comments and questions have helped me clarify many issues.

I remain deeply indebted to the many colleagues who always responded so generously to requests for reprints and references, arguments and details on a range of topics, and who provided suggestions and raised issues I might not have considered otherwise. Lastly, I owe more than I can say to Herbert H. Clark, who listened to many fragments of data and argument, argued for and against positions, and encouraged me throughout. Writing a book is a collaborative endeavor to which family, friends, students, and colleagues have all contributed – whether they know it or not.

Stanford, California

# 1 Acquiring language: Issues and questions

Language is quintessentially human. We use spoken language every day, face-to-face, as a means of communication, while written language allows us to record and hold on to our history across generations. Language itself is very complex. It has a sound system that allows us to use numerous distinct words, a vocabulary of some 50,000 to 100,000 terms for many adults, and a series of constructions for relating these words. It allows us to express innumerable ideas, describe events, tell stories, recite poems, buy, sell, or bargain in markets, administer legal systems, make political speeches, and participate in the myriad other activities that make up the societies we live in. Language allows us to coordinate what we do with others, relay information, find out answers, and carry out everyday activities – gossiping, making puns, writing memos, reading newspapers, learning histories, enjoying novels, greeting friends, telling stories, selling cars, reading instructions – the list is unending. Language use calls for an intricate web of skills we usually take for granted. It is an integral part of everyday life that we rely on to convey wants and needs, thoughts, concerns, and plans. Using language seems as natural as breathing or walking.

But babies are not born talking. They *learn* language, starting immediately from birth. What do they learn? They need sounds and words, meanings and constructions. They need to know what to use where and when, how to integrate language with other modes of communication, how to make themselves understood and how to understand others. How does this process take place? When do children master the skills needed for using language successfully? What stages do they go through as they learn to understand and talk? Do the languages they learn affect the way they think?

This book focusses on children's acquisition of a first language, the stages they go through, and how they use language as they learn. In this chapter, I take up some of the issues in that process. I outline some of the theoretical approaches in the field and the assumptions they make before turning to the overall plan of the book.

## Some issues for acquisition

When children learn a first language, they could build on preexisting notions of what to represent with language as well as prior notions of communication. Or they could start from nothing and discover what is (and isn't) represented in language. And since languages differ, their acquisition might also be affected by the properties of each language. For example, the type of language could influence the order in which children acquire specific parts of the language and could also make some elements harder or easier to acquire. Their acquisition could also be affected by social interaction and cognitive development. Factors like these could also determine whether language-learners follow the same path, detect and use the same patterns, and make the same inferences about meanings during acquisition.

### A tabula rasa?

Do children have to learn everything about language and language use from scratch? Do they start out at birth with John Locke's tabula rasa, or do they come with certain things already pre-wired? Debate over this has led many to draw strict lines between "nature" (any innate capacities and structures children are born with) and "nurture" (what they gain from experience). Biologists would generally argue that this dichotomy is a false one. From conception on, fetal development is shaped by maternal health and nutrition as well as by the fetal cells that are maturing, so to distinguish nature from nurture in development is close to impossible.

Since children are not born speaking, they must learn language. The question then becomes one of what they are born with that is required for this task. Do they come with innate learning mechanisms to get them started? Are such mechanisms general-purpose aids to learning or specific to language alone? What empirical findings could help answer these questions? A related issue is whether children are born with built-in linguistic categories and structures required for learning. Here again, there has been a great deal of debate. Some have proposed that children come with syntactic categories like "noun" or "verb" already wired in, along with certain structural arrays for combining them. The task would then be one of working out what counts as a noun or verb in the speech children hear. Others have argued that children can discover nouns and verbs by looking at all the linguistic contexts each word occurs in. And still others have argued that they can discover nouns and verbs from the kinds of things they designate – nouns are for people, places, and things; verbs for actions. Even if children are born with a learning mechanism dedicated to language, the main proposals have focussed only on syntactic structure. The rest has to be learnt.

In language, children face a particularly intricate task for learning. Compare learning a language to learning how to put on socks and shoes or to brush one's teeth. It is clear that languages demand a lot more. They are highly complex systems whether one considers just the sound system or the vocabulary, or also syntactic constructions and word structure. The structural elements are just half of what has to be learnt; the other half consists of the functions assigned to each element. Learners must master both structure and function to use language.

## Languages differ

Languages aren't all cut from the identical pattern, and this makes a difference in acquisition. They differ in the range and combination of sounds they use – for instance, whether they allow only single consonants to begin a syllable (*top*) or also combinations of consonants (*stop*, *trip*); whether they use pure vowels or also diphthongs (combinations of vowels) in syllables (*heat* vs. *height*). They differ in how many word-classes they have. Some have nouns, verbs, adjectives, adverbs, and prepositions (e.g., English and French). Others place "adjectives" in with verbs. Some use prepositions (*in the boat*), some use postpositions (equivalent to *the boat in*), and some add special case endings, usually suffixes, directly onto the locative noun (here, *boat*) to capture the same meaning. Languages also differ in how they indicate who is doing what to whom. Some use case endings on nouns for this (as in German, Finnish, or Latin), and others word order (as in English or Mandarin). A nominative case ending and a first-position noun may do the same job in different languages.

Languages differ in whether word order serves a grammatical purpose (identifying the subject or object, for instance) or a pragmatic one (identifying information as given or as new). They differ in the meanings that are packaged in words, not only in what they have words for (many kinds of camel, in Somali; many kinds of rice, in Thai; many colors, in most Western European languages) but also in just what meaning-combinations are carried by words (whether verbs of motion include information about manner, as in English *walk*, *run*, *stroll*, *trot*, *meander*, or not, as in languages like Spanish or Hebrew that contain fewer such verbs). Languages differ in how they express causation. They may use a lexical verb like *open* to mean 'cause to open' (*he opened the window*), rely on an auxiliary verb combined with a lexical verb, as in French *faire marcher* 'make walk' (*il fait marcher le chien* 'he makes-walk the dog' = 'he walks the dog'), or add an ending to the verb stem itself to make a verb into a causative, as in Turkish or Hindi.

Languages differ in their basic word orders for subject, verb, and object. They may favor SVO or SOV, for example. And they display considerable consistency with the orders of other elements too. In SVO languages, adjectives usually follow their nouns (English is an exception here), and in SOV languages like Japanese they precede them. The same holds for prepositions that precede their nouns in an SVO language like English but follow (and are called postpositions) in an SOV language like Japanese. Relative clauses fill the same positions as adjectives: In SVO languages, they generally follow the nouns they modify, and in SOV languages they precede them. The basic word order in a language is correlated with the order of elements in many other constructions of that language (Greenberg 1963; Hawkins 1988).

When languages combine one clause with another, one clause may be subordinated and introduced by a conjunction indicating whether the relation between the two is temporal (*when*, *before*, *while*), causal (*because*), or conditional (*if*, *unless*). In some, the subordinate clause can follow or precede the main clause, depending on the general flow of information – what's given and what's new. In others, it may be restricted to a single position relative to the main clause. For example, in Turkish and Japanese, both SOV languages, subordinate clauses must precede the main clause.

Languages are usually consistent both in their basic word order and in the orders favored across a variety of constructions. These statistical universals are important for speaking and listening. The internal consistencies in a language help speakers keep track of what they are listening to and what they are planning to say themselves. They allow predictions about linguistic units and offer predictable frames for the presentation of information. So children need to learn general structural regularities in the language they're acquiring – whether it is an SOV or SVO language, whether relative clauses and adjectives follow or precede the nominals they modify, whether locative phrases are signaled by prepositions or postpositions, and so on. These properties are important because, once speakers have identified them, they can rely on certain assumptions about the kind of information that can come next in an utterance.

Just as languages display consistent structural patterns, they display consistent lexical patterns in the semantic information they bundle together. Some languages combine information about motion and manner of motion, and put information about the path followed elsewhere. The English verb *stroll* conveys 'move in a leisurely manner', while a preposition like *along* marks the path taken in, for example, *stroll along the bank*. Other languages package motion and path together, and put manner elsewhere. The Spanish verb *bajar* conveys 'go/move' plus 'down' and *salir* conveys 'go/move' plus 'out'. To indicate manner of motion, Spanish speakers must add a participle (*corriendo* 'running') or adverb (e.g., *rapidamente* 'quickly') to convey the equivalent of English *run down* (*bajar corriendo* 'go-down running' or *bajar rapidamente* 'go-down fast') (Talmy 1985). Children must learn how their language packages information at word level.

Knowledge of structure and function informs the assumptions speakers make in interpreting what they hear and in choosing how to convey their meaning when they speak. The structures and vocabulary of a language provide choices for speakers. There is no one-to-one mapping of linguistic constructions (and words) to each situation. Instead, speakers must choose how to represent a particular event to someone else. Did Justin chase the dog, or did the dog run away from Justin? Did Sophie come into the house or go into the house? Did Kate teach the children to tie knots, or did the children learn to tie knots from Kate? In each case, the choice of construction and words conveys a particular perspective on the event (Clark 1997). At the same time, the perspectives speakers can take may be limited by what is available in their language.

## Complexity for learning

Languages differ in what is easier and what harder to learn. Researchers have distinguished two sources of complexity for learning: *conceptual* and *formal* complexity (e.g., Slobin 1973, 1985b). Conceptual complexity pertains to the complexity of the ideas being expressed in language. Children probably develop cognitively at about the same rate in similar societies all over the world. This in turn suggests that they should go through stages in cognitive development at the same rate and grasp similar ideas at about the same age. In general, they master simple conceptual distinctions before more complex ones: the notion of more than one (marked by a plural word-ending), say, before notions of truth or beauty, and the notion of an action being finished (marked by a perfective or past tense ending) before the notion of one event being contingent on another (*if X, Y*). In principle, children should master simpler distinctions before more complex ones.

But since languages differ, the same conceptual distinction may be expressed in a variety of forms. One language might opt for a single word-ending for 'more than one' and use this as an invariant form on every noun, much like the *-s* ending for plural in English. Another might make use of ten or more different plural markers depending on the gender of the noun (masculine, feminine, or neuter), the "shape" of the noun (e.g., whether it ends in a consonant or a vowel), its use with a numeral (*five gold rings*) and what numeral (*five, ten, three hundred*), and so on, much as in Russian or Arabic (see, e.g., Gvozdev 1961; Omar 1973). It should take children longer to learn how to express 'more than one' in these languages than in English. For one thing, there are more forms to learn, and then there are conditions on when to use each one. Differences in formal complexity affect rate of acquisition.

While no one language appears to be easier to learn overall, there are many trade-offs from one language to another in what is easy and what is hard. The plural system for nouns in a language that uses just one ending to mark 'more than one' should be easy. Yet the same language may have an elaborate system of verb tenses and verb forms in each tense, which makes verbs hard to learn. Children may find some aspects of a language easier to master than others, and children exposed to different languages may well learn at different rates on equivalent parts of the system. To find out, we need to establish what's hard and what's easy in acquisition for each language.

## Social dimensions

Language acquisition takes place in mid conversation. Adults and children talk to each other; adults expect children to respond to requests and comments, and to indicate to their interlocutors what they are interested in as well as their needs and wants. When adults talk to children, they directly or indirectly offer them extensive information about their language. They set up both tacit and explicit expectations for when children should talk, what they should say, when and how they should respond to adult utterances; what counts as a turn in conversation, when (and when not) to take a turn; and what counts as an appropriate contribution in the ongoing exchange (Berko Gleason 1988). In the course of conversation, adults use the conventional words for objects and actions. This way, they provide words for whole arenas of experience – food, clothing, toys, pets, vehicles, birds, mammals, plants, gardens, farms, the seaside, mountain slopes, and many more. They also offer information about how words within a domain are related (Clark & Wong 2002).

Conversation demands that its participants attend to each other and to whatever is being talked about. This means keeping track of what others know at each point in the conversation. The participants share common ground and add to it with each utterance. Both joint attention and the updating of common ground play a role in acquisition (Clark 2002b). In learning to participate in conversations, children learn more of their language and more about how to use it (Snow 1978). And in tuning in to a language, they tune in to those distinctions that are obligatory; they come to assume distinctions that are *always* encoded in that language but not necessarily in others. They learn to think – and plan – for speaking in that language (Slobin 1996).

Conversation provides a forum for using language. It displays language embedded in larger systems for communication and so should present children with critical material for making sense of language as they try to understand others and make themselves understood. Conversational exchanges between children and adults should also be a forum for learning to become a member of the society and the culture. From birth on, the exchanges children participate in attune them to the language around them. This holds as much for sound patterns as for words or for constructions used to convey temporal and causal relations among events; as much for intonation contours and tone of voice (with positive or negative affect) as for details of constructing words from roots and affixes.

Understanding in conversation may depend as much on what is not said as on what is said. Knowing some of the elements of a language doesn't necessarily allow one to interpret utterances appropriately. One has to learn the conventions on use. For example, the request in English *Can you open the door?* is both a question about ability (*can*) and a request for someone to perform the action of opening. The context of use then determines how the addressee should construe it. What counts as a request or as an assertion and the range of forms that can be used depend on the conventions of the speech community. (These are not necessarily the same even in communities using the same language.) Construals also depend on the inferences that are licensed in context.

How do children learn linguistic conventions? For instance, the expected response to a question can depend on both the context and speaker. If a speaker repeats with question intonation what a child has just said, this conveys that the adult considers what the child said to be wrong. In everyday conversation, this typically leads the original speaker to offer some alternative. But in the classroom, teachers may question what children say to check on whether they really know, and this calls instead for the child to repeat the original utterance, not change it (Siegal 1997).

Language use is not uniform; it depends on who one speaks to. In most communities, people speak to family members and friends differently from strangers; they distinguish formal from informal speech (e.g., with *vous* vs. *tu*); and they use a range of polite forms that differ in terms of address (*Ms. Pipon* vs. *Sophie*), word-choices (*that policeman* vs. *the cop*), and syntactic constructions (*Come here* vs. *Could you come here?*), depending on the language and addressee. Learning what the conventions are, the "rules of use" for different occasions, takes time.

Language is not an autonomous system for communication. It is embedded in and supplemented by gesture, gaze, stance, facial expression, and voice quality in the full array of options people can use for communicating. In learning language, children may first rely on nonlinguistic options, both in their initial understanding and in their own early use. They might understand affect first from adult voice quality and gesture, and infer the locus of attention from adult gaze or stance before they understand that words pick out referents. And they might rely on iconic gestures referring to or anticipating reference to things later named with words. Adults may draw children *in* to language by leaning on nonlinguistic means to signal affect or to direct attention. They may even indicate to young children how things work at first through gestures rather than words.

## Cognitive dimensions

What do children know by the time they start talking at age one? They have already had about twelve months of perceptual and conceptual development. They are adept at perceiving similarities, identifying objects and actions, recognizing faces, sorting like with like. They can orient objects and know where they are kept and how they are used (spoons, cups, bowls, bottle tops; shoes, socks, mittens; balls, dolls, soft toys, books; blankets, chairs, staircases). They know a good deal about their surroundings, about Euclidean space (up vs. down, back [not visible] vs. front [visible], side to side) and topological space (inside vs. outside, contained, attached, supported). They display memory for objects (persisting in looking for keys that have been covered with a cloth); they use "tools" (enlisting adult aid to get a box open); and they make use of pretense in play (moving a block while making car noises). In summary, they are setting up representations of what they see and know. They make use of these for recognition and recall, summoning them first with gestures and reenactments of events, and later with words (e.g., Piaget 1952; Werner & Kaplan 1963; see also H. Clark 1973).

Do children make use of this perceptual and conceptual knowledge as they acquire language? The answer has to be yes. When they learn to speak, they represent their experiences in words. They also draw on conceptual knowledge and its organization as they work out the meanings of new words and constructions. This is a major source of hypotheses about word meanings. Children use words to pick out categories of objects, whether "dog" or "Dalmatian," "pet" or "pest." These categories may be at different levels (compare "dog" to "Dalmatian" [a kind of dog]), or they can be orthogonal to each other (compare "dog" to "pet" or "guard"). Children can use words with these meanings to pick out the same object from different perspectives. They can use other words to pick out actions, where their choices depend on the number of participants, the effects, the manner of acting, and the location or direction involved (compare throwing a ball, opening a door, drinking milk, pushing someone on a swing, walking, sitting down, swimming, and riding a bicycle). Children can also assign words to pick out relations in space (compare putting keys in a box, hanging a picture above the head of a bed, climbing down a ladder, sitting beside the fire, crawling across the floor, or looking at a lid on a box, at tiles above the sink, or at a screen in front of the fire). One issue for language acquisition is how children find out which meanings there are words for; another is just how they map each meaning to the right word.

How do children form conceptual categories in the first place? They start out, it seems, with the ability to group things by how similar they are. These early groupings are also influenced by perceptual Gestalts that highlight "figures" against "grounds." Anything that moves stands out against its background and so is the figure. And when objects move, they move as a whole, so whole objects are more salient than any one part. Once children have represented an object-type, they can go on to attend to the actions and relations that link it to other things around it. These kinds of conceptual organization provide a starting point for what might also be represented in language.

Early conceptual organization also offers clues to how children might learn language. They must be able to use prior experience to recognize when objects or events recur. They need to set up representations of what they see, hear, touch, and taste so that they can recognize recurrences. Without such representations in memory, they couldn't categorize or organize experience. To do this, children must be able to detect similarity or degrees of similarity, a capacity that appears fundamental for all learning.

## Learners and learning

Learners can be conservative or bold, or somewhere in between. When children learn language, they could go step by step, one form at a time, waiting for evidence from adult speech and rarely going beyond it – *go, run, fall, fell, cat, cats, feet*. They could generalize from a few forms to new instances – from *jump/ jumped* to *run/runned*, from *cat/cats* to *man/mans*. They could go item by item then make some limited generalizations, with different children following different paths. Or they could generalize broadly, acting as if all of language is orderly and rule governed (it isn't), and so regularize many irregular forms (e.g., *bringed, sitted, goed, foots, sheeps, mouses*).

Take the plural *-s* in English. It has three variants depending on the final sound of the stem, as in *cat/cats* [-s], *dog/dogs* [-z], and *horse/horses* [-ɪz]. This is the regular plural form that appears on most nouns in English. It could be learnt by *rote*, with children adding one item at a time as they hear it. Their first version of a word could be singular or plural, depending on what they happen to hear first. So they might learn *cat* and then *cats*; *stairs* then *stair*; *dog* then *dogs*. Rote learning depends on children hearing each form so they gradually fill in the paradigm of singular and plural for each word. Rote learning should preclude errors like *mans* for the plural of *man* or *teeths* for the plural of *tooth*. It should also preclude children treating words like *house* and *purse* as if they were already plural. Yet children make both types of errors.

Suppose instead that children learn a few forms by rote and use those as models for deciding on the plural forms for new words: Because of *cat–cats*, the plural of *rat* should be *rats*. Here children would be relying on *analogy* (Gentner & Medina 1998), using information about similar words (similar in, say, sound or meaning or both) in deciding what the plural (or singular) should be. Analogy can start from any point, with children choosing a regular or an irregular form. For instance, analogy from *dog–dogs* applied to *cat* and *sheep* yields *cats* and *sheeps*. Analogy from an irregular word (e.g., *foot*, *child*) runs into problems.

Children might instead consider all the forms accumulated so far and abstract a *rule* for the plural (Pinker 1999). This could be stated as "Add -*s* to nouns to form the plural." When the words are regular, children succeed in producing the correct forms; when they aren't, they overregularize. Just as for analogy, rules fail for irregular words. The rule applied to words like *foot*, *child*, or *mouse* does not result in the conventional *feet*, *children*, and *mice*. These irregular words either require additional special rules or rote learning of each adult form.

Both analogy and rule work by adding a word-ending to the existing word. Children start with a source word, add something, and produce a new form. An alternative is to start from the goal – what the plural form should sound like – and adjust the singular word until it fits. Here children could use a *schema* or *template* for the plural (Bybee & Slobin 1982). The schema could be characterized as requiring a form ending in -*s*, roughly, PLURAL = [word + *s*]. If a word fits this schema (it already ends in -*s*), no change is required; if it doesn't, then the word must be adjusted until it does (by adding -*s*). The schema approach accounts for the same regular forms as the analogy and rule approaches do, and it also accounts for why children fail to add a plural ending to nouns like *horse* or *rose*: They end in an -*s* sound and so already fit the schema for plural.

Do children depend on rote, analogy, rule, or schema? Which account best captures what they do with the regularities they detect in language? The answer depends on careful analysis of the forms children produce: what they get right and what they get wrong. One factor is the identification of recurring patterns and their frequency. Children hear instances of some nouns and verbs more frequently than others (*man* occurs many more times than *field*, and *put* more often than *yell*). This is token-frequency. They also hear some types of nouns and verbs more often than others: There are many more regular nouns (e.g., *book/books*, *cat/cats*, *chair/chairs*) than irregular nouns (e.g., *foot/feet*, *man/men*, *mouse/mice*) in English. The same goes for verbs: Regular verbs (e.g., *walk/walked*, *open/opened*, *jump/jumped*) far outnumber irregular ones (e.g., *go/went*, *bring/brought*, *fall/fell*). To what extent does this token- or type-frequency play a role in children's generalizations?

Researchers agree that children must learn both sound systems and vocabulary. (How they learn them is another matter.) Sound systems are specific to each language, and children must learn the one they are exposed to (Jusczyk 1997; Vihman 1996). And vocabulary presents a formidable challenge. Adults know somewhere between 50,000 and 100,000 distinct words, so the learning required here is extensive (Bloom 2000; Clark 1993). There is much less agreement about the learning of syntactic constructions. Do children rely on innate knowledge for these or do they learn them as they do words? The arguments for innateness have hinged largely on the putative difficulty of learning syntactic constructions from child-directed speech. Researchers have pointed to the ungrammaticality of adult-to-adult speech and also argued that some constructions are either absent or so rare as to make them unlearnable. If children acquire them anyway, they must be relying on some built-in knowledge. Both premises here are in dispute – that child-directed speech is ungrammatical and that certain structures are unavailable in that speech.

What role do children play in learning? They could be passive recipients of the language directed to them, simply absorbing whatever they hear, or they could play an active role, selecting and generalizing about whatever they have taken in so far. To what extent are children miniature scientists, testing hypotheses and checking up on what they know about particular words or constructions? Do they detect patterns and apply them to new cases? Do they make inferences about possible meanings and make use of them in later word use? Overall, the role that *children* play provides critical information about how (and what) they learn at each stage and about the learning mechanisms they rely on.

## Product versus process

Some approaches to language acquisition focus on the *product* – the end state to be achieved – rather than on the *process*. This distinction tends to capture one difference between linguistic and psycholinguistic approaches to acquisition. Linguists tend to focus on the product, for instance, what a relative clause looks like, laid out on the table for analysis. In contrast, the psycholinguist is more concerned with when the speaker needs a relative clause, how he accesses the pertinent structure, the phrases, words, syllables, and sounds, and then produces the utterance itself piece by piece. This has led to differences in emphasis, with linguistic approaches focussing more on the adultlike nature of children's knowledge while psychological ones have focussed more on the changes that occur during development.

One linguistic approach known as parameter-setting proposes that children start out with default settings for *parameters* that capture all the dimensions that distinguish among languages. For instance, languages differ on whether they require subjects to be marked by a pronoun where there isn't a noun subject present. (Where they don't, languages typically mark person [e.g., *I*, *you*, *he*] and number [singular or plural] with endings on the verb, as in Italian.) This is called the Pro-drop parameter, and researchers have assumed that the default value is to drop pronoun subjects (much as in Italian or Spanish). Each parameter has a start-up setting (the default) and children begin there, regardless of the language to be acquired. Then, at a certain point in development, they identify the actual parameter-setting for that language (it is not clear what the critical data are) and from then on make adultlike use of the pertinent forms. What happens before a parameter is set is of scant interest. The main concern is with the parameters themselves, the values for each, and when the correct setting for each is triggered. Setting parameters is regarded by some as something that happens automatically when children reach the right age and stage of development. This leads researchers to ignore everything that happens before a parameter is set (e.g., Borer & Wexler 1987; Radford 1990). Children's errors prior to adultlike use and any continuity in their attempts to convey a particular meaning are simply not relevant.

Other approaches regard *continuity* of expression and *function* as critical clues to tracing the path children follow as they acquire language. This holds for most processing approaches. For example, they may identify a particular conceptual distinction and then trace its expression by children as they learn more about the conventions of a particular language. Take the notion of plurality, more than one. Children acquiring English often start out by using a word like *more* or a numeral like *two* to express this notion, as in *more shoe, two cup*. Only after that do they learn to add the plural ending (*shoes, cups*). The earlier expressions for plurality show that children have grasped the notion but haven't yet worked out how to express it in English. This comes back to the distinction between conceptual and formal complexity. Children may have acquired the pertinent concept (here, plurality) but not the forms that are conventional for its expression.

Processing approaches have also focussed on what children do at one stage compared to the next. One approach has been to look at where children start, what they attend to first, and what they change in their language as they get older. Their preferences and the changes they make can be captured as processing strategies or operating principles. For example, in producing words, children focus on the core word (the stem) first and on getting the initial sounds right. This strategy can be represented as "Pay attention to the beginnings of words." It helps others recognize the words children are trying to say. Their next move is to start producing word-endings (like the plural, say): "Pay attention to the ends of words." But now they need to attend to the range of meanings conveyed by word-endings, so another strategy might be to look for endings that have a stable, identifiable meaning and to use those whenever needed.

Researchers have looked for consistencies in how children interpret and produce words from the earliest stages on and from those patterns have derived the strategies children seem to apply (e.g., Slobin 1985b). This approach relies on looking at both what children get right and what they get wrong. Sometimes they fail to produce a form altogether (*I throw ball*, without *a* or *the* before *ball*); at other times, they apply a form incorrectly (*bringed, foots*). This approach is concerned both with learning and with how changes come about.

Processing approaches take account of the dynamic nature of conversation. Speakers interact with each other. They don't produce isolated sentences that stand on their own. Once someone has mentioned *Kate*, for example, the next speaker will use *she* (not *Kate*) to refer to her again. Or, once someone has asked Rod whether he wants lasagna, he can answer *Just a little*, or *Yes please*. What these utterances refer to requires that we know that there was a prior offer, *Would you like some lasagna?* Without that, we can't give a full interpretation to *Yes please*. What someone says depends critically on what someone else has just said and often can't be interpreted without a whole sequence of contributions to the conversation. Imagine recording a conversation and then transcribing what only one of the speakers said. It quickly becomes difficult or impossible to interpret what that person means. In fact, utterances depend on both conversational and physical context for interpretation (H. Clark 1996). This should hold even more strongly for young children whose utterances may consist of only one or two words.

## The goal of acquisition

The goal is to become a member of a community of speakers. This entails learning all the elements of a language, both structure and usage. Children need to learn the sound system, the *phonology*. This in turn means learning which sounds belong (sound segments like **p**, **b**, **t**, **d**, **s**, **z**, **a**, **i**, **u**, **e**), which sequences of sounds are legal in syllables and words (phonotactic constraints, e.g., ***drip*** but not ***dlip*** in English), stress patterns on words (e.g., *electric* vs. *electricity*), tone on words in a language like Mandarin or Hausa, and the intonation contours in sentences that distinguish a question from a statement (e.g., *Alan is coming at six o'clock?* vs. *Alan is coming at six o'clock*).

They need to learn about the structure of words, their *morphology*: whether they are made up of one syllable, two, or many (compare *pop, slipper, alligator*), along with their meanings. Words can be complex and made up of several building blocks, sometimes with suffixes or prefixes added to root forms (e.g., *write/writer*, *saddle/__un__saddle*, *push-chair*, *sun-rise*, *house-builder*, *complexify*, *physicist*). These building blocks also allow for the construction of new words to express new meanings, meanings for which there is no existing conventional form. Words may form *paradigms*, groups that display regular alternations to mark particular meanings. In some languages, nouns can be singular or plural, for example (English *cat/cats*, *chair/chairs*, *horse/horses*), but not all of them belong to regular paradigms (English *mouse/mice* or *child/children*). Nouns may also have suffixes that show whether they have the role of subject (e.g., *The man was running*), object (e.g., *The dog chased the man*), indirect object (e.g., *The boy gave the book to the man*), and so on, as in German, Greek, or Finnish. These case endings, like plural endings in English, are generally fairly regular, with the same form used on many different nouns. There may be several plural endings for different sets of nouns (e.g., masculine, feminine, neuter; or common and neuter) and therefore several regular paradigms. Verbs may belong to many paradigms too, each one marking tenses differently, for example. In each instance, noun and verb endings add modifications to the basic meaning of the roots or stems.

Speakers don't use just one word at a time. They combine them, and again the possible sequences of words in a language have to be learnt. This is the *syntax*. Just as with sounds, some sequences are legal, others not. In English, adjectives precede the nouns they modify (e.g., *the green vine*, not *\*the vine green*), articles like *a* or *the* and demonstratives like *that* also go before their nouns (e.g., *the whistle*, *that rosebush*). Relative clauses follow their nouns (e.g., *The wallaby that was hopping across the path was a female*). Subordinate clauses introduced by conjunctions like *if, because*, or *when* in English can be placed before or after main clauses (e.g., *When the bell rang, all the children came inside*, or *All the children came inside when the bell rang*), but in Turkish or Japanese, for instance, such clauses must precede the main clause. Some constructions allow a number of different nouns and verbs to be used in them; others may be very restricted. Just as with sounds and words, children have to learn what the possibilities are.

Language is used to convey *meaning*. Words, suffixes, and prefixes all carry meanings that are *conventional* (Lewis 1969). The speech community relies on all its members agreeing that *ball* means 'ball', *throw* means 'throw', and *sand* means 'sand'. These conventions are what make languages work. Without agreements about meanings, one couldn't rely on the fact that the next time someone uses *sand*, say, people hearing the word will still interpret it in the same way. Conventions are critical in language use. They govern both word meanings and construction meanings. In learning a language, children must learn the conventions for that community.

Languages work in large part because they don't use needless duplication. Each conventional word differs from all its neighbors. Each word reflects a choice made by the speaker to convey one meaning rather than another and so *contrasts* with all the others (Clark 1990). If speakers wish to convey a meaning for which there is no conventional word, they can construct a new one to carry that meaning. This new word then contrasts with any previously established ones. For example, the verb *to skateboard* was introduced along with skateboards themselves to talk about a new method of travel. This verb immediately contrasted with all existing verbs for other means of moving (*to bicycle, to sled, to ski, to roller-skate*, etc.) (see Clark & Clark 1979). Language, and especially its vocabulary (the lexicon), is not static. Speakers coin new words as society changes and adds new inventions and new technologies. But each new word is accepted only if its meaning contrasts with the meanings of existing words. Conventionality and contrast are powerful pragmatic principles governing language use (Clark 1993).

Knowing what the conventions are for the elements of a language and knowing how to use them are two different things. Children must learn how each word and construction can be used to convey their intentions. They learn how to make assertions (*That's a tadpole*), requests (*Can you mend my yoyo?*), and promises (*I'll mow the lawn tomorrow*) (Austin 1962; Levinson 1983). They learn what counts as polite (*Pick up the other one!* vs. *Could you bring in the other box?*), and how polite to be on each occasion. They learn how to give directions and explanations, and how to tell stories. In summary, they need to learn to use language effectively, whatever the genre, whoever the addressee, and whatever the goal.

## Stages in acquisition

Infants don't produce their first words until age one or later, but by three or four, they can talk quite fluently about some topics. This development is one we take as much for granted as the infant's transition from lying supine in the first few months to walking and running around by age one to two. Learning to talk is more complicated than learning to walk. Talking plays a major role in social communication and demands a grasp of all the local conventions of use in each speech community. Language use is an integral part of communication; it goes along with gesture, gaze, and other nonlinguistic means used to convey attitude and affect as well as speaker intentions.

As children learn to talk, they go through a series of stages, beginning with infancy, when they are unable to converse and do not yet understand any language. They go from babbling at seven to ten months old, to producing their first recognizable words six to twelve months later. Then, within a few months, they combine words and gestures, and produce their first word combinations around age two. This is followed by the production of ever more complex, adultlike utterances, as they become active participants in conversation, taking turns and making appropriate contributions. They begin to use language for a larger array of functions – telling stories, explaining how a toy works, persuading a friend to do something, or giving someone directions for how to get somewhere. Between age one and age six, children acquire extensive skills in using language and can sound quite adultlike much of the time. By around age ten to twelve, they have mastered many complex constructions, a good deal more vocabulary, and many uses of language.

Comprehension, throughout this process, tends to be far ahead of production. Children understand many words long before they can produce them, and this asymmetry between comprehension and production is lifelong: Consider the number of dialects adults can understand without being able to produce more than two or three at most. For a second language, consider how much better people are at understanding than at speaking. The same holds true for a first language: Comprehension remains ahead of production, but once production reaches a certain level, speakers tend to no longer notice any mismatch (yet it is still there). At the same time, mismatches play an important role in the process of acquisition: Children's representations for comprehension provide targets for what their own production should sound like.

Is there continuity over stages? Do children try to express similar notions at successive points in development – whether issuing one word at a time, longer word combinations, or adultlike phrases? How much consistency is there in the stages children go through as they learn the same language? How much for children learning different languages? Do children from different social classes go through the same stages provided they are learning the same language? Are they all exposed to the same amount and same range of child-directed speech?

### Why study acquisition?

In the late 19th century, the burgeoning study of child development emphasized language, and many researchers kept extensive diaries of their children's development, including language (e.g., Ament 1899; Baudouin de Courtenay 1974; Compayré 1896; Lindner 1898; Major 1906; Preyer 1882; Ronjat 1913; Stern & Stern 1928; Sully 1896; Taine 1870; see also Campbell 2006). Because researchers lacked tools for preserving their observations, these records vary in quality. There was no audio- or videotape to record what happened and no International Phonetic Alphabet to help note children's exact pronunciations. Some, like Clara Stern and William Stern, who kept a detailed diary, though, raised many issues that are still critical in the twenty-first century. These observational studies were followed by extensive records of children's vocabularies in terms of size and content at different ages. In the 1930s and 1940s in the United States, the emphasis remained on vocabulary size and sentence length, with little analysis of structure and no analysis of conversational skill.

In the 1960s, under Noam Chomsky's influence in linguistic theory, researchers renewed their interest in how children acquired language. Chomsky himself argued that children must rely on certain innate structures and mechanisms, specific to language, because it would be impossible for them to learn from adult speech alone (but see Chapter 2). These claims became embedded in the Chomskyan approach, although few of his students did empirical research on language acquisition in children. Among psychologists who took up the challenge of studying language acquisition directly was Roger W. Brown. He in turn drew many of his students as well as others into the field during the 1960s and 1970s, made major contributions himself, and has had a lasting impact.

Initially, many studies of language acquisition were undertaken to assess the psychological reality of a linguistic proposal or to test the predictions of linguistic theory against acquisition data. And here several problems arose immediately. First, linguistic theory for the most part is a theory about product and not process, so it was unclear what the predictions should be. Even when these appeared fairly clear, there was frequent disagreement on how to interpret findings inconsistent with the current linguistic theory, with linguists commonly dismissing acquisition data as irrelevant and, therefore, as no test for the theory. Second, linguistic theories displaced each other with some rapidity, so theoretical claims became even harder to evaluate. These factors led to some divergence in approach, with much of the research on language acquisition being carried out at some distance from theoretical claims in linguistics. This encouraged the development of other approaches to acquisition and may have led researchers to ask broader questions than they might have done otherwise.

Some of the current issues are still those that dominated debates about language acquisition after the publication of Chomsky's *Aspects of the theory of syntax* in

1965. One of these is whether there is a mechanism for acquisition specialized for language alone, independent of other cognitive skills. This claim has generally been accompanied by the claim that some knowledge about language is also innate, with syntactic categories (word-classes like noun and verb) and basic syntactic structure (subject and predicate, along with other basic grammatical relations, for example) being the prime candidates. This in turn has led to discussion of how much of language is learnable and under what conditions (where the focus has again usually been on syntax alone); whether there is a critical period for language learning, after which humans can no longer learn a language, in much the same way that goslings can no longer imprint on a mother goose or white-crowned sparrows can no longer learn the songs characteristic of their species; and how children learn to correct any errors they make, given the supposed absence of corrective reactions from adults.

The problem with many of these debates lies in the virtual absence of empirical findings and testable hypotheses. The premises have all too often been regarded as facts, and the arguments have raged from there on in. What are needed are testable hypotheses and analyses of pertinent data by the researchers making the claims. Ideally, their questions should yield answers from actual findings on acquisition. These debates, largely carried on in the pages of linguistics books and journals, have ranged over nature versus nurture, innateness (what's innate and "special" about human language) versus learning (what might be learnt, or not, from child-directed speech), and, more recently, the social versus cognitive properties of language as a tool for communication or a system for the representation of knowledge.

My own emphasis is on the social setting of acquisition combined with the cognitive foundations children can build on. So I view both social and cognitive development as critical to acquisition. Since it remains unclear how much of language is innate or whether any specialized learning mechanisms subserve it, my stance on this is a conservative one. I prefer to see how much one can account for on more general grounds first. The emphasis here is therefore on how (and how much) children can learn from adult usage, including specially tailored child-directed speech. I also look at evidence for early generalizations versus initially piecemeal acquisition of constructions with specific verbs and other lexical items. I place considerable emphasis on the developmental processes required in learning a language from the first words on and none on arguing that children know (nearly) everything from the start. As a result, I emphasize continuity in development – continuity in the meanings they express as they move from one word at a time to adultlike utterances for conveying their needs, their interests, their attitudes, and their thoughts.

## The plan of this book

Language is social. For language to work, speakers must ensure joint attention with their addressees and then make every effort to achieve and maintain common ground in each exchange. Its successful use depends on collaboration and cooperation among speakers. In this book, I start from that premise as I follow different themes through the process of acquisition. These themes include the roles of social and cognitive factors in language acquisition; the extent to which children learn different languages differently – how the course they follow is shaped by properties of each language; the increasing complexity of the expressions acquired with age; the stability children display in their order of acquisition for meanings and structures within a language; the role of common ground and the flow of information; the speaker's choice of perspective marked through words and constructions; and the importance of pragmatic factors in the acquisition and use of language, and what might constitute plausible mechanisms for acquisition.

Language is an elaborate resource for communication. It is complemented by various nonlinguistic resources – gesture, gaze, facial expression, bodily stance and orientation – that, together with language, make up the general repertoire people draw on to communicate. Language itself depends on a complex set of conventions on the meanings and uses of words and constructions. Without these conventions, speakers couldn't be sure that words, for instance, had the same meaning from one occasion to the next or from one speaker to the next. So, in learning a language, children need to learn both its conventions and how to apply them. The goal in acquisition is mastery of the language in use around them, so analyses of acquisition must be based on the language children hear. This *use-based approach* to acquisition takes actual usage as the target rather than any idealization of language. The words children hear and the constructions those words appear in are drawn from local patterns of usage in the speech community. The social setting where children are exposed to a first language is critical; this is where they hear their language used. This is the material they must learn to recognize, analyze, understand, and produce themselves.

To study acquisition, then, requires that we look at how children use language, what they have learnt about carrying on a conversation – for instance, taking turns, uttering different speech acts, taking account of what the addressee knows, and connecting new information to what has already been given. This approach encompasses both the acquisition of structure (forms and their meanings) and function (what forms can be used for and how they are deployed for each purpose). The same use-based approach must apply where children acquire more than one dialect or more than one language at a time: learning two (or more) at once, and when to use each, again depends on the usage within the community.

This book is divided into four parts. In the first (Chapters 2–6), I begin by looking at children's conversations with adults and the information adults offer them about language use (Chapter 2). Next I turn to how children analyze the speech stream to recognize words (Chapter 3) and then review the content of children's early words – the kinds of meanings they express – and how they learn to pronounce them (Chapters 4–5). I end with how children map meanings onto words (Chapter 6). The emphasis is on how children get started and their earliest uses of language.

In Part II (Chapters 7–11), I focus on children's acquisition of structure. They learn first to combine two or more words in a single utterance (Chapter 7) and modify each word with appropriate endings (Chapter 8). They add complexity to what they say in two ways: (a) by elaborating the information inside clauses (Chapter 9) and (b) by combining two or more clauses (Chapter 10). In each case, children advance from rudimentary expressions of meanings to more elaborate ones that use conventional adult forms. Lastly, I look at how children coin words when they don't have any ready-made for the meanings they wish to convey (Chapter 11). The emphasis here is on how children acquire the adult forms for their meanings. With both constructions and coinages, they gradually build up more elaborate communicative options.

In Part III, I turn to the social skills children need. They take part in conversations quite early, but learning what to say when is complicated, and getting the timing right for taking turns is also hard (Chapter 12). On top of that, learning how to be polite, to be persuasive, to give instructions, or to tell stories all take added skill (Chapter 13). Finally, children exposed to two languages from the beginning have two systems to learn, and are also continually faced with the decision of how to talk – which language (or which dialect) to use. These choices, just as in the case of one language, depend on the addressee, setting, and topic (Chapter 14). All these social dimensions of language acquisition complement the structural ones. Children have to master both to become identified as speakers from a particular community.

In Part IV, I take up biological specialization for language and where in the brain language is processed (Chapter 15). I then review the kinds of mechanisms needed for the acquisition of a system as complex as language, demanding a wide range of skills for use (Chapter 16).

Throughout, I draw on data from a range of languages to underline both similarities in the analyses children do and differences in how speakers do things from one language to another, and, for both cases, the effects this can have on acquisition. I draw extensively on the diary study I kept of my son from birth to age six to illustrate some facets of language development described here. These observations are supplemented by other longitudinal records and by experimental data on the comprehension and production of specific constructions. I also draw extensively on other published findings and on data from the CHILDES Archive, a collection of transcripts from different researchers (MacWhinney & Snow 1985, 1990). Despite a plethora of studies since the 1960s, there are still many gaps in what we know about acquisition, even for well-studied languages, and there are still too few language-types included among those for which we do have data (Slobin 1985a, 1992, 1997). I hope the present overview will inspire readers to ask further questions, look at as-yet unstudied languages, and take up new questions about the many intriguing puzzles of acquisition.

# PART I

## Getting started

*It seems to us that a mother in expanding speech may be teaching more than grammar; she may be teaching something like a world-view.*

Roger Brown & Ursula Bellugi 1964

*[S]peech skills have a tremendous potential for assisting the formation of non-linguistic categories. The total list of such categories that a child must learn is a cognitive inventory of his culture. Speech, therefore, is the principal instrument of cognitive socialization.*

Roger Brown 1958b

The chapters that follow look at the setting in which infants are first exposed to language and in which they take the first steps towards making use of it. This setting is a social one, where language forms part of a larger system for the communication of wants and desires, attitudes and affect, requests and needs. Language itself is a product of social interaction, and in learning a language, infants learn how to interact, initiate social exchanges, respond to others in maintaining such exchanges, and how to end exchanges. In doing this, they receive pragmatic directions, both tacit and explicit, about how to use language – which words are appropriate (conventional) for particular purposes, which expressions, and which constructions. They hear and extract the regularities within a language, for example the correlations of lexical items to constructions, of sound patterns to morphemes and words, and of prosodic contours to structural units within constructions. Children assign meanings to the forms they isolate. They build up semantic domains by adding more words, assigning meanings to unfamiliar words, and attending to pragmatic directions about use.

# 2   In conversation with children

Infants are born into a social world, a world of touch, sound, and affect, a world of communication. They develop and grow up as social beings, immersed in a network of relationships from the start. It is in this social setting that they are first exposed to language, to language in use. This language forms part of the daily communication around them and to them. It regulates what they do. It tells them about the world, events, actions, objects, and relations within it, and presents them with affective attitudes to people and events. In short, language is a central factor in the social life of infants. The users of language they are exposed to provide the context in which children themselves become proficient at communicating wants and desires, affect and interest, requests and instructions, questions and observations, and commentary on all the contents of everyday life.

This chapter explores the social setting in which children are exposed to language, respond to it, and begin to use it. It is in and from *interaction* that children are offered conventional ways of expressing attitudes and of saying things, along with the conventional words and expressions for what they appear to be trying to say. And it is in interaction that children take up these words, expressions, and constructions. Language can be used for talking about needs and desires, or objects and events in the world at large; for talking about how to behave, how to act, what to say in different circumstances; for talking about problem-solving, for expository argument or explanation, for giving instructions; and for pretending, teasing, joking, or telling stories. In all these uses, language always forms part of a larger system for communication. It's therefore important to keep sight of communicative purposes and goals in looking at how children become members of the speaking community and learn in their turn how to talk with the same range of skills as adults. It is in the service of communication that children learn to break up the stream of speech into smaller and smaller elements, learning to identify clauses and phrases, words and morphemes.

Each linguistic chunk or unit carries meaning. So an important part of the analysis that children must do involves working out which meanings are carried by which forms. In solving this problem, they rely heavily on general pragmatic principles that language communities exploit to make sure their communicative systems remain both effective and fairly stable over time. Conventionality captures the fact that speakers expect a particular meaning to be conveyed by a particular form within their community. Members of a language community have in common a large stock of conventions – forms they expect to be used to convey particular meanings. The inflections to use on a verb are conventional (e.g., *-ing* or *-ed*), as are the word-choices for talking about particular entities or events (e.g., *tiger* for talking about tigers, *circus* for talking about circuses), or the forms to use in making polite requests (*May I…* or *Could you…*). Conventionality covers all the agreements that members of a language community tacitly adhere to in using their language (Clark 1993).

Contrast captures the fact that the same speakers assume that any difference in form must mark a difference in meaning. If speakers don't use a conventional form, they must mean something different from what they would have conveyed by using the conventional form (Clark 1990,1993; Croft 2000). I return to these principles and their general role in acquisition in Chapter 6.

## Language in context

When we think about learning a language, our first association is often to language as represented in "the form of grammars and dictionaries, or of randomly chosen words and sentences" (Halliday 1975:20). This view of language is misleading in two respects. First, it removes language from its social setting, and, second, it depicts it as a product rather than as a part of a dynamic system for communication. Language is best viewed as part of a broader communication system that draws not only on the speaker's utterances but also on gesture, stance, facial expression, affective display, and any other factors that contribute to successful interactions – successful in that speakers achieve their goals in conveying their intended meanings to their addressees.

The goals of an interaction, both local and global, are critical to how that interaction is carried on and what resources the participants use in communicating their intended meanings. Learning a first language, under this view, is part of learning to communicate. Other functions of language, as it is used to represent knowledge of the world, for instance, are put to use within a communicative framework. That language is essentially social is critical in considering the settings in which children acquire language and the kinds of language addressed to them at different stages in development.

What properties of language use and language structure distinguish adult–child conversations – and hence *child-directed speech*[1] – from conversations between adults? Child-directed speech presents a major issue in research on acquisition because of the theoretical claims that have been made about its role in acquisition. While all researchers agree that children need to be exposed to language to start in

---

[1] I use the term child-directed speech in preference to other terms that have been used in research on this topic, including "motherese" (mothers are not the only people who talk to babies and young children) and "parentese" (other people also talk to young children). Both of these share an unfortunate echo of words like "bureaucratese" and "journalese." The term "input" lacks the sense of language used in communicative exchanges and any notion of cooperative exchange. And "infant-directed speech" is too limited in scope since the claims made here are not restricted to infants.

on acquisition, there is much less agreement on the form that this exposure must take. The nature of child-directed speech itself has been a matter of debate. For many years, Chomsky and some of his colleagues assumed that adult speech to young children offered at best a degenerate version of a language – such speech was full of errors, hesitations, breaks in construction, retracings, pauses, and other disfluencies, repairs to vocabulary, to pronunciation, and so on, to the extent that children would necessarily have great difficulty both in learning what might be systematic in a language and in discerning what the structures were. This view derived from a 1959 study of language production by Howard Maclay and Charles Osgood, who analyzed the transcripts of a psycholinguistics conference and extracted all the pauses, disfluencies, hesitations, and repairs in the talks and discussions. Their characterization was assumed to be representative of all adult speech. This general argument has come to be known as "poverty of the stimulus" and has been used to support the view that children must therefore be innately endowed with certain kinds of linguistic knowledge.[2] But Maclay and Osgood recorded academics speaking at a conference, not adults talking to young children.

At the same time, sociolinguistic research showed that adults are attentive to their addressees and use different styles or registers accordingly. In general, speakers have control over a variety of different ways of talking – the way they talk to babies, to foreigners, to pets, and so on – and this varies with the addressee, the occasion, and even the topic under discussion. One question here, then, is whether adult-to-adult interchanges at a conference are comparable to exchanges between adults and infants, adults and two-year-olds, or even adults and five-year-olds. Mightn't their language be modified by the nature of their addressees, in particular their age and expertise, and even by the topics talked about? Since the way adults talk to each other depends on how well they know their addressees, their relationship to them, their relative ages, the social setting, and just what they are asking them to do, mightn't this hold just as strongly for adult speech to infants and young children? By looking at just how adults *do* speak to children, one can better assess the force of Chomsky's position versus the sociolinguistic position. It turns out that child-directed speech is often singularly well tailored to its addressees, highly grammatical in form, and virtually free of errors. This makes for a rather different picture of its role in acquisition and the extent to which it presents a plausible source from which to learn a first language.

Even if the language addressed to young children is tailored to their level of skill as speakers, is such tailoring necessary for them to learn a first language? Could they acquire it instead from simply overhearing utterances addressed to others? Could they learn a first language from listening to the radio or watching television? Or do they need to hear language in interactive exchanges? What is sufficient versus necessary exposure for the process of acquisition? (Even if adults do modify their speech in talking to less-skilled speakers, this in itself doesn't tell us whether such modifications are needed for acquisition.) The nature of the exposure, it turns out, is

---

[2] I return to these issues more directly in Part IV.

important for acquisition. Children appear to need exposure to language in inter-active contexts. Merely overhearing does not appear to promote acquisition.

When children make mistakes during the course of acquisition, do they need explicit corrections (feedback) to learn the appropriate forms for what they had intended to say? Here too researchers have taken different positions. Some have assumed that children receive no corrective feedback, so the fact that they do eventually learn the adult versions of things must be evidence for the innateness of (some aspects of) language. Others have argued that feedback can take a number of forms and pointed out that adults often restate what children say, thereby offering conventional forms for the intended meanings and that such indirect corrective information is just as important as explicit rejection of an error combined with a corrected rendition. If children can learn from indirect correction, there should be less need to appeal to innateness here. In short, claims about child-directed speech have theoretical implications for claims about both innateness and learning in language.

## Universal modifications?

This chapter begins by looking at what conversations with children are like, then takes up their most prominent structural characteristics and the prag-matic factors that motivate adult choices when they talk to young children. That child-directed speech differs systematically from adult-directed speech raises the question of whether the modifications adults make might be universal in those societies where adults talk to infants and young children. By modifying their language use, are adult speakers offering mini-language lessons? If so, are such lessons either necessary or sufficient? Are the effects of particular aspects of child-directed speech discernible in the patterns or rates of children's language acquisition? Or are adults simply concerned to make themselves understood as well as possible and to make their child-addressees understood too? What follows, for the process of acquisition, from this communicative goal? Do adult modifica-tions change with the age of the child-addressee? And under what circumstances do adults stop using them? These are some of the main questions that have been addressed in studies of child-directed speech.

## Holding a conversation

Participants in a conversation need to observe a number of general conditions if communication is to be effective:

- Speaker and addressee must share a joint focus of attention during the con-versational exchange and take account of common ground.
- Speakers must take account of what their addressees know and tailor their utterances accordingly.

- Speakers must choose speech acts that are appropriate for the meanings they intend to convey.
- Participants in a conversation must listen to what others say so they can each make appropriate, relevant contributions when they take a turn.

The first condition depends on joint attention, with both speaker and addressee attending to the same focus, whether an object or event, and each aware that the other is also attending (Moore & Dunham 1995). This joint attention enables subsequent communication by allowing for coordination between speaker and addressee. It also identifies some common ground both for a starting point in the subsequent exchange and for coordinating as each participant adds to that common ground with each contribution. In conversations with young children, adults anchor their conversational contributions to objects or events physically present on each occasion. That is, they rely on physical and conversational co-presence as they add to the common ground in the conversational exchange.

The second condition requires that speakers tailor their contributions to their addressees, taking into account what they know – and this will include what they know about communicating, with or without language – and designing their utterances so they will be understood. For the third condition, that speakers choose the appropriate speech acts for the meanings they wish to convey, they need to use the appropriate forms, for that community, when they wish to refer, request, assert, promise, and so on. Finally, the fourth condition requires the speaker to make sure the other has understood, and the addressee to listen and signal understanding, as the exchange proceeds. This allows the participants to ground each utterance (add it to the common ground on this occasion) and so further both local and general goals in a conversation (H. Clark 1996; Grice 1989).

This pragmatic management of coordination in conversation pervades exchanges with young children just as it does those with adults, and it provides the general framework for acquisition of a first language. Conversational exchanges between an infant and an adult may be minimal at first, in the sense that the adult participant may effectively supply all the turns, as in the "exchange" between three-month-old Ann and her mother (Snow 1977:12) in (1):

(1)        Mother and Ann (aged three months)
           ANN:      (smiles)
           MOTHER:   oh, what a nice little smile
                     yes, isn't that nice?
                     there
                     there's a nice little smile
           ANN:      (burps)
           MOTHER:   what a nice little wind as well
                     yes, that's better, isn't it?
                     yes
                     yes
           ANN:      (vocalizes)
           MOTHER:   there's a nice noise

## 2A  Daily routines in the first two years of life

(a) diaper or nappy changes in the first 24 months @ 6 per day = (365 × 6) × 2 = 4,380 (typical accompanying comments: "phew," "let me get this off you," "here we go," "now you're clean," "up with the feet," "lie still," etc.)

(b) naps and bedtimes in the first 24 months @ 2 per day = 365 × 4 = 1,460 (along with: "beddy-bye," "night-night," "in you go," "down you lie," "sleep tight," "tucking you in," etc.)

(c) mealtimes in the second year @ 3 per day = 365 × 3 = 1,095 (along with: "here's your bib," "upsy-daisy," "now get down," "do you want to get up?," "in you go," "another spoon," "here's the spoon," "one more," "let's wipe your mouth," "here's your cup," etc.)

(d) routine games and books with accompanying rhymes or routine utterances, several times a day in the first 24 months @ 5 per day = (365 × 5) × 2 = 3,650 (along with: "look," "here you are," "eensy-weensy spider," "peek-a-boo," "shall I tickle you?," "show me your nose," etc.)

Based on Ferrier 1978

As infants get older, parents raise the criterion for what counts as a contribution from their infants. At seven months, for example, this mother expected vocalizations and consonantal babble for Ann's turns and only continued talking herself after hearing such a contribution. By the time Ann was eighteen months old, her mother expected words (Snow 1977:18), as in (2):

(2)      Mother and Ann (aged 1;6)
         ANN:      (blowing noises)
         MOTHER:   that's a bit rude
         ANN:      *mouth*
         MOTHER:   mouth, that's right
         ANN:      *face*
         MOTHER:   face, yes, mouth is in your face
                   what else have you got in your face?
         ANN:      *face* (closing eyes)
         MOTHER:   you're making a face, aren't you?

At each age, the mother treats the infant's contributions as if they initiated an exchange and then responds to them accordingly.

   The range of topics in such exchanges tends to be rather small, so these exchanges have a highly repetitive flavor, not only when adults comment on repeated enactions of daily routines but also when infants themselves begin to contribute with more explicit content. The daily routines during the first two years of life and the stereotypical adult verbal routines that accompany them are both highly repetitive (Ferrier 1978) and very frequent, as estimated in Box 2A.

   The point is, adults (or, in many societies, older siblings) talk to babies, infants, and young children as they look after them, wash them, feed them, play with them, and carry them around. Much of the speech addressed to these babies consists of short, routine, repetitive utterances produced with great consistency and frequency in the same contexts, day after day. As babies get older and become able to do more on their own, these adult–child or sibling–child conversations encompass a growing range of topics, an ever more extensive vocabulary, and so a greater range of language uses.

Adults use language not only for talking about everyday activities and routines but also for regulating all kinds of behavior. They specify what children should say, how, and when across a range of social situations, from eating a meal at someone else's house to talking to a neighbor ("Say please"), dealing with a child who's taken away a toy ("You need to give it back"), or greeting a visitor or a relative; from thanking someone for a present to playing a game, reading a book ("Can you say *raisin*?"), petting an animal, taking turns on a swing ("You must take turns"), teasing, telling a joke, setting the table, or getting dressed ("Now your shoe"). Regulatory uses of language cover virtually every aspect of becoming socialized, of learning how to behave (see Berko Gleason, Perlman, & Greif 1984; Deffebach & Adamson 1994; Halle & Shatz 1994; Flynn & Masur 2007). Language is a primary vehicle for teaching children how to become members of a society.

Conversations become more elaborate as children understand more and take account of more uses of language. As this happens, children's turns come to contain more content, though the topics they raise may remain fairly limited for the first year or more of talking. These interactions are conversations, and they therefore place a special onus on the adult as the more skilled speaker. For instance, adult interlocutors have to monitor infant addressees with more care than they would six-year-olds or other adults to make sure the infants are attending to what is being talked about.

## Joint attention comes first

In a successful conversation, the two participants must agree on what is being talked about. One way to ensure this is to start with the same locus of attention. But how does one make a one- or two-year-old systematically attend to what one is saying? One solution is for the adult to monitor what the infant *is* attending to and then talk about that (or use that as a starting point for talk) (e.g., Colas 1999; Gogate, Bahrick, & Watson 2000; Schmidt 1996). Alternatively, the adult can *attract* the infant's attention to something, with verbal attention-getters ("Hey!", "Look!") and gaze (Estigarribia & Clark 2007). Indeed, by age one, infants have become quite good themselves at checking on the adult's gaze, stance, and physical orientation, and are as likely to track the adult's locus of attention as adults are to track theirs (Moore & Dunham 1995).

Adults rely first on perceptual information to establish joint attention. If speaker and addressee are attending to the same object or event (say, a toy train), they can both more readily assume that their shared focus of attention is what the speaker is talking about, as both will have the train in mind. In adult conversations, addressees check on what speakers are attending to and coordinate with them to achieve joint attention. But in conversations with young children, adult speakers often monitor what the children are attending to in order to achieve the necessary coordination (Barresi & Moore 1993; Butterworth & Jarrett 1991; Collis 1977; Murphy & Messer 1977; Stern 1977, 1985; Tomasello 1995; Trevarthen 1977). They rely on several perceptual cues in trying to establish joint attention with an infant or young child. They can follow the child's direction of gaze, so both adult and child can then see that the other is looking at the same thing; they can follow the child's pointing, so both adult and child can see that the other is also looking at the object being pointed at; and they can follow the child's body orientation towards something, so, again, both adult and child can see that the other is attending to the same thing (Clark 1997). And even young infants can track adult attention (Hood, Willen, & Driver 1998; Muir & Hains 1999).

Infants also become adept at actively soliciting adult attention. As young as six months of age, they co-opt adults as instruments to satisfy goals (Mosier & Rogoff 1994). By twelve months of age, they can get adults to open things, offer things that are out of the child's own reach, and attain a variety of goals they couldn't achieve on their own. In doing this, they first attract the adult's attention, then communicate what they want with combinations of gestures, vocalizations, and eventually words (Bates 1976; Carter 1978). In addition, as children get older, they attend more to adult intentions: monitoring of adult action and gaze emerges around twelve to eighteen months, along with explicit attempts to shift adult attention to what the infant wants (Leung & Rheingold 1981; Rheingold, Hay, & West 1976; Buresh & Woodward 2007).

Information about the speaker's locus of attention can provide essential information about the intended referent of an unfamiliar word. Baldwin (1991, 1993) presented infants under two with a new word in a situation where the infant played with one object while the adult looked at another as she named it. Unless they made use of the speaker's locus of attention, they could assign the word to the wrong referent. For instance, the adult speaker would focus on one object out of sight inside a bucket and produce an unfamiliar label ("A modi!") while the infant was attending to a different toy near at hand on the table. In these circumstances, infants, from sixteen months on, monitored the adult's locus of attention and so avoided unintended mappings for unfamiliar words. By age two, children can take account of repairs ("Uh-oh, it's not an *X*, it's a *Y*") and also distinguish intentional from unintentional actions ("Oops!") in assessing the speaker's intent (see Clark & Grossman 1998; Tomasello & Barton 1994; Tomasello & Kruger 1992).

Joint attention is supplemented by physical co-presence, the actual presence of the object or event at the locus of attention, and by conversational co-presence, the speaker's explicit reference to the target object or event. Together, these help ensure that speaker and addressee are talking about the same thing. With physical co-presence, the speaker talks about objects or events perceptually available to both speaker and addressee. With conversational co-presence, the speaker refers directly to the object or event that provides the topic of the exchange.

What evidence is there for reliance on physical and conversational co-presence in child-directed speech? First, adults rely heavily on the here and now in many of their exchanges with children. Talk about what is currently happening and about objects that are in use or in view for both adult and child helps ensure that each knows what the other is attending to and talking about. Emphasis on the here and now also limits the number of possible topics to what is physically present. This presumably makes it easier for both adult and child to track what the other is talking about.

Second, in the early stages of language acquisition, adults generally follow up on child-introduced topics rather than the reverse. A comparison of the average number of new topics introduced per hour of recording for one child, Eve, from 1;6 to 2;3, showed that her mother proposed about five new topics per hour to Eve's twenty (Moerk 1983). In effect, the child took the lead in initiating exchanges on new topics (see also Bloom, Margulis, Tinker, & Fujita 1996). And Eve's mother followed up on the topics her daughter introduced, expanding and commenting on what was already conversationally co-present.

Even very young children are persistent in their attempts to establish a new topic, trying a variety of means to get the adult to attend to the target object or event. In one exchange, Brenda (aged 1;8) produced her version of *bus* nine times in succession in an attempt to get her adult addressee to attend to a car going by outside. She had begun by saying *car* four times, which only elicited a "What?" of incomprehension; she then switched to the word *go* (twice), with no better success; and then she tried *bus*, only to have her interlocutor misidentify it as *bicycle*, which she rejected with *no* (Scollon 1976:109). But adults are often more successful, as in the exchange between Ann at 1;6 and her mother (Snow 1977:18–19) in (3):

(3)        Mother and Ann (aged 1;6)
           MOTHER (talking of Ann's nose):   don't know where it is.
           ANN:                              *Titus Titus.* [= cat]
           MOTHER:                           where, I can't see him.
                                             oh, there he is.
                                             yes, he's on the floor.
                                             Titus is …
           ANN (interrupting):               *floor.*
           MOTHER:                           floor.
           ANN:                              *floor.*
           MOTHER:                           yes, Titus is on the floor.

Participation in a conversation requires signs that one is following what the speaker is saying, ratification of what the speaker has said, and contributions of one's own – additions to the topic at hand. This typically results in taking turns. But what counts as a turn in conversations with infants or very young children? When adults take part in a conversation, they expect speaker and addressee to alternate in making contributions and so adding new information, or in ratifying what the other has contributed (Fisher & Tokura 1995; Clark & Bernicot 2008).

Each turn is generally acknowledged by the other participant(s) in some way before the current speaker continues. Acknowledgements may take the form of an "uh-huh" or a head nod, or they may involve more extensive exchanges ("Did you mean *X* or *Y*?" or "That's which *X*?"), or even a full response to a question or request. So what happens in exchanges with babies or one-year-olds?

As we saw in the exchange between three-month-old Ann and her mother, turns are imposed on very young participants. An adult talking to a two- or three-month-old will count a burp, a smile, or a leg kick as a turn; in fact, adults typically say something, then wait for the baby to do something, and then resume talking. But as babies get older and extend their repertoire of actions, adults tend to up the ante. A four- or five-month-old must smile or kick; a six- or seven-month-old must vocalize; an eight- to ten-month-old must babble. That is, adults wait for an appropriate level of reaction before going on talking. Once infants begin to produce their first words, adults raise their expectations still further: now only a word (or perhaps a babble sequence) will do.

As infants begin to make more of a linguistic contribution to what is going on in the interaction, adults ask for more and more explicit expression of the meanings intended. Compare the two exchanges between Richard and his mother while looking at a book, the first in (4), when Richard was 1;1.1, the second in (5), some months later, when he was 1;11 (Bruner 1983:78, 86):

(4)     MOTHER:  Look!
        RICHARD (touches pictures)
        MOTHER:  What are those?
        RICHARD (vocalizes a babble string and smiles)
        MOTHER:  Yes, there are rabbits.
        RICHARD (vocalizes, smiles, looks up at mother)
        MOTHER:  (laughs) Yes, rabbit.
        RICHARD (vocalizes, smiles)
        MOTHER:  Yes. (laughs)

In this exchange, Richard's linguistic contributions are minimal, yet his actions – touching the picture, vocalizing, looking at his mother, smiling – are clearly appropriate to the interaction and are treated as turns. Ten months later, Richard's turns contain identifiable content, as he and his mother actively negotiate over what to call the animals in the picture they are looking at:

(5)     MOTHER:  What's that?
        RICHARD:  *'ouse.*
        MOTHER:  Mouse, yes. That's a mouse.
        RICHARD:  *More mouse.* (pointing at another picture)
        MOTHER:  No, those are squirrels. They're like mice but
                 with long tails. Sort of.
        RICHARD:  *Mouse, mouse, mouse.*
        MOTHER:  Yes, all right, they're mice.
        RICHARD:  *Mice, mice.*

As children learn to make relevant contributions, they become more skilled at taking turns, at acknowledging the contributions of others, and at ratifying them. They learn when and how to make their contributions in relation to other speakers, and how and when to acknowledge the information offered by another. Acknowledgements can take the form of no more than an "uh-huh" or a head nod, or they might involve something more extensive ("Did you mean $X$ or $Y$?" or "Which $X$?"), even a full clarification question, or the supplying of some requested information. The general notion of reciprocity and alternation seems to be established early through a variety of interchange types in "exchange games," notably games of give-and-take and peek-a-boo that emerge around nine months of age (e.g., Rheingold, Hay, & West 1976). The content of the child's turn needs to be pertinent to the topic that has been established. This is probably easier for children when they themselves have initiated the topic than when the adult has done so. Yet even two-year-olds will interrupt exchanges between their parents and older siblings with pertinent comments (Dunn & Shatz 1989). Remember that, from about age two on, more conversational exchanges are initiated by children than by adults, so children more often choose the topics that get talked about.

In summary, the give-and-take of conversation is imposed on babies and young children, as if to show them from the start how to be a partner in such exchanges. Then, as infants become able to make more of a contribution to what is going on, adults ask for more explicit expressions of the meanings intended. Children who begin with gestures and minimal vocalizations gradually approach conventional forms of expression, such as *look*, *that*, or terms for object categories, such as *dog*, as they get older (e.g., Carter 1978, 1979). In effect, children become more and more skilled as conversationalists.

How soon can we be sure that children are intent not just on achieving some goal but also on making sure their addressees have understood them? In many cases, the evidence is difficult to evaluate, and some researchers have concluded that young children have conversational goals but do not necessarily take account of what their addressees do or don't understand (Shatz 1983). Others have argued that even nonverbal infants are intent on making others understand. Golinkoff (1986), for instance, argued that infants initiating negotiations, rejecting incorrect interpretations of their nonverbal signals, and creatively repairing failed signals all suggest they are trying to make themselves understood to others (see also Marcos 1991; Marcos & Kornhaber-Le Chanu 1992). Others have argued that these actions can be explained by infants wanting to change someone's behavior rather than by their wanting to make the adult understand them (Shatz & O'Reilly 1990).

If children are intent on achieving understanding in addition to their expressed goals, they should repair misunderstandings whether or not they achieve their goals. Shwe and Markman (1997) therefore looked at the repairs and clarifications made by two-and-half-year-olds when they either did or didn't get a toy they wanted, and where they had either been understood or misunderstood. They reasoned that if children clarified their requests more when misunderstood than when understood, even if they had got the toy, this would be evidence that they were taking account of the addressee's comprehension over and above their specific goal. Overall, the two-year-olds repeated the term for the toy they had requested more often when the experimenter expressed misunderstanding than when she expressed understanding; and they verbally rejected the toy they were given more often when she misunderstood than when she understood. As expected, they never repeated their request when the experimenter understood them and they got the toy they wanted. They repeated at a relatively low rate when she expressed understanding but didn't give them the desired object. But when she expressed misunderstanding, they persisted in clarifying what they'd wanted more often when they got the right toy than when they got the wrong one. So these children offer clear evidence that they care – not just about the goal but about communicating their intentions.

This concern for communication also leads two-year-olds to modify their requests in accord with what their mothers already know. Consider how two-year-olds asked their mothers for help in retrieving an object out of reach under two different conditions: In one, the mother had seen where the object was placed; in the other, the mother hadn't seen this because she was outside the room or had her eyes covered (O'Neill 1996). They labeled the object, labeled its location, and gestured to its location significantly more often when the mother hadn't seen where it was put than when she had seen this. This tailoring of utterances to what the mothers knew offers further evidence that two-year-olds are intent on communication when achieving their goals. If the goal alone had been paramount, they should always have offered all possible information about the target object and its location, but they didn't. They made use of what they knew the other person did or didn't know (see also Ganea & Saylor 2007).

## Child-directed speech

What structural characteristics distinguish child-directed speech from adult-to-adult conversation? And, to what degree do the modifications that speakers make stem from their attempts to make themselves understood to less-skilled users of the language? If adult modifications depend on reactions and responses from their addressees, those modifications should change as child-addressees become able to provide increasingly appropriate responses and evidence that they have understood. And the modifications offered to one- and two-year-olds would presumably no longer be offered to five- or six-year-olds, since older children would be more likely to understand what is said to them.

### Pitch and intonation

When adults talk to young children, in many languages they appear to favor higher pitch and to use exaggerated-sounding intonation contours. Effectively, they may double the range for intonation – in English from about three-quarters

Table 2.1 *Mean fundamental frequency of adult speech*

| Addressees | Mean fundamental frequency (Hz) |
|---|---|
| Group 1: speech to 2-yr.-olds | 267 |
| Group 1: speech to adults | 198 |
| Group 2: speech to 5-yr.-olds | 206 |
| Group 2: speech to adults | 203 |

*Source*: Garnica 1977:73. Used with permission from Cambridge University Press.

of an octave to one-and-a-half octaves – and produce higher intonational peaks with steeper rises and falls. This gives the effect of exaggerated intonation patterns. Acoustic investigations of infant-directed speech have shown that it typically displays higher overall pitch, wider and smoother pitch excursions in intonation contours, slower tempo, greater rhythmicity, longer pauses between utterances, and greater amplitude than adult-directed speech (e.g., Fernald *et al.* 1989; Grieser & Kuhl 1988).

Do infants pay greater attention to speech with such characteristics? The answer appears to be yes: They show a clear preference for it, from an early age, over adult-directed speech (e.g., Fernald 1985; Panneton Cooper & Aslin 1990; Werker, Pegg, & McLeod 1994; see also Zangl & Mills 2007). Are they attentive to the higher pitch? To the slower tempo? To the more extensive pitch excursions? In studies designed to find out whether infants were attending to the pitch, amplitude, or durational effects in adult-to-infant speech, Fernald and Kuhl (1987) gave infants resynthesized versions of speech to listen to. They found a preference for adult-to-infant speech only when the infants listened to the fundamental frequency "envelopes" of the two types of speech (adult-to-infant vs. adult-to-adult). Infants appear to be more attentive to very high pitch in speech, and the younger they are, the more attentive they are (Werker & McLeod 1989). But high pitch alone can't account for infants' attention since, in some languages, it does not occur in infant-directed speech (Bernstein-Ratner & Pye 1984). Other factors must also play a role here, such as the deliberate use of all sorts of communicative devices to attract and hold infant attention through facial expression, eye contact, touching, pointing, and so on (Stern *et al.* 1983; Werker, Pegg, & McLeod 1994).

Adults continue to use higher pitch with young children. In one study of English speakers, for instance, when adults were recorded talking to two-year-olds versus other adults, they used higher pitch to the two-year-olds than they did to the adults, across a range of speech activities. A second group of adults showed little difference in the fundamental frequency they used to five-year-olds versus adults (Table 2.1).

Why use higher fundamental pitch in speaking to younger children? When four-month-old infants are given the choice of listening to infant-directed speech (higher pitched) versus adult-directed speech, they show a clear preference for the infant-directed speech in that they prefer to listen to the higher-pitched utterances

Table 2.2 *Pitch ranges in adult speech*

| Addressees | Narrowest range (semitones) | Widest range (semitones) |
|---|---|---|
| Group 1: speech to 2-yr.-olds | 14 | 23 |
| Group 1: speech to adults | 6 | 13 |
| Group 2: speech to 5-yr.-olds | 11 | 16 |
| Group 2: speech to adults | 7 | 13 |

*Source*: Garnica 1977:75. Used with permission from Cambridge University Press.

(DeCasper & Fifer 1980). This suggests that sensitivity to higher pitch makes infants more attentive when they hear relatively higher voice pitch. This then allows pitch to act as an attention-getter for infants and young children. As Fernald (1989) pointed out, higher pitch may also distinguish speech directed to the infant from other background talk and noise by making that speech more audible.

The adult speakers in Garnica's (1977) study distinguished both two- and five-year-olds from adults in that they used a wider pitch range (the distance from low to high point in pitch), measured in semitones, to both groups of children than they did to other adults. Their intonation with children was more exaggerated than with adults. In fact, the narrowest range in speech to children was typically the same as the widest range in their speech to adults (Table 2.2). This perhaps is where children begin to learn what the intonational system is for their language, by learning "some of the meanings of the adult intonation system," for example, which contours signal questions and which signal assertions (Cruttenden 1994:145). Exaggerated intonation contours also attract attention by distinguishing adult speech to children from other types of conversation (and addressees).

### Rate, pausing, and fluency

The steep rises and falls in intonation might also mark phrase- or clause-boundaries, along with pauses. Broen (1972), for example, analyzed the locations of pauses in mothers' speech to their two-year-olds and five-year-olds compared to conversation with other adults and found that between 75% and 83% of pauses in speech to the children occurred after terminal contours at the ends of sentences (that is, final falling intonation contours), compared to only 51% of the pauses in conversation with adults. This difference was even more striking when she looked at the sentence-boundaries followed by pauses. In talking to their two-year-olds, mothers paused at the ends of sentences 93% of the time; with their five-year-olds, they paused 76% of the time, and with adults, they paused only 29% of the time. The pauses in speech to young children are consistently longer than the analogous pauses in adult-to-adult speech (Fernald & Simon 1984). The combination of falling intonation and a pause, then, marks the ends of utterances in a highly reliable fashion in speech to young children and so provides clear information about boundaries, both for the utterances as a whole and for the final words in those utterances.

Table 2.3 *Words per minute in speech to children versus adults*

| Addressee (age) | Free play | Storytelling | Conversation |
|---|---|---|---|
| 2;3–3;5 | 69 | 115 | – |
| 3;10–5;10 | 86 | 128 | – |
| Adults | – | – | 132.4 |

*Source*: Broen 1972:6. From Broen, Patricia A. 1972. The verbal environment of the language-learning child. *Monograph of the American Speech & Hearing Association* 17. © American Speech-Language-Hearing Association. Reprinted by permission.

Utterance-final position is salient to infants for another reason as well. In speech directed at infants and young children, adult speakers consistently lengthen the vowels of words they wish children to attend to. Adults talking to two-year-olds typically lengthen the stressed syllables in words they want children to attend to, for instance, when solving a puzzle, but they do this much less in talking to five-year-olds or to adults (Garnica 1977). In another study that compared infant- and adult-directed speech, adult speakers (mothers) were asked to label seven objects when speaking either to the experimenter or to their infant. The target words directed at the infants were both higher pitched and had greater syllable-lengthening than the analogous adult-directed speech (Albin & Echols 1996). Stretching out words as well as raising the pitch both seem to be designed to attract the young addressee's attention. In fact, two-year-olds appear to make use of all these cues as they interpret what adults are saying (Shady & Gerken 1999).

Adults generally speak more slowly to young children than to older ones or to adults. In her detailed study of parental speech, Broen found consistent differences in the number of words per minute in the same mothers' speech to two-year-olds and five-year-olds, in both free-play and storytelling, compared to speech to adults (Table 2.3). (Some of the features of slow speech also show up in the overly careful articulation adults use in human–computer interactions when people are trying to make a computer recognize words (e.g., Oviatt *et al.* 1998).)

The slower rate to young children is achieved through pauses rather than stretched out words. That is, adults pronounce individual words at the same speed as in adult-directed speech, but they insert more pauses (at sentence- and phrase-boundaries) in their speech to younger children. Overall, adults use fewer than four words per utterance to two-year-olds compared to over eight words per utterance to adults (Phillips 1973). The shorter sentences used to two-year-olds are also simpler in structure than those used to older children or adults. For example, Sachs, Brown, & Salerno (1976) found that adults used simpler constructions in telling a story to a two-year-old than to another adult. To the child, they used only a few coordinate and subordinate clauses (introduced by *and, when, if,* or *because*) and hardly any relative clauses (e.g., *The dog that I patted ran away*), complements (*He wants to climb up*), or negations (*They didn't come*).

Table 2.4 *Mean number of disfluencies per one hundred words*

| Addressee (age) | Free play | Storytelling | Conversation |
|---|---|---|---|
| 2;3–3;5 | 0.58 | 0.66 | – |
| 3;10–5;10 | 1.61 | 0.77 | – |
| Adults | – | – | 4.70 |

*Source*: Broen 1972:11. From Broen, Patricia A. 1972. The verbal environment of the language-learning child. *Monograph of the American Speech & Hearing Association* 17. © American Speech-Language-Hearing Association. Reprinted by permission.

Adults are also much more fluent when they talk to young children than when they talk to other adults. They produce many fewer false starts, mispronunciations, or hesitations – about one-ninth of the rate in their speech to adults (Table 2.4).

### Repetitiousness

Adults also repeat themselves a lot in talking to young addressees. One reason is that they rely heavily on a small number of constructions that combine a small "sentence frame" with a noun phrase or a nominal. Some typical examples are listed in (6):

(6)　　Construction　　　　Example
　　　Where's NP?　　　　Where's Daddy?
　　　Here's NP　　　　　Here's (the) kitty
　　　Look at NP　　　　Look at (the) doggie
　　　That's a N　　　　　That's a ball
　　　Here comes NP　　　Here comes Danny
　　　Let's play with NP　Let's play with the blocks

Adults use constructions like these to introduce new words and often produce them with an exaggerated intonation contour and heavy stress on the new word in final position (Broen 1972; Ferguson, Peizer, & Weeks 1973; Clark & Wong 2002). At times they make use of question–answer pairs, both spoken by the adult, as in "Where's the ball? Here's the ball." These adjacency pairs, normally produced across a pair of speakers, are quite frequent. Children soon learn their part, the kind of response needed after the adult produces the first part of such a pair. For example, they respond to *How many*-questions with a number, as in "How many frogs do you see?" – "Two" (regardless of the actual number depicted), or to *What colour*-questions with a colour term, as in "What colour is your ball?" – "Red" (even if it isn't). That is, children learn the appropriate kind of response before they have fixed the reference for terms such as *two* or *red* (Clark 2006; Clark & Nikitina 2009).

Adults also repeat themselves with small variations when they ask young children to do things, as in (7). Repetitions like this in English are three times more frequent in speech to two-year-olds than in speech to ten-year-olds (Snow 1972; see also Shatz 1978a, 1978b).

(7)          ADULT (trying to get a two-year-old to pick up some blocks): Pick up the red one.
             Find the red one. Not the green one. I want the red one. Can you find the red one?

In highly inflected languages like Turkish or Finnish, adults often rely on variation sets, utterances with much the same semantic content and intent, as in (7), but with extensive changes in word order from one utterance to the next. Küntay and Slobin (1996) argued that such variations help children identify the stable elements like verbs that recur from one utterance to the next, and so could offer important information for identifying chunks as words (see also Bowerman 1973a).

In summary, adults consistently produce shorter utterances to younger addressees, pause at the ends of their utterances around 90% of the time (50% in speech to adults), speak much more fluently, and frequently repeat whole phrases and utterances when they talk to younger children. They also use higher than normal pitch to infants and young children, and they exaggerate the intonation contours so that the rises and falls are steeper over a larger range (up to one-and-a-half octaves in English). The grammaticality, fluency, and simplicity of the language addressed to young children shows that earlier assumptions about child-directed speech were simply wrong.

Adults streamline their delivery when they speak to young children, and they appear to do this more the younger the child, with the most careful delivery directed at children just starting to speak. This streamlining may be attributable in part to the greater ease of planning and producing really short utterances. This would also account for the relative absence of speech errors in child-directed speech compared to adult-to-adult speech (Broen 1972).

While this summary captures some of the main structural characteristics that have been observed in speech directed to young children in various Western societies, it does not consider all the modifications adults make, nor why they might make them when and how they do. We turn next, therefore, to some of the main functions that adult modifications seem to serve.

## Functions of child-directed speech

Why do adults speak to infants and young children differently from other adults? What motivates the modifications they make? I will argue here that their modifications help speakers get and keep their addressees' attention. These addressees are young and unskilled as speakers, and have only a limited know-ledge of the language around them. The changes adults make in how they talk seem designed to ease their communication with such addressees. First, they need to make sure they and their addressees are attending to the same objects or events, that there is joint attention on the target topic, so they can then direct it to the relevant event. To do this, they use devices to signal that that addressee and no one else is the intended addressee: They use a vocative (the child's name) or an endearment (*Sweetheart!*); they use a deictic term as a summons (*Here! Look! See!*); and they mark their utterance with higher than normal pitch, for example, to distinguish it from utterances that might be designed for other addressees.

Getting the addressee's attention is the first step. The next is holding it. To do this, speakers seem to focus on getting the child-addressee to attend to the message being communicated. They maintain high pitch and exaggerated intonation, often repeat themselves, with alternative formulations of the same content, presumably all in an effort to keep the child's attention on the intended interpretation.

To make themselves understood, adults have to go further still. They have to tailor their utterances to what their child-addressees can understand. They have to choose appropriate words and present them in such a way that the child can identify them in the speech stream. For the infant or very young child, this may be done best by presenting the target terms at the ends of short utterances or in frames where they are perceptually salient, readily recognized, and so more easily understood. The words chosen should be appropriate to and useful for the specific distinctions being made. Initially, this might mean relying on a small number of baby-talk words (e.g., *bye-bye, night-night, upsy-daisy; kitty, doggy, woof-woof*) or words that are among the first words children attempt themselves. A little later, this may mean choosing words that are at the requisite level of utility (Brown 1958a) for the distinctions required, for example choosing the term *fruit* or *apple*, depending on the context of the offer. On each occasion, the joint attention shared by speaker and addressee will help the child identify the intended target of the adult speaker's utterance, while physical co-presence (talking about objects or events in the here and now) and conversational co-presence (using familiar words for the target information) provide further help for the child in zeroing in on what the adult means. Young children often initiate conversations, and when this happens, adults must work out the locus of the child's attention and then use joint attention along with physical and linguistic co-presence to discern the child's meaning.

Effectively, adults check up on what children have said with clarification questions, with prompts for pronunciation or the provision of further information, presentations of the conventional way of saying things (having made any repairs needed to word order, inflections, agreement, and word-choice), and expansions on what the child has just offered. When they expand, they add further facts (and the words for them) about activities, properties, states, and relations; they bring in nearby objects and events; they compare the present object or event with nearby relations; and they express different affective attitudes. In making sure children can make themselves understood, adult speakers make explicit corrections of pronunciation and of word-choice. Where children make themselves understood but use erroneous forms, adults offer a plethora of tacit corrections, with almost involuntary repeats as they reformulate, in conventional terms, what the child seemed to have said, and so offer children new versions said in the way an adult would have said them (Chouinard & Clark 2003).

In short, adults seem to be concerned with making themselves understood to young children and with making sure that the children, in turn, can make themselves understood to others. They correct uses of forms and meanings, offer conventional ways of saying things, and provide a stream of additional facts and pieces of information about the topics children raise.

## What role does child-directed speech play in acquisition?

Adults may adjust their speech to the perceived needs of their addressees, but that does not necessarily mean that such adjustments are necessary for acquisition. The range of adjustments made and the fact that they change with the age and linguistic sophistication of child-addressees suggests a number of possible roles for child-directed speech.

Are adult adjustments intended as language lessons? Do they reflect tacit efforts to teach children their first language? Many of the things that adults present children with tell them how to use language in various circumstances, for various purposes. Child-directed speech offers potential lessons in how to take turns and in what to say when. It also offers extensive information about how words map onto the world – information on how to talk about different situations, which words to use for what. But adults don't talk to young children to teach them language. Potential language lessons are simply a side-product of the adult concern with being understood. Parents, other adults, and older siblings don't set out to teach young children language; they set out to make themselves understood to these young and rather unskilled users of language. The modifications they make to promote better comprehension have the incidental effect of also providing children with information about language structure and function. And since the adjustments adults make are guided mainly by how much comprehension children display, they tend to keep pace with development. That is, as children offer more evidence of understanding, older speakers make fewer modifications in how they speak to them.

A rather different view is that how adults modify their speech in talking to young children is irrelevant to acquisition. All that children need is exposure to the sounds and sound patterns, and to the mappings of meanings onto forms. Given that exposure, they simply follow their own course, with development of syntactic structure unfolding as a matter of maturation (Radford 1990). That is, the structures are innate rather than learned. Children, under this view, are not sensitive to details of child-directed speech (factors such as the frequency of different word orders, choices of ways to talk about motion, manner, and location). Adult speech simply serves as a general source of information to which children need exposure in much the same way that ducklings need exposure to a moving object (ideally a mother duck) to imprint upon it at the appropriate stage of development.

This account, though, is not maintainable. Although experiments on this topic would be hard to devise, several naturalistic settings offer us a look at what happens, or fails to happen, when the speech children are exposed to lacks social, interactional properties. The hearing children of deaf parents who sign, for example, hear very little spoken language from older speakers until they enter nursery school. One parental solution to this was to turn on the radio and television as much as possible. Sachs and Johnson (1976; Sachs, Bard, & Johnson 1981) studied one child who received such exposure to spoken English. At the age of 3;9, Jim had only a very small vocabulary, possibly picked up from a few playmates, plus a few words from television jingles.[3] While he did produce some multiword utterances using English words, he did not use English word order (e.g., *I want that make*, *Off my mittens*), and he omitted word-endings (plural *-s*, past tense *-ed*) that three-year-olds would normally have already acquired. His language was far behind other children of his age. Although he had overheard a great deal of spoken English, he had had very little direct interaction where he used any spoken language with another person. Once he spoke with a hearing adult regularly, his language developed rapidly. Sachs and her colleagues concluded that simple exposure early on to language intended for others won't necessarily help children acquire a first language.

Another natural experiment in acquisition occurs when children speaking one language are exposed to a second via television. Such children appear not to learn much or even any of the second language even after daily exposure. For example, Dutch children who watch *Sesame Street* in German do not appear to learn any German from it (Snow *et al.* 1976), even though this is a program designed for children. Because it is something to be watched, it lacks the direct interactive properties of language used for face-to-face communication.

Whether on the radio or on television, the language heard can rarely be matched to situations that form a joint focus of attention for the speaker and the child, and little of such speech focusses on objects or events that are physically and con-versationally co-present. It therefore offers little help to very young children in mapping meanings onto forms. In addition, the stream of speech may be harder to segment under such circumstances: All children can hear is rapid speech that hasn't been tailored to them in any way. Finally, of course, exposure to radio or television does not require that the child participate in any exchange: The talk all goes one way, so the child is merely an overhearer. Overheard speech from radio and television is not social in the ways that child-directed speech is, so it should not be surprising if it is therefore more difficult for young children to make use of.

At the same time, children are often active participants in one sense as they watch programs such as *Sesame Street* or *Teletubbies*: They rarely watch TV on their own; they normally watch with a parent or caretaker and talk about what is happening with that person (Naigles & Mayeux 2000). This makes what is visible on the TV screen the focus of their joint attention. It is physically co-present and now becomes conversationally co-present as well. And while there is little evidence that children learn any grammatical structures from TV watching, they may well learn some new words from exposure to TV. Rice and her colleagues (1990) compared children's vocabulary scores on the Peabody Vocabulary test with the amount of *Sesame Street* they had watched over a two-year period and found that children who had watched more made greater gains in vocabulary. However, there was no direct link between

---

[3] This child received relatively little exposure to the American Sign Language used by his parents because they thought he should learn to talk since he had normal hearing (Sachs, Bard, & Johnson 1981).

words used frequently on the TV program and words actually acquired. Children over three or so may well pick up some new words from exposure to TV, and the greater their knowledge of language, the more likely this becomes. (Adults do this too.) But the findings so far further suggest that it is social interaction that is essential in the earlier stages of acquisition proper.

### Participating in conversation

In summary, learning a language requires proficient use for all sorts of everyday purposes – from greetings to gossip, from simple requests at the table to the telling of a joke, from giving instructions to telling a story. To do any of these things requires knowing *how* to use one's language. One has to know the appropriate ways to address others, depending on age, sex, relationship, and status; one has to know how to get the other's attention, how to take turns, and how to talk about the topic in question in that language. These are all skills on constant display in conversation, and it seems reasonable to suppose that children acquire these skills from conversation. In effect, they have conversation imposed upon them and must learn how to participate in it if they wish to communicate with greater detail and precision.

Conversation provides the primary setting for language acquisition, and it is in conversational settings that children display their emerging knowledge together with their skill in using a language (see Part III). Conversations with adults offer children information about word forms and word meanings, about constructions, and about conventional usage. So any language lessons children receive are lessons in language use rather than in language structure. These "lessons" converge on Grice's (1989) Cooperative Principle: Speakers try to be informative, truthful, relevant, and clear in their contributions to a conversation, and their addressees interpret what they say on the assumption that speakers are trying to follow these principles.

In becoming participants in conversation, children need to know how to engage in this joint activity, how to contribute, and how to take turns. They must also know which utterances are intended for them and which for others. Adults and older speakers help by calling for children's attention with a range of attention-getters. Children adopt the same strategy to make sure of their addressees' attention: They may begin by tugging at clothes, touching the parent's face, or even turning it so there is eye contact first, before they begin speaking. Later, they preface their contributions with vocatives or a general *You know what?* as a signal that they are about to make a contribution (Garvey 1975; McTear 1985). Long before this, of course, they had as infants been induced to take turns by the imposition of a turn-taking structure upon all sorts of nonlinguistic acts – burps, sighs, smiles, blinks, and arm or leg movements (Snow 1977).

Parents appear to monitor child usage, frequently repeating with repairs what their child said, retaining the child's word order for content words but placing them in a conventional construction for the meaning the child appears to be aiming for.[4] Adults repeat and repair significantly more often for erroneous than for conventional utterances, but expand for both (Chouinard & Clark 2003; Hirsh-Pasek, Treiman, & Schneiderman 1984).

Conversations serve to introduce new words in many conceptual domains. The here-and-now nature of many conversations with young children helps guarantee joint attention along with physical and linguistic co-presence. (It also helps adults interpret what young children are likely to be saying.) This allows children to make maximum use of contextual cues in assigning an interpretation to unfamiliar words and constructions. On hearing "Can you shut the door?" the one-and-a-half-year-old may only know the word *door*, but when interpreting the adult's request in context, there are only a few options possible. Shutting the door may be the most obvious course (Shatz 1983). This action, if accepted, offers a possible meaning for *shut* for the next time. The same holds for *open* used in a similar context. Children can put together words like *door*, *handle*, *open*, *shut*, *go in*, and *go out*, linked by the uses they hear in specific contexts.

Finally, the structural modifications adults make to young children provide information about how to segment speech. They identify boundaries when they speak more slowly, pause at the ends of utterances (after a word, phrase, or whole clause), make frequent use of frames, and offer frequent repetitions (Shady & Gerken 1999). These techniques for getting information over to less-skilled participants all help children find the edges of words and morphemes in the stream of speech.

## Pragmatic directions about language

Parents offer children pragmatic directions about language use as they talk to them. Aside from giving them general information about when to talk and when to keep quiet, they tell them about how to talk, when, to whom, and what to say on particular occasions – how to greet, to thank, to apologize, to congratulate, to request, to assert, and so on. They give directions on how to be polite (and how polite to be), how to address people, how to behave and just what to say on occasions like birthday parties or Halloween. As they do this, they are simultaneously telling children how to represent the world around them in this particular language. They tell them what things are called and also how objects and events are related to each other (Clark & Wong 2002; Berko Gleason 1988; Berko Gleason *et al.* 1984).

Adults offer children information about words in the language they are acquiring. In particular, they offer the conventional terms for the objects and events that provide the focus of attention on different occasions. These offers may be direct in form (e.g., "This is a *Z*," "That's called a *Y*"), or they may be indirect in that they

---

[4] It's possible there is an element of hit-or-miss here since the adult's interpretations of the child's intentions may be off, because the child's form of expression or pronunciation of the target words is still so far from the adult versions (see also Braine 1971). For example, a child in a high-chair who has just dropped a cup and says *Down cup* could be construed as saying 'I just dropped my cup' or, alternatively, 'I want to get down to get my cup back'. But adult repeats that miss the child's intended meaning are typically rejected on the spot.

occur as corrections or repairs to whatever the child has proposed. The adult in such cases replaces the term the child has proposed by another more appropriate one, and the child often takes this up in the next turn (Clark 2002b, 2007; Clark & Wong 2002; Jefferson 1982). Such offers of conventional terms for the objects or events in question are important for children as they try to work out just what meaning is carried by each form they have isolated or been offered.

Linking a form and a meaning requires also coming to understand both how that combination differs from its neighbors and how it is related to other terms in the same semantic domain. Consider terms like *owl*, *duck*, and *chicken*, or *dance*, *hop*, and *jump*: Just what properties distinguish one from the other? And what makes the terms in each set belong together? Adults often offer very young children explicit information about what distinguishes one term from another – for instance, they may identify one or more properties that distinguish the referents: Sound or shape can distinguish a duck from an owl (e.g., quacking versus hooting); type and speed of motion can distinguish dancing from jumping (e.g., Callanan 1990; Clark 2002a, 2007; Clark & Wong 2002; Gelman *et al*. 1998a).

Adults also tell children in the course of conversation how words are related to each other. They may indicate this by listing two or more terms from the same semantic domain, such as *big* and *wide*, for instance, or they may elaborate on descriptions of properties or relations to indicate this, as in "Little tiny pieces; not too big" (Rogers 1978). They may offer information about set inclusion or membership, as in "Seal is a kind of animal"; about properties or substance, as in "That's a street made out of stones"; about parts, as in "Those are his ears"; or about function, as in "That's a knife for cutting chicken" (see Callanan 1985, 1989; Clark & Grossman 1998; Clark & Wong 2002).[5]

Lastly, adults don't just offer children the conventional words for things; they also display for children the conventional way to do all sorts of things with words. They do this, of course, just by talking to children and using the language of the community. But they go further when they check up on just what their children have said, and such checking occurs frequently in conversation when children make errors. When adult interlocutors do this, they reformulate erroneous child utterances to check on their intended meanings (e.g., a child's "at zoo" reformulated as "at the zoo?"), and in reformulating, adults offer conventional versions, without errors, of what the children appeared to intend (Chouinard & Clark 2003; see also Clark & Bernicot 2008). These reformulations effectively offer children corrective information about their errors. If children did not get any corrections of errors, it has been assumed, they would be unable to learn the morphology or syntax of their language (Marcus 1993; Morgan & Travis 1989). But since they do learn them, they must have some innate knowledge they can call on instead. But children do in fact get corrective information about errors (phonological, morphological, lexical, and syntactic), so it is perhaps unnecessary to claim reliance on innate knowledge of linguistic categories on this score (see Part IV).

---

[5] These offers are considered further in relation to how children acquire meaning in Chapters 4 and 6.

## Social class

Language use varies with social class, with socioeconomic status (SES). What effects might this factor have on children's acquisition? Do adults from different SES levels speak differently to small children, in terms of quality – the kinds of things they say, or quantity – the amount they say?

SES is measured by years of formal education (completion of high school, junior college, undergraduate degree, advanced degree), type of job (car mechanic, bank teller, nurse, teacher, doctor), and earned income. In one early look at social class in language acquisition, Snow and her colleagues (1976) recorded the speech of lower, lower-middle, and upper-middle SES parents to two-year-olds in two settings, reading and free play, and found few differences. Both lower-middle and upper-middle SES mothers used more deictic expressions (e.g., *this*, *that*, *here*) than lower SES ones in free play. Upper-middle SES mothers produced more *wh-* questions and fewer *yes/no* questions than the other two groups. Lower SES mothers used more imperatives than either of the other two groups. The higher the social standing, in other words, the less direct the speech, even to two-year-olds. This finding has shown up in several subsequent studies with possible consequences for acquisition. Newport, Gleitman, and Gleitman (1977), for instance, noted that the number of parental imperatives was negatively correlated with children's subsequent development of verb-phrase and noun-phrase complexity, while uses of deixis were positively related to vocabulary growth and children's later development of noun-phrase constructions.

When researchers compared four settings (mealtimes, dressing, toy play, and reading), they found several differences in how lower versus middle SES mothers talked to their children (e.g., in rate of speech, number of different word-roots, mean length of utterance). But Hoff-Ginsberg (1991) found only two differences related to SES: (a) middle SES mothers were more likely to pursue a topic when a child took it up than low SES mothers; (b) low SES mothers used more directives to control their children's behavior than middle SES ones (see also Miller 1982). The measures for topic continuation and directive use are summarized in Table 2.5.

Table 2.5 *Social class and child-directed speech*

| Measure | Mealtime | Dressing | Toy play | Reading |
|---|---|---|---|---|
| Topic continuers | | | | |
|   Low SES | 35 | 38 | 31 | 44 |
|   Middle SES | 42 | 45 | 38 | 51 |
| Directives | | | | |
|   Low SES | 24 | 24 | 26 | 16 |
|   Middle SES | 13 | 15 | 20 | 15 |

*Source*: Hoff-Ginsberg 1991:791. Used with permission from the Society for Research in Child Development.

In short, middle SES parents followed up on topics in their conversations more than low SES parents did, and low SES parents issued more orders for what to do and how to behave to their children than middle SES ones did.

The negative relation with parental prohibitions and the positive one with parental expansions of topics are consistently associated with SES.[6] In lower SES families, Hoff-Ginsberg found that up to 20% of parental utterances prohibited child activities. Such prohibitions were much less common in middle SES families where children heard many questions (up to 45% of parental utterances) and more frequent elaborations of topics (see also Heath 1983; Hoff-Ginsberg & Tardif 1995; Wells 1985). Hoff-Ginsberg also concluded that outcomes for language acquisition might be affected by quantity – the amount of time parents are engaged in talking to their children as they interact with them. This is further borne out in Hart and Risley's (1992, 1995) longitudinal study of parenting in American families. They made monthly observations of spontaneous adult–child interactions, for two-and-a-half years, in forty families representative of family size, race, and SES, and analyzed parenting along three dimensions: (a) amount of parenting per hour, measured by how much parents were engaged with their children, how much they said to them, and how attentive they were to their children's responses; (b) the nature of the parents' social interactions with their children; and (c) the content of child-directed speech. The first and third of these were strongly related to SES and to subsequent measures of child IQ.

Overall, the amount of talk to children, measured in number of words per hour, differed enormously by social class. Children in middle SES professional families heard around 2,100 words per hour in speech addressed to them; children in low SES, working-class families heard around 1,200; and children in welfare families about 600. Stated differently, the average number of utterances per hour ranged from 197 in welfare families up to 482 in middle-class families (Hart & Risley 1995; see also Roberts, Burchinal, & Durham 1999). The numbers mount up over time.

## 2B Children's cumulative experience with language, measured in words, in a hundred-hour week, a year, and four years

|  | One week | One year | Four years |
|---|---|---|---|
| High SES | 215,000 | 11 million | 44 million |
| Middle/Lower | 125,000 | 6 million | 24 million |
| Welfare | 62,000 | 3 million | 12 million |

Based on Hart & Risley 1995

[6] Other social factors like religious orientation can play a role here too (Wiley 1997).

The amount of child-directed speech was correlated with children's vocabulary size in the first years of development and in the early school grades. As children progressed to third grade at age eight, the differences in vocabulary size widened, with lower SES falling further behind middle SES ones (Hart & Risley 1995). At the same time, vocabulary measures such as the McArthur Communicative Development Inventory (CDI) (see Fenson *et al.* 1994; Arriaga *et al.* 1998) may underestimate lower SES language skills. Vocabulary is only one measure, and a vocabulary list might not be the best way to assess language skills. The vocabulary and syntactic structures children in less literate groups are exposed to in oral narratives (Corson 1995) may not be tapped in standard tests. We need to keep in mind that one-dimensional measures may miss the full range of language experiences children are exposed to. At the same time, classroom vocabularies and language use are closer to middle-class than to lower-class usage.

Yet low SES parents do a great deal of one-on-one teaching of their children. In her case study of three lower SES families, Miller (1982) found that they taught children how to tease, how to talk back, how to assert themselves, and how to respond in different situations. This is another place where there is often some mismatch between home and school settings: How do teachers react to teasing and challenges in the classroom? The norms for who can talk when and how, and what is appropriate to say, often differ by social class (Heath 1983).

Lastly, in a study that looked at both social class and race, Lawrence and Shipley (1996) contrasted black and white middle and low SES parents talking to their three-year-olds at mealtimes, in free play, and in a picture identification task. The two middle SES groups differed from the low SES ones in the information they supplied about objects in all three settings and in how much they directed their children's behavior. And, as in previous studies, middle-class parents expanded more on each topic, while working-class parents were more directive about their children's behavior, independent of race. Social class, then, affects the amount of language children are exposed to early on.

### Language and birth order

IQ declines with increasing family size. In a classic study of birth order and intellectual development, Zajonc (1976; Zajonc & Mullally 1997) showed that child IQ declined with the number of children in the family. Shifts in family size over time predict rises and falls in national achievement tests like the Scholastic Aptitude Test in the United States and Advanced-level examination passes in the United Kingdom. Since most IQ tests rely heavily on knowledge of vocabulary, there would appear to be a link between IQ and children's language acquisition.

How might family size affect the language experiences of children? Hoff-Ginsberg (1998) identified first-born versus later-born children in high SES versus middle SES families and studied the language addressed to them and their rates of language development. By age, first-born children were more advanced in lexical and grammatical development than later-born children; but later-born children were more advanced in conversational skills (see also Huttenlocher *et al.* 1991). These differences seem to arise primarily from the children's linguistic experiences. Adults talk more to first-born than to later-born children, and high SES adults talk more to their children than middle SES adults do (see also Bernicot & Roux 1998; Wells 1985).

These conclusions receive further support from a study of the language addressed to children in crowded homes (Evans, Maxwell, & Hart 1999). In a secondary analysis of the data collected by Hart & Risley (1995), Evans and his colleagues examined the number of people living in the house and the amount of parent-to-child speech. Adults in crowded homes spoke to their children in simpler, less sophisticated, ways than adults in less-crowded homes. And adults in the more crowded settings were less responsive verbally to their children. This finding was independent of SES, but since there tends to be more crowding in lower SES homes, this is likely to impact lower SES children more than higher SES ones.

The effects of early linguistic experiences endure over time. Differences in family SES, children's language production (amount and quality), and child IQ are all related to progress in elementary school (Hart & Risley 1995). In a follow-up of the original study, researchers assessed the children repeatedly between age five and ten, and found that the SES-related differences observed before these children entered school predicted their later verbal skills in comprehension and production of language, and their levels of achievement on standardized tests at age nine to ten (Walker *et al.* 1994). The more language children heard early on, the better their scores and their general progress in school.

### Universals in child-directed speech?

As Ferguson (1977:209) remarked, "In all speech communities there are probably special ways of talking to young children which differ more or less systematically from the more 'normal' form of the language used in ordinary conversation among adults." In his summary of data from a large range of languages, Ferguson pointed to special talk marked by higher pitch, wider pitch range, special pitch contours, favorite word shapes, substitution of simpler for more difficult sounds,[7] and assimilation. These observations have been backed to a large extent by recent experimental work with different languages. But notice that these properties of child-directed speech all have to do with the speaker's delivery and not directly with the pragmatic functions of such utterances.

The consistent appearance of such properties in child-directed speech has been widely reported. For example, Fernald and Simon (1984) found that German mothers' speech to their newborns has higher pitch, a wider pitch range, longer pauses, and more uses of whisper than their speech to older children or to adults

---

[7] Ferguson (1977) pointed out that adult judgements of what constitute easy and difficult sounds vary considerably from one language to another and may bear little or no relation to any general ease of articulation.

(see also Garnica 1977 for English). Grieser & Kuhl (1988) reported the same of Mandarin Chinese, while Fernald and her colleagues (1989) compared prosodic modifications of parents' speech to infants between the ages of ten months and one year two months in French, Italian, German, Japanese, British English, and American English, with measures of pitch height, pitch range and variability, and pause duration. They found that, overall, both mothers' and fathers' speech showed "greater prosody" to infants than to adults.

However, some anthropologists have contested such claims of universality. Heath (1983:75), for example, in her ethnographic study of a black working-class community in North Carolina, reported that "everyone talks *about* the baby, but rarely *to* the baby." Adults there apparently don't use special pitch or intonation patterns. What is unclear is whether older children use any prosodic modifications to their younger siblings, or whether adults make it clear in some other way who they are addressing when they talk to an infant or young child (see Hoff 2006). Both Ochs (1982) and Schieffelin (1979) have made similar observations for infants in Samoa and among the Kaluli (Papua New Guinea). But Schieffelin (1979:86) also noted that Kaluli mothers often "speak for the child in a special high very nasal voice register." In K'iche' Mayan, adults appear not to use higher pitch (it is actually lower), extended pitch range, or any special intonation contours (Bernstein-Ratner & Pye 1984; Pye 1986), but in this society, pitch height is a variable in adult–adult speech, with higher pitch reserved for addressing higher-status people.

In cultures where parents don't speak to infants or young children, one will not find specific forms of language peculiar to that class of addressees. So the general issue is whether adults speak to infants (or whether older siblings speak to them), and if so, how they modify their speech (and hence the characteristic properties of child-directed speech); or if not, at what point parents do start to talk to children and whether this talk diverges in any way from what they use to older addressees or to adults.

Schieffelin (1979) did observe that adults spent a lot of time "talking for" their young children in Kaluli. That is, Kaluli adults typically held the child up, facing the prospective addressee, said what the child should say on that occasion, and then ended the utterance with "ɛlɛma," an expression she glossed as 'say it like this'. Such utterances were also often marked by nasalized intonation and occurred in specific kinds of interactions. Uses of such utterances for the child were particularly common in triadic settings (parent, child, and other), as shown in Table 2.6. That is, adults tell young children directly what they should say, and the words to use, to a third person.

For the three children Schieffelin observed, 86% of "ɛlɛma"-marked utterances from adults were produced during triadic exchanges. (The small numbers of other uses of "ɛlɛma" were all in dyadic interactions with just the parent and child.) For Abi, the percentage of "ɛlɛma"-marked utterances in triadic interactions in three recordings (5.5 hours total) was 68%, with 60% and 50% respectively for the first two sessions, rising to 80% for the third. For Meli, the percentage was consistently higher for uses of "ɛlɛma" utterances in triadic interactions (over five hours of recordings), at 97%. This

Table 2.6 *Frequency of dyadic and triadic "ɛlɛma" interactions at three ages*

| Abi | | | Meli | | | Wanu | | |
|---|---|---|---|---|---|---|---|---|
| Age | Dyadic | Triadic | Age | Dyadic | Triadic | Age | Dyadic | Triadic |
| 2;1.10 | 12 | 18 | 2;0.24 | 0 | 42 | 2;0.7 | 1 | 19 |
| 2;1.27 | 14 | 14 | 2;2.3 | 2 | 53 | 2;1.4 | 3 | 65 |
| 2;3.17 | 11 | 46 | 2;3.21 | 3 | 62 | 2;2.21 | 25 | 130 |

*Source*: Schieffelin 1979:89. Used with permission from Academic Press.

held for all the uses of "ɛlɛma" in her first session, and for 96% and 95% respectively in the second and third observation sessions. Wanu received the same pattern of input, with 88% for the three observation sessions (a total of 7.5 hours); 95% of these uses occurred in triadic interactions in the first session, 96% in the second, and 84% in the third. It is precisely in triadic interactions that it would make sense for the parent to speak for the child to the other person as addressee, as shown in the exchange in (8) between Wanu, aged two (with his mother offering models for him), and Binalia, aged five (Ochs & Schieffelin 1984).

(8)  MOTHER (to Wanu): Whose is it? Say like that. 'ɛlɛma'
    WANU (to Binalia): *Whose is it?*
    MOTHER:    Is it yours? Say like that.
    WANU:    *Is it yours?*
    MOTHER:    Who are you? Say like that.
    WANU:    *Who are you?*
    MOTHER:    Did you pick it? Say like that.
    WANU:    *Did you pick it?*
    MOTHER:    My gramma picked it! Say like that.
    WANU:    *My gramma picked it!*
    MOTHER:    This MY GRAMMA picked. Say like that.
    WANU:    *This MY GRAMMA picked.*

Pragmatically, this may be easier for a child to grasp as speech-for-the-child since the child on such occasions is faced towards the addressee and (presumably) then gets speech back from that person. (Schieffelin did not discuss that aspect of the conversational interactions.)

Although "ɛlɛma" can also be addressed to adults, this is rare compared to its uses to young children. Most adults, it seems, can be relied on to know what is appropriate to say on most occasions. Uses of "ɛlɛma," then, generally mark utterances as designed for the child to say. These utterances have a high-pitched nasalized coloring that further identifies them, from their inception, as utterances that the child should pay particular attention to. Similar exchanges with young children, and uses of prompts combined with what to say in each setting to specific addressees, have been observed in Sesotho (Lesotho), Kwara'ae (Solomon Islands), and in lower socioeconomic status (SES) English-speaking groups (see Demuth 1986; Miller 1986; and Watson-Gegeo & Gegeo 1986a, 1986b).

Schieffelin's (1979) study suggests that researchers need to be careful in observing and assessing each culture for how children are treated, from birth on, in communicative and conversational exchanges (see de León 1998). The actual information about language use that is offered to children in one culture versus another may differ considerably. Yet, in all cases, there seem to be ways of signaling to children when they should attend to what is being said. That is, there are probably many different ways of conveying to children what they should (or shouldn't) say in different contexts, on different occasions, to specific addressees. Overemphasis on differences between cultural groups may obscure what they actually have in common and the common functions of some kinds of conversational exchanges.

## Summary

Language in its conversational settings does social work. Speakers use it to license different kinds of social relations, to mark social occasions – to communicate in all sorts of ways for a range of different purposes. Language serves adults and children alike as a means for making clear what their intentions are on different occasions as they make use of language to communicate. But are the modifications adults make as they talk to young children essential for acquisition? If we could show that acquisition occurs whether or not children hear such child-directed speech, we might conclude that such modifications are not necessary though they might nonetheless be helpful. If we could show that acquisition did not occur without exposure to such modifications, we could conclude that some modifications may not only be helpful but also necessary for acquisition to take place. On balance, the data suggest that children do need to find "a way in" to language and that speech addressed to them directly in conversation fosters their entry into the speech community.

Do children require child-directed speech for learning? Is there a causal connection between the kind of speech that children have addressed to them at different stages of development and the kinds of utterances they go on to produce? The difficulty lies in arguing for cause from correlation. It's possible that parental modifications are driven by the children's level of comprehension (and so partly independent of what the children themselves produce), so adult modifications are reactive and reflect perceived degrees of comprehension rather than being deliberately designed as miniature language lessons. That is, parents effectively teach their children by modifying their language, but they modify it to make themselves understood. And they react to their children's contributions with the same goal in mind: They repeat poorly pronounced words as a way of checking whether they have understood their children as intended; they offer alternative formulations where children have used nonconventional forms – with inappropriate word orders, wrong word-endings, or the wrong words, say. In short, they offer other ways of doing things with words when their children's formulations fail.

# 3    Starting on language: Perception

To what extent are human infants predisposed to attend to speech sounds? This question has been addressed from a number of positions over the last twenty years, with the answers becoming more complex as researchers learn more about how infants (and adults) analyze the speech stream, categorize speech sounds, and process running speech. This chapter looks at what infants start from as they begin to attend to the language around them and how they come to identify units within the stream of sound. What abilities do infants have at birth? Can they detect similarity and difference in successive speech sounds? When are they able to recognize previously heard units? Until children can recognize chunks of speech (words or phrases, for instance) as recurring from previous contexts, they cannot begin to attach meanings to them. The emphasis in this chapter is on how children first *get in* to language through analysis of the speech stream.

In many cultures, adult speakers consistently differentiate how they speak according to the age of their addressees – infants, young children, older children, adults (see Chapter 2). Exaggerated affect in the voice, a higher pitch range, and steeper rises and falls in intonation mark off some speech as directed to infants, who appear to be particularly attentive to such modulations. Indeed, some researchers have suggested that such speech allows infants to attach affective meaning to vocalizations early in their exposure to language (Bloom 1997; Fernald 1992). The modifications adults adopt also serve to display shorter chunks of the speech stream than one might hear in adult-to-adult speech (shorter utterances, clearly articulated, and typically separated by pauses). They also highlight recurring words and consistently display new information, for instance, in either initial or final position in the utterance. The adjustments adults make to different-age addressees are generally geared to children's levels of comprehension, and they have the effect of breaking up the speech stream into what may well be more manageable chunks for analysis.

## Tackling the speech stream: Extracting forms

Whether children listen to the speech addressed to them or to the speech around them, they are faced with some critical problems. One is the *segmentation problem* – how to go about identifying units (phrases, words, morphemes, sound segments) in the speech stream when they have no reason to break it up at any particular point. (Knowing, from the meaning, what counts as a word, for example, allows adults to analyze speech from unfamiliar speakers on unfamiliar topics.) Another problem is that of *invariance*, since spoken language is not invariant: The same speaker may pronounce the same word on different occasions with large acoustic differences and even pronounce the same sounds with different acoustic properties in different contexts. And a third problem is the *language problem*: Infants have to work out which sounds and sound patterns are systematic and therefore belong in the language around them.

### The segmentation problem

Imagine listening to a radio broadcast in an unfamiliar language or overhearing people talking an unfamiliar language. We have no idea what counts as a word or where to place any breaks between words. (Breaks are not marked by pauses in speech in the way they are marked by spaces in writing.) So how do infants come to segment what they hear into appropriate units for that language, whether segments, syllables, words, expressions, or clauses? The puzzle here seems to lie in the fact that adults automatically segment the stream of speech they are listening to into meaning units – but infants don't know what those units are yet. At the same time, by eight months of age, infants can detect recurring sequences of syllables ("words") with a high probability of occurring next to each other in a particular order, and distinguish these from "nonwords" or "part-words" – sequences with a low probability of occurring together in the set heard earlier (Saffran, Aslin, & Newport 1996). This suggests that children tackle the segmentation problem before they begin to link forms and meanings.

### The invariance problem

The acoustic properties associated with a specific sound in a language are not invariant, but depend heavily on the speech context, which other sounds precede or follow. First, for example, what counts as a **k**, say, is actually acoustically different before a high front vowel, **i**, as in *kitchen*, from a high back one, **u**, as in *coop*. Infants must learn eventually that these **k** sounds in English count as the same. Second, particular sounds may vary from one context to another, from one utterance to the next, both for the same speaker and from one speaker to another.[1] In rapid speech, for instance, words are shortened acoustically, and this affects the amount of information available for the recognition of consonants. (Compare **cudja** or even **cuja** for *Could you* in rapid speech.) In fact, subsequent uses of the same word or phrase by the same speaker tend to be less clear acoustically than initial uses (Galati & Brennan 2006). This has led some researchers to argue that adult speech to children is not necessarily clear (e.g., Bard & Anderson 1994), but others have shown consistent use of more extreme vowels in speech to children.

---

[1] This is the reason speech-recognition software for computers can usually cope with only a single speaker.

That is, speakers enlarge the vowel space to clearly distinguish one vowel from the next (Kuhl *et al.* 1997). Overall, loudness, rate, and emotional state can affect how speakers produce speech, regardless of the language being spoken. In addition, speakers may make use of variants of particular sounds depending on a variety of sociolinguistic variables – gender role (male or female), addressee (male or female, older or younger), and topic among others. Use of variant forms in child-directed speech exposes children to the local social patterning associated with different pronunciations of the same sound (see Chambers 2003; Foulkes, Docherty, & Watt 2005).

### The language problem

Infants exposed to language have to identify the set of sounds (phonetic segments) relevant to that language and, eventually, map them onto the phonological categories for that language. For example, in English, the two "l" sounds (light l in *lid*, and dark l in *pill*) are phonetically distinct but belong to the same phonological category in English where the choice between them is completely predictable: Light l always occurs at the beginning of words or syllables and is pronounced with the tip of the tongue against the alveolar ridge with the body of the tongue low in the mouth, while dark l always occurs at the ends of syllables or words and is pronounced with the tip of the tongue against the alveolar ridge and the body of the tongue raised towards the hard palate or roof of the mouth. In other languages, there may be only one l sound (e.g., in French, l is always light), or different l sounds may belong to different phonological categories (e.g., light l versus retroflex l in Hindi).[2] In English, the choice of variant for l doesn't affect word meaning, but in Hindi it does.

Infants don't work on the sound system of a language for its own sake. Rather they appear to discover it in the course of trying to figure out the communicative significance of different utterances addressed to them – that is, as they begin to set up a mental lexicon of recognizable words. Infants, then, must be able not only to discriminate one sound from another – a capacity actually present very early – but also to identify chunks or units, so they can recognize them from one occasion to the next in the speech stream (the segmentation problem), from one context to the next, and from one speaker to the next (the invariance problem). On top of this, they must learn to group phonetic segments into the phonological categories of the language and then learn which phonological sequences are legitimate for that language within words and syllables.

Although it is possible to point to some of the capacities involved (the ability to discriminate similarity and difference, for example), it appears unlikely that children could start by first recognizing segments and then building up to possible sequences of sounds in a language. A number of researchers have proposed instead that children start from some perception and representation of target *words* (chunks), and, over time and through comparisons with other words,

---

[2] The retroflex l in Hindi is pronounced with the tip of the tongue against the center of the hard palate.

discover inside those words the segmental structure of their makeup (Lindblom 1992). The sound segments put to use in the phonology of a language are therefore "discovered" via earlier identification of whole words. This is consistent with the fact that infants are exposed to and learn their first language in a social context where the meanings to be conveyed take priority. From a processing point of view, starting from meaning units would suggest that infants need to begin with a top-down approach, from words to segments, in their analysis of the speech stream rather than with a bottom-up approach, from segments to words. But even if infants first break up the sound stream into chunks rather than sound segments, they could still be working from bottom-up as well, just with chunks of speech larger than a sound segment. For both bottom-up and top-down analyses, infants most likely begin with whole chunks and then break these into smaller units.

## What infants know about language

Researchers have devised several methods to look at what infants can and can't perceive in speech. They all rely on one essential observation – that infants, like adults, (a) react to changes they perceive around them and (b) habituate to or get bored by repetitions of the same event. Changes, in the case of speech, can be changes in a sound or syllable being repeated, in pitch contour (from rising to falling, say), in word shapes (forms heard previously vs. forms that are entirely new), in the sex of the speaker (from male to female, say), and so on. Researchers first collect baseline measures and then look for departures from the baseline that coincide with the infant's being exposed to something new. The main measures that have been used have relied on sucking-rates (infants suck harder and more frequently when they see or hear something new) or on conditioned head-turns (infants readily learn to turn their heads towards a sound accompanied by an image of an animated toy). In each case, departures from the baseline rate are assumed to reflect a detection of difference, of change, in the stimulus being listened to (see Aslin 2007; Jusczyk 1997; Kuhl 1985; Vihman 1996).

The technique used most widely with young infants has been *high-amplitude sucking* (HAS). This procedure generally takes the following form in studies of speech sound discrimination: The infant is placed in a reclining seat and given a nipple without a hole to suck on. This nipple contains a pressure transducer that measures the rate at which the infant sucks while listening to auditory stimuli. First, a baseline level for each infant's sucking rate is established, and then the infant is presented with a speech syllable (e.g., /ba ba ba/) whose frequency of repetition is controlled by the infant's sucking rate, with the rate increasing as the infant learns the contingency between sucking and hearing the sound. The increase is taken to mark increased attention or interest. As the infant gets used to presentations of a particular sound, its sucking rate levels off and then declines. The decline is taken to mark habituation to the current stimulus. Control groups of infants continue to hear a single repeated stimulus, but experimental groups are at this point presented with some minimally different auditory stimulus – a different syllable, a different intonation contour, a different voice. If the infants detect a new stimulus, their sucking-rate should increase again. Sucking-rates can then be compared after the shift in stimulus for the experimental group and for the control group that received no change in stimulus. When there is a difference in the mean response rates, this is taken to show that infants can detect the difference.

This measure can test infants on within-category and across-category boundary differences in adult phonetic categories (e.g., Eimas *et al.* 1971). It has also been adapted for the study of what infants actually encode and remember about speech sounds, in addition to their discrimination of differences. While this is an effective measure for infants under four to five months of age, older infants tend to be more active and less ready to suck and listen. One drawback is that testing sessions take up to fifteen minutes, and many infants fuss, fall asleep, or start crying before the procedure is done. When infants don't show habituation, it is hard to know whether they are unable to detect a difference or simply lack interest in what they are hearing.

The other widely used procedure is the *conditioned head-turn*. Here infants are trained with a visually reinforced head-turn procedure that exploits their natural tendency to orient towards a sound source. The infant first hears one sound several times, then hears a new sound, and then is switched back to the original sound. If infants turn their heads when the new sound comes on, they are "rewarded" with a picture of a lit-up, animated toy. Provided infants turn their heads in response to changes but not when there is no change in the stimulus they hear, they are taken to be detecting a difference between the sounds in question (see Kuhl 1985). This technique appears to be most effective in the six- to ten-month-age range. Just as with HAS, collecting enough data from each infant takes time, and, with difficult discriminations where infants may be rewarded rather infrequently, many infants fail to complete the procedure: Crying, fussing, and falling asleep take a toll.

Other researchers have made use of *head-turn preferences* (e.g., Fernald 1985) and *visual fixation* (Horowitz 1974). The head-turn preference procedure has been adapted, for instance, to study infants' ability to detect familiar words in fluent speech (Jusczyk 1997; Jusczyk & Aslin 1995). Researchers have also monitored infant *heart rate* on the assumption that detection of a new stimulus will lead to an increase in rate, while habituation leads to a decrease and leveling off of heart rate. (This is basically the same assumption as for high-amplitude sucking.) This measure is harder to use because of the instability of infant heart rates, but it offers a way to measure surprise and shifts of attention (e.g., Moffitt 1971). Again, these methods tend to be most useful in infants under a year old.

## Are human infants specialized for speech?

Sounds like **b** (closure of the lips with voicing) and **p** (closure of the lips without voicing), when pronounced in isolation, differ systematically in Voice Onset Time: For **b**, it is zero seconds – that is, voicing starts right away; for **p**, it is +0.06 seconds – voicing begins only with the transition to whatever the vowel is that follows the **p**. In everyday conversation, the phonetic tokens of these consonants vary considerably in their acoustic properties, so how do people recognize which sound is intended? Researchers checked on people's ability to categorize these sounds by giving them synthesized versions that differed by small increments over a continuum from **b** to **p**. People showed 100% agreement except in a very narrow range (somewhere between 0.04 and 0.05 seconds) that formed a boundary between the two sounds. In effect, people imposed discrete categories on this acoustic continuum and identified each sound as either a **b** (voiced) or a **p** (voiceless). This categorical perception of speech sounds allows speakers to ignore all kinds of small variations in pronunciation as well as variations due to the phonetic surroundings provided by other sounds (Liberman *et al.* 1967).

In 1971, Peter Eimas and his colleagues attempted to see whether infants, like adults, treated speech sounds categorically. If certain linguistic abilities were innate, why not the categorical perception of speech sounds? The findings lent support to the view that this ability might be innate: Infants as young as one month old could discriminate the voicing contrast (/ba/ versus /pa/), and, just like adults, their discrimination was categorical (Eimas *et al.* 1971). Subsequent studies focussed on infants' ability to discriminate place of articulation. Five-month-olds could discriminate /ba/ syllables (pronounced with lip closure) from /ga/ syllables (with velar closure between the back of the tongue and the hard palate) (Moffitt 1971). Even two-month-olds could discriminate this place-of-articulation difference (Morse 1972). Later studies showed that two-month-olds could discriminate /ba/ from /da/ categorically (voicing and place of articulation combined) and that such discrimination appeared not to depend on exposure to speech, since even newborns could discriminate place-of-articulation differences (e.g., Bertoncini *et al.* 1987; Eimas 1974).

Researchers also looked at other distinctions between consonants in infant perception: stop versus glide (/ba/ and /wa/), oral versus nasal (/ba/ and /ma/), liquids (/ra/ and /la/; /wa/ and /ja/), and some vowel contrasts (see Jusczyk 1997; Vihman 1996). They also looked at infants' ability to discriminate differences among vowels. At one month, infants discriminate open from closed vocal tract, /a/ and /i/, and also a front–back discrimination, /i/ and /u/. At two months, they can make these discriminations with pitch changes (rise vs. fall) on the vowels and with changes of speaker. And at six months, they can also discriminate differences in vowels within syllables (e.g., Trehub 1973). In summary, infants from birth or soon after appeared to make categorical discriminations for speech sounds. This ability, present so early, strongly suggested that human infants were uniquely specialized for the perception of speech.

Further studies showed that this conclusion could not stand. First, Kuhl and Miller (1975) showed that chinchillas seemed to have categorical perception for voicing differences in speech. Subsequent studies have shown that macaque monkeys, rhesus monkeys, and even Japanese quail show similar effects (e.g., Kluender, Diehl, & Killeen 1987; Kuhl & Padden 1982). Second, a number of researchers reported categorical discrimination for nonspeech as well as speech sounds, in both adults and infants (e.g., Cutting & Rosner 1974; Miller *et al.* 1976). Together, the findings suggest that both human and nonhuman discriminations depend on properties of the hearing system and not on any specialization in humans just for the processing of speech sounds (Jusczyk 1997).

## Breaking into the speech stream

If adults break up the speech stream by identifying the units of meaning it contains, infants must clearly start in some other way: They don't yet have any linguistic meanings to make use of. What alternatives are there? One possibility is that, like adults, infants can detect recurring sequences in the speech stream. That is, they can recognize two (or more) sequences as similar. This would allow them to recognize clusters of adjacent sounds and thereby isolate certain recurring sequences. There is growing evidence that this provides a way in for infants. Saffran and her colleagues showed first that eight-month-old infants, after only two minutes of listening to an artificial language made up of syllables strung together, with no prosodic or acoustic markers at boundaries, could segment out chunks or words just on the basis of statistical relations among the sequences of syllables involved. To test the infants' ability to segment such sequences, they compared their responses to words versus part-words (i.e., sequences that crossed a word-boundary), as in Box 3A. The words and part-words were matched in frequency, but the transitional probability patterns across each sequence-type differed. Infants at eight months reliably discriminated words from part-words. So, even after very brief exposures, infants can segment continuous speech into recurrent patterns (words) on the basis of the transitional probabilities of constituent syllable pairs (Aslin, Saffran, & Newport 1998; Saffran, Aslin, & Newport 1996; see also Maye, Werker, & Gerken 2002).

---

### 3A Breaking into the speech stream

Infants aged eight mths listen to a stream of syllables, with no pauses, no stresses, level intonation,
   bidakupadotigolabutupiropadotitupirogolabubidaku…
   with repeated sequences of syllables that make up recurring chunks or words:
   bidaku, padoti, golabu, tupiro
They were then tested on words (sequences with high probability transitions) vs. part-words,
   e.g., **bidaku** vs. dakupa (daku + pa), or **padoti** vs. titupi (ti + tupi)
Infants recognized the words with repeated groups of three syllables always in the same order (so with high transitional probabilities between syllables) in what they'd heard, but not part-words like daku-pa or ti-tupi

Based on Saffran *et al.* 1996

The ability to pick out clusters of sounds that co-occur with high frequency allows infants to make some initial segmentation of the speech stream. How early they begin to do this is not yet clear. Saffran's studies focussed on eight-month-olds, but still younger infants can discriminate differences among sounds from the time they are only a few weeks old.

## Becoming specialized for a language

What is the time course children follow as they analyze the stream of speech? Let's suppose they start out holistically and first learn to recognize the language around them in terms of familiar-sounding prosodic contours and patterned distributions of sounds. Next, they could attend in more detail to specific prosodic patterns and later still to the phonotactic structure – the permissible co-occurring patterns of sounds. Only after this might they focus on specific sound segments. There is considerable support for this general progression as infants and young children come to identify words in the speech stream and attach consistent meanings to them.

At what point do they start to focus on the distinctions relevant to the language they are being exposed to? Very early, most likely in utero. Newborns, for example, prefer to listen to their mother's voice over that of a stranger (DeCasper & Fifer 1980; Mehler *et al.* 1978). How could such a preference develop so early? One possibility is that even limited exposure to the mother's voice after birth is enough for such a preference to develop. Another is that prenatal experience produces the infant's postnatal preference. Subsequent studies have supported the latter possibility. DeCasper and Spence (1986) showed that infants preferred to listen to a story already heard prenatally to a story never heard before. But in utero exposure to speech is limited. Frequencies above 1 kHz are attenuated by transmission through tissue, whereas intensity and spectral properties are very similar whether inside or outside the uterus. This suggests that newborn preferences for maternal voices and for familiar stories could be based on prosodic information in speech. In fact, when newborns, exposed to a story prenatally, hear either an unfiltered recording of their mothers' voices or a low-pass (1 kHz) filtered version, they show no preference, but infants in a control group who had not heard the story prenatally preferred the unfiltered version of their mothers' voices (Spence & DeCasper 1987). Prenatal exposure to the low-frequency properties of maternal voices, and in particular their prosodic contours, it seems, influence infants' early perception.

Infants also seem able to distinguish their own language from another (foreign) language from as young as four days after birth. When French infants were given taped speech samples of French and Russian to listen to, from the same fluent bilingual speaker, they showed greater arousal (measured by sucking-rates) to the samples of French. But when the four-day-old infants of parents whose native language was not French (the languages represented included Arabic, Chinese, German, Italian, Portuguese, Spanish, Polish, and

Indonesian) heard the same tapes, they gave no evidence of preferring French over Russian. Moreover, their baseline sucking-rates most resembled those of French infants listening to Russian. That is, this second group of infants found both languages unfamiliar and responded much as the French infants did to the unfamiliar language sample (Mehler *et al.* 1988). In a third experiment, four-day-old French infants heard samples of Italian and American English (again from a bilingual speaker), and reacted as the non-French infants had: They showed no preference. However, when the same speech samples were played to somewhat older American infants (two-month-olds), the infants showed a preference for the English over the Italian samples. Equally, when American two-month-olds then heard samples of French and Russian speech, they showed no preference.

Finally, to see just what kind of information infants could have had access to in utero, Mehler and his colleagues (1988) had four-day-old French infants listen to low-pass filtered versions of French and Russian speech. (Use of a low-pass filter at 400 Hz removes any information about individual sounds but leaves information about rhythm, stress, and intonation.) They also had two-month-old American infants listen to low-pass filtered versions of Italian and American English. In both cases, infants attended more to their first language (French in the first case, American English in the second). This suggests that what infants are attending to are the prosodic properties of the speech they were exposed to prenatally. These properties allow them to group utterances that belong to the native language and to ignore utterances that do not. In short, infants can home in on the appropriate set of materials for analysis as they begin to break up the speech stream (see also Moon, Cooper, & Fifer 1993).

## Language-specific discriminations

Werker and her colleagues have found that young infants can discriminate nearly every phonetic contrast on which they have been tested, including ones that do not occur in their language-learning environment. But there is a significant change with age in the ease with which people discriminate many non-native contrasts. This change takes place within the first year of life, so when infants between six and twelve months old are tested on their ability to make various phonetic discriminations, they show a decline in sensitivity with age.

In one study, Werker and Tees (1984) tested Canadian infants from English-speaking households on their ability to discriminate three contrasts: (a) the English place-of-articulation contrast between /ba/ and /ga/, (b) the Hindi retroflex versus dental stop contrast (/ta/ and /ta/), and the Nthlakampx (an Amerindian language) glottalized velar versus uvular stop contrast (/k'i/ and /q'i/). The youngest infants exposed to English (six- to eight-month-olds) could discriminate all three, but by eight to ten months, only some infants could discriminate the non-English contrasts. By ten to twelve months, infants appeared to be sensitive only to the distinction in the English /ba/ ~ /ga/ contrast. Infants exposed to Hindi and

Nthlakampx respectively, at eleven months, *could* discriminate the relevant contrasts for their language. The researchers argued that the change at around ten months results from a reorganization in perceptual biases rather than from any loss of initial auditory capacity.

As a test of this position, Werker and Lalonde (1988) compared adult speakers of English and Hindi for their ability to discriminate a synthetic place-of-articulation continuum, from /b/ through /d/ to retroflex /ɖ/. Adults distinguished categories in accord with the phonemic categories of their first language: English speakers distinguished just two, /b/ and /d/, while Hindi speakers distinguished all three. Werker and Lalonde then used stimuli from the same continuum in two further experiments, first, to replicate the finding that infants reorganize their phonetic perception from "universal" to "language-specific" between six and twelve months of age (they did so), and, second, to see whether infant perception had a phonological basis or whether it depended on the physical similarity of the stimuli. At six to eight months old, infants learning English could distinguish all three categories, but by eleven to thirteen months of age, infants distinguished only two (/b/ vs. /d/) – the two that were relevant to the language they were being exposed to.

Once infants have developed a preference for the ambient language, they start showing a preference for specific prosodic properties of recurring elements in the speech stream. For instance, they attend to the characteristic stress patterns in a language. (This in turn, of course, may help in their further segmentation of the speech stream.) The majority of English words, for instance, place stronger stress on the first syllable, e.g., *báby, líttle*; *róbin, éagle*; *blánket, gárden.* (In Hungarian, there is also a highly consistent assignment of stress to the first syllable in words.) Jusczyk, Cutler, and Redanz (1993) looked at whether infants showed any evidence of listening longer to sequences with a strong–weak stress pattern over those with a weak–strong one (e.g., *bóttle* vs. *awáy*). If they prefer a strong–weak pattern, this could help in their eventual identification of those sound sequences that form words. While six-month-old American infants showed no preference, by nine months they listened significantly longer to words with strong–weak stress patterns. This suggests that the preference for strong–weak develops with greater exposure to the ambient language. Nine-month-olds exposed to English continue to show this preference when the speech is low-pass filtered to remove any segmental information about the sounds that made up the words. And at this age, infants combine this prosodic preference with phonotactic information about high probability sequences in bisyllabic (CVC–CVC) words they are exposed to, so making use, where possible, of multiple cues to potential word-boundaries (Matttys, Jusczyk, Luce, & Morgan 1999; Christophe *et al.* 2001).

If infants attend to predominant stress patterns, this should eventually help them in their identification of word-level chunks. But to identify strong–weak as a predominant pattern (over weak–strong), infants must have heard enough sequences of all strong–weak or enough isolated pieces with a strong–weak pattern to distinguish these from weak–strong sequences. Since this also depends on when in a sequence infants start attending, the actual speech addressed to them may be critical. This, after all, is their primary source of information.

In fact, by seven-and-a-half months, infants listen longer to previously familiarized "words" when these are later presented inside longer sentences than to sentences containing unfamiliar control sequences (Jusczyk & Aslin 1995). In a further study, infants this age were first familiarized with sets of sentences and then tested on "words" from these sentences versus foils: Again, they listened longer to the words they had heard in the familiarization sentences. These findings suggest that infants can segment individual syllables (all the words were monosyllabic) from fluent speech during the second half of their first year. Further studies have shown that, by nine months (but not at six months), infants are also able to discriminate sequences of two or more syllables grouped perceptually by both segmental and rhythmic properties (Morgan & Saffran 1995).

Finally, at nine months, infants prefer to listen to lists of isolated words from the ambient language over lists of words from another language (Jusczyk et al. 1993). This presumably reflects both their recognition of familiar kinds of sequences in the sound patterns of the isolated words and their growing attentiveness to the native language they are being exposed to. At eleven months, infants shift their attention (measured with event-related potentials, or ERPs) to familiar words within 250 ms of presentation onset (Thierry, Vihman, & Roberts 2003; see also Mills et al. 2005). So towards the end of their first year, infants seem to be representing what they hear in memory. This is an important step in their recognition of recurrent sequences in the speech stream.

This focussing in by infants towards the end of their first year on the phonetic categories of the specific language they are exposed to appears to mark the first stages in the organization of a functional phonology, a sound system tied to a particular language. It coincides in its timing with the first evidence of systematic responses from infants to adult words. That is, infants at this stage appear to be setting up representations in memory for recurring stretches of adult speech so they can recognize them on subsequent occasions.

Infant concentration on discriminating native-language categories of sounds, then, goes hand in hand with their early segmentation of word- or phrase-like chunks. Infants have to learn the patterns for recurring sequences of sounds in a language and so come to discriminate possible sequences from impossible ones. They must also attend to other factors helpful in identifying word-boundaries. They must learn about the range of rhythmic patterns (including dominant stress patterns), and they must learn that some words lack strong or stressed syllables altogether. All of this together helps them in segmenting out more words from the speech stream.

Nearly all these studies are of discrimination, of the ability to treat some sounds as the same, and so distinguish them from other sounds. Discrimination of sounds is essential, but it is not the same as identification. Infants may be able to discriminate differences but have little or no ability to identify a chunk of the speech stream as one they have heard before or heard before on some specific occasion. They must go on to *identify* chunks of various sizes as familiar and (eventually) as belonging to specific categories. In summary, they must learn to recognize what they have heard before in particular sequences. They need to assemble information about familiar chunks, along with prosodic properties (like word stress), phonotactic properties (the distributional patterns of occurrence of sounds), and information about boundaries (derivable from distributional properties of sound segments as well as from utterances and pauses in child-directed speech) for use in their initial representations for linguistic chunks. These chunks, with more analysis, will become identifiable as units, such as words and morphemes, as well as larger expressions. Critically, therefore, they need to attach meanings to such chunks in order to be able to make use of them – to understand them and, later on, produce them.

The changes that take place between eight months and twelve to fourteen months are also relevant here: Infants narrow in on and focus more directly on native-language phonetic categories than on other kinds of sounds. This heightened attention to the ambient language also appears directly relevant as young children set up representations in memory so they can recognize chunks (words) they have heard before. The studies that show children prefer to listen to words previously heard within longer sequences of sounds (utterances) also suggest that discrimination, towards the end of the first year of age, is being supplemented by a growing ability to recognize familiar sequences and so identify them when they recur in new contexts. To do this effectively, children must start to make use of any information available about boundaries, boundaries of syllables, morphemes, words – in short, anything that marks off some kind of linguistic unit.

### Finding and using boundaries

How much information can one extract from the speech stream? When adults are exposed to fifteen minutes of an entirely unfamiliar language, they appear to gather a surprising amount of information, albeit tacitly rather than explicitly. Zwitserlood and her colleagues (2002) looked at how much Dutch-speaking adults could infer about Chinese from exposure to a single fifteen-minute tape of continuous speech compared to exposure to the same speech accompanied by a videotape. By comparing the audio and video conditions, they could assess how much people can learn about a language from listening alone compared to when they have simultaneous exposure to speech and some visual reference-world for what was being talked about. They also assessed the effects of repeated words and of the visual highlighting of objects as certain words were heard. Overall, they found that, for recognition of sound sequences as well as for associations of sound and meaning, people need more than speech alone: They need a visible reference-field, and they rely on repeated sequences of sounds and the highlighting of objects in conjunction with specific sound sequences.[3]

People do extract some regularities from speech alone, but they extract more information when speech is supplemented by visual information. What kinds of information did they extract? First, the more often a word was said, the more likely people were to identify it as familiar (vs. new) when they were tested later. People were also good at identifying the possible referents of words that were both frequent and accompanied by highlighting on the videotape. Next best were low-frequency words plus highlighting, then high-frequency words without highlighting. They also extracted a good deal of information about legitimate versus illegitimate sound sequences, and did well on identifying nonwords when segments from the Chinese inventory occurred in illegal positions in a syllable. Even fifteen minutes' exposure to Mandarin Chinese speech allowed adults to extract a surprising amount of information about the sound structure of Mandarin as well as to identify some sound/meaning pairings. But their analyses were implicit rather than explicit, in that they were seldom conscious of what they had learnt.

These findings suggest that it should not come as any surprise that quite young infants are able to extract pertinent information about word-boundaries on the one hand and to assign potential meanings on the other. The kind of language spoken to infants highlights the boundaries of words and phrases in the speech stream (Chapter 2). For instance, adults favor short utterances, with pauses in between, and thereby mark the end-boundary of words produced in final position. They favor highly repetitive constructions or carrier-phrases in which to introduce new words (e.g., *There's a* _____ , *Look at the* _____ ), thereby signaling the initial-boundary of the words that follow. And, in English, they also strongly favor introducing new information at the ends of utterances (e.g., Fernald & Mazzie 1991; Fernald & Hurtado 2006; Clark 2009).[4]

Infants in their turn appear to make good use of such information in the speech addressed to them. When American infants aged seven-and-a-half months were familiarized with two different monosyllabic words that they subsequently heard embedded in sentences, they listened longer to those sentences than to others without those words. Six-month-olds showed no such preference. From the second half of their first year on, infants pay more attention to what they hear. When seven-month-olds are familiarized with forms that differ in their initial sound segment by one or two features from target forms (e.g., /g-/ vs. /k-/, with one feature different, compared to /k-/ vs. /d-/, with two features different), they

---

[3] See also Moeser and Bregman (1972), who showed that the learning of grammatical rules in small artificial languages was enabled when a reference-world was provided along with sentences of the language.

[4] Where speakers place new information in an utterance is determined by a number of factors. In languages where the predominant predicate order is VO (verb followed by object), new information tends to go in last place; in languages where the unmarked predicate order is OV (object followed by verb), new information tends not to appear in final position. In some free word order languages, new or newsworthy information comes first. So placing new information last is by no means universal.

showed no preference for passages containing the target forms when they heard them later (Jusczyk & Aslin 1995). They did not treat the forms they had heard earlier as the same as these target forms. This finding is consistent with all the data on younger infants' ability to discriminate differences among sounds for both place and manner of articulation. Recognition of forms as familiar requires prior discrimination of the relevant sounds and then checking of the sequence being discriminated against what is stored in memory. Before infants can start processing speech, they must be able to discriminate words and other linguistic chunks (recurrent sound patterns of various lengths), and they must have begun to store some representation for these in memory for recognition on subsequent occasions.

By nine months, infants also appear to be sensitive to the legal consonant clusters that can begin and end syllables. Dutch infants, for instance, listen longer to legal Dutch sequences for words heard in isolation; they also listen longer to sequences of syllables with legal clusters than to sequences with phonotactically illegal ones (Friederici & Wessels 1993). Information about legal clusters of sounds in a language offers another set of clues to word-boundaries in ongoing speech. By ten to eleven months, English-speaking infants seem to be using several kinds of information about word-boundaries: prosodic (word-based stress patterns), phonotactic (legal sequences at the beginnings and ends of words), and allophonic (positionally conditioned variants of sound segments) (Morgan & Saffran 1995).

As Jusczyk (1997) has argued, findings like these support the following scenario for early word-segmentation: Infants begin with approximations to word-boundaries, presumably based on information from pauses and constancy in repetitive carrier-phrases in child-directed speech. These allow them to identify certain sound sequences with strong (stress-bearing) initial syllables, and they can then use the occurrence of other strong syllables to isolate other potential word-chunks, sequences that do *not* appear in final position in the utterance. That is, the initial identification of some properties of words in a language allows children to discover further properties that help them segment the stream of speech still further. They can then go on to identify the same words in less-prominent positions as well as recognize words occurring in a larger range of syntactic contexts.[5]

The more infants discover about word-boundaries, the more effective they become at extracting words or word-like chunks from the stream of speech as a whole. They rely first on their ability to detect different kinds of regularity in what they are hearing, but then, as they learn more, they can look for other properties that mark the edges of linguistic units. For example, eight-month-olds segment familiar chunks more readily from the edges of utterances (either initial or final position) than from the middle (Seidl & Johnson 2006). In short, their initial

---

[5] This works for stress-timed languages like English, where there is an equal time interval between stresses on the words being produced. (All multisyllabic words have stress assigned to a specific syllable. The stressed syllable is strong, the unstressed one weak.) But can infants exposed to syllable-timed languages like French apply the same range of analytic strategies as they look for word-boundaries? The answer to this question may require further cross-linguistic research.

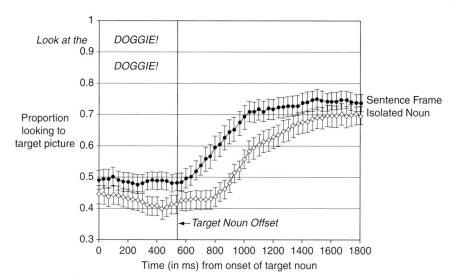

Figure 3.1 *The time course of children's looking to the correct referent in the Isolated Noun and Sentence Frame conditions. Curves show changes over time in the mean proportion of looking to the correct referent (in ms) from noun onset* Source: Anne Fernald & Nereyda Hurtado, Names in frames: Infants interpret words in sentence frames faster than words in isolation, *Developmental Science* 9 (2006): F36. Used with permission from Blackwell Publishing.

ability to recognize recurring patterns in the sound stream as the same is further leveraged by each new type of information they identify for recurring patterns.

When can young children not only recognize familiar sequences – chunks, words – but also map meanings onto newly extracted chunks? In one study, seventeen-month-olds were first given a statistical segmentation task in which to extract recurring sequences (sequences making up chunks with high internal transitional probabilities), and then an object-labeling task. When the infants heard "words" from the first task, they were able to learn the object labels they were presented with in conjunction with a referent. But when they heard nonwords or part-words from the first task instead, they were unable to learn them as labels (Estes *et al.* 2007). This suggests that mere exposure to a sequence of sounds doesn't help in the learning of labels: Children need to segment out the relevant chunk or word first.

At about the same age, infants can also make use of recurring carrier-phrases as signaling upcoming information. In one online processing task, where eighteen-month-olds see two pictures on a screen and listened for a familiar word for one of them, they are faster, by 120 ms, at recognizing familiar words after a carrier-phrase, than they are at hearing the same familiar words said in isolation, as shown in Figure 3.1. In online processing, familiar carrier-phrases appear to alert children to upcoming information better than just a familiar word on its own, or even a separate attention-getter like *Look!* that is then followed, but in a separate utterance, by a familiar word on its own (Fernald & Hurtado 2006). This finding also suggests that carrier-phrases could play an important role in signaling the imminent occurrence of either a familiar word, as in Fernald and Hurtado's study, or of some new word, in final position, after the carrier, at the edge of the utterance.

Final position in the utterance in English (as in many languages) is favored in part because it is where speakers tend to place new information. Certain carrier-phrases then function as flags or cues for new information, including new words for things (Clark & Wong 2002; Clark 2007; Fernald & Mazzie 1991; Fernald & Hurtado 2006). Words in final position receive the main sentential stress and generally convey what is new. Since nouns occur in final position more often than verbs in many languages, this might account in part for why very young children tend to accumulate more nouns than verbs in their initial vocabularies (see Chapter 5). More important though is the fact that final position in carrier-phrases marks what is new. By age two, children seem aware of this and take notice of unfamiliar words presented with final stress in final position. In one experimental study, children aged 2;1 readily learned new nouns for unfamiliar objects when these were presented with final stress, but they failed to learn the word/meaning pairing for new nouns without stress, but in final position (Grassmann & Tomasello 2007; Akhtar, Carpenter, & Tomasello 1996). And parents reading picture books to their fourteen-month-olds, for instance, consistently highlight new words by stressing them (Fernald & Mazzie 1991), just as the parents of two- through five-year-olds stress unfamiliar words they do not expect their children to know. And in addition to stressing these words, they make every effort to place them in final position, regardless of their word-class (Clark 2009).

Finally, children become more efficient at recognizing familiar words during the course of their second year (from 1;3 to 2;1). They get steadily faster at recognizing them while listening to speech that names one of two pictures. The measure is how quickly children look towards the appropriate picture. The mean response time at fifteen months is 1000 ms; by 2;1, this decreases to a mean response time of just under 800 ms (Fernald, Perfors, & Marchman 2006). And analyses of the growth curves for the children studied showed that greater speed and accuracy at 2;1 was correlated with more accelerated vocabulary growth in the second year.

## Storing word shapes in memory

There is little reason to remember a chunk or sequence of sounds unless it conveys consistent information. Meanings motivate children's memory for word shapes and hence for language-specific distinctions among sounds. Shvachkin (1973) argued that children only learn contrasts among sounds (the functional phonology of their first language) when these make a difference to meaning. By studying which contrasts infants could make, he established a developmental sequence for the sound-types of Russian in acquisition from the age of ten months up to two years. The method he used was to teach Russian infants nonsense words for as-yet-unnamed objects. Each pair of monosyllabic words differed only in the

Table 3.1 *Perceiving distinctions among sounds in Russian (between the ages of ten months and two years)*

(1) Discrimination among vowels:
    (i) [a] vs. other vowels
    (ii) [i] vs. [u], [e] vs. [o], [i] vs. [o], [e] vs. [u] (front–back)
    (iii) [i] vs. [e], [u] vs. [o] (high–low)
(2) Presence vs. absence of initial consonants: [ok] vs. [bok], [ek] vs. [bek]
(3) Nasals, liquids, and glides vs. stops and fricatives: [m] vs. [b], [y] vs. [v]
(4) Palatalized vs. nonpalatalized consonants: [n] vs. [ɲ]
(5)   (i) nasals vs. liquids and glides: [m] vs. [l], [n] vs. [r], [n] vs. [y]
    (ii) intranasal distinctions: [m] vs. [n]
    (iii) intraliquid distinctions: [l] vs. [r]
(6) Nasals, liquids, and glides vs. fricatives: [m] vs. [z], [n] vs. [ʒ]
(7) Labials vs. nonlabials: [b] vs. [g], [w] vs. [s]
(8) Stops vs. fricatives: [b] vs. [v], [d] vs. [ʒ]
(9) Alveolars vs. velars: [d] vs. [g], [t] vs. [k]
(10) Voiced vs. voiceless: [p] vs. [b], [f] vs. [v], [s] vs. [z]
(11) "Hushing" vs. "hissing" *s* sounds: [z] vs. [ʒ], [s] vs. [ʃ]
(12) Liquids vs. glides: [r] vs. [y], [l] vs. [y]

*Source*: Shvachkin 1973:124. Used with permission from Holt Rinehart Winston.

segment to be discriminated, for example, /ek/ versus /uk/ for a front–back vowel contrast or /mok/ versus /bok/ for a nasal–oral stop contrast. Shvachkin tested young children repeatedly on each contrast pair by seeing whether they could keep the two meanings they were taught distinct. To demonstrate this, they had to touch, point to, or pick up the correct referent-object when tested. At first, they appeared unable to make many of the contrasts tested, but as they got older, they managed more of them and did so in a consistent developmental order. The sequence he documented is summarized in Table 3.1.

In replications in other languages, Shvachkin's original findings have received general support, but researchers have found variability across children in their order of acquisition. For example, while the overall order in acquisition of stops, then fricatives, and then glides in English is fairly uniform, Edwards (1974) found, for instance, that some children who had mastered the contrast between one stop and fricative pair – /p/ vs. /f/, say – failed to discriminate the same difference in another pair, /b/ vs. /v/ (see also Garnica 1973). This may be further evidence that children start with holistic representations of adult words and only gradually extract the details of contrasting sound segments (Lindblom 1992).

From a quite early age, young children must set up fairly adultlike representations of target words. These stored representations need to contain enough information to be able to recognize each adult form in different contexts, from different speakers, on different occasions, as well as to discriminate each form from others nearby.

How much phonetic detail do children store for familiar words heard from adults? While there has been debate about the amount of phonetic detail children store in their second year, they must clearly store enough to be able to recognize the same word on separate occasions, from different speakers, in different carrier frames and syntactic contexts. What happens if young children hear familiar words that have been distorted in various ways? Preferential listening studies with Dutch infants (aged eleven months) show that they listen longer to words than nonwords, but they don't distinguish words from nonwords if the words are mispronounced at onset or offset (the initial and final sounds). Children prefer correct pronunciations to onset mispronunciations. And when a little older, fourteen to fifteen months, they show similar preferences for forms based directly on adult forms over any distortions, even when the distortions don't interfere with recognition of the target words (Swingley & Aslin 2002; Swingley 2005).

The amount of phonetic detail children appear to store from early on suggests they set up pretty adultlike representations for words from an early age, and store all sorts of phonetic detail in these representations from as young as one- or one-and-a-half years old. The amount of detail they store may explain how children keep track when they learn new words in already dense lexical neighborhoods. Density here refers to the number of words that share phonological forms, perhaps differing from each other in just one segment. For example, there are many words that share the sequence /-at/, as in *cat*, *hat*, *mat*, *rat*, *vat*, *pat*, and *fat*, but very few that share the sequence /-up/, as in *up*, *cup*, and *pup*. So picking up *pup* as a new word might be easier than picking up yet another word ending in *-at*. This proposal is based on the finding that adults are slower to recognize and retrieve words from dense neighborhoods than they are from sparse ones. When seventeen-month-olds are exposed numerous times to new nonwords in either high-density lists or low-density ones (list of nonwords that share segments and sequences with the target words), they look longer at the target referent only in the low-density condition (Hollich, Jusczyk, & Luce 2001). This could be because the children, like adults, find it harder to extract and recognize targets in high-density neighborhoods.

Another possibility is that children are already sensitive to the phonotactic properties of nonwords. That is, they are aware of the probabilities involved in different sequences of sounds in possible words (whether nonwords or real words). When this possibility was explored further, children of seventeen months showed good recognition of the target words in high-density neighborhoods too. In short, children store detailed information about words from early on, and use this information in recognizing familiar words, and in tracking phonotactically possible patterns in new words.

## Storing adultlike targets in memory

The mismatch between how children produce words and how they seem to have represented them in memory is well documented, although only a handful of studies have explored the extent of such mismatches in any detail. If children's representations are based on adults' productions of words, they should be much closer in detail to the adult versions of words than to the versions currently produced by the child. This shows up in the following examples of what Berko and Brown (1960) called the *fis* phenomenon:

(1)    One of us, for instance, spoke to a child who called his inflated plastic fish a *fis*. In imitation of the child's pronunciation, the observer said: "This is your *fis*?" "No," said the child, "my *fis*." He continued to reject the adult's pronunciation until he was told, "This is your fish." "Yes," he said, "my *fis*."   (Berko & Brown 1960:531)

(2)    An example of this was provided in the author's experience by a child who asked if he could come along on a trip to the "mewwy-go-wound." An older child, teasing him, said "David wants to go on the mewwy-go-wound." "No," said David firmly, "you don't say it wight."   (Maccoby & Bee 1965:67)

(3)    FATHER: Say "jump."
       CHILD: *Dup.*
       FATHER: No, "jump."
       CHILD: *Dup.*
       FATHER: No, "jummmp."
       CHILD: *Only Daddy can say **dup**!*   (Smith 1973:10)

In (1), the child is clearly aware of the adult contrast between /s/ and /ʃ/ even though he can't produce it himself, and he consistently corrects the adult when she fails to produce *fish*. The little boy in (2) is similarly aware of the difference between /r/ and /w/ although he himself produces /w/ for both. (Jakobson [1968] and Elkonin [1971] cite similar examples from French and Russian.) And the child in (3) can distinguish between his own production of the cluster /-mp/ and the adult's. The common ingredient in these instances is the child's rejection of his own pronunciation when it is (re)produced by the adult. This suggests that the child's representation for a word like *fish* is actually much closer to adult *fish* than to *fis*, the version produced by the child.

Children also distinguish pairs of adult words that they themselves pronounce alike. Neilson Smith (1973) observed that his son Amahl perceived the difference between *mouse* and *mouth*, for example, long before he was able to produce it: When asked for one or the other, he would fetch the appropriate drawing on a card from the next room. After he began to talk, he continued to perceive this distinction although he produced only one form, "mouse," for both. Other pairs of words that he pronounced alike at this stage included *cart* and *card*, both "gart," and *jug* and *duck*, both "guck." But in comprehension, he consistently distinguished these pairs. Smith argued from this that Amahl must already have stored fairly adultlike representations of the relevant words in memory for recognition.

This child's adultlike representations also took priority in word identification (Morton & Smith 1974). For example, whenever Amahl's own production coincided in form with the representation of some other adult word, he would retrieve that first. So when Smith asked him (aged 4;2) about his pronunciations of the words *shirt*, *shoe*, and *ship*, all still produced with an initial /s-/, he only identified his own words where there wasn't an adult word of that form, as shown in the exchange in (4).

(4)      FATHER: What is a sirt? [= shirt]
         AMAHL (immediately points to his shirt)
         FATHER: What's a soo? [= shoe]
         AMAHL (immediately points to his shoe)
         FATHER: What's a sip?
         AMAHL: *When you drink.* (imitates action)
         FATHER: What else does sip mean?
         AMAHL (puzzled, then doubtfully suggests *zip*, though pronouncing
             it quite correctly)
         FATHER: No: it goes in the water.
         AMAHL: *A boat.*
         FATHER: Say it.
         AMAHL: *No. I can only say* **sip**.     (Smith 1973:136–137)

Notice that Amahl identified his own forms right away for *shirt* and *shoe*, but with *sip* he first retrieved adult *sip* and then had difficulty in coming up with *ship* as well. Again, these observations are quite explicable if (a) the child's representations are closer to the adult forms of these words than to his own productions of them and (b) adult-based representations take priority in word identification.

Experimental evidence that children base their representations for comprehension (and hence for the identification of words) on adult forms comes from research on word recognition in young children. In one study of minimal pairs like *bear* versus *pear*, where the words differed on just one sound segment, Barton (1978) found that children aged 2;3 to 2;11 who already used the words themselves (regardless of pronunciation) succeeded 89% of the time in pointing at appropriate pictures as referents for each term. But when the words in minimal pairs had been taught just before testing, they did less well (48% correct) (see also Swingley, Pinto, & Fernald 1999). This suggests that, by this point in development, children include segmental information about sounds in their representations for comprehension. But vocabularies for younger children contain few minimal pairs already familiar to them, which limits this type of investigation.

Another approach is to look at whether young children find mispronunciations of familiar words harder to process than correctly pronounced forms. Swingley and Aslin (2000) had children aged 1;6 to 1;11 listen to words that were either pronounced correctly or slightly mispronounced (e.g., *baby* vs. *vaby*, *dog* vs. *tog*). They heard the words in short sentences (*Where's the –?*) while looking at pairs of pictures, one representing the referent of the target word. The researchers used visual fixation as the measure: If young children are looking at the picture of a baby when they hear the word *baby*, they typically stay on that picture; but if they are looking at the other picture, they promptly shift away from it to the picture of the baby and fixate that instead. The speed of this shift and the length of their subsequent fixation both offer evidence that the children have processed the target word in what they heard (see Swingley & Fernald 2002).

If children's representations for familiar words are at first vague or under-specified, they should not respond any differently to small changes in pronunciation. But if their representations are accurate (i.e., closely based on adult pronunciations of the target words), they should treat correct pronunciations differently from mispronunciations. Because mispronunciations are harder to recognize, children should take longer before either fixating on or shifting to the target picture. Swingley and Aslin (2000) found that the children's accuracy (the amount of time they fixated on the target picture) was significantly greater for correct words (73%) than for mispronounced ones (61%), but in both conditions, they recognized the intended target. They were also faster in shifting to the target picture with correct words (718 msecs) than with mispronounced ones (850 msecs). These results offer further support for the view that children set up representations for recognizing words that are directly based on the adult pronunciations they hear (see also Ballem & Plunkett 2005). They are also consistent with the finding that, by this stage, infants can discriminate and remember information about the relative order of sounds in pairs of sequences such as [pœt] and [tœp] (Bertoncini & Mehler 1981).

Further evidence for early adultlike representations comes from a study of three-year-olds that followed up Smith's observations. Dodd (1975) found that English-speaking three-year-olds are usually much worse at recognizing their own productions of words and at identifying the target words said by other three-year-olds than they are at recognizing the same words uttered by an unfamiliar adult. She asked three-year-olds to name a large set of pictures and then, first, had them listen to the tape of their own productions and identify each entity being named; next, listen to the tape of another three-year-old doing the same task; and last, listen to the tape of an unfamiliar adult again doing the same task.

The children failed to identify their own words 52% of the time and failed to identify those of a peer 48% of the time. But when they heard the adult tape, they correctly identified the words in it 94% of the time. Moreover, those child productions they did identify were consistently closer to the adult pronunciation than those they failed to identify. Consider the examples in Table 3.2. Forms identified correctly include the pronunciations shown in the center column; among those they failed to identify are forms in the right-hand column. The unidentified forms typically lacked the correct initial segment found in the adult version; they sometimes even lacked the whole first syllable, particularly where this was unstressed (as in *giraffe*); and they often contained single consonants in place of clusters (as in *skipping*). The more distant such pronunciations were from the adult forms, the less likely the three-year-olds were to recognize them. Dodd concluded that children store adult pronunciations for word identification but that they do not store their own deviant pronunciations, since otherwise they should have been able to identify the adult target words on the basis of their own productions. If they had stored their own productions, the degree of mismatch

Table 3.2 *Three-year-olds' recognition of their own versus adult versions of words*

| Adult target | Identifiable pronunciations | Unidentifiable pronunciations |
|---|---|---|
| umbrella | ʌmbɛlə | nenə |
| skipping | skipiŋ | kipiŋk |
| giraffe | əræf | raft |
| zebra | zɛvrə | ʒɛbrə |
| shoe | su | sə |
| flower | fæːə | æːə |

*Source*: Barbara Dodd, Children's understanding of their phonological forms, *Quarterly Journal of Experimental Psychology* 27 (1975):171. Reprinted by permission of The Experimental Psychology Society.

between child and adult pronunciation should not have affected their recognition of the target words.

As children hear more speech from both familiar and unfamiliar people, they must add to their memory-store of word forms. They can gradually add information about the forms of more and more words, and also add in information about how to normalize different accents of their first language so that they correctly identify words from speakers with a slightly different vowel system, for example. That is, in addition to learning how to take into account variation in a single speaker, they learn what range of pronunciations count as instances of the same word across different speakers (see Foulkes *et al.* 2005). Greater exposure to the language also allows them to increase their store of forms for comprehension. It offers them more material for further analysis of words and phrases into smaller units of meaning. Finally, children also store information about individual words and what else they occur with.

In summary, children must add continually to their memory-store so they will be able to recognize forms already encountered when they hear them again. They must store not just forms that recur but also any meanings they have managed to associate with each form. These additions to their memory-store play an important role when it comes to children's own productions: They offer a template or target version of the form being attempted when children try to produce that word themselves. What children store is based on the speech they hear from others, probably primarily child-directed speech. Any mismatch with their adult-based forms stored in memory serves to signal what they still need to streamline in their own productions so that they will be consistently understood by others.

## Representations for comprehension

The data from children's own ability to recognize words suggest that they base even their early representations for comprehension on adult forms of the target words or phrases. But how much of an adult target gets stored as a representation for comprehension? Do these representations correspond directly with the adult's? This would assume that children have already analyzed all they need to know about the phonology of their first language by the time they begin to store word forms in memory for later recognition. And while children may be fairly sensitive to the sounds of their first language and even to some of the phonotactic details by the end of their first year, it is unclear whether they have really mastered the sound system in terms of all the variants for individual sounds or the range of adjustments made in each phonological context as well as in rapid versus careful speech.

One view is that at first children base their representations on their own productions of the adult target words (e.g., Waterson 1971). If this were the case, since children's forms in production are pretty distant from the adult targets, how would they recognize what an adult was saying? To store only one's own productions seems to offer no route for development. Children would have difficulty recognizing what adults say and, without any adultlike representations as a guide, also lack any templates against which to compare their own faulty productions with more adultlike ones. In short, they would have no representations to provide targets for what their productions should sound like.

Another view is that what children store reflects only what they know so far about the phonology of the language they are learning. Under this view, one might expect children to sometimes include more detail than necessary for some forms and not enough for others. One consequence is that children could fail to recognize words where they have stored too much detail, because a particular speaker might not include all the detail found in another's utterance of the same forms. Or they may have too many forms associated with a single representation, because they have not included enough detail to be able to keep them apart. If children are to be able to make use of representations in memory, they must be able to recognize a form produced by the same speaker on different occasions and also that form produced by different speakers. If so, the best targets for such storage are the adult forms used in speech to children. The closer children's representations are to those forms, the better able they will be to recognize them (Swingley 2005). At the same time, it seems likely that these representations in memory may change over time as children's phonological knowledge becomes more systematic and as they learn to abstract away both from specific speakers and from idiosyncratic pronunciations.

Children need to represent everything that could be considered relevant to word recognition for their language. This includes all kinds of information about possible word forms. For instance, they must be able to recognize the phonetic segments, syllables, and stress patterns (e.g., weak–strong vs. strong–weak stress assignments) found in a language like English. They must be able to recognize tones on words and how individual tones contribute to combinations of tones in a language like Chinese. They must recognize how vowel harmony applies within words in a language like Turkish. And they must come to recognize which sequences of sounds are legal where, within each language (see, e.g., Messer 1967). They must be able to deal with every detail of the sound system that plays a systematic role in how others produce their words. But notice that the representations needed for comprehension do not correspond to those needed for production. Comprehension depends on the addressee's identifications of words from acoustic information, combined in varying degrees with visual information (e.g., lip shape), in addition to all sorts of top-down information about the probable topic of conversation. It may also depend in part on the perception of intonation contours – over words, phrases, and whole clauses (Hirsh-Pasek *et al.* 1987), since these can also mark boundaries in the speech stream. But none of these representations need include information on how to *produce* the utterances in question (see Chapter 5).

## Summary

For infants to get started on language, they must break into the speech stream. They need to do this so they can isolate words along with any smaller units (morphemes on the one hand; syllables and segments on the other) in order to arrive at generalizations about possible word forms in their first language. This comprises a critical step for identifying units of meaning that may range in size from single morphemes up to combinations of several morphemes in complex words, idioms, phrases, and constructions, all varying in size and complexity. None of these will be accessible without this initial analysis of the speech stream.

# 4    Early words

Once children break into the speech stream, they have two problems to solve. First, they have to map meanings onto words and phrases. For each conceptual domain, they have to find out, first, how to express particular meanings via the words and phrases available in the language spoken around them, and, second, how best to use language to communicate their intentions to others. They must discover how to tailor their utterances for each addressee, taking common ground into account, marking social distinctions appropriately, in order to convey what they mean on each occasion. In solving these two problems, children must look for consistent pairings of situations with utterances or parts of utterances in adult speech. They need to take detailed account of what adults say when and for what purpose. Learning to convey their own intentions is inseparable from learning how to interpret the intentions of others. The prerequisite to this, of course, is breaking into the speech stream to identify recurrent chunks and attach preliminary meanings to them (Chapter 3).

What is the content of children's first utterances – the single words they pick up on and the first meanings they attach to them – in early expressions of their intentions? What is the nature of early vocabularies and their relation to eventual (adult) vocabulary size? And what paths do children follow as they add new words to their repertoires? Do they add words at a steady pace or in spurts? Do they all progress in the same way? Finally, how do they use their early words? What meanings do they assign, and to what extent do they supplement these words with other devices in their attempts to communicate?

What is the general trajectory for children as they acquire words and build up their vocabulary? Few children produce any words before age one. Most say their first recognizable words in the next three months or so. By age two, they may be able to produce anywhere from 100 to 600 distinct words. By age six, they have a vocabulary of around 14,000 in comprehension, with somewhat fewer in production. These numbers imply that they acquire words between age two and age six at a rate of nine to ten words a day. For each year in school, they add some 3,000 more words to their vocabulary (for an additional 36,000 in twelve years of schooling), and between the ages of twelve and seventeen, it is estimated that they are exposed to up to 10,000 new word-root-plus-affix combinations just in school textbooks. At a minimum, children may have learnt some 50,000 words by the time they leave school. English-speaking adults have an estimated vocabulary in the range of 50,000 to 100,000 words (see Anglin

1993; Clark 1993; Nagy & Anderson 1984; Templin 1957). Estimates for the speakers of other languages are probably very similar.

Notice what an enormous task this presents: Learning a word requires assigning it a meaning, finding out which grammatical category it belongs to, and identifying the constructions it can appear in. But this can't all be done in one step. Many words have more than one meaning and, even with one meaning, may have several different nuances associated with them when they occur in different constructions. Many appear not only in a range of constructions but also in various idioms. Take a few uses of three common English terms used as both nouns and verbs. The term *brush* can be used as a noun to denote an implement with bristles for brushing and thereby tidying or cleaning things, as in the expressions *use a brush*, *a hairbrush*, or *a brush and pan*. The same term can be used to refer to the action of brushing, as in *brush one's hair*, *brush something aside* (or *away*), or *brush past someone*. And it appears as either a noun or verb in various idioms, among them: *have a brush with* (= encounter), *brush up on* (= renew knowledge about), or *brush over* (= ignore). The term *run* has a similar range. As a noun, it denotes any episode or event of running, as in *go for a run*. As a verb, it denotes the activity itself, as in *run fast*, *run away*, *run about*, or *run a race*. And it appears in such idioms as *run across* (= meet by accident), *run into* (= meet, or collide with), or *run through* (= consume). Or take the term *spill*. As a noun, it denotes an event with a fall or tumble, the quantity spilt, or a slip of wood or long match, as in *take a spill*, *make a spill on the tablecloth*, or *use a spill to light the fire*. As a verb, it denotes the activity, as in *spill water* or *spill crumbs on the floor*. And it appears in idioms like *spill the beans* (= reveal a secret) or *cry over spilt milk* (= express useless regret).

Children could not acquire this range of meaning all at once. In fact, acquiring the conventional adult meanings of a word involves the gradual accumulation of information as children learn more about each term and the constructions it can appear in. They start to use words, of course, as soon as they have *some* meaning attached to them. Inferences about early word meanings, then, afford us only small glimpses of the general process of meaning accretion, but they can also reveal considerable consistency across languages at specific ages in what children do and in how they may limit their hypotheses about word meanings. (This is taken up further in Chapter 6.)

## Early vocabularies

What do young children talk about? What do their early vocabularies consist of? A survey of the first 40–50 words reported in diary studies for a variety of languages showed that children's first 50 words fall into a fairly small number of categories (Clark 1979): people, food, body parts, clothing, animals, vehicles, toys, household objects, routines and activities or states. Century-old diary reports coincide fairly closely with the first 50 words produced today by at

Table 4.1 *Early word production: First words said by at least 50% of the monthly sample (at each month from 1;0 to 1;6)*

---

*People*: daddy (1;0), mommy (1;0), baby (1;3), grandma (1;6), grandpa (1;6)
*Food/drink*: banana (1;4), juice (1;4), cookie (1;4), cracker (1;5), apple (1;5), cheese (1;5)
*Body parts*: eye (1;4), nose (1;4), ear (1;5)
*Clothing*: shoe (1;4), sock (1;6), hat (1;6)
*Animals*: dog (1;2), kitty (1;4), bird (1;4), duck (1;4), cat (1;6), fish (1;6)
*Vehicles*: car (1;4), truck (1;6)
*Toys*: ball (1;3), book (1;4), balloon (1;4), boat (1;6)
*Household objects*: bottle (1;4), keys (1;5)
*Routines*: bye (1;1), hi (1;2), no (1;3), night-night (1;4), bath (1;5), peekaboo (1;5), thank you (1;6)
*Activities (sound effects, motion, state)*: uh oh (1;2), woof (1;4), moo (1;4), ouch (1;4), baa baa (1;4), yum yum (1;4), vroom (1;5), up (1;5), down (1;5)

---

*Source*: Fenson *et al.* 1994:93. Used with permission from the Society for Research in Child Development.

least 50% of the sample for the first six months of language production measured by the McArthur infant and toddler (1;0–1;6) communicative development inventories (Fenson *et al.* 1994:92–93) (Table 4.1).

Not surprisingly, young children talk about what is going on around them: the people they see every day; toys and small household objects they can manipulate; food they themselves can control; clothing they can get off by themselves; animals and vehicles, both of which move and so attract attention; daily routines and activities; and some sound effects. The terms for all of these are used first as single-word utterances, so it is not possible to assign them yet to any grammatical word-classes such as noun or verb.

Several researchers have proposed that children go through a one-word stage before they learn how to combine two or more words in a single utterance (e.g., Dromi 1987). But children differ in the rate at which they learn to produce their first words. In one study of six infants, researchers tracked their trajectories in word production, using a strict criterion for what counted as a word compared to a nonword vocalization (Robb, Bauer, & Tyler 1994). They found considerable variation in age for when children reached the ten-word (between 1;0 and 1;4) and then the fifty-word mark (between 1;5 and 1;10) as well as in the average length of utterance for each infant at those two points. Since children also differ in motor skill, whether for walking or picking up small objects, they should differ just as much when it comes to the fine motor movements required for speech. This suggests that the single-word period is not a discrete stage in development but rather a period when children learn to produce larger and larger numbers of intelligible vocalizations. The children produced as many recognizable words as they did nonword vocalizations in the period from 1;1 to 1;9. But as their vocabularies got larger, they began to produce up to twice as many intelligible words as they did unintelligible vocalizations. Children continue to produce nonword forms throughout their first months of acquisition, even though their ratio of words to nonwords is typically over 3:1 by the time they hit the fifty-word mark in production (see also Peters 1983). This is consistent with the view that producing a word takes motor skill, and that in turn may take a good deal of practice.

### Vocabulary spurt, or not?

The first words children learn to produce tend to be used in highly restricted ways, often in very limited contexts. They may say *hi*, for example, only when standing in a particular doorway or *shoe* only for shoes inside a cupboard. These uses have been characterized as context-bound, but they rarely last more than a few weeks and rarely affect more than two or three words (Barrett 1995). After several weeks or months of adding rather slowly to their initial repertoire, many children appear to increase their rate of production rather suddenly. This increase typically occurs around 1;5 to 1;8 as they approach the fifty-word level in production (Bloom 1973; Nelson 1973) and often consists of an increasing number of words for objects.[1] Several researchers have argued that this spurt in words produced marks a significant step forward in acquisition because it marks the point at which children show they have recognized the symbolic value of words, when they realize that everything has a name (see, e.g., McShane 1980).

But identifying this first vocabulary spurt in young children has often been difficult. What counts as an increase in rate – a move from two new words produced per week to four new words per week? Or from 4–5 new words a week to 10 new words a week? The criterion Goldfield and Reznick (1996:242) offered for identifying this spurt was "three to five contiguous 2.5-week intervals in which 10 or more new words were added per interval." In their 1990 study, they identified a vocabulary spurt in a sample of eighteen children followed with diary records and short vocabulary checklists from age 1;2 to 1;10, with analysis of the cumulative diary entries every 2.5 weeks. Thirteen of the children gave evidence of a spurt lasting up to three months. The spurt showed as many as 60 new words added in one 2.5-week interval. For two of the thirteen, the spurt began around 1;2; for another five children, it took place between 1;5 and 1;7; for the remaining six, it didn't occur until 1;8 to 1;10. For these children, the proportion of nouns (words for objects) increased with the overall number of words produced. But the remaining five children gave no evidence of a spurt. Instead, they followed a path of steady increase, adding words from all word-classes (rather than mainly from nouns), throughout the whole period.

---

[1] I am deliberately avoiding the terms "noun" and "verb" for the moment since it is impossible to know what the grammatical status of these words is in early child speech (see also Stern & Stern 1928).

To what extent, then, is the early vocabulary spurt attributable to the insight that words refer to things? When children show no spurt in production, is it because they acquired this insight early, whereas others who acquire it somewhat later signal it with a spurt at that point? Goldfield and Reznick (1990, 1996) looked at the correlations between the presence or absence of a word spurt and birth order and found that first-borns were slightly more likely to show a spurt in production. (Of the thirteen first-borns, eight showed a vocabulary spurt; and the five steady-increase children were all second-born.) They proposed that exposure to other children's speech might result in an earlier grasp of the symbolic function of language, hence the absence of vocabulary spurts for their later-born children.

Another view is that an early vocabulary spurt reflects changes in children's skill at producing words. It marks advances in articulatory motor skill rather than insight into the symbolic value of words. For example, some children's initial attempts at words are a long way from their adult targets and may at first go unrecognized. These children appear to practice intensively on each new word attempted before they try another. Other children manage to get closer to the adult target on their first try and show little evidence of practice after adding a new word. In a comparison of two such children (both first-borns), the practicer gave clear evidence of a vocabulary spurt just prior to her first production of two-word combinations, while the nonpracticer showed no signs of a spurt but demonstrated steady acquisition of new words and produced word combinations early, within a few weeks after production of his first word (Clark 1993; Dromi 1987). In short, whether or not there is a discernible point at which children recognize the symbolic function of language (of words), motor skill clearly plays a role, from the start, in how easily and how recognizably children *produce* words.

But vocabulary spurts in production may not actually be spurts at all. Consider the fact that, as soon as children begin to talk, they steadily add more words to their repertoires. This requires them to construct representations for multiple words that differ along several dimensions in difficulty. The degree of difficulty may depend on the meaning of each word – how accessible a first mapping for this is from the adult context of use; on the form of each word to be produced – how complex it is from an articulatory point of view; on the syntactic frame each word is introduced in, and the child's level of skill in accessing and producing each word just added. Since words differ in difficulty along a variety of dimensions, they should take different amounts of time to acquire, and since children are adding new words all the time, at a certain point they will begin to produce many more than they had earlier. Computational modeling of these factors shows that, in effect, a vocabulary "spurt" is simply the natural product of parallel learning combined with variations in difficulty (McMurray 2007). This suggests that the variations seen in the vocabulary growth of children between age one and two is just that: variation in the amount and difficulty of the extensive parallel learning necessarily involved in the learning of vocabulary (see also Anisfeld *et al.* 1998; Redford & Miikkulainen 2007).

Can we reliably assess children's growth in vocabulary simply from observing what they produce? Since production generally lags behind comprehension, production-based measures of vocabulary size seem likely to underestimate what young children may actually know. One puzzle for assessing how much children understand in the early stages lies in how to measure the size of their comprehension vocabulary. Goldfield and Reznick (1992), for example, checked what infants looked at when they were shown pairs of pictures and heard a word for the object in one of them. They checked on only 15 words at each two-month-interval test between the ages of 1;2 and 1;10, but by 1;8–1;10, for instance, some children may understand several hundred words (Goldfield & Reznick 1992). In fact, the McArthur norms suggest that, at 1;4, infants at the fiftieth percentile for production may understand 151–200 words even though they only produce around 18 (Fenson *et al.* 1994:66). Oviatt (1980) assessed comprehension in nine- to seventeen-month-olds by looking at how reliably they responded to recently taught words for objects and actions. Children under one year old learnt relatively little; to elicit comprehension took considerable time and repetition on the part of parents; and any comprehension was limited to terms for highly salient objects and activities. By 1;3 to 1;5, though, nearly all the infants she tested showed both immediate- and longer-term comprehension of newly acquired terms for objects and actions. Comprehension at this stage appears far ahead of production.

In summary, several factors suggest that the emergence of a symbolic insight into language does not explain children's vocabulary growth. Rather, it depends on the increasing number of words children are trying to represent in memory combined with the degree of articulatory skill each child brings to language. Less-skilled children may need to spend more time on practice initially, but once they master certain sound contrasts, they find themselves in a position to add new words more rapidly (in a spurt) because they already know so many words. But the new words they start to produce are only produced once children have attached a stable enough meaning to them. The degree of difficulty here differs from word to word. At the same time, children who start out with greater articulatory skill need spend less time on practice so are more likely to attempt longer sequences (word combinations) at an earlier age. This account would favor continuous models of vocal development, based in part on motor development, rather than on models with discrete stages, from one word at a time to two words combined, from one-syllable words to two-syllable ones, and so on.

## Object words before action words?

The notion of vocabulary spurt has sometimes also been tied to an increase in the number of object words (nouns) found in children's early vocabularies. But there has also been independent research on the composition of early vocabularies (typically at the 50–100 word level in production). In a now classic paper, Gentner (1982) surveyed reports of early vocabularies and found that children seemed to use more object words than action words in languages as different as English, German, Japanese, Kaluli, Mandarin, and Turkish. She proposed that this reflected a bias towards objects that were bounded perceptually and conceptually, in comparison to events. Objects were more readily identifiable and therefore more readily associated with linguistic expressions. The result, she argued, was a bias towards object words (a "noun bias") in children's early vocabularies. Because verbs are relational in nature and take account of participants in an event, they are more complex than nouns for objects and are therefore harder to acquire.

This proposal provoked both interest and argument. Subsequent studies of languages like Tzeltal, Korean, and Mandarin, which all allow more extensive ellipsis of arguments than languages like English, had mixed results: Some researchers found that children produced more action words (verbs) than object words (nouns) at around 1;8 to 1;10 in these languages (e.g., Brown 1998; Choi & Gopnik 1995; Tardif 1996; Tardif, Shatz, & Naigles 1997). But others reported there was no evidence of an action word (verb) bias, for example, in Korean (Au, Dapretto, & Song 1994). Reanalyses of the English data have also suggested there is less of an object word or noun bias than was originally claimed (Bloom, Tinker, & Margulis 1993; but see Gentner & Boroditsky 2001). Disagreements over the facts in different languages also suggest that spontaneous speech samples and maternal checklists of vocabulary may simply yield different results.

Finally, both child speech and child-directed speech in different contexts typically contain different proportions of object and action word uses, even within a single language. When children read books with their parents, they produce more object words than when they play with mechanical toys in both English and Mandarin (Gelman & Tardif 1998). Gelman and Tardif also compared the word-type proportions in children's spontaneous speech with the proportions found in maternal recall using the McArthur inventory checklists to identify child vocabularies (Fenson *et al.* 1994). For both languages, mothers underreported the number of action words (verbs) their children used. Somewhat younger children (1;4 to 1;8) learning either English or Korean at the fifty-word level all had more nouns than verbs (Kim, McGregor, & Thompson 2000). But the children learning Korean learnt significantly more verbs than the children acquiring English. They heard more activity-oriented utterances from caregivers, more verbs, and more salient cues to verb meanings (see also Choi 2000; Ogura *et al.* 2006; Kauschke, Lee, & Pae 2007).

What can we conclude from this? Languages indeed differ in the amount of ellipsis they allow and hence in the relative proportions of verbs to nouns in spontaneous (adult) speech. At the same time, speakers of all languages typically have a range of means for talking about both objects and events, and children must learn this vocabulary in learning a first language. Whether any long-term cognitive consequences stem from overall differences in the proportions of noun-to-verb use in child-directed speech across languages may be difficult, if not impossible, to establish. Where speakers of one language may use a verb, speakers of another may use a noun, perhaps in combination with an auxiliary or light verb. There is also a further problem when it comes to children under age two who often use just one word at a time: Can we reliably assume that what are nouns for adults are also nouns for children?

Consider the following question: Can we assign words to part-of-speech categories when children are producing only one word at a time? In one study of English, some children (aged 1;7 to 2;5) had picked up the word *door* and used it consistently for opening things and for getting access to things – opening boxes, taking lids off jars, removing nuts from bolts, taking clothes off dolls. But other children the same age used *open* in the same range of contexts to express the same range of meaning (Griffiths & Atkinson 1978). That is, some had chosen what for adults was a noun, and others had chosen a verb, but the child uses for the two terms appeared identical. One solution is to wait until children start to produce utterances in which the structure reliably identifies the words in question as nouns or verbs. But this means waiting until children use both the appropriate word-endings to distinguish nouns from verbs and consistent word order in predicates, verb before direct object, say – at least in a language like English (Bowerman 1973b).

Child uses can often diverge from adult uses, as the observations of *door* and *open* show. At the same time, children may well use a larger number of adult nouns for talking about objects and of verbs for talking about actions, just because these are the terms that have been offered and made most accessible to them for talking about those things. When adults talk to small children, they are more likely to use nouns for objects and verbs for actions, so it should be no surprise if this is reflected in children's early word uses. At the same time, for those languages with more (pronoun) argument ellipsis, children will hear proportionally more utterances containing only verbs, or verbs with fewer noun arguments, and this too is reflected in child usage. Finally, to label the terms in single-word utterances as nouns or verbs attributes additional knowledge about these word-classes to very young children, knowledge they are still unlikely to have (Stern & Stern 1928).

### Early word extensions

Children's earliest word uses often coincide with adult usage but may also depart from it in quite striking ways. Both nineteenth- and twentieth-century diarists, for example, noted numerous occasions where young children *overextended* their words and used them for referring to things that would not be covered by the adult word. For example, a two-year-old might overextend the word *dog* to refer to cats, sheep, horses, and a variety of other four-legged mammals. Why do children do this? One possibility is that they do not yet distinguish among the mammal types they are referring to this way. However, since one-year-olds can readily distinguish cats from dogs, for example, and both from other animal types,

Table 4.2 *Early word uses: Overextensions based on shape*

| Word | First referent | Domain of (over)extensions |
|---|---|---|
| *mooi* | moon (Eng.) | > cakes > round marks on windows > writing on windows and in books > round shapes in books > tooling on leather book covers > round postmarks > letter O |
| *nénin* | breast (Fr.) | > button on garment > point of bare elbow > eye in portrait > face in portrait > face in photo |
| *buti* | ball (Serb.) | > ball > radish > stone spheres on park gates |
| *ticktock* | watch (Eng.) | > clock > all clocks and watches > gas meter > fire hose on spool > bath scale with round dial |
| *gumene* | coat button (Serb.) | > collar stud > door handle > light switch > anything small and round |
| *baw* | ball (Eng.) | > apples > grapes > eggs > squash > bell clapper > anything round |
| *kottiebaiz* | bars of crib (Eng.) | > large toy abacus > toast rack > picture of building with columned façade |
| *tee* | stick (Eng.) | > cane > umbrella > ruler > [old-fashioned] razor > board of wood > all sticklike objects |
| *kutija* | cardboard box (Serb.) | > matchbox > drawer > bedside table |
| *mum* | horse (Eng.) | > cow > calf > pig > moose > all four-legged animals |

*Note*: The symbol > indicates the next (over)extension for the word in question.
Based on Clark 1973a.

this explanation seems implausible (Mandler & McDonough 1993). Another possibility is that children overextend words for communicative reasons. They may well know that their word is not the right one, but they don't have or can't readily access the right word, so they make do with a term close by.

Overextensions appear most commonly in children's speech from about age 1;6 to 2;6 and may affect as many as 40% of children's early words until they reach a production vocabulary of around one hundred (Rescorla 1980). Some overextensions last no more than a day, but others may persist for several weeks or even months. The majority appear to be based on some similarity of shape between the adult referent for the term overextended and the child target on a particular occasion (Clark 1973a; see also Anglin 1976). Some typical examples of overextensions based on shape, observed in children acquiring different languages, are listed in Table 4.2. Overextensions are sometimes based on other physical similarities, most often characteristics of movement, sound, taste, size, or texture (Table 4.3). (Color is notably absent, perhaps because it is less reliable as an indicator of category membership.)[2]

---

[2] Color is also absent from most dictionary definitions, perhaps for the same reason.

Table 4.3 *Overextensions based on movement, size, sound, and texture*

| Word | First referent | Domain of (over)extensions |
|------|----------------|----------------------------|
| *sch* | sound of train (Ger.) | > all moving machines |
| *ass* | toy goat on wheels, with rough hide (Ger.) | > sister > wagon (things that move) > all things that move > all things with rough surface |
| *fly* | fly (Eng.) | > specks of dirt > dust > all small insects child's own toes > crumbs of bread > toad |
| *em* | worm (Eng.) | > flies > ants > all small insects > heads of timothy grass |
| *fafer* | *chemin de fer*, sound of train (Fr.) | > steaming coffee pot > anything that hissed or made a noise |
| *wau-wau* | dog (Serb.) | > all animals > toy dog > soft house slippers > picture of old man in furs |

Based on Clark 1973a

Evidence in favor of the communicative view of these overextended word uses comes from the asymmetry observable between children's production and comprehension. Words overextended in production are rarely overextended in comprehension. Take a one-year-old who overextends a word like *ball*, say, to refer to other round objects like doorknobs, lamps, pieces of soap, apples, and oranges. The same child, presented with a picture of a ball and a picture of an apple, and asked "Show me the ball," points to the picture of the ball. That is, in comprehension, children show a much closer match to adult uses than they do in their production of the same target words (Thomson & Chapman 1977).

While shape, category membership, and lexical knowledge are clearly all factors in children's early overextensions, few studies have tried to disentangle them. Notice that shape and taxonomic category are usually highly correlated in the world (cats and dogs are both four-legged, mammal-shaped animals), and words can serve to identify category membership for two-year-olds even where surface similarity is lacking (see Gelman & Coley 1990). With overextensions, it is often unclear whether children are overextending a term on the basis of overall shape and size, or taxonomic category, or both. In a study of both the production and comprehension of overextended terms, Gelman and her colleagues (1998) first elicited overextensions from children aged 2;0, 2;6, and 4;6. These were typically based on a combination of shape and taxonomic category, and the two younger groups produced many more than the four-year-old group. They then checked on the same children's understanding of the terms *dog* and *apple*, commonly overextended, in a task designed to find the boundaries of these two words. Children consistently gave more accurate responses in comprehension than production for the same pictured items. (They also became more accurate with age.) But their responses were affected by the familiarity of the items pictured: children did better overall on familiar instances than on unfamiliar ones, and with unfamiliar ones, they were less likely to use shape

Table 4.4 *Narrowing down domains by adding new words*

| Word | Initial and subsequent referents | More appropriate word |
|------|----------------------------------|----------------------|
| *papa* | father/grandfather/mother 1;0 | **mama** 1;3 |
|  | any man 1;2 | **Mann** 1;5 |
| *Mann* | pictures of adults 1;5 any adult 1;6 | **Frau** 1;7 |
| *baby* | self/other children 1;2 pictures of children 1;4 | **boy** 1;8 |
|  | any child 1;8 |  |
| *ball* | balls 1;0 balloon, ball of yarn 1;4 | **balloon** 1;10 |
| *Wauwau* | dogs 1;1, stone lion 1;1 | **dog** 1;11 |
|  | horses (bronze bookends)/toy dog/ | **hottey** [horsie] 1;10 |
|  | soft slippers with face 1;3 | **shoe** 1;6 |
|  | fur-clad man in poster 1;4 | **Mann** 1;5 |
|  | porcelain elephant 1;6 |  |
|  | picture of sloth 1;8 |  |
| *cake* | candy 1;6 | **candy** 1;10 |
|  | real cakes and sand cakes 1;9 |  |
| *cookie* | cookies and crackers 1;6 | **cracker** 1;10 |
| *candy* | candy 1;10 |  |
|  | cherries/anything sweet 1;11 |  |

Based on Barrett 1978

alone and did slightly better by choosing taxonomic category or both shape and category. Young children's overextensions therefore probably don't depend on similarities of shape alone but rather on shape combined with other properties, in particular those that help identify the taxonomic category (Gelman *et al.* 1998b).

The communicative view of overextended uses is also supported by observations of what happens when children start to produce words for objects that had formerly been in the overextension of an earlier word. Take the case of a child who overextends *ball* to talk about apples, say. What happens when he starts to produce *apple* as well as *ball*? He promptly restricts his earlier overextension of *ball* so it no longer includes apples. This pattern of use with the addition of new words is illustrated in Table 4.4, with data from Leopold's (1939–1949) diary study of his daughter Hildegard. As this child learnt to produce words for things in the domains of various overextended words, she removed the pertinent referents from her earlier overextensions. Once Hildegard acquired a more appropriate word (in the right-hand column), she ceased to overextend the word in the left-hand column to that part of the domain.

Logically, child word uses could also be underextended, could fail to match, or could coincide with adult usage. Children may underextend words in comprehension as they first start to establish their extension, but this is difficult to observe because underextensions (unlike overextensions) are always included in the set of appropriate adult uses, even if they are more limited in range (Dromi 1987). Consider a child who only produces the word *car* when she sees cars moving on the street below but never says it when she is at street level and sees cars going by (Bloom 1973). Does she realize that cars in the street are the same kind of thing and so belong to the same category as cars seen from above? Part of learning a word meaning is also learning what the extension of each term is, by learning what counts as a possible referent in different settings. Children also try out some words in ways that are hard to link to any adult use. The target word itself may not even be identifiable, and the general absence of adult comprehension typically leads to the word's being quickly abandoned. Such mismatches, though, perhaps because of their complete failure to communicate anything, have rarely been reported. Most of the time, children's uses in production appear to coincide rather directly with adult usage in the contexts where they *are* used (Huttenlocher & Smiley 1987).

## Where do early meanings come from?

Children appear to draw on two major sources in their initial assumptions about the kinds of things words can be used for. First, they attend to what the adults talking to them are talking *about*. They draw on the words and utterances addressed to them, by making the readiest inferences possible about referents, on the basis of joint attention combined with physical and conversational co-presence. From this, they find out that adults talk about kinds and individuals. This in turn allows them to make certain generalizations about the objects, properties, and activities being referred to. These inferences are buttressed by the ontological categories children have available. They already have experience, for example, of a range of types – objects, actions, relations, and properties. Among object-types, they have encountered kinds that are individuals (dogs, chairs, spoons), that are countable (dogs, etc.), and that can be identified by shape (as demonstrated by their sorting skills and by their early overextensions) (Namy & Waxman 2000; Prudden *et al.* 2006). They have encountered certain substance-types (milk, rice, earth, sand), and certain activity-types that regularly involve one participant (motions like running or changes of location like sitting), two participants (causative actions like breaking or opening), or even more than two (putting an object somewhere or giving something to someone) (Buresh, Woodward, & Brune 2006). They have also encountered a range of relations in space and time (containment, support, or juxtaposition in space; sequence or simultaneity in time). And they hear adults talking about these in ways that may divide up space differently from one language to the next, as shown in Box 4A (e.g., Bowerman 1996b; Choi 2006). Finally, the greater their experience with object- and activity-types, the more readily they can distinguish some of the properties that appear to group some kinds of objects or some kinds of activities.

**4A Cross-cutting categories in Korean and English: Korean *kkita* 'fit tightly/interlock' vs. English *put in* and *put on***

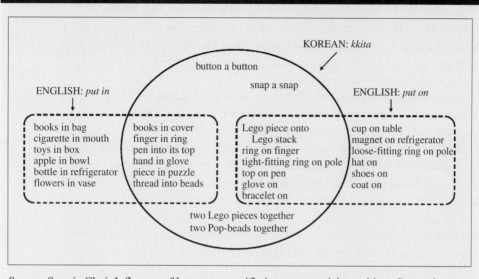

*Source*: Soonja Choi, Influence of language-specific input on spatial cognition: Categories of containment, *First Language* 26 (2006): 211, reprinted with permission from Sage Publications Ltd.

In summary, children's initial hypotheses about word meanings arise from the conjunction of social and conceptual knowledge. The people around them direct their attention and offer them utterances about what is at the locus of that joint attention; and in doing this, adults tend to focus on objects and events in the here and now since these are highly accessible and allow them to ensure that they and their children are both attending to the same things. Children bring to these interactions whatever conceptual categories they have already identified, plus their emerging knowledge about language. But finding out exactly how these two sources mesh takes careful attention to just what is being encoded by the language and what is not. Solving the mapping problem takes time.

### Making do

As children start to use language, they generally make do with minimal means. They may wish to talk about many more things than they have words for. This communicative impulse, it seems, lies behind some of the options they favor as they stretch their linguistic resources to their limits. One way in which they do this is to overextend some of their early words to talk about things for which they don't yet have the necessary words (Tables 4.2 and Tables 4.3). They also rely heavily on both deictic and general-purpose terms. They use deictic terms like *that* to pick out all kinds of objects and events, and they make use of general-purpose verbs like *do* to pick out different kinds of activities (Clark 1978b, 1978c; Rodrigo *et al.* 2004). In context, with the aid of joint attention, it is normally quite clear what children are talking about when they do this. Without contextual details, though, it is usually impossible to interpret such utterances as they were intended at the time they were produced.

Children also rely on one further resource, especially during the earlier stages of acquisition: gestures that communicate about the speaker's intentions. They take account of gaze (especially for purposes of joint attention) and of gestures of the head, hand, or body that indicate what speakers are attending to and hence talking about, or what they want their children to attend to (e.g., Behne, Carpenter, & Tomasello 2006; Harris, Barlow-Brown, & Chasin 1995; Moore & Dunham 1995; Woodward 2003; Woodward & Guajardo 2002). Children also attend to gestures that demonstrate an action, since these too may offer hints about what the speaker expects – whether in the form of what object to attend to (the locus of gaze or hand gesture), what action to perform on it (iconic gestures of manipulating, moving, tipping, etc.), where to put something (movements towards a container or customary storage place), and so on (e.g., Moll *et al.* 2006; Thoermer & Sodian 2001; Zukow 1986). Infants and young children not only attend to adult gestures of all kinds, they often gesture themselves, especially during their second year. Infant gestures may supplement early word production and so extend children's communicative options when the linguistic means they control are still rather meager.

## Gestures, intentions, and words

Towards the end of their first year, infants begin to use two broad classes of gestures: pointing and reaching. With pointing, infants typically try to direct the attention of others, while with reaching they indicate things they want (Werner & Kaplan 1963). More recent studies of infants' early communicative gestures have considered them as marking acts of communication that *indicate* (mostly pointing-type gestures) or *request* (mostly reaching-type gestures, often open-handed or with an opening-and-closing hand) (e.g., Capirci *et al.* 2005; Franco & Butterworth 1996; Guidetti 2002; Liszkowski *et al.* 2006; Zukow-Goldring & Rader 2001). As such, they have been characterized as protospeech acts, the forerunners of the speech acts with those functions (Bates, Camaioni, & Volterra 1975; Bruner 1975).

Infants seem to follow a clearly demarcated path in their use of gestures. They begin to show objects to adults at around seven to eight months of age and to take part in games of exchange by giving and taking back. At around nine months, they start to make use of open-handed reaching, sometimes accompanied by opening and closing of the hand, and then, between ten and fourteen months, they produce better-defined gestures of pointing (generally with distinct extension of the index finger),[3] showing or displaying, and giving, along with a steady increase in the tendency to vocalize along with the gesture (Leung & Rheingold 1981; see also Carter 1978, 1979).

Some children rely on a number of representational gestures alongside their uses of deictic gestures for establishing the locus of attention. Their representational gestures appear to be used to refer to objects and events in much the same way that words refer. Consider some of Caselli's diary observations (Casadio & Caselli 1989). She found that deictic or pointing gestures (which remained more or less unchanged over the months) first emerged around ten months of age and were at times accompanied by vocalization. What she called referential gestures emerged about two months later. Her son's earliest referential gestures, all produced with consistency by age one, included BRAVO[4] (meaning 'good boy' and expressed through hand clapping), BYE-BYE (expressed through waving), and REQUEST-RADIO (expressed by dancing). These gestures, Caselli suggested, emerge from early interactional routines through gradual separation from specific contexts. In the next month, her child also produced referential gestures combined with a deictic point as requests; for example, PACIFIER (expressed by a sucking action) and SHAMPOO (expressed by ruffling hair). In further studies of Italian children, Caselli and her colleagues found that such reliance on referential or representational gestures alongside deictic gestures and early word uses appeared widespread in the early months of the second year (Iverson, Capirci, & Caselli 1994). However, children differed considerably in how many representational gestures they made use of.

Similar variability across children appears in the observations of young American children at the same stage of communicative development (Goodwyn & Acredolo 1993).[5] In their initial studies of symbolic gestures, Acredolo and Goodwyn found that in retrospective interviews with the parents of thirty-eight infants, 87% of the children (aged 0;11–1;8) were reported to have used symbolic gestures, mainly to name things and ask for things (a mean of 3.9 gesture-types). These gestures, used early in the second year, were later replaced by the corresponding words (Acredolo & Goodwyn 1988). Most of the representational gestures infants used had some nonarbitrary, metonymic (part-for-whole) relation to the meaning being represented; for example, FLOWER (expressed by a sniff), DOG (expressed by a pant), FISH, HOT, or BEAUTIFUL (expressed by blowing,

---

[3] The emergence of highly distinctive pointing-with-a-finger gestures in Western cultures has led some researchers to assume that such developmental pointing is universal (e.g., Butterworth & Cochran 1980; Butterworth & Jarrett 1991). But anthropologists caution that many societies do not point with fingers; they may use the whole hand or use the chin or face to point instead (e.g., Sherzer 1973). Do one-year-olds in such societies start by pointing with fingers and then learn the conventional way of pointing, or do they start out with the conventional pointing gesture favored by adults in each society? For further discussion see Wilkins (2003).

[4] I use capital letters to indicate meanings expressed through gestures.

[5] Of fifty-four children studied longitudinally, all produced representational gestures, typically starting around 1;2–1;3. Five of them produced between twelve and seventeen such gestures, while the remaining infants produced fewer than nine each (Goodwyn & Acredolo 1993).

from different children), BOUNCE-BALL (expressed by patting the air several times). Acredolo and Goodwyn suggested that the relation between the gesture and the entity designated might provide some support in memory for children at a stage when the demands of setting up a symbolic representational system in the form of words were still rather heavy.

Lastly, for children who use representational gestures during the earliest stages of acquisition, the meanings of their gestures seem to complement the meanings of their first words. At this stage, representational gestures and words appear to form a single lexicon. Acredolo and Goodwyn (1988; Goodwyn & Acredolo 1993) noted that children did not use a gesture where they could already produce a word. And, as they got older, the two-year-olds replaced their representational gestures with words. When children aged 1;6 and 2;2 are taught either gestures or words in reference to novel objects, the younger ones respond as if gestures and words can serve equally well to refer to instances of object categories (Namy & Waxman 1998). At 2;2, though, children readily interpret new words, but not new gestures, in this way. (With additional teaching and practice, the older children would still treat gestures as symbolic, but they didn't do so spontaneously in the way children did at one-and-a-half.) So by age two, children appear to have developed an appreciation of words as symbols (see also Namy & Waxman 2000; Preissler & Carey 2004) . This may well play a role in their increasingly rapid acquisition of words for talking about their surroundings.

## Doing things with words

When children start to use their first words, they use them, even one word at a time, for particular purposes. They make requests for actions and objects, they comment on what is happening, and they accept or reject adult proposals. Like adults, they make use of their words in trying to convey their intentions to others within the context of the ongoing interaction. But since at first they produce only one word at a time, these intentions on their own may be hard to interpret. Their interpretation becomes a little easier when the words are supplemented by gestures and other information about the child's locus of attention and apparent purpose in context. But once children begin to produce longer utterances, with the relevant grammatical information (e.g., inflections for case, tense, person, number, etc., and consistent word orders), their intended meanings become easier to discern.

In general, children appear to use their first words either for making requests, typically accompanied by their request gesture, or for commenting on events, typically accompanied by a deictic gesture. But within these domains, children may choose among different words for what they are requesting or commenting on. Some researchers have suggested that children's choices here are governed by some measure of informativeness. That is, they are more likely to mention information they identify as new than something that is already known or given (previously mentioned) in the current conversation (e.g., Greenfield 1979). So they choose a word for whatever part of the event contributes new information in the current context. This would suggest that even one-year-olds are good at assessing what their interlocutors know and at keeping track of what is given and what is new in conversational exchanges. This may be hard to establish, though, since children's words are taken as marking what they consider to be new, but, without an independent judgement about each event in context, this can make for a certain circularity in definition.

Researchers have also suggested that, in selecting elements within events to talk about, children develop the ability to talk about different semantic roles or functions in a consistent order. Greenfield and Smith (1976) observed two children for whom they kept detailed diaries and found a similar developmental sequence for both. The children commented on agents of actions, as in (1); on actions or states associated with agents and with objects, as in (2); and on objects affected, as in (3):

(1) a.    NICKY (1;1.3, hearing someone come in): *dada*.
    b.    MATTHEW (1;1.3, hearing father come in the door and start up the
            steps): *dada*.
(2) a.    NICKY (1;2.21–1;3.18, whenever he sits or steps down): *down*.
    b.    MATTHEW (1;1.16, responding to "Do you want to get up?" by reaching up
            and saying): *up*.
(3) a.    NICKY (1;4.19–25, asking for a fan (/bar/) to be turned on or off): *bar*.
    b.    MATTHEW (1;0, having just thrown a ball): *ball*.

Only after this did the children also talk about objects associated with places, recipients, and possessors, and about modifications of events, as when a child requested that an action or event be repeated.

Both children appeared to attend to and talk about the same kinds of roles within events as they started to use single-word utterances. Interestingly, the things they talked about first were generally animate objects (people, animals) or else small inanimate objects (often things that they themselves were manipulating). They talked also about the actions in question and the states that resulted. This suggests that actors, their activities, and the objects affected by activities of various kinds stand out, for example, over places and properties associated with objects. This in turn suggests that some types of things might be more salient to really young children, and so more worth talking about (e.g., Prudden *et al.* 2006). Indeed, children seem to talk more about things that move (that are animate) and that are movable or manipulable, and these do have properties that attract the attention of infants. But we have to be wary of circularity here too: We need an independent assignment of salience in each context and then a study correlating such assignments with the things children actually pick out with their words. This has yet to be done.

This research raises a number of questions. First, when we identify certain utterances as talking about agents, is the notion of agent here the same as that for adults? And is the agent of an action of breaking the same as the agent of an action of dropping or of cutting? Is the actor participating in the activity of running the same as the actor swimming or waving? That is, do children identify general roles across event-types, or do they identify more specific kinds of actors, initially specific to each individual activity-type? The same question applies to all such roles – agent (actor), object affected, recipient, location, or possessor, for instance (see Schlesinger 1974). Second, does the sequence of emergence observed by Greenfield and Smith (1976) in the roles children first talk about with single words hold for other children, other languages? Third, how does their view of roles picked out in one-word utterances relate to what counts as given versus new in a particular conversational context? We will return to these questions when we look at how children's utterances become more complex with the addition of more words and of inflections (Chapters 7 and 8), as well as how this increasing complexity is scaffolded by adults within conversation (Chapter 12).

## Choosing a perspective

As children add to their vocabularies, they have more options available as they decide to talk about a particular object or event. That is, they can take different perspectives on the object or event and mark the perspective chosen through the words they decide to use. For example, a cat can be *the cat*, *the animal*, *the Siamese*, *the family pet*, or *the scratcher*. While children still have only a small vocabulary, they may have few choices of perspective available. The cat might be just *cat* or *animal*; a doll might be *doll* or *toy*; and an apple might be *apple* or *fruit* or possibly *food*. Speakers, adult or child, can have different reasons for choosing one perspective over another as they present an object to their addressees. The same goes for events. Adults may present an event from the perspective of the agent, the object affected, or the recipient. Compare *I gave Jan the ball*, *The ball was given to Jan*, and *Jan got the ball* (Clark 1990). But when producing only one word at a time, children might only use a term for the agent (*dada*), the action (*give*), the object affected (*ball*), or the recipient (*Jan*), because they lack the ability to put two or more of these together into a single syntactic construction and so can't exploit structure yet to mark perspective.

How do children choose a perspective? In part, they are limited by the terms and expressions they have available. Once they have two or three relevant nouns in their vocabulary along with at least one general-purpose verb (e.g., *do*, *get*, *make*), they can do more. Their selection of a word to use may also reflect in part the way in which they segment the event itself into activity and participant(s) (see, e.g., Tomasello & Brooks 1999; Tomasello 2000). This may lead them sometimes to focus on the activity and so talk about that, and, at other times, to focus on one of the participants, the agent, say, and so talk about that role instead. But it is really only once children can invoke grammatical information – for instance, in the form of word order and inflections – that we begin to see how they use constructions to mark different perspectives on the same event.

Word-choice also marks perspective. The same toy may be a *horse* on one occasion as the child pulls it along on its string, but on another occasion, as the child seats himself on it, it is a *chair* (D, 1;6.24; Clark, unpublished diary data). Even one-word utterances show that children can conceive of the same referents in different ways. They may represent one referent at two distinct levels (*bear* and *animal*) or as belonging to two distinct domains (*dog* and *pet*) (Clark & Svaib 1997). As soon as children have the words to pick out different perspectives, they make use of them for that purpose (Clark 1997). This finding has important implications for claims about how children assign meanings to unfamiliar words and about the kinds of information they take account of. First, they appear early on to recognize that there are conventional terms for things and they elicit those from adult speakers, with interminable *What's that?* questions. More than that, they act from the start as if any difference *in form* marks a difference *in meaning*. This does *not* mean a difference in reference. That children can and do use two (or more) different words for the same referent shows that they are aware that one can, for instance, talk about the same person as *my son*, *the little boy*, *the bicyclist*, and *the reader*, without finding such multiple perspectives confusing.

The terms they acquire must involve both meaning and reference. They must also involve the pragmatic notions of convention and contrast, factors that allow languages to be maximally communicative (Clark 1987, 1993). Within speech communities, speakers agree on the conventions for their language, the conventional meanings assigned over time to particular expressions. When speakers use these, they do so in the expectation that their addressees will assume that the conventions hold for interpreting that utterance; otherwise that expression would not have been used (Grice 1989). Since any difference of form marks a difference of meaning, addressees infer that speakers have a different meaning in mind each time they use a different term. (The reverse does not hold since several meanings can be expressed by the same term; e.g., *a line on a page*, *a line of trees*, *to line a suit*, etc.) Children can identify the referent as the same, as the locus of attention, even when speakers take different perspectives and talk about the family dog both as *the spaniel* and *the dog*, or as *the dog* and *the animal*. (I return to these issues in Chapter 6.)

## Summary

Children's first words and the uses to which they put them are limited. They add relatively slowly to their vocabulary in production and often use gestures as they begin to communicate. Because their resources are still limited, they may overextend their early words or use general-purpose terms for talking about what is in the focus of attention. They also rely on gestures to make their utterance clear – pointing to direct attention at something of interest, reaching to make a request. And their utterances at this stage typically consist of just one word at a time.

# 5    Sounds in words: Production

When children start to talk early in their second year, it is often difficult to identify their first words. Their earliest attempts typically fall far short of the adult forms. Take one one-year-old's first production of the English word *squirrel*: **ga**. Upon reflection, we can trace the processes that probably led to this simplified pronunciation. First, children typically omit liquid sounds like **l** and **r**; they simplify consonant clusters, usually retaining only the stop if there is one, so in the initial cluster **skw-**, they drop both the glide **w** and the initial **s-**, keeping only the velar stop **k**; and they often voice initial stop consonants, here changing the **k-** into a **g-**. Finally, vowels in children's earliest words are typically produced with little or no narrowing of the vocal tract, here the **a**. In this case, we know what the target word was. But this is often not the case.

Young children are also inconsistent in how they produce the same word on different occasions. Their pronunciations vary more than adults' do from one occasion to the next, and, in their first few months of talking, they may produce multiple versions of the same word (Ingram 1974; Maekawa & Storkel 2006; Sosa & Stoel-Gammon 2006). One child, Philip, used as many as five different versions of *blanket* within a month. At age 1;9, he had multiple versions of 50 of the 125 words in his repertoire. Another child, Fernande (learning French), at one stage used five different pronunciations for *chaise* 'chair'. And at age 1;5, she too had multiple versions for nearly half her words, 47 out of 114. Since children continue to babble until several months into their second year, it is hard to tell at times whether they are producing a short babble or attempting a word. Together, these factors – simplified forms, varying pronunciations, and overlap with babble – all make it hard to draw a clear line between children's babbling and their first productions of words.

One assumption here is that children make use of what they already perceive as they start trying to *produce* words. That is, they rely on stored representations of words and longer expressions heard in the adult speech around them. These stored forms provide readily available models of the targets they are aiming at, models against which they can compare their own productions (Clark 1982, 1993). These models can serve as guides when children produce unrecognizable forms and need to repair their pronunciation until it better approximates the adult target (see Käsermann & Foppa 1981; Scollon 1976). Mastering adultlike articulation seems to require both time and practice.

As children produce more words, they observe more and more carefully any restrictions on the forms of words in their language. These restrictions in a language are captured by phonotactic rules that characterize possible words in terms of different kinds of units. These include *syllables*, with specification of the sounds and sound combinations that can appear in legal beginnings and endings of the syllable-types allowed in each language; *word stress* in multisyllabic words (in languages like English or Spanish, say); *tone* (in languages like Mandarin or Yoruba); *timing* or the relative length of syllables in complex versus monosyllabic words; and so on. That is, children learn the prosodic phonology of the language they speak and all that it entails for different manners of speaking – fast or slow, formal or informal. How do children learn to match their own word productions to the pronunciations around them? What relation is there between babbling and the shapes of their first words? Do children focus on whole words or on sound segments in their first productions? How do they build up to longer sequences of syllables and words? Do all children exhibit the same patterns in development? These are some of issues this chapter focusses on as we consider children's first productions of single words and their transition to producing combinations of words.

## Babbling

Infants produce crying sounds from birth on and start to make cooing sounds as well, from around two months of age. Up to about five months, most infant vocalizations consist of crying and cooing, sometimes characterized as sad and happy sounds respectively. However, even parents can't distinguish these very reliably without further contextual information (Muller, Hollien, & Murry 1974). Most infants begin to babble between six and eight months, though some don't start until as late as ten months or so.

The earliest babbling tends to consist of a single "syllable" repeated, for example, **babababa** or **gagagaga**, where the syllable consists of a consonant-like sound (here a **b** or **g**) combined with a vowel-like sound produced with an open vocal tract, some kind of **a**. Canonical babbling consists of short or long sequences containing just one consonant-vowel (CV) combination that is reduplicated or repeated. As these babble sequences become longer and more frequent, infants may display a preference for one consonant-type over others, with some favoring mainly **m**- sounds, others **b**- sounds, and others still **g**- sounds.

They soon vary the intonation contours of babble sequences too, matching the rises and falls of intonation patterns in the language around them. They also start to vary the syllables within a babble sequence, for example, **bababa-mamama**, **mememe-dede**, **baba-dadada**. It is harder to tell whether infants vary vowel-like sounds systematically because there tends to be more variability in these than in consonant-like sounds. For consonants, there is distinct closure for stops (e.g., **p**, **b**, **t**, **d**, **k**, **g**) at different places in the mouth and discernible near-closure for fricatives, where the sound is produced with audible friction (e.g., **s**, **f**, **v**), so it is possible to identify the general place and manner of articulation for babbled syllables (Elbers 1982). By ten to twelve months of age, many babbled sequences sound compatible with the surrounding language, using similar sound sequences, rhythm, and intonation contours (de Boysson-Bardies & Vihman 1991; Vihman 1996).

## The relation of babbling to first words

What relation is there between infants' babbling and their first recognizable words?[1] Is there continuity of vocalizing from six months up to and past the age when children first produce words? Or, is there a break between babbling and talking? Researchers have taken different positions on this. Some have argued for continuity because both babbling and speech involve vocalization. They assume that babbling is a direct precursor to speech. At the same time, since infants produce a number of sounds in babbling that are not represented in the language around them (e.g., uvular **r** sounds produced in the back of the throat and fricatives like the final sound in *loch* in the babbling of infants exposed to English), these researchers have sometimes also assumed that parents must selectively encourage or reinforce their children to produce just the right sounds, so they will narrow them down eventually to just those in the target language (e.g., Mowrer 1960). However, parents don't appear to be selective: They tend to encourage all infant vocalizations regardless, so any narrowing down must reflect the growing attention infants pay to the surrounding language (Chapter 3). The absence of a full match in infants' babble versus speech repertoires presents a further problem: Some sounds that appear in babbling (e.g., **l** sounds) may not emerge in their words until two or three years later.

These observations about babbling have led other researchers to assume discontinuity instead and to argue against any connection between babbling and early words. Jakobson (1968) argued strongly for this view on the following grounds: Infants typically make use of different repertoires of sounds in the two activities (babbling and first words); they sometimes stop babbling for a short period (typically while starting to walk) before they produce their first words; and the system of sounds infants use in their first words requires attention to phonological contrasts, unlike the sounds used in babbling.[2]

More recent analyses offer support for continuity over discontinuity. First, babbling typically continues until well after the appearance of children's first words, and a number of analyses have shown that there are strong similarities between the phonetic sequences in babbles and early words (Oller *et al.* 1976).

---

[1] In observational studies, researchers have typically ignored all babbling once infants begin to produce recognizable words, but in fact there are usually several months of overlap.

[2] Jakobson based his arguments on analysis of published studies of children's general development; however, the observers relied on the orthography of each language to represent the sounds (there was no agreed-on system for doing this available at the time), and records differ in the detail they offer about form in both babbling and early words. These records may also have presented a discontinuity between babbling and first words because they focussed only on words as soon as these began to appear.

Many infants use intonation contours carried by babble sequences to mark proto-requests and rejections, for instance, before the emergence of recognizable words. Work by Elbers and Ton (1985) also suggests that, although parents do not reinforce infants for using some sounds over others, young children themselves show considerable continuity from babbling to early words in their choices of the sound sequences attempted in their first words. In addition, they appear more likely in their first words to attempt sounds that had appeared previously in their babbling and to avoid sounds that hadn't. Finally, young children continue to produce babbled sequences alongside words until as late as age two or two-and-a-half (see also Robb, Bauer, & Tyler 1994). Babbling, then, seems to lay a foundation for producing words.

## The shapes of early words

The targets of children's earliest attempts at words may be hard to recognize. Around age one, young children start to use consistent vocalizations in specific contexts.[3] They are often associated with systematic gestures and appear to carry a consistent meaning. Consider the stable early vocalizations produced by David between the ages of 1;1 and 1;4 (Carter 1978, 1979). They were consistently produced with specific gestures. For example, David's pointing or showing gestures were accompanied by vocalizations with an initial **d-**, where the adult target may have been some form of *there*; and his exchange forms, with a reaching gesture towards the person giving or receiving something, were consistently accompanied by vocalizations with initial **h-** forms, possibly based on *here*. His disappearance schema with its initial **b-** vocalizations may have had its origins in early parental attempts to inculcate a hand-wave and *bye-bye* routine.

Carter identified some eight prelinguistic schemas in David's repertoire. Their uses accounted for 91% of the communicative episodes she observed over a four-month period (Carter 1979). Table 5.1 summarizes the relevant gestures, vocalization-types, communicative goals for each schema, and their frequencies. These gesture–vocalization schemas were later replaced as David gradually came to use recognizable conventional words in these communicative episodes.

### Whole words or single sounds?

As children begin to speak, do they focus on producing whole words or individual sounds? Each approach has both advantages and disadvantages. If children target whole words, they are zooming in on chunks with meaning,

[3] Researchers have called these first meaningful vocalizations "pre-words," "vocables," "proto-words," "phonetically consistent forms," "quasi-words," "sensorimotor morphemes" (associated with specific gestures), or "call-signs" (Vihman 1996:130). They have also included consistent uses of effort grunts as possible precursors to words (e.g., McCune *et al.* 1996).

Table 5.1 *David's communicative schemas in the period 1;1 to 1;4*

| Schema | Gesture | Sound | Goal | Number of instances |
|---|---|---|---|---|
| (1) Request Object | reach to object | [m]-initial | get help in obtaining object | 342 |
| (2) Attend to Object | point, hold out | [d]- or [l]-initial | draw attention to object | 334 |
| (3) Attend to Self | sound of vocalization | phonetic variants of "David," "Mommy" | draw attention to self | 142 |
| (4) Request Transfer | reach to person | [h]-initial | get object from, give to receiver | 135 |
| (5) Dislike | prolonged, falling intonation | [n]-initial, nasalized | get help to change situation | 82 |
| (6) Disappearance | waving hands, slapping | [b]-initial | get help in removing object | 32 |
| (7) Rejection | negative headshake | nasalized glottal stop sequence | get help to change situation | 20 |
| (8) Pleasure – Surprise – Recognition | (smile) | flowing or breathy [h] sounds, especially *hi*, *ha*, *oh*, *ah* | express pleasure | 20 |

*Source*: Carter 1979:132. Used with permission from Academic Press.

so when they produce an identifiable form, it will immediately help them communicate. But the disadvantage is that, since each word consists of a sequence of phonetic segments, children will have to be able to produce enough of them, with enough accuracy, for adults to be able to recognize the word in question. If, instead, children first target single sounds, they could concentrate just on producing a **b** sound or just on producing an **o** sound; the disadvantage is that single segments don't normally carry any conventional meaning. They only carry meaning when they contribute to the overall form of a word.

In either case, children could simply focus first on establishing a system of contrasts for sounds in whatever word forms they can produce. This was the essence of Jakobson's (1968) theory of emerging contrasts in acquisition. He proposed that children gradually master an increasingly complex set of contrasts in production, from the simplest possible to rather more complex ones. With vowels, for example, children could start from a basic vowel-versus-consonant contrast. Jakobson represented this protovowel, produced with a fully open vocal tract, as [A]. This contrasts with any consonant made with closure of the vocal tract. The contrast here is between an open vocal tract (the vowel) and a closed vocal tract (the consonant). Jakobson did not specify which sounds children might use to exemplify any early contrasts; he was concerned primarily with identifying the initial dimensions of contrast among sounds in early production.

After the initial vowel-versus-consonant contrast, children could add contrasts among vowels, on the high–low dimension for instance, represented by low [A] versus high [I], and on the front–back dimension, represented by front [A] versus back [U]. Or they could elaborate contrasts from open [A] to the more closed [E] and then from relatively open [E] to closed [I]. In short, Jakobson proposed not that children learn particular phonetic segments but that they set up oppositions using dimensions such as high–low or back–front as they start to use more than one vowel.

His proposal for contrasts among consonants followed similar lines. The first consonant-type, he suggested, was an archetypal bilabial closure of the end of the vocal tract, represented as [P-B]. This could then be elaborated through an oral–nasal contrast among bilabials [P-B] versus [M], and these in turn could be elaborated through a contrast of bilabial versus dental among the oral consonants [P-B] and [T-D] on the one hand and the nasals [M] and [N] on the other. With a relatively small set of such contrasts, children could produce a range of contrasting word forms that might include such word shapes as *ba, pa, ma, baba, papa, mama, dada, tata, nana*, just with the archetypal vowel [A] alone. Use of additional vowels allows for a more elaborate set of word shapes, as does use of different consonants within words.

Jakobson's proposal, then, is a theory about contrasts among sounds, *not* a theory about the acquisition of sound segments. Theoretically, this approach leaves open the question of how children actually realize such a system of contrasts: whether they treat consonants in medial or final position in the same way as they do consonants in initial position; whether they apply a specific contrast just to one pair of segments or to groups of sounds with similar properties; what they do with different consonant–vowel (CV) and vowel–consonant (VC) combinations or with forms that contain more than one consonant, as in CVC or CVCV word shapes, and so on. In this account, it remains unclear how children relate specific phonetic segments to systematic phonological contrasts in the target language. It also leaves unclear what children take as their primary targets in working out such a system – segments or whole words.

Do children begin with individual sound segments? There is considerable evidence against this. First, in many well-documented cases, children produce a sound appropriately at one stage and then later appear unable to produce it in that word any more. For example, many children start off pronouncing adult *dog* or *doggy* first as [do], then with a reduplicated consonant **d** as [dodi]. But once they become able to produce the **g** sound, they start to pronounce *doggy* as [gogi] instead, and only some time later master the adult sequence *doggy*. One question such shifts raise is whether children's perceptions of adult words – and hence their representations of those words in memory for comprehension – are always a faithful reflection of the adult forms. For instance, if their perception of certain words or word-types was initially erroneous, this might account for apparently regressive errors, as in the production of [gogi] after several weeks of [dodi].[4]

Representations based on occasionally faulty perception of some segments might also account for children at times pronouncing some words with a wrong segment but managing to produce the missing segment elsewhere, as when Amahl produced *puddle* as *puggle* (phonetically [pʌgəl]), yet said *puzzle* as *puddle*, [pʌdəl]. One possibility here is that children initially misperceive certain sounds in some words and so set up erroneous representations in memory. If they use these representations as targets against which to match their productions, they will produce the words wrongly. However, once they correct their earlier misperception and change those representations, they would have appropriate targets to aim at in production (see further Macken 1980). For a small number of words, children may need to make changes in how they represent them in memory as they correct earlier misperceptions.[5]

Suppose instead that children's representations in memory for comprehension are closely based on the adult forms (although some details may take time to establish fully) but that producing some sound sequences is harder than others. Adjustments in how they produce specific sequences could make children appear to go back on sounds they had produced correctly earlier, as in the shift from [dodi] to [gogi], with initial **g**- now in place of initial **d**-. This could occur, in part at least, because sounds children could produce appropriately in a single CV syllable, even when reduplicated, may be harder to maintain in longer CVCV sequences where they attempt two different consonants in succession (Kiparsky & Menn 1977). While Smith (1973) assumed that correct representations for comprehension would call for rapid across-the-board changes as soon as a child mastered the production of a specific sound sequence, this view may be mistaken. Sometimes children have such well-practiced erroneous pronunciations for certain words that it can take weeks before they reliably manage to produce the more adultlike form. During this time, though, they appear able to judge that the adult form is the "right" one, and they often make spontaneous repairs after they produce their old (erroneous) version (see, e.g., Clark & Bowerman 1986; Slobin 1978). Children's changes in the production of the appropriate set of word forms take place in exactly the right set of words, but it may take them some time to instantiate: They first have to streamline their access to the new sequences of articulations for these expressions.

---

[4] The assumption here is that the version closer to the adult target is the one with the correct initial segment, namely [dodi].

[5] One source of misperceptions, Macken suggested, could be misanalysis of morpheme-boundaries where the child does not yet know the elements that make up complex words; for instance, a child might not know the word *quiet* and so fail to analyze *quietly* as containing a boundary between the **t** and **l**.

## Path, preference, and avoidance

How do children build up appropriate articulatory programs for producing the words they are trying to say? Building up such programs and then practicing them until they can produce the intended goal – the target word – takes time. From a communicative point of view, children would appear to be better off trying to say words rather than segments. And that indeed seems to be what they do. But in doing this, children must also find ways to produce and maintain contrasts among word shapes, so they can get other people to recognize what they are saying. This requires that their productions eventually match those of the speakers around them. What must children find out about production and about how to articulate sequences of sounds to achieve this? How much practice do they need? Do they all tackle this job in the same way?

Children seem to start out somewhat slowly with only a handful of recognizable words produced in their first few weeks or, occasionally, months of talking. But some then start adding further words steadily and rapidly to their repertoires, while others may advance a step at a time, adding a few words, then practicing those and adjusting their forms to bring them closer to the adult targets before adding the next few (Clark 1993; Dromi 1987). Other children still may spend an extended period of time working hard on generalizations about phonological form and contrast, without adding much to their production vocabulary.

Consider Jessie, between the ages of 1;3 and 1;8 (Labov & Labov 1978). In her first five months of one-word utterances, her speech was dominated by just two words, *cat* and *mama*, with over 5,000 recorded uses of each term. From 1;5 to 1;8, she experimented sporadically with a handful of other words as well (including *hi, dada, blow, apple,* and *there*). Throughout this period, Jessie revealed "continuous exploration, experimentation, practice, and intense involvement with linguistic structure" (Labov & Labov 1978:817). Although she made no progress in the number of sounds or words produced, she exhibited a growing control of some linguistic processes. Jessie worked first on producing the vowels and consonants in *cat, mama, hi,* and *there* (Period I); then she experimented with initial **d-** and bilabial **β-**, and with the final labial consonants **-l, -p, -m** (Period II). (The phonetic symbols used here are shown in Figure 5.1, with illustrations for each.) Next she spent about six weeks experimenting with and developing control over the vowels **u, ʌ, a, o, ɪ** (Period III). In the last six weeks, she experimented with final **-d** and free **a** but otherwise dropped all her previously established contrasts and abandoned the system she had been working on for five months.

Jessie's first organization of phonetic segments into phonological categories followed two main contrastive principles. First, she used oral vowels for words and kept nasal vowels for requesting and complaining. Second, she used mid central vowels as general deictic terms, and peripheral vowels (high, low, front, or back) for all other words. She kept to the first principle throughout her five-month *cat*-and-*mama* period, although, around 1;5, she briefly connected "wanting" and "food" (with a nasal-to-oral vowel continuum). She maintained the

**Vowels**

| Front | peel, pin |
| Back | pool, book |
| High | peel, pool |
| Low | cat, part |
| Mid | pet (front), buck (center) |
| Central | the, postman |
| Nasal | (Fr., cinq, tante, train) |

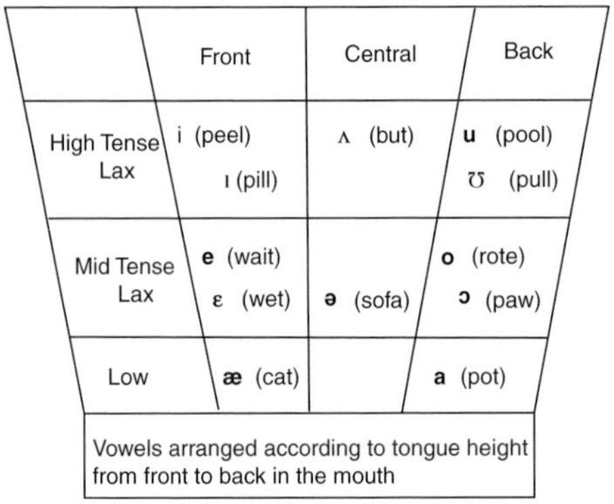

|  | Front | Central | Back |
|---|---|---|---|
| High Tense Lax | i (peel) / ı (pill) | ʌ (but) | u (pool) / ʊ (pull) |
| Mid Tense Lax | e (wait) / ɛ (wet) | ə (sofa) | o (rote) / ɔ (paw) |
| Low | æ (cat) | | a (pot) |

Vowels arranged according to tongue height from front to back in the mouth

**Consonants**

|  | Stop | Fricative | Affricate | Liquid | Glide |
|---|---|---|---|---|---|
| Labial | pill | fig | | | wake |
| | bone | vase | | | |
| | mail | sup | | | |
| Alveolar | tile | | jug | fill | vell |
| | dent | | chubby | rake | |
| | nail | | | | |
| Velar | kitten | | | | |
| | goal | | | | |
| | thong | | | | |
| Nasal | made | | | | |
| | nail | | | | |
| | thong | | | | |

Figure 5.1 *Examples of vowels and consonants*

second principle throughout the first half of her *cat*-and-*mama* period. By 1;6, though, the vowel she used for pointing or calling attention to something was lowered so it was often hard to tell whether she was saying *there* or *cat*, both now produced as [ʔæ]. In fact, her experiments with consonants appeared to focus more on the art of articulation than on the exploitation of contrast. She also expanded the range of syllable-types she could produce as she grew more expert with different stop consonants. In summary, what might be regarded as a rather flat plateau in Jessie's development, upon closer inspection, revealed a constantly changing series of small experiments where she progressively scrutinized and tried out different phonological options.

Jessie began with just two words and a limited number of sounds. Her basic or canonical word shape changed from CVC and reduplicated CV-CV to CV and then CVCVC. She experimented with a range of initial consonants and contrasted them. And she developed target vowels as the nucleus for each of her word shapes. She also tried to elaborate final consonants. While she succeeded with the final labial **-m**, in *mam*, she was unable to produce a final **-d** in *dad*. Instead she produced a final nasal, **-n**, or a stop followed by a nasal, **-dn**, with same place of articulation as **d** alone (see Clark & Bowerman 1986). While Jessie's intensive analysis here concentrated on a very small domain, her experimentation and practice showed that she was extracting general principles.

The different paths children follow in the production of their first words reflect differences in their initial analyses of the phonological structure involved. This was one of the main findings of Ferguson and Farwell (1975) in their study of production data from one-year-olds. They examined all the word productions by three children over several months. To their surprise, they found variability in all three children's word forms. Although the children tended to be quite accurate in their first productions, their accuracy often declined over time, so later versions of the same words were further from the adult targets. And all three children favored certain sounds and selected words with those sounds as ones they were more willing to attempt. Effectively, these children each constructed their own phonology or sound system, with each one of the three following a slightly different path.

The specific path chosen reflected the various strategies that that child applied in trying to produce identifiable words. Each child, as a result, had a somewhat different and different-sounding initial lexicon of word forms. Ferguson and Farwell emphasized two points. First, children choose *words* as their primary targets and hence as the domain relevant to phonological development. Second, the children they studied all went through an initial, presystematic period of piecemeal learning, followed by a period of discovery and more systematic generalization of patterns in their productions of word forms.

Children often appear to be selective in which words they try to pronounce, and hence which they avoid, during the early stages of language production. These differences seem to reflect preferences for some sounds, and even for some word shapes, over others (e.g., Elsen 1994; Ferguson & Farwell 1975; Labov & Labov 1978). These preferences probably have their roots in earlier babbling. Elbers and Ton (1985), for instance, analyzed six weeks of recordings from Thomas between the ages of 1;3 and 1;5. They focussed on place of articulation (front vs. center vs. back of the mouth), and on manner of articulation (stop with complete closure vs. nonstop) in both words and babble. During this time, Thomas produced four distinct words, which emerged successively. The first word he produced had a front stop consonant, **p**, and was based on the adult Dutch *hap* or diminutive *hapje* 'bite, mouthful'. Thomas used it for food or drink. The forms it appeared in are shown in (1):[6]

(1)          [ap(ə)] or [ab(ə)], [hap(ə)], [hab(ə)]

He used this word frequently from week one onwards. His second identifiable word contained a center stop consonant, **t**, and was based on adult *auto* 'car', used for cars. Its forms are listed in (2):

(2)          [at(ə)] or [aut(o:)], [o:t(o:)], [o:t(ə)]

His third word contained a sequence of stops, front **p** followed by center **t**, and was based on adult *paard(je)* 'horse, horsey', with the variants shown in (3). Like *hapje*, this word was very frequent from the moment of its emergence in week four.

(3)          [pa:t(ə)] or [ba:t(ə)]

Thomas' fourth word contained a sequence of front **b** then back **x** (the sound in Scottish English *loch*) where the two consonants now differ in manner, with the first a stop and the second not. This word shape appeared to be based on adult *poes* (or diminutive *poesje*) 'cat, kitty' and was produced in the forms shown in (4):

(4)          [bəx] or [pəx], [bux], [pux]

Each word was produced with some variations in form but, in each case, with a clearly identifiable place and general manner of articulation for the consonants.

Evidence for a parallel between babble and speech could play out as phonological preferences in the child's word shapes for those sounds and syllable sequence-types most frequent in his babbling, and as practice of the relevant word shape-types in both words and babble. They found evidence for both. Overall, Thomas had a clear preference for front consonants (**p, b**) in his babbling. This had also been true for the two previous months of prelinguistic babbling (see Elbers 1982). But in the period when his first word with a center stop (**t**) appeared, there was also a rise in center consonant babbles from 15% to 40%, while the proportion of babbles with front consonants remained constant (at about 40%). Next, in the fourth week of recording, at the point where Thomas first began to produce the word *paardje* 'horse', in the form [pa:tə], he also produced babbles containing consonants at two places of articulation, front followed by center. This babble-type increased in frequency from 5% to 11% over the last two weeks of recording (weeks five and six). This child's babbling preferences appeared to reflect just the kinds of practice called for by the word forms he was then trying to produce.

---

[6] The vowels in parentheses in Thomas' productions were produced on some occasions and not others. For some words, these vowels may reflect choices of diminutive forms as the child's target (e.g., *paardje* rather than *paard*, or *hapje* rather than *hap*).

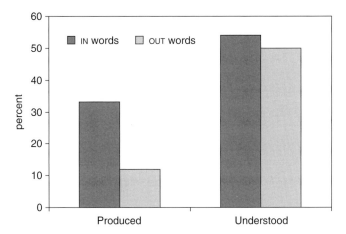

Figure 5.2 *Percentages of* IN *and* OUT *words produced by one-year-olds.*
Based on Schwartz & Leonard 1982

More systematic evidence of avoidance in early language production comes from an experimental study by Schwartz and Leonard (1982). They examined a group of one-year-olds with small vocabularies to determine the consonantal inventories and syllable structures for each child's current words. They then constructed a set of new words (unfamiliar forms), corresponding to unfamiliar referent-objects and -actions, for each child, such that half the words contained consonants that the child used (IN words) and half consonants that the child didn't use (OUT words). They then presented IN and OUT words equally frequently to each child in play sessions over several weeks and observed all the spontaneous productions the children made. They produced a significantly greater number of IN words during the play sessions, and they produced them more rapidly, than OUT words (Figure 5.2). At the same time, tests of comprehension showed no differences between IN versus OUT words (see also Schwartz *et al.* 1987).

In summary, young children are selective in what they try to say. This choosiness is correlated with earlier preferences for particular consonant- and syllable-types in babbling. Essentially, children appear to tackle early word production by working first on what they can already do and only after that moving on to harder problems with sounds inside word shapes.

## Simplifications in production

Until they master the full range of articulatory programs necessary for the variety of legal word shapes in their language, children often fall short of adult pronunciations in their own production. They omit some sounds altogether and substitute some sounds for others. There is considerable consistency in the problems children encounter in production, so their own forms can often be described in terms of characteristic substitutions, assimilations, and omissions, by comparison with the adult targets they are attempting.

### Substitutions

Children tend to voice consonant sounds in initial position but find it difficult to voice them in final position. As a result, they often voice voiceless initial consonants, as in [bay] for *pie*; and they appear to devoice final ones, as in [nop] for *knob* (Joan 1;9; Velten 1943). Some children compensate for their inability to voice stop consonants in final position by using a nasal consonant after the stop at the same place of articulation, as in [dadn] for *dad* (Labov & Labov 1978), or by combining a nasal consonant with a voiceless stop, as in [pɪŋk] for *pig* or [bɛnt] for *bed*. Since voiced nasals like **n** or **m** are easier to produce in final position, they seem to offer a convenient way, early on, to maintain voicing at the appropriate place of articulation (Clark & Bowerman 1986).

Another common substitution is to use a stop in place of a fricative (Ferguson 1978; Olmsted 1971), as in [tæwiʃ] for *sandwich* (with initial **t-** for **s-**), [nayb] for *knife* (with final **-b** for **-f**), [bʌd] for *bus* (with final **-d** for **-s**), or [dun] for *soon* (with **d-** for **s-**). Or occasionally the reverse: A final stop may become a fricative, as when *up* is produced as [ʌf] (Menn 1971).

Other common substitutions include fronting, where the child produces a consonant further forward in the mouth than the intended target, as in [ti] for *key* or [fit] for *thick*; and gliding, where children produce the glides **w** and **y**, typically in place of the liquids **l** and **r**, as in [wæbɪt] for *rabbit*.

### Assimilations

Assimilation refers to the effect of sounds on those preceding or following them within a word or across word-boundaries. The commonest assimilation in young children's productions is probably reduplication,[7] where children simply repeat the syllable they are articulating, as in [baba] for *bottle*, [kiki] for *kitchen*, or [dada] for *daddy* (Ingram 1974). They may also use partial reduplication, either keeping the vowel the same across syllables (vowel harmony), as in [lidi] for *little*, or keeping the consonant the same (consonant harmony), as in [babi] for *blanket*. A third type of assimilation is to add nasality to non-nasal consonants, as in the production of [nam] for *lamb*, where the initial **l-** is produced as **n-**.

### Omissions

Children often omit the final consonant, or even final syllable if it is unstressed, in their early words. Examples like the following are very common:

---

[7] Reduplications here have been included under the heading of assimilation because, within the word, young children at first typically hold the consonant fixed or the vowel, or both, when they attempt to produce two syllables rather than just one.

[ba] for *ball*, [ti] for *kick*, or [bu] for *boot*. Leopold also noted forms like [bu] for German *Blumen* and [pi] for *Pipe*. They may continue to do this as late as age two-and-a-half or three (Leopold 1939–1949: vol. I). By age three, however, children make fewer than 10% such omissions in word-final position (Winitz & Irwin 1958).

Children also find clusters of adjacent consonants difficult to pronounce and generally attempt only certain parts of them. For instance, in initial clusters with an **s** plus a stop, for example, **st**- or **sm**-, children generally produce just the stop, as in [top] for *stop* (2;8), [mo:] for *small* (2;4), [laid] for *slide* (2;7), and [dɛk] for *desk* (2;8). Where a stop is combined with a liquid, they again produce just the stop, as in [gok] for *clock* (2;2), [mɪk] for *milk* (2;2), or [bɪŋ] for *bring* (2;2). And if a stop is combined with a nasal, they again focus on the stop, as in [bʌp] for *bump* (2;2) or [tɛt] for *tent* (2;2). Finally, where a fricative is combined with a glide, they tend to produce only the fricative, as in [fom] for *from* (2;2) or [fu:] for *few* (2;2) (Smith 1973).

At first sight, children's patterns of substitutions and omissions appear to follow tendencies similar to those observed in consonant inventories across languages (Jakobson 1968). That is, ease in production appears to account both for early acquisition by children and for presence in basic inventories of sounds in the sound systems of languages. For example, the presence of fricative consonants in a language implies that it also possesses stop consonants (but not the reverse). Likewise, affricates imply stops; and affricates also imply the presence of fricatives. Children generally master some stop consonants (**p, g**) before fricatives (**f**) or affricates (**ch**), and they also generally learn to produce some fricatives before any affricates.

But Jakobson's theory is a theory of contrasts, not phonological acquisitions. So we still need an account of why children master specific target sounds in production in the ways they do. For example, universal patterns that show stop consonants (**b, d, k**) in languages that also contain fricatives (**f, v**) appear consistent in some sense with children's substitutions of stops for fricatives in early word production. But these typological patterns say nothing about inconsistencies in children's mastery of the general contrast between voiced and voiceless stops: Some children may produce **b** versus **p**, for example, but not **d** versus **t**, among their stops. They may be able to produce stops with consistent voicing (a voiced–voiceless contrast) in initial position in words but be unable to produce any voiced stops in final position (Clark & Bowerman 1986). Nor does Jakobson's account explain why children avoid certain sounds. Finally, this account doesn't distinguish between comprehension and production, but, as we have seen, children appear able to make the necessary distinctions in perception for comprehension (Chapter 3) well before they come to master them in production.

Children also show consistent differences in their articulatory skill depending on where a particular segment appears in a word form. While children manage to produce word-initial singleton sounds before they manage to produce word-final ones, the reverse appears to be the case for consonant clusters. Word-initial consonant clusters are harder to produce than word-final clusters. For example, two-year-olds acquiring English do better in producing word-final clusters (as in *cups*, *box*, *nest*, or *lamp*) than they do in producing word-initial clusters (as in *spoon*, *snow*, *plum*, or *crab*). Overall, they do best on final nasal + **z** (as in *drums*) and final stop + **s** clusters (as in *boots* or *fox*). They are consistently more accurate, for example, on word-final stop + s (79%) than on word-initial s + stop (45%). (They don't do well on all final clusters: for example, they evinced considerable difficulty with nasal + stop clusters, as in *pink*, *jump*, or *tent*; see also Clark & Bowerman 1986.) After evaluating structure, morphology, and frequency in search of an explanation for these asymmetries, Kirk and Demuth (2005) argued that ease of articulation for specific sound sequences in clusters offered the best account. Although by age two children can produce many final segments (single-tons), they vary in how well they do this. They are fairly accurate on codas (final segments) in monosyllabic words (CVC), but tend to do poorly on final segments in medial unstressed syllables. One explanation for this is that the longer duration of prominent (stressed) final syllables in words gives children more time to articulate the final consonants, and this in turn leads to greater accuracy in production (Kirk & Demuth 2006).

## Templates for word shapes

Children's first word shapes in production tend to be CV syllables, in which a small number of consonantal sounds contrast with each other, as in [ga] versus [da] versus [ba], or [ma] versus [na]. As a result, they may produce large numbers of homophones, words with the same form, among their protowords (e.g., Smith 1973). A survey of the commonest syllable-types in children's words between age 1;2 and 1;6 showed that, in the first year of speech, children heavily favor CV (32%), reduplicated sequences of CV syllables (25%), and, to a lesser extent, CVC (14%) in their early word shapes (Winitz & Irwin 1958). Children seem to draw on what they can already do in their babbled sequences when they try to produce their first words.

Their next step is to elaborate the range of word shapes. One way to do this is to build up more elaborate syllable-types. Children initially tend to favor CVC word shapes with the same place of articulation for both the initial and the final consonant. For example, early CVC forms tend to contain only coronal con-sonants, as in a form like [tɪn], where both the **t-** and the **-n** are pronounced at the alveolar ridge (behind the teeth); or only labial consonants, as in [pom], where both the **p-** and the **-m** are bilabials. Then they start to form more elaborate CVC syllables by allowing two distinct places of articulation for the two consonants. Alongside [pom], they may also produce a form like [pok], with an initial labial **p-** followed by a velar **-k** in final position. Similarly, a syllable-type like [tɪn] with an initial **t-** may be contrasted with [pɪn] with an initial **p-**, as children add to their repertoire of CVC word shapes (see Levelt 1994; also Branigan 1976).

Children also start to contrast the vowel from one word shape to another. In effect, they are discovering the range of possible phonological contrasts available in legal word shapes as they start trying to produce some of the more elaborate adult targets to which they have already attached some consistent meaning (Jusczyk 1992; Lindblom 1992).

They must set up representations for production as "packages" or "envelopes" of information about the properties present so far in the relevant whole words. These packages include information about (a) the intonational or prosodic contour, including word stress; (b) the syllable structure of each word shape, with information about the onset, nucleus, and coda of each syllable; and (c) features of each segment (e.g., voicing, nasality).

Take the prosodic contour of words. Children acquiring Germanic languages appear to have strong preferences, within two-syllable word forms, for strong–weak (S–W) sequences (e.g., *dóggy*) over weak–strong (W–S) ones (e.g., *helló*). This preference in production appears to mirror an earlier preference in perception, where, at nine months of age (though not at six months), infants prefer listening to S–W sequences over W–S ones (Echols, Crowhurst, & Childers 1997; Jusczyk *et al.* 1993). And, in early production, they often omit weak or unstressed syllables in initial or final position, as in these spontaneous word productions (Menn 1971; Smith 1973):

(5)     **bye**-bye  >  [bab] (1;4)
        he**llo**   >  [hwow] (1;7)
        **Ste**vie  >  [iv] (1;10)
        a**way**    >  [wei] (2;0)

In one study of 616 word forms elicited from three children aged 1;5 to 1;11, Echols and Newport (1992) found that those syllables that were either stressed or final in adult words were retained much more often and produced much more accurately than unstressed, nonfinal ones. This suggests that such syllables are more salient for young children and therefore more likely to be extracted, represented, and attempted in early word productions (Echols 1993).

This attention to stressed syllables often leads young children to omit grammatical information as they begin to produce longer utterances. Many grammatical morphemes, such as articles, pronouns, and prepositions, are monosyllabic and unstressed relative to content words (nouns and verbs) in the same utterances. Children are more likely to omit weak syllables when they occur just before a strong syllable in the same word or phrase than when they occur just after a strong syllable. So in a sentence like *The* LAMB KISSED *the* BEAR, two-year-olds more often omit the first *the* than the second. In a sentence like *He* KICKS *the* PIG, they typically retain *the* before PIG (84% of the time), but in a sentence like *He* CATCHes *the* PIG, they retain *the* much less often (52%) since it no longer follows immediately after a strong (stressed) syllable. Gerken showed in systematic imitation tasks that children more often omit unstressed than stressed syllables, and do so more often in W–S sequences than in S–W ones (e.g., Gerken 1991, 1994a;

Gerken & McIntosh 1993). Children acquiring English seem to make extensive use of trochaic S–W sequences in their own production, and this leads them to make systematic omissions of unstressed syllables that fail to fit a repeating S–W pattern within utterances (Gerken 1996).

While adherence to a trochaic metrical template accounts for much at the sentential level of children's early production, the range of word shapes children produce en route to adult mastery suggests that they must rely on other things as well. This becomes particularly clear when one tracks children's productions of multisyllabic words. Demuth (1996), for example, suggested that children's productions follow a hierarchical order of development, so they first expand their earliest word shapes from core CV syllables into minimal words using core syllable combinations, (C)VCV, closed syllables, (C)VC (ending in a consonant), and vowel length. Then, as they attempt multisyllabic forms, they assign one stress per word (per metrical foot) and finally learn to produce phonological words that include unstressed syllables that don't fit the trochaic pattern.[8] Other researchers like Gerken (1994a) have proposed a metrical template account of word shapes and syllable omissions, with children treating multisyllabic words (with sequences of stressed and unstressed syllables) as they do sequences of words in an utterance. Others still, like Fikkert (1994), have focussed more on how children might extract prosodic units (phonological feet) from adult targets and then map them onto their own metrical templates for words (see also Archibald 1995). All these approaches assume children set up trochaic templates for themselves and pay particular attention to stressed syllables in their own early word productions.

In a comparison of these proposals, Kehoe and Stoel-Gammon (1997a) looked at how well each could account for a large corpus of multisyllabic word forms produced by children between 2;3 and 2;10.[9] In all words consisting of weak followed by strong syllables, WS (e.g., *giraffe*), children produced the stressed syllable; in SS (*shampoo*), SWS (*dinosaur*), and SWS (*kangaroo*) words, they produced both the stressed syllables; in WSW (*potato*), SWW (*animal*), and WSWW (*binoculars*) words, they produced the stressed syllable plus the unstressed syllable in final position; and in SWSW (*helicopter*), SWSW (*avocado*), and SSWW (*rhinoceros*) forms, they produced both the stressed syllables and the final unstressed syllable (e.g., *he'co'ter* for *helicopter*). So children generally preserved stressed syllables on the one hand and unstressed syllables in final position on the other.

This early focus on prosodic properties of words and syllables can be illustrated with some examples from D's early productions of multisyllabic words like *blanket, monkey,* and *slinky* (Clark, unpublished diary data). In the first set given in (6), this child relied on a ´CV-CVC template, with stress on the first syllable and production of two different consonants in the second syllable. The

---

[8] These syllables are usually called "extrametrical."
[9] The data included both spontaneous and elicited multisyllabic word forms, collected cross-sectionally.

initial consonant of the first syllable was repeated at the start of the second one, which ended in a velar consonant (**-g, -k, -ŋ**). He assigned all candidate multi-syllabic words with stressed first syllables to this template over a period of several weeks, beginning at 1;7.1.

(6)      *blanket* [ˈbæ-bɪk] (D, 1;7.1)
         *monkey* [ˈmʌ-mɪk] (D, 1;8.1)
         *slinky* [ˈji-jɪŋk] (D, 1;8.3)

Further additions over the next few days included *basket* [ˈbæ-bɪk] (1;7.9), *bucket* [ˈbʌ-bɪk], and *donkey* [ˈdɒ-dɪk]. During the same period, [ˈbæ-bɪk] for *blanket* became [ˈbæ-kɪt] (1;7.10 on). *Basket*, at first [ˈbæ-bɪk], by 1;10.29 had become [bakɪt]. Velars like **g** or **ŋ**, favored in D's early babbling too, played a central role in the assignment of words to this template, with candidate words identified by the presence of either a velar alone or a nasal + velar sequence in the second syllable of the adult form.

D set up a more complex template, again involving velars, for the word-types shown in (7), starting with his version of the four-syllable name *Veronika* (1;11.6). Here he relied on a four-syllable pattern CV-ˈCVN-CVN-CV, in which the nasals were homorganic (articulated at the same place) with the following velar con-sonant, with reduplication of the nasal–velar sequence. When he first tried *harmonica* (2;0.1), he used the same template:

(7)      *Veronika* [vɛˈrɒŋkiŋka]
         *harmonica* [hɑˈmɒŋkiŋka]

Next, beginning at around 2;4, D added a further template for additional four-syllable words, this time with stress on the first syllable. In this case, the template did not preserve all four syllables but instead dropped the second one. (This weak syllable began with a liquid in all the candidate words.) The template structure here was ˈV-CV-CV, as in (8):

(8)      *alligator* [ˈæ-geitə]
         *elevator* [ˈɛ-veitə]
         *helicopter* [ˈɛ-gɒtə]

D's multisyllabic forms all preserved stressed syllables and also final unstressed syllables, consistent with Kehoe and Stoel-Gammon's (1997b) findings.

Children do not just adhere to trochaic stress patterns in setting up their own templates for adult forms. They also attend to other stress patterns. As Kehoe and Stoel-Gammon pointed out, children seldom make stress errors with word-types that do not conform to a trochaic (SW) template. They did not, for instance, produce SW sequences in trying to say adult words with W<u>S</u>, <u>SS</u>, or SW<u>S</u> forms. In addition, because they tended to preserve the stressed syllable and the final unstressed syllable in adult **S**WW forms (e.g., *elephant*), children produced nonadjacent syllables (*e-phant*) from the adult target. And in **SS**W forms (e.g., Dutch ***stofzuiger*** 'vacuum-cleaner'), they preserved the two stressed syllables rather than retain just the second S and the W. In short, child productions like these do not conform to Fikkert's (1994) or Archibald's (1995) predictions about development.

While children rely on templates for multisyllabic words, it is less clear how they construct these templates or how they map from the adult targets to their own templates. They attend to stressed syllables – these are acoustically salient – but they also preserve unstressed syllables provided they occur in final position and follow a stressed syllable.[10] Just which syllables they preserve also appears to depend on which consonants or clusters of consonants begin and end syllables in the adult target forms (Kehoe & Stoel-Gammon 1997a). Different children favor different consonants or groups of consonants from babbling onwards, and these preferences influence which words they try early in production (and which they avoid) as well as their construction of templates containing certain sound-types or sequences of sounds. As a result, children do not all follow the same path as they learn to produce words.

## From words to segments

Researchers have made a number of proposals about how and when children master the sound segments they need. Some have assumed children work on one sound (or perhaps a class of sounds) at a time, so that, once mastered, they can simply pronounce the right sound wherever it belongs. But, as we have seen, this kind of account would be unable to explain why children who had been able to say [do] or even [dodɪ] might then switch to [gogɪ] in their efforts to say *doggy*. The shift from initial **d-** to initial **g-** is explicable in word-based approaches to production but not in segment-based ones. Others have assumed that children start from a small set of universal contrasts and then add to those as they work out which further contrasts belong in the particular language they have been exposed to. But mastery of a contrast (voiced vs. voiceless, for example) is not the same as mastery of the relevant target sounds (voiced **d**, voiceless **t**, or voiced **b** and voiceless **p**), although these approaches both assume some primacy of sounds over words in the process of production.

According to other researchers, children discover sound segments only after they have begun to say words. They come to identify individual sounds by comparing sets of similar words – minimal pairs that differ in only one or two segments, like *pin* versus *bin*, or *cat* versus *hat* versus *hit* versus *hot*. This approach suggests that children's inventory of systematic sounds in their language is an emergent property of the lexical forms acquired so far. It also suggests that knowledge of the sound system for production develops in part in response to factors such as pronounceability (for the child) and discriminability (for the

---

[10] It is only later that they add unstressed (pretonic) syllables just before stressed ones (see further Peters & Menn 1993).

addressee).[11] For example, vowel qualities in children's attempts at words appear to be selected to be discriminable for others – a condition implicitly imposed by the online nature of processing in interactions between speaker and addressee.[12]

Lindblom (1992) considered production in terms of its functional properties and economy of storage. His concern was with what information, and how much, was needed for production so that sound segments could emerge from the words they occurred in. In his model, children would need to be able to (a) break down articulatory "scores" into anatomically distinct pieces (lips, tongue tip, tongue body, jaw, etc.) within motor patterns and (b) identify motor programs for words in the lexicon. (Linguistically speaking, this implies that there must be minimal pairs.) They must also be able to (c) store the activity pattern for each anatomical channel separately.[13] Having done this, children would be able to compare the words they were producing and discover (via their articulations) that the same segment was produced at the beginning of *cat* and *cup*, or at the end of *hat* and *bit*.

Another factor that may affect children's discovery of the segmental structure of words is vocabulary size. In one study of precocious two-year-olds Smith, McGregor, and Demille (2006) compared them (a) to their exact age-mates with average-size lexicons and (b) to older 2;6-year-olds, also with average-size lexicons equivalent to the lexicons of the precocious group. They measured the children's production ability in terms of the number of target consonants attempted and produced correctly, and found that children in the precocious group matched their lexicon-mates on most measures, and both these groups were ahead of the average two-year-olds who had smaller lexicons. For instance, precocious two-year-olds produced significantly more final consonants in closed syllables than their age-mates (60% vs. 42%). This suggests a link between vocabulary size and articulatory skill – the more words in use, the more practice, and hence greater accuracy in production. But as children learn more words, some lexical neighborhoods become denser than others, with a number of different words beginning with the same sound, or with the same segment and the same nucleus (the medial vowel). More words also share final segments. As phonological neighborhoods become dense, children appear to organize them by both initial segment (onset) and nucleus, and nucleus and final segment (rhyme) (Storkel 2002; Edwards, Beckman, & Munson 2004).

### "Practice makes perfect"

Talking is a motor skill, and producing words so they are recognizable takes a great deal of practice. And practice children do. However, there are large

---

[11] Notice that what goes on in production, therefore, is quite distinct from what children need to be able to perceive in order to *recognize* words (Chapter 3).

[12] As Lindblom (1992:155) pointed out, "The functional value of an articulation is not context-free, but is defined only in relation to its system neighbors."

[13] "When these conditions are met by the model, a 'segmentation' will be automatically imposed on the stored motor scores" (Lindblom 1992:147).

individual differences here too, just as there are in the onset of walking and in general manual dexterity. Children whose early words are far from their adult targets take out quite a lot of time in the first few weeks or months of word production to practice individual words until they become recognizable. Where first pronunciations are close to the adult forms, children may need less practice. That is, their articulatory skill seems to be related to the amount of practice and rates of vocabulary growth in production (see Dromi 1987; Locke 1993).

Children practice sounds. This can happen in babbled sequences once they have started to produce words (e.g., Elbers & Ton 1985). They also focus on specific words in this practice and systematically contrast nearby sounds, for instance, as in the following extract from a bedtime monologue. This child, Anthony, had recently been introduced to raspberries, which he liked (Weir 1962:108):

(9)     back *please* / berries / *not* barries /
        barries barries / *not* barries / berries / ba ba

Like many children, Anthony talked to himself before he fell asleep. Analysis of his bedtime monologues from 2;4 to 2;6 revealed extensive practice and play with particular sounds in words containing specific sound structures (labials and velars, for example), along with deliberate repairs of faulty pronunciation. He also practiced combining words in what Weir called "build-ups" and "break-downs." In a build-up, as in (10), the child began with a word or phrase and then added to it, elaborating it. In break-downs, as in (11), he did the reverse – starting with a longer utterance and then reducing it to smaller pieces (Weir 1962:82).

(10)    Build-ups: *block / yellow block / look at the yellow block light / see yellow blanket / up there in yellow light*

(11)    Break-downs: *Anthony jump out again / Anthony jump another big bottle / big bottle*

He also practiced grammatical patterns (Weir 1962:109), as in (12):

(12)    *what color / what color blanket / what color mop / what color glass*

and made substitutions in what sound like extracts from mini-language drills (Weir 1962:111–112), as in (13):

(13)    *I go up there / I go up there / I go / she go up there*
        *put on a blanket / white blanket / and yellow blanket / where's yellow blanket*
        *there is the light / where is the light / here is the light*

Practice like this also occurs in daytime monologues where the child has no addressee and is unconcerned with communication. Consider these typical examples:

(14)    Child (1;9; Bohn 1914:586)
        *Daddy walk on grass / R* [child's name] *walk on grass – no /*
        *Daddy walk on grass – yes / Daddy walk on snow / snow deep /*
        *know that word*

(15)        Child (2;9; Snyder 1914:421)
            *Train go on track / car go on track / wheel go on track / little*

How widespread such practice is can be seen in the studies by Kuczaj (1983) and Nelson (1989).

As children get older, they often announce that they can (now) say a word that they were unable to say earlier. When one Danish child, Frans, finally mastered the initial **fl-** cluster at 2;11, he went around to his parents saying words that began with this sequence and asking them whether they could say them. "When asked if he could say *blad*, Frans answered, 'No, not yet; Frans cannot say *b-lad'* (with a little interval between the **b** and the **l**)." Five weeks later, when he mastered initial **kl-**, he announced, "Frans can say *kla* so well" (Jespersen 1922:111). Another child, Amahl, about the same age, after nearly a year of pronouncing English *quick* as *kip*, announced, correctly: "Daddy, I can say *quick*" (Smith 1973:10). Leopold (1939–1949: vol. IV:57) reported similar observations from his daughter Hildegard, who was also interested in her own improved pronunciation. She had previously pronounced English *merry-go-round* as [mɛkəriraʊnd], but at 4;1, she announced mastery of the right pronunciation: "Watch my mouth: *merry-go-round*." In German, she had had difficulty with *Verzeihung* (confusing it with *Zeitung*), but, around age four, said one day: "Look at my lips: *Verzeihung*" (now correctly produced) (Leopold 1939–1949: vol. IV:57).

In summary, some children take time out to practice different aspects of their language during the day and in their bedtime monologues. They play with language, with sounds and sound sequences; they make repairs; they announce achievements. It seems as if they are focussing on language and its elements, not only in their own everyday usage but also in an increasing range of metalinguistic reflections on language (Clark 1978a; Slobin 1978).

## From one word at a time to longer sequences

The development of articulatory skill does not end with single words. Children learn how to plan and produce longer sequences too. The achievement this represents can be seen in the transition from single-word utterances to utterances containing two or more words. After a few weeks (occasionally months) of one-word utterances, children start to combine words into longer sequences. This usually begins between age 1;3 and 1;8. This transition is often marked by children's beginning to produce strings of one-word utterances. The transition occurs gradually, in roughly the steps shown in Box 5A (Bloom 1973; Fonagy 1972; Leopold 1939–1949: vol. IV).

So as children learn to produce longer sequences, they must work both on extending the intonational envelope or contour so it covers more than just one word, and on making the final word in a sequence more prominent. This requires

## 5A  Steps in combining words under a single intonation contour

(a) Children produce single words with separate intonations, with longish pauses between each one, and equal stress on each word.

(b) Children produce a shift in intonation contour. Instead of separate falling contours on each word, they produce the first word with an incomplete fall, then pause, then produce a complete fall on the second word. As before, the two words have equal stress.

(c) Next, children shorten the pause between two words produced in succession and shift to uneven stress, with the second word receiving heavier stress than the first.

(d) Finally, they produce full combinations of two words, with virtually no pause between, with a single intonation contour, and with heavier stress on the second word. (In longer sequences, the final word receives heavier stress.)

adjustments in timing, in planning sequences for articulation, and in utterance-level stress assignment. Further support for this account comes from single words, successions of single words, and multiword utterances where analysis of spectograms – displays of the intonation contour and timing of each word – are consistent with earlier observations. Branigan (1979) argued for a single intonational envelope placed over two successive words as children move from one word at a time to longer sequences. In his analyses of utterances from three children, he compared the locations of (a) the terminal pitch contour and (b) the durations of words across the three utterance-types. Successive single words shared suprasegmental patterns with multiple-word utterances, namely the same contour fall from nonfinal to final term (see also D'Odorico & Carubbi 2003; Fonagy 1972; Scollon 1976, 1979).[14]

Overall, it is the presence of a pause between words that has led observers to characterize sequences within a turn as single-word utterances. But in terms of contour and duration, Branigan found that sequences of single words typically belong with more fluent multiple-word utterances, not with the earlier single-word ones. The duration of a word (or its compression) and the assignment of a single intonational contour are both evidence for the planning of a single unit. Compression of a word marks anticipation of further words in the same utterance, and maintenance of a nonterminal contour indicates likewise that the speaker knows the utterance still has some way to go (Levelt 1989). The difference between successive-one-word and multiple-word utterances is, therefore, at least in part, a matter of fluency of articulation.

Children appear to work hard to combine articulatory routines in utterances that consist of word combinations rather than just single words. The effort they invest in various transitions, from babbling to words and from single words to longer utterances, has been related by some researchers to attention (e.g., Clark 1982; Elbers & Wijnen 1992). At various transition points in development, children

---

[14] Bloom (1973), contra Branigan, proposed that successive single words had no underlying organizational basis, while multiple-word utterances did, in the form of an underlying syntax.

appear to turn their attention selectively to particular problems they have to solve and to work hard on one problem or one aspect of a problem. It is as if they turn on a spotlight selectively to focus on one place at a time during development. Once they have solved that problem, they move the spotlight to somewhere else.

Acquisition of fluency also shows up in the trade-offs observable in two-year-old speech. When accuracy of consonant production is considered for single words versus the same words in word combinations, children tend to produce isolated words more accurately (Nelson & Bauer 1991). Effectively, children this age simplify their pronunciations of words when they produce them in word combinations, and the longer the utterance, the more they simplify (see also Plunkett 1993).

In moving from one word at a time to longer utterances, children can also take advantage of the fact that, within a conversation, turns in dialogue serve to link one-word utterances into a larger "whole," as in this example from a child learning French (Veneziano, Sinclair, & Berthoud 1990:636):

(16)     CAMILLE (1;7.18, putting a baby doll into a toy cradle): *dodo*. 'sleep' (As she completes the action): *la*. 'there'

Veneziano and her colleagues suggested that such sequences at the one-word stage are good candidates for later combinations in similar contexts (see also Scollon 1976). In conversations with others, in fact, children repeat words to endorse the intention they had expressed initially, and these repetitions are often an integral part of their first combinations, as in the following exchange (Veneziano *et al.* 1990:641):

(17)     CAMILLE (1;7.18, handing her mother a little bottle): *bwa*. 'drink'
         MOTHER: Oui. 'yes'
         CAMILLE (putting her finger on the opening of the bottle): *lo. bwa*. 'water. drink'
         MOTHER (as Camille again holds the bottle out to her): ah tu veux de l'eau toi! 'ah, so you want some water!'

As Camille attempted more word combinations, she also became more likely to link them to words in her mother's intervening utterances. Children learn how to construct combinations, Veneziano and her colleagues argued, precisely from seeing how to build up longer sequences in alternating turns. Furthermore, children who can coordinate with another speaker to some extent can start to attend to more of the details of form in the language addressed to them. In this case, this was signaled by an increase in the number of utterances starting with a filler vowel, that is, with attempts at producing the articles that must be used in French with nouns. Uses of these protoarticle forms increased from around just 5% at 1;6 to 45% a month later, at 1;7, and increased again, in the following month, to around 73% (Veneziano *et al.* 1990; see also Bassano & Eme 2001).

Children acquiring English also give early indications that they are trying to produce certain grammatical morphemes, again around the time they begin to combine single words into longer utterances. But how they do this seems to depend on their analysis of the forms in question (Peters & Menn 1993). One child, Seth, produced a variety of filler syllables, mainly uses of the neutral vowel schwa, [ə], and syllabic [n], and moved fairly steadily into more adultlike forms that differentiated his uses of pronouns, prepositions, modals, and the copula. Another child, Daniel, followed a different path, yet both, Peters and Menn argued, offer strong evidence for a general "phonology first, morphology later" strategy. Both children tried to produce appropriate-sounding sequences, perhaps at the syllabic level, before they had fully analyzed the component forms (and meanings) of the grammatical elements involved – terms like *the*, *for*, *in*, and *to* (see also Carter & Gerken 2004; Elbers & Wijnen 1992).

One last point: Children appear to distinguish new information from given information by how clearly they articulate the relevant words. When asked to describe a series of pictures where some elements remained the same (given information) but others changed (new information), they consistently articulated expressions for new information more clearly than expressions for given information (Goffman, Schwartz, & Marton 1996). This finding also holds for adult speakers in conversation: Even in using different expressions to refer to given information, they do not articulate as clearly as when they convey new information (Fowler 1988; Fowler & Housum 1987). Producing a word may be affected not only by the child's developmental stage but also by the conversational context and the status of the information being expressed.

## Production from comprehension

Representations for production must differ from those for comprehension. While children start right away on storing representations for comprehension – representations that allow for recognition and hence comprehension on the basis of word forms stored in memory – they take much longer to set up appropriate representations for production (Clark 1993). For production, one needs to be able to retrieve from memory not only the relevant word for the notion to be expressed but also the relevant articulatory specifications for producing an auditory sequence that will be recognized. To produce recognizable words, children have to discover the correspondences between articulatory movements and adjustments to the vocal tract and the particular auditory patterns that result. Getting sounds and sound sequences right takes time. And producing multisyllabic words and longer expressions requires that children attend, check their own current productions against their representations for comprehension, and try again whenever they detect a mismatch between them.

The large asymmetry between production and comprehension in young children can be clearly seen in one study of two-year-olds (Goldin-Meadow, Seligman, & Gelman 1976). The children were tested on their ability to

Table 5.2 *Nouns understood and produced at age 2;0 by twelve children*

| *Body parts* | *Animals* | M (4,4) |
|---|---|---|
| foot (12,5) | fish (11,8) | heart (0,0) |
| head (12,5) | cat (10,10) | |
| hair (11,7) | rabbit (9,9) | *Food* |
| mouth (11,5) | bear (9,8) | banana (10,9) |
| hand (10,5) | cow (8,7) | orange (10,8) |
| teeth (10,3) | pig (7,6) | grape (10,6) |
| finger (9,4) | giraffe (5,5) | cake (9,7) |
| arm (9,3) | butterfly (2,2) | cereal (8,5) |
| lips (7,1) | | sugar (8,4) |
| tongue (7,1) | | mustard (4,2) |
| knee (5,2) | *House parts* | |
| elbow (4,2) | clock (12,9) | *Miscellaneous* |
| thumb (4,1) | chair (12,9) | ball (12,11) |
| armpit (0,0) | table (12,9) | pillow (11,6) |
| | door (11,7) | scissors (10,8) |
| *Clothing* | window (11,5) | flower (10,7) |
| hat (12,9) | house (10,6) | crayon (10,4) |
| sock (11,7) | floor (10,1) | money (9,9) |
| button (9,8) | wall (8,5) | paper (9,8) |
| belt (9,5) | sink (7,4) | plate (9,5) |
| pocket (7,6) | lamp (5,4) | mirror (8,4) |
| scarf (4,1) | pot (3,3) | ladder (8,3) |
| badge (1,0) | couch (1,1) | ring (6,4) |
| | | cigarette (3,3) |
| | | broom (7,6) |
| *Vehicles* | *Letters/shapes* | flag (3,2) |
| train (10,9) | A (5,5) | tire (1,1) |
| airplane (11,10) | star (5,4) | stamp (0,0) |

*Note*: The first number in parentheses is the number of children (out of twelve) who understood each item; the second is the number (out of twelve) who produced it.
*Source*: Goldin-Meadow, Seligman, & Gelman 1976:192. Reprinted from *Cognition* 4, Susan Goldin-Meadow, Martin E. P. Seligman, & Rochel Gelman, Language in the two-year-old, 189–202, copyright 1976, with permission from Elsevier Science.

understand and produce some 80 terms for objects (adult nouns) and 30 terms for actions (adult verbs). Overall, they showed understanding of 61% of the terms but produced only 37% of them. Moreover, as other researchers have noted, they only produced terms that they also understood. The data for nouns is given in Table 5.2 and for verbs in Table 5.3.

The asymmetry was larger for verbs than for nouns. While children gave evidence of understanding the verbs 74% of the time, they produced them only

Table 5.3 *Verbs understood and produced at age 2;0 by twelve children*

| Transitive | Transitive | Intransitive |
| --- | --- | --- |
| eat (12,7) | pick up (10,1) | sit (11,6) |
| throw (12,3) | shake (9,2) | jump (11,5) |
| open (11,7) | touch (9,1) | run (11,3) |
| close (11,6) | wash (8,4) | stand (11,2) |
| kiss (11,4) | step on (8,0) | lie down (11,1) |
| drink (11,3) | kick (6,2) | fall (9,5) |
| blow (11,1) | push (6,1) | turn around (9,1) |
| drop (10,2) | pull (5,1) | dance (8,1) |
| hug (10,1) | point to (4,0) | fly (7,2) |
|  |  | cry (5,2) |
|  |  | smile (5,0) |
|  |  | crawl (3,0) |

*Note*: The first number in parentheses is the number of children (out of twelve) who understood that term; the second is the number (out of twelve) who produced it.
*Source*: Goldin-Meadow, Seligman, & Gelman 1976:192. Reprinted from *Cognition* 4, Susan Goldin-Meadow, Martin E. P. Seligman, & Rochel Gelman, Language in the two-year-old, 189–202, copyright 1976, with permission from Elsevier Science.

21% of the time. With nouns, they gave evidence of understanding 56% of the time and could produce them 37% of the time.

This asymmetry remains even for adults. It simply becomes less obvious for most everyday purposes. Take our ability to understand different dialects of our first language: However good we are in comprehension, we can never match this level in production; speakers control only two, or maybe three, different dialects, a fraction of the number they can understand. Or take a version of your first language from a century ago or three centuries ago: These varieties of the language are typically still easy to understand. They are neither easily nor readily produced. Or take second-language learning: It is commonplace to observe that one's comprehension is always far ahead of one's skills in production. What holds for two-year-olds here also holds for adults.

For children, the asymmetry appears critical for the process of acquisition. Their retention in memory of representations for comprehension, starting at around nine to ten months, allows them to recognize words, starting with familiar chunks in the speech stream. As these are isolated and associated with consistent meanings across occasions of use, they become able to fill in more details about both the meanings and forms of words. They then have these representations available to serve as the targets when they begin trying to produce the words themselves. Notice that if, instead of being able to rely on such representations in memory, they had to wait on hearing the word they had intended to say from some nearby adult, say, they would take much longer to get going since adult speakers would hardly be a reliable source of output just when needed. Logically, of course, this would also be a barrier for children's recognition of recurring forms in adult speech. Somewhere, they have to store representations for comprehension, or they will never learn how to use language. These representations for comprehension provide targets against which children can always check their own outputs. When their own productions don't match these representations for comprehension, they can try again – and they do.

## Summary

Why learn to produce language? If children are to participate in conversations, making their own wishes and claims known to others, and responding to other participants, they must learn how to be speakers as well as addressees (and, often, listeners or even overhearers) in conversational exchanges. One essential ingredient in this is managing to make oneself understood – as a speaker. To become a speaker requires mastery of conventional forms of words and expressions in both formal and rapid speech. So children must find out early how to produce the sounds and sequences they need to be heard and understood. But becoming a fluent speaker takes time and practice.

# 6    Words and meanings

In *Words and Things*, Roger Brown (1958b:194) described what he called "the original word game." His account went as follows:

> The tutor names things in accordance with the semantic customs of the community. The player forms hypotheses about the categorical nature of the things named. He tests his hypotheses by trying to name new things correctly. The tutor compares the player's utterances with his own anticipations of such utterances and, in this way, checks the accuracy of fit between his own categories and those of the player. He improves the fit by correction.

He noted further that "[w]e play this game as long as we continue to extend our vocabularies and that may be as long as we live." In this account, Brown recognized the essentially social nature of the exchanges between tutor and player. Effectively, tutors are the adult experts, and the players the children learning language. Adults offer both words and information about word meanings, and children try out their hypotheses about word meanings in their own uses of the words, with adults offering corrections when needed. These exchanges take place in the everyday conversations between children and adults (Clark 1999).

Consider the following exchanges in (1), where an adult offers a new word and the child picks up on the offer (Clark, diary data):

(1)      D (1;8.2, points to some ants on the floor and says): *Ant. Ant.*
         FATHER (indicating a small beetle nearby): And that's a bug.
         D: ***Bug***.

The adult's *bug* for the other insect on the floor is ratified by the child's repetition. In the next two exchanges, the child's initial proposal is tacitly rejected in the adult's counteroffer in the next utterance:

(2)      MOTHER (asking son aged 1;9 about a shape): What does it look like?
         CHILD: *A eight.*
         MOTHER: It looks like a square, doesn't it?
         CHILD: ***Square***.

In this exchange from Garvey (1984), the tutor (here, the mother) ignores the child's proposal and continues in her next turn with the offer of *square*, which the child then ratifies. In the third exchange (from Kuczaj, CHILDES Archive data), with a slightly older child, the mother does much the same thing, offering the conventional term in place of that proposed by the child. Her correction is embedded in the next utterance.

(3)          A (aged 2;4, wanting to have his orange peeled): *Fix it.*
             MOTHER: You want me to peel it?
             A: *Uh-huh.* **Peel** *it.*

In the exchanges in (2) and (3), the adults (or tutors) provide the conventional words (*square* and *peel*), and these are immediately taken up by the two child-players. This ready uptake is characteristic in children's acquisition of unfamiliar words (see Bloom *et al.* 1996; Clark 2002a, 2007; Réger 1986; Veneziano 1985).

In this chapter, I assess the social and cognitive contributions to children's mapping of meanings onto forms as they acquire new words. I first consider proposals about a priori constraints on children's hypotheses about word meanings and then weigh these against an alternative, pragmatic approach based on children's grasp of speaker intentions and their ability to make inferences licensed in context, including inferences based on their current conceptual knowledge. I take up some consequences of the relations between conceptual perspective and lexical choice next, and then take another look at child-directed speech and the pragmatic directions adults offer about words and meanings. I end by looking at the coping strategies children also rely on as they map meanings onto forms.

## A priori constraints on meanings

When children assign a meaning to an unfamiliar word form, they must take into account all kinds of information: the locus of attention at that moment, the kind of object or event that is physically co-present, other terms that may contrast with the new word, plus any other information seen as pertinent. This encompasses many things: children's perceptual and conceptual categories so far, any preferences children display when they hear unfamiliar words, their knowledge about social interaction and about the inferences licensed in different contexts. In what follows, I weigh the contributions of both conceptual and social factors to children's solutions for the mapping problem in early acquisition.

Several researchers have proposed that children simplify the task of assigning meanings to forms in early acquisition by relying on a priori, built-in constraints on the hypotheses they are willing to entertain. The constraints proposed have in common a perceived need to simplify the mapping task for children. The problem of mapping meanings onto forms is regarded as so formidable as to be unresolvable without limiting what children are willing to consider as possible meanings. The need for this is generally justified by appeal to Quine's (1960) indeterminacy problem: If a child hears his mother use a word like *gavagai* as she points at a rabbit, what meaning should the child assign to it? Notice that it could refer to the rabbit, to some part of the rabbit, or to any of a host of properties or details pertinent to that particular rabbit on that occasion.

How does the child know which assignment to make? In the original word game, of course, whatever assignment the child opts for will be adjusted in light of the adult tutor's reactions to child uses, as well as the child's anticipations[1] (met and unmet combined) of further adult uses of *gavagai*. In the constraints view, if children don't yet have a word for rabbits as a type, they rely on one or more constraints to decide what meaning to assign to the unfamiliar term. These constraints are assumed to hold very generally and from a very early age (Golinkoff, Mervis, & Hirsh-Pasek 1994). They limit the hypothesis-space that children can consider as they assign meanings to unfamiliar words and expressions. Later, they have to give up some or all of these constraints, which are incompatible with many of the semantic relations inherent in the adult lexicon. Some constraints bias children to pick up terms for objects in preference to terms for parts, collections of parts, properties, relations, or actions. This should result in an early preference for acquiring (adult) nouns over other word-classes.

Which constraints might children observe, and when? As they begin to map meanings onto linguistic expressions, they appear to make certain assumptions about how speakers use words to refer. With object categories, they seem to assume that speakers use words to pick out whole objects, not just a part or a property of what is being talked about (Markman 1989; Mervis 1987). This *whole-object assumption*, of course, presupposes that children already have categories of objects, such that objects can be represented as whole entities distinct from their locations or from their relations to other objects or places. In fact, when children hear a term for an as-yet unlabeled object, they do appear to assume that the unfamiliar word picks out the whole object. This finding holds for children as young as one-and-a-half, although it has been demonstrated most extensively for three- and four-year-olds (e.g., Macnamara 1982; Markman & Wachtel 1988; Mervis & Long 1987; Woodward 1992). Viewed as a constraint on children's hypotheses about word meaning, the whole-object assumption presupposes that children have a built-in bias towards assuming that the adult is picking out an object as the intended referent when introducing an unfamiliar word.

A second constraint that has been proposed is the *taxonomic assumption*. According to this constraint, speakers use words to pick out categories of objects, say, rather than associated clusters of objects. That is, children appear to assume that a term like *squirrel* picks out just squirrels and not complexes of squirrels-on-branches or squirrels-eating-nuts, just as a term like *swing* picks out just swings, and not swings-with-children-on-them or swings-and-trees (Markman & Hutchinson 1984). And the categories of "squirrel" and "swing" are quite distinct from their neighbors in their respective conceptual domains.

---

[1]  Quine did not take the child's or addressee's role into account in his discussion of indeterminacy. Nor did he deal with joint attention, and its corollaries – physical and conversational co-presence.

This assumption is consistent with a general design feature of the lexicon: Many terms pick out single categories with internal coherence. Combinations of such categories and relations among members of different categories are designated through appropriate noun phrases and other constructions. For example, the expression *that swing* picks out a specific instance of the type "swing" that the speaker is concerned with on that occasion. If the speaker wants to comment on the fact that the swing has more than one child on it, then she must add the right modifiers, as in *that swing with two boys on it*. If *swing* instead designated a category of "swing-R-boy" (i.e., with some unspecified relation, R, holding between the category types "swing" and "boy"), one would then need separate words for swings in relation to girls, to babies, to adults, and to trees, for example, in addition, perhaps, to a term for swings alone. But the number of such potential combinations is both large and unpredictable because a new combination could arise every day. To base all word meaning on such combinations or clusters would be far too unparsimonious. And indeed, no language does this, except with certain terms for culturally significant combinations.[2] The general combinatorial work in languages is done instead through syntactic combinations of smaller lexical elements, in nouns phrases, in clauses, and in their combinations (see Part III).

Two other constraints that have been proposed are the *basic-level assumption* and the *equal-detail assumption*. The basic-level assumption captures the fact that the categories of whole objects favored by one- and two-year-olds tend to be categories at what psychologists have identified as the basic level (Rosch 1973). Conceptually, members of such categories are easier for adults to categorize than objects either above or below this level. Compare "dog" at the basic level to "animal" (above the basic level) or "dachshund" (below the basic level). Members of a basic-level category generally have more parts in common with each other than with members of a higher-level category, and they are more readily distinguished from members of neighboring categories in the same domain than are instances of lower-level categories (Tversky & Hemenway 1984). Conceptually, basic-level categories are privileged: They cohere internally, so their members are readily perceived both as members of their category and as distinct from nearby categories. The basic level is also privileged linguistically: The terms assigned to basic-level categories tend to be simpler in form than those assigned to lower levels and so are easier to learn and to remember (Berlin, Breedlove, & Raven 1973). And a certain proportion of children's early vocabulary consists of what would be basic-level terms for adults (Mervis 1987). Yet what counts as basic level depends not only on the actual term used but also on what it is being used for.

As children represent what they know about categories within a conceptual domain, they also seem to look for equal detail in any alternatives they consider

---

[2] However, this is still a simplification. Many terms designate complex states of affairs (e.g., nouns for events, such as *circus* or *party*), and societal and religious institutions (e.g., *trial, school, temple*), in addition to the many verbs that necessarily link various participants in the kinds of event designated (e.g., *put, give, chase, break*).

(Shipley & Kuhn 1983). Children who already produce the term *dog* for dogs, according to this assumption, should look for a category at the same level of specificity when trying to map the newly heard term *cat* and so are more likely to assume that *cat* refers to cats in general (as experienced so far) and not just to some subgroup of cats – Siamese cats, say, or Manx cats, both subkinds of cats and therefore offering more detailed points of comparison than are needed. This assumption also depends on some temporal proximity in uses of a familiar term like *dog* next to an unfamiliar one like *cat*. Otherwise there would be less basis for children to suppose that dogs and cats belong in the same general domain.

## Are constraints conceptual in origin?

All these assumptions appear to be derived from the structure of children's current *conceptual* categories. The extent to which these should be regarded as constraints specific to children's *lexical* development is therefore unclear. The whole-object assumption would seem to play a rather general role both perceptually and conceptually in distinguishing figures from grounds: Whole objects move as units, do not change their essential nature under rotation or with motion through space, and are therefore all the more readily identified and categorized against different types of ground (Spelke, Gutheil, & Van der Walle 1995). Does this assumption actually constrain the meaning children might assign to an unfamiliar word? Notice that the whole-object assumption is incompatible with large sectors of the lexicon of any language – none of the terms for actions, events, and relations denote whole objects, nor do terms for parts and properties.

Similarly, although both the basic-level and the equal-detail assumptions appear to play an important role in the way children structure and organize their conceptual categories, it is less clear that they constrain the meanings children assign to unfamiliar words. First, adults do not restrict themselves to basic-level terms in talking to children, but use whatever term is most useful for current purposes – basic, superordinate, or subordinate (Brown 1957). That is, adults will use a term like *fruit* (superordinate) when pointing out a bowl with several kinds of fruit in it, but *apple* or *orange* (basic level) when asking two-year-olds if they want some fruit for lunch. The equal-detail assumption also plays a role in structuring conceptual categories, so any constraint it places on meaning may be derived from its role in conceptual organization.

The taxonomic assumption likewise plays an organizational role in memory for those categories that belong to hierarchical taxonomies, with two or more levels, such that member categories within a single level do not overlap with each other. This holds, for example, for natural kinds such as animals, birds, or plants. It is less clear that it also constrains the meanings children are willing to assign to terms for such categories. This assumption was proposed to account for the observation that children who were asked to choose *another dax* when presented with pictures, say, of a dog (earlier called *a dax*), a cat, and a bone, chose the cat (a taxonomic choice) rather than the bone (a thematic choice) (Markman & Hutchinson 1984). But, depending on the number and type of choices they are offered, four- and five-year-olds shift from taxonomic to thematic assignments for unfamiliar words, or the reverse (e.g., Dockrell & Ralli 1996). This suggests that the taxonomic assumption per se is not a primary determinant of children's initial decisions about possible meanings.

Another constraint that has been proposed is the *mutual exclusivity assumption* (Markman 1987; Markman & Wachtel 1988; Merriman & Bowman 1989). This assumption captures the observation, based on experimental findings, that young children appear not to allow more than one word to pick out the same referent. If children know the term *dog* for dogs, they will not also accept reference to a dog with the terms *animal*, *spaniel*, or *pet*. In effect, this constraint stipulates that children apply each term exclusively as if all categories belonged at a single level with no overlap, and as if the lexicon allowed speakers to take only one perspective, conceptually, on any particular object. However, the findings supporting mutual exclusivity are at odds both with data on children's early spontaneous usage and with other experimental studies of new word acquisition (e.g., Clark 1997; Clark & Grossman 1998; Haryu & Imai 2002; Savage & Au 1996; Waxman & Hatch 1992).

### When and where do constraints apply?

The constraints that have been proposed are intended to hold only for a limited amount of time. But where do they come from and when do they take effect? Are they innate or are they learnt, and, if so, from what sources? Are they constraints designed solely to simplify children's early word-learning, or do they originate in general categorization abilities and conceptual development? That is, do children build on what they know about conceptual categories and the conceptual organization of such categories when they look for ways to talk about category-members?

According to Golinkoff and her colleagues (1994), some constraints take effect around ten or twelve months of age and are abandoned within the following year, while others take effect between twelve and eighteen months and are dropped at some less-determinate point later on. Constraints like the whole-object and mutual exclusivity assumptions have been used to account for data from two-year-olds and from three- to five-year-olds, and different researchers have argued for different onset points (e.g., age two vs. age four). There has been little agreement on when constraints start taking effect and even less on when they stop. Yet although researchers agree that they do stop taking effect once children make use of information that overrides each constraint, there has been little attempt to specify what information counts and under what circumstances. If one postulates built-in constraints incompatible with the adult lexicon, it becomes essential to specify the age and circumstances under which such constraints can be overridden.

Lastly, several researchers have characterized some constraints in terms of defaults. That is, they have stipulated that the constraint applies unless the child has information that would override or replace the limitation(s) it mandates (e.g., Woodward & Markman 1991; see also Behrend 1990; Nelson 1988). What does this imply? First, constraints are intended to account for some initial, basic ways of assigning meanings that can be modified with additional information, or with other information. But what counts as pertinent information for overriding any particular constraint has yet to be spelt out. Second, children could draw on a variety of alternatives to a particular constraint when they assign meanings. This in turn suggests that there are specifiable conditions under which children can ignore or abandon constraints. Again, these have not been specified. Third, since constraints have a developmental role – they apply as an aid to acquisition in order to simplify the first mappings of meanings to forms – it should be possible to identify the developmental changes that lead children to abandon particular constraints, whether on a one-time basis or for good. This too remains to be done.

In summary, while a variety of proposals have been made about constraints on early meaning assignments, there is little agreement on (a) where they come from, (b) when they start to apply and how long they last, and (c) why they are abandoned. An alternative to this approach is to look at how children might build on conceptual categories in combination with pragmatic information in context, making use of pragmatically licensed inferences in assigning meanings to forms. This approach, which combines cognitive with social information, yields a different interpretation of the experimental data available and is consistent with observations from spontaneous speech.

## The social context of meaning acquisition

Language acquisition is embedded in a social context. Children learn language as they interact with people in conversation (Chapter 2). This assumes that children rely on several important abilities. They have the ability to track someone else's locus of attention to achieve joint attention. They can pick out the entities, actions, relations, or events around them when these provide the locus of joint attention with the current speaker. And they can segment the speech stream to interpret some of what the speaker says by identifying familiar sequences and by separating out unfamiliar words.

Children rely on a variety of physical cues in identifying what someone else is attending to. Primary signals here are direction of gaze and gestures like pointing. Children themselves start to use pointing, between ten and twelve months of age, as a means of directing attention to things for other people, and, from about age one onwards, they respond to the pointing of others (Lempers, Flavell, & Flavell 1977; Leung & Rheingold 1981; Rheingold, Hay, & West 1976). By age two, children readily infer from someone's gestures where to search for a hidden object (e.g., Tomasello, Call, & Gluckman 1997).[3] So from about age one on, children

---

[3] Two-year-olds readily make generalizations based on pointing gestures that are independent of distance, for example, where chimpanzees appear unable to (Povinelli *et al.* 1997; Tomasello *et al.* 1997). By this age, and possibly even younger, children, unlike chimpanzees, appear to understand the communicative intention of the person who is pointing.

can – and do – make use of the gaze, gestures, physical stance, and orientation of the speaker to identify what the speaker is attending to (Moore & Dunham 1995).

Since adults tend to talk with children about what is currently happening in the immediate vicinity (e.g., Harris, Jones, & Grant 1984/1985; Messer 1978; Sachs 1979), the locus of joint attention and the physical co-presence of what is being talked about coincide in many mother–child conversations. Moreover, with very young children, adults often adopt the child's locus of attention to ensure that they share joint attention (Collis & Schaffer 1975). This ensures that physical and conversational co-presence coincide too. But adults can also capture young children's attention and get them to switch their attention to something else. Again, they are systematic in doing this with verbal attention-getters, gaze, and gestures (Estigarribia & Clark 2007). Adults talk about what is physically present, at the locus of joint adult–child attention. The general conditions that hold for adult–child interactions help license the inferences children need to make in assigning meanings to unfamiliar forms.

With language use, it is a truism that much of what an addressee understands is inferred from his knowledge of the speaker, from the common ground shared on that occasion between him and the speaker, from their shared knowledge about the conventions of the language being spoken (which words and expressions are conventionally used for what), and about the conventions of use in that language community (e.g., the usual way of asking for food). All these factors license general inferences about the speaker's intended meaning, as do any departures from the expected or usual expression for something. Such inferences help the addressee reconstruct what the speaker intended in saying something (Levinson 2000). In acquisition, the picture is complicated by the fact that children are using language while learning it. Most studies of acquisition have focussed on the acquisition of forms. Few have emphasized children's changing knowledge about the conventions on use. But this is essential for the assignment of meanings to forms. In fact, the study of word acquisition should be the study of the pragmatic inferences children make about language use.

### Inferences licensed by conceptual knowledge

What information might children use in assigning meanings? The simple answer is, whichever conceptual categories and relations might form the basis for and license initial inferences about possible meanings. This approach to meaning acquisition, like earlier ones, emphasizes the universal nature of perceptual and conceptual primitives. One- and two-year-olds' overextensions of words (Chapter 4) suggest children attend closely to similarity in shape in deciding to extend a word to new referents. Analysis of early word uses led researchers to propose the semantic feature hypothesis (Clark 1973a). Under this view, children built up word meanings piece by piece from a universal set of meaning components or semantic features. These features are initially identified with perceptual and conceptual information, and children display considerable uniformity in their first word uses regardless of the language being acquired. For example, analysis of overextensions cross-linguistically showed that children depend on shape first, followed by properties like sound, size, taste, and texture.[4] As they get older, they rely on other information as well, and shape plays a less prominent role (e.g., Gelman & Ebeling 1998).

Shape itself is not really assimilable in a straightforward way to the notion of semantic feature or component of meaning, since complex shapes can often be analyzed further but languages typically don't represent this detail. Compare a rubber ball or a thin stick with an abacus or a table. Perceptual and conceptual categories are encoded only indirectly by words and constructions. As Slobin (1979:6) pointed out, "Language *evokes* ideas; it does not represent them. Linguistic expression is thus *not* a straightforward map of consciousness or thought. It is a highly selective and conventionally schematic map."

The semantic feature hypothesis was originally proposed to account for certain patterns in children's early spontaneous word uses (Clark 1973a). The analysis of word use identified properties such as shape or size as semantic features, but conceptual information does not map in any direct fashion onto meanings. Although this approach to meaning acquisition offered a quite general account of early word uses and of some consistent errors of interpretation by children, it was only partially successful in predicting order of acquisition. And it offered no account where word meanings could not be decomposed into smaller elements (Clark 1983).

The semantic feature hypothesis assumed that all meanings are composed of smaller elements. (The same assumption has been made in other accounts of meaning and meaning acquisition.) But only some word meanings can be broken up into components or features that can be tracked in acquisition. Compositionality, then, can play only a limited role in explanations of the order in which children acquire terms in particular domains. Researchers studied several domains on the assumption that children start with only one or two meaning components and then add to these systematically as they acquire more of the adult meaning for each term. These domains include dimensionality – terms like *big*, *tall*, *long*, *deep*, and their opposites, *small*, *short*, *shallow* (e.g., Brewer & Stone 1975; Clark 1972; Donaldson & Wales 1970; Ebeling & Gelman 1994); relative amount, as in *more* and *less* (e.g., Donaldson & Balfour 1968; Wannemacher & Ryan 1978); kinship, as in *grandmother*, *uncle*, *cousin*, or *daughter* (e.g., Benson & Anglin 1987; Chambers & Tavuchis 1976; Haviland & Clark 1974); and time, as in *before* and *after* (e.g., Clark 1971; Ferreiro 1971; Johnson 1975).

Other researchers have focussed on the acquisition of a single component, such as CAUSE. This component is widely attested across languages. As part of the meaning of causative transitive verbs, it is often marked with a special ending

---

[4] The primacy of shape in categorization, as well as in decisions about word use, has also been attested in more recent studies (e.g., Anglin 1976; Baldwin 1989; Clark 1977; Landau, Smith, & Jones 1998).

Table 6.1 *Causative errors in young children's speech*

---

(a)  C (2;3, pulling a bowl closer to her as she sits on kitchen counter): *I come it closer so it won't fall.* (= make it come close; bring it closer)

(b)  C (2;6, trying to hold refrigerator door open, having difficulty): *Mommy, can you stay this open?* (= make this stay open; keep this open)

(c)  C (2;8, sitting in a toy chair that spins; mother had been spinning her but stopped; C looking hopefully across room towards father): *Daddy go me round.* (= make me go round)

(d)  C (2;9, holding a piece of paper over sister E's head): *I'm gonna just fall this on her.* (= make this fall on her; drop this on her)

(e)  C (2;11, trying to smooth down paper on her magic slate): *Make it nice and flat.* (brings it to mother): *How would you flat it?* (= make it flat; flatten it)

(f)  Mother (holding a broken musical cow toy; music no longer plays): The cow would like to sing but he can't. C (3;1, pulling string that used to make the music play): *I'm singing him.* (= making him sing)

(g)  B (2;7, making stuffed toy dance): *I'm dancing Jeremy Fisher.* (= making Jeremy Fisher dance)

(h)  J (3;1): *Yuck! It coughs me ... The thing coughs me ...* (= makes me cough) *I cough when I put it in my mouth.*

(i)  J (3;6, sitting on a metal stool): *It colds my bottom.* (= makes my bottom cold)

(j)  J (3;8): *I can't inside this out.* (= make it turn inside out)

---

Based on Bowerman 1974; Lord 1979

added to the verb-root. In her study of early verb uses of English, Bowerman (1974) argued that children's errors in using intransitive verbs like *fall* or *come* as causatives (e.g., *he falled it, I come it closer*), together with uses of periphrastic causative verbs like *make* and *get* (e.g., *he made it fall*) are critical in showing that children have realized that causative verbs contain CAUSE as part of their meaning (see also Bowerman 1982a, 1982b; Figueira 1984). Examples of common errors in causativization are given in Table 6.1.

These studies all assumed, probably correctly, that meaning acquisition is gradual, even though children start to use a word as soon as they have associated it with *some* meaning. But early usage may make it hard to discern whether a child has acquired the full adult meaning or not. They also assumed that words with related meanings might be confused with each other during acquisition, precisely because they share meaning components. However, while certain words do seem to be confused, many others that would appear to have just as much meaning in common appear not to be confused. Even where there are confusions, their basis may be hard to identify and even depend on different factors on different occasions (see Bowerman 1982b).

In summary, approaches based on semantic components fail overall because only part of the lexicon is compositional. The semantic feature hypothesis also has a mixed record in its predictions about order of acquisition. Finally, although this approach assumes a cognitive basis for universal semantic features, it pays no attention to social aspects of language use. It lacks all account of how interaction might affect meaning acquisition through choices of the right words, and how speakers can negotiate meanings. In short, it takes no account of pragmatic factors in language use and acquisition.

## Pragmatics in meaning acquisition

In everyday use of language, speakers and their addressees make a number of assumptions about which expressions are appropriate, and what inferences are licensed under particular circumstances. Speakers tend to take for granted that, in communicating, they are conveying their intentions to their addressees, and addressees likewise take for granted that they are in the business of trying to discern what the speaker's intentions are. All this takes a lot of skill. But since inferring a speaker's intentions is central to communication, this plays a critical role in children's acquisition of meaning.

To communicate at all, infants have to be able to make their own intentions clear and assess the intentions of others. They develop both these skills as they participate in communicative exchanges, both nonlinguistic and linguistic. From around ten to twelve months of age, they start to convey their own intentions in the form of protorequests and protoassertions (Bates, Camaioni, & Volterra 1975; Bloom 1997; Bruner 1975). They rely first on gestures to make requests, indicating what it is they want (stretching towards a toy, a book, a cookie). They also use gestures to indicate what they are interested in, what has caught their attention, but here they typically point rather than reach or stretch towards the chosen target (Bates, Camaioni, & Volterra 1975; Ingram 1971; Werner & Kaplan 1963).

In attending to others, infants start to use the other's direction of gaze as an indicator of attention from around ten months on. They will look at where another is looking. They will also follow gestures, often pointing gestures, to find a locus of attention (Rheingold, Hay, & West 1976; Tomasello 1995). Given the adult's propensity to adjust to what the infant seems to be focussing on (Murphy & Messer 1977), this makes it all the more likely, by around the age of one year, that infants and their adult interlocutors share their focus of attention when one of them is trying to communicate with the other. Infants appear highly adept at using gaze to indicate what another person is attending to, and are good at making use of gaze or pointing to make further inferences about where something is hidden. Primates, in comparison, require extensive training before they make use of gaze or gesture in the same way, and often fail to extrapolate to new situations (Povinelli *et al.* 1997; Tomasello *et al.* 1997). This reliance on joint attention plays a central role in allowing speaker and addressee to start out from the same point and then add to their common ground (Clark 2002b; H. Clark & Marshall 1981). Speaker and addressee also rely on their knowledge of physical co-presence (the location of the object or event that provides the focus of their joint attention) and on conversational co-presence (use of the relevant terms or expressions to pick out the object or event in question) in communication.

## Two general pragmatic principles

Users of language observe two general pragmatic principles. First, they assume conventionality in the system they are using. That is, if a particular meaning is conventionally associated with a particular form, then speakers will use that form to convey the meaning in question. When they do this, they can be pretty sure that their addressees will interpret them as intended. When they don't, their addressees assume that, because the speakers used some other expression, they must mean something else (Clark 1987, 1990, 1993; Clark & Clark 1979). Conventionality can be defined as follows:

> *Conventionality:* For certain meanings, speakers assume that there is a conventional form that should be used in the language community.

In essence, speakers give priority to any already-established, conventional forms for the expression of particular meanings.

This pragmatic principle has an important corollary. Speakers also assume that different forms differ in meaning. If they use two different forms, they must intend two different things. And if they use a form different from the one anticipated, they must intend something else. This is the principle of contrast, which can be defined as follows:

> *Contrast:* Speakers assume that any difference in form signals a difference in meaning.

Conventionality and contrast interact in that speakers are expected to use conventional, already-established forms. When they don't (when they coin new terms, for example), their addressees assume that they must therefore be trying to express some other meaning, one not currently captured by a conventional term (Clark & Clark 1979). The consistency over time conferred by conventionality offers speakers a reliable way of denoting object- and event-types.[5] And the difference of meaning associated with each difference in form offers extensive networks of both subtle and gross distinctions speakers can draw on in using language. Language-users need a certain stability in the conventional meanings they can

---

[5] Conventionality and contrast depend on children assuming that speakers use words to designate types rather than individuals. This holds not only for words for objects and events, but also for words for actions, relations, and properties. Speakers, of course, can refer to types or to specific individuals belonging to the relevant type, but this distinction will be marked explicitly in various ways, depending on the language being spoken. In English, speakers rely on definite articles or demonstratives (*the*, *that*) in referring to an individual, as in *that squirrel* or *the cup*. But notice that the words *squirrel* and *cup* always denote the types in question (Clark 1993).

convey, along with contrasts among those meanings, to make languages effective for communication (Clark 1993; H. Clark 1996; Lewis 1969). Notice too that if contrast is combined with the single level and no overlap assumptions that form part of mutual exclusivity, mutual exclusivity itself is no more than a special case of contrast. But unlike contrast, mutual exclusivity is inconsistent with lexical structure (e.g., any taxonomic hierarchy or any overlapping terms) and with general usage.

Children observe conventionality and contrast from an early age (Clark 1983, 1993). For example, they take as their targets in producing words the conventional forms they hear from adults; they are sensitive to differences between adult misproductions versus on-target productions of words (as when adults adopt a child-pronunciation like *fis*); and they make spontaneous repairs to their own pronunciations from age one onwards. They treat different words as having different meanings and rely critically on this as they build up semantic domains (Clark 1983, 1995). Their reliance on these pragmatic principles supports their inferences about the meanings of unfamiliar terms.

### Inferences from adult word use

When children hear an unfamiliar word, they can readily make several inferences. First of all, they can normally infer that it picks out something at the locus of attention shared jointly with the speaker. Second, depending on what is in joint attention, they can make inferences about what the speaker is picking out with it – a type of object, a type of action, or a type of state, and so on.

In doing this, children draw on conventionality and contrast on the one hand and on whatever conceptual knowledge seems pertinent on the other. For example, if the child and the speaker are attending to an as-yet-unnamed kangaroo jumping, the child infers that *kangaroo* must be something to do with the object-type rather than the action. He tacitly reasons that, if the speaker were talking about jumping, he would have used the conventional (and familiar) term *jump* and not some unfamiliar term. At the same time, since the child does not yet have a term for the kangaroo, the entity at the locus of joint attention, he infers that the new word picks out that creature. In addition, he can use syntactic cues to part of speech to identify the unfamiliar word as a noun (**the** *kangaroo*), a verb (**is** *jump**ing***), an adjective (*stick**y***), or a preposition (*it's* **beside** *the table*). Word-class membership provides added clues to the kind of meaning at issue (e.g., Fisher 1996; Fisher, Klingler, & Song 2006; Gleitman 1990; Hall & Graham 1999; Hall, Quantz, & Persoage 2000; Klibanoff & Waxman 1999; Waxman & Booth 2001).

Children make use of joint attention and common ground as they make inferences in context about the meaning of a new word. This ability is demonstrably present from an early age. By one-and-a-half to two, children follow and take account of an adult's focus of attention as she introduces new words (Baldwin *et al.* 1996). Moreover, young two-year-olds can accurately assess what their mothers do or don't know depending on whether the mothers have or haven't seen the experimenter put objects into a container. Where the mothers hadn't seen what happened, the children were more likely to use pointing gestures and to name the object or the location than when the mothers were present and had seen what happened earlier (O'Neill 1996; see also Akhtar, Carpenter, & Tomasello 1996).

Common ground assumes children make use of physical co-presence. They can build on the fact that speaker and addressee have a common focus of attention on some referent that is in sight. But because they are good at attending to the speaker's locus of attention and to affective information about success and failure in a search, they can also make appropriate inferences even when a target referent (an object or an action) is concealed from sight (e.g., Baldwin 1993; Goodman, McDonough, & Brown 1998; Tomasello & Kruger 1992; Tomasello, Strosberg, & Akhtar 1996). In short, infants as young as one-and-a-half can make use of both joint attention and physical co-presence in inferring meanings. To do this, they must draw on both social and conceptual resources.

On other occasions, children may already have words for both object and action, or words for neither, and then they reason differently. Take the case where they already have words for both object (e.g., dog) and action (running): They must then work out whether the speaker could be picking out some further property of the object (a part like fur or nail, say) or some property of the action, such as its manner of performance (e.g., patter, trot, race). To do this, children draw on what they know about the structure of their language and how the new term could be connected to familiar ones. Is it linked to the word for the object in question (as in *the dog*'s *tail*) or to the word for the action (as in *it raced into the yard*)? What other information appears pertinent in light of what the speaker said earlier and also in light of what he said in the next utterance?

Or take the case where the child doesn't have words for either the object or the action that child and speaker are both attending to: Then the child must try to decide whether the new term picks out the object (a spaniel) or the action (clawing at a gate) (Tomasello & Akhtar 1995). Here again, several kinds of knowledge play a role. Children can use the fact that the word is preceded by an article to infer that it must be a term for the unfamiliar object rather than the action; or they can use the fact that it occurs after a pronoun and with a verb inflection on it to infer that it must denote the action (Dockrell & McShane 1990; Hall, Quantz, & Persoage 2000; Klibanoff & Waxman 1999; see also Brandone *et al.* 2007; Imai, Haryu, & Okada 2005).

Whatever else the adult says may offer additional information about what a new word may denote. For example, the speaker may draw attention to similarities with other objects (*It looks like a snake*, *It's like a horse but smaller*) or contrast the first action with another (*Can it roll over?* or *It can beg too*). Speakers often allude, implicitly or explicitly, to contrasting categories from the same domain. Dockrell (1981; Dockrell & Campbell 1986) asked three- and four-year-olds to help her put away some small plastic animals lying on the table, with successive requests like "Can you give me the cow/the pig/the gombe/the horse?" The terms for other animals indicated the domain the new word belonged to, and the listing contrasted *gombe* with familiar animal terms, so the children could look at the plastic animals, identify the unfamiliar one, an anteater, say, and reason that the unfamiliar word must, on this occasion, denote that type (see also Diesendruck & Markson 2001).

Explicit contrast was invoked in much the same way when Carey and Bartlett (1978) introduced four- and five-year-olds to the unfamiliar word *chromium*. They relied on requests like "Give me the chromium tray, not the red tray, the chromium one." This told the children that *chromium* belonged in the same domain as *red* and that they must therefore pick out some color, even if they were unsure which one (see also Au & Markman 1987).

This reliance on conversational co-presence is probably commonplace for young children. For example, when parents talk about dimensions (*tall*, *big*, *wide*, etc.), they tend to use a number of contrasting terms that offer alternate perspectives on the same object. They may describe a toy truck successively as *big*, *bigger than that one*, *too tall to go under the bridge*, *short enough to fit in the garage*, and so on, as the child and adult are playing with the truck and moving it around (Messer 1978; Rogers 1978).

Children can use their own knowledge of conventional terms, where they either do or don't already know various terms that seem pertinent. They can also rely on the fact that any difference in the form used by the speaker signals a difference in meaning. They can then draw on both their current linguistic knowledge about word-classes, for example, in deciding whether a new word denotes an object or an action, or something else. They can also draw on their knowledge of a domain and its members (often called up through conversational co-presence) in trying to decide what it is the speaker is talking about. Imagine that an adult has just pointed at a monkey in a new wild animal puzzle, using the term *monkey* (at this point unfamiliar to the child). Just before this, though, the adult pointed out a tiger and an elephant, using the terms *tiger* and *elephant*. Because the child is already familiar with those terms, he readily infers that *monkey* belongs in the same domain – so it must be another animal term. Children make use of both conceptual and social resources as they assign meanings to unfamiliar terms.

Children appear to make such preliminary assignments quite rapidly when they hear an unfamiliar word, and they also seem to retain something of their rapid mapping over quite a long time. In a first study of this, Carey and Bartlett (1978) noted that, even several weeks after their initial exposure to the term *chromium* (presented as a color term for an olive shade), nursery-school children remembered it as a word for color and assigned it variously for shades from dark green to brown. This suggests not only that children make rapid inferences about possible meanings but that they remember them quite tenaciously, even after only a few exposures (see also Heibeck & Markman 1987). This retentiveness for preliminary meanings is valuable for young children as they gradually work out what the full (conventional) meanings are of the new terms they encounter. They need to be able to accumulate inferences from different occasions and look for consistency over time.

These moves are basic to the acquisition of meaning. They are guided by what infants and young children already know about the pragmatics of communication, combined with their general knowledge (so far) of the world around them. But children must not only acquire words for objects or events; they must also learn how different words can apply to the same objects or events to mark alternate conceptual perspectives.

### Conceptual perspective and word-choice

Speakers can present objects and events from different conceptual perspectives by making different lexical choices. They may talk about a dog as *the dog, the spaniel, the pest,* or *our other family member,* depending on the conceptual perspective chosen. The lexical choices speakers make have clear effects on how well their addressees remember details in pictures – with more specific terms eliciting better memory than more general terms (e.g., Jörg & Hörmann 1978); how they reconstruct line drawings labeled in different ways – with people distorting the original to correspond more closely to the term used (e.g., Carmichael, Hogan, & Walter 1932); and even how they give estimates of speed in videotapes of accidents – with people offering higher estimates after hearing verbs that connote greater force (*crash* compared to the less forceful *hit*) (Loftus 1979). In effect, speakers can present the same object to their addressees in a variety of ways by choosing different terms for referents, as shown in Box 6A. They could even talk about a rabbit, for instance, as *the rabbit* or (as Quine put it) *that collection of undetached rabbit parts.*

Children seem able to take multiple perspectives on objects and actions as soon as they have the necessary words (Clark 1997). They spontaneously make reference to the same object in different ways and, by age two, may already have a variety of terms that they can apply so as to present different perspectives on the same referent. These perspectives may mark a difference in the level of categorization (as in *dog* vs. *spaniel* or *food* vs. *cereal*), or a difference in domain membership (e.g., *dog* vs. *pet* for the family dog, or *pencil* vs. *dinosaur* for a dinosaur-shaped pencil) (Clark 1997). A few typical examples from D are given in Table 6.2.

Children can also switch conceptual perspective when asked. Just over age two, they can interpret terms from different levels (e.g., *animal, cat*) and from different

### 6A Taking different perspectives on the same referent

| Referent | Some lexical choices | | | |
|---|---|---|---|---|
| BOY | boy | son | mischief | student |
| DOG | dog | guard | pet | dustpan |
| BRICK | brick | doorstop | shelf support | path edge |
| PERSON | neighbor | teacher | mayor | violinist |
| NEWSPAPER | newspaper | trash | birdcage liner | wrapper |
| BOWL | bowl | flower vase | soup tureen | container |

Table 6.2 *Using more than one expression for the same referent*

---

(a) D (1;7,1, looking at his bowl of cereal at breakfast): *Food*.
(A little later, still at the table, looking at his own and then his parents' bowls of cereal):*Cereal*.

(b) D (1;7,20, doing his animal puzzle; D named each animal type as he took it out [e.g., *lion, tiger, zebra*], then, on completion, with all of them back in, pointed and said): *Animal back*.

(c) D (2;1,27, when his mother asked what D was usually called)
Mother: Are you 'lovey'?
D: *No, I 'Damon', I 'cookie', I 'sweetheart'! Herb 'lovey'.*

(d) D (2;2,24, playing with several small dolls)
Mother: Do you call them people?
D: *They not people, they childrens. They kids.*

(e) D (2;5,4, putting the wastebasket, usually called basket when he throws anything into it, down over his head): *That's a hider. Hide me in there.*

---

*Source*: Clark, unpublished diary data

domains (*postman*, *bear*) as having the same referent. They can also produce two or more terms for a single referent to mark differences in level or domain (Clark & Svaib 1997). By age three and four, they readily answer questions that require talking about the same referent in three different ways – from three perspectives – as when they talk about a rose as *a rose*, *a plant*, and *a flower*. In one study, most three-year-olds (75%) and all but one four-year-old (92%) produced more than one term for the same referent at least half the time (Waxman & Hatch 1992; see also Deák & Maratsos 1998). This is consistent both with Clark and Svaib's findings for young two- and three-year-olds, and with observations of children's spontaneous speech from as young as one-and-a-half (Clark 1997).

Finally, adults use multiple ways of referring to a single object or action even when talking to one-year-olds. When asked to introduce terms for members of an unfamiliar domain (whales), parents used two or more terms for a single referent 17% of the time to children aged 1;4 and over 35% of the time to children aged 1;11 (Callanan & Sabbagh 2004). With children who had a very small vocabulary, parents used both *beluga* and *whale* (or even *fish*) as they labelled and related subkinds of whales to each other. As Brown (1957) pointed out, parents-as-speakers choose the terms that are most useful for current purposes – *fruit*, for instance, in an utterance intended as a warning, "Don't touch the fruit," but the more specific *orange* in an offer, "Do you want an orange?"; *money* in designating a pile of coins, but *coin* in picking one out from a collection of objects; and so on. Speakers rely on being able to mark perspective through lexical choice in a way that is relevant to the current conversational goal.

Assigning a meaning to an unfamiliar word requires finding out which perspective it calls up. Is it at a more specialized level of categorization that calls attention to particular details or parts? Is it a superordinate that allows fairly disparate things to be grouped together? Does it mark membership in some orthogonal domain? Does it pick out a part or property? Children have to learn how terms within a domain are related in meaning. These relations reflect the connections among different perspectives on the same object or event.

### Directions about meaning relations

Adults not only provide children with conventional words for objects, actions, and relations; they also offer information about semantic relations. They give information about a relation like class inclusion in utterances like "This is a kind of dog" (said of a poodle) or "An oak is a tree." They present relations like part of, looks like, belongs to, and is made of in connecting new words to others that are already familiar (Clark 1997; Clark & Wong 2002). Some typical examples of such relations are shown in Table 6.3.

Moreover, adults are rather consistent in *how* they present information about such semantic relations. They offer extensive information about terms that refer to categories organized into taxonomic hierarchies, for example, in explicit sort-of and kind-of statements (Callanan 1985, 1989). And, in the case of the part-of relation, they introduce a term for a part only after presenting a term for the whole; for example, "This is a rabbit," followed by "These are his ears." Children as young as two readily infer from such juxtapositions that an unfamiliar term picks out a part of a known object (Masur 1997; Saylor, Sabbagh, & Baldwin 2002; Saylor & Sabbagh 2004). Parts of objects may be salient and so play an important

Table 6.3 *Directions about meaning relations*

---

(1) Inclusion: *X* is a kind of/sort of *Y*
    "Oaks are kinds of trees"; "A pug is a kind of dog"
(2) Set membership: *X* is a *Y*
    "A cat and a dog are both animals"; "These trees make a forest"
(3) Comparison: *X* looks like/is similar to *Y*
    "Tusks are like teeth"; "A zebra looks a bit like a horse"
(4) Property identification: *X* has *Y*, *X* is made of *Y*
    "A walrus has tusks"; "The ball is made of rubber"
(5) Part identification: *X* is part of *Y*
    "Your thumb is part of your hand"; [hammer] "You see this part? It's called a claw"
(6) Listing: [with *X* and *Y* known] This is an *X*, this is a *Y*, and this is a *Z*
    "This is his paw, this is his toe, and this is his claw"; "This is a bear, this is a lion, and this is a leopard"
(7) Function: *X* is for/is used for *Y*
    "Do you know what you do with a wrench? You tighten pipes"; "It's a wick. You can't burn a candle if you don't have a wick"

---

*Source*: Clark 1997:11. Reprinted from *Cognition* 64, Eve V. Clark, Conceptual perspective and lexical choice in acquisition, 1–37, copyright 1997, with permission from Elsevier Science.

role in the identification of category instances (Mervis & Greco 1984). This salience in fact appears to affect how readily children learn terms for the objects themselves. In one word-learning task, children aged 1;8 learned the words for object-types with salient parts (as judged by adult raters) more readily than words for objects without salient parts (Poulin-Dubois, Graham, & Riddle 1995).

Children also take up information about semantic relations from an early age. They attend to inclusion statements offered about unfamiliar words. In one study, young two-year-olds heard a single utterance of an inclusion statement ("a *dax* is a kind of *ruk*") during a task where they were taught *dax* and *ruk* for two sets of objects somewhat similar in shape and function. Later, when tested on the words *ruk* and *dax*, they consistently treated the objects that had been called daxes as a kind of ruk but not the reverse. So when asked to pick out all the *ruks* on the table, they consistently chose both daxes and ruks, but, asked to find all the *daxes*, they chose only daxes (Clark & Grossman 1998). A real-word analogy to this learning situation would be where children learn the words *car* and *van*, and then are told that *vans* are a kind of *car* (see also Waxman & Senghas 1992). If asked for all the cars, children should pick up both cars and vans. But if asked for all the vans, they should pick out only vans.

The same children were also able to interpret adult self-repairs and to ignore information presented prior to the repair in favor of information offered later. The repair in this case was to the word being taught, for which the speaker then substituted a different word: That is, the child was first taught one word for a set of objects, then the adult glanced at a piece of paper, exclaimed "I made a mistake! This is not a *ked*. It's a *dob*," and then proceeded to teach the second new word, *dob*, in place of the one just taught. Upon later testing, the two-year-olds reliably chose the appropriate referents for the second word (*dob*) only and claimed not to know what the first word (*ked*) meant.

Children this age are also attentive to nonspecific indications of repair. They take account of affective reactions ("oops" or "wrong!," for example), followed by a new action or demonstration involving the target action or object in word-learning. Again, as in the case of repairs to specific words, they take up the information that follows the repair (e.g., Tomasello & Barton 1994). Both types of repair require that children be able to make inferences about speaker intentions and take into account the pragmatic information being offered that signals that intent.

Children also use the words they already know to make inferences about co-occurring words that are unfamiliar. When two-year-olds are asked to identify the referent (from among four pictures) of an unfamiliar noun like *ferret*, after hearing *The mommy feeds the ferret*, they can nearly all pick out the animal. And they retain this information about the meaning of *ferret* a day later (Goodman *et al.* 1998). That is, children soon learn the kinds of entities that one can feed, the kinds of stuff one can eat, the kinds of things that can move on their own, and so on. This knowledge in turn adds to the inferences they make about new words. Indeed, it is in learning which domains specific nouns and verbs belong to that they learn permissible combinations for nouns and verbs – birds eat seed, but flowers don't, cats miaow but dogs bark, cars drive, airplanes fly. One opens doors, bottles, briefcases, and jam jars, but (in English) not radios, light switches, or taps (Bowerman 2005). That is, children can use the common co-occurrence relations between words to make further inferences about meanings.

Children encounter many situations in which there is no explicit information about semantic relations. They may hear, or be taught, one or more new words but not receive any information about how they are related to other already familiar terms. Where they lack such information, they rely on general coping strategies when they need to make inferences about possible connections among word meanings. Those are important for the clues they offer to the inferences children make and hence to how children connect words on the basis of partial knowledge about the conventional meanings.

### Strategies for coping with unfamiliar words

On the conceptual side, children can take into account what they know about the objects or actions in the current locus of attention – the general properties and the possible relations they can enter into. For instance, spoons can be used for eating, for picking up pieces of food, and for stirring around in liquids; cups can be used for drinking from; blocks can be stacked on top of one another or lined up side by side; and balls can be dropped, rolled, or thrown.

The specific conceptual information that appears pertinent will depend on the actual referent on that occasion. Take a word like *soft*: What counts as soft for blankets or cuddly toys is rather different from what counts for skin, peaches, or mattresses. The same goes for *tall*: Whether something is picked out as tall depends on the surroundings. In a street of bungalows, a three-story house is tall, but the same house next to a skyscraper is not tall. Or take the preposition *in*: This can be used for various kinds of containment in space,[6] as in the following phrases: *the tape in the cassette case, the orange in the box, the flowers in the garden*, or *the people in the house*. The first encounter that children notice could lead them to try out hypotheses about the meaning of *in*, including tight or loose fit, support and enclosure, close contact, or enclosure with little or no contact (Choi & Bowerman 1991; Choi *et al.* 1999).

In short, the context in which children first encounter a word may play an important role in the first meaning assigned and in how children subsequently go on to use that word. Here there are liable to be large individual differences. Eventually, children converge on the conventional meaning, but this may take quite some time. Just where children start, for any one word that is unfamiliar, is a haphazard affair. The first referent may be typical or atypical, and so give rise to mappings that vary in appropriateness. To overcome this, children need to attend

---

[6] I am ignoring other uses of *in* here – for states and for time, as in: *in a huff, in a rage, in laughter, in delight; in two minutes, in a month*, etc. Some of these uses are acquired much later than spatial uses; others appear in the third to fourth year.

Table 6.4 *Coping strategies for placements in space*

Ordered choices for spatial location

(1) If the Reference Point is a container, place *X* inside it.
(2) If the Reference Point offers a supporting surface, place *X* on it.

*Source*: Clark 1973b:168. Reprinted from *Cognition* 2, Eve V. Clark,
Nonlinguistic strategies and the acquisition of word meaning,
161–182, copyright 1973, with permission from Elsevier Science.

to a range of exemplars and to accumulate what they observe in the usage of
others, as well in reactions to their own uses. Throughout this process, children use
words long before they have the full conventional meanings established. Since
they cannot know their preliminary meanings are incomplete, they have no reason
not to use them. (Adults do this too.)

Despite this variation, there is considerable consistency in what children
do either before they have mapped any meaning to a new word or after they
have made a preliminary mapping in certain types of context. This consistency,
I suggest, stems from the cognitive categories and organization children can draw
on. Take the locative relations encoded by the prepositions *in*, *on*, and *under*:
When children aged one-and-a-half to two are presented with small objects that
can be placed with respect to locations like small boxes lying on their sides,
miniature tables, or toy cots, they exhibit remarkably consistent choices. They
place the small movable object *inside* anything that can be treated as a container
(e.g., the box and the cot) and otherwise place it *on top of* anything that has an
extended supporting surface (e.g., the table) (Clark 1973b; see also Grieve,
Hoogenraad, & Murray 1977; Johnston & Slobin 1979; Wilcox & Palermo
1974/1975). These choices reflect ordered preferences where containers always
take priority over surfaces (Table 6.4).

## 6B  An early misassignment of meaning

"Deleterious" may not be in the vocabulary of most preschoolers, but it's a word I've known since
I was very young. For many years, however, I – and I have learned, at least some of my siblings – had a
mistaken impression of its meaning.

My parents were quite strict about nutrition. Cake, cookies, and other treats that they deemed
to be unhealthy, at least for regular consumption, were tagged as being "deleterious" – perhaps a bit of
an overstatement, but a not inaccurate use of the word.

However, over years of asking, "Can we buy some cookies?" and hearing, "No, they're
deleterious," my siblings and I came to the conclusion that "deleterious" meant something that
was sweet and really tasty!

I can't recall how old I was before I was disabused of that notion, but even today, when I
encounter the word, my mouth begins to water.
D. C. Grossman, AWAD mail issue 275, 7 October 2007

Once children work out the meanings of *in* and *on* in English, they can make contrasting placements in response to the relevant preposition in an instruction. But they appear to retain the strategy for dealing with other relations in space prior to working out those word meanings. Three- and four-year-olds rely on the same strategies in dealing with pairs like *on top of–underneath*, *above–below*, and *in front of–behind* (e.g., Clark 1977, 1980; Kuczaj & Maratsos 1975).

These strategies for dealing with relations in space are not specific to English. Children learning Korean and American Sign Language rely on them too. They reflect what children know, conceptually, about general relations between locations and objects being located: Some locations can serve as containers or enclosures with some degree of support, and others offer supporting surfaces without any degree of enclosure. In addition, young children appear to have a strong preference for putting smaller objects inside anything that is container-like (Gesell & Thompson 1934). For a language like English, this will make it seem as if children learn the meaning of *in* rather earlier than *on*, and both of these earlier than *under*. But, in fact, these children are simply relying on their conceptual knowledge to provide a basis for some response to the adult request to act. The request "Put the mouse in the box" elicits 'Do the most obvious thing to the mouse in relation to the box', where "obvious" is filled in by the child's conceptually based preference for a specific type of spatial relation.

Children also rely on their general conceptual preferences in dealing with differential amounts. Given a choice between two piles of coins and asked for the one with *more* or the one with *less*, three-year-olds and even many four-year-olds typically choose the pile with the larger amount (Donaldson & Balfour 1968). But this strategy is moderated by children's reliance on contrast when they hear two different words, *more* and *less*, in the same session. They consistently treat them as if they differ in meaning, even when they may be unsure what the precise difference is (Wannemacher & Ryan 1978).

Strategies analogous to choosing the larger of two piles also show up for other dimensions. When children are asked to choose a longer or shorter plank for a bridge or to decide whether someone should climb the taller or the shorter of two trees in order to see something, they consistently opt for the entity with greater extension – in height, width, or length (Donaldson & Wales 1970). In response to requests like "Point to the short plank," children consistently respond as if to 'Choose the longer of the two planks', where this reflects their conceptual preference for greater extension. That is, before children work out the exact meanings of dimensional terms like *high–low*, *tall–short*, or *wide–narrow*, they rely on a conceptual preference for greater extension (Klatzky, Clark, & Macken 1973). Some of the preferences that have been identified are summarized in Box 6C.

### Hypothesis testing and the original word game

Brown's (1958b) original word game assumed hypothesis-testing on the part of child-players. That is, children, in context, come up with a preliminary

## 6C  Some coping strategies for different situations

(1) *Location:* Assume smaller objects go inside containers, but, in the absence of containers, put them on supporting surfaces.
(2) *Extension:* Assume greater extension takes priority over lesser extension for amount, volume, height, length, width, etc., and choose the more extended exemplars.
(3) *Event order:* Assume clause order mirrors actual event order, such that the first clause describes event 1, the second describes event 2, and follow instructions to act out events accordingly.
(4) *Agent identification:* Assume usual or canonical relations hold among participants in an event, and interpret utterances accordingly (e.g., dogs chase cats, mothers feed babies, cars go on roads, etc.).
*Source*: Clark 1997:29. Reprinted from *Cognition* 64, Eve V. Clark, Conceptual perspective and lexical choice in acquisition, 1–37, copyright 1997, with permission from Elsevier Science.

hypothesis about the meaning of a term and then test this hypothesis. They can use that term in what they predict should be an appropriate way. More expert speakers then either accept or reject the children's uses. Acceptances ratify the hypothesis; rejections indicate that the hypothesis is wrong or needs adjusting.

Adults may accept child uses tacitly, but they also often follow them up by using either the child's term or else a form like *he* or *that* to indicate the same referent. These continuations all mark acceptance. When they reject the child's term, they may be direct or indirect. Direct rejections aren't very common, and when they do occur, they may be hedged, as in "It does look like a snake but it isn't really." Indirect ones appear as embedded corrections, where the adult speaker ignores the child's term and offers another word instead (e.g., the offer of *peel* in lieu of *fix* in talking about peeling fruit).

On the basis of their hypotheses, children can predict when and where other speakers should use the same terms. When their predictions are met, they receive support for the meanings hypothesized. When they are not met, they need to adjust their hypotheses or start again. So children can gain information both from reactions to their own uses and from their predictions about uses by others. In both cases, they can also make use of information from other terms speakers produce in order to restrict or refine their hypotheses about the meanings they are currently trying to map.

Hypothesis testing, then, depends on children being able to keep a tally of uses by adult speakers and of adult reactions to child uses of specific terms. Without such a record, children would have a hard time keeping track of whether they had in fact hit on a more or less appropriate meaning for any particular word, and an even harder one in trying to decide what adjustments to make to the meaning they had initially assigned. This suggests that meaning acquisition requires a tallying mechanism similar to that required as children start to match their own pronunciations of words in production to the adult-based forms they have stored in memory (Chapter 5). I return to more detailed discussion of such tallying and where it seems to be needed later on (Chapter 16).

What children say – how they use a word – reveals what their current hypothesis is about its meaning. But word uses can be hard to evaluate: A child's use may appear quite appropriate on one occasion, then inappropriate two days later. The appropriate uses may reflect instances where the child's meaning overlaps with the adult's but doesn't yet fully coincide with it. This shouldn't be surprising given the differences in experience for adults versus two- or three-year-olds. And, of course, identifying the relevant dimensions that lead children to use the same word on two different occasions, once appropriately and once not, may not be all that easy. To assume that what children say reflects exactly what an adult would intend in using the same expressions can all too easily induce us to overestimate how much children know about conventional meanings.

One solution to this is to combine observations of what children say spontaneously with what they understand. Ideally, children's comprehension of a term can be tested in settings where a discrepancy between child and adult meanings will show up in how children interpret instructions or requests. Take the case of locative *here* and *there* in English. Children produce both terms from an early age, often producing *here*, say, as they hand something to someone else and *there* as they place the last block on a tower. While both uses are appropriate, they do not reveal whether these children know that *here* and *there* also contrast deictically – that *here* picks out a space near the speaker (with a boundary that is infinitely extendible) and *there* picks out a place beyond that, away from the speaker. In systematic checks on comprehension of *here* and *there*, many three-year-olds take *here* to pick out a place near themselves: *here* is 'near me' rather than near the speaker. When child and speaker are next to each other, the child's use appears adultlike, but when the child is seated opposite the speaker, it becomes clear that the child is using himself rather than the speaker as the reference point.

Only around age four do children acquire the deictic meanings of *here* and *there*. Other deictic pairs – *this* and *that*, and *come* and *go* – take even longer to acquire fully (Clark & Garnica 1974; Clark & Sengul 1978). While children make a number of errors in production, especially with the verbs *come* and *go*, it is only when one combines observations of production and comprehension that one can see that children are using these terms with only part of the relevant adult meaning.

Another indication that children have not yet fully mastered the conventional adult meanings of words appears in their "late errors." As Bowerman (1982b) noted, children may make apparently error-free use of some forms for as much as a year or two, and then start to produce occasional errors. She suggested that such errors arise as children analyze the meanings of the relevant forms in more detail and, as a result, start trying to reorganize parts of their lexicon. Some typical late errors in children's uses of such verbs as *make*, *let*, and *get* are given in Table 6.5.

So one has to be careful not to attribute full adultlike knowledge of word and construction meanings to children too soon. Appropriate uses in one context don't necessarily connote mastery of the adult meaning. A stronger indication of acquisition is consistent adultlike use across a range of contexts. In much the

Table 6.5 *Some typical "late errors" with* make, let, give, *and* put

---

*Make* and *let*

(a) C (3;6, disagreeing with mother's use of the word *puppet* for dolls with toilet paper roll bodies): *But usually puppets make – let people put their hands in.*

(b) C (3;9, begging father to let her watch a TV show): *Make me watch it.*

(c) C (3;6, after mother has told her she must go to bed): *I don't want to go to bed yet. Don't let me go to bed.*

(d) C (3;8, as mother puts C's shoes on; she'd wanted another pair): *How come you always let me wear those?*

*Give* and *put*

(e) E (2;4, to father, after mother has told C and E that it's time to give him his Father's Day presents): *We're putting out things to you.*

(f) C (3;4, request for mother to give her the pink cup): *You put the pink one to me.*

(g) E (2;7, pointing to ice-crusher): *Give some ice in here, Mommy. Put some ice in here, Mommy.*

(h) C (4;1): *Whenever Eva doesn't need her towels she gives it on my table and when I'm done with it I give it back to her.*

---

*Source*: Bowerman 1985a:389. Used with permission from Lawrence Erlbaum Associates.

same way, appropriate use of one verb with a particular construction (e.g., *want to go out*) doesn't indicate that the child has learnt how to use complements like *to go out* or has identified those verbs that, like *want*, can take this construction. Uses of the same construction with several different verbs offer firmer evidence for the acquisition of complement constructions introduced by *to*.

## Summary

Children acquire words and their meanings in conversational settings. They take up words they hear in conversation and make inferences from the conversational context, along with other sources of information, about possible meanings. A critical factor in their identifications of conventional meanings are the reactions of other speakers. As Brown (1958b:228) argued with respect to a player of the original word game (the player, of course, being the child):

> Whether or not his hypothesis about the referent is correct the player speaks the name where his hypothesis indicates it should be spoken. The tutor approves or corrects this performance according as it fits or does not fit the referent category. In learning referents and names the player of the Original Word Game prepares himself to receive the science, the rules of thumb, the prejudices, the total expectancies of his society.

But social interaction tells only part of the story. The other part is told by what children bring to the interaction – what they have learnt so far about the objects, actions, properties, and relations in the world around them. This growing store of conceptual knowledge provides the basis for their coping strategies as they respond to unfamiliar terms. Through joint attention in each exchange, it also provides a source of hypotheses about possible word meanings. In combining what they know about the world and about social interaction, children rely critically on pragmatic knowledge to interpret the intentions of others.

# PART II

# Constructions and meanings

*[E]ven within a single language, grammar provides a set of* options *for schematizing experience for the purposes of verbal expression. Any utterance is multiply determined by what I have seen or experienced, my communicative purpose in telling you about it, and the distinctions that are embodied in my grammar.*

Dan I. Slobin 1996

*Words are not coined in order to extract the meanings of their elements and compile a new meaning from them. The meaning is there FIRST, and the coiner is looking for the best way to express it without going to too much trouble.*

Dwight Bolinger 1975

The focus in these chapters is on the steps children take as they express more elaborate meanings, beyond one word at a time. They must find out which constructions to use for particular meanings and which words go in each construction. They work out which inflections can be applied to different word-types (nouns, verbs, and adjectives) and what meaning each one adds; how to present information to the addressee and what perspective to use as speaker; how to combine clauses in talking about complex events; how to analyze complex words and coin new ones. As children become increasingly skilled at communicating what they want and what they think, they learn which constructions convey which conventional meanings.

# 7    First combinations, first constructions

As children add to their first words, they add specificity and detail to how they express what they want and what they are interested in. This all entails including more information, and hence more complexity, in each utterance, as in the move from *More block* to *I need another block* or *They've got all the blocks*. This in turn requires the learning of structure: structure in the form of contrasting inflections added to words and in the form of constructions reflected in the combinations of words. To do all this, children have to start learning to think for speaking in their first language (Slobin 1996). That is, they must start to use the conventional constructions for expressing particular meanings.

The focus of this chapter is on the move from single-word utterances to longer utterances, the emergence of multiword combinations, and the meanings children use these combinations to express. In doing this, do children begin from formulaic forms that they then analyze into the component parts, much as they try whole words and only later extract the segmental details (Chapter 5)? Or do they build up utterances one element at a time, with each word or affix that they add? That is, what do longer utterances tell us about emerging structures and the uses children make of them at this stage in speaking?

## One word at a time

One-year-olds don't speak very often. When they do, they typically say one word at a time and produce their words at extended intervals, with long pauses between utterances. Some researchers have proposed that there is a single-word stage during the first few months of language production, a stage in which children never produce more than one word at a time. In a remarkably detailed case study, Dromi (1987) followed the progress of Keren up to the point where she began to produce word combinations. For the five to six months prior to this point, Keren exhibited a consistent pattern in her uptake of new words in production. Her first attempts were generally far from recognizable, and she would then spend several days in intensive practice until her productions of each new word approximated the adult pronunciation rather more closely. Only then did she add a few more new words. That is, her progress showed a pattern of additions followed by intensive practice that resulted in much greater intelligibility. Over the first three to four months of such additions, her first attempts at new words became better, so by the time she had been doing this for about five months, even her first attempts at a new word were likely to be fairly close to the adult pronunciation. Soon after she reached this point, two things happened. First, she began to add new words in larger numbers (around 40–50 in place of 5–6 per week), and, second, after some three weeks of this, she produced her first multiword combinations (Dromi 1987).

Keren's general pattern of development suggests that, in language production, there may be certain trade-offs in development between articulatory skill and word combination. To produce an interpretable multiword utterance, children need to be able to articulate longer sequences in a recognizable way, and that requires more fluency than the production of just one word on its own. If children produce their words in more recognizable fashion from the beginning, we would expect to see the emergence of multiword sequences earlier and a less clearly defined one-word stage. This, in fact, is just what one finds in some children who begin to produce multiword utterances only five or six weeks after the production of their first recognizable words (Clark 1993). This difference appears to reflect an initial difference in articulatory skill analogous to differences in dexterity with fine motor control of the finger or in balance with early walking (Thelen & Smith 1994). Given the large range in motor control within development in general, it shouldn't be surprising to find differences in the development of articulatory control, a domain that requires rather fine discrimination of the movements for particular sounds.

But does the production of word combinations depend on children's individual words being interpretable? Could they be attempting combinations much earlier that simply go unrecognized? Peters (1983) noted that children differ in whether they focus mainly on producing single words or on larger "phrases" early on. Children who produce intelligible words also produce longer babble-like sequences or phrases. These phrases, which are generally dismissed as unintelligible, as nonsense sequences, or as babbling, may in fact be attempts at producing larger chunks of speech. While these often carry distinct intonational contours, they may not be intelligible. Since researchers, like children's interlocutors, favor what is interpretable over what is not, these longer phrases have been ignored in most accounts of syntactic development.

### Sequences of single words

When children produce just one word at a time, they give each word its own intonational contour. At a certain point, children start to produce a few sequences of single words, typically focussed on a single event. These sequences are produced without intervening adult utterances and seem to occur shortly before the emergence of multiword utterances proper. Some typical examples from two children, Allison and Nicky, are shown in Table 7.1.

What is the status of such sequences? Do they mark the first evidence of structure in children's utterances? Researchers have differed on this. Bloom

Table 7.1  *Sequences of single words*

---

(a)  Allison (1;6, after eating two pieces of peach her father had cut for her, in the bowl
     of a spoon, she holds out another piece of peach): *peach / Daddy /*
     (then she picks up the spoon): *spoon /*
     (and as she gives both peach and spoon to her father): *Daddy / peach / cut /*
(b)  Allison (1;7, after taking a pot from the shelf in the toy stove, she "stirred" it with
     her hand): *cook / baby /*
     Mother: Is the baby cooking?
     Allison (extending the topic she had introduced): *pot /meat /*
(c)  Nicky (1;6, wanting the fan to be turned on): *fan /*
     (when nothing happened, he made a follow-up request): *on /*
(d)  Nicky (1;9, just after he had left his bear on the trolley): *bear / trolley /*

---

Based on Bloom 1973:41; Greenfield & Smith 1976:123, 152

(1973) argued that sequences of single-word utterances are just that, single words, with no underlying structure. They may reflect an increase in the child's ability to call up more than one word for a specific event, but they don't offer evidence per se of underlying structure to link them. There is no consistent word order (in English at least), and therefore, according to Bloom, such sequences offer no evidence that children are trying to express structural relations.

What if such sequences showed evidence that individual words were planned together, as opposed to separately? Earlier observers argued that children on the verge of producing multiword utterances gradually shorten the distance between their words and simultaneously extend a single intonational contour over more than one word. So the nonfinal term in a two-word sequence, for instance, no longer has final (falling) intonation (Fonagy 1972). Having the same intonational "umbrella" stretched over two words rather than over just one suggests that the production of the two words must have been planned at the same time because they are treated as a single unit. If two words are treated as a unit, this in turn suggests they are linked in some way in the child-speaker's mind.

Do nonfinal words in such sequences look more like isolated single words (pronounced with longer duration) or more like nonfinal words in multiword combinations? Spectographic analyses of single words, successive single-word sequences, and multiword utterances from three children strongly suggest that their sequences of single words are in fact planned together and that such sequences do therefore mark the emergence of structured relations in young children's speech. Branigan (1979) compared (a) the terminal pitch contour and (b) the durations of words across these three utterance-types for a series of recordings of three children made over a five-month period. He found that sequences of single words shared intonational patterns with multiword utterances but not with single-word ones: Both the single-word sequences and the multiword utterances exhibited the same contour level in nonfinal terms (Figure 7.1). And both of these utterance-types had a fall on the final word, to means of 198 Hz and

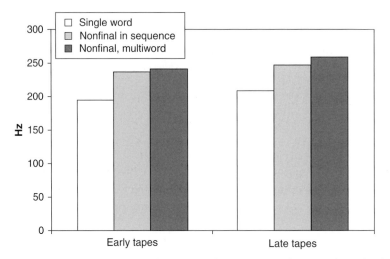

Figure 7.1 *Mean values for $F_0$ in Hz for early versus late recordings for three children.* Based on Branigan 1979

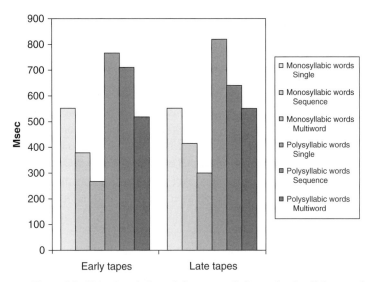

Figure 7.2 *Mean length (in ms) for monosyllabic and polysyllabic words in isolated single words, sequences of single words, and multiword utterances from three children.* Based on Branigan 1979

194 Hz respectively on the early tapes and to 203 Hz and 204 Hz respectively on the late tapes.

When Branigan measured the durations of single words, he found that nonfinal words in two-word combinations were significantly compressed compared to single words, and nonfinal words in multiword utterances were still further compressed (Figure 7.2). In both sequences and multiword utterances, nonfinal monosyllabic words were significantly more compressed than single words in isolation. There was a similar trend for polysyllabic words, but these showed greater variability than monosyllabic ones.

Overall, the presence of a pause between successive words has led some observers to characterize sequences of single words as single-word utterances, but in terms of intonation contour and duration, these sequences appear to be the immediate antecedents of more fluent multiword utterances. Their relative duration (compression) and intonational contour both offer evidence of coordinated planning. The compression of a word marks anticipation of further words in the same utterance, and a nonterminal contour also indicates that the utterance has not been completed. The difference between sequences and multiword utterances appears to be a matter of fluency. As children become more fluent, their articulation time for a word is shortened, and this compression shows up in their multiword combinations.

Similar results have been found for other languages. In Italian, precursors of word combinations – two single-word utterances – take longer to produce than later combinations of the same two words. With single-word utterances, children lengthen the final syllable of each word, but in word combinations, they lengthen only the final syllable of the second or last word (D'Odorico & Carrubi 2003). In German, research on the acquisition of a single prosodic contour over two words rather than just one has shown that children's control of such phonetic parameters as pitch, loudness, and duration takes time to master. In an analysis of two-word utterances produced by one child between 2;0 and 2;3, Behrens and Gut (2005) found that different types of multiword utterances became fluent at different points, and that the child displayed high variability in pausing and stress pattern at the onset of word combination. So the degree of fluency in early two-word utterances may not always be a good indicator of whether the child is still producing single-word utterances or is actually attempting a two-word combination.

### Word and gesture combinations

To compensate for lack of fluency, children may have recourse to gestures. This strategy appears quite prevalent in a gesture-rich culture like Italy's. Capirci and her colleagues (1996) videotaped twelve children acquiring Italian at 1;4 and again at 1;8 to see whether they relied on gestures in the transition to multiword utterances. They analyzed these tapes for deictic or pointing gestures, for representational gestures, and for deictic and representational words (e.g., *this*, *there*; *fish*, *bread*). They found a general increase in GESTURE + word combinations produced prior to an increase in word + word combinations. This suggests that children who might still have difficulty producing the longer articulatory sequences required for a two-word combination could instead produce a GESTURE + word combination (Table 7.2).

The children also combined two deictic terms, as in *eccoli qua* 'here-they-are here'; a deictic and a representational term, as in *questa pappa* 'this food'; or two

Table 7.2 *Some typical* GESTURE + *word combinations*

| DG & rw | POINT (to flowers) & *fiori* 'flowers' |
|---|---|
| DG & rw | SHOW (a cup) & *acqua* 'water' |
| DG & dw | POINT (to toy) & *questo* 'this' |
| DG + rw | POINT (to drawing of pigeon) + *nanna* 'sleep' |
| DG + dw | POINT (to game) + *te* 'you' |
| RG + rw | ALL-GONE + *acqua* 'water' |
| RG + dw | YES + *questo* 'this' |

*Note*: POINT was generally with the index finger extended, SHOW was an object being held out in the adult's line of sight, and REQUEST was an extended arm, sometimes with repeated opening and closing of the hand (Capirci *et al.* 1996:654). DG indicates a deictic gesture; dw a deictic word. Representational gestures included a number of gestures iconically related to actions on or by the referent: opening and closing the mouth for FISH, flapping the arms for BIRD, wriggling the nose for RABBIT, and so on (Capirci *et al.* 1996:654). RG marks a representational gesture; rw a representational word.
*Source*: Capirci *et al.* 1996:652–653. Used with permission from Cambridge University Press.

representational terms, as in *piccolo miao-miao* 'little kitty'. And they produced some gesture combinations, as in POINT (to drawing of fish) + FISH, or POINT (to closed box) + OPEN. On average, the number of GESTURE–word combinations doubled from 1;4 to 1;8, from a mean of 15 to a mean of 33. The increase held for most of the children. There was also a clear increase in the number of two-word combinations, from a mean of 0.42 at 1;4 to 13 at 1;8, and of multiword forms, from a mean of 0.42 to 7 (Capirci *et al.* 1996; see also Acredolo & Goodwyn 1988; Caselli 1983). Gestures, then, appear to help young children communicate before they can pronounce the longer phonological sequences required for combining words.

Do children systematically replace gestures with words? And how is this process related to the onset of word combination? Gestures could simply be something that precedes language, or gestures themselves might bear a more fundamental relation to language. In one study of ten children, Iverson and Goldin-Meadow (2005) studied the transition from single words to two-word combinations and found that gestures played an integral role. First, many of the "words" produced initially in gestural form were later replaced by actual words. And second, those children who first produced GESTURE + word combinations like POINT (bird) + *nap* were also the first to produce two-word combinations (*bird nap*). Changes in their gestures predated and also predicted changes in their language.

Just how do children move from gestures to words in the first place? What role do children's gestures play in the actual process of acquisition? One possibility is that children's gestures elicit the requisite words from their parents and caretakers. In this way, adults could supply just the words children need at this point in order to move on from a GESTURE + word combination, for instance, to a word + word one. Researchers therefore examined all the maternal responses to the gestures and speech produced by the same ten children during the period when they produced just one word at a time. All ten mothers "translated" their children's gestures into words. These offers of words provide timely models for how to express the child's notions in words, whether in place of a single gesture, or in place of a GESTURE + word combination (Goldin-Meadow *et al.* 2007; see also Iverson *et al.* 1999).

## Early word combinations

Across languages, children's early word combinations take a remarkably similar form and cover a similar range of functions. Children produce two-word combinations as they make requests, describe locations and actions, as they negate some state of affairs, and as they talk about possession and modification. They also ask questions, usually with *where* or with a *yes/no* marker of some kind (Slobin 1970). Some of the similarities from one language to the next can be seen in the two-word utterances from English, Luo (Kenya), and Finnish, languages from three very different language families, given in Table 7.3.

These early word combinations are very similar in content. Do they reflect salient scene-types? Do children look for recurrent event-types that might be considered prototypical of self-instigated motion, say, or of causal changes involving an agent? Do they identify the different kinds of participants across event-types – agents, objects affected, objects possessed, locations, actions – and simply

Table 7.3 *Two-word utterances from three languages*

|  | English | Luo | Finnish |
|---|---|---|---|
| *Request* | more milk | adway cham | anna Rina |
|  |  | 'want food' | 'give Rina' |
| *Locate* | there book | en saa | vettä siinä |
|  |  | 'it clock' | 'water there' |
| *Negate* | no wet | beda onge | ei susi |
|  |  | 'my-slasher away' | 'not wolf' |
| *Describe* | hit ball | odhi skul | takki pois |
|  |  | 'he-went school' | 'cot away' |
|  | mail come | omoyo oduma | talli 'bm bm' |
|  |  | 'she-dries maize' | 'garage "car"' |
| *Possess* | mama dress | kom baba | täti auto |
|  |  | 'chair father' | 'aunt car' |
| *Modify* | big boat | piypiy kech | rikki auto |
|  |  | 'pepper hot' | 'broken car' |

Based on Slobin 1970

use the words they have available to say what they wish about them? Do they recognize the abstract similarities that hold across participant roles in different kinds of events? And, finally, to what extent do these utterances, like one-word utterances, result from children's participation in conversation? Do they reflect the fact that children are trying to make appropriate contributions and are attentive to what is given versus new within an exchange? What they have not yet mastered are all the conventions of how to say what they wish to say – the grammatical structure, the relevant morphological inflections, and the right words for conveying specific meanings.

Children who wish to talk about events need to be able to analyze what they observe to decompose scenes into the constituent parts relevant to linguistic expressions in the language they happen to be learning. They have to work out what kind of language they are learning in terms of how to talk about agent versus patient, location versus instrument, or beneficiary versus recipient. They must find out how to mark grammatical relations such as subject and direct object. And they must also learn how to indicate that the elements in a constituent (a noun phrase or a predicate, for instance) belong together, through agreement or adjacency, or both, depending on the language.

One- and two-word utterances could indicate that children focus initially on conveying what is most salient to them about each scene or event. They may try to talk first just about participants that are salient – because they move, for instance – and about salient actions. Then they could fill in details about less salient aspects and look for ways to talk about those too. Later still, they should use consistent linguistic expressions for whole events (see Tomasello 2000) as they master more of the conventions of the language.

The next move in research was to take more account of what children seemed to intend in terms of the roles and actions denoted in each two-word utterance. The general framework was Fillmore's (1968) notion of case relations associated with specific verbs. For example, the transitive verb *to open* in English in a sentence like *The boy opened the door with a key* is associated with an Agentive argument denoting the actor carrying out the action (here *the boy*), an Objective argument denoting the entity affected by the action (*the door*), and, optionally, an Instrumental argument for the instrument used in effecting the action (*the key*). These roles are marked in different ways in different languages, but as underlying cases associated with specific verbs, they serve to represent generalizations about participant roles across a variety of event-types.

Consider the corpus of two-word utterances in English from Kendall, aged 2;0 (Table 7.4). These utterances have been analyzed in terms of the participant roles in the events talked about, where the nouns Kendall produced denoted the agent of the action (the agentive), for example, or the object affected (the objective), the place (the locative), or the possessor (the experiencer). Kendall produced 88 two-word combinations in one hour of recording, plus numerous one-word utterances and a few three-word utterances during the same session

Table 7.4 *Two-word utterance-types in the speech of Kendall, aged 2;0*

| | |
|---|---|
| (1) *Verb and Agentive* (28) | (5) *Verb and Objective* (23) |
|     Kendall swim |     Kendall look [look at K] |
|     Kimmy come |     Kimmy kick [kick K] |
|     doggie bark |     shoe off |
|     Mommy read | (6) *Agentive and Objective* (5) |
|     pillow fall |     Kendall spider [is looking at] |
| (2) *Verb and Experiencer* (1) |     Kendall book [is reading] |
|     see Kendall [K sees] | (7) *Experiencer and Objective* (14) |
| (3) *Verb and Goal* (1) |     Kimmy bike |
|     writing book (L or O?) |     Papa door |
| (4) *Verb and Locative* (3) |     Kimmy pail |
|     play bed | (8) *Locative and Objective* (13) |
|     sit pool |     Kendall water |
| |     towel bed |
| |     there cow |

Note: The numbers in parentheses indicate the number of two-word utterances classified as belonging to that category.

*Source*: Bowerman 1973a:Appendix R. Used with permission from Cambridge University Press.

(Bowerman 1973a). Most of these utterances consisted of combinations of a verb and a noun for either the agent of the action or the object affected by the action (58%). A further 31% of her two-word utterances consisted of two nouns, generally for the possessor and object possessed or for the object and its location. These utterance-types accounted for the large majority (89%) of her two-word combinations on this occasion.

The analysis of Kendall's utterances reflects a shift from earlier purely distributional analyses of early word combinations to semantically based analyses taking into account the apparent meaning of each utterance. Earlier analyses had focussed on the distributions of word-types in word combinations. For example, Braine (1963) looked at positional regularities in two-word combinations and proposed, on purely distributional grounds, that children's words at this stage could be divided into two classes, a small *pivot* class and a large *open* class. Pivot words included terms like *more, no, again,* or *it*. These were few in number and typically had a fixed position (either always first or always last) in word combinations. Open words included terms like *jump, hit, play, eat, ball, cup, dog,* and *chair*; they generally consisted of adult nouns, verbs, and adjectives. Most early two-word combinations were made up of two open class words or of a pivot plus an open class word. Combinations of pivot words were rare. Different children typically favored different pivot words in early combinations. Compare an English-speaking child who produced many combinations with *more* plus different open class words (Braine 1976):

(1)       *more car* [= drive around some more]
          *more cookie*
          *more high* [= there's more up there]
          *more read*
          *more sing*
          *more juice*, etc.

with a French-speaking child who used a form of *mettre* 'put on' combined with open class words (Bloch 1924):

(2)       *bóló mè* [robe mettre 'dress put-on']
          *papo mè* [chapeau mettre 'hat put-on']
          *man mè* [ruban mettre 'ribbon put-on']

Both children relied on what could be thought of as protoconstructions, where one term contributes a stable meaning across events, and the others fill in additional information about the desired activity or the object affected.

Purely distributional analyses, though, paid little attention to the intended meaning of children's utterances and typically ignored the contexts in which they occurred. That is, children's word combinations were analyzed without regard to their role in the flow of conversation. From a theoretical point of view, it was also unclear how children moved on, developmentally, from a pivot and open word classification, say, to more adultlike word-classes.

While identification of the roles denoted by children added a more semantic dimension to the analysis of two-word utterances, it also raised issues of interpretation. Is the child's notion of agent (the Agentive argument) the same as the adult's? More serious still, is the notion of agent a coherent one holding across event-types, or should we distinguish the type of agent in events of hitting from those in events of opening, loading, or building? Does the child's notion of location coincide with the adult's? And how clearly defined are adult notions of such general roles as agent or instrument (Schlesinger 1995)?

Another set of questions concerns the grammatical information being expressed in early word combinations. To what extent do children use word order for grammatical relations and to what extent does their word order reflect the learning of specific word combinations? If word order is the main device used in a language to mark grammatical relations like "subject of" or "direct object," then we need to be sure that children are using word order for that purpose before we can impute to them knowledge of the pertinent grammatical relations. But in many languages word order serves a pragmatic rather than a grammatical purpose, indicating information as given versus new, while grammatical relations are indicated, for example, through case endings on nouns and through agreement patterns that link the subject and the verb it governs.

## Patterns in early combinations

What general patterns can be detected in early word combinations? And to what extent do different children's combinations resemble each other? We have already seen that the general functions of two-word utterances are similar across languages (Table 7.3), and they are also quite similar within languages across children. But not all children follow the same path as they begin to produce longer utterances. Some consistently combine two (or more) open class or content words, while others tend to combine one open class word with a demonstrative or pronoun like *that* or *it* (Bloom, Miller, & Hood 1975; Nelson 1975). The latter may at first be easier for children who have yet to streamline their articulation of longer sequences of words.

In one view, the earliest productive combinations are actually formulas of limited scope that children use for expressing specific meanings. Each formula expresses only a limited semantic content. For instance, children may use one formula for location by mentioning first the object being located and then its location, as in Andrew's *kitty down there, more down there, cover down there*. They may have another formula for expressing completion of an activity, as in his *all broke, all buttoned, all done, all dry,* and *all fix*. And another still for commenting on or requesting that something be repeated, as in *more cereal, more read, more sing,* and *more toast* (Braine 1976). In different children, such formulas tend to emerge in different orders, even if all the children express the same kinds of content (agent–action, action–object, object–location, object–quality, possessor–object, and so on).

For some relations, children's word order varies in response to conversational factors (what the previous speaker had already mentioned). In some combinations, word order marks differences in pragmatic importance and serves to reflect what is given and what new; in other combinations, word order (just as for adults) marks grammatical relations such as subject-of or direct object-of. But for children, there is little evidence that word order has any grammatical role at this stage.

At the same time, children appear to be quite attentive to word order in the speech around them, and they reflect this in their own utterances. In Finnish, adults use word order pragmatically and in talking to young children may vary it in trying to get the children to attend to or to understand what they are saying. Bowerman (1973a) found that Finnish children's choices of word order were highly correlated with parental choices, and, for example, their dominant word orders for agent + action or action + object affected reflected the dominant word orders in their mothers' speech for the same semantic relations.

Researchers studying other languages with flexible word order have also found that children's uses of word order match parental patterns. In a study of spontaneous conversations between mothers and young children learning Turkish, Küntay and Slobin (1996) found a high correlation between child and adult orders in three-word utterances, as shown by the percentages in Table 7.5. As in Finnish, grammatical relations are indicated in Turkish by suffixes that mark the grammatical relation on the noun (subject, direct object) plus subject–verb agreement. By age two,

Table 7.5 *Percentage of each word order in parent–child conversations for children aged 2;2 to 3;8 in Turkish*

| Word order | Children (n = 14) | Mothers |
|---|---|---|
| SOV | 46 | 48 |
| OSV | 7 | 8 |
| SVO | 17 | 25 |
| OVS | 20 | 13 |
| VSO | 10 | 6 |
| VOS | 0 | 0 |

*Source*: Küntay & Slobin 1996:269. Used with permission from Lawrence Erlbaum Associates.

Turkish children can deal with all six of the word orders for subject, verb, and object shown in Table 7.5. In act-out tasks, they appear to rely on case endings as reliable cues to the actor (the grammatical subject) versus the object acted upon (the direct object), regardless of the word order used in each instruction (Slobin & Bever 1982).

## Given and new information

What do children do with their first multiword utterances? They link them to preceding utterances, and they use them to add new information. In this, children are relying on common ground with the adults in conversations. When adults do not possess the relevant knowledge for understanding what the child is talking about, they may fail to establish the necessary common ground. Compare Meredith (1;6) talking to two different adults, the first an outside observer present with her in the living room while her mother was in the kitchen, then her mother a few minutes later, about the same topic (Snow 1978:254–255):

(3)     MEREDITH: *Band-aid.*
        OBSERVER:  Where's your band-aid?
        MEREDITH: *Band-aid.*
        OBSERVER:  Do you have a band-aid?
        MEREDITH: *Band-aid.*
        OBSERVER:  Did you fall down and hurt yourself?

Meredith's mother then entered, and Meredith reinitiated the same topic:

(4)     MEREDITH: *Band-aid.*
        MOTHER:    Who gave you the band-aid?
        MEREDITH: *Nurse.*
        MOTHER:    Where did she put it?
        MEREDITH: *Arm.*

Because her mother knew the background to Meredith's interest in the band-aid, she and Meredith shared the necessary common ground for the ensuing

Table 7.6 *Utterances where mention of the agent is informative*

---

(a) *Agent is not visible*

Matthew (1;1.3), upon hearing his father, not yet visible, come to the outside door and start up the steps to the apartment, says: *Daddy.*

(b) *Conflict over agent*

Matthew (1;10), as his mother butters some bread for him, in a bid to be allowed to do it himself, says: *Self.*

(c) *Seeking a change of agent*

Matthew (1;7.4), having been trying unsuccessfully to cut his meat with a knife, then hands the knife to mother, saying: *Mommy.*

Matthew (1;8.10), again trying unsuccessfully to cut something; his older sister Lauren says: Let me do it.

Matthew: *Mommy.*

---

*Source*: Greenfield 1979:165–166. Used with permission from Academic Press.

exchange to take place. This was not the case for the observer, and Meredith's skills were still too rudimentary to manage an unexpected set of questions about the topic she had introduced. Mutual knowledge established as common ground plays a critical role in conversations between children and adults.

Mutual knowledge also provides the starting pointing as children produce longer utterances: What they say adds to what has already been established, what is already common ground, for the participants in the conversation. In fact, what children decide to say even at the one-word stage, Greenfield (1979) proposed, is what is most informative in context. For example, in response to a question, the most informative action is to offer an answer. Under this view, the words young children provide in many contexts typically designate what would be counted as "new" information for adults in the same circumstances. Greenfield analyzed two short dialogues, relating what the child said to what had happened previously or to what was happening currently. She argued that whenever children referred to either an object, or to a state or action that the object was undergoing, they were offering material that was informative. She proposed rules for different situation-types, for instance, the agent–action scenario, where someone is doing something. In such scenarios, she suggested, children generally take the agent for granted and so are more likely to mention the action because it is less certain in context. Saying the word for the action will therefore be more informative than designating the agent.[1] There are other agent–action situations where offering information about agents could be more informative, as shown in Table 7.6. In the first example, Matthew identifies an agent who is not yet visible; in the second, he

---

[1] The problem here is the absence of any independent criterion. Since Greenfield based her analysis on what the child actually said, validation of her "rules" for describing particular situation-types needs to be tested across a large range of instances, in a new corpus, to see how well they actually predict children's single-word utterances in general.

names himself as agent in place of his mother; and, in the last two, he proposes changes of agent. In summary, Greenfield proposed that, with single-word utterances, children verbalize what is currently less certain or new in context and leave unexpressed what is known, established, or relatively certain. Once children advance to two-word combinations, they can tie their own utterance to the preceding speaker's and add some new information to it. This can be seen in their growing skill as conversational partners (e.g., Clark & Bernicot 2008), and, for instance, in their ability to supply lexical subjects at the two-word stage in a language like Italian where the subject doesn't normally receive separate expression. But Italian children supply lexical subjects in just those places where they are needed pragmatically because they are new (Serratrice 2005).

One device for marking information as new in English is stress on the word or phrase that presents the new information.[2] Wieman (1976) studied the relation between stress and semantic role in children's early combinations in an analysis of data from play-session recordings for five children (aged 1;9–2;5, with Mean Length of Utterance [MLU] of 1.3 to 2.4). First, she extracted all the two-word utterances, excluding any obvious imitations, and asked two trained phonologists to rate each utterance for its stress pattern. The utterances were then sorted by the semantic relation being expressed. In the Verb + Location combinations, the children always stressed the locative element (23/23), regardless of word-class or word order, for example *play MUSEUM, goes HERE, coming UP*; and *HERE goes* and *goes HERE* (both meaning 'it goes here'). In their Modifier + Noun combinations, they produced one pattern for possessive combinations and another for attributive ones. In 27/28 possessives, they placed primary (heavier) stress on the possessor element, for example *MY boot, RABBIT house, ELEPHANT's foot*, while in the attributive phrases, they put heavier stress on the second-place nouns (63/78). In their Verb + Object utterances, they stressed the object noun more heavily in 26/27 instances. And finally, in their Agent + Verb combinations, they always stressed the verb (21/21).

These findings reflect a hierarchy of stress assignments. Highest in priority, that is, most likely to be stressed, were locative and possessor elements; then, in order, came objective, attributive, verbal, and agentive elements. This ordering is nearly identical to Chafe's (1970) hierarchy for the position of new information in English utterances.

Exceptions to these patterns in the assignment of sentential stress, according to Wieman (1976), were all consistent with the stress being placed on what was new in the conversational context. For example, David placed stress on two occasions on the object noun rather than on the locative one; in both instances, he was

---

[2] Stress can also distinguish among meanings. Miller and Ervin (1964) noted that the child they recorded, Christy, used CHRISTY *room* for possessive meaning (meaning 'Christy's room') but *Christy* ROOM for the locative meaning (meaning 'Christy is in the room'). And Bowerman (1973a) reported that Kendall stressed the object noun more heavily than the subject noun in fourteen out of seventeen instances in subject–object combinations but stressed the possessor noun in ten out of twelve instances in possessor–possessed combinations.

answering a *what* question, so the object noun encoded the new information, as shown in (5) and (6):

(5)       MOTHER (pointing to letter "A" on truck in picture): What's that on the side of the milktruck?
          DAVID: *milktruck* **B**.

(6)       MOTHER: What's in the street?
          DAVID:    FIRETRUCK *street*.

The pattern of placing stress on the object rather than the verb was also broken once by Mark, who produced the sequence of utterances in (7) while playing with some marbles:

(7)       MARK: MORE *marble*. (drops one) *Marble* DOWN. (marble rolls away on floor) *One marble* MISSING. (finds marble) SEE *marble*.

Assignment of heavier stress to the new element also accounted for four exceptions to the assignments of sentential stress from Seth. These four, cited in (8)–(10), were all instances where he had produced the noun first and then added the adjective in his next utterance, so the information carried by the adjective was new:

(8)       SETH: *Man*. BLUE *man*.

(9)       SETH: *Ball*. NICE *ball*. ORANGE *ball*.

(10)      SETH: *No sock*. BLUE *sock*.

Children acquiring a language like English have to learn at least three things about the information being expressed: (a) the basic word orders for different kinds of propositional content; (b) how word order marks grammatical relations; and (c) how to use stress to mark new information in an utterance. The children studied by Wieman had fairly good mastery of sentential stress and of some basic word orders. It is unclear whether they were trying to mark any grammatical relations yet.

   If word order combined with stress can be used to identify information as given versus new in an utterance, this raises some questions about what Braine (1976) called "groping patterns" – patterns children tried out as they constructed two-word combinations. Their groping patterns consisted of limited uses of fixed word orders for some two-word combination-types, orders that either do not conform to the adult order or that reflect only one of several adult orders. Braine suggested that children were still trying to work out which orders were possible, but he based his analyses on corpora of child utterances only. Perhaps the children were actually using word order to indicate given versus new information. To establish this, one would need the full conversational record, not just the children's two-word combinations. So even when children produce combinations that appear fixed (with certain words always co-occurring, say), it is important to take into account the communicative interaction to see what children are doing with such utterances in the conversation.

Finally, in a detailed study of one child, Jill (aged 2;5), taped for about fifteen hours over one month, Weisenburger (1976) tried to account for what the child did and didn't say, given that she had enough vocabulary for several words pertinent to each occasion. With the aid of detailed contextual notes, she established that Jill was more likely to use terms for things not mentioned before and not present in the current context. That is, she appeared intent on making herself understood, so information she omitted was typically recoverable (already "on stage," or given, for the participants in the conversation) compared to information that she did express, even in her one-word utterances. What she produced typically picked out new information not yet known to the addressee and important to the child. Jill was also more likely to express information that was not redundant in context.

Children, then, don't choose their words at random. Even when they are using just one word at a time, they try to contribute to the conversation and present information that is new. They take the current situation as given, known jointly to themselves and their addressees. Then, with their utterances, they add new information. As their utterances get longer, they mention given information in addition to what is new. The given information links their utterance to prior contributions; the new information advances the conversation. The conversational context of early word combinations is critical for assessing what such combinations can reveal about children's growing knowledge of syntactic structure.

One further issue here is how much information children try to express in a two-word utterance. Are they talking about a single event or about a complex of two events, with one word for each? Consider the utterances in (11) and (12) (Clark, unpublished diary data):

(11)        D (1;6, wanting to get out of his high chair and looking at his toy cart on the floor, about two meters away): *Get-down cart.*

Here D's intended meaning is something like 'I want to get down in order to get my cart'. That is, the child is expressing two propositions with his two-word utterance. (Note that the utterance was produced with a single intonation contour and no pause between words.)

(12)        D (1;9, wanting his hand to be held under the cold water tap, after he got it pinched as he shut a kitchen cupboard): *Hand sore water.*

This utterance also appears to express a complex event in that the child is both stating that his hand is sore and (therefore) asking for a remedy in the form of cold water. The use of two- and three-word utterances to talk about complex as well as simple events further complicates the analysis of early word combinations as one tries to unravel their meanings and structure.

## From word combinations to early constructions

Children's first word combinations reflect their efforts to express what is salient, to link their contributions to what is already given, and to add something new. At the same time, they suggest that children are still quite far from adultlike knowledge of word-classes. When children use what for adults would be a verb or a noun, we tend to take for granted that they are making use of adultlike word-classes. But this assumption is far too strong. Even in such combinations as *hot* + *X* or *big* + *X*, where *X* is almost always a noun, this is not because children already have a category "noun" but because the meanings expressed by these patterns call for reference to an entity in the *X* slot. It is a fact about the world that entities that can be hot or big are typically concrete objects, and, in adult English, words denoting concrete objects are characteristically nouns (Braine 1976:76–77; see also Stern & Stern 1928).

Evidence for word-classes such as noun or verb becomes easier to gather only after children produce the relevant word-endings (see Chapter 8). But contrastive uses of noun inflections for number (e.g., singular vs. plural) and case (e.g., nominative vs. accusative), for instance, often do not appear until after the first word combinations. The same goes for early verb inflections – for tense (present vs. past), person (first, second, or third), and number (singular vs. plural). Early word combinations by themselves, then, offer little or no evidence for either syntactic word-classes or grammatical relations.

Word-classes like noun and verb probably emerge from two sources of information. First, children can draw on the correlations between the entities in the world and the categories at the core of syntactic word-class definitions in many languages (see Croft 1991). In a language like English, the names of persons, places, and things are typically nouns; the names of actions are typically verbs; the names of properties and qualities are adjectives; and the names of relations in space are typically prepositions. The correlation of semantic with syntactic properties, combined with a general adult propensity for talking about observable events in the joint locus of attention, offers children one way to establish syntactic word-classes. If they attend to such correlations for objects and actions, for instance, at the same time as the properties of each word-type and its inflectional suffixes (Maratsos & Chalkley 1980), they should be able to set up some preliminary word-classes. As they learn more vocabulary and more about distributional patterns, they can extend these word-classes beyond their initial semantic basis to a more general definition of noun or verb based on distributional and inflectional properties across a wider, and eventually more abstract, semantic range (Valian 1986; see also Brent & Cartwright 1996; Schütze 1994). When three- and four-year-olds are asked to select from a set of pictures the most appropriate choice for an utterance like "Show me sibbing" (activity) versus "Show me some sib" (substance), they consistently choose pictures of hands kneading something for the activity, versus a bowl of some undefined substance.

Table 7.7 *Some common English constructions*

| Construction | Meaning | Form |
|---|---|---|
| Intransitive motion | *X* moves to *Y* | Subject V Oblique |
| *The bird flew into the room* | | |
| Transitive | *X* acts on *Y* | Subject V Object |
| *Jan rode the scooter* | | |
| Double object | *X* causes *Y* to receive *Z* | Subject V Object Object 2 |
| *Kate sent Rod the picture* | | |
| Caused motion | *X* causes *Y* to move *Z* | Subject V Object Oblique |
| *Alan threw the kite into the air* | | |

*Source*: Goldberg 1999:199. Used with permission from Lawrence Erlbaum Associates.

They are able, in short, to use the information in inflections like plural *-s* or present *-ing* to decide whether the nonsense stem *sib* is being used as a noun or a verb (Brown 1957).

Second, word-classes may also emerge from consistent patterns within the constructions children pick up and extend. Particular words can occur in only certain construction types. For example, *dog* can occur in various noun-phrase types, from the relatively simple *the dog* to more complex demonstrative expressions like *those black-and-white shaggy dogs* to quantified expressions like *some of those dogs* or *all six of the dogs*.[3] Among verbs, *kick* can occur in several constructions in English: as an intransitive verb in *The horse kicked*; combined with a particle like *out*, with or without an object affected in *His father kicked out the tenants* or *The horse kicked out*; or as a transitive verb with a direct object, in *He kicked the step*. And *look* can appear with particles like *at*, *to*, or *for*, combined with an affected object, as in *Look at the sea-gull*; with other locative particles that specify direction, as in *Look around you*, *Look up*, or *Look inside*; and with a *wh*-clause as complement, as in *Look where he is* or *Look what I'm doing*. It also occurs in certain idioms, such as *Look out!* In general, the identification of construction-types depends on analysis of both event-types and participant roles.

What counts as a construction? Goldberg (1999:199) defined a construction as "a pairing of form and function such that some aspect of the form or some aspect of the function is not strictly predictable" from the component parts. Table 7.7 lists some common constructions in English, including intransitive motion, transitive action, and caused motion. In each case, the form and its associated constructional meaning are not predictable just from the words that can appear in the construction. For children, identifying the constructions that a particular word appears in

---

[3] But the count noun *dog* cannot occur with the quantifiers *some* or *a lot of* (e.g., *\*I saw some dog*) unless the referent of *dog* is construed as a mass or substance. (The asterisk indicates that the linguistic form is ungrammatical.)

Table 7.8 *The emergence of construction-types in early syntax*

|  | Lexical partition of events | Specification of participant roles | Categorization of specific event-types |
|---|---|---|---|
| Single-word utterances (1;0+) | − | − | − |
| Word combinations (1;6+) | + | − | − |
| Verb-island constructions (2;0+) | + | + | − |
| More adultlike constructions (3;0+) | + | + | + |

Based on Tomasello & Brooks 1999

depends on how adult speakers use that word. Moreover, the constructions each verb can appear in, for instance, will depend on the meaning of the verb. Terms with similar or related meanings tend to appear in the same set of constructions.

What do children need to do to identify constructions as well as the meanings of the words in each construction? First, they must attend to how adults use constructions as well as words in those constructions; second, they need to attend to the events adults talk about. In doing this, they must learn how to identify candidate events, sort them into event-types, and then partition each event into action or relation and participants. The analysis of events into their component parts may take time, with children sometimes learning to map some words onto parts of events before they grasp the syntactic constructions appropriate to the encoding of different event-types. They may also learn just one construction for a particular verb at first and only later identify other constructions it occurs in. Table 7.8 shows one route children might follow as they map events to words and constructions. First, they begin to offer some lexical encoding of selected aspects of events with single-word utterances, and then with word combinations. Next, they provide some syntactic marking of actions with certain roles, but this may be limited to a small number of constructions – often just one – already learnt for a specific verb. Tomasello (1992) called such limited construction uses "verb islands," because each verb first appears in only one or a very small number of constructions, so its uses are highly restricted compared to the adult range. Only as children learn to use adultlike constructions do they give evidence of consistent categorizations of event-types.

Children's early verb uses may be limited to one particular noun, for example, that may pick out the role of the agent, of the object affected, or of the location of the action in question. And this noun may occur in a fixed position, just before or just after the verb. Such verb-island uses may then be elaborated in two ways: First, children may go on to combine the same verb with different nouns, so a verb like *hold* might occur with several agent nouns, and a verb like *find* might occur with several object nouns; and second, they may start adding to the arguments they produce with each verb. In their early word combinations, they typically produce a verb with just one argument, but as they elaborate such utterances, they may produce verbs with two arguments, for example, an agent and an object affected. The next step is to combine each verb with other constructions for still more elaborate encodings of event-types (Tomasello 1992).

This sequence of development suggests that children learn construction-types in relation to specific lexical items. They learn for each particular verb which constructions it can occur in, on the basis of compatibility between the meanings of the verb and the relevant construction (Goldberg 1995). Indeed, children appear to attend closely to the speech directed to them in picking up on just the constructions represented there for use with each specific verb (de Villiers 1985; Naigles & Hoff-Ginsberg 1998). So children's notions of semantic roles such as agent or location may indeed be more restricted than those of adults. For instance, the agent of an action of holding differs from an agent of hitting or an agent of splashing. Yet one generalization they will need to make, for linguistic purposes, is that agents who do different kinds of actions are treated alike, as are different kinds of locations and different kinds of instruments.

The general meanings of the constructions in Table 7.7 appear to be related to the meanings of highly frequent general-purpose verbs (sometimes called light verbs), such as *go*, *do*, *give*, and *put*. These verbs are widely used across languages; they are among the first verbs acquired and are frequent in young children's speech (Clark 1978c; Edwards & Goodwin 1986; Goldberg 1999; Huttenlocher, Smiley, & Charney 1983). Young two-year-olds use *go* and *put*, for example, more than twice as often as any other verbs for talking about intransitive motion and caused motion. They also use *do*, *make*, and *get* at least twice as often as any other verbs for talking about transitive actions (Bloom, Miller, & Hood 1975). General-purpose verbs like these may lead the way for children in that they occur with specific argument arrays in core constructions and are frequent in adult usage, and so might provide the first models for acquisition of core constructions like those in Table 7.7 (see Ninio 1999a, 1999b). As children are exposed to a greater range of verbs and the constructions they occur with, they discover which verbs convey the action in transitive action versus caused motion events, for instance, and which are used for intransitive motion.

Are general-purpose verbs like *do* and *go* really the first to appear with new constructions in children's speech? The answer is still unclear, but there are at least two further issues here. First, the constructions children learn depend on which constructions adults use (de Villiers 1985), and it has not yet been established (a) whether adults use general-purpose verbs with a larger range of constructions than they do verbs with more specific meanings, or (b) whether they might even introduce some constructions first with general-purpose verbs and only later with more specific ones. It seems unlikely that adults would start with general-purpose verbs if only because they are not good at restricting themselves to a subset of the words and constructions they would normally produce. In conversation, even with a two-year-old, their focus is on what they need to say on each occasion to achieve the goal of the exchange. Second, although many languages make use of at least some general-purpose verbs, adults also use verbs with very specific meanings in talking to children. Given that, one would expect children to acquire verbs with specific meanings early on as well, and they do. In some languages, children's earliest verbs all have specific rather than general meanings and are used appropriately, in limited contexts, from early on (see, for instance, Brown 1998 for Tzeltal; Choi & Bowerman 1991 for Korean). So whether adult uses of general-purpose verbs lead the way for children to acquire certain constructions remains to be seen. Children might instead learn each verb first in one construction and then gradually add others.

One way to look at this is to see when children begin to make productive use of a construction, using it with more than one verb and filling in the different arguments needed. Intransitive motion, for instance, demands a verb of motion and an argument to identify the entity that is moving (e.g., *The dog is running away*), while transitive actions require a transitive verb and two arguments, one denoting the agent of the action and one the object affected (e.g., *The boy broke the cup*). Many of the earliest combinations children produce are limited in scope: They contain an agent mentioned with only a small set of actions, locations mentioned with only a few objects, and so on. The limited nature of children's early combinations may stem in part from the size of their vocabularies. In one study of two-year-olds, researchers found that precocious talkers with vocabularies that matched those of two-and-a-half-year-olds also produced word combinations earlier than their age-matched peers. The precocious group's combinations also matched those of the older group (McGregor, Sheng, & Smith 2005). This suggests that vocabulary size and early combinations are closely linked.

Can one distinguish fixed two-word combinations from productive uses of combinations? Researchers have long noticed what have been characterized as individual differences, or differences in style, as children start to produce two-word combinations. Some children combine any open class words already in their vocabulary (noun + noun, say, or noun + verb), while others go instead for a noun or verb combined with some kind of pro-form (a pronoun like *me* or *it*, a demonstrative like *that*, a locative like *there*). Bloom *et al.* (1975) characterized these children as "nominal" versus "pronominal," and Nelson (1975) related these early combination-types to whether children had earlier on been "expressive" (attending more to social routines in early vocabulary acquisition) or "referential" (attending more to words for things), with expressive children at first producing more pronominal-type combinations, and referential children opting for nominal ones. That is, referential children may begin by building up constructions from constituent parts already in their vocabularies, while expressive children may start by varying the content of just one slot in a previously unanalyzed phrase (see also Braine 1976). By age two-and-a-half, though, differences between these two groups have vanished.

These two patterns for early word combination, then, probably mark alternative routes to the production of longer utterances. Pine and Lieven (1993) proposed that early word combinations should be analyzed in relation to the first one hundred words or expressions children add to their lexicons. One can then characterize multiword combinations as (a) *frozen forms*, where part or all of the expression has appeared only in that one form in the child's speech to date; (b) *intermediate forms*, where the constituent elements have appeared separately in the child's speech before, but none have occurred in the same position in two previous multiword combinations; and (c) *constructed forms*, which contain forms already used independently, combined with some word or phrase that has appeared in at least two earlier word combinations.

With these criteria, one can identify patterns of frozen, intermediate, and constructed word combinations in children's early utterances. Pine and Lieven could account for 77% of the word combinations produced once they had identified the first ten positional patterns used by each of the five children they studied from 0;11 to 1;8. A further 17% of early combinations just failed to reach the criterion for constructed combinations, leaving only 6% of word combinations unaccounted for in this lexically based analysis. In a study of eleven additional children (Lieven, Pine, & Baldwin 1997), 92% of their utterances appeared either in the first twenty-five patterns noted for each child or as frozen forms not yet linked to any pattern. When children added a new word combination, they relied on an existing pattern. That is, the constructed forms identified as productive patterns were indeed productive: Children produced further combinations that fitted them (see further Lieven *et al.* 2003).

The earliest productive patterns for word combination may vary considerably from one child to the next. This can be seen, for instance, in the first ten productive patterns identified by Pine and Lieven (1993) (Table 7.9). Although a few patterns are common to more than one child, no pattern was common to all five. At the same time, there were some commonalities in the content they expressed. Four children used a pattern for talking about absence or disappearance (e.g., Martin's *Dummy gone*; Elaine's *No birds*; Yvonne's *No ducks*; and Anne's *Cat gone*). Three of them had a pattern for talking about possession (e.g., Martin's *Mummy car*; Leonard's *Me got shoe*; and Elaine's *That Daddy's*). And three had a pattern for talking about object location (e.g., Leonard's *Coat in there*; Yvonne's *Hat on*; and Anne's *Book on there*).[4]

The lexical specificity of children's early constructions can also be followed by looking at successive uses of each verb in the child's speech. This is what Tomasello (1992) did in his diary-based study of his daughter T's verbs. He observed that T gradually extended her uses of each verb as she added different arguments, then arrays of arguments, and also constructions like complements. For *spill*, T first used it as a single-word utterance, typically in the unanalyzed form *spill-it*, after someone spilt something (Table 7.10). About two months later, she began to combine *spill-it* with nouns, but the nouns designated the place of the

---

[4] Use of these patterns offers little evidence for such broad semantic categories as "location" or "possessor" underlying children's speech at this early stage of utterance construction.

Table 7.9 *The first ten productive positional patterns for five children*

| Yvonne (1;6) | (1) **X + stairs** | (6) There + X |
|---|---|---|
| | (2) **X + on** | (7) **X + cat** |
| | (3) Mummy + X | (8) **Come on + X** |
| | (4) Oh + X | (9) **No + X** |
| | (5) X + there | (10) **In there + X** |
| Anne (1;8) | (1) Up + X | (6) X + up step |
| | (2) **More + X** | (7) **X + gone** |
| | (3) **Bybe bye + X** | (8) Daddy + X |
| | (4) X + please | (9) Drink + X |
| | (5) X + on | (10) X + on there |
| Martin (1;8) | (1) X + gone | (6) Daddy + X |
| | (2) All + X | (7) There's the + X |
| | (3) **X + Mummy** | (8) More + X |
| | (4) X + car | (9) No more + X |
| | (5) **Mummy + X** | (10) X + there |
| Leonard (1;7) | (1) **Oh don't + X** | (6) Daddy + X |
| | (2) X + stairs | (7) Me got + X |
| | (3) Oh + X | (8) X + shoe |
| | (4) It's a + X | (9) The + X |
| | (5) Wanna + X | (10) X + in there |
| Elaine (1;8) | (1) **Big + X** | (6) **X + bird** |
| | (2) No + X | (7) X + Charlotte |
| | (3) I + X | (8) **X + Daddy** |
| | (4) Where + X | (9) **That + X** |
| | (5) There + X | (10) X + **bus** |

*Note*: The first instance of patterns in boldface involved two words already in that child's
vocabulary used as single-word utterances.
Based on Pine & Lieven 1993

spill only (e.g., *beard, leg, couch, table, tummy*, etc.). A month later, she combined
*spill* for the first time with a noun for the agent doing the spilling, and then, a few
days later, she combined it for the first time with a noun for the direct object, the
thing that had been spilt. That is, over several months, T combined *spill* with
nouns first only for the place of a spill, then for the agent who did the spilling, and
then for the thing spilt. And at this point, she began to produce more complex
utterances with *spill*, where she designated two distinct roles rather than just one.
This pattern of additions to each verb with the concomitant build-up of constructions was typical of her early verb uses.

Gradual acquisitions like this, along with the limited verb-based patterns
observed by Pine and Lieven (1993; Pine, Lieven, & Rowland 1998) suggest
that children are initially conservative in their acquisition of constructions. They
add only slowly to the forms that can co-occur with each verb, and they take a long
time to build up a repertoire in which the same construction occurs with several

Table 7.10 *Successive uses of* spill *from T*

---

(a) *Single-word use*: during or just after a spill, *spill-it*
    1;7.25 *spilled-it* [after spilling a liquid]
(b) *Use in combinations*:
    1;7.22 *spilled-it a beard* [spilt juice on chin]
    1;7.23 *mommy spill-it on leg* [telling mother about spill]
    1;7.23 *spill-it couch* [spilt juice on couch]
    1;7.23 *spill-it leg* [telling father about spill]
    1;7.23 *spill-it table ... made-this ... spill this ... fall-down* [telling someone
       about spilling juice]
    1;7.23 *spill-it tummy* [telling father about spill]
    1;9.1 *I never will spilled-it* [after being warned not to spill drink]
    1;9.6 *spilled wheezer milk* [spilt cat's milk]
    1;10.5 *spill something over mommy's coat* [sees stain on mother's coat]
    1;11 *I spilled it* [did so, twice]
    1;11 *I spilled the blackboard* [??]
    1;11 *won't spill it anymore* [promise]

---

Based on Tomasello 1992

different verbs. Children do not seem to make generalizations about a single construction and then plug in any and all candidate verbs right away. Rather, they work from each specific verb to the range of forms each occurs with, building up groups of constructions compatible in meaning with each verb. And although they produce some verbs very frequently early on, they typically produce them in only one or two of the constructions actually possible with that verb in adult speech.

## Moving on to larger units

As children use more words and constructions, they mark more of the conventional distinctions made in the language they are acquiring. But for each such distinction, children first have to discover that it *is* made in their language, and next how and where it is made. They also add to the informativeness of their utterances by including both given and new information. Where earlier they focus on providing new information in their contributions to the conversation, they later anchor their contributions by first mentioning information that is given, already known to the other participants. This leads to greater elaboration of the utterances they produce as turns. This elaboration may show up in a variety of domains, depending on the language being acquired. For example, children start to make argument structures explicit (see Clancy 1996 and Choi 1999 for Korean); to use aspect marking to distinguish event-types (see de Lemos 1981 for Portuguese); and to produce definite and indefinite articles (see Veneziano 1988 for French).

Children learn these distinctions through conversation. In the same way, they find out how to talk about motion and path in space (e.g., Choi & Bowerman 1991), how to distinguish given from new information in their references (e.g., Bresson 1977; Warden 1976), and how to distinguish completed from noncompleted actions (Smoczyńska 1985). The conversational context, with exposure to adult usage, is probably the major source of information children draw on as they build up a repertoire of constructions. As Roger Brown observed (1968:288), "The changes produced in sentences as they move between persons in discourse may be the richest data for the discovery of grammar."

# 8    Modulating word meanings

The utterances children hear don't consist of bare words strung together. Rather, depending on the language, words are usually modulated to include further information about the specific meaning to be conveyed. These modulations take the form of inflections, usually suffixes, added to word-stems, and of freestanding grammatical forms like prepositions. Some languages indicate the roles played by the referents of each noun phrase (e.g., agent, recipient, place, instrument) through word-endings added to the noun. They mark the doer of the action with nominative case, or where the event took place with locative case. On verbs, they can mark when an action took place with tense marking on the verb, or the general temporal "shape" of an action – whether it was completed, reiterated, or lasted for some time – with an aspectual ending on the verb, and so on. They may also mark gender on nouns (e.g., masculine, feminine, neuter) as well as on articles, adjectives, and sometimes verbs; and they can mark person (e.g., first, second, or third person on the verb) and number (e.g., singular or plural on nouns, verbs, and adjectives).

Modulations like these are generally provided by the inflections of a language, but languages differ in how they add such information to nouns and verbs, the regularity of the forms they use, and the division of labor between grammatical particles (inflections or free grammatical morphemes) versus reliance on word order.

## Inflections and typology

Languages differ a great deal in how they manage these modulations. Typologically, some languages are *analytic* (with little inflectional morphology, as in Mandarin Chinese); some are *synthetic* (with extensive reliance on inflections that mark several distinctions simultaneously, as in Spanish or Hebrew); and some *agglutinative* (with highly regular inflections, each one marking a separate distinction, as in Turkish or Hungarian).[1] In analytic languages, a specific distinction may be unpacked, so to speak, so the notion of first person plural, expressed in

---

[1] Note that English is more analytic than synthetic, but like many languages, it presents a mixed picture. It is highly atypical as Western European languages go in that its morphology is markedly impoverished.

English by the pronoun *we*, may be conveyed by a combination of a first-person form plus a plural marker, as in Mandarin *wo3.men2* (first person + plural, or [1P + PL]). Synthetic languages typically mark more than one distinction with each inflection. On a verb, for example, a single affix may mark third person, singular number, and simple past tense, as in Spanish *caminó* 'he walked', where the *-ó* ending marks third person and singular and past (or [3P/SG/PAST]) simultaneously.[2] Some synthetic languages that use case on nouns lack prepositions or postpositions, and rely on case inflections alone; other case-marked languages use both case marking and prepositions or postpositions. Lastly, in agglutinative languages, each distinction is added cumulatively to the word-stem, with one morpheme per meaning, as in these successively more elaborate forms in Turkish:

(1)     *el* 'hand'
        *el-ler* 'hands' (hand + PL)
        *el-im* 'my hand' (hand + 1POSS)
        *el-ler-im* 'my hands' (hand + PL + 1POSS)
        *el-im-de* 'in my hand' (hand + 1POSS + LOC)
        *el-ler-im-de* 'in my hands' (hand + PL + 1POSS + LOC)

Languages differ in whether they are analytic, synthetic, or agglutinative. They also differ in which grammatical distinctions they make. Do they mark relations among the participants in events through case, for instance, and if so, through how many cases – the accusative, genitive, and dative of Modern Greek, or the twenty-one cases of Finnish? Do they mark plural with an affix on the noun, as in many Western European languages, or through a classifier and numeral system as in Thai? Is the subject marked through case, word order, or both? To what extent does language typology affect the process of learning? What helps or hinders children's acquisition of inflections? Cross-linguistically, inflectional morphology presents many different options, and children appear to find different aspects of each system harder or easier depending on such factors as semantic complexity, formal complexity, regularity, and frequency.

## Getting started

For children, the initial domain of morphology appears to be the word. They add inflectional affixes to words, or rather word-stems, as in English *dog* versus *dogs* (dog + PL). To do this, they must identify each inflectional affix and its meaning (e.g., the suffix *-s* on nouns in English for 'more than one'). Children acquiring English or Spanish learn that nouns denoting more than one are used in plural form (i.e., with the addition of the relevant plural suffix), as in *The flowers* or *Las flores*. In Spanish, children also learn to mark any adjective and article accompanying a plural noun with plural inflections too (e.g., *las flores pequeñas*

---

[2] In polysynthetic languages, the same stem may be used with derivational suffixes to form a nominal or a verbal form, and several stems, some with verbal and some with nominal force, may be combined in the same word, effectively forming a long "one-word" sentence.

'the small flowers'). Their first verbs are either an uninflected form (e.g., English *want*, *throw*, *sit*) or a single inflected form (e.g., French *tombe*, *vais*) for each verb. These forms remain the only ones in use for several weeks or months. Since number links subjects and verbs, a singular noun phrase subject requires a singular verb. So the domain for each inflection may extend beyond the word to mark agreement over several different words.

Before children can make productive use of inflections, they need to know what they mean, where they can be added – at the ends of words in most languages, or at the beginnings in a few – and whether specific inflections belong on nouns or verbs, for instance. For this, children also need to have distinguished word-classes.

## Word-classes

Children could begin identifying word-classes from two distinct angles. First, they attend to the categories picked out by different words – objects, actions, relations – and may rely on shared properties of the referents to group certain words together, for instance, words for people, places, and things. Simultaneously, they attend to when and where such words occur and so identify some of their distributional properties (Mintz, Newport, & Bever 2002; Pinker 1984). Among these properties are the inflections carried by each word-class. But in many languages, identifying a word as belonging to a particular word-class may not be enough to tell which inflections it can take. Within word-classes, terms are often further organized into paradigms. For instance, whether a noun takes the regular plural affix or, in some languages, one of two or three distinct regular plural forms, versus an irregular form, depends on the paradigm the noun belongs to. Paradigms typically group together like phonological forms, with further divisions in some languages on the basis of a dimension like gender. Some languages have one highly regular paradigm and a scatter of small irregular ones, as for English plurals; others may have several regular paradigms, with a variety of smaller, less regular ones. Children have to learn which words belong to which paradigms before they come to use inflectional affixes in a conventional way.

Children who have not yet learnt this could regularize irregular forms by assigning them to a major paradigm in the relevant word-class. At issue here is the extent to which children learn an inflection like the plural on a word-by-word basis versus a constructional, rule-like basis. If children learn inflections word by word (e.g., *cat/cats* but *man/men*), one would not expect them to make errors, since they should base their own productions on what they have heard for each individual word. But if they identify major paradigms and then assign unfamiliar words to these paradigms, they could produce errors of overregularization (e.g., *good/gooder*, *foot/foots*) whenever they assign a term to the wrong paradigm. As we will see, children do produce overregularization errors, but when, why, and how often are all issues under dispute.

Some paradigms are productive, in the sense that each slot in the paradigm is filled with forms predictable from the paradigm itself. Major regular paradigms offer templates for the use of specific inflections. Since most nouns in a language can add the same inflections (e.g., English *cat/cats, thing/things, truth/truths*), for instance, inflectional affixes are usually assumed to be fully productive. There are few unfilled slots in any paradigm (but compare *cat/cats* with *sheep/sheep*). Children's recognition of this during acquisition may affect their identification of the major paradigms in a language. Where languages have two or more major paradigms for verbs, say, it may take children time to recognize the differences and assign verbs appropriately to one or the other. In fact, they may initially favor just one and overuse it when adding inflections to unfamiliar verbs.

Languages also use free morphemes to mark grammatical meanings. These include morphemes to mark definiteness (e.g., the articles *a* and *the* in English, *un/ une* and *le/la* in French), grammatical relations (prepositions like *to*, *for*, and *with* in English), relations in space (e.g., Spanish prepositions like *en* 'in~at~on', *sobre* 'on top of', or *hasta* 'towards'; the Mandarin general locative marker *de* 'in~at~on', etc.); or given versus new information (e.g., Japanese postpositions *wa* and *ga*, for given and new, respectively). Overall, such modulations of meaning generally consist of a mix of bound inflections attached to words and free grammatical morphemes. And the order in which children learn these grammatical elements appears to depend on their semantic and formal complexity in the language.

## Learning inflections

Is learning done by rote first, with children picking up inflected forms from adult speech without analysis?[3] If children learnt inflections only by rote, using only forms for which they had evidence in the speech addressed to them, we would never see erroneous uses. But children make errors of two kinds – omission and commission. In some languages, they at first may omit inflections altogether. Errors of omission may continue to affect newly acquired words even after children make consistent use of some inflections on words they do know. Later on, children make errors of commission as well: They apply regular inflections to irregular noun- and verb-stems. These overregularizations reveal the extent to which children have analyzed inflectional affixes and their meanings. They also show that children have yet to learn the details of paradigms for irregular forms.

---

[3] Some researchers have assumed that children do not start to work on inflectional morphology or on grammatical morphemes more generally until after they have begun to combine two or more words (Brown 1973). This is probably not the case. While it may hold for some children, data from others learning the same language (English) have shown that they may master several inflectional affixes for nouns and verbs before producing any word combinations (e.g., Mervis & Johnson 1991). Children could simply follow different routes in this respect, with some elaborating first on the content of what they want to say by combining content words, and others elaborating first by adding modulations of meaning to a single content word.

Regularization errors have been taken as evidence by two distinct positions: (a) that children rely on a template or schema for producing a stem and inflection, or (b) that they make use of an abstract rule for adding the relevant affix whenever they wish to express that meaning.

Many observers, from at least Rousseau on,[4] have noticed that children tend to regularize irregular forms. This suggests they are applying a general rule to all instances. Berko (1958) was one of the first people to offer experimental evidence for this. She showed that, by age five to seven, children had identified different inflectional affixes and were able to add them to nonsense stems they had never heard before. To elicit knowledge of the plural suffix in English, she presented children with a picture of a small unfamiliar birdlike creature and the information: "This is a wug." She then showed each child another picture, with two such creatures: "Now there are two of them," "Now there are two_____" and waited for the child to finish. The results showed that five- and seven-year-olds had productive knowledge of a range of inflections. Berko concluded that children this age must have abstracted rules for adding the suffixes. Had they instead just learnt each inflected noun form by rote, they should have been unable to add affixes to unfamiliar forms never heard before.

At the same time, children were not able to produce the more difficult variants or allomorphs of plural and past tense inflections for unfamiliar nonsense words – the phonological variants of each affix that depend on the form of the stem they attach to. They couldn't add the appropriate variant to many of the nonsense syllable stems they were presented with but could do so when they heard a familiar word-stem. For the syllabic plural (/-ɪz/), for example, they did much better with a familiar word like *glass* (plural *glasses*, 91%) than with the unfamiliar nonsense word *tass* (plural *tasses*, produced only 36% of the time). So familiarity does play some role in the production of inflections (Akhtar & Tomasello 1997; Hecht 1983).

As children start to produce inflections, they go through several stages. At first, they may use words, in a language like English, with no inflections at all, producing bare stems only.[5] Cazden (1968) observed that they usually went through some three stages before mastering irregular as well as regular verbs, as shown for the English past tense -*ed* in Table 8.1. First, children made sporadic use of a few irregular past tense forms (e.g., *went, bit, broke*), but it is unclear whether they realize that these irregular forms are connected to the present tense stems *go*,

---

[4] In *Emile* (1792), Rousseau pointed out that "D'abord, [les enfants] ont, pour ainsi dire, une grammaire de leur age, dont la syntaxe a des règles plus générales que la nôtre; et si l'on y faisait bien attention l'on serait étonné de l'exactitude avec laquelle ils suivent certaines analogies." (At first, [children] have, so to speak, a grammar suited to their age, a grammar whose syntax contains rules more general than ours; and if one pays close attention to their language, one is amazed at how well they follow certain analogies.)

[5] In many languages, though, where one has to use some inflection on every form, children tend to pick up just one inflected form for each word and at first produce only that form (e.g., for Hebrew: Berman & Armon-Lotem 1997; for Turkish: Ketrez & Aksu-Koç 2003; for Spanish: Gathercole, Sebastián, & Soto 1999).

Table 8.1 *Stages in the acquisition of past tense* -ed *in English*

| Stage | Pattern of use |
| --- | --- |
| 1 | Sporadic uses of irregular past tense forms (e.g., *went, broke*); no regular past tense uses |
| 2 | Intermittent use of *-ed* on regular verb-stems |
| 3 | General use of *-ed* on both regular and irregular verb-stems (e.g., *jumped, brushed*; *buyed, bringed, goed*) |
| 4 | Correct use of regular (*jumped*) versus irregular forms (*went*) |

Based on Cazden 1968

*bite*, and *break*. Next, they produced the *-ed* suffix on regular verb-stems (*jumped, spilled, cleaned*) to express the meaning of past time but did not always use it when it was needed. At the third stage, children used the *-ed* suffix on an increasing number of regular verbs (e.g., *pushed, climbed, wiped*) and also on irregular ones (e.g., *bringed, goed, buyed*). From then on, children took several years to learn, one by one, the conventional past tense forms for irregular verbs like *bring, go*, and *buy* (Brown 1973).

There are two observations to make about these stages. First, in Stage 1, it is unclear whether children use such irregular past tense forms as *went* and *broke* with any "past" meaning. That is, they may simply have identified irregular forms like *went* and *broke* as verbs, even as stems, but not yet as past tense forms. Indeed, many children add inflections to such forms, to produce *broking* and *broked* for the presumed present tense *broke*, or *wenting* and *wented* for present tense *went*, and so on. (Notice how easy it is to assume instead that, when a two-year-old says *went*, she means just what an adult would mean in using the same form.) The identification of irregular past tense forms as verb-*stems* would be quite consistent with the emergence, in Cazden's third stage, of general reliance on the *-ed* suffix to mark past time on both regular and irregular verb-stems. This suggests further that forms like *wented, thoughted*, and *broked* are not instances of doubled past marking but simply further evidence that children mistakenly identify irregular past tense forms in English as verb-stems in their own right (Clark 1987, 1988). This offers an alternative to the view that children first use irregular past tense forms with past meaning (e.g., *went*), then replace them, temporarily, with incorrect regularized forms in *-ed* (e.g., *goed*) before reinstating the appropriate irregular forms (e.g., *went*) (see further Strauss 1982).

Even when children assign some meaning to an inflection, they may still only produce it sporadically rather than on every occasion where adults expect to hear it. For instance, even when they attach a meaning like 'already past' or 'completed' to the suffix *-ed*, they don't use this suffix for talking about all past events (Kuczaj 1978). The type of event matters: Children are more likely to use *-ed* on accomplishment verbs where there is some result or change of state that follows

Table 8.2 *Order of acquisition for fourteen grammatical morphemes for three children acquiring English*

| Rank order | Meaning | Example |
|---|---|---|
| 1. **-ing** | ongoing process | He's sitt***ing*** down. |
| 2. **in** | containment | It's ***in*** the box. |
| 3. **on** | support | It's ***on*** the chair. |
| 4. **-s** (PL) | number | The dog**s** bark. |
| 5. irreg. past, e.g., **went** | earlier in time | He ***went*** home. |
| 6. **-'s** (POSS) | possession | The girl***'s*** dog ran away. |
| 7. uncontractible copula (**was, are,** as in questions) | number, earlier in time | ***Are*** they boys? |
| 8. **a, the** (articles) | nonspecific/specific | Jan has ***a*** book. |
| 9. **-ed** (reg. past) | earlier in time | He jump***ed*** the stream. |
| 10. **-s** (3P SG reg.) | number; earlier in time | She run**s** fast. |
| 11. 3P irreg. (**has, does**) | number; earlier in time | ***Does*** that dog bark? |
| 12. uncontractible auxiliary verb (**is, were**) | number; earlier in time (ongoing process) | ***Is*** he coming? That's Tom, that ***is***. |
| 13. contractible copula verb | number; earlier in time | That**'s** a spaniel. |
| 14. contractible auxiliary verb | number; earlier in time (ongoing process) | They***'re*** running fast. |

Based on Brown 1973

for the action in question than on verbs for activities (e.g., *He's running*), achievements (*She finished the race*), or states (*He was happy*).

To assess mastery of each inflection in production, one criterion is 90% use in obligatory contexts for three successive recording sessions (see Brown 1973; de Villiers & de Villiers 1973). For example, certain contexts require a past tense form. After an adverbial like *last year*, the speaker must follow up with a past tense verb (e.g., *Last year, he visited the Hebrides*). Other contexts require a plural: In English, the speaker must follow all numerals except *one* with the plural, as in *There were three wrens in the tree*. When Brown (1973) analyzed obligatory contexts for some fourteen grammatical morphemes in English, he found that children appeared to followed a rather consistent order of acquisition (Table 8.2).

## Order of acquisition

What factors determine order of acquisition for inflections and other grammatical morphemes? There seem to be at least two main contributors: (a) the *semantic complexity* of the distinction being made and (b) the *formal complexity* of the expression for that meaning in each language (Slobin 1973).

The cumulative complexity of semantic distinctions makes the best predictions about order of acquisition (Brown 1973). In effect, some inflectional meanings include elements of meaning conveyed by other inflections as well. For instance, the past *-ed* marks 'earlier in time' ($X$) while the auxiliary *were* includes 'earlier in time' ($X$) and 'number' ($Y$). Overall, meaning $X$ is consistently acquired before $X + Y$, and $X + Y$ is consistently acquired before $X + Y + Z$. Take the notion of 'ongoing process' expressed by use of the suffix *-ing*: Children master this well before other morphemes that mark such distinctions as number and earlier in time in addition to ongoing process ($Z$), namely auxiliary *be* (in *He is running*) and copular *be* (*They are brothers*) in English (see Table 8.2).[6] The greater the semantic complexity of a grammatical morpheme, the later it appears to be acquired. Semantic complexity can be computed in terms of the amount of overlap among related meanings, but it can't be measured for unrelated meanings.

How a particular distinction is expressed may also vary in formal complexity. Take number – the concept of one versus more than one. This should be similar across children regardless of the language being learnt. (It is generally acquired between 1;6 and 2;3.) But languages differ in how they express it. Some use just one inflection to mark plural on nouns and may have only a handful of exceptions to be learnt by rote, much as in English. Others make systematic distinctions between two types of plural – forms that denote collections of entities (e.g., *forest*, *family*) and forms that denote individuals (e.g., *trees*, *children*). In addition, plural nouns may fall into two or more groups according to the inflection used (e.g., plurals in *-s* vs. plurals in *-en*, as in Dutch); into many small groups, each with a different plural form (as in Egyptian Arabic); into subtypes depending on the gender and phonological form of the noun (as in Russian); and so on. The forms to be acquired to mark each specific distinction and the conditions under which each is called for differentiate languages in terms of formal complexity (Slobin 1973, 1985b).[7]

Consider the acquisition of expressions for location in bilingual children learning Hungarian and Serbo-Croatian (Mikes 1967). Since the same children were learning both languages, the conceptual distinctions they could draw on, and hence the semantic complexity, was constant across the two languages, but the formal complexity for talking about location differed. Hungarian is an agglutinative language, with a rich system of invariant suffixes for talking about location

---

[6] Order of acquisition comparisons, of course, can only be made for those morphemes that include as part of their meanings a meaning (or meanings) that can otherwise be expressed by some other morpheme.

[7] Notice that formal complexity is not a characteristic of a whole language, but rather of a specific semantic domain, or even of a single semantic distinction. So what is complex for the expression of a certain meaning in language $X$ may be quite simple in language $Y$, while for another meaning, language $Y$ may make use of a much more complex form than language $X$ (Slobin 1973).

and direction (Mikes 1967; Pléh 1998). For instance, the suffixes in (2) (in boldface), among others, can be used on all nouns for locations:

(2)     *hajóban*  [boat + in]                     'located in the boat'
        *hajóból*  [boat + out-from]               'moving out from inside the boat'
        *hajótól*  [boat + away-from-next-to]      'moving away from next to the boat'

Serbo-Croatian, a synthetic language, relies instead on combinations of prepositions and case inflections to mark location and direction, as in (3):

(3)     ***u kucu***  [*u* 'in' + accusative case = into]   'into the house'
        ***u kuci***  [*u* 'in' + locative case = inside]   'inside the house'

Several prepositions in Serbo-Croatian, like *u*, take two different cases, one to mark direction towards or away from, the other to mark static location at a place. Others take only one case, but there may be no clear connection between the case required and the kind of spatial relation expressed. For instance, the prepositions *blizu* 'near', *do* 'as far as', and *iz* 'from, out of', all take the genitive case; *k* 'towards' takes the dative case, and *pri* 'at, near' takes the locative case.

Children bilingual in Hungarian and Serbo-Croatian, around age two, marked location reliably only when speaking Hungarian. There they made consistent reference to the relevant location, using the appropriate suffix on the locative noun. In Serbo-Croatian, they omitted the relevant prepositions, and although they used case-inflected nouns to denote locations, they did not always choose the right case. It took them many months before they combined case marking and prepositions correctly. Hungarian, it appears, offers a much less complex system, formally, for talking about location. This is attested by how early bilingual children can talk about location.

Within a language, one can see both formal and semantic complexity at work. Take plural number. Children have typically grasped the notion of one versus more than one before age two, but it may take them months – even years – to learn how to produce the appropriate forms for marking plurality on each noun-type for each gender and case. Even in English, where the plural morpheme on nouns has just three variants or allomorphs, children master the voiced and voiceless versions (/-z/ and /-s/) well before the syllabic variant (/-ɪz/) (Hecht 1983; see also Berko 1958).

## Frequency

Another factor in acquisition is frequency. Children take account of frequency in several ways. They are sensitive to which allomorphs are the more productive ones among all those they hear. The more productive forms are those that appear on the largest number of stem-types. They tend to use more productive forms more often than less productive ones early on, and only later master less productive forms. Overall, children are more attentive to *type*-frequency than *token*-frequency: They are more likely to use the inflections that appear on many stems than those that appear on only a few, even when tokens of the latter

Table 8.3 *Frequency (%) of verb tokens versus verb-types in the speech of two- to four-year-old French children*

| Conjugation | Types | Tokens |
|---|---|---|
| 1st (*-er*), regular | 76 | 36 |
| 2nd (*-ir*), regular | 6 | 6 |
| Other, mixed | 18 | 58 |

*Note*: Guillaume's third- and fourth-conjugation verbs are combined in "Other"; many of the verbs in this group have some irregular forms. Based on Guillaume 1927

are much more frequent overall. In an early study, Guillaume (1927) compared the numbers of verb tokens versus verb-types in the speech of French children aged two to four and noted that their regularizations of inflections followed the number of types, where the highest number was for first-conjugation verbs (76% of the types produced), rather than the number of tokens, where the most frequent verbs were irregular third-conjugation ones (58% of the tokens produced) (Table 8.3). So children acquiring French take their main paradigm for verb inflections from the highly regular first conjugation (e.g., *donner* 'to give', *sauter* 'to jump'), even though, individually, these verbs are far less frequent than irregular third-conjugation ones.

In more recent work, Marchman and Bates (1994) have argued that children only begin to add regular inflections to verb-stems (including irregular ones) at the point where regular verb-types outnumber irregular ones by about 55% to 45% in children's early vocabularies. They argued that this proportion (55%) represents a critical mass for children's identification of a past tense paradigm in *-ed*. The idea is that children need to observe an inflection on enough different verb-types before they can extract it and analyze its probable meaning. Irregular verbs will not offer enough types for the extraction of a consistent inflectional morpheme to which they can assign a meaning, so children should not take even highly frequent irregular verbs as models for how to inflect verbs in general.

This conclusion has to be modified in light of results from studies of Italian. Orsolini and her colleagues (1998) showed that older children's performance with productive and unproductive inflections were hard to distinguish from each other. When children aged four to ten made errors with root-changing verbs (verbs with at least two stems) in Italian, they used the highly transparent morphological patterns found in one unproductive class of verbs and generalized this to other verbs. And with another semiproductive class, commonly used for verbs derived from adjectives, they applied the appropriate inflections more accurately for forms with a high token-frequency. The line between productive (rule-based) and unproductive (rote-learned) verb forms appears not to affect children's long-term learning of inflectional paradigms as they get older.

In summary, early on, children attend to those inflections represented across the greatest number of types to which they have been exposed. But as they learn more of their language and master smaller (less regular) paradigms, they must also pay attention to those tokens that they hear frequently but on very few types.

## Producing grammatical morphemes

What form do children's earliest attempts at grammatical morphemes take? At first, they produce them only sporadically, or, in some languages, not at all. And they often begin by simply producing a pseudo-morpheme or filler syllable in the form of a neutral vowel (schwa) or a syllabic **n** sound, say, rather than a recognizable morpheme (Peters & Menn 1993). Take *a* and *the* in English: Children's first attempts at them typically consist of a schwa before nouns (e.g., [ə] *dog*), so it is impossible to tell whether they are aiming at definite *the* or indefinite *a*. Equally, their first attempts at prepositions like *in* often consist of either a schwa as place-holder before locative nouns, or a syllabic **n** sound that is indeterminate between *in* and *on* (e.g., [n] *dere*). Reliance on such filler syllables in production may also mirror children's uncertainty, at this stage, about differences in the meanings and hence the functions of some grammatical morphemes.

Children acquiring English produce their first filler syllables towards the end of the second year, and these may not take on any more adultlike form for several months. By two-and-a-half or three, most children can produce something close to *the* for the definite article and a schwa, just like adults, for *a*. But it remains unclear whether these contrasting forms reflect appropriate usage. Children's grammatical morphemes, including inflections, are rarely checked up on. (Even where child uses are inappropriate for what was intended, they may still be interpretable.) The findings for French are similar: Children rely on filler syllables there too. Their first uses of articles with nouns, for example, typically take the form of a schwa attached to the beginning of the word. In conversation, adults treat some of these as if they were definite, others as indefinite (and some as masculine, others as feminine) and follow up children's utterances accordingly (Veneziano *et al.* 1990).

The inappropriateness of these early articles is only apparent in settings where the form required is not the one children usually produce. When children are shown a short three-panel cartoon strip, for instance, and asked to tell the story it shows, they overuse the definite article in contexts that require the indefinite (e.g., Bresson 1977, Bresson *et al.* 1970 for French; Warden 1976 for English). This suggests that production of some grammatical morphemes precedes mastery of appropriate usage (see also Bassano & Eme 2001, Karmiloff-Smith 1979, Veneziano 1988, Veneziano & Sinclair 2000 for French; Demuth 1994 for Sesotho).

Similar findings have been noted for number. In many languages (but not all), number is marked on nouns with an added inflection, as in English *cat* (singular) versus *cats* (plural). In English, the plural is among the earliest grammatical morphemes to be acquired.[8] Plural forms can also be elicited quite readily from children aged three and up in naturalistic settings (Hecht 1983) and from older children in more structured games (Berko 1958). But children's comprehension of plural -*s* may depend on more than use of the -*s* alone: They may also rely on additional markings of plurality in numerals (***two*** *cats*), demonstratives (***those*** *cats*), or both (***these two*** *cats*) (Nicolaci-da-Costa & Harris 1983, 1984/1985). Use of such redundant marking for plural appears to be frequent in adult speech (Hecht 1983).

## Word-classes

For children to add noun inflections to nouns and verb inflections to verbs, they need to know which words fall into which classes. They are helped in this by the meanings they have assigned to individual words and by the distributional properties of the terms in child-directed speech. At this stage, meaning and form are highly correlated, in that many nouns are terms for people, places, and things, while many verbs are terms for actions. Once children have become aware of the correlation, they can assign preliminary meanings to unfamiliar terms from their recognition of the word-class and make inferences about word-class from the apparent meanings of new terms. Then, as children add to their knowledge of grammatical morphemes, they can use these as well to identify word-class membership.

In fact, three- to five-year-old English speakers generally use nouns for things and verbs for actions to a greater degree than adults do. In addition, children this age are able to infer part-of-speech membership from the inflections used on nonsense syllables (Brown 1957). Dockrell and McShane (1990), following up Brown, showed that children aged three and four were highly consistent in their use of inflectional information. To check on their knowledge of singular and plural forms for nouns, they asked the questions in (4a) and (4b), using nonsense words in the blanks, as they showed the children pictures from which to choose:

(4) a.    Do you know what a _____ is? In this picture you can see a _____ . Can you show me another picture with a _____ in it? [Noun singular]
    b.    Do you know what _____ s are? In this picture you can see _____ s. Can you show me another picture with _____ s in it? [Noun plural]

As Table 8.4 shows, children hearing a singular nonsense form in these questions reliably chose pictures of single objects; the same children hearing a plural form reliably chose pictures containing several objects.

---

[8]  In an analysis of plural inflections and vocabulary size, Robinson and Mervis (1998) found that plural growth only began after a threshold was reached in vocabulary. At that point, lexical growth slowed while use of plurals increased (see also van Geert 1991).

Table 8.4  *Percentage of choices of referents for nonsense nouns in singular versus plural form*

|              |      | Picture chosen | | |
|--------------|------|--------|----------|------------|
| Noun form    | Age  | Action | 1 object | 2+ objects |
| Singular     | 3;5  | 23     | 60       | 17         |
|              | 4;2  | 29     | 62       | 8          |
| Plural *s*   | 3;5  | 19     | 2        | 79         |
|              | 4;2  | 8      | 0        | 92         |

*Source*: Dockrell & McShane 1990:133. Used with permission from Alpha Academic.

To check on the same children's knowledge of the verb inflections *-s* and *-ing*, they asked questions like those in (5a) and (5b), again with nonsense stems filling the blanks:

(5) a.   Do you know what it is to _____ ? In this picture he _____ s. Can you show me another picture with someone who _____ s in it? [Verb present]

 b.   Do you know what _____ ing is? In this picture you can see _____ ing. Can you show me another picture with someone _____ ing in it? [Verb progressive]

Notice that one of the verb inflections (the generic present tense in *-s*) is identical in form to the English plural *-s*. The children must therefore have been using more than the word-ending alone in choosing a picture; they could also draw on the additional syntactic information offered by the phrases containing the inflected nonsense words. These were marked for verbs, for instance, by use of *to* (as in [5a]) and by mention of the doer of the action (*he*, *someone who*, *someone*, in both [5a] and [5b]).[9] By age three or four, these children had had several years exposure to English morphology. But how do children get started on their analysis of inflections and other grammatical morphemes? How do they come to identify the relevant word-classes or parts of speech?

## Getting started on word-classes

Children could take several different approaches in arriving at the word-classes of their language. First, they could rely on any conceptual categories distinguished so far, plus any new ones, to identify types of objects, activities, relations, and properties, say, and then look for correlations between these types and the lexical choices made by adult speakers in talking about those types. This they appear to do (Brown 1957). Young children build on their conceptual

---

[9]  Phrases with nouns mark them as nouns by means of a preceding article (as in [4a]) and may have the noun follow the verb as its direct object (as in [4b]).

categories (types of objects, relations, properties, and activities) as they set up word-classes. This has been characterized as semantic bootstrapping (Grimshaw 1981; Pinker 1984). Semantic bootstrapping itself depends on several assumptions about children's conceptual categories and the connections between these categories and the semantic categories of a language. The conceptual categories children set up in their first year are assumed to be categories that map directly onto the notional categories used in defining parts of speech (e.g., "Nouns are words that pick out people, places, and things"). This assumes word-classes are universal, and while this may be true for nouns and verbs, it doesn't necessarily hold for other word-classes. There are also many nouns that fall outside the notional definition for "noun" – nouns for events (*a jump*), for ideas (*freedom*), for abstract qualities (*honesty*). The main point of semantic bootstrapping is that it offers a way in, a means of getting started on word-classes.

Second, children could rely on distributional information, identifying the affixes on different word-stems and discovering their patterns of occurrence. This would allow them to arrive at groupings of words that co-occur with different clusters of inflections and, in some languages, groupings tied to specific positions within phrases and clauses. Clusters of inflections across different word-stems might serve to identify verbs as a class, or nouns as a class (see Brent & Cartwright 1996; Maratsos & Chalkley 1980). Different word-types may even differ overall in phonological structure – in the occurrence of specific segments or segment clusters, for example, as well as in syllable structure (Shi, Morgan, & Allopenna 1998).

This route depends on languages having a reasonably extensive set of nominal and verbal inflections. For English, this route might be difficult to follow because there is little inflectional morphology from which to make inferences about word-class membership. But if children combine semantic bootstrapping with distributional properties, they would be in a better position to identify different word-classes. They could use the preliminary meaning assigned to a term in context together with any inflections this term occurred with, and its position relative to other grammatical elements like definite articles or prepositions, in assigning it to a word-class. Distributional information would include (a) all grammatical morphemes (inflectional affixes and free morphemes), (b) consistent patterns of co-occurrence, and (c) consistent ordering within phrases or larger units (Brent & Cartwright 1996; see also Elman 1993; Schütze 1994). In English, children seem to make use early on of both inflections and free grammatical morphemes, and they attend to the structure of noun and verb phrases (Akhtar & Tomasello 1997; Dockrell & McShane 1990; see also Behrend, Harris, & Cartwright 1995).

Third, attention to some distributional information is consistent with the view that children make use of structural information to arrive at possible meanings for unfamiliar terms. They could then use what they know about grammatical morphemes and phrase structure to assign new terms to the categories of noun, verb, or adjective. This approach takes the syntactic categories as given ahead of time because they represent part of the child's innate knowledge about language structure. They do not have to be inferred from the language around them. Rather, syntactic word-classes merely have to be instantiated for each language, and, from then on, children can make use of the relevant syntactic information to assign preliminary meanings to new words (Gleitman 1990). Notice, though, that this syntactic bootstrapping relies heavily on whatever meanings children have already assigned to other terms in the utterance with the unfamiliar term, so it may be hard to give credit for inferences about a meaning only to immediately neighboring syntactic information.

These approaches to identifying word-classes all rely on imperfect correlations. None gives the right answer all the time, and each one on its own gives the right answer only part of the time. If they were all put to use simultaneously, they could provide children with a wealth of information. The evidence suggests that children in fact make use of more than one kind of information as they move beyond one-word utterances.

## Inflections and phrase structure

As children acquire inflectional affixes, they are at first quite selective in where they use each inflection. Bloom, Lifter, and Hafitz (1980) noted, for example, that English-speaking children tended to use *-ing* (indicating ongoing duration) on activity verbs like *run* but not on accomplishment or achievement verbs like *break* and *build*, or *finish* and *reach*; nor did they use *-ing* on stative verbs like *want* or *know* (Brown 1973). (Activity verbs may make up 50% of the verb-types produced up to age three (Clark 1996).) Children made use of *-ed* on both accomplishment and achievement verbs, but the meaning seemed to be 'completed action' rather than the adult 'past tense'. (Achievement verbs with a change of state, where *-ed* is the first inflection used, make up as much as 36% of the verb-types used before age three.) And children rarely used the past tense *-ed* on activity verbs. That is, they appeared to be sensitive to whether a verb denoted an ongoing activity or an activity with a clear end point and tended to observe compatibility of meaning between the verb-stem and the inflection.

These tendencies may reflect general correlations observable in child-directed speech, but notice that both *-ing* and *-ed* can appear on most verbs since these mark the event as ongoing, *-ing* (the contour of the event), or in the past (*-ed*) relative to the moment of speech. These patterns of early inflection use on verbs are consistent with uses noted for inflections in other languages like Turkish and Italian (Aksu-Koç 1988; Antinucci & Miller 1976). Children distinguish activities from accomplishments in their choices of inflections, and they also distinguish both of these from achievements and from states.

Verbs differ in the events they denote. Activity verbs pick out event-types where actions can continue with no clear beginning or end to the activity; accomplishment verbs pick out actions that have some result (e.g., *build*) and may effect a change of state or location on the object affected (e.g., *break*, *lift*).

Achievement verbs pick out the end points of certain actions (e.g., *finish, reach*) and therefore denote inherently punctual event-types. And stative verbs denote states rather than actions (e.g., *want, know, like*). These event-types are susceptible to different temporal modifications (e.g., *in an hour* vs. *for an hour*), and the verbs used to denote them license different inflections (Vendler 1967).[10]

In general, children appear to be rather conservative in where they first add inflections. When taught new nouns and verbs, they are more cautious in adding inflections, whether the plural on nouns or the past tense on verbs, than they are for words already familiar to them (Tomasello *et al.* 1997). They are equally conservative in their extension of consistent word orders to word combinations that contain newly learnt terms. When taught a novel verb in isolation, children appear unwilling to combine it with other already familiar terms. That is, they do not assign any constructions to the new verb without evidence for such constructions. This contrasts with their response to newly taught nouns, which they appear willing to combine with other, familiar nouns and also with familiar verbs (Tomasello *et al.* 1997; see also Akhtar & Tomasello 1997). This suggests that new nouns may be easier to characterize as nouns, so children are more willing to add them right away to various constructions. Another possibility is that nouns in general occur in fewer constructions than verbs, constructions that are also more predictable than constructions for verbs.

But children are also conservative in their initial uses of inflections with nouns. For example, they add conventional plural inflections initially noun by noun (Clark & Nikitina 2008), and, as they begin to identify the meanings of case inflections in languages like Latvian or Russian, they use certain nouns only with case markings that are semantically compatible with the noun-stem. They produce nouns for instruments (e.g., the equivalents of English *hammer* or *spoon*) only with instrumental case marking, and nouns for places (e.g., the equivalents of English *school* or *kitchen*) only with locative case marking. They may also limit plural marking to nouns for pairs or groups of objects (e.g., shoes, blocks) (for Latvian, see Ruke-Dravina 1973; for Russian, see Gvozdev 1961; for Spanish, see Gathercole *et al.* 1999; also Slobin 1973).

The initial conservatism children display in the learning of inflections is also apparent in their early noun phrases like *these books*, *an old woman*, or *the tall beanstalk over there*. In an analysis of the overlaps in uses of determiners (e.g., *the, some, that, a*, etc.) in the speech of eleven children in the early stages of multiword utterance production, Pine and Lieven (1997) found little evidence that the children were using a category of "determiner." Rather, they began by using *that* only with certain nouns and *a* or *the* only with certain others. Their uses of each determiner were best characterized as a set of limited-scope formulas (Braine 1976), since they appeared only with a subset of child nouns. Acquisition of the

---

[10] Event-type classifications depend on more than just the verb; in addition to temporal modifications (compare *in an hour* vs. *for an hour*), event-types also differ in their argument arrays (e.g., *push the cart* vs. *push the cart to the barn*) (see further Jackendoff 1983; Verkuyl 1993).

Table 8.5 *Three most productive patterns of determiner use and the percentage of determiner use accounted for in the speech of eleven children under three*

| Children | Productive determiner patterns | Percentage of use accounted for |
|---|---|---|
| Anna | *a + X; in the + X; in a + X* | 60 |
| Alan | *a + X; on the + X; (in) the + X* | 56 |
| Charles | *a + X; in the + X; want a + X* | 52 |
| Helen | *that's a + X; a + X; like a + X* | 62 |
| Irwin | *a + X* | 62 |
| Karen | *a + X; want a + X; that's a + X or in the + X or on the + X* | 35 |
| Laura | *a + X; in the + X; where's the + X* | 52 |
| Leonard | *a + X; there's a/that's a/the + X* | 62 |
| Lionel | *a + X; want a + X* | 54 |
| Margaret | *a + X; get a + X; there's the + X* | 41 |
| Molly | *a + X; where's the + X; there's the + X* | 79 |
| Mean: | | 56 |

*Note*: Irwin used only one pattern more than once, and Lionel used only two.

*Source*: Pine & Lieven 1997:132. Used with permission from Cambridge University Press.

adult category of determiner was quite slow, as children gradually extended the range of lexically specific frames in which they produced each determiner. The three most productive patterns of determiner use for each child are shown in Table 8.5, together with the percentage of uses accounted for by just these patterns in that child's speech (see also Pine & Martindale 1996). Effectively, at 2;1, children used both *a* and *the* with only 10% of their nouns. By 2;6, this rises to around 20%. But parents use both articles with twice or three times as many nouns in their speech at both ages.

In assigning meanings to terms for objects and actions, relations, and states, children build on their conceptual categories and observe the distributional properties of these terms and what co-occurs with them in the speech they hear. It seems plausible to assume that they could learn in this way what the word-classes and phrase-types of their language are. So what is the advantage of positing innate knowledge of syntactic word-classes? One difference between semantic and syntactic bootstrapping lies in the assumptions about what is innate. Syntactic bootstrapping supposes that children come equipped with syntactic word-classes. These just have to be instantiated (however that is done), and then children are all ready to make use of them in assigning possible meanings. Semantic bootstrapping supposes instead that children can derive word-classes from conceptual categories plus some distributional analysis. Even if one posits innate word-classes, it is unclear *how* what is innate gets mapped onto the available categories and distinctions in the target language. So it seems preferable to assume that children can learn from the available data unless we can find strong evidence against this view.

One way to test such an approach is to look at computational models and their outcomes. Can one, in principle, discover the major word-classes (noun and verb, say) from distributional analyses of the target language? While some of the first such tests were based on written text only (e.g., Schütze 1993, 1994), several studies have now been carried out on child-directed speech (e.g., Cartwright & Brent 1997; Mintz *et al.* 2002). The most extensive of these compared the outcomes of four different distributional analyses of speech addressed to children under 2;6 for the discovery of major word-classes. The first analysis simply took into account one word each side of the target word; the second compared the effects of looking at two words each side of the target with eight words each side of the target; the third analysis looked instead to the nearest phrase-boundaries before and after the target word; and the fourth reduced the amount of information available from closed class words by treating them all as if they were the same.

All four models allowed successful extraction of nouns and verbs as word-classes. The one that used phrase-boundaries (working from the beginnings and ends of noun phrases, verb phrases, and prepositional phrases) did better than the models looking at an arbitrary number of adjacent words (Mintz *et al.* 2002). These results support the view that children could use distributional analysis to find word-classes. These models, of course, also rely on specific assumptions about the computational abilities available to children and about any biases they might exhibit in applying those abilities. From a learning point of view, the existence of both abilities and biases is quite consistent with the capacity required for learning in other domains. This suggests one should be cautious before assuming that anything is innate, already "given," in the process of acquisition (see Part IV).

### Stressed and unstressed syllables

As children add grammatical morphemes to their utterances, they attend to the metrical templates common in the adult language (Chapter 5). Children acquiring English appear to omit unstressed syllables in order to maintain a metrical template of trochaic or Strong + Weak (S–W) feet. They prefer to produce syllables in a S–W pattern within words, with repeated S–W sequences within utterances (Gerken 1994b). When asked to imitate sequences that begin with a weak (unstressed) syllable, two-year-olds regularly omit that syllable. They also omit other weak syllables that violate the trochaic pattern. They usually retain weak syllables as long as they fit the S–W template (Gerken & McIntosh 1993; see also Demuth 1994).[11] And comparison of noun phrases used in subject position

---

[11] And when presented with familiar words in such tasks, children this age are able to retain even extrametrical unstressed syllables (Boyle & Gerken 1997). This suggests that they rely on some

with those used in predicates predictably shows much less article use for subject noun phrases, with an W–S pattern (McGregor 1994). Metrical templates, then, appear to play a role in children's early productions of word forms (Chapter 5), in their production of familiar words (compared to unfamiliar ones), and in their production of grammatical morphemes as they elaborate their utterances. This reliance on metrical templates appears to account for which grammatical morphemes children do and don't produce prior to adultlike mastery.

### Rules or schemas?

When children learning English add *-ed* to a verb-stem, what are they actually doing? They could be applying the implicit rule: "Add *-ed* to the end of any verb-stem to mark past meaning." If they do this, they may well include irregular verb-stems along with regular ones and so regularize the latter by adding *-ed* there as well. This would yield errors like the attested *buyed*, *comed*, and *thinked*. It predicts that children should add the same endings to all verb-stems.

Or could children be making use of a schema or template for past meaning for verbs? The schema could be characterized as in (6), with the meaning on the left and the phonological form on the right:

(6)          verb-stem + PAST → [——t/d]PAST

This schema is to be read as requiring that any verb-stem combined with the meaning 'past' in English should result in a form that ends in an alveolar stop consonant, namely /-t/ or /-d/ (Bybee & Slobin 1982).

The rule and schema accounts make different predictions about the errors children will produce. The rule-based account predicts that, when children over-regularize their marking of past tense, they should do so by adding *-ed* to *all* verb-stems alike, with regard only for whether a stem requires /-t/ (after final voiceless consonants, as in *jump/jumped*), /-d/ (with final voiced consonants and vowels, as in *sew/sewed*, *rub/rubbed*), or /-ɪd/ (after final alveolars, as in *melt/melted* or *side/sided*). The schema-based account makes the same predictions for the first two types of verbs: Those with a voiceless final consonant will take the final voiceless alveolar stop (/-t/), and those with a final voiced consonant or a final vowel will take the voiced alveolar stop (/-d/). It makes a different prediction for the third group of verbs. Because these stems end in a /-t/ or /-d/ and already fit the schema, children should make no change in the verb form when they intend to convey a past meaning. This is just what Bybee and Slobin found when they elicited past tense verbs with a range of stem shapes. Children under six or seven tended to treat the final /-t/ or /-d/ of the stem as if it satisfied the template for past meaning. They had not yet fully established the further schema needed for verbs

form of canonical word template when attempting new material and that they make use of such templates (presumably derived from the most general patterns detected in the target language so far) until they have had sufficient practice with new words to be able to set up articulatory programs that (where necessary) go beyond the basic trochaic sequence in production.

with stems that already end in a /-t/ or /-d/. These findings support the view that children may rely on schemas or templates rather than rules, at least in their initial generalizations about noun and verb paradigms.

Additional support for schemas comes from data on noun plurals. In Berko's original study of inflections, she found that children often simply repeated the nonsense words she offered (e.g., *tass*), with no change in form. Responses like this were most likely to occur with nonsense words that already fitted the plural schema (Köpcke 1998). A similar study of German showed the same pattern: Children were most likely to just repeat target words that already fitted a plural schema. Analysis of spontaneous speech from seven children (2;1–2;9) acquiring the plural system offered further support for such reliance on plural templates. Children seemed to test word forms against the schemas they knew to see whether they already fitted a plural schema or not. If they didn't, children inserted those forms into the relevant template. If they did, they simply used those forms just as they were (Köpcke 1998). In summary, children appear to rely on schemas in their acquisition of inflectional morphology. In addition to the errors children produce as they add inflections to irregular verbs and nouns, one other set of data appears consistent with the schema-based account, namely adult slips of the tongue (Fromkin 1971; Garrett 1975). And some patterns observable in language change are also consistent with reliance on templates of the type proposed here (Bybee 1985; Zager 1981).

Once children have acquired the full set of schemas needed, say, for irregular as well as regular verbs, it may be difficult to distinguish between schema- and rule-based accounts, since the products will be the same. At one level, schemas and rules represent equivalent generalizations. Where they differ is in whether children are attending to the source-form, the verb- or noun-stem, and then adding the inflection to it, or whether they are attending to the goal-form and checking whether the stem they have fits it or not. Since the relevant schema already contains the phonological information about the target form, the child has only to insert any stems that don't already fit that schema to produce the desired product.

## Representations in memory

Just what information children (and adults) use in producing inflected forms should have consequences for what they store about word forms in memory. Do they list stems and then the applicable inflections separately? Do they store each inflected form, that is, stem + inflection, individually? Or do they store both inflected forms and those same forms decomposed into their parts? Does such double storage depend on the frequency of specific modulations of noun- or verb-stems? These questions are important for both acquisition and processing. There is growing evidence that adults store both the modulated form and the decomposed parts, depending on the regularity of paradigms and the frequency of inflections (Baayen 1994; Niemi, Laine, & Tuominen 1994).

What makes a form count as regular or irregular? Most discussions of English have tended to identify specific verb- or noun-stems as regular. *Jump* is a regular verb while *bring* is irregular. But most English verbs have only one stem form. The issue is more complicated when we consider other languages. It may be harder to link regularity with specific verbs or nouns, since the paradigms are more complex, with many inflected forms and more than one stem.

Take French verbs. The first conjugation in French, with the infinitive in *-er*, as in *donner* 'to give', contains the largest number of types.[12] But many of the most frequent verbs (measured by token-frequency) belong to the third conjugation, the main repository for irregular verbs. Both regular and irregular verbs may make use of several stems in French. *Finir* 'to finish' uses two stem forms in the present tense: *fin-* and *finiss-*; *vouloir* 'to want, wish' uses three stem forms, two in the present, *veu(l)-* and *voul-*, and another in the future and conditional, *voudr-*. *Avoir* 'to have' uses *ai*, *a(s)*, and *av-* in the present, *aur-* in the future and conditional, *av-* in the imperfect, and *eu(-)* in the historic past and in the past participle. Another common verb, *prendre* 'to take', uses two stems in the present, *prend-* and *prenn-*, another in the future and conditional, *prendr-*, and a fourth, *pri(-)*, in the historic past and past participle. In languages like this, it seems simpler to identify the tense or the form where a particular verb is irregular, rather than the verb as a whole. In short, should a verb with one irregular form or one irregular tense be counted as irregular or as regular?

This question is central for the dual encoding hypothesis put forward by Marcus and his colleagues (1992) in their account of the acquisition of regular versus irregular past tense forms in English. Regular verbs, they proposed, are stored as stems with rules for adding the allomorphs of the past tense inflection *-ed*. But irregular verbs have to be stored as both a present tense stem and a past tense form (e.g., *sit* and *sat*; *bring* and *brought*) because these forms have to be learnt one by one and cannot be constructed with a rule, as in the regular case. In memory, therefore, each verb has to be tagged as regular or irregular, and stored accordingly for processing in recognition and retrieval (see also Kim *et al.* 1994).

They proposed further that children "extract" the rule for past tense formation in English early on but learn irregular forms through one-by-one associations of stem and inflected form until they have mastered the relevant pairs for each irregular verb. But since verbs don't come tagged as regular or irregular, children may assume at first that all verbs work the same way in conveying a past-time meaning. This would account for children's overregularization errors on the one hand and their failures to link related verb forms with different stems (e.g., *think* and *thought*, *break* and *broke*) on the other.

At first glance, the dual encoding hypothesis offers a persuasive analysis of acquisition data for past tense forms in English. But it becomes less compelling for other languages. Where does a French verb like *aller* 'to go' belong? Should it be stored as a stem (or set of stems) with rules for regular inflection for each tense,

---

[12] Grevisse (1964) estimated that 98% of French verbs belong to this conjugation.

say, or should it be stored with a full set of inflected forms as an irregular verb? *Aller* is irregular only in the present tense; it is entirely regular in the imperfect, the perfect past, the historic past, and the past participle; it is also regular, with a different stem, in the future and conditional. The same question arises for all irregular verbs in French, since all are regular in most tenses and only irregular in certain subparts of the overall paradigm they belong to.

Is regularity assessed from the specific forms (schemas) for the expression of particular inflectional meanings? If so, it is often difficult to decide whether a verb is stored as a stem plus rules for adding inflections, or as a full set of inflected forms (see Elsen 1997 on German; Orsolini *et al.* 1998 on Italian). Or could a verb be stored in two places – with the specific irregular inflected forms in one place *and* a stem-plus-inflection listing elsewhere? This, however, would run counter to the implicit economy of storage assumed in the dual encoding account. If one drops criteria based on economy (there is a lot of memory storage available), an alternative approach might be to list all forms, regular and irregular, and also store decomposed forms, with the stem and inflections separate. This is the solution advocated in an increasing number of processing studies of adult speakers (e.g., Sandra & Taft 1994; see also Ramscar 2002).

In acquisition, there are some additional questions for the dual encoding hypothesis. First, do children really start out with a regular rule-based approach to the addition of inflections and only later switch over to forms now tagged as irregular (i.e., with separate but associated representations for each form of the irregular word)? As we have seen, much of the evidence favors a schema-based starting point, where children set up schemas for the target word shape for each inflected form. These data don't support a rule-based view. And in languages where there are several past tense schemas, or several plural schemas depending on gender, the evidence also seems to favor schemas over rules.

### Overregularization

How often children overregularize during their acquisition of inflections varies considerably. It depends, of course, on how many irregular noun- and verb-stems children have already attached some meaning to and begun to use. The period of greatest overregularization for the past tense in English is from around age two to three-and-half. At this point, children may overregularize up to 50% of the time when they produce an irregular verb-stem in the past tense (Kuczaj 1977; Maratsos 1993, 2000). Some researchers have calculated much lower rates, below 5%, with data averaged over a longer age span, from two up to age five (Marcus *et al.* 1992). But as children get older, they produce many more correct irregular past tense forms for irregular verbs, so the number of overregularizations decreases steadily.

At issue, in part, is how children stop regularizing an irregular verb. Marcus and his colleagues appealed to an account in which the existence of a past tense form like *fell* or *went* in the language is sufficient to block use of regularized past tense forms like *falled* or *goed*. But the presence of blocking on its own is not enough.

Children need to know that the two forms belong to the same verb, for example, *fall* and *fell* or *go* and *went*. They also need to realize that the relation between *go* and *went*, for instance, is the same as that between *jump* and *jumped* or *open* and *opened*. And they must register that wherever they produce the regular version of the past tense for such verbs, for example, *falled* or *goed*, adults produce a different form, namely *fell* or *went*, instead. From these observations, they need to infer that the *meanings* conveyed by *fell* and *went*, say, are identical to those they are trying to convey with the forms *falled* and *goed*. Then, because there is no meaning difference between *fell* and *falled*, children must choose just one form for the past tense. They opt for the one used by adult speakers. The dropping of a regularized form for an irregular verb, then, is motivated by contrast (or rather the lack of contrast between the meanings of two distinct forms), while the eventual choice of a specific form is motivated by conventionality – the form used by adults (Clark 1987, 1993; Harris & Shirai 1997; Kuczaj 1981; Shirai 1997). Establishing the meaning of each irregular past tense form is what is critical.

## Summary

Children follow similar paths as they master the inflectional forms of different languages. They typically begin with fixed forms, used in every context, taking only the meaning of the word-stem into account. When they use a second or third inflected form on the same stem, they must establish a difference in meaning for each inflection. In effect, they maintain contrast. Once they have identified the meaning of a specific inflection, they may also overapply it in place of the conventional allomorphs called for instead. For instance, once Russian-speaking children learn the masculine singular instrumental case ending (*-om*), they may add it for a while to all nouns, regardless of gender and number, whenever they wish to express instrumental meaning (Gvozdev 1961). Children take longer to acquire inflectional systems that use a number of variants for different nouns and verbs (see Ferguson & Slobin 1973; Slobin 1985a, 1992, 1997). The variations found in inflectional systems depend in part on the formal complexity of the forms used to convey specific meanings, and these reflect typological properties of the languages being learnt. Variations can also reflect the conceptual complexity of the distinctions being marked. And children acquire less complex distinctions first.

Learning to use inflections allows children to modulate meaning at the word level. Children may latch onto an inflectional contrast while still producing only one word at a time. (This is commonplace in inflected languages like Russian or Hungarian.) Or they may start in on inflectional modulations once they combine words to form more complex utterances (Chapter 7). But since inflections tend to be specialized for nouns versus verbs versus adjectives, their uses offer insight into children's analyses of what to treat as a noun, a verb, an adjective. So analysis of inflections on unfamiliar words may provide children with information over and above what is inferable from common ground about the meanings of new forms.

# 9    Adding complexity within clauses

As children pack more material into a single clause, they become able to convey more information in each utterance. This additional complexity comes at some cost: Children have to master the range of constructions conventionally used to convey each shade of meaning they are trying to express. They add to their repertoire by indicating more consistently whether information is given in the discourse (already known to the addressee) or new, and so keeping track of information flow. They add greater precision for the addressee by adding adjectives to noun phrases. They also add demonstratives and quantifiers, as in (1), with occasional errors as the combinations become more complex, as in (2) (Clark, diary data):

(1) a.    D (2;2.26, eyeing shredded wheat at breakfast): *I want some of these. I want some of those* …
    b.    D (2;3.26, in the car, having drunk his milk): *I want some more milk.*
(2) a.    D (2;2.14, holding two toy buses): *All both my buses.*
    b.    D (2;3.4, at supper): *We all both got pie.*

They also start to use relative clauses to pick out the referents when there are several possible candidates, as in (3), where the relative clauses identify a specific building and a specific doll:

(3) a.    D (2;0, looking at the institute where his parents work): *I see [ə] building Eve go.*
    b.    D (2;0,1, picking up a doll): *Here [ə] doll Shelli give Damon.*

Children elaborate verbs and verb phrases by adding inflections and auxiliary verbs; they become more adept at tracking referents, substituting pronouns for lexical noun phrases; and they make use of more constructions with each verb. Their general progress towards more adultlike usage is illustrated in the utterances in Table 9.1. Those in the top half come from diary observations of D, aged 1;6–1;7, while those in the bottom half come from the same child six months later (aged 2;2). Added complexity is not simply a matter of length – more words and more morphemes. It is also the acquisition of new constructions and expressions. Children extend their range not only with the acquisition of more words but also with phrases and constructions that can be combined to express both more precise and more complex meanings.

In the present chapter I look at several types of complexity within the clause and the course children seem to follow as they master them. I consider first how

Table 9.1 *Adding complexity: Some utterances from D at 1;6 and 2;2*

---

(1;6.12, trying to fit a key into a keyhole): *Key door, key door.*

(1;6.13, trying to fit a ball into a form-box hole): *Put ball. Put back.*

(1;6.19, request to be put into his high-chair): *Me up.*

(1;6.28, request to be lifted into his high-chair): *Me chair.*

(1;6.28, after he dropped his blanket): *Fall, blanket fall.*

(1;7.0, wanting his pyjamas taken off): *Pyjamas off.*

(1;7.0, request, upon seeing his father eating a banana): *Me banana.* (then moved a stool to the table so he could reach): *Stool banana eat.*

(1;7.3, expressing intention): *Get down floor.*

(1;7.6, talking about the swimming pool): *People water, swimming.*

(1;7.6, request for water): *Water cup!*

(1;7.7, playing with a cork in the sink): *Cork float.*

(1;7.7, asking to have pen top put back on his finger): *Me back finger.*

(2;2.1, as father finished cereal D had been taking): *You eat my flakes away!*

(2;2.1, at the table): *Big people don't wear bibs. Only little boys.*

(2;2.2, of his doll, Danny): *Danny don't getting all wet.*

(2;2.3, wanting his cup for orange juice): *Where my orange-cup?*

(2;2.3): *I taking food out of my hair. Know why? You might wash it, with shampoo.*

(2;2.4): *I want milk afore read book.*

(2;2.4): *I turned the light on.*

(2;2.4): *Where this goes?*

(2;2.5, hearing a truck on the road): *I go outside see a truck may have dirt in it.*

(2;2.5, drinking with a straw): *I drink afore any bubbles.* THEN *I blow bubbles.*

(2;2.6, toy boat in the kitchen sink): *It sink down. Make it sink up.*

(2;2.7, vitrine turtle on the side of his dresser): *It might fall down.*

(2;2.9, Cheerios at breakfast): *I did eat my rings.*

(2;2.10): *Wait [ə] get dark outside, then turn [ə] light on.*

---

*Source*: Clark, unpublished diary data

children present information as given and new in an utterance, and how they link semantic roles like agent or location to a grammatical role like subject. Then I turn to how they ask questions and express negation. Lastly, I take up several constructions used to express alternate perspectives on an event. These constructions all exemplify developments within the clause in children's ability to convey different meanings.

## Early constructions

On what basis do children elaborate their earliest word combinations? Besides adding inflections, children take account of which constructions their parents use with each verb, for example, and make use of those as they extend their own repertoires. They also exhibit increasing awareness of how to manage

Table 9.2  *Children follow their parents in construction use*

|  | Adam 2;3–2;8 | Adam's mother | Eve 1;6–1;11 | Eve's mother |
|---|---|---|---|---|
| Adam | 1.000 | | | |
| A's mother | **0.67** | 1.00 | | |
| Eve | 0.51 | 0.35 | 1.00 | |
| E's mother | 0.48 | 0.48 | **0.70** | 1.00 |

*Source*: de Villiers 1985:593. Used with permission from Cambridge University Press.

the flow of information in terms of what is given and what is new in each exchange. In their earliest word combinations, children simply tend to assign given information to one position and new information to the other, usually in the sequence GIVEN + NEW. But as their utterances become more elaborate, they rely on what has been called Preferred Argument Structure, the favored pattern for presenting information within a language to manage the flow of information. Each added option allows children to convey more finely differentiated meanings through their choices of words and constructions.

### Constructions in adult speech

How do children learn different constructions? There is growing evidence that they attend closely to lexical usage in adult speech and to the range of constructions used with individual words in parental speech. And they appear to extend their own uses only to ones they have heard and not beyond. In a detailed study of one set of verbs in the speech of two children and their mothers, de Villiers (1985) focussed on all the constructions the verbs appeared in as the children moved beyond two-word combinations. Both children used the target verbs only in constructions they heard attested in their own mothers' speech. As a result, their usage was more highly correlated with that of their own mothers (correlations of 0.67 or more) than with each other (a correlation of 0.5) or with the other child's mother (0.35 or 0.48), as shown in Table 9.2. These correlations suggest that children are conservative learners and only combine words with constructions heard from their parents.

In another study of the twenty-five most frequent verbs addressed to fifty-seven young children, the set of syntactic frames offered children reliable information about the semantic class of each verb. For example, a verb with a prepositional phrase was most likely to be a motion verb (e.g., *go into the house*), and a verb with a direct object was typically a causative verb with an agent and patient (e.g., *the boy is chasing the dog*). Moreover, each of the twenty-five verbs could be uniquely specified by the set of syntactic frames it appeared with, so there was a correlation between a verb's meaning and its constructional options

(Naigles & Hoff-Ginsberg 1995).[1] This suggests that children could make use of both context-based inferences about verb meanings and the range of constructional options for each verb form to keep the meanings of closely related verbs distinct from each other.

Naigles and Hoff-Ginsberg predicted that the verbs the parents used most frequently, in final position, and in the most syntactic frames would be most likely to appear in the utterances of the fifty-seven children ten weeks later in those constructions (Naigles & Hoff-Ginsberg 1998). As in de Villiers' study, the children's use of verb frames was similar to that of their mothers. For instance, they used direct objects with transitive verbs more than half the time but hardly ever did so with intransitive verbs; and they used prepositional phrases with motion verbs like *go* or *run* more often than with internal state verbs like *need* or *hear*. The frequency with which parents had used particular verbs ten weeks earlier was highly correlated with children's later uses of those verbs, and the parental diversity of constructions for each verb was also highly predictive of both the frequency and the diversity of frames for those same verbs in the children's speech. In short, these two factors made robust predictions about order of acquisition for verbs. So children keep track of the co-occurrence of forms, whether these are single words or words used in constructional frames.

Children also seem to build on constructions that are already established in their language. In German, for example, Abbot-Smith and Behrens (2006) examined the acquisition of two passive constructions with auxiliary *sein* 'to be' and auxiliary *werden* 'to become'. They showed that prior acquisition of copular *sein* 'to be' facilitated acquisition of the *sein*-passive construction, so children learnt the *sein*-passive before the *werden*-passive. And the later-acquired *werden*-passive then supported, in its turn, the still later acquisition of the copular *werden* construction. In short, existing constructions can facilitate the acquisition of more complex constructions, or, on occasion, inhibit them.

### Preferred Argument Structure

Children also make early use of what Du Bois (1987) called Preferred Argument Structure. He argued that Preferred Argument Structure reflects the management of information flow in discourse. That is, whenever possible, speakers appear to place given information in the Agent slot (A) of transitive verbs, and reserve the Object slot (O) of transitives and the Subject slot (S) of intransitives for new information. This also leads them to favor pronouns or zero (no pronoun at all) in the given slot (A), compared to content words in the two new slots (O and S). This allows speakers to present given and new information in predictable slots within clauses, and, in general, to provide addressees with given information

---

[1] This type of correlation has been well documented in those languages that have been studied from this point of view. For example, Gross (1975) found that differences in verb meaning in French predicted differences in the range of constructions possible with each verb.

Table 9.3 *Referential forms in two children's Korean: A, O, and S*

| Role | Nominals | | Pronouns | | Ellipsis | |
|---|---|---|---|---|---|---|
| | Hyenswu | Wenceng | Hyenswu | Wenceng | Hyenswu | Wenceng |
| A role | 12 | 14 | 10 | 12 | 77 | 73 |
| O role | 30 | 42 | 23 | 14 | 43 | 35 |
| S role | 28 | 24 | 17 | 16 | 54 | 57 |

*Source*: Clancy 2003: Fig. 1. Used with permission from John Benjamins.

before new information. Du Bois would predict, then, that the Agent role should be a preferred site for ellipsis (for given information) and that the Object and Subject roles should be preferred for content words (for new information).

Children's acquisition of preferred argument structures appears to reflect a convergence of word-choice, referential form, and grammatical role (Clancy 1996, 2003). This convergence arises in conversation, where children learn to introduce new information with particular verbs (a small set of verbs used very frequently by young two-year-olds) in specific argument slots. In Korean, for instance, speakers can choose among three options in making a reference: a noun (or nominal expression), a pronoun, or ellipsis where they use neither. In a longitudinal study of two children, Clancy (2003) found that the verbs they produced most frequently displayed marked asymmetries in the referential forms for different argument roles. For both children, ellipsis (no pronoun or noun) in the Agent role with transitive verbs was very high (77% in Hyenswu's speech and 73% in Wenceng's), and nominals were rare (12% and 14%). In the Object role for transitive verbs, the children used somewhat less ellipsis and made use of more nominals than in the Agent slot. The distribution of referential forms in the Subject slot of intransitive verbs fell between the levels for the Agent and Object roles. Both children used more ellipsis for S than for O, but less than for A, and they used more nominals for S than for A, as shown in Table 9.3. This pattern is consistent with Du Bois' predictions.

With new information, Clancy found that the highest percentage appeared in the O slot (61% for Hyenswu and 52% for Wenceng), a lower percentage in the S slot (35% and 41% respectively), and only a few instances in the A one (4% and 7%) (Clancy 2003). Overall, new information typically appeared as the core argument of the verb. With intransitives, it appeared as a nominal in the S slot, the only argument of the verb. With transitive verbs, it appeared as a nominal in the O slot. All the other arguments of verbs were marked either with pronouns or with zero anaphora (neither pronoun nor noun).

Lastly, the verbs produced most frequently by the children, whether intransitive or transitive, readily lent themselves to providing the introduction for a new referent (e.g., *issta* 'exist', *ota* 'come', or *hata* 'do'). The Agent role, with ellipsis (i.e., no overt mention of the agent), was typically filled by the child-speaker or by the addressee (as the actor in the action being talked about), while the Object role contained references to new actions or to inanimate objects on which to perform the actions.

In summary, children are more likely to use nouns where these are more informative, and what is informative is generally information that is new in context (see also Choi 1999; Guerriero, Oshima-Takane, & Kuriyama 2006; Salazar Orvig *et al.* 2006). Similar observations have been made for children acquiring other languages, including English and Inuktitut (see Allen & Schröder 2003). Other languages also display asymmetries in where either full ellipsis or pronoun subjects are preferred (e.g., Adone 1994 for Mauritian Creole).

## Getting in the subject

What happens in languages that lack the ellipsis possible in Korean? Even in English, Dutch, or French, where subjects must be mentioned with a nominal or a pronoun, young children at first omit them as much as 30% of the time. (These subjects are typically the agents of the action being talked about.) So when these children produce their first transitive verbs, they are more likely to make consistent use of a nominal for the direct object than for the subject.

Researchers have proposed several explanations for this omission of subjects. Some have assumed a deficit such that children's grammar doesn't yet fully match the adult grammar. In this view, all children begin acquisition with a series of what have been called parameters or settings for particular phenomena. With the Pro-drop parameter, children start out by assuming that they need not mention subjects (as in Italian), but they later discover that, in languages like English or French, subjects are obligatory. But until they hear enough relevant data, it has been argued, children tend to treat all languages as Pro-drop languages (not needing to have subjects mentioned), and only later reset the parameter to require subjects in certain languages. For languages like Italian or Mandarin, children can stick with the original setting, since there mention of subjects is not obligatory (Hyams 1986). In this account, then, children's mental representations of language structure lack some of the information present in adults. This lack is remedied as soon as children detect the need to reset the parameter.[2]

Other researchers have appealed to performance limitations to explain the absence of subjects in children's utterances (e.g., Pinker 1984; Valian 1991). Children omit subjects because they are not yet able to access and produce them in longer or more complex utterances. Valian and her colleagues (1996) used a sentence imitation task with children aged 1;10 to 2;8 to pit this view against the

---

[2] However, since such proposals are not concerned with developmental change, they offer no account of how the resetting of such a parameter occurs, beyond pointing out which data are considered critical in how a parameter gets reset. In addition, they assume that resetting a parameter makes for an across-the-board change in the child's system wherever that parameter applies. Acquisition data are often inconsistent with such a view (see Fletcher 1985; Ingham 1992).

grammatical account. According to the grammatical account, children producing short utterances (less than three morphemes) should rely, for instance, on given information from earlier in the conversation and therefore omit subjects more often than children who can produce longer utterances (e.g., Rizzi 1994). Since both younger and older children (with short and long utterances) relied equally on given information, their omission of subjects was inconsistent with the grammatical account. In contrast, performance limitations predicted that they should omit subjects more often in longer than shorter utterances and that this effect should be more pronounced for younger children. Imitation data supported this view, with younger children more likely than older ones to omit pronoun subjects (Valian *et al.* 1996; see also Theakston *et al.* 2001).

Other researchers have focussed on metrical structure to explain children's omissions not only of pronoun subjects but also of other unstressed syllables (e.g., Gerken 1991). They have assumed that (a) speakers group syllables into prosodic feet, with one strong syllable per foot; (b) these prosodic feet can be iambic (weak–strong) or trochaic (strong–weak) in form; and (c) children are more likely to omit initial weak syllables (in iambic feet) (see Chapter 5). Because speakers are more likely to place given information in the A and S slots than in the O slot, they are more likely to use pronouns in the A slot and, to a lesser extent, the S slot in a language like English. And since pronouns are unstressed, young children are likely to omit them. The pronoun *he* in (4), for example, is omitted by most two-year-olds who are asked to imitate this sentence (Gerken & McIntosh 1993):

(4)        he CALLED + ALL the + DOGS[3]

And since children more often omit unstressed (weak) syllables in initial position in a metrical foot, definite articles before a strong syllable are more likely to be omitted than definite articles after a strong syllable. In (5), for example, the first *the* is more likely to be omitted than the second:

(5)        the BOY + CALLED the + DOG

At the same time, notice that elements in utterance-final position generally refer to new information and therefore tend to be nominals rather than pronouns in English. In addition, new information typically carries heavier stress than given information in the utterance as whole. In short, Gerken's (1991) findings, summarized in Figure 9.1, suggest that metrical factors also contribute to the frequent omissions of subjects in children's two- and three-word utterances.

In imitation tasks, two-year-olds were much more likely to omit subjects that were pronouns than subjects that were nouns (Gerken 1991). This was in marked contrast to the object position: There, they never omitted lexical noun phrases and they omitted pronouns only 1% of the time. But the (unstressed) article preceding noun objects was omitted quite frequently, 18% of the time. So children appeared

---

[3] The capital letters indicate the strong syllables, and lowercase the weak syllables.

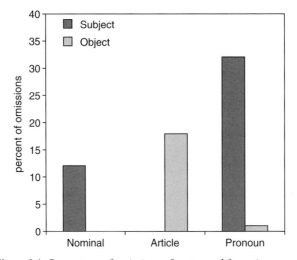

Figure 9.1 *Percentage of omissions of unstressed forms in two-year-olds'*
*imitations of nominals, articles, and pronouns in subject vs. object position*

to retain new information in preference to given information, but this interacted with the form in which this information appeared. This is consistent with how children aged 2;6–3;6 answer different types of questions. In response to a specific question like "Where is the broom?" they use pronouns or ellipsis in response: *It's on the shelf* or *On the shelf*. But with general questions ("What do we need?") or contrast questions ("Do we need a mop?"), they rely on lexical noun phases: *A broom* or *No, a broom* (Wittek & Tomasello 2005b). That is, they attend to whether they are offering given or new information.

Children at this stage do not always omit the subject in the A or S slot. They are more likely to do so when they are talking about their own actions (Huttenlocher, Smiley, & Charney 1983). But when they introduce contrastive information about the agent or doer of the action – when the doer is *you* (the addressee), for instance, or a third person (e.g., *Daddy*) – children typically mention the subject even in two-word utterances. These utterance subjects are usually nominals, so they also carry strong rather than weak syllable stress within the relevant metrical foot.

Overall, children may omit subjects in their early utterances for reasons of language type, discourse, and phonological structure combined. The typological influence comes from the patterns in the language they hear from their interlocutors in conversation. Some languages allow the subject to be dropped altogether because it is marked on the verb through number and person inflections (as in Italian or Spanish, for example). Discursive influence comes from the marking of given versus new information in utterances: Pragmatically, what is given is already in common ground. Given information can be omitted while new information can't be. And unstressed elements (weak syllables) carry less weight and are more likely to be omitted than stressed ones. Together, these factors appear to account for why children omit pronoun subjects but keep nominal ones.

### Canonical linking rules

In English, each utterance can be considered in terms of the argument roles it contains – Agent, Recipient, Location, Instrument, Theme, all the participants in an event – and the grammatical relations it expresses – Subject, Direct Object, Indirect Object or Oblique. If an utterance contains an Agent, it is said to be canonically linked to the grammatical relation Subject, as in *Jan* [Agent and Subject] *climbed the tree*. If the Agent doesn't appear as the Subject (as in *The tree* [Theme and Subject] *was climbed by Jan* [Agent]), the link between argument and grammatical roles is said to be noncanonical. Since adults make use of both canonical and noncanonical linking, any privileged status for canonical linking, some researchers have argued, could only stem from a priori (innate) connections (Pinker 1989). But if argument roles are based on the general conceptual categories to which specific referents belong, there would seem to be little reason to assume any special linkage of argument roles with grammatical relations (Dowty 1991). That is, canonical linkage would not be privileged in any way. Choices of Subject will depend, on each occasion, on the perspective the speaker has chosen.

The canonical linkage hypothesis predicts that children should give priority to canonical over noncanonical linking. This should show up in preferences or biases in favor of word orders that are consistent with canonical linking patterns. For example, in utterances containing just a Theme (the argument role for the object affected by the action) and a Locative, either the Theme or the Locative could be linked to the Subject. When the Theme is the Subject, the linking is canonical (e.g., *The vase is on the table*); when the Locative is the Subject, the linking is noncanonical (e.g., *The table has a vase on it*). If canonical linking has priority, children should first learn verbs with Theme Subjects and only later those with Locative Subjects. Bowerman (1990) compared all uses of these two verb-types in her diary data for two children and found that both types were produced from the same early point. For example, Eva began to use *got* and *have* (both verbs with Locative Subjects) at the same point in development that she produced her first verbs with Theme Subjects (e.g., *go, come off, fell off*). Canonical linking, therefore, shows no advantage over noncanonical linking (Bowerman 1988, 1990, 1996a).

In summary, children appear to be more attentive to information flow in their choices of what to place first and what later in their utterances than they are to canonical linking of argument roles and grammatical relations like Subject. At this early stage in acquisition, this is perhaps not surprising. Theoretical claims about built-in linkages between arrays of argument roles and grammatical relations need to be reevaluated against existing acquisition data (see also Bowerman 1982a; Clark, Hecht, & Mulford 1986).

### Asking questions

Children start to make requests from a very early age and readily adopt the appropriate intonations to accompany their request gestures (see Chapter 5). But

Table 9.4 *Order of acquisition of* wh- *question-forms in English*

| In comprehension | In production |
|---|---|
| where | where, (what) |
| where, what | where, what |
| why | why |
| who | who |
| when | when |

Based on Ervin-Tripp 1970; Tyack & Ingram 1977

they take time to master the adult forms of questions. In their spontaneous speech, they display a rather stable order of emergence for different question-types (e.g., *what*, *where*, *when*, etc.; *wh-* questions for short), an order that appears to follow their understanding of each *wh-* question word, as shown in Table 9.4.

Production of a form doesn't necessarily imply understanding since children rely heavily on formulaic utterances in asking questions. And identification of the *wh-* element becomes elusive when one transcribes child speech carefully (see Johnson 1981, 2000; Vihman 1980). The phonetic forms of early *wh-* words (like all other words) may be hard to identify, yet adults regularly construe children's questions according to the contexts in which they are produced. Use of the term *one* leads to the question being treated as "what," while use of *go* leads to its being treated as "where." Consider the sequence of questions phonetically transcribed in Table 9.5 (they were interspersed with maternal replies) as Jane (2;8.30) tried to fit shapes into a Tupperware ball – mixing *what's this* with *where's this one go*. Inspection of her successive question-forms at the beginning of each utterance shows little or no difference in her pronunciation of these two *wh-* forms – *what* and *where*. The glosses on the right give an approximate version of what she appeared to be saying.

Johnson (1981, 1983) made careful longitudinal recordings of eight children talking to their mothers, with two children starting at each of four age levels (1;6, 2;0, 2;6, 3;0), and each child recorded five times over the course of about two months. She then transcribed all the children's utterances and extracted those that appeared to be questions and were treated that way by the parents. Johnson hypothesized that children would initially rely on unanalyzed formulaic utterances to ask questions and only later analyze the forms that went into each question-type. This general hypothesis was strongly supported by her data. Of 581 early *what* questions, 70% consisted solely of the formulaic *what's this* or *what's that*, used across a range of communicative situations.[4] They were reliably used in a small number of interactional routines, for example, pulling toy animals out of a

---

[4]  *What's that* was the earliest and most frequent *what* question-form (n = 282), with *what's this* ranked second (n = 123).

Table 9.5  *A sequence of questions from Jane (2;8.30)*

| | |
|---|---|
| (a) [wʌðɪswʌŋɔmam] | 'wh- this one go mom' |
| (b) [wədɪwo] | 'wh- dio' |
| (c) [wəsdɪswʌŋɔmam/ɪnhir] | 'wh's dis one go mom/in here' |
| (d) [wʌtsdɪswʌŋɔmam] | 'wh'ts dis one go mom' |
| (e) [ɪdɪswʌn] | 'i dis one' |
| (f) [wʌsɪswʌŋɔmam] | 'wh-s iss one go mom' |
| (g) [wʌsdɪswʌn/ɔmam] | 'wh-s dis one/go mom' |
| (h) [wʌdɪswʌn] | 'wh- dis one' |
| (i) [wʌsdɪtswʌn] | 'wh-s dits one' |
| (j) [wʌsɪfəɔgo] | 'wh-s if-n go' |
| (k) [ʌsðɪsfowʌn] | 'iss this fo' one' |
| (l) [wʌsdɪswʌn] | 'wh-s dis one' |
| (m) [owasdɛ] | 'o wha-s da' |
| (n) [wʌtsɪswʌgɔmam] | 'wh- ts'is o(ne) go mom' |
| (o) [ʌtsjɛ/wʌtsədætʃarpsɪŋɔmam] | 'i-tcha'/wh-ts a dat sharp sing go mom' |
| (p) [wʌsɪswʌn/gɔ] | 'wh-s iss one/go' |
| (q) [wʌsɪsðəwanəgɔ] | 'wh-s iss the one a go' |

*Source*: Johnson 1983:113. Reprinted by permission of the Department of Linguistics, Stanford University.

bag, looking at a picture book. In addition, nearly one third of all the utterances interpreted as *what* questions by the parents lacked any phonetic trace of an initial *wh-* sound (e.g., [sæt], [sɪs]).

After their early uses of such formulaic forms, according to Johnson, children might start to use these formulas as elements in a wider range of contexts. As they extend the range of functions for a particular question-form, one might hear *What's that?*, for example, in place of adult *What color is that?* (a new interactional routine):

(6)     MOTHER: What color's that one?
        GRAHAM (2;4.20): *That's a green one.*
        MOTHER: Don't think so.
        GRAHAM: [wʌsæt]
        MOTHER: Looks like red to me.   (Johnson 1983:110)

Another child, Lindsay (aged 3;2.8), asked *what's that?* after she tried to fit a section of plastic pipe onto a pipe structure; yet her intention, in context, would have been more appropriately expressed by something like *Why won't this piece fit?* (Johnson 1983:110). What children produce often seems to lag behind what they understand. For instance, they may continue to produce *where* for *when* even though they understand both *wh-* forms (Ervin-Tripp 1970).[5]

---

[5] Before they understand *when*, they typically respond to *when* questions as if *when* must mean *where* (e.g., Clark 1971; Ferreiro 1971).

Table 9.6 *Increasing the complexity of formulaic interrogative frames*

| Frame-type | | | | Utterance |
|---|---|---|---|---|
| I. | { *what's that* / *what's this* } | { *one* / *thing* / N / loc / *called* } | | *what's this one?* / *what's this thing?* / *what's that car?* / *what's that over there?* / *what's that called?* |
| II. | { *what's that* / *what's this* } | { *one* / *thing* / N } | { loc / VP / S } | *what's that thing right there?* / *what's this one say?* / *what's that one is all finish?* / *what's this thing you make?* |

*Source*: Johnson 1983:110. Reprinted by permission of the Department of Linguistics, Stanford University.

Reliance on formulaic uses across a growing range of contexts has also been closely documented for second-language learners, who begin to use interrogative forms before they do any analysis of the linguistic elements involved (Wong Fillmore 1979). In first language acquisition, children demonstrate the same progression from simpler, formulaic frames for asking questions (Frame I) to more elaborate interrogative frames (Frame II), as shown in Table 9.6. Notice that any one child may produce only one or two such formulas during the earlier stages of acquisition. In Johnson's study, for instance, only two of the eight children ever asked *what's this called*.

Once children have several frame-types in place, they can analyze the elements that make up each formulaic frame. Evidence for such analysis can be found in their shifts from singular *this* or *that* to the occasional plural form (*these* or *those*) and their extraction of *is* and *are* in place of contracted forms of the verb *be*. But children still remain very limited in the amount of new material they insert into any one frame for their spontaneous *what* interrogatives. Even with the added frame-types shown in Table 9.7 (III, IV, V, and VI), children consistently underproduced, with each child tending to favor just one or two versions of each new frame. The only verb children produced in *what* questions (until use of Frame IV) was the copula *be*. In Frames V and VI, they occasionally used *make* or *do*, and one child produced a few instances of *happen* (*what's gonna happen*).

Use of Frames I–VI accounted for over 95% of all eight children's *what* questions. From a developmental point of view, these frames bore an implicational relation to each other. A child who produced Frame IV-type *what* questions also produced I-, II-, and III-type *what* questions. The most highly analyzed forms emerged only after uses of Frames I and II had appeared as combining forms in larger combinations, and after the emergence of Frames III and IV (which required analysis of the copula *be*).

Reliance on this small number of frames was seen in all the children: They consistently produced these few forms even when a more elaborate, and more

Table 9.7 *Using additional interrogative frames*

| Frame-type | | | | Utterance |
|---|---|---|---|---|
| III. *what's* | $\left\{\begin{array}{l}\textit{that}\\ \textit{(this)}\\ \textit{those}\\ \textit{these}\\ \text{NP}\end{array}\right\}$ | $\left\{\begin{array}{l}\text{loc}\\ \text{(VP)}\\ \text{S}\end{array}\right\}$ | | *what's these?*<br>*what's those?*<br>*what's in here?*<br>*what's a shape?*<br>*what's your name?* |
| IV. *what* | $\left\{\begin{array}{l}\textit{'s}\\ \textit{(is)}\\ \textit{are}\\ \textit{'re}\end{array}\right\}$ | $\left\{\begin{array}{l}\textit{that}\\ \textit{this}\\ \textit{(those)}\\ \textit{these}\\ \text{NP}\end{array}\right\}$ | $\left\{\begin{array}{l}\text{loc}\\ \text{(VP)}\\ \text{S}\end{array}\right\}$ | *what is it?*<br>*what is this? what is that?*<br>*what're those?*<br>*what're those here?*<br>*what are they?* |
| V. *what's* | $\left\{\begin{array}{l}\textit{'s}\\ \textit{'re}\end{array}\right\}$ | pro *(gonna) do*<br>*(with this ...* $\left\{\begin{array}{l}\textit{thing})\\ \textit{Mom}\end{array}\right\}$ | | *what you do?*<br>*what we do with this thing?*<br>*what we do with this, Mom?*<br>*what're we gonna do?*<br>*what we make, Mommy?* |
| VI. *what* | pron | *makin(ing) (Mommy)* | | *what we making?* |

*Source*: Johnson 1983:111. Reprinted by permission of the Department of Linguistics, Stanford University.

specific, question-form was called for. But only once children can segment out the *wh-* element in their interrogative frames can they assign a more specific meaning to each *wh-* word (*where* vs. *what* vs. *who*, for instance), and only at this point do children produce creative syntactic constructions for asking questions. Each of the *wh-* forms Johnson (1981) observed followed a similar course in development, from a single formulaic structure to compositions of formulaic sequences to gradual analysis of each formula.

Why this reliance on formulaic utterances? There may be certain advantages to acquiring structure this way. First, reliance on formulas provides children with a small set of structures to store in memory. And once stored, these formulas are more accessible for analysis than any ongoing utterances that fly by in the course of conversation (Wong Fillmore 1979). Second, formulas are real syntactic constructions, as opposed to the loose pragmatic juxtapositions children sometimes rely on early for communicative purposes (Givón 1979). Formulaic constructions could help children learn any restrictions on possible word combinations. They might also help in their acquisition of conjunctions.[6] In other words, reliance on formulas in the early stages may help children acquire syntactic constructions – the breaking down of large units (formulas) into smaller elements that, once analyzed, can be related to similar elements in other constructions.

---

[6] Adults also rely on such formulas (Bolinger 1976, 1977; Fillmore 1979).

Children's reliance on formulas is pervasive, not just in interrogatives. But this presents a problem for the study of acquisition: Their early production of adultlike constructions by no means guarantees that they have acquired those forms. They could simply be relying on as-yet unanalyzed formulas. We therefore need to exercise caution in attributing knowledge of syntactic constructions to young children. At the same time, studies like Johnson's (1981) show that, in domains where children begin with a small number of fixed formulas, they display a consistent pattern in their acquisition of the target constructions: (a) analysis proceeds in small steps; and (b) analysis is limited to small domains and is repeated all over again for the next-door domain. For example, the progression summarized for *what* is recapitulated for *where* and then for *who*, and then for each of the other *wh-* words. In *yes/no* question formulas, children may gradually extract the verb *want* (*Want this?*, *D'you want this?*) and then do the same for *see* (*See that?*, *Can I see that?*), and so on (see also Dabrowska 2000).

For both *wh-* and *yes/no* question-types, researchers have assumed that children acquiring English need to master auxiliary verbs (e.g., *be*, *do*, *can*, *will*). These verbs help mark questions as questions with inversion of the sentence subject (in boldface) and the auxiliary verb (underlined), as in *Where is **the boy** going?* Acquisition of these inverted auxiliary forms also appears to proceed gradually, one auxiliary verb form at a time. Children may begin with inverted *can* as their only inverted form in *yes/no* questions (*Can we go?*). Next, they produce the inverted copula *are* (e.g., *Are you ready?*), say, followed by auxiliary *is* (*Is he going?*), and, later still, inverted *will* (*Will it break?*) (Kuczaj & Maratsos 1983; Rowland & Pine 2000). Again, children only slowly analyze each element in early formulaic frames, and they repeat the process for each element within a domain, here for each *wh-* word and each auxiliary verb (see also Stromswold 1989).

This account of question-forms offers a more complex view of what is required for acquisition than the three stages originally documented by Klima and Bellugi (1966). There, the stages were defined by Mean Length of Utterance, as shown in Table 9.8, with the first stage generally marked by the absence of auxiliary use in early word combinations; the second by the appearance of a limited set of (negative) auxiliary forms, without inversion; and the third by the appearance of further auxiliary forms, with inversion apparently only in *yes/no* questions.[7]

While children's mean length of utterance (MLU) will reflect the increasing complexity of their utterances, as in Table 9.8, it doesn't distinguish among the different types of complexity being added and fails to distinguish formulaic utterances from utterances constructed for the occasion. As a result, length of utterance offers only a preliminary guide to the child's stage of development. To find out more, one needs to scrutinize what both adults and children are saying

---

[7] Klima and Bellugi's stages represent a compilation, for each stage, of utterances from three different children.

Table 9.8 *Increasing complexity in question-forms*

| MLU 1.75 | Fraser water? | where Ann pencil? | what(s) that? |
|---|---|---|---|
| | see hole? | where kitty? | where horse go? |
| | sit chair? | what cowboy doing? | who that? |
| MLU 2.25 | see my doggie? | where my mitten? | what book name? |
| | dat black too? | where me sleep? | what me think? |
| you want eat? | | where baby Sarah rattle? | what the dollie have? |
| you can't fix it? | | why you smiling? | why not me sleeping? |
| MLU 3.5 | does lions walk? | | can't it be a bigger truck? |
| | oh, did I caught it? | | can't you work this thing? |
| | will you help me? | | can't you get it? |
| | can I have a piece of paper? | | |
| where small trailer he should pull? | | where my spoon goed? | |
| where the other Joe will drive? | | why kitty can't stand up? | |
| why he don't know how to pretend? | | which way they should go? | |
| how that opened? | | how he can be a doctor? | |
| what I did yesterday? | | what he can ride in? | |
| Sue, what you have in your mouth? | | what did you doed? | |

Based on Klima & Bellugi 1966

and how they are saying it. Fine-grained transcription of children's early question-forms reveals, for example, that *wh-* words are often completely missing and that children rely for nearly all their questions on only a handful of question formulas. These serve children well in the beginning, and their different construals by adults, in context, are probably one factor that contributes to children's eventual analysis of different formulas (Johnson 2000; Valian & Casey 2003). By around age three, they have analyzed the *wh-* words, auxiliary verbs, and other details that allow them to freely construct the appropriate questions to elicit just the information they need.

The acquisition of *yes/no* questions has also been reevaluated, in large part in light of adult usage where auxiliary verbs and subjects are often omitted, as in "Going?", or "You going?" compared to the canonical "Are you going?" (Estigarribia 2007). When all types of adult *yes/no* questions are considered, rather than just those with subject–auxiliary inversion (canonical *yes/no* questions), it is clear that the different types must be considered in children's speech too. This requires the analysis of data that before had been ignored. The adult question-types can be ordered from simpler ("Going?") to more complex ("You going?") to the most complex ("Are you going?"). The simpler forms generally emerge first in children's *yes/no* questions, with the more complex forms emerging later. In effect, children generally "build" *yes/no* questions from right to left, first adding subjects, and then auxiliaries too (Estigarribia 2007). The variation in adult speech, then, helps children acquire the range of *yes/no* question-forms used in English. This is yet another place where adult usage appears to play a crucial role in children's acquisition of structure.

## Being negative

Children learn to say *no* very early. Their negative constructions rapidly take over from earlier gestures of rejection and add content to headshakes. In general, children have to learn how to add a negative element to negate, deny, or reject what is otherwise being expressed. The earliest words used for this purpose typically include *off, allgone, no-more*, and *byebye* (Bloom 1970). Quite early on, children pick up negative terms used alone to negate some preceding proposal (e.g., *no, nein*, or *non*), and they also learn how to negate propositions with utterance-internal negatives such as *not, nicht*, and (*ne …*) *pas*. In some languages, negative constructions are simple structurally, with the negative element always preceding the main verb. In others, the negative element has to be combined with an auxiliary or modal verb form, so those have to be acquired too before children can master the adult forms for negation.

Negative utterances containing *no* on the one hand and *not* or *don't* on the other have significantly different distributions in children's uses (Drozd 1995). Children make early use of *no* in exclamatory negations, as in (7) and (9):

(7)    NICHOLAS (2;1): *No Mommy do it* [= I don't want Mommy to do it]
                                                                    (de Villiers & de Villiers 1979:61)

(8)    MOTHER (to P cutting bologna, holding the knife upside down): Do you want
            me to cut it?
       PETER (2;2): *No Mommy cut it.*   (Bloom, CHILDES)

In rejecting his mother's proposal, Peter echoes her *cut it* but makes clear he doesn't want her to do this. Children contrast *no* in these uses with uses of internal *not* or *don't*, as in (9) and (10):

(9)    KATHRYN (2;0.14): *That not [ə] rabbits house.*

(10)   KATHRYN (2;0.14): *I don't need pants off.*   (Bloom, CHILDES)

Utterances with *no* are more likely to echo the preceding utterance while rejecting it, as in (7) and (8), while those containing *not* or *don't* are significantly less likely to repeat the preceding adult utterance, as shown in Figure 9.2. *Don't* seems more likely to appear initially as an imperative, while *not* is used in assertions. These different functions are quite consistent with contrast and would allow children to distinguish their earliest negative forms from each other, even if they don't do this on the same grounds as adult speakers (see Bloom 1991:144).

Earlier analyses had assumed that children's early uses of *no* resulted from substitution of *no* for internal *not*. Initial or final *no* was assumed to be the most

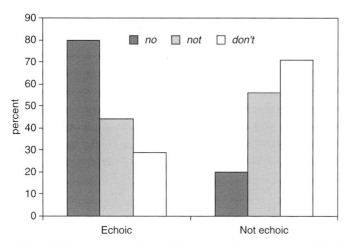

Figure 9.2 *Percentage of uses of the negative forms* no, not, *and* don't *that are echoic*

primitive negation type, the earliest stage of sentential negation (Klima & Bellugi 1966). But analyses like those by Bloom (1991) and Drozd (1995) suggest instead that children start out with two main negation types: *exclamatory negations*, marked in English by *no*, which reject the contents of the preceding utterance and are typically echoic in form; and *predicate negations* with an internal negative such as (unanalyzed) *don't* or, later on, *not*.

As the data in Table 9.8 suggest, children make use of two or three distinct negative forms by the time their average utterance length is over two morphemes. At this point, forms like *can't* or *don't* contrast in meaning with *not* (used internally but without a copula or auxiliary verb in place) and with *no*. Early uses of *can't* generally pertain to the ability to do something and may be used for inanimates as well as animates (e.g., *It can't fit here*, said of a puzzle piece, meaning 'It won't fit here'). *Don't* typically emerges first in imperatives and is then extended to nonimperative uses. At this point (MLU 2.25), children make no use of the positive counterparts to *can't* and *don't*: These negative forms have not yet been analyzed as contractions of a modal verb with the negative *not*. Notice that children make no errors on where to place internal *not*: They always put it in front of the main verb. What they appear to lack still, at MLU 3.5, is recognition that sentence-internal negation must always be accompanied by a modal or auxiliary verb. If one doesn't use a modal, an auxiliary, or the copular *be*, then one must use *do*.

By the time children produce utterances that average 3.5 morphemes in length, they have analyzed *can't* and *don't* into *can* + *not* and *do* + *not*, and now make use of several modal verbs and auxiliary *do* in both positive and negative utterances. They also use both copular and auxiliary *be* but still omit the copula in some contexts, as can be seen in the lower half of Table 9.9. In English, auxiliary *be* and copular *be*, especially in contracted form, are among the later grammatical

Table 9.9 *Emergence of sentence-internal* not *in English*

| MLU 2.25 | I can't catch you | I don't sit on Cromer coffee |
|---|---|---|
| | that not O, that blue | don't bite me yet |
| | that no fish school | don't wait for me … come in |
| | I no want envelope | |
| MLU 3.5 | Paul can't have one | that was not me |
| | this can't stick | he not taking the walls down |
| | Donna won't let go | I isn't … I not sad |
| | no, I don't have a book | this not ice cream |
| | I didn't caught it | I not hurt him |
| | you don't want some supper | I not crying |
| | don't kick my box | Paul not tired |

Based on Klima & Bellugi 1966

morphemes to be acquired (Chapter 8). In many other languages, acquisition of utterance-internal negation is no more complicated than acquisition of echoic exclamatory negation, because children do not have to master auxiliary and modal verbs first (see Volterra 1972, Antinucci & Volterra 1975 for Italian; Grimm 1973 for German).

What is still missing from some of the negative utterances in Table 9.9 are forms like *no one, nowhere, never,* and *nothing*. These are used for more specialized types of negation, as in *No one went outside* or *Nothing appealed to them*. Children also have to master *any* and its companions, for example, *anyone, anything, anywhere*. These are licensed by a negative elsewhere in the utterance or by certain negative contexts, including *yes/no* question-forms. (Consider *They didn't see anyone outside* and *Did they see anyone outside?*) And there is more: Children must eventually learn the range of so-called negative polarity items, elements that occur only in negative, but not positive, contexts, as in uses of such idioms as *lift a finger, care a fig for, bear* (meaning 'tolerate'), *hold a candle to,* and so on. These expressions require contexts that are overtly negative or implicate some form of negation.

When do children start to acquire such expressions? And how do they limit their use to negative contexts? (Why can't one say *I'll lift a finger to help him?*) In a study of children acquiring Dutch, van der Wal (1996) found that they acquire negative polarity items early. They begin with just one or two expressions (the ones used most frequently by adults to children), always in negative contexts (where the negative elements itself might consist of a headshake rather than a *niet* 'not'). This suggests they are initially unanalyzed combinations of a negative plus a polarity item, for example, *niet meer* 'not anymore' with the negative always before and adjacent to *meer*, or *hoeft niet* 'don't need to' (1;11.21) with the negative always immediately following the verb.

As Dutch children's utterances become more complex, they show they have now analyzed these forms by using *meer* with other negatives besides *niet*, as in *zie niks meer* 'see nothing anymore' (2;7.24) and using *geen* 'no' (rather than just *niet* 'not') as the negative with *hoeft*, as in *meisje hoef geen slab om* 'little-girl not-need any bib on' (2;8.11) (van der Wal 1996:59, 68, 122). She also established, through tests of comprehension and judgements of what puppets said, that children slowly extend the possible contexts of such expressions to other negatives and also add in other negative polarity forms. But this acquisition takes many years and may not be fully in place even as late as age eighteen. What is important, though, is that children link polarity items to negation from the start and are conservative about extending their uses of such items to further contexts. As a result, they appear to make few or no errors in use.

## Choosing a perspective

Speakers can mark the conceptual perspective they are taking on an entity or an event through their lexical choices (Chapter 6). But they can also mark it through the construction they opt for. For example, when the speaker focusses on the agent of an action, already known, the favored construction is likely to include a transitive causative verb, as in *The boy opened the door*. But if the speaker didn't know who the responsible agent was, but did see the resultant event, then the construction favored is more likely to be something like *The door opened* or *I saw the door open*, with no mention of an agent. In English, many verbs have the same stem in both intransitive and causative forms, such as *open*, but not all (e.g., *eat* vs. *feed*, *fall* vs. *drop*, *come* vs. *bring*). Some lack a causative form altogether and have to express the causative with a periphrastic verb (e.g., *disappear* vs. *make disappear*). The choice of a causative versus an intransitive verb form, then, can be used to represent two different perspectives on the same event.

Other verbs also allow other alternatives in how an event is represented. The speaker can take either location or theme as the entity directly affected, as in the contrast between *She sprayed paint* [theme as direct object] *on the wall* [location], versus *She sprayed the wall* [location as direct object] *with paint* [theme]. This contrast, called locative alternation, appears with other verbs, for example, *He stuffed the bag with books* versus *He stuffed books into the bag*. But many verbs do not allow such an alternation. Take *fill*, in *He filled the jug with cider*. In English, most speakers can't also say *\*He filled cider into the jug*. So *fill* only has the location-as-direct-object form. But the verb *pour* only has the theme-as-direct-object, as in *They poured water into the tub* and not *\*They poured the tub with water*.

Another choice lies in whether the agent or the theme of an event is treated as already known to the addressee. Here, the choice is marked in the *voice* of the verb – active, as in *The scouts lit the fire*, versus passive, as in *The fire was lit by the scouts*. However, use of the so-called agent *by*-phrase in the passive is relatively infrequent in adult speech,[8] so the active probably contrasts more

---

[8] According to Svartvik (1966), it occurs only about 10% of the time in passives in adult-to-adult speech.

often with a truncated passive, as in *The fire was lit*. In addition, although the passive is usually formed with the verb *be*, it can also be formed with *get*, as in *The birds got frightened*, *The car got damaged*, or *The job got finished*. When there is some adverse consequence involved, *get* is more likely to be selected, but it doesn't always carry a negative connotation.

These choices – causative versus intransitive verb forms, locative alternation verb forms, and active versus passive voice in the verb – all involve choices that mark the speaker's perspective. All three also involve choices of construction made within the clause (Levin 1993). I will take up each in turn and briefly review the evidence for children's gradual acquisition of these constructions.

## Causative/noncausative alternations

Children distinguish among event-types not only in the inflections first attached to accomplishment versus activity verbs (Bloom *et al.* 1980; Clark 1996; Shirai & Andersen 1995; see Chapter 8), but also in terms of actions that do or don't involve an agent. At around age two, children recognize, for verbs like *open* or *break*, that the transitive verb form, with agent and theme, has a causative meaning and that the intransitive one, with theme only, does not. Once children realize this, they can form novel causatives from intransitive stems like *fall* or *eat*, on analogy with *open* or *break*. To do this, they "must have recognized the causative member of a pair as implicitly containing the meaning of the noncausative member of a pair plus an additional component suggested by the term CAUSE" (Bowerman 1974:150). While this relation is usually implicit in English, languages like Turkish make it explicit by adding a causative morpheme to the intransitive verb-stem (e.g., *-dır-*, and its variants, as in *öl-* 'die' vs. *öl-dür-* 'kill/ cause-to-die'). Children can also mark the CAUSE component by relying on a periphrastic verb like English *make* or *get* to express that part of the causative verb meaning (e.g., *He made the stick break*) or French *faire* 'make, do' (e.g., *Elles font sourir les enfants* 'they-FEM-PL make-smile the children' = 'they make the children smile'). Whatever the device used to mark CAUSE, the speaker must include the agent when using the causative verb, as in the shift from the English intransitive *The door opened* to the causative *The boy opened the door*.

Children begin to express causation in the verb between two and two-and-a-half. This is evident both from their use of periphrastic verbs in causative contexts and from their (erroneous) uses of noncausative verbs as causatives. Some typical uses are given in Table 9.10. A few other verbs often used in English as if they were causative include *disappear* (e.g., *I'm gonna put the washrag in and disappear something under the washrag*, 3;7, = make disappear), *bleed* (e.g., *Did she bleed it?*, 3;6, = make bleed), and *ache* (e.g., *You ached me*, 4;1, = make ache) (Bowerman 1974, 1982a).

Early accounts of causative errors focussed on the noncausative to causative forms children produced, but children also produce causative to noncausative errors (Lord 1979; Figueira 1984; Braunwald 1995). This happens when they

Table 9.10 *Using noncausative verbs as transitive causative verbs*

(a) John (2;3): *You sad me.* [= sadden, make sad]

(b) E (2;4, screwing the nipple on her bottle): *Don't tight this 'cause I tight this.* [= tighten]

(c) D (2;2.23, holding out his hands to mother): *Jump me down.* [= make/let jump down]

(d) Kendall (2;3, after she dropped a toy on the floor): *Kendall fall that toy.* [= drop]

(e) D (2;4.21, building with blocks): *I'm going these chimneys on too, on top.* [= make go on, put on]

(f) John (2;6): *Who deaded my kitty cat?* [= kill]

(g) C (2;9, pulling bowl closer to her as she sits on counter): *I come it closer so it won't fall.* [= bring]

(h) Jennifer (3;1): *Yuck! It coughs me ... The thing coughs me ... I cough when I put it in my mouth.* [= make cough]

(i) E (2;1, holding an object in the air and wiggling it as if it were swimming): *I wanta swim that.* [= make swim]

(j) E (2;2, pulling string on bird-shaped music box): *I'm talking my birdie.* [= make talk]

(k) Benjy (2;5): *I'm dancing Jeremy Fisher.* [= make dance]

(l) C (3;1, handing mother an orange half and waiting expectantly for mother to squeeze the juice into her mouth): *Drink me. Uh ... put it in.* [= make/let drink]

(m) E (3;2, wanting mother to help her climb a pole): *Will you climb me up there and hold me?* [= make/have climb]

Based on Bowerman 1982a; Lord 1979

use a causative verb as an intransitive, with the theme or patient affected as the subject of the verb (and no mention of any agent), as in Table 9.11. Similar uses of intransitive forms as causatives, and the reverse, have been reported for Hebrew (e.g., Berman 1982), Cantonese (Cheung 1998), Portuguese (Figueira 1984), Japanese (Morikawa 1991), and Thai (Yumitani 1998) (see also Slobin 1985a, 1992, 1997).

Children's overgeneralizations about causative and intransitive verb forms, though, are asymmetric. They are more likely to turn intransitive verbs into causatives than the reverse. In one diary study of Portuguese, the two children observed used 29 intransitive verb-types as causatives, but only 4 causative types as intransitives (Figueira 1984). In English, Lord (1979) reported 71 intransitive verb-types used as causatives, versus 55 causatives used as intransitives, from two children. Lord proposed a syntactic basis for these errors and characterized them in terms of adding an agentive subject (for intransitive to causative shifts) or subtracting the agentive subject (for causative to intransitive ones). Such an account seems to assume symmetry, though, in children's willingness or ability to add or subtract arguments. In Bowerman's account, in contrast, children derive causatives from noncausative verbs by adding the

Table 9.11 *Using causatives as intransitive verbs*

---

(a) D (2;4.6, at breakfast, playing with a small bell in his spoon): *I not going to eat it. It doesn't eat. Only some food.* [= be eaten]

(b) D (2;8.11, as mother looked at flowers growing): *That flower cuts.* [= can be cut, picked]

(c) D (2;8.21, getting new diaper on, one that covered his belly button): *This one covers.*

(d) C (3;0): *Bert knocked down.* [= get knocked down]

(e) Benjy (3;3): *We have two kinds of corn: popcorn, and corn. Popcorn: it crunches. And corn doesn't crunch; its eats!* [= get/be eaten]

(f) Benjy (3;7): *I think I better put it down there so it won't lose.* [= get lost]

(g) Benjy (3;8, B and mother looking for B's sandals): *They don't seem to see. Where are they?*

(h) Benjy (3;9, looking at dial of toy gauge): *What does it read about?*

(i) Jennifer (2;9): *I can't hear it.* (puts clock to her ear) *It can hear now.*

---

Based on Bowerman 1982a; Clark, unpublished diary data; Lord 1979

semantic component CAUSE. The rarer causative-to-intransitive errors she characterized as back-formations. In the majority of cases, children chose to go from an intransitive form to a causative (Bowerman 1974, 1982a).

Is there in fact an asymmetry in children's errors here? One difficulty is that these observations come primarily from diary data collected by parents. But when one is participating in conversation, one can often miss "errors." So any asymmetry might simply reflect a failure of observation. Interestingly, the failure has a consistent direction, intransitive to causative, across languages. At the same time, even regular recordings, an hour every two to three weeks, often miss the full range of uses observable by diarists keeping a daily record.

One way to check on the apparent asymmetry is to ask children to judge correct and incorrect causatives and intransitives as appropriate or not (Hochberg 1986). For English causatives in one study, children aged 3;4 to 5;5 heard adult (correct) versus child (incorrect) utterances, such as:

(11) a.     I'm gonna make the frog jump.
     b.     I'm gonna jump the frog. [intransitive used as causative]

or, for verbs with two different stems (e.g., *fall/drop, come/bring*):

(12) a.     I'm gonna drop the rock.
     b.     I'm gonna fall the rock. [intransitive used as causative]

For intransitives, the children heard pairs of correct adult transitive verbs alongside incorrect child intransitives:

(13) a.     I'm putting on my clothes.
     b.     My clothes are putting on. [causative used as intransitive]

Table 9.12 *Percentage of incorrect choices of verb form by age*

| Age | Intransitive as transitive | | Transitive as intransitive | |
|---|---|---|---|---|
| | Same stem | Different stem | | Mean |
| 3;4–3;10 | 52 | 22 | 16 | 30 |
| 4;1–5;5 | 32 | 8 | 0 | 13 |
| Mean | 42 | 15 | 8 | 22 |

*Source*: Hochberg 1986:323. Used with permission from Cambridge University Press.

They simply had to choose which of two puppets had said something "silly" and which one said something "okay" for each pair.

The children made few errors in their choices of intransitive forms as appropriate (only 8% on average), as shown in Table 9.12. They made many more errors on intransitives used incorrectly as transitive causative verbs which they accepted as okay 42% of the time. This asymmetry favors Bowerman's semantic account over Lord's syntactic one. Children are not just adding or subtracting an argument role, but are focussing on the idea that verbs differ in causativity, as in pairs like *open/open* or *break/break*. Once they have assigned the meaning CAUSE to an intransitive verb, they then use that verb with the same syntax as other causative verbs they already know.

This is not the whole story, though. A full account of the verb-types involved needs to include both semantic and syntactic information, as proposed by Figueira (1984) in her account of causative and intransitive errors in Portuguese. Certain errors, where children make use of noncausative, transitive verbs, suggest that the degree of transitivity plays a role (Hochberg 1986): Some verbs are more transitive than others, depending on the type of agency, whether the event is complete, whether the action was intentional, and so on (Hopper & Thompson 1980). In addition, the existence of verb pairs with two different stems (e.g., *eat/feed, come/ bring*) seems to encourage earlier causative uses of the intransitive stems (e.g., *eat* and *come*). (This can be seen in the second column of Table 9.12.) Finally, it may be harder to arrive at adultlike judgements of verbs that require a periphrastic form (e.g., *make*) because there is a gap in the verb paradigm, which lacks a causative with the same stem as the intransitive verb (see further Brooks *et al.* 1999; Bowerman & Croft 2008). In summary, children use information about verb meaning, verb-type, the presence of intransitive/transitive pairs already known, and word order as they acquire causative verb uses.

Children use periphrastic causative forms within weeks of producing their first lexical causative errors (Bowerman 1974; Figueira 1984). And it has been suggested that, at first, children do not distinguish lexical from periphrastic meanings, even though lexical causatives generally mark direct causation and periphrastic ones indirect causation, often with a less conventional manner of causation (Shibatani 1976). But children as young as 2;8 associate lexical causatives in

English with conventional manner pictures (direct causation) of causal events when they are asked to match lexical and periphrastic causatives to the pictures in an array. For example, they choose a picture of someone squeezing a toothpaste tube for the lexical causative *squirts toothpaste*. And by 3;8, they reliably associate periphrastic causatives like *makes the toothpaste squirt* with an unconventional manner such as hitting a toothpaste tube with a hammer, as well (Ammon 1980, 1981).

Different languages mark causativity in the verb in different ways. Does this affect children's acquisition of causative verbs? Take the commonest periphrastic form with *make* in English and compare it to the equivalent constructions in other types of languages. In (14), one finds a Noun-Verb-Noun-Verb sequence, with the first noun marking the agent and the second one the patient affected; the first verb is causative, the second one infinitival:

(14)    The horse makes the camel run.

In Italian, the word order in the equivalent form, in (15), is Noun [agent]-Verb-Verb-Noun [patient]; again the first verb is causative and the second infinitive:

(15)    Il cavallo fa correre il cammello, 'the horse makes to-run the camel'

In Serbo-Croatian, the word order is similar to that in English, but the two nouns are marked with case endings: the first (the agent subject) is nominative and the second (the patient or object affected) accusative:

(16)    Zdrijebe tjera devu da trči, 'horse-NOM drives camel-ACC PARTICLE runs'

Lastly, in Turkish, there is also case marking of the two nouns, with the agent as nominative and the patient as accusative, and a single verb, with an added causative morpheme:

(17)    At deveyi kos**tur**sun, 'horse-NOM camel-ACC **cause**-run'

When children aged 2;0 to 4;4, learning each of these languages, were given these kinds of causative constructions to interpret, they differed considerably, depending on the language they were acquiring (Ammon & Slobin 1979), as shown in Table 9.13.

These findings show two main effects of language-type. First, children learning the two inflectional languages (Serbo-Croatian and Turkish), where the agent of the action is distinguished from the object affected by case marking, mastered causative forms earlier than children acquiring the two word-order languages (English and Italian).

Second, three of the languages can mark causativity with a periphrastic verb construction, while Turkish inserts a causative morpheme into the verb. Is the overt periphrastic verb easier to process than the causative morpheme inside the Turkish verb, or harder? The overall performance for Turkish was consistently higher than for the other three languages, which suggests that periphrastic verbs

Table 9.13 *Percentage of correct interpretations by age and language*

| Age | Language | | | | |
| | English | Italian | Serbo-Croatian | Turkish | Overall |
| --- | --- | --- | --- | --- | --- |
| 2;0–2;4 | 7 | 8 | 68 | 37 | 30 |
| 2;8–3;0 | 33 | 60 | 61 | 94 | 62 |
| 3;4–3;8 | 72 | 67 | 82 | 96 | 79 |
| 4;0–4;4 | 70 | 64 | 95 | 95 | 81 |
| Mean | 38 | 50 | 77 | 81 | |

*Source*: Ammon & Slobin 1979:9. Reprinted from *Cognition* 7, Mary Sue Ammon & Dan I. Slobin, *A cross-linguistic study of the processing of causative sentences*, 3–17, copyright 1979, with permission from Elsevier Science.

like *make* are acquired later than causative marking directly in the verb. Ammon and Slobin suggested that verb marking, standard SOV word order, and a highly regular case-marking system all combine to make the Turkish causative construction easier to acquire than the causative constructions in the other three languages. Overall, children are particularly sensitive to inflections that mark the roles of specific words (e.g., case marking on nouns, particles adjacent to verbs). They have greater difficulty with constructions that rely on word order alone to mark both semantic roles and grammatical relations. These languages require them to keep track of the whole clause in order to determine the role of each noun, instead of being able to assign roles locally, through case inflections (Ammon & Slobin 1979).

## Locative alternations

Like other languages, English has many verbs for talking about motion and location in space. Many of these focus on how the action being performed affects the entity being located (e.g., *He poured water into the jug*, where *water* is the figure [F] being located and *jug* the location or ground [G]); others focus on the ground and make that the direct object of the verb (e.g., *They filled the shelves with books*, where *shelves* is G and *books* F). Still others allow alternation between these two options, with either F or G as the direct object, as with the verbs *spray* and *stuff*, shown in (18) and (19):

(18) a.   He sprayed paint (F) on the wall (G).
     b.   He sprayed the wall (G) with paint (F).

(19) a.   He stuffed books (F) into the bag (G).
     b.   He stuffed the bag (G) with books (F).

The problem for children is how to align each candidate verb with the appropriate locative construction or pair of constructions. This turns out to be difficult, and

Table 9.14 *Locative alternation errors in figure and ground assignments*

---

(a) E (3;0): *'Cause I'm going to touch it* (F) *on your pants* (G).

(b) E (4;5): *I'm going to cover a screen* (F) *over me* (G).

(c) C (4;9): *She's gonna pinch it* (F) *on my foot* (G). [= pinch my foot/G with a toy/F]

(d) E (5;0): *Can I fill some salt* (F) *into the bear* (G)? [G = salt shaker]

(e) E (2;11): *Pour, pour, pour. Mommy I poured you* (G). [waving empty container near mother]

    Mother: You poured me (G)?

    E: *Yeah, with water* (F). [= poured water/F on you/G]

(f) E (4;11, after mother asked if she was going to finish her toast): *I don't want it because I spilled it* (G) *of orange juice* (F). [= spilled orange juice/F on it/G]

(g) E (4;1): *I didn't fill water* (F) *up to drink it; I filled it* (F) *up for the flowers to drink it.* [= filled watering can/G up with water/F]

(h) E (5;3): *Terri said if this* [= rhinestone on shirt] *were a diamond then people would be trying to rob the shirt* (F). [= trying to rob me/G of the shirt/F; or = steal the shirt/F from me/G]

(i) C (3;11): *Eva is just touching gently on the plant* (G). [= touching the plant/F]

(j) C (4;2, giving instructions to mother): *Pinch on the balloon* (G). [= pinch the balloon]

---

*Source*: Bowerman 1982b:338. Used with permission from Cambridge University Press.

children make errors in their choice of construction. After an initial period of apparently appropriate usage, they may treat some verbs as alternators, when in fact those verbs allow only one of the constructions. This results in errors like those in Table 9.14, where the positions of F and G are reversed, as in (a)–(f), or where G is omitted or is demoted to an oblique argument position, as in (g)–(j). In some cases, these errors might be attributed to momentary confusions among related verbs, such as *rob* and *steal*, or *fill* and *pour*. But the same errors occur with verbs that have no near neighbors, such as *touch*, *feel*, and *pinch*. If children are making a syntactic generalization, they limit it to just those verbs that mention agent, figure, and ground.

In making such errors, children could be overregularizing one pattern where F is the direct object of the verb, at the expense of the other, where G is the direct object. Alternatively, these errors could reflect the speakers' attempts to change the perspective on a specific event or even reliance on some default pattern consistent with the desired perspective (Braine *et al.* 1990). Bowerman suggested that earlier errors were more consistent with an overregularization account, while later ones – once children have established a fairly large repertoire of such verbs – are more likely to mark shifts in perspective. Late errors, from around age five, also coincide with when children's choices of syntactic forms in storytelling become sensitive to the speaker's perspective and build on what has already been recounted (e.g., Karmiloff-Smith 1981).

Another view of these verbs is that the choice of F versus G as direct object depends on which one is the entity affected by the action. Some verbs specify, as part of their meaning, the manner of motion affecting the content being moved. For example, *pour* specifies the manner in which the content is moved. Other verbs specify change for the container rather than the content. For example, *fill* specifies a change of state (from not-full to full) for the container. The same goes for *cover*, *top up*, or *empty*. Still other verbs specify change in both content and container, for example, *spray* and *stuff*. These are the verbs that allow alternation. Gropen and his colleagues (1991) argued that the perceived affectedness of the contents or container was critical in children's uses and interpretations of locative alternations (but see Brinkmann 1995).

When children (aged 2;6–5;11) were shown sequences of pictures that either emphasized the manner in which some content was transferred or the end state of the container involved, they showed a stronger preference for manner-based interpretations of episodes of dumping, pouring, filling, and emptying, overall, than for end-state interpretations. They identified the contents as the object affected three times more often than they did the container as affected. In a more detailed study of the verb *fill*, Gropen and his colleagues (1991) also tried to establish the extent to which 'pouring' (i.e., manner) was part of the meaning of *fill* for young children and the extent to which its meaning was just 'filling'. They found a significant increase in the number of children (aged 3;5–8;9) who were sensitive to the end state of the container for *fill* – and in the number of children who required the container to be at least three-quarters full, if not completely full, at the end of the action. With age, more children identified pouring as a better means than dripping for the action of filling. (Adults showed the same preference.) But this, of course, doesn't show that pouring is part of the meaning of *fill*, only that pouring is a better method.

Children's errors with such verbs raise a number of questions. Do they begin on them conservatively, using them only in constructions they have heard them used in by others? (This would be consistent with other early syntactic acquisitions.) When they make errors, the most widely attested one seems to be with the verb *fill*. And some dialects of English in fact treat this verb as a contents-affected verb (*fill water into*) rather than, or as well as, a container-affected one (*fill the glass with*). Finally, getting rid of errors remains an issue: Can children do it by careful observation of the conventional forms used by more expert speakers? Does the elimination of errors depend on full analysis of the verb meaning? But how does one arrive at this except by attending to those uses from others that depart from the child's own predictions? Can data from other languages cast added light on just what is involved in such acquisition?

In summary, children make errors with certain locative verbs, in part because they have to learn what the appropriate construction(s) are for each one. This requires working out whether a verb meaning contains information about manner in affecting the content, about end state in affecting the container, or both. The presence of these elements of meaning in turn determines the choices of syntactic

Table 9.15 *Errors in the forms of active/passive voice alternations*

---

(a) D (2;2.3, looking at pieces of a sandwich he'd pushed off the edge of his plate): *These fall down from me.*

(b) Julia (2;2, recounting a visit to the doctor):*I took my temperature from the doctor.*

(c) C (2;2): *I want see my bottle getting fix.* [= getting fixed]

(d) E (2;7): *If Deedee don't be careful, she might get runned over from a car.*

(e) E (3;3): *I just got pinched from these pointed stuff.*

(f) C (3;6): *Also it can be putten on your foot.*

(g) C (3;9): *They got spanken.* [= spanked]

---

Based on Clark & Carpenter 1989a; Budwig 1990

construction. At the same time, children are probably trying to use what they already know about these constructions to mark either content or container as given compared to the other, which they wish to highlight as new. This factor in discourse may be the ultimate determinant in children's choices of construction where a choice is available.

## Voice alternations

Finally, another option that can be used with certain verbs is voice in the verb. In *The boys built the fire*, the speaker begins with the given information, the agent of the action. But in *The fire was built by the boys*, the speaker begins instead with the entity affected by the action. In English, choice of verb voice involves differences in word order, in the subject of the verb, in the form of the verb, and in the assignment of the agent role to a *by*-phrase. Finally, the passive may also be selected when the speaker is unaware of the agent's identity or not interested in it (*The fire was built …*).

At what point do children contrast active and passive forms to convey these perspectives? Their early uses of a passive or a passive-like construction may precede their mastery of the passive in English (Table 9.15). In utterances like these, the children are presenting the entity affected by the action as given, in the subject slot, rather than presenting the agent as given (Budwig 1990; Clark & Carpenter 1989a, 1989b). Such choices appear from age two onwards in English and in other languages (see Demuth 1989). Voice, therefore, with its accompanying changes in word order and optional agent, is exploited quite early in conveying the speaker's perspective on an event.

In English, children can mark their utterances as passive with *be* or *get*. These two forms contrast for children: They use *get* when focussing on actions that have painful or negative outcomes and otherwise use *be* (Budwig 1990). In her analysis of all the passive forms from Bowerman's diary data for her two daughters, Budwig found that the verbs used with *be* overlapped only minimally

Table 9.16 *Passives with* be *versus* get *in Eva's speech*

| Verbs with *be* | | Verbs with *get* | |
| --- | --- | --- | --- |
| ashed | messed up | bumped | stinked up |
| bandaided | picked/up | burned | striked |
| blowden up | pictured on | buried up | untucked |
| bushed up | played with | drowned | **usened** |
| called | putted on | **eaten/aten** | washed up |
| changed | readen to | fastened | |
| cooled | scrunched | floated | |
| cut bald | **splashed** | gone out | |
| descripted | stepped on | hurt | |
| dried/up | sticked on | kill | |
| **eaten/up** | throwed up/off | lightninged | |
| fired | throwned away | losed | |
| glued | tooken away/out/down | pinched | |
| goened in | **used/up** | pricked | |
| ground | voted | sent (to jail) | |
| hided | whipped toppinged | **splashed up** | |
| invaded | written | staled | |

*Source*: Budwig 1990:1235. Used with permission from Cambridge University Press.

with those used with *get*: Eva produced passive forms with 53 different verbs – 34 with *be* and 22 with *get*, and only 3 of these appeared with both auxiliary verbs (see boldface entries in Table 9.16). Christy produced passives with 50 different verbs – 35 with *be* and 22 with *get*. Out of the 50 verbs, only 7 appeared with both auxiliary verbs. Overall, 65% of the children's passives with *get* were used for events with negative consequences, while 74% of their *be* passives were used for neutral events (Budwig 1990).

Most other studies of passives have focussed on form rather than on function. For example, elicitation of passives in response to pictures that highlight one participant suggests that younger children rely more on truncated passives than older ones do (Horgan 1978). Another restriction on passivization may reside in the semantics of the verbs: First, adults talking to young children use passives only with certain verbs. Second, children appear to understand passives better with action verbs with a volitional agent (e.g., *find*, *hold*) than with mental verbs for internal states (e.g., *forget*, *hear*) (Maratsos *et al.* 1985). Maratsos and his colleagues proposed that children learn the passive first for verbs with high transitivity (i.e., with an agent, a patient affected by the action, and an action that produces a change of state) and only later for other verb types. An alternative view is that children first learn the passive for canonically transitive events (those with an agent, action, and patient affected [see Slobin 1981]), and then, on a one-by-one basis, add other verbs that license the passive (see Pinker, Lebeaux, & Frost 1987). Both these accounts emphasize the form of the passive and the verbs it can be used with, rather than the functions it might serve in conversation. Finally, case marking may also facilitate the acquisition of active over passive forms, but although children acquiring German have good control of nominative (subject) vs. accusative (object) case marking before age three, this does not lead to any earlier mastery of passives than in children learning word-order marked languages (Wittek & Tomasello 2005a; Abbot-Smith & Behrens 2006).

Children can make use of alternative word orders for talking about the entity affected rather than the agent from age two to two-and-a-half onwards. Moreover, analysis of children's narratives shows that they make use of voice in keeping to continuity of topic, as well as in presenting events from different points of view, from as young as 3;6 (Slobin 1994). But they take time in English to master the auxiliary verb required by the passive, the marking of the agent with *by* (often using *from* rather than *by* at first [Clark & Carpenter 1989a]), and the full semantics of those verbs that do or do not allow the passive. As a result, they make errors in comprehension, at times relying on what they know from world knowledge rather than from an interpretation of particular structures (e.g., Strohner & Nelson 1974). They also make numerous errors in the forms they need to present events to their addressees in a manner consistent with whatever has already been said.

## Summary

In this chapter, we have explored the ways in which children add complex information within the clause. In addition to the modulations added as they acquire inflections and other grammatical morphemes (Chapter 8), they acquire the conventional means for marking utterances as questions and negatives. They also work on how to map such argument roles as agent, location, or instrument onto grammatical relations like subject, direct object, and indirect or oblique object. Different mappings allow them to present different perspectives on the same event. But verbs are often limited in the options they allow, so children need to learn the possibilities for each verb – which constructions are licensed and whether alternations in causativity, location, or voice can be used as well.

# 10    Combining clauses: More complex constructions

Speakers can add complexity in another way, by combining two or more clauses into a single utterance. This allows for linking clauses through coordination (where neither clause is syntactically dependent on the other) or through subordination. In subordinate constructions, one clause (the subordinate clause) is embedded in the matrix or main clause. This embedding can take one of two main forms. In the first, the embedded clause fills one of the grammatical roles in the matrix clause and acts as the subject or object, for instance, of the matrix verb (e.g., *That Tim arrived early* shocked them, Nan invited them *to go skiing*, Bill thought *that they had already eaten*). This is a type of complementation. In the second, the embedded clause modifies one of the constituents of the matrix clause. It can modify a noun phrase, for instance with a relative clause (e.g., *The house that was covered with ivy* stood back from the street*), or modify a verb phrase with a temporal clause (e.g., *Kate opened the door *when she heard the cat outside*). These modifications typically allow for more elaborate identifications of referents in conversation and for identifications of events as related in time (sequential or simultaneous, for instance), as related by cause and effect, or as related through contingency.

All these devices allow speakers to convey more complex information in a single utterance and to produce coherent sequences of utterances when, for instance, recounting an adventure, telling a joke, or explaining how a toy came to be broken. To get to this point, children must learn how to talk about the causal and temporal relations that can connect events. They must also learn how to structure information and decide what belongs in a main clause versus a subordinate clause and what should be said first versus later. How speakers package information affects how their addressees interpret what is said. Notice the different meanings conveyed by the following utterances:

> Tom threw the stick before the dog ran away.
> After Tom threw the stick, the dog ran away.
> Tom threw the stick and the dog ran away.

Part of learning more complex forms and how to use them involves learning how to package the information to be conveyed.

Why use more complex forms like this? There appear to be at least three factors at work here in development. First, access to a larger range of forms allows for more options in the *flow of information*. It lets speakers mark different kinds of information as given and in particular allows speakers to characterize information about event-types via noun phrases (e.g., *the circus, the lunch meeting*), noun phrases modified with prepositional phrases or relative clauses (e.g., *the circus in December, the lunch that the teachers went to*), or whole clauses (e.g., *After the circus arrived in December*, or *Because Justin wanted to play outside*). Second, the use of more complex forms allows for the linguistic expression of more complex events and relations: Speakers can talk about specificity, time, cause, and contingency, for example, by using the relevant conjunctions (e.g., *who, that; after, until; because; if*) to link the descriptions of the events being talked about. And third, mastery of complex linguistic forms allows speakers to talk about more complex events with an increasingly subtle use of information flow for a larger range of purposes. They can use these options in telling jokes, giving stage directions in play, arguing for their point of view, persuading people to do things, and telling stories. In each case, knowing the more complex linguistic forms as well as simpler ones adds to the range speakers can call on to present coherent, structured accounts of events, alongside descriptions of perceptions, feelings, and attitudes.

In this chapter, I focus on how children combine clauses, from their first word combinations onwards. I look in some detail at the course of acquisition for coordinate, complement, relative, temporal, causal, and conditional constructions. For each construction-type, children must learn how to combine two or more clauses into a single construction to express a specific meaning. The acquisition of these constructions is motivated by their functions, and so, for each one, children must learn the appropriate forms to use.

## Combining propositions: The first stages

Even in two-word combinations, children may actually be combining two distinct propositions or protoclauses (Chapter 7). As children's utterances become more complex, their references to two or more events within a single utterance become more clearly discernible, even when they do not yet use adult constructions and omit all connectives for linking one clause to another. Consider the following utterances from D around age two:

(1) a.     D (1;11.11, as father tested the car door to see if the child lock was on): *Car driving. Don't open. Don't open. Don't open.*

    b.     D (1;11.23, playing with toy car, pushing it and letting it run; as it slowed down):
        [ə] *race-car stopping,* [ə] *red light.*
        *I(t) waiting* [ə] *red light.*

    c.     D (2;1.11, watching his parents at breakfast): *I get bigger I have tea.*

On each occasion, he juxtaposes two events to indicate they are connected, but the precise connection can only be inferred in context. In (1a) and (1b), the connection is causal; and in (1c), it is temporal. One of the next steps is to add the relevant connectives, often at first in the form of a schwa-vowel as place-holder (see Chapter 8). By age two-and-a-half to three, children begin to produce *and*, *because*, *when*, and *if* to link one clause to another.

## Coordination and subordination

Speakers can combine clauses either through coordination, where each clause can carry the same weight, or through subordination, where one clause (subordinate) depends on the other (main). Speakers' choices of coordinate versus subordinate constructions depend on a number of factors – for instance, the kinds of events being talked about, the genre of speech (narrative, persuasive, instructive), the status of the addressee, and the formality of the occasion.

The primary markers of relations between clauses are conjunctions. The first to appear in children's production is *and*. But how do children interpret different forms of coordination – coordinations with transitive or intransitive verb phrases (e.g., *He picked up the stick and threw it*, *He shouted and cried*), with subject or object noun phrases (*The sheep and the cows were grazing*, *They chased the rabbit and the hen*), or with "gapped" verbs (*Duncan ate the peas and Helen the broccoli*), for example? Do they produce different kinds of coordination for different event-types? Ardery (1979, 1980) argued, from her findings, that children's comprehension of coordinate structures is best considered in terms of surface constraints and processing strategies. As Table 10.1 shows, children

Table 10.1 *Order of acquisition: Understanding coordinate construction-types*

| Order of acquisition | Example coordinate form | % correct | Mean age |
| --- | --- | --- | --- |
| Intransitive verb | The frog ran and fell. | 100 | 3;11 |
| Object noun phrase | The giraffe kissed the tiger and the cat. | 99 | 4;0 |
| Sentential intransitive | The dog ran and the cat fell. | 97 | 4;3 |
| Verb phrase | The dog kissed the horse and pushed the tiger. | 95 | 4;5 |
| Subject noun phrase | The tiger and the turtle pushed the dog. | 75 | 4;9 |
| Sentential transitive | The turtle pushed the dog and the cat kissed the horse. | 67 | 5;0 |
| Gapped verb (+ particle) | The horse bumped into the cat and the dog into the turtle. | 42 | 5;0 |
| Transitive verb | The turtle kissed and pushed the frog. | 24 | 5;2 |
| Gapped verb (- particle) | The giraffe kissed the horse and the frog the cat. | 10 | 5;7 |
| Gapped object | The cat kissed and the turtle pushed the dog. | 4 | 5;9 |

*Source*: Ardery 1980:313–314. Used with permission from Cambridge University Press.

aged two-and-a-half to six show systematic comprehension of some coordinate constructions before others.

When children made mistakes in comprehension, they did so most often with sentential transitive coordinations. They transposed the noun phrases, acting out an event with the wrong agent, for example, or they omitted one or other whole conjunct. These errors are probably better attributed to their difficulty in remembering the full content of the coordinate construction than to difficulty with the coordinate construction itself. In gapped-verb coordinations, for instance, children often omitted the content of the second of two conjuncts; they never omitted the first. And they sometimes treated both the subject and object nominals of the second conjunct as additional objects of the first verb. Ardery observed similar errors with other coordinations. But whether the coordination involved backward or forward deletion appeared to have no discernible effect on their comprehension.

The same children were asked to describe a series of acted-out events (with the experimenter using the comprehension events as "tacit directions"). Ardery scored children for the appropriateness of their lexical choices for objects and actions, and, when they used a coordinate construction, for the type of coordinate structure elicited. The coordinate type children produced most frequently (and correctly) was a conjunction of two transitive-verb clauses (80% of all coordinate forms elicited) (see also Lust 1977). They also produced coordinations of subject noun phrases but relied on a plural pronoun *they* in place of two conjoined NPs 24% of the time. Their transitive-verb coordinations were rare (4%), and they preferred by far to produce verb phrase coordinations (69%). Finally, they produced no gapped-verb or gapped-object coordinations, only combinations with two full clauses (see also Ardery 1979).

Overall, the coordinate structures best understood were the ones the children seemed able to produce most easily. Those they found harder to understand were replaced in production by structurally simpler forms. Ardery proposed three factors to account for these findings: (a) *verb primacy* – the verb serves as the primary unit of clausal structure; (b) *linear sequencing* – declarative sentences in English should consist of an initial subject immediately followed by a verb that, when transitive, is immediately followed by an object; and (c) a *coordination strategy* – any sequence of two or more phrases joined by *and* should be interpreted as a single larger constituent with the same function as the individual phrases.

*And* serves a variety of functions for two- and three-year-olds. Clauses linked by *and* may be additive, temporal, causal, or even adversative in meaning (see Bloom *et al.* 1980; Clark 1970, 1973c). The conjunction itself merely links two clauses or constituents; the larger context then licenses pragmatic inferences about the precise connection between the descriptions of the events so linked. (Compare *He fell down the steps and broke his arm* with *He broke his arm and fell down the steps.*) Coordinate *and* is generally the first conjunction children produce. Next to appear are relative clauses marked by *that* or *who*, typically used for specifying the referent being talked about. Next comes temporal *when*, followed shortly by

Table 10.2 *Early connectives and semantic relations in child speech*

| Mean age of emergence | Connective and its meaning in context |
| --- | --- |
| 2;2 | **and**: additive, temporal, causal |
| 2;7 | **and then**: temporal |
| 2;8 | **when**: contingent (epistemic) |
| 2;8 | **because**: causal |
| 2;8 | **what**: notice |
| 2;9 | **so**: causal |
| 2;9 | **then**: temporal |
| 2;10.15 | **if**: contingent (epistemic) |
| 2;11 | **but**: adversative |
| 3;0 | **that**: referent specification |

*Note*: These meanings were productive for at least three of the four children observed.
*Source*: Bloom, Lahey, Hood, Lifter, & Fiess 1980:249. Used with permission from Cambridge University Press.

*because* (*'cause*) and *if*. The emergence of connectives in the speech of four children observed by Bloom and her colleagues, together with the meanings these connectives expressed in context, is summarized in Table 10.2.

Up to age 2;9, the connectives children produced most frequently were *and*, *because*, *what*, *when*, and *so*. Somewhat less frequent were *and then*, *if*, *that*, and *where*. When children produced a connective, it added cohesion to the child's own speech. Such cohesion was observed for two of the connective meanings marked by *and* (additive and temporal), used for specifying the referent and for complementation, as shown in (2) (Bloom *et al*. 1980:244–245):

(2) a.  ERIC (2;5,21, going towards disks): *Get them **cause I** want it*. [causal]
    b.  GIA (2;10,15, using a toy telephone)
        MOTHER:  Who did you call?
        GIA: *The man **who** fixes the door*. [referent specification]
    c.  PETER (3;2, telling about a friend who hurt her foot): *She put a band-aid on her shoe **and** it maked it feel better*. [causal]

When the two parts of a semantic relation were distributed across two different speakers, though, the cohesion linked the child's utterance to an adult utterance, as in (3):

(3)     ADULT: maybe he'll ride the horse.
        CHILD: *yeah, **when** he comes in*.

Only two of the relations children expressed involved adult–child cohesion more than 20% of the time, namely causal and adversative relations (Bloom *et al*. 1980).

To look more closely at the forms children use to relate one clause to another, I start by taking a more detailed look at relative clauses.

## Relative clause constructions and referent specification

Children begin to produce relative clauses at around age two. Typical examples from one child are shown in Table 10.3. The function of these clauses was to *specify* the entity referred to – whether it was a particular building, doll, place, or person. That is, from the earliest uses on, this child used relative clauses to restrict the reference he was making. But children's early relative clauses typically lack relativizers, the elements introducing the relative clause itself. Initially, the specifying information is simply adjoined to the relevant noun phrase, usually in final position in the utterance. Not until several months after production of his first relative clause did D produce a relative in medial position, as in example (l) in Table 10.3.

The placement of early relative clauses attached to the last noun phrase in the clause fits with Slobin's (1973) observation that young children generally seem to avoid interrupting linguistic units. Relative clauses are produced at first only in utterance-final position and are attached, typically, to the object noun phrase (rather than the subject) of the main clause. This observation is supported both in children's spontaneous speech, as in Table 10.3, and by children's imitations of relative clause constructions (Slobin & Welsh 1973). Table 10.4 gives some examples of imitations from Echo, aged 2;2. A willing imitator, she "unpacked"

Table 10.3 *Typical relative clauses in D's speech*

(a) D (1;11.22, showing off a cookie he'd been given): *Look I got!*
(b) D (2;0.0): *I see [ə] building Eve go.*
(c) D (2;0.1, picking up his doll): *Here [ə] doll Shelli give Damon.*
(d) D (2;0.6, reading Jersey Zoo book, page with a map): *That [ə] map gorilla live.*
(e) D (2;0.9): *Herb work [ə] big building have [ə] elevator 'n it.*
(f) D (2;0.14, looking at a picture in a book): *That [ə] birdhouse [ə] bird lives.*
(g) D (2;0.9, after discussion of his birthday a month earlier, but no mention of Shelli): *Where Shelli gave [ə] doll [ə] Damon?*
(h) D (2;1.30, after talking about the dark, D brought up something he'd seen the evening before): *I see swimming-pool have lights on.*
(i) D (2;2.5, after deciding he'd heard a truck, not a car, outside): *I go outside see [ə] truck may have dirt in it.*
(j) D (2;2.16, looking for his thimble that he'd mislaid)
    Mother: Where did you have your thimble?
    D: *I leave it over there where I eat supper.*
(k) D (2;4.19, of a toy): *I'm going to show you where Mr. Lion is.*
(l) D (2;5.16, touching a wet spot on the front of the newspaper): *That paper what Eve got fell into a tiny puddle.*

Note: The schwa, [ə], represents the indeterminate vowel D used as a filler at this stage for various grammatical morphemes. He later replaced it by a form of the determiner.
*Source*: Clark, unpublished diary data

Table 10.4 *Some relative clauses imitated by Echo, aged 2;2*

| Adult model | Echo's version |
|---|---|
| Mozart who cried came to my party. | *Mozart came to my party.* |
| | ***Mozart cried*** *and he came to my party.* |
| The owl *who eats candy* runs fast. | ***Owl eat a candy*** *and he run fast.* |
| The man *who I saw yesterday* got wet. | ***I saw the man*** *and he got wet.* |
| The man *who I saw yesterday* runs fast. | ***I saw the man*** *and he run fast.* |

Based on Slobin & Welsh 1973

sentences with medial relative clauses into their two clausal constituents, which she then repeated as coordinate constructions. Her imitations reveal that she typically interpreted the content of subject relative clauses appropriately, regardless of whether the main clause subject functioned as the subject or as the direct object within the relative clause.

Echo managed to repeat the content appropriately as long as the relative clauses she heard contained relativizers like *who* or *that*. But when she heard a relative clause like the one in *The boy the book hit was crying*, she had great difficulty in repeating it. (This one she reproduced as *boy the crying*.) That is, when she didn't hear a relativizer, she appeared not to analyze the relative clause as such and had great difficulty interpreting the target utterance at all. Further studies have shown that overt marking of relative clauses with *that*, *who*, *which*, or *what* facilitates children's comprehension (Brown 1971). In addition, relative clauses appear easier to understand when the subject of the main clause is also the subject of the relative clause, as in *The dog that chased me crossed the road*, where *the dog* is the subject of both clauses. They are also easier to understand when the relative clause is attached to the object (or final) noun phrase of the main clause, as in *The dog crossed the road that goes uphill*. But relative clauses may be harder to understand when they interrupt the main clause, as in *The dog that we stroked ran away*, or when the object of the main clause is also the object of the relative clause, as in *The dog ran to the tree that the cat was in* (for English, see Sheldon 1974; for French, Cohen-Bacri 1978; for Japanese, Hakuta 1981).

In English, relative clauses can be marked by *who*, *which*, *that*, or, in some cases, by no relativizer at all; in other languages, relative clauses must be marked with a relativizer. Regardless of language type, children may on occasion use the wrong relativizer. In French, for example, children tend to overuse *que* as a relativizer in place of both *que* 'who' (object-relative) and *qui* 'who' (subject-relative) (Bouvier & Platone 1976). Or they may overuse *où* 'where' for both 'where' and 'who'. At the same time, children produce relative clauses in French, as in English, to specify the referent, as in the examples in (4) from five-year-olds who had to distinguish two otherwise identical objects:

(4) a.  *la voiture que le monsieur arrête* 'the car that the man is stopping'
    b.  *\*la voiture que le monsieur met une roue* 'the car that the man is putting a wheel'
        (for adult: la voiture à laquelle le monsieur met une roue 'the car on which the man
        puts a wheel')
    c.  *le camion où on met d'l'essence* 'the truck where someone's putting in gas'
    d.  *\*la voiture où l'gendarme l'arrête* 'the car where the-policeman it-stops' (for
        adult: la voiture que le gendarme arrête 'the car that the policeman stops')

These French-speaking children had clearly grasped the function of the relative
clause construction for identifying referents through features like perceptual
properties, historical facts, or current location. But they still hadn't fully mastered
the different relativizers – *qui*, *que*, *où*, *quand*, etc.

In a rather similar task in English, Tager-Flusberg (1982) varied the event-
types in terms of the number of participants (two vs. three) and the role filled by
each one (subject/agent, direct object/patient, indirect object/beneficiary). For
each scene, there were two almost identical characters or objects on stage, but
only one of each pair participated in an event. Tager-Flusberg asked three-, four-,
and five-year-olds to describe each enacted scene to someone who had looked at
the objects on stage and then put on a blindfold. To allow this person to know
which of each pair had participated, children had to include the relevant information in their descriptions for scenarios like those in (5), where the expected role of
the target referent, underlined, is indicated in parentheses:

(5) a.  girl with pail + girl alone; girl with pail kisses dog (agent)
    b.  clown in wagon + clown alone; girl gives clown in the wagon to bear (patient)
    c.  boy standing + boy sitting; elephant gives clown to the boy standing (beneficiary)

Children produced several different forms in specifying the target referents,
including adjectives (e.g., *the yellow bear*, for the bear wearing a yellow ribbon),
prepositional phrases (e.g., *the girl with the pail*, *the boy on the cow*), coordinate
clauses (e.g., *the girl is holding the pail and she kissed the dog*), and relative
clauses. The percentage of each response-type, by age, is shown in Table 10.5.

Table 10.5 *Response-types by age in referent specification*

| Response categories | 3;4 | 4;7 | 5;7 |
|---|---|---|---|
| Prepositional phrases | 71 | 42 | 22 |
| Adjectives | 0 | 12 | 11 |
| Coordinations | 14 | 23 | 18 |
| Relative clauses with relativizer | 14 | 19 | 46 |
| without relativizer | 0 | 4 | 3 |

*Source*: Tager-Flusberg 1982:110. Used with permission from the
Department of Linguistics, Stanford University.

Three-year-olds produced few relative clauses; in fact, all came from just two of twelve children. Both three- and four-year-olds favored prepositional phrases, but by age five, children were more likely to use relative clauses for referent specification.

Comparisons of two-participant scene descriptions showed that children produced relative clauses equally for agents and patients. With the more complex, three-participant, scenes, when agent, patient, and beneficiary were compared, three-year-olds produced no relative clauses. Four- and five-year-olds did produce relative clauses but were more likely to do so for specifying the beneficiary than the agent or patient. These relative clauses were always in utterance-final position since they followed the noun phrase for the beneficiary (the indirect object).

Finally, the typology of the language being learnt also affects the acquisition of relative clauses. In languages where the phrase to be modified occurs before the modifying element (here, the relative clause construction), children appear to acquire such structures considerably earlier than they do in languages where it appears *after* the modifying element. As a result, children acquiring languages like English or French master relative clauses earlier than children acquiring Turkish or Japanese (Aksu-Koç & Slobin 1985; Hakuta 1981).

In summary, in acquiring relative clauses, children must identify both function (specification of the referent) and form, and learn how to interpret and use this type of modification in a range of different syntactic positions. This appears to be simpler in some language-types than others and so appears to become available for use in the specification of referents at an earlier age for some languages than others.

## Complement constructions and attitudes

Complement constructions in English consist of finite clauses (i.e., with an inflected verb) or nonfinite clauses (with an infinitive verb) embedded in one of the argument slots of the main verb, as in *I thought that he would be late* (with a finite, tensed verb in the complement) or *I wanted them to clean up their rooms* (with a nonfinite, infinitival verb in the complement). Both these complement-types allow the clause describing one event to be embedded as part of another event, represented by the main-clause verb. Each complement-type occurs only with certain main verbs, so lexical specificity plays a role in clause combinations with complement constructions (see also Chapter 9). I begin by considering some of the findings for finite complement constructions and then turn to the acquisition of some nonfinite complement forms.

One way to express belief or commitment to a claim or statement in English is to make it the complement of a main clause verb like *know* or *see*, as in *I know (that) X* or *I see (that) Y*. But such complements typically lack the complementizer *that* in children's speech (e.g., Bloom *et al.* 1989), as in the child utterances in (6) with main verbs *think, know, bet*, and *mean*:

Table 10.6 *Forms of parenthetical verbs in child speech*

| Verbs | 1-person | 2-person | 3-person | Lexical noun | Total |
|---|---|---|---|---|---|
| guess | 36 | – | – | – | 36 |
| bet | 36 | – | – | – | 36 |
| mean | 13 | 12 | – | – | 25 |
| know | 30 | 47 | 5 | 3 | 85 |
| think | 315 | 50 | 5 | 1 | 371 |
| Total | 430 (78%) | 109 (20%) | 10 (2%) | 4 (0.7%) | 553 |
| wish | 30 | – | 1 | – | 31 |
| hope | 15 | 2 | – | – | 17 |
| Total | 45 (96%) | 2 (4%) | 1 (2%) | – | 48 |

*Source*: Diessel & Tomasello 2000. Used with permission from the Berkeley Linguistics Society.

(6) a.     SARAH (3;2): *And I think <pause> we need dishes.*
    b.     SARAH (3;2): *I know he sit right here.*
    c.     ADAM (4;6): *I bet I could play it.*
    d.     ADAM (3;9): *Down <pause> I mean <pause> I have to do all <pause> of this.*

Analysis of all the potential *that*-complements produced, marked either by *that* or zero, in one longitudinal study of six children, shows that they used *that* as a complementizer in only fourteen of 1,224 instances (1.2%) (Diessel & Tomasello 2000). So are these constructions really complement constructions, with one clause embedded in another, or something else? In 98% of all their utterances containing *guess*, *bet*, *mean*, *know*, or *think* as the apparent main verb, these children nearly always produced those verbs only in first- (78%) or second-person (20%) form, and in the present tense. This strongly suggests that the verbs are actually being used as parenthetical verbs to express the speaker's attitude to the content of the adjoined clause. The children also produced the verbs *wish* and *hope* almost entirely with first-person present form (96%) and used them too to convey their attitude about the content of the rest of the utterance. The overall distribution of each form of these verbs in the children's speech is shown in Table 10.6.

Effectively, these verbs are being used like evidential markers: They reflect the speaker's attitude, or commitment, to the content of the adjoined clause (see further Aksu-Koç 1988; Aksu-Koç & Alıcı 2000). At the same time, children pick up just one or two of these attitude verbs at first and only later add others (Diessel & Tomasello 2000). Even at four-and-a-half to five, they produced few or no complements introduced by *that*. Verbs like *think*, *know*, and *bet* or *guess*, then, are being used to add some shade of meaning – an allusion to the speaker's attitude – to the adjoined clause.

Why would children begin by using complement-taking verbs as parentheticals or discourse markers rather than as true complement constructions? Maybe because this is also what they hear from their parents. In over 4,000 examples,

Table 10.7 *Stages in the acquisition of* to *complements*

| I. | Verbs used without any *to* | |
|---|---|---|
| | want: | *want the man stand up* |
| | | *I want open it* |
| | | *wanna go playground* |
| II. | Verbs with [ə] | |
| | want: | *she wants [ə] get it* |
| | have (oblig): | *he has [ə] go home* |
| III. | Verbs with *to* | |
| | want: | *want me to do it?* |
| | wait: | *I wait for you to fix it* |
| | need: | *need something to eat* |
| | show how: | *I'll show you how to work it* |

Based on Bloom, Tackeff, & Lahey 1984

parents produced these verbs 97% of the time with no *that* marking the following clause. The main verbs that can take *that* complements are therefore readily construable as parentheticals rather than as main verbs for embedded complements. If the zero-marked forms differ in meaning from those with a *that* complementizer, children are simply not hearing the complement forms yet, so it shouldn't be surprising that they don't produce them either.[1] While different matrix verbs in adult speech differ in meaning (compare *know*, *think*, *guess*, *bet*), it is not clear at this point just when children arrive at the full adult meanings of these verbs, whether used as parentheticals or as complement-takers (see also Thompson 2002). What is clear, though, is that children acquire these verbs one by one, and their acquisition of the parenthetical use comes first. The complement construction comes later and is associated with each particular verb in turn.

Lexical specificity can also be seen in children's acquisition of nonfinite *to* complements in English, for example, *I want to go out*. This complement type appears with several subgroups of verbs in English, including verbs of *intention* (e.g., *want to*, *be going to* [future], *have to* [obligation]), verbs of *inception* (e.g., *try to*, *be ready to*, *need to*), verbs of *invitation* (e.g., *like to*, *be supposed to*), verbs of *instruction* (e.g., *show how to*, *know where to*, *ask to*), and certain verbs of *negation* (e.g., *forget to*, *used to*, *not nice to*).

Children acquiring English at first produce *to* complements only after the verb *want*, as can be seen for Stage I in Table 10.7. Bloom, Hood, and Lightbown (1974) followed the production of *to* complements in the speech of four children from 1;7 to 3;0. Over the course of several months, as the children begin to mark the place of the *to* first with a schwa, a couple of them added one further verb (the *have* of obligation), and, some months later, all four

---

[1] Bolinger (1972) argued that finite complements with zero versus *that* differ in meaning (see also Dor 1996).

children used at least two verbs followed by a *to* complement. In short, their main use of the *to* complement for several months involved just one verb, *want*. They then added additional verbs with this complement construction one by one over many months.

Children also have to learn about certain exceptions in verbs with *to* complements. If one compares *ask* or *tell* with *promise*, it is clear that *promise* is the only verb where it is the speaker who is under an obligation to carry out any action mentioned:

(7) a.    Jan promised Ed to shovel the driveway. [expected: Jan shovels it]
    b.    Jan asked/told Ed to shovel the driveway. [expected: Ed shovels it]

For other verbs of communication, the subject of the main verb is *not* the subject of the verb in the complement. But for *promise*, the subjects of the matrix verb and the verb in the complement are the same. To be able to assign roles appropriately in their interpretation of *to* complements, children have to learn the meaning of each verb. For an exception like *promise*, children take several years to acquire the relevant meaning. They rarely interpret it correctly before age eight or nine (see Chomsky 1969; Kessel 1970).

In summary, children have to learn which verbs can take *that* and *to* complement constructions, the meanings of those verbs, and the relation between their meanings and the construal of the complement clause. Acquisition of these constructions proceeds verb by verb, and mastering the adult meanings of some of the matrix verbs takes many years.

## Temporal constructions and events in time

When people talk about events, they can place them on a time line and talk about their sequential organization, their simultaneity, or their overlap. They can also take different points of view, placing themselves – as speakers – at some particular point in time and then presenting other events in relation to this point or to each other. The speakers' choices determine which conjunction to use. The focus here is on adverbial clauses introduced by a temporal conjunction.

When children first talk about more than one event and link them in time, they simply juxtapose them, as shown in Table 10.8. While the relation between the two events is a temporal one, the two events may co-occur, as in (a) and (c), or be sequential, as in (b) and (d). The intended relation becomes easier to interpret once children use conjunctions like *when*, *before*, or *after*. But early uses of these conjunctions are sometimes hard to interpret because children haven't yet worked out exactly what they mean.

As children describe events, they also attend to the flow of information. They generally describe the event already known first (the given information) and then introduce the new event in second place. In describing *sequences* of events, they (like adults) prefer to present them in the order in which they occurred. Their order

Table 10.8 *Early temporal clauses in D's speech*

---

(a) D (1;11.16, alluding to the morning before when his father had gone
    running very early): *Damon sad Herb go* [ə] *walk, say bye-bye.*
(b) D (2;0.18, to father who had just been picked up in the car): *I get out Eve stops.*
(c) D (2;1.11): *I get bigger, I have tea.*
(d) D (2;1.23, sitting in his car-seat): *I get out!*
    Mother: Not yet!
    D: *Get home, get out.*
    Mother: Yes. Then you'll get out.
(e) D (2;2.19, fantasizing): *You get a tiny baby, and I get bigger, I carry you*
    *back home.*
(f) D (2;4.26, at breakfast, to father): *The toast make a noise when you put butter on.*
(g) D (2;5.3, as he was being put down for a nap): *When you close the door, then*
    *I can kick all my blankets off.*
(h) D (2;5.17, shaking a rattle mother had bought as a present): *When I was a*
    *little baby, I used* [ə] *do that. And then I drop it down.*
(i) D (2;6.18, after putting the book Henny-Penny on the table): *Once I get up,*
    *I'm going to show you Foxy Loxy an'* [ə] *crown.*
(j) D (2;6.20, picking up a stick he used for drumming): *This makes my knuckle*
    *don't hurt when I run.*
(k) D (2;6.22): *I going* [ə] *bring this pile of books to the table, after I aten my*
    *supper, then I can read them.*
(l) D (2;6.27): *You wear gloves when it's snowy-time.*

---

*Source*: Clark, unpublished diary data

of mention typically follows the order of occurrence, except where this conflicts
with the flow of given and new.

By age three, children have begun to produce temporal descriptions with *when*
to mark both co-occurrence (8a–8b) and sequence (8c–8d) (Clark 1970):

(8) a.　　I was crying when my mummy goed away. [= 'at the time']
    b.　　*When I was a baby, I got washed in a basin.*
    c.　　*I'm coming up when Nicola's jumped.* [= 'after']
    d.　　*I'll pick it up when I've made this.* [= 'after', of a book on the floor]

Many of their spontaneous uses of *before* and *after* appear in possibly formulaic
descriptions of common routines (putting on clothes, e.g., socks before shoes;
getting up, e.g., dressing before breakfast, and so on). As a result, it is often
unclear which conjunctions children really understand and use appropriately.

One way to find out is to compare how children interpret conjunctions in
unfamiliar instructions with how they themselves describe events they have
watched. When children aged three to five are asked to act out events after hearing
a description like "The boy patted the dog before he kicked the stone," they
respond very consistently. Where the order of mention corresponds to the actual
order of the events, as here, children of all ages acted out the two events in the

Table 10.9 *Three-year-old children rely on order of mention*

| Order of mention | Order acted out (%) | Order of occurrence |
| --- | --- | --- |
| Event 1 **before** Event 2 | Event 1, Event 2 (96) | Event 1, Event 2 |
| Event 2 **after** Event 1 | Event 2, Event 1 (83) | Event 1, Event 2 |
| **Before** Event 2, Event 1 | Event 2, Event 1 (80) | Event 1, Event 2 |
| **After** Event 1, Event 2 | Event 1, Event 2 (90) | Event 1, Event 2 |

Based on Clark 1971

correct order. But when the same children heard "The girl jumped the fence after she rode the horse," the younger ones treated the first event mentioned as the first to occur (for English, see Clark 1971; for French, Ferreiro 1971). In short, three-year-olds ignored the conjunction (*before* or *after*) and attended only to the order of mention of the two events, as shown in Table 10.9. As a result, three-year-olds' responses were correct over 90% of the time when order of mention coincided with order of occurrence, but they were wrong over 80% of the time when the two didn't coincide.

The same children observed two events acted out by someone else and were then asked questions like "What happened before/after the boy patted the dog?" (where the question referred to either the first or second of the two events). They relied on the order of occurrence they had observed. Three- and four-year-olds, for example, typically described the two events in the order they occurred in, regardless of the question asked. They used *and* or *and then* rather than a temporal conjunction, for example, *The boy patted the dog and (then) he jumped over the fence*. They also relied on heavy stress to mark which of the two events was the new one (i.e., the one that provided the answer to the question they had been asked). For example, in response to a question about the first of two events in the form "When did the boy pat the dog?" they might reply with *First he patted the dog and* then *he jumped the fence*. Both tactics allowed them to avoid using conjunctions whose meanings they were unsure of. They also made mistakes with conjunctions and used *before* in place of *after*, and vice versa. Interestingly, children acquiring English and French relied on the same options and made similar errors in their comprehension and production of these temporal conjunctions (Clark 1971; Ferreiro 1971).

Most children acquire the meaning of *before*, whether introducing a clause in first or second position, before that of *after* (Clark 1971). The concept of priority (one event seen as occurring before another) seems to take precedence over the concept of one event's following another. The result is that children start to get instructions containing *before* correct while still relying on order of mention for *after*. By 4;6 to 5;6, most children interpret both conjunctions appropriately. But they still have to master other temporal conjunctions, such as *while, during, until*, and *since*. Finding out just how these conjunctions contrast with *when, before*, and *after*, as well as with causal and conditional conjunctions, takes time (e.g., French & Nelson 1981; Keller-Cohen 1987).

The speaker's choice of a temporal conjunction depends on at least two factors – the temporal relation between the events talked about (sequential, simultaneous, or overlapping, for example) and the starting point of the utterance with the initial event in a sequence, some medial event, or the ending event. The starting point chosen depends in turn on what has been talked about already in the conversation. That is, the information flow in terms of what is currently given and what will therefore be new to the addressee affects the vantage point the speaker takes on particular pairs of events. Whether one says "The boy patted the dog before he jumped the fence" or "The boy jumped the fence after he patted the dog" depends on whether patting dogs (the first event) or jumping fences (the second) has already been mentioned. The prior mention marks the event as given and so is taken up first, leaving the other to be presented as new (Clark 1970).

## Causal constructions and causal sequences

Children begin to express causation *within* events from around age two to two-and-a-half on. They use a causative verb for what the agent does in causing a change of state in the patient or theme (Chapter 9). They also begin to talk about causal sequences *between* events by presenting one event as the cause and another as the effect or outcome. They talk about causal chains from one event to another. Just as in temporal sequences, children here too rely initially on simple juxtapositions of the clauses describing cause and effect, with no conjunction to mark the causal relation. In fact, it is sometimes unclear whether, in early juxtapositions, very young children are talking about a temporal, causal, or conditional sequence. To see which, the (adult) addressee must depend on context. Some typical examples of early causal sequences in one child's speech are listed in Table 10.10.

Although most early uses of the connective *because* appear quite appropriate, others are less so, as can be seen in the exchanges in (9):

(9) a.      D (2;4.17): *I'm tired.*
              MOTHER: You're tired?
              D (looking at his doll "asleep" in his cart): *'cause I'm going to go to bed.*
    b.     D (2;4.18): *Those lights on 'cause it getting light.*
              MOTHER: You mean dark?
              D: *No, it getting light.*
              MOTHER: Oh, they make it light?
              D: *Yes.*

In both cases here, D seems to be using *because* instead of *so*. On other occasions during the first few months of use, he also produced *because* where a temporal conjunction would have been more appropriate. Errors like these, and children's

Table 10.10 *Typical early causal utterances in D's speech*

---

(a) D (1;11.16, to mother after he managed to climb over a gate at the bottom of
the stairs to follow her up, explaining why he'd been crying): *Damon crying
mummy go upstairs.*

(b) D (1;11.18, after he dropped a toy bus on mother's toe, and mother said "ow")
> D: *Eve ow, Eve ow, Eve ow, Eve ow, Eve ow.*
> Mother: I said "ow" because you dropped your bus on my toe.
> (D retrieved his bus and went round the table to report to his father)
> D: *Eve ow [ə] drop [ə] bus [ə] toe.*

(c) D (2;2.3, to father): *Eve going change me because I wet.*

(d) D (2;2.23, to father): *Eve drop his toast.*
> Father: Eve dropped her toast?
> D: *Because it is hot. Eve a bad boy.*
> Father: Now, why is she a bad boy?
> D: *She a bad boy, know why? He dropped his toast.*

(e) D (2;3.4, trying to squeeze his way past a chair): *You better move this chair.
You better move this chair.*
> Mother: Why? Why had I better move this chair?
> D: *Because, because I can't move out this side.*

(f) D (2;3.30, as father began to clear the breakfast table): *You don't get my
bowl because ... I still eating.*

(g) D (2;4.12, his father teasing)
> Father: I'm gonna drop you in the dishwasher …
> D: *No.*
> Father: Why not?
> D: *Because I not some glasses, some cups and some bottles.*

(h) D (2;4.17, after he stood his toy dog up and said it should say "woof-woof"; then,
of his doll Danny): *Danny can't say woof-woof because he got his mouth shut.*

(i) D (2;4.30): *You can't eat it because I just ate it.*

(j) D (2;5.11, father asking him what different things are called in a Richard Scarry
book)
> D (as father pointed at a truck): *A cow-truck.*
> Father: Why's it called a cow-truck?
> D: *Because it's got cows on the back.*

(k) D (2;7, playing with blocks, with father): *You build me a tower?*
> Father: You see how big a tower YOU can make.
> D: *I can't because it might knock down.*

(l) D (2;7.3, putting a pan back in the kitchen cupboard): *I'm putting this back in
here because I finished my working.*

---

*Source*: Clark, unpublished diary data

occasional confusions among temporal forms, suggest that they take some time to
work out the meanings of such conjunctions.

When children's descriptions of causal sequences are examined, they are
generally appropriate. In one analysis of 2,220 causally interpretable statements

from eight children (from 2;0 to 3;5), 618 contained *because* (28%) and 310 contained *so* (14%). *Because* was nearly always followed by a cause and *so* by an effect. This held for 93% of these children's uses (Hood & Bloom 1979). It is possible, though, that most talk about causes involves routine sequences, and these generally elicit appropriate usage from quite an early age (French & Nelson 1981). It is when children answer questions or talk about less-routinized sequences that they reveal what they don't yet know.

Children may describe either internal causation or external causation. With internal causation, the cause is presented as some internal state, such that the effect or result depends on this (Donaldson 1986). Presentations of internal causes typically take the form of *'cos I sad, 'cos I want to*, or *'cos he tired*. With external (usually physical) causes, an initiating causal event is presented as bringing about some result. Children describe internal states as causes quite early (typically between 2;3 and 2;6) and may at first offer them in explanations more often than they do physical causes. Although they talk about both internal and external causes, they don't always use the same conjunction to mark both types of cause as causes. Some children use *because* for internal states and justifications:

(10)      CHILD (3;4.19, justifying the request): *Could I have another gingersnap 'cos I want to put it in my mouth and drink at the same time?*

They contrast *because* with another term, such as *from*, to mark external causation (Clark & Carpenter 1989a, 1989b). They also tend to use *from* to mark nonsubject agents within causal events, as when D (2;2.3) pushed a piece of sandwich off his plate while saying *This fall down from me*. Some typical examples of *from* used to introduce physical causes include the following:

(11) a.      D (2;6.12, reporting an incident of three months earlier): *Then I cried a bit from you go get him.*

     b.      S (2;8.3, explaining how a block became stuck on top of his toy garage): *That's fro' <repair> that's from I put a thing on it.*

     c.      D (2;10.23): *If I talk too much, I be tired from doing that.*

By age three to three-and-a-half, though, children appear to have established *because* for both external and internal causes (Clark 1970, 1973c). Causal clauses may be offered to explain a resultant state of affairs or given as a justification for carrying out a desired action, as in (12a) and (12b), both from three-and-a-half-year-olds:

(12) a.      Child inside playhouse: *They can't come here 'cos we're sweeping up.*

     b.      Child wanting fresh paper on an easel: *Take it off 'cos I'm going to paint on it.*

By age four, children offer a variety of explanations and justifications using *because*, both spontaneously and in response to questions (Donaldson 1986).

In summary, by three-and-a-half to four, children can talk about causal connections between events, in temporal order or not, as they justify their own actions or offer explanations with either internal or external causation. Understanding of causality in many domains can take many years, but three- and four-year-olds have already mastered some of the linguistic means for talking about one event causing another.

## Conditional constructions and contingency

What do children need to know to describe contingency? Contingency is generally conveyed by modal verbs and various conditional constructions (e.g., *He'll come if he can*; *If they had been ready, they wouldn't have missed the train*). These emerge in children's speech soon after temporal and causal constructions, but the full range takes children a long time to master. These constructions can be analyzed in terms of the cognitive complexity of the notion of contingency, the pragmatic conditions on use of a conditional, and the formal complexity of the construction itself (Bowerman 1986). In this approach, the main difficulty they have appears to stem largely from having to imagine counterfactual conditions and their consequences when these don't match what children already know about the events (Reilly 1986).

Grasping the meaning of the conditional construction has several cognitive prerequisites: contingency, hypotheticality, inference, and genericity. First, children need to recognize that one event may be *contingent* on another. This recognition is apparent in many of the juxtapositions children offer in their early utterances. Kate (aged 2;4), for instance, was clearly aware of the contingency involved when she produced the sequence in (13) (Reilly 1986:317):

(13)     KATE (2;4, climbing into her crib): *Climb in. Be fun.* (as she toppled in, laughing)

Second, children need to recognize when an event is *hypothetical* rather than actual. This is established very early in pretense. Children as young as one or one-and-a-half can pretend that one object is another; for instance, when they hold a spoon to their ear and say *hello* yet the next minute use the spoon for eating. Or when they pretend that a block is a car, moving it along the table edge with accompanying sound effects such as *vroom-vroom*. Within a few months, they also begin to talk about hypothetical events, marking them with terms like *almost*, as in (14):

(14)     CHRISTY (1;10, to mother, who had just caught a pitcher Christy put down on the edge of the sandbox): *Almost fall*.

Third, children need to be able to *infer* that two events are connected. This too is an ability that seems to be well established by around age two. Consider the next two exchanges, first from Christy (1;10):

(15)       CHRISTY (1;10, as she was about to go play in some tubs of water outside,
              looking at her mother): *Mommy shirt wet.*

Christy was able to infer a possible consequence and express it in anticipation of
what was about to happen. In the next, from D (1;11.28), the child infers that a
move made by his father is intended to draw his attention to the act of eating (in
lieu of talking):

(16)       D (1;11.28, as father tapped D's bowl with a spoon): *Herb hitting* [ə] *bowl.*
              FATHER: Why was I hitting your bowl? Why was I hitting your bowl?
              D (as picked up spoon and finally took a mouthful): [ə] *eat* [ə] *corn flakes.*

Fourth, children need to understand the *generic* nature of certain events and
combinations of events. Here too children clearly have the necessary cognitive
understanding in place by two to two-and-a-half. It is then that they start to
make generic statements based on their observations about how things are in
the world. These early generalizations typically take the form of timeless
statements (in the simple present in English) often with plural subjects, as in
(17a) and (17b):

(17) a.    D (2;0, in the car, talking about his toy puppy dog that produced a barking
              sound when pulled along by a leash with a handle): *Puppy dog go wuff-
              wuff. Hold* [ə] *handle, puppy dog go wuff wuff.*
     b.    D (2;5.16, at a local playground, to mother): *This a ladder for kids to climb up,
              and some ladders for ... mens to climb up.* (then turning to the slide, as he
              slid down himself): *And some kids slide on slides.*

In short, cognitive complexity alone does not account for why conditional constructions appear so late.

Pragmatically, there are few restrictions on conditionals. Although McCabe and
her colleagues (1983) found that the largest category of conditionals produced by
sibling pairs (aged 2;10–7;3) were bribes or threats (e.g., *If you want a cup you
have to play my games*), these conditionals are not the first type to emerge. Rather,
the first uses of conditionals, across languages, tend to be future predictives; they
comment on familiar, predictable two-event situations (Bowerman 1986). Some
typical early conditionals are listed in Table 10.11. As in other early clause
combinations, the earliest ones lack any explicit conjunction in the form of *if*
(or *when*). But by 3;6, this child had begun to produce some counterfactual
conditionals in relation to present states.

The forms used in conditionals – notably the conjunction and the specific tense
or mood of the verb – have to be linked to the particular meaning to be expressed
by each conditional type. Particular choices of forms in conditionals divide up the
relevant domain within a language. Do children show any preferences in the forms
they favor in their earliest conditional constructions? The answer is yes; they seem
to start from the semantic pattern used for future predictives, where the first of two
events is possible but uncertain and the second is contingent on the first, as in (18)
(Bowerman 1986; Reilly 1986).

Table 10.11 *Early conditional constructions in D's speech*

(a) Mother: If it starts raining, I'll open the umbrella.
     D (2;2.10): *You open umbrella starts raining.*
(b) Mother: Okay, would you like to climb on your plate– your seat?
     D (2;3.4): *I too big to climb on my plate. I might fall and cry.*
(c) D (2;4.26, pressing button on edge of oven door): *When I press this button, the light goes off. Where, where is the light?*
(d) D (2;8.13, commenting on the routine of picking up the newspaper and bringing it in from the driveway each morning): *If somebody takes the newspaper, I'll be sad.*
(e) D (2;8.16, in the car): *When I get bigger into a man, I will sit in the front seat.*
(f) D (2;8.21, being dressed): *I used to wear diapers. When I growed up–* (pause)
     Father: When you grew up?
     D: *When I grewed up, I wore underpants.*
(g) D (2;8.26, asking for specific T-shirt): *If it doesn't have writing on it, it's not my Levi's shirt.*
(h) D (2;9.3): *If I dropped something, I might cut my hand, but I'm not going to do it now.*
(i) D (2;9.5, in the bath, cracker in hand): *If I get my graham cracker in the water, it'll get all soapy.*
(j) D (2;9.6, trying to use tongs to pick up blocks): *If you help me I can do it better.* (pause) *If you don't help me I can't do it better.*
(k) D (2;9.9, after getting father to tie doll's bow tie): *If it comes undone again, you do it up again.*
(l) D (2;9.11): *If you put the egg on here, it might fall down and somebody will say "Whose egg is that?" and I will say "That's my egg."*
(m) D (2;11.18): *What if I stayed in the shopping cart all day?*
     Mother: I think you'd get a little sad and maybe bored.
     D: *The shoppers would bring me home.* [= people who own the shop]
(n) D (3;6.30, arriving at the top of one of the two staircases): *If we had one step instead of two steps, our house would have been small.*

*Source*: Clark, unpublished diary data

(18) a.   CHRISTY (2;4, on a rainy Sunday): *If we go out there we haf' wear hats.*
     b.   EVA (2;8): *If Christy don't be careful, she might get runned over by a car.*
     c.   D (2;7, going on a picnic, noticing sheep in a field): *The sheep might run away if I don't pat them.*
     d.   KATE (2;6, at bedtime, after collecting bugs in a jar): *I go see jar then go to bed.*
     e.   KATE (2;6): *Can I have some gum?*
          MOTHER: No, we don't have gum.
          KATE: *I have gum when I'm older?*

In English, future predictives take *if* when the future antecedent is uncertain (as in *If Rod comes, we'll go out*) and *when* when it is certain (as in *When Rod comes, we'll go out*).[2] English-speaking children master this distinction very early. Bowerman analyzed diary data from three children for all the future predictives where the relative certainty or uncertainty of the antecedent event was clear from the context. All three children used *when* in the certain cases and *if* in the uncertain ones, as shown in the following 2 × 2 tables (Bowerman 1986:301):

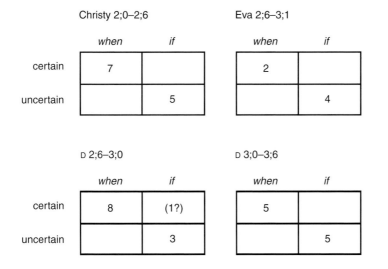

Christy 2;0–2;6

|            | when | if |
|------------|------|----|
| certain    | 7    |    |
| uncertain  |      | 5  |

Eva 2;6–3;1

|            | when | if |
|------------|------|----|
| certain    | 2    |    |
| uncertain  |      | 4  |

D 2;6–3;0

|            | when | if    |
|------------|------|-------|
| certain    | 8    | (1?)  |
| uncertain  |      | 3     |

D 3;0–3;6

|            | when | if |
|------------|------|----|
| certain    | 5    |    |
| uncertain  |      | 5  |

Essentially, these children used *when* for the next instance of a reliably recurrent event or for an act currently planned for immediate implementation (Table 10.11). Otherwise they produced *if*. The other early conditionals Bowerman observed included some expressions of pure hypotheticality, of present contingency, and of generic contingency. These three children produced few or no past (counterfactual) conditionals.

Children go through several stages before they can produce the full range of conditional constructions available in English (Reilly 1982, 1986). Reilly based her conclusions on a combination of diary observations from children aged 1;0 to 4;4 and of elicitation experiments with children between 2;6 and 9;0. To assess children's understanding of conditionals, Reilly asked them *what if* questions that fell into five categories: (a) *What if* questions asked in the context of a story; e.g., "What if you eat three ice-creams?" (to elicit such responses as *you get sick* or *you will get sick*). (b) *What if* questions asked about *The three little pigs* and *The three bears*, both stories with familiar, known outcomes; questions in this context were counterfactual, e.g., of a picture of the straw house blown down by the wolf, "What if the straw house had been made of bricks?" (c) *What if* questions about pretense, where the child was asked to pretend to be or do various things and to tell about it. (The child heard models from the adult first; e.g., "If I ate a hundred

---

[2]  Many languages rely on the same conjunction for both uncertain and certain antecedents, e.g., Dutch *als*, German *wenn*, Polish *jak* [+ indicative].

marshmallows, I would get sick.") (d) *What if* questions designed to elicit *when* sentence completions: Here children were given *when* clauses with different verb tenses (present, past, punctual, stative, durative) and asked to complete a sentence; e.g., "When you get home …" or "When your Daddy was at work …" (with "Tell me" used as a prompt). (e) *What if* questions designed to elicit generic *when* clauses. Here, children were asked about familiar items used in specific, well-defined, contexts; e.g., "What do you do with rain-boots?" (prompts: "All the time?"; "Every day?").

At first, children simply juxtapose two clauses; next, they begin to use the conjunctions *if* and *when*, mainly for future predictives. Then they extend predictive *when* to relate objects to familiar contexts in protogeneric utterances, as in (19):

(19)        ADULT: What are umbrellas for?
            LAUREN (2;7): *When rain comes, we put an umbrella on top of us.*

But two- and three-year-olds often reject the presupposition of the antecedent when asked a *what if* question, as in (20):

(20)        ADULT: What if a snake bites?
            LAUREN (2;7, objecting): *Snake have any mouthes and teethes.* [any = no]

In the next stage, according to Reilly, children produce their first hypothetical and their first predictive *if*'s, as in (21):

(21)        ADULT: What if you fall in the water?
            LAUREN (2;8): *I'll get eaten by a shark.*

And although children still reject the presuppositions of *what if* questions, as in (22a), they now begin to produce *when* in fantasy pasts, as in (22b):

(22) a.     ADULT: What if Ilse [= dog] bites you?
            LAUREN (2;8): *Her doesn't bite me.*
     b.     ADULT: Right this minute, you're this teeny? [hands 20 cm apart]
            AMANDA (2;11): *I was that/this little when I was when I wa, when I was that small and then, um … um … um … that that, um that, um that, um that, that– the panda bears bite me.*

At this point, this same child used *when* in both predictive and protogeneric expressions, as shown in (23a–b):

(23) a.     AMANDA (2;11): *When I older than Lindsay, then I'm the big sister.*
     b.     ADULT: Do you go to bed at night?
            AMANDA (2;11): *We go to bed when it's dark.*

It is only after this point that children use their first hypothetical conditionals:

(24)        RYAN (2;10): *If Bulldozer man saw a fire, he would call the fire department.*

Yet children who can now produce hypothetical conditionals still reject the presuppositions of adult *what if* questions, at times quite vehemently, as in (25):

(25)         ADULT: What if your car broke on the way?
             RYAN (2;10): *Well, but when we drove here, our car didn't broke.*
             ADULT: Well, what happens, what if your car did break?
             RYAN: *It doesn't break. I told you!*

In Reilly's sixth stage, children take their first steps in differentiating fact from supposition, thereby fully differentiating their uses of *when* and *if*. (This occurs between 3;6 and 4;0; notice that children distinguished *when* and *if* for marking the relative certainty vs. uncertainty of the antecedent up to a year earlier.) By this stage, children become willing to accept the antecedents in *what if* questions and can give appropriate responses to many of them, as in (26):

(26)         ADULT: Molly, what if you ate three chocolate cakes?
             MOLLY (3;6): *You would have a tummy ache.*

Finally, beginning around age four, children clearly differentiate *if* from *when*, relying primarily on *if* for hypothetical states of affairs. This shows up, for example, in their spontaneous repairs:

(27)         GRANT (3;10): *When I was <repair> if I was a tiger, I would cook pa– <repair> popcorn.*

Overall, children produce future hypotheticals (typically predictives) before they produce past hypotheticals (see also Kuczaj & Daly 1979). This stage also marks the point at which children succeed in answering *what if* questions in counterfactual elicitation tasks, and show increased sophistication with counterfactuals in causal reasoning tasks (Harris, German, & Mills 1996). While three-year-olds offered appropriate responses only 36% of the time, Reilly's four-year-olds did so 93% of the time. Children at this stage also use more counterfactuals in their spontaneous speech.

(28) a.      KATE (4;1, in a sedan car with eight people): *We shoulda taked the grey car 'cuz it has a way-back.* [grey car = a station wagon]
     b.      D (3;6.14, appearing with his father's shoes)
             FATHER: Where were my shoes?
             D: *Upstairs in the logs.* [= beside the fireplace]
             FATHER: I looked all over for them last night.
             D: *If you looked all over for them, you would have found them.*

By age four, many children make use of future, present, and counterfactual conditions in talking about how one event is contingent upon another. But they still have many structural details to learn for counterfactuals, especially in mastering the appropriate verb forms in both clauses. Consider some typical counterfactuals produced by six- to eleven-year-olds who were describing a picture of a girl watching a rabbit run away from its cage (Crutchley 2004):

(29) a.      If she's shut the door, the rabbit wouldn't have escaped.
     b.      If she didn't let the rabbit out, the rabbit wouldn't have run away.
     c.      If she hadn't of let the rabbit out, it wouldn't have got out.

>    d.        If the girl would have put her rabbit in the cage, this wouldn't have happened.
>    e.        If she didn't leave the rabbit's cage open, the rabbit wouldn't run away.

(These forms are ordered from the most favored form, in *a*, to the least favored, in *e*.) Children clearly still have a number of structural details to master (for instance, the appropriate sequences of tenses in such constructions), but they have grasped what it means for one event to be contingent on another both in reality and in some hypothetical world by around age four.

## Summary

        When children learn how to combine clauses, they can talk about more complex events, and they gain additional tools for managing the flow of information. They can use coordination to link or contrast events. They can use complementation to convey information about dependent events and, in their main verbs, for instance, reflect attitudes towards those subordinate events. They can add detail to specify referents more precisely by using relative clauses to modify noun phrases. And they can talk about relations between events in terms of time, cause, or contingency. In this chapter, I have reviewed some of the major types of clause combinations. These add to the repertoire of clause-internal elaborations that children can use (Chapter 9) and expand the constructional options they can call on.

In acquiring these constructions, children can be more precise about what they mean and incorporate into their utterances what they need, for instance to specify the intended referents of each utterance. Having more options, both within the clause and for clause combination, allows speakers greater efficacy in conveying their intentions. It provides more choices in the amount of information and range of detail they can readily convey. This in turn allows them to locate one event in time relative to another, to connect an event to its cause or result, and to identify the contingency between one event and the next – in actual fact or hypothetically.

Acquisition of options for clause combination also increases the possibilities for speakers as they "think for speaking." Languages offer different possibilities for within-clause and between-clause elaborations. In some, causation in the verb may be best analyzed as clause combination, with some form of periphrastic causative verb, analogous to English *make* or *get*, as the main verb, with the action being caused expressed as the verb in the embedded clause. In English, causation in the verb is usually a within-clause modification. The point is that the options reviewed in Chapters 9 and 10 are not necessarily expressed with the same structural devices across languages. Some languages make distinctions where others don't. So within each language, speakers must learn to think for speaking in that language to express what they want to say (Slobin 1996). In some languages, they must learn to attend to how to express the temporal contour for each event (ongoing, completed, iterating, etc.). In others, they must learn to be attentive to whether events are known through direct observation or through some form of hearsay. In still others, they must attend to the grammatical gender of every noun and mark it on all elements "agreeing" with that term within the clause. In others, they must attend to how object-types are classified for counting or for making reference, and in still others, they must attend to whether properties are temporary or inherent to the entity being talked about.

Finally, all these structural options are put to use by speakers to further their goals in conversation. Children learn how to use such options in adjusting for different addressees and for different purposes as they talk. They treat a two-year-old addressee differently from a peer and differently from an older child or an adult (e.g., Shatz & Gelman 1973). They choose different options for a sibling or other family member from a teacher or an unfamiliar adult. They also learn what is effective in persuading someone to do something compared to giving directions or instructions on how to work some toy. And they learn what counts as polite, with degrees of politeness for achieving different goals under different circumstances (e.g., Kyratzis 1993).

Before I turn to children's acquisition of these social skills in language use, I examine one more domain of elaboration. The next chapter takes up what children know about the internal structure of complex words and how and when they use this knowledge in coining words to express meanings for which they haven't yet acquired the conventional terms in their first language.

# 11 Constructing words

As children learn more words, storing them in memory and producing them as needed, they begin to identify and analyze the meanings of *parts* of complex words – affixes (prefixes, suffixes, infixes) and roots or stems. Once children can analyze the internal structure of words, they can make use of stems and affixes as building blocks for new words to convey new meanings. To exploit this resource, though, children must be able to analyze words into their constituent parts, assign meanings to those parts, and learn which combinations of parts are allowed in the language they are acquiring. Coining words represents another type of complexity in acquisition.

Languages differ in which types of stem and affix combinations they license and in the meanings conveyed by different types of word-formation. Some languages rely extensively on compounding or the combination of word-roots, as in *sun-dial* or *rabbit-hole*; others rely on derivation or the combination of word-roots with affixes, as in *green-ish* or *re-read;* and many rely on both, as in *shoe-maker* or *watering-can*. If some options are easier to acquire than others, children acquiring different language-types should reflect this in their acquisition of word-formation.

The focus in this chapter is on children's acquisition of compounding and derivation in word-formation, as displayed in their coinages to fill gaps in their current vocabulary. After a brief review of the options for compounding and derivation, I look at evidence from several languages on when children analyze and understand specific word-formational options and when they begin to use them in the coinage of new words.

## Compounding and derivation

Within a language, *compound forms* are usually divided into types according to their syntactic class. In English, one finds compound nouns formed from roots only (often called root compounds), as in the established forms *sun-rise*, *push-chair*, and *dog-sled*. One also finds some compound adjectives (e.g., *grey-eyed*, *wine-dark*) and compound verbs (e.g., *to side-step, to dry-clean*). Compounding in new adjective and verb formation is rare compared to new noun formation. Compounds in English may also combine affixes and roots, as in the established terms *clock-mender* or *washing-machine*. (These are called synthetic compounds.) Compound nouns like *snow-flake* contain a head (here *flake*) and a modifier of that head (namely *snow-*); the head element carries number marking, and, in many languages, case and gender marking too. In compound verbs like *to white-wash*, the head (*wash*) carries tense and aspect as well as any agreement for person, number, and (in some languages) gender. In English, the head is the rightmost member of the compound (*flake* in *snow-flake*), and compounds generally have primary stress on the modifier followed by tertiary stress on the head.

*Derivation* in the formation of words relies on affixation to a root or an existing word. Affixes – prefixes, suffixes, or infixes – can maintain or change the syntactic class of the resulting word. Compare addition of the prefix *re-* (with no change in word-class) in the verb *redraw*, with the suffix *-ize* for a noun-to-verb change in *hospitalize*. In many languages, derivational affixes can be divided into two main groups, depending on whether they require some modification of the root they are added to (Group I affixes) or not (Group II affixes). In English, Group I affixes include *-ous*, *-ive*, *-ory*, and *-ify*: Their addition to a root may be accompanied by a shift in word stress (e.g., from *electric* to *electricity*), a change in the pronunciation of a vowel (from tense to lax, for example, in the shift from *opaque* to *opacity*), and a change of certain consonants (as in the shift from **k** to **s**, also audible in *opaque* to *opacity*). In contrast, Group II affixes have little or no effect on the roots they are added to. In English, they include the following nominal, verbal, and adjectival suffixes: *-ness*, *-less*, *-er*, *-ize*, *-y*, and *-ish* (e.g., established *penniless*, *farmer*, *hybridize*, and *darkish*). Group I affixes are normally added to the root form before any Group II affixes in words that contain both. For instance, the verb *to nationalize* contains Group I *-al* before Group II *-ize*, but there are no verbs like *\*to nationlessify* with a Group II suffix (*-less*) followed by a Group I suffix (*-ify*).

Lastly, in English (and in many other languages), derivation can occur without affixation, with a simple shift of word-class, as in the move from noun to verb (from *a captain* to *to captain*) or from verb to noun (from *to jump* to *a jump*). This type of derivation is usually called either zero derivation (to mark the parallel to affixal derivation despite the absence of any affix) or conversion (to emphasize the shift in word-class).

These two types of word-formation – compounding and derivation – characterize many words in the conventional lexicon. Together they offer ways of creating new words when speakers perceive a need for them. Adult speakers both create and interpret such coinages every day: When they coin a word, they fill a gap where there is no ready-made word available for just that meaning; and when, as addressees, they encounter a coinage, they are often unaware that they have never heard it before. (The speaker has designed the meaning to be readily computable on that occasion.) The formation of new words, then, offers a means for conveying new meanings when they are needed. Ultimately, this represents a way of renewing and extending the lexicon as a whole over time (see Adams 1973; Bauer 1983; Marchand 1969).

Once children start to analyze parts of words and to assign meanings to those parts (roots and affixes), they attend to consistencies in the forms of combinations (their relative order and the combinatorial possibilities) too, and to the meanings expressed by particular word-formation patterns. They also attend to the relative productivity of different word-formation options for specific kinds of meaning, and, like adults, where possible favor more productive over less productive possibilities. So children must first identify each affix and assign a meaning to it, and only after that can they make use of that pattern to express a new meaning.

Just as with syntactic constructions, children tend to master the simpler options in word-formation before more complex ones. For instance, they master root compounds before synthetic compounds. But the complexity of the word form is only part of word-formation: Children also have to make sure that the meaning they intend is transparent relative to other meanings conveyed by those roots and affixes and that they are using a productive word-formational pattern. In what follows, we also consider transparency and productivity as factors in what children learn as they master constructions for creating new words.

## Analyzing complex words

Evidence about when children begin to identify specific roots and affixes comes first from their spontaneous comments on words, word-parts, and their meanings. Some analyses from one child are given in Table 11.1. These spontaneous comments appear from age two on, and, as in the examples in the table, tend to concern root elements rather than affixes. That is, children appear to start discerning familiar root elements in complex combinations of two or more roots, or in combinations of roots and affixes.

By age three or so, children appear to comment quite readily on words newly encountered or parts of words just noticed, as in (1):

(1) a.     D (3;2.15): *Egg-nog comes from "egg"!*
    b.     D (3;2.15): *Hey, "golden" begins with Goldilocks in one of my books!* [= 'is at the beginning of']

They are also able to segment words into their parts, whether roots and affixes, or syllables, or even individual segments (Slobin 1978). But their spontaneous coinages can also reveal failures of analysis, as in one three-year-old girl's triumphant claim as she was playing: *I'm spiderman-woman!*

The second major source of information about children's analyses of complex word forms and their meanings comes from systematic studies of their interpretations of innovative word forms. These interpretations depend on children's ability to identify the constituent parts of the unfamiliar words.

### Interpreting complex words

Children's analyses of the internal structure of words allow for a close look at aspects of acquisition that may not be as visible in other domains. Their analyses often reveal what they know about the meanings of prefixes, suffixes,

Table 11.1 *Spontaneous analyses of word-parts*

(a) D (2;4.3, looking at a toy car): *That a motor-car. It got a motor.*

(b) D (2;4.13, after mother pointed at a picture of a lady-bug and asked him what it was): *A lady-bug! That like "lady."*

(c) D (2;6.20, to father, about a favorite stick): *This is a running-stick.*
   Father: A running-stick?
   D: *Yes, because I run with it.*

(d) D (2;7.1, in the bath, after father said, "You're making a cake?"): *It's a water-cake.*
   Father: Why do you call it water-cake?
   D: *I made it in the water.*

(e) D (2;9.10): *You know why this is a HIGH-chair? Because it is high.*

(f) D (2;9.24): *Does cornflakes have corn in it?*

(g) D (2;9.24): *Eve, you know what you do on runways? You run on them because they start with "run."*

(h) D (2;10.23, offering a pretend present to father): *I brought you a tooth-brush and a finger-brush.*
   Father: What's a finger-brush?
   D: *It's for cleaning your nails.*

(i) D (2;11.2): *Windshield! Wind goes on it. That's why it's called a windshield.*

(j) D (2;11.28, looking at flowering ice-plant on hillside): *What's that called?*
   Mother: That's ice-plant.
   D: *Does it grow ice?*

*Source*: Clark 1993:40–41. Used with permission from Cambridge University Press.

and roots, how these elements are ordered inside words, and the meanings different combinations can express. All this can tell us a good deal about what they attend to when, and how, they build up their general knowledge about word construction.

Much evidence here comes from elicited comprehension tasks, where children are asked about the meanings of unfamiliar words. They have to supply a potential meaning based on their current knowledge about parts of words and how they are usually put together. Take compound nouns. In English, the head of the compound appears in second place, to the right of, or after, the modifier in a linear representation, as in the innovative *pencil-tree*, coined to refer to a kind of tree. The head identifies the category (here a tree) being designated by the root compound. But in Hebrew, the head comes first, rather than second, and is followed by the modifier. How soon do children recognize which element is the head and which the modifier? And how soon do they make use of this information with unfamiliar compounds?

English-speaking two-year-olds frequently construct novel root compounds when they talk about subcategories, as in the innovative *house-smoke* (smoke from a chimney) or *dalmatian-dog* (kind of dog). This suggests that they have already mastered the modifier versus head distinction within root compounds. One way to test this is to offer children novel compound nouns and ask them to identify the intended referent (in a choice of picture, say). For each compound in one study, young children saw sets of four pictures that tested either for their identification of the head noun (e.g., choices of a tree, a flower, a pencil, and a pen, as a referent for *pencil-tree*) or for their identification of head and modifier combined (e.g., choices from pictures of a tree with pencils in lieu of leaves, a tree with cups on, a bunch of pencils alone, or a tree alone) (see Clark, Gelman, & Lane 1985). Their choices showed that by 2;6 to 3;0 they could reliably identify which element in an unfamiliar root compound is the head and which the modifier, as shown in Table 11.2.

Are these findings specific to English, or might they reflect a general strategy in which the final element in a noun phrase is assumed to denote the category being talked about? Do children grasp the modifier–head relations of the language they are learning by age two to three? To check these possibilities, a similar study was carried out with children acquiring Hebrew with its head–modifier order (Berman & Clark 1989). If what the English-speaking children did reflected a general processing strategy, one would expect a large number of errors in Hebrew. But if children attend to the structure of the language they are acquiring, they might work out rather early how heads and modifiers are ordered. And then Hebrew-speaking children should show skill similar to English speakers in identifying the ordering of heads and modifiers. And they do. They reliably picked out pictures depicting the intended referents of novel root compounds, as shown in Table 11.3.

Table 11.2 *Percentage of identifications of head and modifier-head referents for novel English root compounds*

| Age | Head noun | Modifier + Head |
| --- | --- | --- |
| 2;4 | 48 | 49 |
| 3;4 | 82 | 85 |
| 4;0 | 92 | 96 |

*Source*: Clark, Gelman, & Lane 1985:86. Used with permission from the Society for Research in Child Development.

Table 11.3 *Percentage of identifications of head and modifier-head referents for novel Hebrew root compounds*

| Age | Head noun | Modifier + Head |
| --- | --- | --- |
| 2;5 | 78 | 86 |
| 3;5 | 90 | 80 |
| 4;8 | 98 | 98 |

*Source*: Berman & Clark 1989:254. Used with permission from Alpha Academic.

Another source of information about how children analyze unfamiliar compounds is the paraphrase or gloss they offer in trying to explain their meanings to someone else. When asked what a *box-opener* is, for example, children might say *someone who opens things*, *he opens boxes*, *a boy who opens*. These show that they understand that *box-* is the modifier, here standing in the relation of direct object to the action, and that *-opener* is the head. They are also aware that in *-opener*, the suffix *-er* designates the agent of the verb *open*, so an *opener* is a person who opens something (Clark & Hecht 1982).

In one paraphrase task with unfamiliar synthetic compounds in Hebrew, four-year-olds identified the head correctly 87% of the time, and by age five, they were right 96% of the time. (Even three-year-olds [mean age 3;2] identified the head noun appropriately 43% of the time.) Three of the four head-noun types in this study took some kind of inflection or else a change in the form of the root, so children had to be able to extract the relevant (basic) forms for their paraphrases (Clark & Berman 1987). And in a study of synthetic compounds in English, four-year-olds identified the head noun appropriately 66% of the time, while five-year-olds did this 80% of the time (Clark 1984). In short, by around age three, children can identify the heads of both root and synthetic compounds quite accurately and soon after give adequate paraphrases or glosses when asked what unfamiliar compounds might mean.[1]

These findings are language-specific. Children as young as 2;6 acquiring English and Hebrew show distinct preferences in which element (first or last) they identify as the head noun in a root compound. In English, they pick the last element as the head, while in Hebrew they pick the first. By age three, children are also able to offer glosses for some affixes in innovative word forms. In English, they are good at glossing unfamiliar agentive and instrumental nouns in *-er*, and in Hebrew, by age four, children do very well in glossing several agentive forms (Clark & Berman 1984; Clark & Hecht 1982). These glosses show, for synthetic compound nouns, that children can identify both the verb base and the affix (in English) from which the novel noun has been constructed. The percentages of verbs correctly identified in their English glosses are shown in Table 11.4.

By age three, children can reliably identify the heads of unfamiliar compound nouns, and extract verb-roots and certain affix meanings from unfamiliar derived nouns. This is just the start. In any one language, children have to learn how to interpret the set of compounding patterns available in that language, along with the repertoire of affixes in derived forms (prefixes, suffixes, and, in some languages, infixes).[2] They appear to store their repertoire of word structures in memory; they

---

[1] The actual meanings offered can differ considerably from one child to the next. Although the component roots contribute to an innovative meaning, they do not specify the precise relation that could hold between the two (or more) elements in a novel compound. Effectively, one compound form can be used by speakers to express a range of different meanings, depending on the discourse context and the content of the prior conversation (see further Clark & Clark 1979).

[2] In Semitic languages like Hebrew, children must also learn the repertoire of nominal patterns or *mishkalim* that can be used for coining new nouns. This in turn requires understanding of how to intercalate vowel combinations into consonant roots (Berman 1985).

Table 11.4 *Percentage of verb-bases extracted from unfamiliar agent and instrument nouns in children's glosses (English)*

| Age | Agent glosses | Instrument glosses |
|---|---|---|
| 3;4 | 93 | 79 |
| 4;0 | 98 | 81 |
| 4;10 | 98 | 97 |
| 5;8 | 99 | 96 |

*Source*: Clark & Hecht 1982:11. Reprinted from *Cognition* 12, Eve V. Clark & Barbara F. Hecht, Learning to coin agent and instrument nouns, 1–24, copyright 1982, with permission from Elsevier Science.

then make use of this store in interpreting unfamiliar forms, whether conventional or novel. Such information can also serve as a template for the *production* of novel forms. This asymmetry goes beyond a simple lag in mastery: In their coining of new words, children reveal that comprehension and production may be qualitatively, as well as quantitatively, different. And, as in other domains, comprehension is consistently ahead of production.

Three- and four-year-olds acquiring English reliably identify the head noun versus the modifier in their glosses of novel compound nouns. But when they are then given similar glosses (to elicit new word forms) and asked what one could call such a person or thing, at a certain stage they make errors in their production of synthetic compounds. For instance, when one child who had produced *pull-wagon* (someone who pulls wagons) and *throw-ball* (someone who throws balls) was presented with other novel forms constructed on the same plan (e.g., *kick-box, fill-bottle*), she nonetheless interpreted the rightmost element – here, *box* and *bottle* – as the head. For her, the template for identifying the head in *interpreting* novel compounds (Choose the rightmost element) was different from the template for *producing* such compounds (Place the head first). Indeed, children also added the agentive suffix *-er* to that first element, as in *kicker-box* or *filler-bottle* (Clark 1984; Clark, Hecht, & Mulford 1986).

## 11A Comprehension and production differ

**Comprehension**: What d'you think a wall-builder is?
*A man that builds walls, Someone that builds things*
**Production**: What could you call someone who pulls wagons?
*A pull-wagon, A puller-wagon, A wagon-puller*

Based on Clark 1984

So, while three- and four-year-olds may be almost perfect at understanding unfamiliar or novel synthetic compounds, they lag behind in production. The lag here is both quantitative and qualitative in nature. Their main error in production is to rely on the word order of the verb phrase in English, where the verb is the head of the verb phrase, followed by any modifying material (e.g., a direct object noun phrase). This results in adultlike comprehension contrasting with nonadultlike production: The same children who take the *rightmost* element as the head in interpreting a novel compound place the head element in the *leftmost* slot when they coin and produce a novel compound noun themselves (Clark 1984; Clark *et al.* 1986). (These coinages always carry primary stress on the modifier and tertiary stress on the head.) But when the children who make these errors in production are presented with additional novel compounds, constructed on their own erroneous pattern, to interpret, they consistently identify the rightmost element as the head.

Word-formation studies, then, throw added light on the asymmetry between comprehension and production. Although children may understand that the head in synthetic compounds is the rightmost element in English, in production they appear to rely instead on the head-followed-by-modifier order from the verb phrase. Children learning languages with consistent modifier–head ordering across constructions appear to show only a quantitative lag (Clark & Berman 1987) without any accompanying qualitative difference. In languages where modifier–head order varies with the construction, children must learn that, in compound nouns, say, the head is always the rightmost element, even when it is constructed from a verb-root.

## Acquisitional factors in word coinage

When children coin words, they attend to conventionality and contrast in much the same way adults do. Coinages fill lexical gaps, so if they already know a word for something, they won't coin a new word for it. At the same time, children know much less of the conventional vocabulary than adults do and their vocabularies are much smaller. As a result, they often coin words that are illegitimate because there are already words with those meanings in the conventional lexicon. Young children don't yet know them. Children's coinages, therefore, tend to be a mix of legitimate and illegitimate forms.

While children grasp some of the conditions on coinages very early, they may take a long time to master others. Several factors affect order of acquisition in word structure – how transparent the meaning of the new form is, how easy it is to construct, and how productive that option is in the language community. Conventionality and contrast also play a basic role in novel word-formation.

## 11B  Preemption in the lexicon: Nouns

| Source | Regular paradigm | Preempting form |
|---|---|---|
| curious, tenacious | curiosity, tenacity | |
| glorious, furious | *gloriosity, *furiosity | *glory, fury* |
| sweep (V) | *sweeper[1] | *broom* |
| drill, bore (V) | *driller, *borer | *drill* (N), *bore* (N) |
| ride, drive (V) | rider, driver | |
| cook, spy (V) | *cooker, *spyer | *cook* (N), *spy* (N) |
| apply, inhabit | *applier, *inhabiter | *applicant, inhabitant* |

*Note*: Preempted forms are marked with an asterisk; preempting forms are in italics.
[1]*Sweeper* is acceptable provided it contrasts in meaning with *broom*.

## Conventionality and contrast

Speakers give priority to words that are already established in the lexicon for their community. They don't coin words if there are words already available for the meanings they are trying to express. Boxes 11B and 11C give examples of established, conventional words that preempt new words that could otherwise express those same meanings. For instance, although adjectives in *-ious* generally form nominals in *-icity*, *glorious* and *furious* are exceptions because of the existence of *glory* and *fury*. Similarly, although English speakers can normally form any noun into a verb to denote an activity connected with the referent of that noun, the existence of the verbs *to fly* and *to drive* preempt the formation of *to airplane* or *to car* for those exact meanings. Since the existing form already carries the relevant meaning, it preempts, or blocks, use of what would otherwise be the regular noun- or verb-formation in the paradigm.

## 11C  Preemption in the lexicon: Verbs

| Source | Regular (denominal) paradigm | Preempting form |
|---|---|---|
| bicycle, jet (N) | to bicycle, to jet | |
| car, airplane (N) | *to car, *to airplane | *to drive, to fly* |
| stable, jail (N) | to stable, to jail | |
| hospital, prison (N) | *to hospital, *to prison | *to hospitalize, to imprison* |
| chauffeur (N) | to chauffeur | |
| baker (N) | *to baker bread | *to bake* |

Note: Preempted forms are marked with an asterisk; preempting forms are in italics.

Why give conventional terms priority? This helps speakers maintain stability in the conventional lexicon. If everyone agrees that meaning-a is carried by form-1, and meaning-b by form-2, then failure to make use of the conventional term implicates that the speaker intends to convey some other meaning. If the speaker wants to convey a meaning that contrasts with the conventional meaning of *glory*, for instance, then use of *gloriosity* would become justified, precisely because its meaning will now contrast with that of *glory* (Clark & Clark 1979). The conventional vocabulary has a large store of agreed-on meanings, but these can be supplemented for new meanings by the coining of further words from the available roots and affixes.

Young children start with very small vocabularies, so they have many gaps to fill. One option is to coin new words, making use of familiar roots and affixes in derivations and compounds. Indeed, as children's coinages show, when they don't yet know the conventional term for a meaning, they often coin one. They produce terms like *spyer* (for *spy*), *cooker* (for *cook*), and *driller* (for *drill*), or *to car* (for *to drive*), *to piano* (for *to play the piano*), and *to bell* (for *to ring*) (Clark 1993). They coin many terms that would be preempted by existing words for adult speakers. But they give up these forms as they learn more vocabulary. They replace verbs like *to sand* (2;4.13, 'to grind into powder') or *to crack out* (2;6.11, 'to crack a shell and get out [of chicks]') with conventional *to grind* and *to hatch*; and they replace innovative nouns such as *sleepers* (2;6) or *climber* (2;5.24) with conventional *pyjamas* and *ladder* (Clark 1987).

How long such replacement takes depends on the circumstances. Children who use their own coinages (e.g., a verb like *to oar* in lieu of *to row*; an agent noun like *cooker* in lieu of *cook*) will hear the conventional terms from other speakers in just those contexts where they produce these innovations. Before they give up a coinage, they must work out that the meanings of their own word (say the verb *to oar*) and of the adult word (*to row*) are identical. At that point, since the conventional (adult) forms take priority, they can give up *to oar* in favor of *to row*. The amount of time this takes will depend on each child's experience with the conventional term: how many times it is used in appropriate circumstances where the child would predict use of the coinage but hears the adult term instead. In one study of children's judgements, child innovations were paired with their conventional counterparts, as in the choice between *The boy scaled the apples* versus *The boy weighed the apples*, along with a picture of a boy weighing some apples on a scale. By age four to five, children were more likely to prefer the conventional adult forms over child innovations for many of the verb pairs tested (Clark, Neel-Gordon, & Johnson 1993). What seems critical is that children must recognize that two forms have exactly the same meanings before they can choose just one, the conventional one, as the term to use in their speech community.

How do children decide which roots and affixes to combine in a new derived or compound form? One proposal is that they rely on certain principles designed to maximize transparency of meaning and simplicity of form along with productivity of word-formation in any new word.

## Transparency of meaning, simplicity of form

The meaning of a complex word is *transparent* when children already know the meanings of its component parts (roots and affixes). This makes the internal structure of some complex words easier for children to interpret and also tells them which elements to use in constructing a form for a new meaning. Take two terms that differ in register but have similar meanings: *analgesic* versus *pain-killer*. The latter is more transparent because it is constructed from familiar elements – the roots *pain* and *kill* plus the suffix *-er*. The form of a word is *simple* when the elements to be combined in it require either no changes or only minimal changes as a result of combination. Compare the root compound *dog-sled* (*dog* + *sled*) with *electricity* (*electric* + *ity*). In *dog-sled*, neither word needs adjustment in form; but in the derivation of *electricity* from *electric*, the adjective *electric* needs to have its final **k** sound softened to an **s** sound, and the primary stress has to move from the second syllable of *electric* to the third syllable of *electricity*. Transparency and simplicity are evident in children's choices in coining new words. As they get older and learn more about options for constructing new words, these factors play a lesser role.

Transparency of meaning predicts that children rely first on known roots in coining words. When they learn the meanings of affixes, they make use of those too. Their earliest coinages, as predicted, consist of one root form or a combination of roots, but later coinages combine roots and affixes. Evidence for this prediction is given in Table 11.5, with examples of novel verbs formed from noun-roots and novel nouns from combinations of noun-roots.

Table 11.5 *Early innovative verbs and nouns in English*

Novel verbs from noun-roots
*to button* (2;4) 'to press the button(s) [on a calculator]'
*to sand* (2;4) 'to grind [into powder]'
*to flag* (2;5) 'to wave like a flag'
*to fire* (2;6) 'to light [a candle]'
*to horn* (2;6) 'to touch with a [toy] horn'
*to rug* (2;8) 'to vacuum the rug'

Novel nouns from combinations of noun-roots
*crow-bird* (1;7) 'crow'
*baby-bottle* (1;11) 'bottle used when Speaker was a baby'
*cup-egg* (2;0) 'boiled egg' (vs. *plate-egg* 'fried egg')
*coffee-churn* (2;0) 'coffee-grinder'
*spear-page* (2;1) 'page with picture of people with spears'
*car-smoke* (2;4) 'car exhaust' (vs. *house-smoke* 'smoke from chimney')

Based on Clark 1993; Clark, Gelman, & Lane 1985

Further evidence for transparency comes from children's later uses of affixes. Once they identify an affix, combinations of known roots with that affix become transparent. In fact, once children map the meaning of an affix, they may overuse it on all potential candidates. For example, D (aged 2;2) began to add the suffix -*y* to all the adjectives already in his repertoire, such as *nice, dark, cold, stuck*, to produce such forms as *dark-y, cold-y*, or *nice-y*. Then, within a few weeks, he began to construct novel adjectives by adding -*y* to familiar noun-roots such as *crumb* (for *crumby* 'covered in crumbs') and *crack* (for *cracky* 'with a big crack'). His novel adjectives were all marked as such with this adjective-forming suffix. Other suffixes and prefixes, once identified, are applied with a similar consistency in marking an agentive meaning, for instance, with -*er*, or a reversal-of-action meaning with *un*- (Clark, Carpenter, & Deutsch 1995; Clark & Hecht 1982). Overall, as children come to understand more roots, affixes, and compounding patterns, the more transparent any unfamiliar complex word they encounter is likely to be.

Where one affix carries more than one meaning, children may learn just one meaning first and the other meaning only later. English -*er*, for example, conveys both agentive and instrumental meaning. Young children often produce it first only on novel agent nouns. It is sometimes several months before they use it for novel instruments as well (Clark & Hecht 1982). D, for example, coined nouns like *brusher* (for his mother brushing tea leaves out of the sink), *climber, gunner* (of himself, having just announced that his block was a gun), and *cooker* (for real cooks and pictures of cooks) from age two on. Not until 2;5 did he use -*er* for novel instrument nouns as well, as in *hider* (for an inverted waste-paper basket placed over his head) or *sharper* (for a pencil-sharpener).

Transparency of both compounding patterns and affixes pushes children towards the construction of paradigms – use of the same pattern to link related meanings. For instance, the suffix -*er* connects all agent nouns that end in that form, the suffix -*y* all adjectives, and so on. Paradigms link small or large groups of words related in both form and meaning; they make explicit certain regularities in the lexicon. Paradigms in word-formation are susceptible to overregularization much like those for inflections.

When children produce words, they seem to start out with just one shape per word. In inflected languages like Russian or Hungarian, for instance, they produce only one form of a particular verb (e.g., the third-person singular present) and a different form of another verb (the second-person singular imperative); or they produce only one form of one noun (e.g., in the accusative case) and another form of another noun (the genitive case). In less inflected languages like English or Swedish, they may use only bare noun- and verb-roots at first, without any inflections at all. Reliance on a single inflected form per word, or on bare roots only, is an effect of simplicity of form. In the construction of new words, simplicity (like transparency) predicts that children will rely first on bare roots or combinations of roots before they modify them by adding affixes, shifting word stress, or adjusting vowels and consonants.

Simplicity of form is relative to the options within a language and can't be assessed in an absolute manner across languages. Some languages offer only derivational suffixes for new coinages; others offer both derivation (with suffixes and prefixes) and compounding; still others offer patterns of intercalation (where vowels are inserted between consonants) along with derivational affixes and compounding. Children have to work out the options available and proceed from there. The morphological processes typical of each language will affect what counts as simple versus complex as children learn all the ways to change a root to reflect changes in meaning.

Both simplicity and transparency are dynamic. What counts as transparent changes with what children know. What counts as simple is the degree to which they have, so far, identified possible variants in form for any one word-root, along with any modifications that accompany word-formation patterns. Again, while a preference for making the least change possible prevails early on, as children become better versed in the forms of the language, such a preference carries less weight and has less influence on their choices in word coinage.

Simplicity and transparency can diverge on the acquisition of affixes. The simplest forms for new words are those based on roots alone – for example, uses of zero derivation with noun- or verb-roots, and the construction of root compounds. Adding an affix makes forms more complex; and vowel changes or stress shifts add still more complexity. But as soon as children master the meaning of an affix, it is added to the repertoire of elements that are now transparent. So transparency, unlike simplicity, differentiates among affixes, depending on whether they are already known or not. And affixes in a language tend to be acquired in order. What is transparent, then, may not always be simple. But forms that are simple are transparent.

## Productivity

Another factor that children are sensitive to is the relative productivity of options in the adult language, for example, *-er* versus *-ian* in English *writer* versus *librarian*. Productive patterns in word-formation are those favored by adult speakers when they coin new words. Data on children's lexical innovations across languages show that they attend to the major options available early on and identify productive options before unproductive ones. For example, children acquiring French or Hebrew identify and start using derivational options before they learn the much less productive compounding options. But children acquiring Germanic languages often start with compounding (with root compounds), a highly productive option (Clark 1993). Children learning both language-types use their first affixes for word-formation around age three.

Compounding may be more or less productive than derivation. And within each of these major options, some patterns of compounding are more productive, just as some affixes are. In English, for instance, there are three agentive suffixes – one type I suffix, *-er*, which can be added to any verb-root and also to noun-roots (e.g., *runner, lifter, farmer*); and two type II suffixes, *-ist* and *-ian*, which can be added to a more restricted set of roots, usually Greek or Latin in origin (e.g., *chemist*, *violinist*; *librarian*). The *-er* suffix is the most productive (and the most frequent) of the three in English and is the first to be acquired. Children use it to mark novel agents at around age three and by age four do so consistently (Clark & Hecht 1982). By age four to five, they also produce occasional innovative uses of *-ist* (e.g., *trumpetist* or *drummist* for *trumpeter* and *drummer*).

In one study of productivity, children aged four to six were exposed to sets of six novel words at a time for various "circus groups" (illustrated with pictures of different yoga poses), where each set of words all ended in *-er*, all in *-ist*, or all in *-ian*. Then the children were reminded of the novel (nonsense) word-roots, offered with a prompting intonation, and had to supply the word-endings (Clark & Cohen 1984). They recalled *-er* better (53%) than either of the other two endings (35% and 20%). Four-year-olds substituted *-er* for both *-ist* and *-ian* (19% of the time each) but did not use *-ist* or *-ian* in place of *-er*. Five-year-olds, who were beginning to use the other two suffixes, made substitution errors with all three suffixes (*-er* produced for *-ist* 15% and *-ian* 24%; *-ist* for *-er* 8% and *-ian* 7%; and *-ian* for *-er* 13% and *-ist* 21%). In summary, the more productive of the three suffixes was better remembered and was the most frequent substitute for the other two.

The findings for near-synonymous affixes or word-formation patterns in other languages are very similar: Children learn more productive forms earlier and make wider use of them in their own lexical innovations (Berman 1987; Clark 1993; Clark & Berman 1984). Over time, of course, adults may change the options most favored for coinage. One would therefore expect to see children rely on different options in different eras, and they do. Records from both French- and Polish-speaking children show that their preferences shift along with adult preferences. Children in the 1890s, for example, favored French *-ier* in novel agent nouns, while children nowadays favor agentive *-eur* (Aimard 1975; Compayré 1896; Egger 1887; Grégoire 1947). In Polish children's coinages, there is also a shift from the affixes favored in the 1890s to those in the 1960s (Baudouin de Courtenay 1974; Chmura-Klekotowa 1970).

Overall, these findings show that children track specific patterns in word-formation and their relative frequencies (see further Chapter 16).

## Setting up paradigms

Children have a keen ear for regularity, not only in inflectional morphology (Chapter 8) but also in word-formation. They attend to and later exploit consistent patterns in the language addressed to them. In word-formation, these consistencies guide choices of new word forms for the expression of new meanings. They attend to productivity and readily exploit the patterns they detect, from the occasional single instance as a model – as in *coffee-churn* (for *coffee-grinder*; cf. conventional *milk-churn*) or *yesternight* (for *last night*; cf. conventional *yesterday*) – to widespread use of root compounds. They use these, for instance, for contrasting subcategories, as in *tea-sieve* versus *water-sieve*, for small and large strainers

(2;2.0); *car-smoke* (= exhaust) versus *house-smoke* (from a chimney) (2;4), or *flower-kite* versus *snow-kite*, for kites decorated with flowers and snow-flake patterns (3;2.18).

Children rely on the paradigms they know, particularly when trying to contrast two objects, actions, or properties that are near neighbors. This shows up when they coin words to distinguish subkinds for which they lack a conventional vocabulary. In some cases, there may be no conventional, agreed-on, word, so the child's innovation is quite legitimate. In others, the child is filling a gap, but the term is actually preempted by the conventional adult word, not yet known to the child. In both cases, when children coin a word, they usually make use of an appropriate affix in a derived form, or an appropriate compounding pattern, so the coinage fits into an existing paradigm that uses the same template and where there are already other instances in the same semantic domain. One factor here is how familiar children are with existing compounds. They do better, for example, in offering definitions for compounds that share constituents with other compounds (and so belong to large constituent families) than where they do not share any constituents (Krott & Nicoladis 2005). This suggests that children's analysis of newly encountered compounds may be helped by what they already know about other compounds in the language.

In summary, paradigms in a language reflect general organizing tendencies children adhere to. (Adults use these too.) Wherever possible, they favor patterns of compounding and derivation similar to those found in other terms with nearby meanings. In coining words, children make use of what they know at each stage about the internal structure of words – the roots already identified, familiar affixes, and ways of combining elements to convey a specific meaning. Their skill changes with age as they identify and learn more suffixes and prefixes. They also develop greater skill in constructing complex words, no longer restricting themselves to the simplest ones, as they do at earlier stages. And, in all this, the frequencies of word-formation patterns also play a role. In essence, children use word-formation to make their meaning clear. They coin words to convey meanings where they've not yet acquired the conventional terms.

## Using derivation

Children's earliest attempts to coin words depend on which language they are learning. Different languages offer different options, with some favoring derivation (with or without affixation) and others compounding. Many rely on both. Children coin words from around age two on, and in English a good number of these coinages make use of derivation, at first without and later with affixation. Among the earliest child coinages, in English and other languages, are denominal verbs – verbs coined from nouns that denote some entity associated with the action they wish to talk about. Conventional denominal verbs in English include terms like *to brush* (from the noun *brush*, the instrument used for brushing with), *to dust* (from the noun *dust*, meaning to remove dust from something or some place), and *to captain* (from the noun *captain*, meaning to act as the captain) (see Clark & Clark 1979).

Innovative denominal verbs allow children to talk about specific actions associated with particular roles. These actions are frequently associated with instruments and locata (objects that are located somewhere), as in the typical child innovations *to scale* (= to weigh [with a scale], 2;4), *to broom* (= to hit with a [toy] broom, 2;7), and *to nipple* (= to nurse [an infant], 2;11) among instrument verbs; or *to trouser* (= to put trousers on someone, 2;3), *to pillow* (= to throw a pillow at, 2;6), and *to band-aid* (= to put a band-aid on, 3;4) among locatum verbs (Clark 1982, 1993; also Becker 1994; Bowerman 1985a). Although most of their novel denominal verbs fall into the same categories as adults', they also coin verbs for characteristic activities, e.g., *to buzzer* (said of a buzzer going off, 2;3), *to bell* (said of a bell the child wanted rung, 3;0), and *to truck* (said of a truck going by, 3;0), a type not found in adult usage. They construct novel verbs from adjectives like *flat, dark,* or *straight,* again with zero derivation, and sometimes coin verbs from onomatopoeic exclamations like *pow!, squush,* or *ow!* Tables 11.6 and 11.7 illustrate typical early verb coinages in English. Children acquiring other languages produce innovations very similar to these (see Clark 1982, 1993).

Table 11.6 *Innovative denominal verbs in D's speech*

---

(a) D (2;4.18, waiting in his car-seat, having refused to let his father unbuckle him): *Mom, you buckle me? I can't get out.* [= undo the buckle]

(b) D (2;8.4, to mother in the shower, wanting to paddle in the water in the bottom): *Leave a puddle in there so I can water in it.* [= paddle in water]

(c) D (2;8.4, in the car; the window open in the back, blowing on D, who had some sleep in one eye): *I have my window open so that sleep can wind away.* [= blow away by means of the wind]

(d) D (2;9.1, of a sock): *And did you needle this?* [= mend with a needle]

(e) D (2;9.10, after talking about seeing some boats): *And we might see a man oaring a boat with oars.* [= row]

(f) D (2;11.28, of a car dropped on the floor, to father): *Car me! I want my car.* [= give/hand a car to]

(g) D (3;0.8, playing with new construction toy)
    Mother: And here's a wrench for undoing them. [them = nuts]
    D: *How do you wrench them?* [= use a wrench on]

(h) D (3;0.21, digging a hole on the beach with mother and discussing whether it'll have water in the bottom; D wondering if it'll come in from above): *Will it wave in?* [= come in from/via a wave]

(i) D (3;2.9, picking up the Cuisinart blade mother had left in the sink)
    Mother: You shouldn't take that. It's VERY sharp.
    D: *But I didn't blade myself.* [= cut with the blade]

(j) D (3;4.5, handing mother a small yo-yo on its string): *Eve, will you wind this up for me so I can yo-yo it down?*

---

*Source*: Clark, unpublished diary data

Table 11.7 *Innovative de-adjectival and onomatopoeic verbs in D's speech*

Verbs coined from adjectives

(a) D (2;5.4, in his mother's study, as she demonstrates a small pencil-sharpener)
   Mother: You want to watch me? Remember the picture of Huckle sharpening
   pencils in your school book? Well, I'm going to sharpen some pencils.
   D (holding up some pencils he picked up off the floor): *Sharp these!*

(b) D (2;9.24, PanAm badge, fastened onto and then taken off D's shirt): *No, no, I was tighting it. I tighted my badge, and you should untight it.* [= loosen]

(c) D (2;10.13, explaining, with gestures, why there was peanut butter coming out around the edges of his sandwich): *You flatted and flatted and flatted it and the peanut-butter came out.* [= flatten]

(d) D (2;10.23, first to mother, and then to father one minute later, making his hand flat): *Straight your hand out like this and let me hit it.* [= straighten]

(e) D (3;3.26, wanting to see how a picture on the wall looked with the lights out): *Now turn off the lights and see if it darks it.* [= become dark]

Verbs coined from onomatopoeic expressions

(f) D (2;8.30, watching father comb his wet hair): *That comb is very ...* <repair> *it ows.* [= hurts, < "ow"]

(g) D (3;3.25, mashing up mashed parsnips): *Smush. Smush. Smush. Smush. Smush. I smushed the potatoes.* (then, accompanying the action): *Smush. Smush. Smush. Smush. Smush. Smush.*

(h) D (3;4.2, asking for a second bowl of yogurt and fruit):
   Mother: Your tummy'll say "I've had too much."
   D (uncertain intonation): *No.*
   Father: It doesn't talk, does it?
   D: *It grrrs when your tummy gets hungry.*
   Father: What?
   Mother: Grrrs.
   D: *That's what bears say – grrr – with their claws like this.*

*Source*: Clark, unpublished diary data

In English, nouns have long been the most productive source for new verbs, and children are clearly sensitive to this productivity. Their denominal types, with one exception, fall into the same categories as adult types (Clark 1982). But many of their verb coinages are preempted by existing verbs with just the right meanings. For example, a coinage like *broom* (= sweep) is preempted by adult *sweep*, *needle* by adult *mend*, and *oar* by adult *row*. Verbs from adjectives are often preempted by a different form from the same source, for example, the verb *flat* is preempted by *flatten*, *dark* by *darken*, and *straight* by *straighten*.

By about two-and-half, or sometimes earlier, children start to make use of the first affixes. The earliest of these are typically suffixes like the English diminutive *-ie* or agentive *-er*. Some typical early uses of novel agentive nouns in D's spontaneous speech are shown in Table 11.8. Agentive uses of *-er* appeared several weeks before his first instrumental uses, and they outnumbered instrumental uses by 10:1.

Table 11.8 *Typical innovative derived agent nouns in D's speech*

---

(a) D (2;2.22, to mother who'd just been brushing tea leaves out of the sink with her hand as D sprayed with water from the small hose): *Come here, brusher.*

(b) D (2;3.21, suspended between the table edge and the sofa in the living room): *Look-it at me ... I a climber!*

(c) D (2;4.7, father reading from the "When I'm grown up" page, in *Oh What a Busy Day*, picture of someone typing)
  Father: And what about this one?
  D: *A typewriter.*

(d) D (2;4.14, after extracting a bristle-block from his pocket): *This a gun. You a bad guy, and Herb a bad guy, because I a gunner.*

(e) D (2;5.13, at supper)
  Mother (teasing): Are you an eye-blinker?
  D (began to clap his hands): *I a clapper.*

(f) D (2;5.26, reaching over to put some meat in a bowl at the counter, helping father cook): *I reached right over. I'm a big reacher.*

(g) D (2;6.10, D and mother in the garden; D playing with a trowel while mother planted impatiens): *I'm a big digger. We both diggers.*

(h) D (2;6.27, as came downstairs after mother, to fetch father): *We are both runners. We are both DRIVERS. I drive in the back and YOU drive in the front.*

(i) D (2;7.0): *I'm gonna RUN, and RUN, and RUN, 'cos I'm a BIG RUNNER.*

(j) D (2;7.2, as got out of the car, of the car door): *I'm going to shut that door hard because I'm a shutter.*

(k) D (2;8.5, playing with the tea ball and a mug in the sink): *I have tea in there.*
  Mother: Did you take a sip?
  D (as took out tea ball): *I have a sip. I am a sipper.*

(l) D (2;9.10, on the beach with mother, D raking sand with his toy rake): *I'm a raker.*

---

*Source*: Clark, unpublished diary data

When English-speaking children are asked to coin agent nouns in response to probes like "This man opens things. What could you call him?", they reliably produce verb-roots with *-er* from around age four on (e.g., *opener*). Younger children make some use of *-er*, but they also rely on compounding, combining a noun- or verb-root with a head noun like *-man* (Clark & Hecht 1982). As noted earlier, children grasp the agentive meaning of *-er* before they identify its instrumental meaning. The same lag is evident in other languages where the same suffix serves to mark both agent and instrument meanings (see further Clark 1993).

The advance of agent on instrument uses can be seen in the décalage found both in spontaneous coinages and in systematic elicitation from large numbers of children. Table 11.9 summarizes the patterns of use for all the four-year-olds in parallel studies of English, Icelandic, and Hebrew (Clark & Berman 1984; Clark & Hecht 1982; Mulford 1983). The differences among the three languages appear to be attributable to the number of options available, especially for instrument nouns. In English, children favored *-er* for agents and relied on other forms as well

Table 11.9 *Asymmetries of agent and instrument uses of the same suffix in English (-er), Icelandic (-ari), and Hebrew (-an)*

|  | Agent uses | Instrument uses |
|---|---|---|
| English (3;9–4;5) | 90 | 71 |
| Icelandic (3;9–4;5) | 83 | 49 |
| Hebrew (4;2–4;9) | 62 | 43 |

Based on Clark 1993

for instruments. In Icelandic, many instrument nouns are constructed with zero derivation, and, in fact, four-year-olds relied on this option 41% of the time. In Hebrew, children had to choose among several noun patterns (*mishkalim*) in forming both agent and instrument nouns, but they favored the suffix *-an* for agents over instruments. Four-year-olds also made quite extensive use of nearby, existing instrument nouns (26% of the time). Overall, all three languages offered a mixture of options for instrument nouns and fewer for agent nouns. The first device children picked up on was typically the most productive one for forming new agents – *-er* in English, *-ari* in Icelandic, and *-an* in Hebrew.

Another early affix is the negative prefix *un-* for verbs in English. This prefix marks the reversal or undoing of the original action, as in conventional *untie, unfold*, or *unsaddle*. As Horn (1988) pointed out, use of *un-* connotes return to some prior state of affairs – when a parcel was *tied*, some paper *folded*, or a horse *saddled*. Children's earliest uses of *un-* emerge just before age three and in many cases are applied to the reversal of prior actions of enclosing, covering, or attaching (Clark *et al.* 1995). Some typical early spontaneous uses in English are shown in Table 11.10.

Elicited coinages have a similar pattern of development. When taking part in a game that calls for contradicting someone, English-speaking children rely first on negative particles like *out* or *off* and, from around 3;6 on, on the prefix *un-*. They readily produced particles to reverse actions described with verb-and-particle combinations: *turn on* elicited *turn off*, *hold on* went to *take off*, *tuck in* to *tuck out*, and *plug in* to *plug out*. But they did so more readily when the particle was negative (*off, out, down*) than when it was positive. At age three, they supplied *un-* about 50% of the time for verbs that required it for reversal (e.g., *lock* to *unlock*, *wrap* to *unwrap*, *snap* to *unsnap*) and also some 40% of the time for verbs with suppletive reversal forms (e.g., *bury* to *\*unbury* [for *dig up*], *bend* to *\*unbend* [for *straighten*], *squeeze* to *unsqueeze* [for *let go*]). Very similar errors are produced in Li and MacWhinney's (1996) connectionist model for the acquisition of English *un-*. But children virtually never added *un-* to verbs where the action was irreversible in the world (e.g., *hit, burn, scratch*) (Clark *et al.* 1995), as shown in Table 11.11.

German lacks a reversal prefix like *un-*. In a replication of this task in German, children relied instead on particles to express reversal (return to a prior state). But

Table 11.10 *Typical early spontaneous uses of* un- *for reversal*

---

(a) D (2;8.22, after D had pulled his mother's belt undone)
  Mother: Did someone undo my belt?
  D: *No no, I unpulled it because it wasn't tied yet!*
(b) D (2;9.11, opening the plug in the bidet, to mother outside): *It's unflowing.*
  [= water is flowing out]
(c) D (2;9.24, of his PanAm badge that had been fastened onto and then taken off
  his shirt): *No no, I was tighting it. I tighted my badge, and you should untight it.*
(d) D (2;10.8, wanting to know who'd emptied his money box): *Who took it unfilled?*
(e) D (2;10.20, with his thumbs hidden in his fists): *They've disappeared.*
  Mother: Can you make them appear again?
  D: *No, I can't make it undisappear.*
(f) D (3;1.12, to family friend B who was proofreading, pointing at pencil
  marks on the pages): *Are you going to ungrow those?* [= erase pencil marks]
(g) D (3;3.28, as mother took the decorations off the tree; D looking up
  at the lights): *How do you untake those?*
(h) D (3;4.3, at the table, with his socks off, filling them with nuts from
  his tin; pretending to be Santa Claus as he filled the socks, then taking on
  he role of recipient): *I don't know what's in my stocking.* (feeling it): *I'll have
  to unhang it.* (puts his hand inside): *I know what's in there, it's a bus 'n a
  toy 'n a firetruck …*
(i) D (3;4.8, getting things out of his cubbyhole): *That's a picture and you
  have to uncrumple it to see what it is.*
(j) D (3;5.8, of untaped diaper)
  Mother: I think that's my fault. I didn't tape it properly last time.
  D: *And then it untaped.*
(k) D (3;5,9, out of the blue, to mother): *Show me how you uncatch your necklace.*
(l) D (3;8.11, talking about a castle he'd built): *It doesn't have a door.*
  Father: Then how do you get in?
  D: *I just have to unmake it and put the people in.* (showing how he could
  take a block away)

---

Based on Clark 1981; Clark, Carpenter, & Deutsch 1995

just as in English, German-speaking children did not try to reverse irreversible
actions. Instead, they resorted to forms like *stop* (stop burning that) or *don't* (don't
hit). So, as young as age three, children acquiring these languages are well aware
that some actions can be reversed and others can't, and this knowledge was one
factor that guided them as they tried to express notions of reversal.

In summary, where zero derivation offers a productive option for coining
words, children start to make use of it very early. But the acquisition of affixes
takes time. Just as with inflections, children tend to master suffixes before
prefixes. Again, for both suffixes and prefixes, children acquire relatively productive ones first and only later master less productive ones in the same semantic
domain. In languages that make little use of zero derivation or of compounding,
children produce few lexical innovations before age three or four – they have to

Table 11.11 *Percentage of elicited uses of* un- *by age*

| Age | *un-* verb | Suppletive verb | Irreversible verb |
|-----|-----------|-----------------|-------------------|
| 3;2 | 54 | 44 | 2 |
| 3;8 | 70 | 32 | 3 |
| 4;4 | 94 | 74 | 3 |
| 4;8 | 80 | 64 | 4 |
| Mean | 74 | 54 | 3 |

*Source*: Clark, Carpenter, & Deutsch 1995:649. Used with permission from Cambridge University Press.

wait until they have learnt to produce the relevant affixes for constructing derived word forms.

### Using compounding

Compounding is the other major word-formation process for the construction of new words. Recall that, in English, compounds can be divided into two main classes – root compounds (combinations of two or more root forms, e.g., *snow-tire*, *white-wash*, *sun-rise*) and synthetic compounds (combinations containing at least one verb-root and a derivational affix, e.g., *shoe-maker*, *washing-machine*).

One common function for compound nouns is to identify subcategories of a familiar category. This is one of the first functions assigned to root compounds, as shown by some typical innovations from D's speech (Table 11.12). Compounding serves much the same function in other languages. Children acquiring German, Swedish, and Icelandic construct new root compounds from as young as age two (Clark 1993). In these coinages, they are consistent in placing the head noun – the noun that designates the kind of category being talked about – in the appropriate head slot, and the modifier in the modifier slot. They hardly ever make errors in the order of elements in new root compounds. In English, they are also highly systematic in assigning the appropriate stress pattern, placing primary stress on the modifier (in first position) and much weaker stress on the head noun (in second position) (Clark *et al.* 1985).

With synthetic compounds, they have a much harder time. In these compounds, speakers need to combine a verb-, noun-, or adjective-root and an affix. One of the most productive patterns in English is the *clock-mender* type (Adams 1973; Marchand 1969). The conventional *glass-blower* is for someone who blows glass, or *book-marker*, for the object used to mark the page reached in a book. In both instances, the noun-root appears in modifier position (*glass-* and *book-*) and the verb-root in head position. The head is marked as an agent or instrument with the suffix *-er*. When children are asked to coin synthetic compounds in English, they make two kinds of errors. Young children at first omit the relevant suffixes, and, as

Table 11.12 *Typical early compound nouns in D's spontaneous speech*

(a) D (1;9.27, at breakfast, as mother shook the cream carton): *Milk all gone.*
    Mother: Yes, it's all gone.
    (mother put down the cream carton in front of the half gallon carton on the table)
    D (very pleased tone): *Baby-milk!*
(b) D (1;10.5, looking up at cousin's towel and facecloth on the shower rail above the bath, as mother was running water): *Justin towel.*
    Mother: Yes, that's Justin's towel.
    D (pausing, then pointing up at facecloth): *Baby-towel.*
(c) D (1;10.10, looking at the carpenter who'd come to fix the trellis and who had very curly hair): *Bubble-hair.*
(d) D (1;10.13, as he drank from a 4-oz bottle instead of his usual 8-oz one): *Damon drink* [ə] *milk* [ə] *baby-bottle.*
(e) D (1;11.28, to father): *Read* [ə] *lion-book!*
(f) D (1;11.30, removing *Pigs Go Oink* from mother's knee; book open at a picture of ducks): *I read a Babar-book. Not* [ə] *duck-book.*
(g) D (2;0.15): *Where where my orange-juice-cup?*
(h) D (2;0.21): *Where where yogurt-box?*
(i) D (2;1.9, sitting inside a box that had just been emptied of oranges): *I reading* [ə] *book in* [ə] *orange-box.*
    (then to father): *Herb, I sitting in* [ə] *orange-juice-box.*
    Father: What? In what?
    D: *I sitting* [ə] *box right here, reading.*
    Father: Oh, you are!
(j) D (2;1.18, pointing at muffin bag): *What's that?*
    Father: Well, what is it?
    D: *That* [ə] *bread-bag.*
(k) D (2;2.0, at the sink after he got home): *That* [ə] *tea-sieve.*
    Mother: What?
    D (pointing at the small sieve in the sink): *That* [ə] *tea-sieve.*
    (then pointing at the larger one used for straining vegetables):
    *That* [ə] *water-sieve.*
(l) D (2;3.0, rejecting striped T-shirt in favor of one mother'd told him the day before had little boats on it): *I want my boat-shirt.*

*Source*: Clark, unpublished diary data

late as age four to five, they make order errors, producing the verb-root before the noun-root in the compound. As a result, children acquiring English go through several stages, shown in Table 11.13, before they master the structure of synthetic compounds. The errors that characterize these stages of the highly productive *clock-maker* pattern show that children learn to identify the head appropriately (e.g., by adding -*er*) before they master the correct word order.

Why the order errors in these compounds but not in root compounds? The answer probably lies in an inconsistency in the structure of English. In the verb

Table 11.13 *Stages in the acquisition of English synthetic compounds of the type* clock-maker

| Stage 1 | *V + N | wash-man, open-man |
|---------|-----------------|--------------------|
| Stage 2 | *V + N[object] | hug-kid, break-bottle |
|         | *V-ing + N[object] | moving-box, throwing-ball |
|         | *V-er + N[object] | cutter-grass, puller-wagon |
| Stage 3 | N[object] + V-er | water-drinker, wall-builder |

*Source*: Clark, Hecht, & Mulford 1986:21. Used with permission from Mouton de Gruyter.

phrase, the verb goes first, followed by the direct object and any other arguments or adjuncts (e.g., *make a clock*). But in synthetic compounds, the verb head goes in last or rightmost position (*clock-maker*). The verb-as-head, then, has two different positional assignments, depending on whether it appears in a verb phrase or a compound noun. Children's order errors suggest they initially assign verb heads to the position the verb would have in the verb phrase. One test of this is to look at a language where there is consistency in head placement across the verb phrase and the compound noun. In those languages, children should not make order errors. Hebrew is one such language, and, as predicted, children do not make any order errors in synthetic compounds (Clark & Berman 1987).

Why use compounding rather than derivation? Or why combine the two options, with compounding patterns that include derivational affixes? The draw seems to be that compounding enables speakers to include more material (additional roots, for example) in a novel word form and so add more precision or specificity to its intended meaning. Take an agentive noun like *mender*: It is less precise than *bicycle-mender* (for a person who mends bicycles); similarly, an instrumental noun like *opener* is less specific than *box-opener* (for a tool that opens boxes). In context, the addition of a modifier or two can direct the addressee with even greater specificity to the intended meaning. The amount of information conveyed, of course, is critical when speakers wish to pick out subcategories of known categories. The child coinages, *dalmatian-dog* and *boxer-dog*, pick out subtypes of dogs; and, in each case, the modifier noun adds critical information for distinguishing which subtype is intended. The same goes for compounds like *car-smoke* versus *house-smoke* (for car exhaust vs. smoke from a chimney).

But compounding is not an option in every language, and even where it is an option, it is less productive in some languages than others. In such languages, children tend to wait until age three or four before they make much active use of novel word-formation. Compounding is simply not an option earlier on. They start to use derivational affixes at much the same time as children learning languages that offer both compounding and derivation. But children who rely primarily on derivation also make use of certain constructional alternatives to compounding. They may add specificity and precision to their coinages by attaching additional root forms with prepositional phrases introduced by French *à* or *de* (as in the conventional *rouge à lèvres* 'lipstick' or *vin de pays* 'local wine') or Hebrew *shel* (as in *ben shel gamadim* 'child of smurfs'). They make extensive use of such constructional alternatives in languages where compounding is a less-favored option (Clark & Berman 1987).

Children's coining of words offers general insights into the construction of word forms. It allows us to track what children attend to in the word forms they hear from others, and to follow them as they put together roots and affixes in new combinations. It allows us to ask whether and when they attend to surface order, to the attachment of affixes to a root with a specific role (head versus modifier, say) or to a root in a particular position (leftmost vs. rightmost). It is often easier to check on children's comprehension and to elicit novel word forms than to track their comprehension and production of larger constructions in syntax. Word-formation offers constructions in miniature for study, constructions that nonetheless rely on many of the same factors at work in syntactic constructions.

## Summary

One general goal in speaking is to find the right words, the words for what the speaker wishes to convey to the addressee. Children begin with a small vocabulary and limited resources. They stretch these resources as far as possible: Children under two-and-half or so may overextend words and rely heavily on deictic terms to identify target referents for their addressee (Chapters 4 and 6). Or they may turn quite early on to the construction of word forms to convey their meanings for terms they lack. So when they can't find a word already in place, they coin one. This allows them to fill lexical gaps. What is a gap for one two-year-old, of course, may not be one for the next two-year-old; and gaps for three-year-olds are likely to be much more numerous than gaps for seven- or eight-year-olds. Filling these gaps typically involves nonce uses, just as it does for adults. But such uses also fit regular paradigms, and it may take children some time before they realize that their own coinage carries just the same meaning as some established adult term. Until they arrive at that point, they may hold on to some innovations (e.g., *cooker* for conventional adult *cook* for the person), just as they retain some overregularizations in inflectional morphology for months or even years before replacing them with the adult forms.

When children construct the words they need, they consistently rely on word-formation options from the language being acquired. They don't try out just any random combination of roots and affixes. They use well-established patterns that are productive in adult speech. This results in close adherence by children, from the first, to the word-formation rules of their language. At the same time, since languages favor general word-formation options like derivation versus compounding to different degrees, children learning different language-types follow somewhat different paths (Clark 1993).

Children differ in how much they rely on coinages during acquisition. The coinages in their spontaneous speech suggest there are considerable individual differences in how willing they are to coin words. Some children offer a primer for productive word-formation. Others produce few or no innovations. Despite such individual differences, structured elicitation tasks reveal considerable consistency in what children know when about word forms. They typically master certain root-compounding patterns before any derivational affixes and derivational patterns. They make use of zero derivation before affixes in derivation. And they attend first to those patterns that are productive in adult speech.

# PART III

# Using language

*[L]anguage acquisition is to a great extent the learning of how to make conversations.*

Jean Berko Gleason 1977

*Language is a social art. In acquiring it we have to depend entirely on inter-subjectively available cues as to what to say and when.*

Willard v. O. Quine 1960

Speakers need to make use of different skills to participate fully in conversation. They need to acquire a range of skills, from telling stories to persuading someone of their point of view; from giving instructions to telling jokes; from adjusting one's speech to the level of the interlocutor to translating from one language to another. The focus in these chapters is on children's emerging skills in conversation, as they learn how to talk to different people about different things and how to adjust their speech to accommodate to their addressees as they accumulate common ground in each exchange. Children learn how to present topics and choose goals in conversation. And when they learn two languages at once, they are faced with additional choices – which language to use when.

# 12   Honing conversational skills

What do children need to know and do to participate successfully in conversation? First, they must learn to observe some basic conditions for conversation:

- Speaker and addressee must share a joint focus of attention during the conversational exchange and take account of common ground.
- Speakers must take account of what their addressees know and tailor their utterances accordingly.
- Speakers must choose speech acts that are appropriate for the meanings they intend to convey.
- Participants in a conversation must listen to what others say so they can each make appropriate, relevant contributions when they take a turn.

Establishing joint attention requires speakers to make sure that the addressee is attending both to the speaker and to whatever the speaker is attending to. This condition is essential to successful reference, whether by a child or an adult. Joint attention is supplemented by both physical and conversational co-presence (H. Clark 1996). Physical co-presence is particularly important for young children, since, together with joint attention, it helps solve the mapping problem when they encounter unfamiliar terms. And conversational co-presence gains in importance as children's lexical knowledge and general linguistic skills expand, since they become better able to use whatever linguistic as well as nonlinguistic information speakers offer in the course of conversation.

Speakers also need to be able to convey their intentions, and this requires that their addressees be able to recognize the speech acts they produce. To be successful, speakers need to assess what their addressees already know (their common ground) and tailor their utterances on that basis. In addition, they need to make clear whether they are asserting or commenting on some state of affairs, making a request for information or for action, or presenting some other speech act (a promise, a threat, a greeting, and so on) or a combination of speech acts. Lastly, all the participants in a conversation need to make their contributions relevant, appropriate to the topic at hand at each stage in the exchange.

Speech acts can be classified into several types (Searle 1975). The main categories that have been described are assertives, directives, commissives, expressives, and declarations. First, with an *assertive*, speakers convey their belief that a proposition is true. The commonest assertives are straight assertions (e.g., *Rod left yesterday*), but they can also be introduced by verbs like *suggest*, *hint*, *swear, flatly state*, and so on (e.g., *I swear Rod left yesterday*). These verbs qualify the strength of speakers' beliefs in or commitments to what they are saying (as does the intonation they use). Second, with a *directive*, speakers try to get their addressees to do something – carry out an action in response to *ordering*, *commanding*, *begging*, or *pleading*, or provide information in response to *asking*. The main types of directive are requests and questions (e.g., *Could you open the skylight?*, *D'you know where the stamps are?*). Third, with a *commissive*, speakers commit themselves to some future course of action (e.g., *I will be on time*; *If you lose that, I'll be angry*). They may *promise*, *vow*, *pledge*, or *guarantee* something, or alternatively they may *threaten* something. Promises and threats can be conveyed through intonation and tone, without use of an overt verb like *promise* or *warn*. Fourth, with an *expressive*, speakers convey, within certain social bounds, how they feel about some event. Expressives mark socially sanctioned feelings involved in such acts as *apologizing*, *welcoming*, *congratulating*, or *deploring*. These are all events that carry a specific value in society and are to be expressed in socially acceptable ways. Finally, with a *declaration*, speakers bring about a new state of affairs simply by virtue of saying the relevant words. Consider *I resign*, *I name this child Miranda*, and *I sentence you to ten years*. It is the act of producing these utterances that results in a new state of affairs, for example, one where the child is named Miranda. Most declarations, it turns out, are specialized parts of conventional ceremonies or rituals in law, religion, or government.

As participants in conversation, children must also learn to take turns. This requires appropriate contributions at the right moment in the exchange. Children need to get both the content and the timing of their turns right on each occasion, and this takes considerable skill. Each turn should be designed to add new information to what is already given. Effectively, turns allow each participant to add to common ground, to what is now mutually known, and also to ratify whatever someone else just added. This may be done by repeating some or all of what the other just said, by acknowledging it (*uh-huh*, *yes*, *okay*), or simply by building on that information in the next turn. In taking turns, children will discover some general patterns in conversational exchange: Greetings elicit greetings (*Hello / Hello*, or *How are you? / Fine thanks*), thanks elicit disclaimers (*Thank you for coming / You're welcome* or *No problem*), and questions elicit answers (*Where's the boat? / Over there*). Some of these exchanges have become routinized and always take the same form (many greeting exchanges, for example); others have more variable content. In each case, the next contributor is expected to build in some way on what has already been placed in common ground.

## Speech acts

From around the age of ten months, infants indicate objects they appear to be interested in by pointing at them. Their pointing gestures are readily recognizable, with the index finger extended and the remaining fingers curled into

Table 12.1 *Early speech acts*

| Speech act type | Utterance + gesture(s) | Context |
|---|---|---|
| assertion | **recor(d)** + point | pointing at record player, with record on |
| assertion | **car** + look | turning to window, car passing outside |
| request | **recor(d)** + whine (× 2) | record player just turned off; child wants it on |
| request | **car** + look + whine | wanting toy car that had just fallen on floor |

Based on Greenfield & Smith 1976

a fist. These gestures contrast with a different kind of gesture, less fixed in form, that marks not interest but desire. Infants this age reach persistently towards something they want. Such communicative gestures, typically present before the first words, have been documented by many researchers (Werner & Kaplan 1963) and in recent years have been viewed as the precursors or protoversions of assertives (points) and directives (reaches) (e.g., Bates *et al.* 1975; Bruner 1975).

Early points and reaches become combined with single words and later with combinations of words as children become more skilled. Typical examples from one-year-olds are shown in Table 12.1. The child producing these utterances relied on both gestures (point, look, reach) and intonation (ordinary falling contour, whine). She also differentiated her utterances in terms of the response required: She appeared satisfied (i.e., she stopped repeating the protospeech act) when her assertions were acknowledged by the adult but would persist with her requests until the adult said "yes" or acceded in some other way. This suggests that children this age (around one) are indeed expressing different intentions with these combinations of words and gestures.

Infants under twelve months are already quite attentive to positive and negative affect marked in intonation, to exaggerated intonation contours, and to attention-getters like pointing and gaze (Fernald 1989; Moore & Dunham 1995). This attention to others, along with adult management of interaction, enables infants to achieve the joint attention needed for communication (Chapter 2). Between nine and twelve months, infants themselves actively start to attract adult attention to what interests them (pointing and gazing) or to what they want (reaching, often with plaintive vocalization). Sometimes these efforts involve more active enlisting of adult attention, as when they catch at adult clothing and pull in the direction of something they wish to have opened or something they want reached down off a shelf (Bates 1976). Although adults initially manage joint attention, infants this age begin to take part more fully in interactions, and by about one-and-a-half, they are equal participants with adults in achieving joint attention (see further Estigarribia & Clark 2007; Liszkowski *et al.* 2004; Rowe 2000). At the same time, what infants can do, as late as age two to three, may still be limited by their minimal knowledge about language.

This raises questions about whether children can understand the speaker intentions behind an utterance. How consistent are they in making relevant inferences in response to what adults *say* to them? To what extent do their responses suggest they have understood the speaker's intent and are attempting to reply appropriately? Consider the exchange in (1) between a father and his son, nearly two years old (Clark, diary data):

(1)        D (1;11.28, talking instead of eating at breakfast; father taps the edge of D's
              bowl with a spoon): *Herb hitting* [ə] *bowl.*
           FATHER: Why was I hitting your bowl? Why was I hitting your bowl?
           D (grinning as he picked up his spoon): [ə] *eat* [ə] *cornflakes.*

In drawing the child's attention to the bowl by tapping it, the father seems to have implied something was wrong. This inference is supported by his subsequent question. And the child draws the intended inference, as he makes clear in the next turn. Are children systematic in making pragmatic inferences like this?

A preliminary answer can be seen in young children's responses to requests. Two-year-olds consistently respond to requests for information or action by acting. If asked "Where's the door?" they typically open the door if it is shut or shut it if it is open (Shatz 1978a, 1978b). That is, they look for some way (relevant to the request) to change the current state of affairs and then do it. Since their vocabularies are limited, it is unclear how well they actually understand the requests in full; they appear to rely on what they can construe of each situation, helped by whatever terms they understand and then compute a possible change in state. Shatz characterized the responses two-year-olds offered as supporting the view that children at first treat language as "a specifier of requisite actions appropriate to the context" (1978b:295). Their inferences about the speaker's intentions, then, may initially depend more on their interpretations of the current context than on real understanding of the speaker (see also Blake *et al.* 2003; Marcos, Ryckebusch, & Rabain-Jamin 2003).

One-year-olds are already rather adept at construing situations: They already appear to take an "intentional stance" in interpreting goal-directed behaviors of rational agents. In one study, Gergely and his colleagues (2002) had fourteen-month-olds watch an adult turn on a light-box by bending forward and touching it with her forehead. In one condition, the adult is holding a shawl round her shoulders, so her hands are not free; in the other, her hands are free. In the shawl condition, 69% of the infants used their foreheads in imitating the adult's action, but in the hands-free condition, only 21% did so. The remainder used their hands to turn on the light-box (see also Gergely & Csibra 2003; Csibra *et al.* 2003).

The ability to make inferences in context is critical because it affords children a basis for interpreting the speaker's intentions at a stage when their knowledge of language is very limited. It also provides a basis for the coping strategies they adopt in the early stages of mapping meanings onto words (Chapter 6) and helps them accumulate information across contexts as they gradually fill in details about meanings for words and constructions, and hence also about speaker intentions.

Children begin to participate in conversation early in acquisition. They contribute one-word utterances both in response to adult prompts and questions, and in initiating exchanges with adults. In fact, some two thirds of adult–child conversations with very young children are initiated by the children (Bloom *et al.* 1996). While the earliest "turns" in preverbal infants are imposed by adults who count smiles and babbles as turns (Snow 1977), by age one, children often take a more deliberate role in contributing to conversation.

## Taking turns

When children contribute to what is being said, they may at first need help from other speakers in the form of scaffolding (e.g., Pratt *et al.* 1988; Rome-Flanders, Cronk, & Gourde 1995). The adult presents a *scaffold* of information about the pertinent event and thereby prompts the child to supply just the piece of information needed at that moment, as in the exchange in (2). This exchange also shows how dependent the participants are on common ground as D is encouraged to tell his father about an earlier episode when Philip (aged ten) had let out his budgerigar; it had flown around, then landed on D's head, and this had frightened him (Clark, diary data).

(2)        MOTHER: Did you see Philip's bird? Can you tell Herb?
           D (1;6.11): *Head, head, head.*
           MOTHER: What landed on your head?
           D: *Bird.*

The scaffolding by the adult also makes clearer the accidental (rather than deliberately organized) nature of turn-taking. The person to speak next is whoever believes he has pertinent information to offer, following the speaker who is just completing a prior utterance (H. Clark 1996).

One way to assess children's skill in conversation is to look at whether they can offer pertinent information when asked or when they interject something into an ongoing exchange. This skill has been studied from several different perspectives – answering parental questions and getting responses to child contributions; joining in conversations between other family members; and contributing to conversations between a parent and an older sibling. This skill also attests to children's ability to track the current topic and to draw on information relevant to it.

In one study of three mother-and-child dyads, Lieven (1978) examined two claims: first, that children are learning to take turns in both vocal and nonvocal interactions from an early age, and second, that they express various intentions systematically prior to speaking. Although all three children appeared equally responsive to adult utterances, one mother responded about twice as often as the other two. Six months later, all three mothers responded to fewer of their children's utterances, while the children responded to more of the adults' utterances (Figure 12.1). After documenting individual differences in the three dyads, Lieven suggested that conversation between mother and child is related to how well organized the child's utterances are and to the sophistication with which the

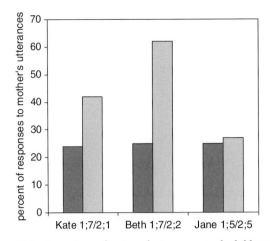

Figure 12.1 *Percentage of maternal utterances each child responded to, at each age. Based on Lieven 1978*

child uses language (see also Lieven 1997). While Lieven looked at child responses to adult utterances, she did not look at the details of turn-taking per se, nor at what made for success or failure in children's attempts to contribute.[1]

Another measure of skill in turn-taking is how successful children are in interrupting the current speaker. As they get older, children get better at timing their interruptions (Ervin-Tripp 1979). Children under 4;6 entered at syntactic or prosodic boundaries 25% of the time when they interrupted a single speaker, but they got the timing right only about 12% of the time when they interrupted an ongoing dyad. Older children (from 4;6 to 6;0) did better, with appropriate timing about 27% of the time, regardless of whether they were interrupting a single speaker or a dyad. The younger children appeared to take more time processing an ongoing conversation, so when they did try to take a turn, they were often late. In a further analysis, Ervin-Tripp found that two-year-olds produced delayed responses 27%–55% of the time following their interruptions, compared to four-year-olds, who responded with a delay 9%–20% of the time after interrupting.

Ervin-Tripp argued that no deliberate shaping is needed for children to learn to take turns in conversation. A child's interest alone in what the speaker is saying suffices to focus attention on the speaker. She noted that there were orderly dyadic interchanges in children as young as age two, who could reply to greetings, *yes/no* questions, confirmation questions, control questions, or commands and offers (see also Wellman & Lempers 1977). But two-year-olds often lack "tying devices" to link their utterances to what went before; they allow long gaps between speakers, and their mistiming gives an impression of incompetence when bidding for the

---

[1] Other factors that might play a role here are parental attitudes to child-rearing and hence to adult–child interaction, social class, and perhaps religious affiliations (see Heath 1983; Miller 1982, 1986; Wiley 1997). See also Chapter 14.

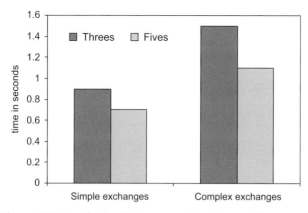

Figure 12.2 *Length of switching pauses for three- and five-year-olds in simple and more complex exchanges. Based on Garvey 1984*

next turn. Their mistiming, in fact, can result in their contributions appearing less relevant and their interruptions being ignored by other participants (see also Dunn & Shatz 1989).

If children are much slower than adults in formulating their contributions to a conversation, they may take longer to switch speakers. Garvey (1984) called this interval between turns the "switching pause." She measured the length of this pause as children successfully switched from one speaker to the next using a question or some other turn-transfer technique. For three-year-old dyads, the median switching pause duration was just under one second (0.9 sec) for the simplest exchanges (greetings or requests for repetition), while the median duration was 1.5 seconds in more complicated exchanges (e.g., answering a *wh*-question, as in *What's that noise? – Maybe it's a typewriter*). For five-year-old dyads, switching pauses were significantly shorter at 0.7 second in simpler turn-transfers and 1.1 seconds in more complex ones, as shown in Figure 12.2.

Young children actively track what other people are saying. When two-and-a-half-year-olds overhear their own names in conversations between others, they consistently look at the addressee, possibly expecting to be addressed in the next turn (Forrester 1988). Children aged two to three often offer relevant intrusions into conversations between parents and older siblings, further evidence that they are attending. In their analysis of regular recordings of family interactions over more than a year, Dunn and Shatz (1989) found that intrusions were quite frequent even when the younger children were just two and became more so in the course of the year. Some typical exchanges are given in (3) and (4) (Dunn & Shatz 1989:402–403):

(3)         Older sibling to mother (about a picture): *I don't know where to stick it.*
            MOTHER to sibling: On your door. Stick it on your door.
            CHILD (2;9): *I'll stick it for her.*

Table 12.2 *Rate of intrusions during the third year*

|  | Age (years; months) | | | | | |
|---|---|---|---|---|---|---|
|  | 2;0 | 2;2 | 2;4 | 2;6 | 2;9 | 3;0 |
| Intrusions per 100 child turns | 22 | 19 | 23 | 22 | 25 | 21 |
| Intrusions per 100 child-to-other turns | 12 | 13 | 19 | 20 | 22 | 25 |

*Source*: Dunn & Shatz 1989:405. Used with permission from the Society for Research in Child Development.

(4) Older sibling is playing a pretend game with mother about a pretend shopping trip; she gets confused about where she has put her bag down:

> SIBLING to mother: *Did I leave my bag there?* [i.e., at the "shop"]
> MOTHER to sibling: You didn't leave your bag at Sainsbury's did you?
> CHILD to sibling: (pointing out bag at pretend "home"): *No! At home!*

Intrusions per se could simply be bids for adult attention, so although an intrusion provides evidence of attention, it doesn't give evidence of understanding. But if an intrusion contains information pertinent to the current topic, then one can infer that the younger child is both attending to and understanding the ongoing conversation. An intrusion, then, can be used to simply interrupt (attention), or serve to join the conversation (attention + understanding). Over the course of the year, the overall rate of child intrusions didn't change. But the rate of intrusions *addressed to others* doubled, as shown in Table 12.2. This suggests that the younger children understood more of the conversations they were tracking as they got older, so their interruptions became more pertinent.

There was a steady increase with age for intrusions that contained new information, from 41% at age two to 68% at age three. The relevance of this information depended on whether the preceding turn was about the child. Where the topic was the child, the relevance was generally very high (97% at age two, and rising); where the topic was something else, the relevance was much lower (between 36% and 61%). At the same time, the number of irrelevant intrusions declined steadily with age, from 29% at two to 10% at three.

Young children, then, do pay attention to language in their presence even if it is not being directed at them. It is unclear whether one-year-olds attend to much speech from others, but by age two, they are attending at least some of the time to speech from older siblings and to older siblings in conversation with parents. This in turn suggests that they become attentive to a growing range of information about language use as they get older (see also Akhtar, Jipson, & Callanan 2001; Akhtar 2005).

Children who are even younger (one-and-a-half to two) can participate in triadic conversations with a parent and an older sibling (aged four or five) and do so more often as they get older (Barton & Tomasello 1991). These triadic conversations are typically three times longer than dyadic ones, not because the mothers and older siblings make larger contributions, but because the younger siblings produce nearly twice as many turns. In fact, the younger children are as likely to make a relevant contribution after a turn addressed to another participant as they are to an utterance addressed to them. (The younger children in these conversations took about 25% of the turns, the mothers about 50%, and the older siblings the remaining 25%.) Barton and Tomasello suggested that there was less conversational pressure on younger children in triadic conversations than in dyadic ones, and this made it easier for the younger children to participate. But young children take longer to plan their utterances and so often mistime their contributions, which suggests that triadic exchanges are harder to take part in than dyadic ones.

### Being informative

Do children's first contributions to conversation make sense? How can this be assessed? One option is to look at how informative they are in terms of what can be assumed in context and what not, or what is certain versus uncertain. If children are being informative, their contributions should be about what is *not* assumed or *not* certain within an exchange (Greenfield 1979:160). Take the situation where the child might or might not be in possession of something. When an object is not in the child's possession, its identity becomes uncertain in context. Under these circumstances, Greenfield proposed, the child becomes more likely to mention that object. But when the object is securely in the child's possession but undergoing a change, the identity of the object is certain, so the child will be more likely to talk about the change instead. Effectively, children should encode what is uncertain, so it then becomes part of what is certain or known, and therefore added to common ground. If the child continues to talk about the situation, he will now express some other aspect of it, up to now unmentioned. Greenfield's analysis assumes only that the child thinks that what he has in his hands need not be mentioned (certain), processes of change are important, and the least certain part of any situation gets mentioned first.

Can this proposal be related to the notions of given and new in an utterance once children are past contributing just one word at a time? If what is uncertain constitutes new information with one-word contributions, what happens as children start to use longer utterances? Greenfield attached considerable significance to the child's initial utterance containing information that was uncertain and hence more informative. But with longer utterances, other observational studies have suggested that children place given information first and follow it with what is new (e.g., Bates 1976; see also Chapter 7). This view is supported by children's consistent assignment of focal stress in longer utterances to new information (Fernald & Mazzie 1991; Wieman 1976).

The notions of given and new are relative to what the speaker judges that addressees do or don't know (Prince 1981). Can children as young as two take into account what their addressees know? To assess this, one needs to set children up so the actual information available about the situation can be accurately measured. This is what O'Neill (1996) did in her study of how well two-year-olds kept track of what their parents knew. In a first study, the children (mean age 2;7) were shown a toy by the experimenter; the toy was then placed in a box or cup on a shelf out of reach. They had been told that their mother was going to help them in the game and that they needed to drop the toy into another container. (This game was readily grasped after a few practice trials.) During this initial phase, the mother was either present in the room, watching what was going on, or else absent, outside the room or seated with eyes closed, unable to see where the toy was placed. What happened when the children requested help in getting the toy back? As predicted, they offered significantly more information about where the toy was – they named the location, or gestured towards it – in trials where the mother did *not* know the location than in trials where she did.

In a second game, children had to enlist their mothers' help to retrieve stickers dropped into one of two identical opaque containers, out of reach at the corners of the table where the child was seated. The experimenter dropped each sticker into one of the containers, and the child had to retrieve it to stick it on a picture on the table. Again, the mother was designated as the helper; on two trials she was present, observing, and on the other two she sat with eyes closed and ears covered. Again, the children – this time aged 2;3 – used significantly more gestures to indicate the target location in the closed-eye trials than in the open-eye ones. They also alternated their gaze between parent and target container more often in closed-eye trials. These findings strongly suggest they were taking into account whether knowledge of the location could be assumed, and therefore part of mutual knowledge, or not (see also Moll *et al.* 2006).

Overall, these findings offer strong evidence that children as young as 2;3 can assess what the other person knows and supply the information needed for the current goal in the game. Notice that the information needed was the location of the relevant container, and the children supplied this much more often when the parent *didn't* know which container was used than when the parent did. Effectively, these children are supplying *relevant, new* information. This is consistent with Maratsos' (1973) finding that three-and-a-half-year-olds gave additional information to their addressees, provided it is clear that they need it (see also Nayer & Graham 2006).

How skilled are two-year-olds at engaging others in conversation, adapting messages to addressees and situations, and responding to feedback? Wellman and Lempers (1977) videotaped ten children (aged 2;2 to 3;0) for ten hours, with one child the main focus in each hour of tape. Of 300 conversational interactions initiated by the children, 79% (236) were directed at adults, and 21% (sixty-four) at other two-year-olds. Overall, 79% of the children's messages elicited an adequate response from their addressees. In 54% of the cases where child-speakers received no response, they reformulated their initial message and tried again. (This compared to just 3% of reformulations by children where they had received an adequate response.) Very few of the children's utterances received negative verbal responses, but on every occasion where this happened, the children rephrased what they were trying to say.

Slightly older children display still more skill. In one study of four- to five-year-old dyads, children were placed in pretend-play settings where their general knowledge about the relevant event was either the same or different. All the children were first assessed for what they knew about four activities or *scripts*: taking a plane trip, baking cookies, doing the laundry, and going to the dentist. Children were then paired up with other children they did not know on the basis of a match in knowledge for one script and a mismatch for another, and were then recorded as they played at each script event for ten minutes, with a break between play sessions (Short-Meyerson & Abbeduto 1997).

Children with matching knowledge should find it easier to maintain play, while those mismatched in knowledge should take longer to establish the appropriate play. Indeed, mismatched pairs took more turns to establish common ground (24%) than matched ones did (14%). Children also made more clarification requests in mismatched pairs than in matched ones. And the proportion of turns maintaining the topic within a script was greater for pairs matched in knowledge than in pairs who were mismatched. So where participants start with some common ground, communication is easier: Matched children who both knew about trips on planes talked more about that script in their play than mismatched children did. Lastly, the fact that play was maintained successfully by both matched and mismatched pairs shows, in addition, that by age four children were relatively skilled at accommodating to their partners' lack of knowledge.

When do children take account of given versus new in a systematic fashion? By taking up whatever was new in the preceding speaker's utterance, the child can (a) indicate that that information is now given, in common ground, and (b) add new information. One- and two-year-olds can add new information with the help of scaffolding (e.g., Veneziano *et al.* 1990; see also Rozendaal & Baker 2008), but have difficulty presenting given and new information within the same utterance. They repeat new information to ratify it and so add it to common ground, but rarely add something new of their own. By three-and-a-half, though, they both ratify and add their own new information in exchanges with adults (Clark & Bernicot 2008). Four- and five-year-olds do better still in tracking what is given and what new for their addressees (Saylor, Baird, & Gallerani 2006).

At the same time, negotiating the frame of reference to be used as common ground can be complicated. The speaker may need to establish in detail what the interlocutor knows about the geography of a city, say, to give successful directions so the addressee can reach a particular goal. Or the speaker might give route directions where speaker and addressee must first establish the same starting point on their respective town models and find ways to resolve ambiguities introduced by symmetry of design (e.g., two bridges, two large buildings, two statues, etc.) before they can coordinate further (e.g., Weissenborn 1986; Iverson 1999). In giving directions, these speakers have to choose what will be most informative to their addressees – which streets to follow, which landmarks to note (and distinguishing candidate landmarks that both fit the description given), and how to use terms like *left* and *right*. Between the ages of seven and fourteen, children go from offering route directions that take account mainly of what the speaker sees, to anticipating what could cause the addressee difficulty and articulating precisely the factors the addressee must attend to. That is, the speaker needs to be able both to encode the relevant linguistic information, and to take the other's perspective in tracking what's in common ground so far. In summary, assessing the addressee's needs in such circumstances requires a range of skills that takes many years to achieve.

## Constructing utterances across speakers

The contributions of each participant in a conversation rarely have clear boundaries. Speaker and addressee often collaborate to arrive at an expression of the intended meaning. Child and adult may jointly construct a proposition, as when an adult offers a scaffold for the child's contributions in talking about a specific event known to both of them. Several researchers have suggested that collaboration on the production of utterances may be fundamental to children's acquisition of linguistic structures (e.g., Garvey 1979; Ochs, Schieffelin, & Platt 1979; Scollon 1976; Veneziano *et al.* 1990). Ochs and her colleagues (1979) looked at the steps used in opening an exchange in young child–child and in adult–child conversations. The sequential construction of a proposition, they argued, involves four steps, any one of which can be repeated within the sequence:

1.    The speaker gives evidence of noticing some entity $X$.
2.    The speaker attempts to get the addressee to notice $X$.
3.    The addressee offers evidence of noticing $X$.
4.    The speaker or addressee provides or elicits additional information about $X$.

### Step 1: The speaker gives evidence of noticing some entity $X$

This step may be initiated nonverbally or verbally (use of pointing, shift in gaze; use of a deictic term like *there*, *that*; use of a referring expression as in [*the*] *horse*; or use of an exclamation like *uh-oh* or *hey*, as in the exchange in (5) (see Ochs *et al.* 1979; Estigarribia & Clark 2007):

(5)    Allison (1;8.21, noticing that mother's juice has spilled)
       ALLISON: *uh-oh*.
       MOTHER: Uh-oh.
       ALLISON (smiling, looking at juice spilled on floor): *mommy*.
       MOTHER: What did mommy do?
       ALLISON: *spill*.

### Step 2: The speaker attempts to get the addressee to notice $X$

Here the speaker can rely on one of two strategies. Strategy 1 is to repeat Step 1 (indicate what you have noticed), and Strategy 2 is to use a

Table 12.3 *Two attention-getting strategies and their possible expressions*

| Strategy 1: Indicate that you have noticed $X$ | |
| --- | --- |
| Nonverbal | Verbal |
| 1. pointing<br>2. looking at object | 1. name<br>2. deictic pronoun or adverb<br>3. expressive particle<br>4. greeting term |

| Strategy 2: Attract your addressee's attention | |
| --- | --- |
| 1. touching hearer<br>  a. pulling<br>  b. tugging<br>  c. tapping<br>2. showing $X$ to hearer, holding up $X$<br>3. giving $X$ to hearer<br>4. initiating eye contact<br>5. movement toward hearer | 1. vocative<br>2. locative directives, e.g., look at $X$, see $X$<br>3. interrogatives<br>4. prosodic devices<br>  a. whining<br>  b. screaming<br>  c. increased pitch or amplitude<br>  d. whispering |

*Source*: Ochs, Schieffelin, & Platt 1979:257. Used with permission from Academic Press.

communicative device to attract the attention of the addressee. Ways to instantiate these two strategies are summarized in Table 12.3.

Step 2 is illustrated in (6) and (7). The first exchange is from Brenda (1;7), who was trying to get her mother to attend to the shoe she is holding up and relied, successively, on gestures, use of a vocative (*mama*), and a series of attempts to produce the word *shoe* in a form recognizable to her addressee (her mother) (Scollon 1979:215):

(6)      B held up mother's shoe and looked at it
        B: *mama. mama. mama. mam.*
        B: *sh. shi. sh. shiss. shoe. shoesh.*

The second exchange is from G (2;11), who was trying to get his mother's attention (Ochs *et al.* 1979:258). G began with a vocative (*mummy*) and then named the toy (*choo choo*) before repeating the vocative, turning to gesture (holding up the train), and again using the vocative before he finally got his mother's attention:

(7)      G has been handed a toy train by another adult
        G: *mummy.*
        G: *choo choo.*
        G: *mummy.*
        (G holds up train to mother)
        G: *mummy.*
        MOTHER: What's that?

### Step 3: The addressee offers evidence of noticing *X*

When addressees do this, they indicate that *X* is now a joint focus of attention. From this point on, *X* can be considered as given. Evidence for this is (a) repetition of part or all of a prior turn, (b) an expansion, or (c) a predication relevant to *X*.

The exchanges in (8) and (9) illustrate this step, the first with a partial repetition, where Toby repeats the last two words of the adult's utterance and thereby marks the activity referred to as given (Ochs *et al.* 1979:259; see also Clark & Bernicot 2008):

(8)    Toby (2;9), in kitchen with nanny
       NANNY: And we're going to cook sausages.
       TOBY: *cook sausage.*

In (9), Ronald offers an expansion by commenting on one aspect of *X* until his mother acknowledges his comment by repeating it, and so places it in common ground (Ochs *et al.* 1979:260):

(9)    Ronald (2;0) and mother playing with dog, Sheshe
       R: *yard.*
       R: *mom.*
       MOTHER: What?
       R: *yard.*
       MOTHER: Yard. Yeah, Sheshe's out in the yard.

### Step 4: The speaker or addressee provides or elicits additional information about *X*

Just as Step 2 entails Step 1, so Step 4 entails Step 3. Both steps can be accomplished at once by Step 4, or else Step 3 can be done separately. In the exchanges in (10) and (11), the second speaker's response to the previous speaker constitutes an acknowledgement of what was said. In (10), the mother acknowledges the child's utterance by repeating it and then asks a follow-up question (Bloom 1973:179):

(10)    ALLISON (1;7.14, pointing to box): *box.*
        MOTHER: Box. What do you think is in that box?

In (11), the first speaker's contribution is rejected and thereby acknowledged (Ochs *et al.* 1979:261):

(11)    Toby and David (twins, 2;10, eating spaghetti)
        DAVID: *skabetis.*
        TOBY: *no skabetis.*
        TOBY: *makaronis.*

A similar analysis applies to questions and assertions relevant to the first speaker's contribution: Both offer evidence that the second speaker is attending to what the prior speaker has said. Consider the parental acknowledgements and follow-up questions in (12) and (13), in exchanges between two two-year-olds and their mothers (Ochs *et al.* 1979:262):

(12)        RONALD (2;0, attending to a car coming down the street)
            R: *dat.*
            MOTHER: What is that?
            R: *car.*

(13)        ANGELIQUE (2;0): *mommy doll here/*
            A: [?].
            A: *mommy button off.*
            A: *mommy button off.*
            A: *button off.*
            MOTHER: OK, just a second. You want to take it off?
            A: *uh-huh.*

Ochs and her colleagues suggested that repetition in such exchanges offers an interactional, pragmatic device, distinct from syntactic options, such as use of an anaphoric pronoun, a definite article, or a relative clause, to highlight the information that both participants can, from now on, regard as given, namely what is in their joint focus of attention in the current exchange.

Shifts in this locus of attention are often achieved through questions, something that might account for the prevalence of adult questions in child-directed speech. Consider the next exchange in (14), between Allison and her mother, where the mother's question serves to shift the child's attention from the truck to the bag of toys. Once the child has given evidence of the shift (by her gaze), the mother follows up with an instruction to get the bag, which the child follows (Bloom 1973:190):

(14)        MOTHER: Do you think there's another baby in your bag? Allison.
            (Allison, 1;7.14, steps in truck but looks towards bag)
            MOTHER: Do you think there's another baby in your bag?
            MOTHER: Go get the bag.
            ALLISON (goes to bag, pulling out another doll): *more.*
            ALLISON: *there.*
            ALLISON: *there!*

Adult questions and directions in such exchanges can also offer a partial scaffold for the child's fragmentary contributions. The adult's contributions often offer a framework into which the child's contribution can be slotted. This framework may contain all but one argument of the verb ("The cat climbed what?") or all but one or two elements of the target utterance for describing the current event ("The little boy peeped into the …") (see also Chapter 7). Such shared construction of utterances offers children a way of contributing turns to a conversation long before they know very much about the conventional constructions available in their language (see Scollon 1976; Veneziano *et al.* 1990).

## Repetition and its functions

In conversations with children, the child frequently proposes a term, the adult counters it in adding a further comment, and the child then *repeats* one or more words from the adult's most recent utterance, much as in (15) (Bloom, Hood, & Lightbown 1974:380):

(15)     PETER (1;9.7, opening the cover of tape recorder): *Open. Open. Open.*
          ADULT: Did you open it?
          PETER (watching the tape recorder): ***Open it.***
          ADULT: Did you open the tape recorder?
          PETER (still watching the tape recorder): ***Tape recorder.***

Repetitions like this appear to serve several functions, sometimes simultaneously. They help speaker and addressee establish common ground; they allow the current speaker to ratify what the previous speaker proposed; and they mark uptake of information about words (or relations among words) offered by the previous speaker.

Child utterances that repeat part of a previous utterance have often been characterized as imitations, especially for children who are still producing only one or two words at a time. (This may stem from the long-term emphasis on the role of imitation in learning.) But notice that what has often been called imitation in adult–child exchanges as in (15) is *not* called imitation in an adult–adult exchange. Essentially, the functions of repeats by children have generally been ignored. When children say something the adult has just said, it is labeled as an imitation, with imitation being regarded as fairly self-explanatory. But the kind of repeat such exchanges exemplify has a distinct function in conversation. By repeating, that speaker accepts and ratifies the expression proposed by the other speaker. In the case of children, they are often accepting terms they have been offered, sometimes in lieu of their own word for that reference. Since their vocabulary often lacks the words needed, they frequently take up the adult term offered instead. A repeat under such circumstances attests to the child's uptake of the new word on that occasion (Clark 1998, 2002a; Clark & Wong 2002; Clark 2007).

If children repeat to mark their uptake, when do they do so? The obvious place to repeat a term would be in the turn just after it was introduced by the adult. Yet studies of imitation commonly assume an expression is being imitated as long as it occurs within five turns of the adult's introduction. How often, then, is the child's repeat in the next turn? In a study of six children, Bloom and her colleagues (1974) observed that four of them were very likely to "imitate" immediately after the adult's utterance. Inspection of the numbers of imitations from these children (observed from around 1;7–1;9 until 1;11–2;0) showed high rates of *immediate* imitations, in the next turn (between 60% and 80%). Two other children, Gia and Allison, "imitated" immediately after the adult's utterance about half the time, on average, but overall produced many fewer imitations than the other four.

Table 12.4 *Percentage of repeats of familiar words (at two points in time) compared to repeats of new words, for five children*

| Child | Time 1/repeat rate | Time 2/repeat rate | New word/repeat rate |
|---|---|---|---|
| Eve, 1;6–2;3 | 23 | 16 | 54 |
| Naomi, 1;1–5;1 | 26 | 23 | 62 |
| Adam, 2;3–4;1 | 33 | 22 | 54 |
| Sarah, 2;3–5;1 | 34 | 12 | 56 |
| Abe, 2;4–5;0 | 15 | 14 | 29 |

Based on Clark 2007

These children, by repeating, are ratifying the term offered by the adult in the preceding turn. This should happen mostly with terms unfamiliar to children, since those are the ones where children are most in need of the right word (Clark 2007). With familiar terms, children should be more secure about their own choices and so more willing to hold on to them. (They may even reject [rather than endorse] the adult offer in the next turn.) This view is supported by the finding that children are significantly more likely to repeat new words they are offered than to repeat new information, as shown in Table 12.4.

Repetitions, then, appear to have at least two functions for children. First, they connote acceptance or ratification of the adult term; second, they offer children an opportunity to try to produce the target term in a recognizable fashion and thus practice the as-yet unfamiliar term. How often children choose to ratify new terms this way may vary. It depends on the vocabulary the child already knows as well as on skills for the structuring of turns and the contents of turns in conversation.[2]

Whether repeats in conversation are answers or whether they ratify what the previous speaker just said, they should be more frequent after adult questions than after other types of adult utterances, and they are. Réger (1986) studied the discourse functions of repeats in longitudinal data collected from two children acquiring Hungarian. At first, both children were equally likely to repeat part of the adult's utterance whether in response to questions or in following up non-questions (around 1;7). But as they got older, they began to use repeats twice as often after questions compared to nonquestions (around 2;3). These repeats were clearly to be taken as responses that ratified information in questions. Réger also analyzed her data to see whether the children's repetitions contributed to their acquisition of unfamiliar words. She counted words as *lexically new* if they had never appeared prior to the child's repeat. For both children, a high proportion of

---

[2] In evaluating the contents of a turn, there is also a general sampling problem for observations relative to the child's current vocabulary. Diary studies, for example, with daily observations undoubtedly offer a more accurate record of just what words children have attempted and can produce, with the apparent initial and subsequent meanings (e.g., Dromi 1987), but to assess usage quantitatively, one needs regular recordings. Diary data, though, offer a better assessment of just what children do and don't know about the conventional vocabulary.

repeated words were lexically new – for Balázs, 43% of his repeats between 1;7 and 2;0, and for Vilma, 37% of her repeats between 1;10 and 2;0.

Researchers have disagreed about the extent to which repetition plays a role in the learning of grammatical structure. Ervin (1964), for example, found no spontaneous imitations that were grammatically progressive (but see Bloom *et al.* 1974). Others have argued against a structure-learning view because of repetitions where the participants do not appear to fill the roles of expert and novice, but are instead participants on an equal footing. Take the adult exchange in (16) cited by McTear (1978:295):

(16)     A: What's yours?
         B: A pint of bitter.
         A: A pint of bitter. Okay.

Speaker A isn't learning a new phrase with the repeat of B's utterance but *is* ratifying or confirming what B said he wanted. Adult-to-adult repeats can mark a request for clarification, emphatic agreement, solidarity, or they can confirm understanding, and so on. Likewise, in symmetrical child–child interactions, repetition often serves communicative or interactional ends rather than a learning function (Keenan 1974b; Keenan & Klein 1975). The point here is that repetition in conversation has multiple functions, and each one may play a different role in acquisition.

McTear (1978:295) tried to distinguish between imitation and repetition. "In imitation, the observer perceives a preceding utterance as a model, intends to copy it and manifests the novel behavior in the process." Repetitions, in his view, "serve as communicative speech acts" and their nature changes as children acquire more rules of conversational interaction. He looked at three functions of repetition in conversation, namely (a) repetition to express agreement or interest, (b) repetition as a form of verbal play, and (c) repetition of the other's questions. Observations come from his daughter, Siobhan, aged 2;6–3;1, with a few more at 3;7 (see McTear 1978, 1985).

### Repetition as agreement

The ability to engage in conversation assumes a capacity for joint attention and action. One way to mark this joint attention is to repeat the utterance just issued by the other speaker. This often occurs at boundaries in a sequence, as in (17):

(17)     FATHER: Right then.
         SIOBHAN: *Right then*.

(Adults do this too.) Children also use repetition to acknowledge the preceding utterance. In Keenan and Klein's (1975) study of early-morning conversations between twin boys aged 2;9, 59% of the responses to assertions were repeats. By three, this number had dropped, and the twins instead began to rely on more complex forms of acknowledgement. Besides the learning of new words (Clark 1998, 2002a, 2007; Réger 1986), repetitions can mark the acquisition of general facts, as in the exchange in (18) (McTear 1978:297):

(18)          SIOBHAN: *... putting the milk in the cows.*
              FATHER:   Oh no, they're taking it OUT of the cows.
              SIOBHAN: **Taking it OUT of the cows.**
              FATHER:   ... People can drink the milk then.
              SIOBHAN: **People can drink the milk then**.

Repetition also serves to establish discourse topics: What is repeated by the second speaker becomes given information (the topic) and is then available for further comment by the first speaker.

### Repetition as verbal play

This type of repetition is common with the return of an insult, say, accompanied by added stress on the pronoun *you*, as in the exchange in (19) between Siobhan, aged 3;0, and her father (McTear 1978:299):

(19)          FATHER (jocularly): You're a wee tough / a nice wee girl / a wee scruff.
              SIOBHAN: *you **a wee tough / a nice wee girl / a wee scruff**.*

Such play exchanges are marked by laughter, pointing at the recipient of the insult, challenging postures, and exaggerated gestures (see also Garvey 1977; Goodwin 1990).

### Repetition of questions

Up to 3;7, Siobhan often repeated questions addressed to her. If she knew the answer, she typically replied quite appropriately, as in the question–answer exchange in (20) (McTear 1978:304):

(20)          FATHER: Do you want to go down to the swings?
              SIOBHAN (doing jigsaw puzzle): *I finish the bits first.*

But if the requests were taken as being "for display," Siobhan typically supplied some appropriate information, just as she would have to a request for information, repeated the question, or repeated the question and supplied the answer. Instances of the last two are shown in (21) and (22) (McTear 1978:305):

(21)          FATHER: What are they doing?
              SIOBHAN: **What they doing?**

(22)          FATHER (indicating tape recorder cable): What's that?
              SIOBHAN: **What's that?** *That goes in there.*

*What's that* questions, McTear proposed, draw attention to something ("look at that") and assign the role of respondent to the addressee ("tell me what that is"). Siobhan's repeats without answers to such questions, he suggested, are rejections of the respondent role that reassign the speaker role to the original speaker. After about 3;7, her repeats of questions became rare, and she instead began answering with *Don't know*.

In summary, repetition can have many roles in conversation. An important one is to acknowledge and ratify what the other speaker has said. Children may thereby signal the addition of some information to common ground, signal uptake of a new word just offered, or acknowledge that an adult interpretation was correct (Chouinard & Clark 2003; Clark 2002a). Overall, repetition often adds coherence (Benoit 1982), indicating that both child and adult are keeping track of common ground in the exchange.

## Requests and offers

In any conversation, the participants need to assess what the current speaker's intention is. Is the speaker making a request for action or for information? Is the speaker making an offer and therefore now waiting for an acceptance or rejection? Is he making a promise or threat, a future commitment on his part? Is he marking a social exchange with a greeting, an apology, a thank you? Is he carrying out some act coextensive with his actual utterance, as in *You're it, I resign*, or *I name this ship the Nereid*? (See further Austin 1962; H. Clark 1996.) To assess speaker intentions, children must identify the speech act and work out which utterance forms can carry which functions.[3] However, since a single construction can be used with several functions, children have to infer the speaker's intention both from what they already know about form and function in the language, and from the content of the utterance itself.

When young speakers of English are asked to make judgements about offers and requests, they appear able, by age three, to distinguish some of the conditions associated with different speech act types. Reeder (1980) focussed on two questions. First, which features, linguistic and pragmatic, constitute cues for discriminating the speaker's intended meaning? Second, how can young children distinguish requests from offers? He set up contexts where children heard variants of "Would you like to do *X*?" and then had to judge whether this utterance was equivalent to either "I <u>want</u> you to do *X*" (in request contexts only) or "I'll <u>let</u> you do *X*" (in offer contexts only). On each trial, children heard a sentence followed by the two variants that they were to judge, as in (23):[4]

(23)      "Would you like to play on the train?"
          I want you to play on the train.
          I'll let you play on the train.

---

[3] Early on, children may rely on a one-to-one match of form and function. For example, one two-year-old consistently used utterances of the form *more* + *N* as requests (demands), and utterances of the form *two* + *N* as assertions of fact (Ervin-Tripp 1974). Another child, Dory, used an invariant *see* to mark assertions and *want* to mark requests in her first nine weeks of multiword utterances (Gruber 1973).

[4] All initial sentences were recorded with a high-fall terminal contour, and the two alternatives to be judged with a mid-fall contour so as to avoid any prosodic bias in children's choices (see further Reeder 1980).

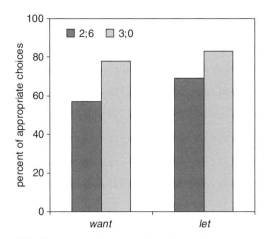

Figure 12.3 *Percentage of appropriate choices for* want *(request) compared to* let *(offer), by age. Based on Reeder 1980*

In OFFER trials, the child addressee A stood near the toy and the adult speaker S stood at a neutral distance from it. In REQUEST trials, S stood near the toy and A at some distance from it. These scenarios, Reeder argued, were adequate to license the pragmatic inferences that could distinguish offers, as in (24), from requests, as in (25):

(24)        OFFER O1 A wants to do act *X*
                        O2 No indication that S wants A to do *X*
                        O3 No indication that S objects to A doing *X*

(25)        REQUEST R1 S wants A to do *X*
                        R2 No indication that A wants to do *X*
                        R3 No indication that A objects to doing *X*

At 2;6, children generally chose the "let" variant for offers (69% of the time), but didn't yet show a preference for the "want" variant for requests. By age three, they chose the appropriate variants most of the time for both offers and requests (Figure 12.3). Just how were the children identifying the relevant speech act? They were probably using a simple pragmatic strategy: When A is close to the toy, A wants to play with it; and when S is closer, S can let A play. This, of course, requires that children keep track of S with some care. In fact, the younger group (2;6) did better on the scenarios when S was close to the toy than when A was.

Children's knowledge of speech acts has also been studied by eliciting utterances designed to express particular intentions from children themselves. Grimm (1975) set up a series of scenarios designed to elicit specific speech acts from children aged five and seven. She included acts of asking, ordering, forbidding, and allowing (all directives), and of promising (a commissive). Sample scenarios designed to elicit requests (with *ask*) and prohibitions (with *forbid*), both directives, are given in (26) and (27):

(26)      To get a child to *ask* for something:
      "You're at the playground with Felix [a large toy cat]. He's sitting on the swing and you're on the slide. Now you'd like Felix to let you swing too. What do you say to him?"

(27)      To get a child to *forbid* something:
      "You want to visit someone and you've put on your best clothes. Felix is smearing paint everywhere and would like to get some on you too. You don't want him to get paint on you. What do you say?"

To elicit several directives on each occasion, the experimenter made Felix refuse to comply with the first three requests the child made. This allowed her to find out how many different forms (up to four) the child could come up with in trying to get the cat to comply. Consider a typical exchange between a seven-year-old and Felix the cat (whose voice was supplied by the experimenter), shown in (28):

(28)      CHILD: *Felix, will you let me swing too, just once, please?*
      FELIX: I don't want you to swing. [refusal 1]
      CHILD: *But then you can slide down the slide.*
      FELIX: I'd rather not let you swing. [refusal 2]
      CHILD: *I'd like to swing just once, not you all the time.*
      FELIX: I'd still rather not let you swing. [refusal 3]
      CHILD: *But you must!*

Overall, children found it easier to make certain requests (*ask, order, forbid*) than to allow something or to make a promise about something (a speech act where the speaker commits to doing something). The percentages of utterances counted as adequate instantiations of the target speech act are shown for two age groups in Table 12.5. Five-year-olds did well on three of the four types of directive[5] but less well when the target was *permit* (directive) or *promise* (commissive). Since all directives place the obligation for the outcome on the addressee (the addressee is the one who will carry out the action requested), while commissives place it on the speaker, the pattern of acquisition in Table 12.5 suggests that children find it easier to grasp speech acts that require addressees to act than speech acts where speakers are obligated to act. The older children in Grimm's study did well on the directive-types but, like the five-year-olds, still knew less about making promises (see also Chomsky 1969; Grimm & Schöler 1975).

---

[5] James (1978) compared the politeness of four-year-olds' request forms to different-aged addressees in situations designed to elicit either positive requests (for someone to do something) or negative ones (for someone not to do something). She found that children were politer when they made positive requests; they were also politer to adult addressees than to peers, and politer to peers than to two-year-olds. One small measure of this can be seen in their uses of *please*: It appeared in 84% of requests to adults but in only 37% of requests to two-year-olds.

Table 12.5 *Adequate utterances for each speech-act type by age*

|  | Directives | | | Commissives | |
| --- | --- | --- | --- | --- | --- |
| Age | ask | order | forbid | permit | promise |
| 5;0–5;6 | 82 | 92 | 86 | 51 | 57 |
| 7;0–7;6 | 95 | 92 | 93 | 86 | 55 |

Based on Grimm 1975

## Breakdowns in conversation

Finally, children early on become adept at repairing their communications when they go awry. When one- and two-year-olds fail to make themselves understood when they mispronounce words, they often try again, "fixing up" at least part of the problem word. They rely extensively on gesture to supplement their small vocabularies (Golinkoff 1986; Marcos 1991; Marcos & Kornhaber-Le Chanu 1992), and they may try out other words from a nearby semantic domain in their efforts to get adults to understand them (Scollon 1976).

From as young as age one, children regularly reject misinterpretations on the part of the adult addressee and reword, maintain, and adjust their meaning over several turns as they try to make themselves understood. Consider the extended exchange in (29) between a preverbal child, Jordan (aged 1;2), and his mother, in which the child persists until his mother figures out what he really wants (Golinkoff 1983:58):

(29)     JORDAN (vocalizes repeatedly until his mother turns around)
         MOTHER (turns around to look at him)
         JORDAN (points to one of the objects on the counter)
         MOTHER: Do you want this? (holds up milk container)
         JORDAN (shakes his head no)
              (vocalizes, continues to point)
         MOTHER: Do you want this? (holds up jelly jar)
         JORDAN (shakes his head no)
              (continues to point)
              [2 more offer-rejection pairs]
         MOTHER: This? (holds up sponge)
         JORDAN (leans back in high-chair, puts arms down, tension leaves body)
         MOTHER (hands Jordan sponge)

With language, children exhibit a similar persistence in making themselves understood, but their pronunciations may be hard to understand because they fall far short of the target forms. As a result, they often repair what they have just said. And when they make repairs to their own words, they generally manage to produce a version that is closer to the adult target than their own original attempt (Clark 1982; Käsermann & Foppa 1981). Such repairs are often triggered by adult signs of noncomprehension or active miscomprehension, conveyed for instance by the adult's misidentification of the intended target (Scollon 1976). Children this age are also sensitive to who their addressee is: They are more likely to repair their utterances for unfamiliar adults than for familiar ones. The latter can more readily deal with imperfections in children's pronunciations, but unfamiliar adults have a harder time identifying the intended targets (Tomasello, Farrar, & Dines 1984).

Finally, children as young as two already have a good understanding of how to deal with adult repairs. They are aware that they need to discard information that has been repaired and replace it by the speaker's more recent offering. In one study, young two-year-olds were taught a new word, *dax*, for an unfamiliar object-type; then, after all the learning trials were finished, the experimenter made an explicit repair like "Oops, these aren't daxes; they're ruks" and then proceeded to teach the word *ruk* as the target term for the same objects (Clark & Grossman 1998). At the end, nearly all the children realized that they did *not* know what *dax* meant (the first term they'd been taught). And they did know *ruk*, the second term. Similarly, children this age are able to distinguish intended from accidental actions performed in teaching them a new word. Verbal signals marking accidental actions (*uh-oh*, *oops*, etc.) effectively lead two-year-olds to ignore those events in favor of others (e.g., Tomasello & Barton 1994).

At age two, then, children are already quite skilled at tracking the speaker's intentions in a variety of settings. The speaker's intentions can be obscured by language that is too complex, but in the tasks studied, children showed good understanding of the pragmatic consequences of speaker repairs. These abilities are not unique to humans: Orangutans modify their gestural signaling in response to the addressee's degree of comprehension (Cartmill & Byrne 2007). Young children are also responsive to requests for clarification, whether from peers (Garvey 1979; Aviezer 2003) or adults (e.g., Corsaro 1977; Gallagher 1977). These requests keep interactions running smoothly and repair possible disruptions. They come in three main forms: (a) a simple clarification marker (e.g., *huh?*, *hum?*, *what?*); (b) repetition of the child's utterance (whole or part) with question intonation added; and (c) repetition with a modification that expands what the child said. These requests clear up misunderstandings from not hearing or from misinterpreting the child, and they acknowledge the child's contribution. Children are responsive to such requests: They may repeat themselves, make repairs to pronunciation, reword what they were trying to say, or speak more loudly. Their repair often zeroes in on the "trouble" that led the adult to ask for clarification (see also Chouinard & Clark 2003).

## Summary

Children are eager to communicate and in their first two years of talking learn how to contribute to conversational exchanges and how to take turns. They learn to contribute information that is pertinent and new for the addressee. This in turn depends on their ability to track what others do and don't yet know, and to tailor their own contributions accordingly. The next chapter looks in more detail at how children learn to express their intentions, how they use language to mark social roles, and how they start to distinguish different genres – to give directions, to persuade, to tell stories.

# 13    Doing things with language

As children become more skilled at using language, they use it in more ways for greater effect. They make use of a growing array of linguistic options to mark social roles for both speaker and addressee. They learn what features identify speech as appropriate for a child compared to an adult, a girl compared to a boy, a teacher compared to a student, a doctor compared to a patient. They learn how to mark membership in different communities in society, from family to classroom, band, computer lab, tennis team, and adventure camp. As children grow up, they become members of other communities and learn how to mark their membership linguistically in each. They also learn how to do things with language: They learn how to be polite and how to be persuasive. They learn how to negotiate to resolve conflicts. They learn to distinguish actual events from play. They learn how to talk inside the classroom as well as outside. And they learn how to tell stories, becoming increasingly adept at presenting protagonists and their motives, and at tracking those events that move the action along.

To manage this, children must extend their repertoires of speech acts. Speech acts have often been represented as a matter for the speaker alone (e.g., Searle 1975), but in conversation, speaker and addressee often collaborate in the production of a single act, so traditional descriptions mislead in leaving out addressees (see H. Clark 1996). And in mastering the many words and constructions for each speech act, children must realize that there is no single match of form and function. Specific forms can be used for many functions depending on the speaker, addressee, setting, and preceding conversation. And specific functions can be conveyed by many forms. As children add to their repertoires of both forms and functions, they become more effective in how they use language (Budwig 1995; Slobin 2001b). This chapter focusses first on language skills that mark social roles and then on the genres of language use that speakers exploit to achieve their goals.

## Social roles

Speakers use language to present themselves. They use language to identify the role they take in one context versus another – a father, a teacher, a tour guide, a pianist. They use language to signal intimacy and distance. And they use language in ways that mark gender or status or power. When do children master these dimensions of language use?

## Style or register

A major part of learning to talk is learning *how* to talk, on different occasions, with different addressees, for different purposes. To do this, children need to master different styles or registers of speech, tailored to specific social roles and social circumstances. Style or register is a way of speaking that is marked by its use rather than by its users. Ferguson (1994:20) characterized the notion of a register this way: "People participating in recurrent communication situations tend to develop similar vocabularies, similar features of intonation, and characteristic bits of syntax and phonology that they use in these situations." Consider how one speaks to childhood friends, to an older relative versus a younger sibling, to a stranger versus a friend, to a teacher in the classroom versus a clerk in the post office, and so on. Language use clearly does not come in just one variety: It can take on many different guises depending on both the current social role the speaker is projecting (e.g., friend, parent, teacher, waiter), the role of the addressee in the current setting, and any relation that holds between speaker and addressee.

For children, it is important to learn different registers and what determines their choice in the larger speech community. This in turn requires attention to different kinds of interaction (e.g., instructing, teasing, narrating), different settings for interaction (e.g., home, school, clinic, airport), different (sub)groups in which one is marking membership or solidarity (e.g., social groupings in schools), and different addressees (e.g., adult, child, family, friend, stranger). These distinctions contribute to a highly preliminary list, because speakers belong to many groups, which may change over their lifetimes, and they each take on many roles depending on the group, the context, and the addressee on each occasion. In short, the skills children will learn, as speakers, are extensive and take many years to master. There are also individual differences in how well any one person learns to deploy the options for specific roles in particular settings.

## Social categories and linguistic choices

Every speaker belongs to a range of speech communities. Gumperz (1982) defined speech community as a group of speakers that shares rules and norms for using language. That means that each member must learn the relevant practices in using language for marking the role relevant on each occasion. But since communities differ widely on what their rules and norms are, the practice used to mark a role in one community is not necessarily used in another, even *within* the same language (French, Hungarian, or English, say). That is, social practices in language use are always relative to a speech community. Moreover, particular roles – teacher, parent, doctor, bus-driver – and gender categories – male, female – are also manifested in language *relative* to each community. There is probably no single practice that marks a specific role in an invariant way across all communities (Eckert & McConnell-Ginet 1992). Children must learn how to adopt the practices for each role they take on, so they need exposure to a variety of roles and communities as they grow up.

In most societies, people, including very young children, are assigned to a particular gender. While this is done on a biological basis, biology and society are intricately connected, so part of learning language is learning how to construct one's identity as male or female through local language practices. Other categories salient to young children are those of adult versus child, one of the general dimensions of power in society; of father versus mother within the family, and of older sibling. Young children are likely to come into contact early with the roles of doctor, nurse, and teacher. If they take notice of the language used in such roles, this may show up in play. At the same time, one might expect that only frequently used, stereotypical features of speech associated with a role appear at first. Variations in how a specific role is marked in different communities take longer to acquire and need sustained observation with membership in those communities. That can only come much later in development, possibly not until adolescence (Eckert 2000).

How do young children enact roles like mother or father versus baby or child? How do they distinguish doctor from patient from nurse? Or teacher from child? Researchers have looked in some detail at which linguistic means children first use to mark such roles and how well they can keep two or more roles distinct (Andersen 1990). One highly successful technique for tracking this knowledge is what Andersen has characterized as "controlled improvisation." In her study, children did the voices for puppets in three settings – the home, the doctor's office, and the classroom. In each setting, children did the voices for at least two puppets at a time and usually produced contrasting "voices" for all three puppets (e.g., father, mother, and child in the home setting, or doctor, nurse, and child-patient in the doctor's office). The puppets, in effect, differed on such dimensions as age (parent vs. child), sex (male vs. female), professional status (doctor vs. nurse), and linguistic skill (adult vs. baby). Voices for these roles were elicited from children aged 4;7, 5;4, and 6;10.

Andersen's analyses focussed on the amount of speech for each "speaker" to each "addressee"; the functions of utterance-types in each role; and the syntactic, semantic, and phonological devices used to mark particular registers. Overall, children appeared sensitive to the relative power of each speaker. For example, more powerful roles made use of less polite request-types, and less powerful roles used politer request-types. In the three settings, greater power was associated with the roles of father, doctor, and teacher. When doing the voices for roles with less power, children were also more likely to use indirect requests and need-based comments that did not entail loss of face if the request were ignored or refused, as shown in Table 13.1.

When doing the voices of child-to-mother and child-to-father, children were sensitive to differences of power. Speech for child-to-mother was more likely to contain "need" statements and to use imperatives as requests, e.g., *I need some ice cream* or *Gimme some ice cream*, while speech for child-to-father was more likely

Table 13.1 *Request-types elicited in the family setting*

| Directive type | Parent-to-child | Child-to-parent |
|---|---|---|
| 1. Hint (*Sweetie, time to wake up*) | 42 | 3 |
| 2. Need (*Mommy, I want a drink of water*) | 2 | 51 |
| 3. Imperative (*Go home!*) | 39 | 13 |
| 4. *Let's* (*Let's turn to page 3*) | 4 | 9 |
| 5. *You ...* (*Now you push the button*) | 4 | 1 |
| 6. Request (*Would you take me home?*) | 9 | 23 |

*Source*: Andersen 1990:130. Used with permission from Routledge.

to contain indirect requests and often relied on less direct forms, for example, *Ice cream tastes nice doesn't it?* and *Might we be able to get some ice cream?*

In marking specific roles for their puppets, children also made consistent use of prosody. They used high voices for small children, and low voices for adult males. (One child contrasted the role of father [a low voice] with that of doctor by giving the doctor a foreign accent.) They used an extended pitch range in doing adult speech to a young child and very slow speech in talking to a baby or a foreigner. And in talking for a young child, they tried to simplify word forms, for instance, substituting some sounds for others and simplifying clusters (e.g., *wid* for *with*, *bwefis* for *breakfast*). Although four-year-olds relied on such cues in their speech to distinguish one role from another, they often failed to maintain the roles: Their use of low pitch, for example, often slipped after the first word or so, and four-year-olds were less likely than older children to reinstate that prosodic role marker. But by age six to seven, children were quite good at maintaining roles throughout each scenario.

Children also made extensive use of lexical and morphological marking. Speech from a small child, for instance, was often marked by the omission of function words – articles and prepositions. In all three settings, children opted for specialized vocabulary for the relevant domains. The younger children, four- and five-year-olds, typically had only scanty knowledge of the relevant vocabulary for the doctor session but used what they had. Typical terms produced by the children included *temperature* and *thermometer* (often confused), *cast*, *broken*, *cut* [operate], *damage* (in the throat), *medical* [medicine], *shot-things* [syringes], *stitches*, *X-ray*, and *aspirin*. This is captured in the following offering from one six-year-old who was doing the voice for the doctor: *I'll have to operate – scalpel, screwdriver, and uh, what else can we use?* These children are just beginning to acquire the specialized vocabulary for this domain, but full mastery can take many years.

In summary, Andersen's controlled improvisations show that children grasp some critical features of language use by age four to five. They are aware that the speaker's choices of forms (constructions, vocabulary, address terms) depend on the speaker's role, and this in turn reflects status, age, and gender. Each of these dimensions, examined separately, can be distinguished by choices of how to talk in that role. So as children do the voices for puppets, they reveal what they have observed so far about language for different roles in different settings. But they still have a long way to go. They will discover more and more roles and learn how to mark those too. The social practices behind the construction of each role in a community demand careful attention to what marks an insider, a member of the community, and a real instantiator of each role (see further Eckert 2000; Milroy 1980).

## Constructing social roles: Gender

One aspect of such role construction involves learning to mark gender and status. Children, like adults, construct social roles through their choices of how to talk – the words and expressions to use, the pronunciations to favor, and the specific dialect or language to opt for – in particular settings and on particular occasions (Goodwin 1990; Ochs 1992). This applies as much to the social construction of gender – how to talk as a boy versus as a girl in the elementary school classroom, say – as it does in the social construction of status arising from expertise – how to talk as a doctor to a patient, for example. But few aspects of language appear to be used exclusively to index gender. When speakers make choices, they typically mark both gender and status at the same time (Ochs 1992).

Choice of how to make a request, for instance, often simultaneously indexes the speaker's gender and status. Requests made in imperative form (*Gimme that*, *Get in the car*) index both male gender and greater status, depending on the context. Ochs (1992) proposed that the imperative indexes status first and then offers a secondary index for gender (male). Requests made with questions and mitigating forms (*Do you want to give me that?*, *Could you get in the car please?*) often index female gender and lesser status. But politer forms (requests as questions, with mitigating phrases) can also be used to mark higher status. In short, there is no one-to-one connection of such choices and the linguistic marking of particular social roles.

Both parents and teachers offer children models of requests that differ in gender and power. Fathers, for example, address more imperatives to their children than mothers do (38% vs. 19%), and male day-care center teachers use more imperatives than female ones (11% vs. 2%) (Berko Gleason & Greif 1983). So request-type is one dimension that children can make use of as they construct their social roles in the classroom, and indeed they do.

In some accounts of conflict and cooperation, the kinds of communication favored by girls and boys differ at a fairly young age (Goodwin 1990; Sheldon 1990). Despite teacher efforts to neutralize gender in nursery schools, stereotyping by gender appears to be well established by age five. It emerges, for example, in children's play, in the activities they choose, and in how they talk about those activities (Cook-Gumperz & Scales 1996; Paley 1984; Sheldon & Rohleder 1996; also Andersen 1990).

In play-story settings, for instance, boys spend less time than girls in narrating the story and more time in negotiating on the events to go into the story. At age four, the narrative of the play takes 36% of the time for girls compared to 22% for boys, and at age seven, the narrative takes 65% of the time for girls compared to 38% for boys. Negotiations also differ by gender, with boys using more challenges and refusing proposals put forward by others; they also tend to leave subordinate clauses unmarked by connectives like *because* or *if*, and simply offer the reason, condition, or justification on its own. Girls, in contrast, use more persuasive forms in their negotiations about a story (*Let's ...*, *Pretend that ...*). They also make more use of subordinate clauses, with the relevant connectives, than of the simpler, bare clauses favored by boys (Kyratzis 1993; Ochs & Taylor 1995).

In short, children are sensitive to differences in language that correlate with gender and status from an early age. Learning what kinds of talk are appropriate for specific roles and identifying their status in different settings, of course, takes time. While most people have good control over the language for the social groups they frequent the most, it is less common to find speakers who have the skills to fit in everywhere. Few speakers control a large number of speech styles, just as few speakers control more than two or three dialects, or more than two or three languages. And many speakers may have control over only one dialect in only one language.

## Making use of expertise

As children learn about how to use their language, they often have recourse to experts, namely to adults and older siblings who provide words and phrasing to convey particular meanings. Young children take adults as their source in deciding on appropriate words for things, but they reject potential experts if they offer information that conflicts with what the children already know, or if they display signs of uncertainty or lack of knowledge in proposing options for what something unfamiliar might be called. In one series of studies, adults offered sixteen-month-olds either true (conventional) or false (nonconventional) labels for common objects with labels already known to the infants. They looked significantly longer at the adult in response to false labels than true ones, and they were more likely to correct false labels produced by an adult they could see than false labels produced from an audio speaker (Koenig & Echols 2003).

Both three- and four-year-olds rely on knowledgeable speakers over ignorant ones, and do so for both verbal and nonverbal information. And four-year-olds, but not threes, use information about an adult speaker's accuracy to make predictions about future reliability as a source of expertise. When exposed to previously accurate versus inaccurate informants who provided conflicting names for new objects, the older children consistently endorsed the labels offered by the accurate adult speakers (Koenig & Harris 2005; see also Koenig, Clément, & Harris 2004). At the same time, three-year-olds appear more willing to attend to adult speakers who exhibit certainty in naming odd-shaped objects such as a key-like object designated as a spoon, "This is a spoon," than to adults who express some uncertainty, "I think this is a spoon" (Jaswal & Malone 2007). And they are even less taken by adult errors when these are combined with distraction. In short, both language use and behavior on the part of potential experts affect young children's reactions.

When three- and four-year-olds have a chance to assess adult accuracy, by watching films of two people who label familiar objects with differential accuracy (100% versus 0% accurate, 100% versus 25%, 75% versus 0%, or 75% versus 25%), and then see a second set of films in which the same two people offer labels for unfamiliar objects, they differ by age in whose labels they accept. Three-year-olds trusted the adult speaker only where the adult was 100% correct on familiar labeling, but four-year-olds gave a more graded judgement. They went with the more accurate adult speaker in all four conditions tested (Pasquini *et al.* 2007).

In short, children expect adults to give information that is consistent with what they already know, and when they don't, they become cautious about trusting them as experts on language use. Effectively, they observe the Cooperative Principle in conversation from early on, and expect other (adult) speakers to do the same. And at the core of this principle is the assumption that speakers are truthful, so any information they offer can be trusted.

## Distinguishing among addressees

Four-year-olds are quite skilled at distinguishing among addressees. For example, four-year-olds speak to younger siblings differently from adults (e.g., Shatz & Gelman 1973). They use short utterances, many attention-getters in the form of the addressee's name or uses of *Look!* or *Hey!*, a lot of repetition, and extensive imperatives in giving instructions to two-year-olds. When offering instructions about the same toys to adults, their utterances are considerably longer; they use few imperatives and virtually no attention-getters. They also make use of some politeness markers and hedges (e.g., *I think this is lamb*, said of a toy lamb). Analyses of spontaneous conversations with other four-year-olds and with adults showed that they adjusted a lot for two-year-olds (and did so more, the younger the two-year-old), but treated their peers, who would be at their same level of development, in the same way as adults (Shatz & Gelman 1973; see also Sachs & Devin 1976).

These distinctions among addressees by age are consonant with their growing skills in doing voices for others. Sachs and Devin (1976) recorded four children (aged 3;9 to 5;5) talking to an adult, a peer, a baby, and a baby doll, as well as role-playing "a baby just learning how to talk." The speech addressed to adults and peers versus babies replicated earlier findings. Children distinguished younger addressees by shortening their utterances, using attention-getters, and modifying their speech along other dimensions, as shown for Sally's speech in Table 13.2.

Sally used longer utterances to her mother than to the baby doll. These utterances contained more material prior to the verb. She also used more

Table 13.2 *Differences in Sally's speech at 3;9 to different addressees*

| Measure | To mother | To peer | To baby | To baby doll | As baby |
|---|---|---|---|---|---|
| Length of utterance | 4.35 | 3.84 | 3.98 | 3.35 | 2.83 |
| Preverb length | 1.46 | 1.65 | 1.25 | 1.03 | 1.00 |
| Nonpresent tense | 0.34 | 0.29 | 0.21 | 0.05 | 0.00 |
| Name use | 0.03 | 0.09 | 0.11 | 0.22 | 0.00 |
| Imperatives | 0.08 | 0.16 | 0.38 | 0.20 | 0.00 |

*Source*: Sachs & Devin 1976:86. Used with permission from Cambridge University Press.

nonpresent tenses to the adult, more name use to the baby doll, and more imperatives to the baby. As the last column of Table 13.2 shows, when Sally spoke as if she were a baby, she followed the same trends, but more so, as she did in talking to the baby or baby doll.

Children also talk differently to mothers and fathers. This probably depends on how much time each parent spends with the child and on how well each parent understands what the child says. Familiarity is a factor here, with the more familiar parent being addressed less formally (and less politely) than the other parent. This distinction typically matches the difference in status and gender that shows up in children's role-play (see also Newcombe & Zaslow 1981; Read & Cherry 1978).

Finally, children as young as two begin to tailor their utterances to their addressees in order to take advantage of common ground (Chapter 12). They appear to be already aware that information known to be available to both speaker and addressee can be assumed, while information not available to the addressee must be added to the conversation before it too can be taken for granted (e.g., O'Neill 1996).

### Distinguishing *given* from *new*

As children become more skilled linguistically, they start to mark information in their utterances as given (assumed to be already known to participants in the conversation) compared to new (assumed to be, up to now, unknown to the addressee). From adults, they consistently hear information partitioned in this way: Repeated words (given) are quieter, shorter, lower-pitched, and less variable in pitch than first-mentioned (new) words, just as they are in adult-to-adult speech. Given information is also less prominent syntactically (usually non-final) compared to new information, which is usually in final position, louder, and uttered with clause-final stress (e.g., Fisher & Tokura 1995). Children make use of stress in word-learning tasks, focussing on words that are stressed and so more prominent over ones that are not stressed (Grassmann & Tomasello 2007), and they make use of sentential stress themselves to mark new information (see Chapter 7).

When children are asked to match utterances to pictures, do they attend more to given information in choosing a match, or more to new information, when the pictures match utterances only on given or only on new information? In a study of six- to ten-year-olds, Hornby (1971) found that, with age, children were more likely to choose pictures that matched given information. When they were asked to fix the sentences to match pictures on both given and new information, children at all ages produced appropriate forms and marked new information with focal stress (see also Hornby & Hass 1970).

Another common device for distinguishing given from new is the use of definite and indefinite articles. The first mention of new information calls for an indefinite article (as in *a boy*), while subsequent mentions call for definite articles (as in *the boy*). This pattern is illustrated in the hypothetical exchange in (1):

(1)      A: There was a boy in that tree yesterday.
         B: So?
         A: The boy climbed up to see if he could reach the squirrel's nest.

Children start to use articles around age two, but their early uses are often indeterminate between definite and indefinite since they take the form of a schwa [ə] (see also Peters & Menn 1993; Veneziano & Sinclair 2000; Rozendaal & Baker 2008). By age three, children contrast definite and indefinite forms but tend to overuse the definite article. As a result, they seem to treat some new information as given instead of new. When three- to nine-year-olds were asked to tell a short story based on three cartoon pictures with repeat appearances of some characters, they made very few errors and displayed no changes with age in their uses of definite articles. But in contexts calling for indefinites (first mentions and hence new), they used the definite article over half the time (54%) at age three and continued to misuse it as late as age nine, as shown in Figure 13.1 (Warden 1976, 1981; see also Maratsos 1974, 1976).

Children acquiring French make the same error. Bresson and his colleagues found that six-year-olds used definite *le* (masculine) or *la* (feminine) 38% of the time where adults used indefinite *un* or *une*. With the plural, they did even worse and used definite *les* 76% of the time in contexts calling for indefinite *des* (Bresson 1977; Bresson *et al.* 1970; see also Karmiloff-Smith 1979, and, for Turkish, Küntay 2002).

Overuse of definite forms in indefinite contexts suggests that children could be misassessing what their addressees actually know. This could be because they are not yet very skilled at assessing differences between what they know compared to what their addressees know. Or they could be going just by what they themselves know in choosing a definite article where, for the addressee, the information is actually new. Yet children as young as two can on occasion take good account of what an addressee knows (O'Neill 1996), so the apparent misattribution of too much knowledge more likely reflects both lack of skill in using articles to mark information as given versus new, and uncertainty about what the speaker and the addressee each know.

Use of an article goes along with use of a lexical noun phrase in referring to a specific entity. And speakers typically rely on lexical noun phrases like *a hoop* or

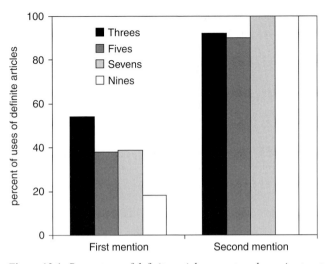

Figure 13.1 *Percentage of definite article uses at each age in storytelling.*
Based on Warden 1976

*that rabbit* in first mentions, and then shift to pronouns for subsequent mentions of
the same entity. Again, the choice of a lexical noun phrase versus a pronoun tends
to mark what is new followed by what is (now) given. To what extent do children rely
on perceptual availability and prior discourse in choosing referring expressions?
Matthews and her colleagues found that three- and four-year-olds chose lexical
nouns in their referring expressions when the addressee couldn't see the referent,
and pronouns when they could see it. In a more neutral setting, even two-year-olds
made more use of lexical noun phrases when there had been no previous mention of
the referent, while three- and four-year-olds consistently distinguished referents that
had already been mentioned (they used pronouns) from those that had not (lexical
noun phrases) (Matthews *et al.* 2006; see also Matthews, Lieven, & Tomasello 2007).

When young children hear pronouns, do they assume that they refer to someone
or something already mentioned? The answer appears to be "yes" (Song & Fisher
2005). When three-year-olds hear stories where the last sentence contains either a
pronoun (given) or a lexical noun phrase (new), they consistently treat the
pronoun as referring to the character that had already been mentioned (see also
Karmiloff-Smith 1981).

In summary, as children learn more constructions, they also learn more ways to
present information as given versus new. This goes hand in hand with their increasing
skill in assessing what their addressees do and don't know on each occasion.

### Going beyond what is said

When people talk, they often license inferences that go beyond the
actual words used. For instance, in (2), speaker B implicates, without saying so
directly, that he has not in fact read the book mentioned by A:

(2)     A: Have you read *A beautiful mind*?
        B: I've read chapter 1.

B achieves this by mentioning just part of the book, rather than responding with a straight "yes" or "no." Notice that the meanings of quantifiers like *some* and *all*, in everyday use, can be related either as *some, but not all*, as in (2), or, on occasion as *some, and maybe all*, as in (3):

(3)     A: Did you find the books?
        B: Well, I did find some.

The acquisition of such scalar implicatures appears to be a rather late development (e.g., Noveck 2001), but a few researchers have argued that children are good at making inferences, and that the focus on entailment scales (e.g., *some, all*; *may, must*) combined with true/false judgements in each setting has resulted in tasks that are too difficult. What if one focusses on more familiar settings to compare such scales? Papafragou and Tantalou (2004) looked at the three types of scale, illustrated by scenarios like those in (4)–(6), where, in each case, the speaker may implicate that he did not complete the task assigned, and is therefore ineligible for a "reward":

(4)     Quantifier scale: *some* vs. *all*
            The tiger is told he has to eat 4 oranges and if he does, he'll get a reward; he retires inside a doll's house to eat in peace. When he comes out, he is asked, "Did you eat the oranges?"
        TIGER: *I ate some.*
(5)     Encyclopedic scale: part vs. whole
            The frog has to paint the house, and if he does, he gets a reward. He goes off to paint, and when he returns, he's asked, "Did you paint the house?"
        FROG: *I painted the roof.*
(6)     Ad hoc scale (established in context)
            The bear has to wrap two gifts, a toy parrot and a doll. He goes off to wrap them. When he returns, he's asked, "Did you wrap the gifts?"
        BEAR: *I wrapped the parrot.*

These scenarios were compared to others where the animals completed the task, as in (7), and were therefore to be given the reward:

(7)     The frog has to fix a broken chair. He goes off to do this and when he returns, he is asked, "Did you fix the chair?"
        FROG: *I fixed it but it was hard.*

Four- to six-year-olds do quite well in making judgements about such scenarios. They are very good at identifying cases where the action is fully completed and hence to be rewarded, but also good at judging when the animals have not completed the task requested, as shown in Figure 13.2.

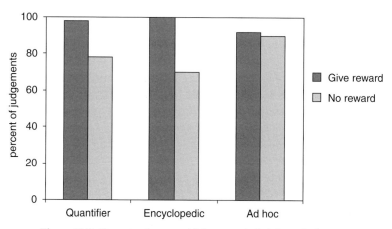

Figure 13.2 *Four- to six-year-olds' success in judging whether actions satisfied scalar implicatures (give a reward) or not (no reward).* Based on Papafragou & Tantalou 2004

## Genres of talk

How do children learn the forms and uses that connote politeness? When do they learn how to persuade, how to induce someone to do something they want? When do they master the discourse of the classroom, as opposed to everyday conversations? When do they start to tell stories and how do they elaborate that skill, setting up characters, fleshing them out, organizing the narrative to highlight critical events, introducing suspense, filling in details of the setting, mood, and attitudes of each protagonist?

### Being polite

To make appropriate use of politeness, children must master several different dimensions of use. First, they need to know what the linguistic forms are for making polite requests. Second, they must identify the pragmatic conditions on making requests in any social setting and hence take into account the status, age, and sex of their interlocutors. Third, they need some general understanding of the costs versus benefits of gaining (or losing) face in relation to others, and the desirability of keeping things equal or balanced within an exchange (Brown & Levinson 1987).

What do young children know about making requests, and how to do so politely? Bates (1976) looked at spontaneous requests in Italian children and identified three stages. Up until about age four, children rely mainly on direct questions and imperatives as requests. Then, from age five to six, they become able to produce all the syntactic forms needed but are not yet skilled at modulating their requests to achieve their goals. By around seven, they vary both the form and the content of their requests and can be quite polite.

While young children rely extensively on imperative forms, they also use other forms in their requests, and soon add expressions like *per favore* 'please', give reasons for the request, add softeners, and become more likely to state their wishes in generic form, as in (8):

(8) a.   CLAUDIA (2;0): *Io voglio il vino, che ci ho sete.*
        'I want wine 'cause I'm thirsty'

   b.   FRANCESCO (2;10): *Ci voglio provare un pochino io.*
        'I want to try a little bit myself'

   c.   CLAUDIA (2;8): *Qua ci vogliono le chiavi.*
        'here the keys are needed'

   d.   FRANCESCO (2;10): *Ma io devo fare Babbo Natale, se no …*
        'but I have to do Santa Claus, otherwise …'

Garvey (1975) observed comparable developments in children acquiring English.

Italian children this age also make some use of the imperfect past (e.g., *wanted*) where adults would use the conditional (e.g., *would like*), as in (9):

(9) a.   FRANCESCO (2;9): *Io volevo attaccare il carro attrezzi.*
        'I wanted to attach the tow truck'

   b.   FRANCESCO (3;2): *Io volevo vede se il vinaio è aperto perche se no, io voglio andare a piglià la gomma che ci ho fame, eh!*
        'I wanted to see if the
        bar was open, because if not, I want to go get me some gum because I'm hungry, yeah!'

They also produce emphatic, unsoftened wishes, as in (10a). And by age three, Francesco used questions as indirect requests, as in (10b):

(10) a.   FRANCESCO (3;3): *Io voglio tutte le fragole, me le mangio tutte io.*
         'I want all the strawberries, I'm going to eat them all up myself'

    b.   FRANCESCO (3;2): *Perché voi non mangiate il caffe?*
         'why aren't you drinking your coffee?'

To complement her observations of spontaneous usage, Bates asked children to judge how polite a request was, first in a task where they had to ask for a piece of candy and were told that the old woman would give them one if they asked very nicely, and, second, in a task where the child and experimenter together were in charge of the old woman's candy and would give it to whichever of two frogs asked for it in the nicest way. Children judged eight pairs of requests in this setting and were also asked to explain their judgements.

The children's choices of what to count as polite forms are summarized in Table 13.3. Use of *please* was identified as polite earlier than use of question intonation. Children wavered on the relative politeness of interrogative versus imperative verb forms, and not until age six did they judge conditional forms politer than indicative ones. They were also uncertain whether the formal form of address (third person *Lei*) was polite until age six or so (see further Axia and Baroni 1985; also Bates & Silvern 1977 for comparable findings for English).

Table 13.3 *Children's choices of polite forms for requests in Italian*

| Age | +please (–please) | +intonation (–intonation) | interrogative (imperative) | conditional (indicative) | formal (informal) |
|---|---|---|---|---|---|
| 3;0–4;0 | 79 | 65 | 70 | 48 | 42 |
| 4;0–5;0 | 100 | 80 | 50 | 61 | 55 |
| 5;0–6;0 | 95 | 95 | 70 | 66 | 68 |

Note: The boldface request-type at the head of each column is the more polite by adult standards, and the percentages indicate how often this form was chosen.
*Source*: Bates 1976:301. Used with permission from Academic Press.

What are the social rules behind choices of polite forms, and when do children come to appreciate them? Axia and Baroni (1985) were particularly interested in whether children recognized the "cost" of a request for the speaker versus the addressee. In situations where the adult did not respond to requests, they found that first requests from five-, seven-, and nine-year-olds all tended to be impolite. (They classified all initial requests as either polite or impolite.) But both older groups produced repeat requests that were politer after encountering resistance. After deaf-ear refusals, five-year-olds simply increased the volume, while older children opted for greater politeness. After motivated refusals, five-year-olds gave very few politer requests; seven-year-olds gave more, and nine-year-olds gave the most. In their repeat requests following a deaf-ear, nines added mitigators, used *please*, and opted for question forms or the conditional tense, as in the sequences of requests in (11):

(11) a. *Il giallo.*    >> 1a. *Il giallo per piacere.*    'the yellow/the yellow please'
  b. *Uno rosso.*  >> 2a. *Me ne dai uno rosso?*  'a red/give me a red one?'
  c. *Uno verde*  >> 3a. *Uno verde vorrei.*  'a green/I would like a green'

In response to motivated refusals, nine-year-olds often negotiated in their repeat requests – producing indirect request forms and altering the nature of the request itself, as in (12):

(12) a. *Dammi un chiodina verde* 'give me a green peg'
  b. *Ah, be', no importa, dammi un chiodino blu.* 'oh well, it doesn't matter, give me a blue peg'

Seven-year-olds evinced the same tendency but less often, and with less discrimination of the refusal-type (see also Baroni & Axia 1989; Becker 1982).

Studies of younger children have reported similar findings. Newcombe and Zaslow (1981) looked at the range of directive request forms that two-and-half-year-olds use with adults. These children produced both hints and questions as directives. And when the adult didn't comply with the children's initial requests, the children persisted 82% of the time. They repeated their original utterance, often restating it in a variant that was also a hint or a question used as a request

(83% of persistent cases), or they produced a more explicit directive (17% of persistent cases). So even very young children have an extensive repertoire of forms for requests.

When asked to make requests of Cookie Monster (who then refused the request twice), children aged 2;6, 3;6, and 4;6 produced a similar range of directive-types overall (Read & Cherry 1978). But the younger children relied more on demonstrative gestures to indicate what they wanted, as in (13):

(13)     DEANNE (2;7, asking for some juice): *Put it in my cup.* (extends her glass to the Cookie Monster puppet) (puts her glass next to the juice; points to the juice, then to her glass; pretends to drink then puts her cup next to the juice): *I want. Get some juice. I want some. I want some juice.* (points to the juice then touches the pitcher): *I want.* (leans forward to touch the juice pitcher)

The older children used more indirect requests and more politeness markers on repeat requests. However, even for four-and-a-half-year-olds, the politeness markers produced sometimes conflicted with the tone of the request, as in (14), where the intonation and use of threats are at odds with the child's use of *please*:

(14)     JANIE (4;6): *Pretty please.*
              *Pretty please, Coo-kie.* (shouts)
              *Pretty please or I'm gonna git out.*
              *I am 'less you gimme some juice.*
              *Pretty please.*

Read and Cherry (1978:243) concluded that "the children knew they had to change their tactic to obtain compliance with their directive, but they opted for more explicitness, rather than politeness," even at age four.

Like the Italian children, children acquiring English use politer forms only around age seven when they are trying to get the addressee to comply. One study of six-year-olds in small reading groups found that children tended to use direct requests for action or information, and were more likely to aggravate than to mitigate subsequent revisions of their initial requests (Wilkinson, Calculator, & Dollaghan 1982). (Aggravation usually meant repetition of the same form, with a rise in pitch and the number of accompanying gestures.) Annie's request sequence to Judy in (15) is quite typical:

(15)     ANNIE: *Judy.*
              *Judy, what's this word?*
              *Judy. Judy. Judy.*
              *Judy, what's this word?*
              *Judy, Judy, Judy, Judy.*
              *Judy, Judy, Judy, Judy, Judy.*
              *What's this word?*
        JUDY: *"Only."*

Children this age did use some mitigations, as in June's *I can't get it. Why don't you read this page too, please?* They also offered reasons for compliance, as in

*Michelle, can I have the pen? I need the eraser for it. I did something wrong* (Wilkinson *et al.* 1982:170–171). And their addressees postponed compliance in various ways, as in the exchange in (16) between Lisa, making the request, and Stephanie, who refuses to comply (Wilkinson *et al.* 1982:174).

(16)    LISA:                         *I don't know how, what to do on this stupid thing. Can you help me?* (to Stephanie)

STEPHANIE (nods):    *I don't know how to do that cause I didn't get that one done.*

LISA:                         *Did this one. Did you get this?*

STEPHANIE:               *Yeah, I got that.*

LISA:                         *Well then.*

STEPHANIE:               *Well, I got that one in my other book.*
*There's two books like this.*
*One's skinny and one's fat, 'n this is a fat one.*

In summary, many six-year-old requests to peers were unsuccessful, and the children appeared to make little use of politer forms in their repeated requests. (For more peer exchanges, see Garvey 1975, 1984.)

What is deemed polite in one culture doesn't always carry over into another (Brown & Levinson 1987). Politeness is a matter of convention, and, in every group, children have to learn what the conventions are. For example, children acquiring Chinese or Japanese must learn to use the appropriate address term for the person they are talking to (Clancy 1985; Erbaugh 1992; Nakamura 2001). Children learning Malagasy must learn what is appropriate language for a male versus female speaker (Keenan 1974a). Children learning Norwegian must learn to use hints (comments or remarks about the desired object) rather than elaborate requests, whereas Hungarian children must learn the opposite (Hollos & Beeman 1978). In each culture, children have to learn what counts as polite in different settings, with different addressees, and must adopt the prevailing norms for how to persist in order to persuade their addressee to accede. Politeness is an important ingredient in achieving one's goals, and children appear to recognize this quite early.

### Asking questions, giving justifications

How good are children at eliciting information, asking questions when needed, and at offering justifications or reasons for why certain things are the way they are? In making successive requests, children are able, on occasion, to justify their requests but they don't always do so consistently. But when four-year-olds were given a short training procedure (ten minutes a day for four days, supported by the researcher) to encourage use of *why* questions in response to claims and *because* statements in justifications, they became a lot more consistent. The procedure, which focussed on three puppets and a toy space-ship, is illustrated in (17):

(17)    A: *I am an alien.*
B: *Why?*
A: *Because I come from another planet.*

On the fifth day, the researchers videotaped the children to record all the questions and justifications used, and found a distinct increase in both challenges to claims (*why* questions) and in the justifications offered (McWilliam & Howe 2004). A typical exchange is given in (18):

(18)    GR: *I've crashed the space-ship.*
        LE: *Why did it crash?*
        GR: *'Cos it falled.*
        LE: *'Cos he wasn't a very good driver.*
        GR: *He's crashed again!*
        LE: *Why did he crash again?*
        GR: *'Cos he was so excited about going to hospital.*

Notice that, like adults, four-year-olds don't question the obvious, but they rely on opposition (19a) or one-upping (19b) to challenge blatantly false or exaggerated claims:

(19) a.    DA: *My name's Toby.*
           AD: *Your name's not Toby ... You stupid!*
     b.    EM: *Aghh ... he's biting my finger.*
           SH: *Well ... he's biting my* HAND.

The training used by McWilliam and Howe apparently alerted the four-year-olds to the contexts where questions and justifications were desirable. Finally, justifications of course also play a role in persuasion and negotiation.

### Being persuasive

Persuading someone to do something, to grant a favor, or to adopt a different view often requires considerable ingenuity. And it typically requires that the speaker minimize the costs to the addressee (any loss of face, say) while maximizing the benefits (any gain of face). One way speakers can do this is by using the relevant polite forms. Researchers have studied the emergence of persuasive skills in young children in two main settings: first, where children try to persuade an adult to do something for them, and second, where they use persuasion to resolve conflicts.

What goals call for persuasion? Preschool children may want a playmate to share a toy or join in a game, or they may want a parent to do something or buy something for them. In one study of role-playing, Weiss and Sachs (1991) looked at the kinds of persuasion used by children aged 3;9 to 6;4 in two role-playing tasks. The children had to convince their "mother" (the experimenter) or their "playmate" to buy or share a toy. The addressee refused to comply five times in succession, following two scripts of specific reasons for noncompliance. In the mother scenario, the mother/experimenter rejected the child's efforts to persuade the mother to buy a toy, as follows: (a) simple refusal; (b) mother doesn't have enough money with her; (c) child doesn't clean up toys; (d) the toy is of bad quality and would break easily; (e) mother becomes annoyed at the child's persistence. In the playmate scenario, the playmate/experimenter offered these successive rebuffs: (a) simple refusal; (b) appeal to the mother's being unwilling to let the child share new toys; (c) the child doesn't want to share toys with others; (d) the other child might break the toy; (e) the playmate becomes annoyed at persistence. The exchanges in (20) are fairly typical (Weiss & Sachs 1991:64):

(20) a.    E (mother):    Y'know it doesn't look like a very good toy. I bet it'll get broken fast.

        CHILD (3;10): *No it won't because his feet are glued ... 'cause his feet are glued onto here.*

    b.    E (mother):    You know I don't like it when you keep asking me over and over again.

        CHILD (4;3):   *I know that, but ... we don't have enough toys.*

The children relied most often on *bargains* and *guarantees*. With age, they made increased use of positive sanctions (offers, bargains, politeness) and reduced their reliance on assertions of rights. That is, they moved towards emphasis on the benefits and away from the costs to the addressee. Boys tended to evoke norms with appeals to rules, fair play, and reason more often than girls, but all the children appealed to some norms. Finally, girls made more requests, through statements or questions, and did so more often than boys.

But what do children's spontaneous attempts to be persuasive look like? In an ingenious study, Axia (1996) unobtrusively recorded eighty-eight adult–child pairs entering a large store where customers had to pass through the toy department to reach the supermarket section. None of the adults had entered the store intending to buy their child a toy. (The children in this study divided into three age groups clustered around ages four, six, and eight.) Axia hypothesized that younger children would take a more egocentric perspective in expressing their desire for a toy, whereas older children would negotiate with the adult, taking into account the adult's perspective as well as their own. She also assumed that older children would use politer forms than younger ones. The results bear this out (Figure 13.3).

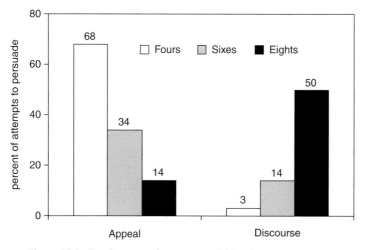

Figure 13.3 *Two linguistic functions in children's attempts at persuasion. Based on Axia 1996*

Younger children made more use of egocentric appeals (68%) than older ones. But more elaborate discourses were used only 3% of the time by the younger children, compared to 50% by the older ones. The remaining exchanges consisted of bargaining rather than negotiations that take into account the other's point of view.

Typical appeals are utterances in which the child tries to take control but fails to respond to adult reactions, as shown in (21) (Axia 1996:306–307):

(21)  a.    GIOVANNA (6;4): *Guarda mamma, che belle le Barbie. La voglio.* 'look, mum, what beautiful Barbies. I want one'
            MOTHER:    *Dai, andiamo.* 'come on, let's go'
      b.    LUCA (6;0):    *Mamma guarda questi Lego! a me mi piacerebbe averlo!* 'mum, look at these Legos! I'd like to have one!'
            MOTHER:    *Ma questo costa tanto.* 'but this one is too expensive'
            LUCA:    *Ma io devo averli tutti i Lego!* 'but I must have all the kinds of Legos!'

The oldest children were more likely to try to overcome adult objections by taking the adult's point of view. The discourse in (22) is typical:

(22)    ANGELA (8;2, looking at dolls): *Questa quanto costa? un sacco di soldi, eh?* 'how much does this one cost? a lot of money, eh?'
        MOTHER:    *Eh, sì, questo è proprio un'esagerazione.* 'eh, yes, this one really costs too much'
        ANGELA:    *E questa?* 'and this one?'
        MOTHER:    *Anche.* 'that one too'

Did children differ by age in how they opened these exchanges? In the forms of requests they started out with? In the degree of politeness and indirectness in the requests they made in this situation? Axia analyzed all the first requests children made. The type they produced most often was an attention-getter like *Guarda* 'look', without further elaboration. The second type they favored resembled advertisements, focussing on the value and desirability of the object, as in (23):

(23)  a.    MICHELE (7;0): *Mamma, aspetta. Guarda* (pointing at some monsters) *ce li hanno tutti!* 'mum, wait. Look – everybody's got them!'
      b.    SILVIA (9;3, touching a small puppet): *Guarda, mamma, così piccoli non li vendono mai.* 'look, mum, they never sell such small ones'

The percentages of each request-type are shown in Table 13.4. Younger children relied heavily on attention-getters. Six-year-olds favored bare imperatives, and both six- and eight-year-olds used need statements frequently. The oldest children used more interrogative forms, probably because they were politer overall. (Interrogatives are politer than indicatives or imperatives in Italian, as in English.) Truly polite requests, marked with *please* for example, were also commoner in eight-year-olds than in the two younger groups. So older children

Table 13.4 *Spontaneously initiated request-types at three ages*

| Request-type | Fours | Sixes | Eights |
|---|---|---|---|
| Attention-getter | 58 | 31 | 18 |
| Imperative | 10 | 17 | 4 |
| Advertisement | 3 | 14 | 11 |
| Need statement | 13 | 17 | 18 |
| Interrogative | 10 | 7 | 29 |
| Polite request | 7 | 14 | 21 |
| Total | 100 | 100 | 100 |

*Source*: Axia 1996:314. Used with permission from Alpha Academic.

start out more strategically in trying to persuade their parents to buy them a toy (see also R. Clark & Delia 1976).

The art of persuasion takes years to master. Piché, Rubin, and Michlin (1978) looked at the skills of American eleven- and fifteen-year-olds trying to persuade a parent, a teacher, a best friend, and an unfamiliar peer to buy a school-class newspaper. The targeted interlocutors differed in status (parent and teacher had higher status than the persuaders, friend and peer had the same status); they also differed in intimacy (parent and best friend were highly familiar; teacher and other peer were unfamiliar). The main findings were as follows:

(a)     Children addressed more imperatives to lower- than to higher-status addressees. (Imperatives here included commands, threats [*If you don't subscribe to it, I might punch you out*], pleas [*Oh please just buy it*], and bribes [*If you get it, I'll even make supper tonight*].) Fifteen-year-olds did this more often than eleven-year-olds.

(b)     Both ages addressed more imperatives to intimate than to nonintimate addressees.

(c)     Fifteen-year-olds used more "positional appeals" than eleven-year-olds. (Positional appeals seek compliance on the basis of conforming to norms or rules plus some aspect of status, role, or position; e.g., *In this class, see, I've gotta see how many subscriptions I can get*; *Well, you're my friend and if you're my friend you'll buy one*; *Your whole class oughta do it. They owe it to the school.*)

In summary, as children get older, they rely on politer forms for persuasion. And they adopt a discourse style where they take account of the other's objections and negotiate for alternatives in order to attain their goals. The skill of persuasion, though, grows slowly, and even fifteen-year-olds are not always very good at it.

### Resolving conflicts

Children learn early on to negotiate in the face of conflict. This often requires persuasion, particularly in offers of alternatives in the face of requests or demands they are unwilling to meet. Consider the exchange in (24) between two three-year-olds (adapted from Eisenberg & Garvey 1981:149), where the first child, Ken, announces his intention of playing with the truck, which in fact belongs to Dan:

(24)     (Ken goes to truck as Dan plays with blocks.)
         KEN: *I'm drive on truck.*
         DAN: *But this is my truck.*
         KEN: *Can I drive on it?*
         DAN: *No, you can ride on the back.*
         (joins Ken at truck)

When Dan objects, Ken asks permission (thereby acknowledging Dan's owner-ship). While Dan refuses permission, he does offer an alternative, namely that Ken can ride on the back. In short, by age three to four, children are already displaying socially adaptive language as they interact cooperatively in adversative encounters.

Adversative encounters arise whenever someone opposes a request, rejects an assertion, or blocks an action. Such encounters require resolution, and in their resolutions, children (like adults) have extensive recourse to both reasons and justifications. These are offered with both the opposing statements that initiate a conflict (children justify their not complying with a request) and the countersuggestions that follow a refusal (children give reasons supporting their requests), as in the exchange in (25) (adapted from Eisenberg & Garvey 1981:152).

(25)     (Anna and Ben are playing with plastic dishes.)
         ANNA: *I need a knife.*
         BEN:   *You have a knife.* [refusal]
         ANNA: *No, I don't. This is a spoon.* [justification for request]
         BEN:   *Well, I've got all the knifes.*

Justifications or reasons can also be used to top earlier ones, as in (26) (Eisenberg & Garvey 1981:153):

(26)     CHRIS (holding a long stuffed snake): *This is a hose.*
         DAVE (holding out hands):          *I'll take care of the fire, 'kay?*
         CHRIS:                             *Well, I will cause I'm the fireman.*
                                            [justification 1]
         DAVE:                              *Well, I'm the fireman cause I want to*
                                            *be the fireman.* [justification 2]
         CHRIS:                             *Okay, then you can have that.*

Uses of reasons and justifications show that both parties understand the conditions on requests – that the initiating speaker has a reason for wanting the addressee to do something or agree to something. And offers of alternatives, along with compromises, likewise reflect understanding that the requester needs to have the request met in some way, as in the exchange in (27) between four-year-olds (Eisenberg & Garvey 1981:155):

(27)        (Annie has taken the ladder away from Rachel.)
    RACHEL:                    *Annie, gimme that ladder.*
    ANNIE:                     *No, I don't have to.*
    RACHEL:                    *I wanna play with it.* [justification]
    ANNIE:                     *Well, I got it first.* [counterjustification]
    RACHEL:                    *I gotta put it on here. Now you gimme it.* [reason; reiteration]
    ANNIE (offers truck):      *You can have this.* [alternative offer]
    RACHEL:                    *No, if you gimme ladder, I'll give you this* (offers flashlight) *if you gimme ladder.* [counter to alternative]
                               (Annie drops ladder and picks up flashlight.)

Eisenberg and Garvey (1981) analyzed the strategies used in exchanges in play between pairs of children. (The age range observed was from three to five-and-a-half.) Overall, children who offered compromises were the most successful in reaching a resolution (77% success). Also fairly successful were conditional proposals (53% success), counteroffers (41% success), and reasons (34% success). Less successful were insistence, with simple reiteration of the request, aggravation or mitigation, and ignoring the refusal.

Children who negotiated with their peers, then, were more successful in getting what they wanted than those who simply continued to insist on what they wanted (see also Ervin-Tripp, Guo, & Lampert 1990; Grimm 1975; Piché *et al.* 1978). But the resolution of conflicts takes different forms in different communities. In their study of three- and four-year-olds in nursery school, for instance, Cook-Gumperz and Corsaro (1977) argued that specific areas in the nursery school are the product of conventional expectations that guide children in the kinds of play accepted as well as in the behaviors that can be negotiated. These may differ from one group to another, depending on local assumptions about socialization in nursery school and kindergarten teaching. This makes it important to consider the customary context of each interaction. For example, children in Italian and American nursery schools quarrel over the same kinds of things (toys and play, mainly), and most of their disputes remain unresolved although children in both cultures appear to make significant efforts to find shared solutions (Corsaro & Rizzo 1990). But, compared to Americans, Italian children rely on a larger range of verbal routines. And they rely more on language in play overall.

Other studies of interaction and dispute have focussed on the ways children look for support from their peers, or point their fingers at offenders. In her research on disputes during play in the street, Goodwin (1993) observed that boys used stories to redirect an ongoing dispute by aligning the audience with the storyteller and against the offender. Girls, though, seemed to use stories to depict offenses by absent parties and so anticipate future disputes. Goodwin suggested that boys used stories locally to restructure current quarrels, while girls used them to identify types of behavior socially unacceptable to the group. At this stage, we don't know how general such observations are, nor the extent to which they hold across social class or ethnic group. Patterns of language use, long taken for granted for adults and for children, require extensive local documentation of how everyday exchanges are really used to achieve recurrent goals.

## Giving stage directions

When children play together, they often enact complex scenes with a variety of roles. This takes planning and requires children to distinguish the play world from the real world as they specify what is to be done and said by each character. What is striking about their stage directions – which emerge around 3;6 to 4;0 – is that they are clearly distinguished, linguistically, from the play itself. In English, for example, children use the past tense for stage directions, even though they are planning *future* actions, as in the exchange in (28) between two children playing Cinderella (Lodge 1979:365), where each speaker's stage directions are in italics:

(28)     A: Where are you going tonight?
         *You said you were going to the ball.*
         B: I'm going to the ball.
         A: Is the Prince going too?
         B: Yes, and I'm going with him.
         *You got cross and argued about it.*
         A: Oh no you're not – I am.
         B: We'll see about that. Mother!
         *You were mother and she didn't want you to go.*
         A (as mother): You're not going to the ball tonight!
         B: There you are, see.
         A: I'll never speak to you again!

In some episodes of make-believe, the same child may give the stage direction and then enact it immediately, as in the joint storytelling in (29) by Jamie (5;6) and a five-year-old friend (Martlew, Connolly, & McCleod 1978:87), again with stage directions in italics:

(29)     FRIEND: *He bumped his tail.* Oh my tail.
         JAMIE:  Wah wah. I've killed everything.
         FRIEND: *But you was wrong. Turtle was alive.*
         *And you said: "Ah I'll cut your head off."*

The stage directions themselves can be quite elaborate, with contributions from more than one child, as in (30) (Martlew *et al*. 1978:93):

(30)     FRIEND: *And you don't know that another one was there. If it pushed you back*
         *it means there was some changes in front.*
         JAMIE:  *But that was a one-way street. But you had to push him back because*
         *it was a one-way street.*

What is striking across the different children is their frequent recourse to a verb that denotes a nonactual time in the stage direction itself. Lodge (1979) proposed that the past tense, for instance, marked off the content of the utterance as currently unreal (*irrealis*). That is, stage directions describe future acts that have yet to be realized in the play, and the past tense offers one way of marking that. English-speaking children also make use of modal forms like *can* and *could*, as well as the explicit *Pretend ...* or *Let's pretend ...* to mark the alternative reality in play, as in the following instances (Kaper 1980:213–214):

(31) a. *Dis could be a ... his house.*
   b. *Dis could be the mother.*
   c. *Dis'll be the blanket –*
   d. *Where can the river be?*
   e. *Pretend that's a car.*
   f. *Pretend turtle found it in the water.*

Children acquiring other languages mark stage directions in similar ways. They may use modal, conditional, or subjunctive forms, or future or past tense forms, as in the following utterances from French, Italian, Dutch, and German respectively (Kaper 1980:214–215):

(32) a.   FRENCH: *Tu étais le gendarme et moi voleur.* 'you were the policeman and me [the] burglar'
   b.   ITALIAN: *La porta era qui.* 'the door was here'
   c.   DUTCH: *Ik was de vader en ik ging een diepe kuil graven.* 'I was the father and I was going to dig a deep hole'
   d.   GERMAN: *Dies ist ein Pferd and das wäre der Stall.* 'this is a horse and that would be the stall'

(See also Andersen 1990; Bretherton 1984; Sawyer 1997.)

In summary, children distinguish actual enactments in play from their stage directions about the enactments. While they opt for somewhat different forms in different languages, the distinction they mark is constant – between current reality (*realis*) and what they anticipate will be in the play (*irrealis*). Their skill in distinguishing these layers emerges between age three and four, and, for stage directions, is typically marked by contrasting verb forms. Children also make quite skilled use of other linguistic forms, such as pronouns and demonstratives, to indicate whether they are in the play scene or outside it (e.g., Strömqvist 1984).

### Talking at school

When children start school, they take with them the skills and expectations about language they have learnt at home. But they soon discover that language in the classroom follows different rules. The classroom differs drastically from the home: Each child must compete with thirty to forty others to get the teacher's attention and must also learn to bid for that attention (by raising a hand) in answering the teacher's questions. The teacher takes at least half the turns and the remaining turns are divided among all the students. The teacher is all-powerful compared to the children, and this makes the classroom very different from the home (Cazden, John, & Hymes 1972; Sinclair & Coulthard 1975; Stubbs 1976). Yet language is still the primary means for communicating new information and for assessing how much children have learnt.

Classrooms contain experts – the teachers who know what is being taught and the answers to any questions – and that makes most classroom language different. At home, for example, one asks a question because one does not already know the answer – otherwise, why ask the question? There are exceptions, of course, as when parents ask questions designed to display their children's knowledge. In fact, children often refuse to answer such "test" questions, which suggests that they detect that they are different from usual. And some families never ask such questions (Heath 1983). At school, though, teachers already know the answers to the questions they ask. And the children know this. Teachers also evaluate the answers given, as in (33) (Wells & Montgomery 1981:223):

(33)    TEACHER:    And what's on the hill?
        ROSIE (4;10):  *Ice.*
        TEACHER:    Ice, good.

Children must learn how to deal with these kinds of questions. While this may not seem difficult,[1] another aspect of questioning in school may lead to serious misrepresentations of what children actually know.

In the classroom, teachers frequently ask a question, receive an answer they regard as inadequate or unsatisfactory, and so repeat the original question in an effort to elicit a better answer. As a result, children become accustomed to assuming that the repeat of a question implies that the answer just proffered was wrong and that they must therefore find another. But a question may also be repeated to test a child's certainty about an answer or the stability of a conceptual representation. If children assume the repeat of the question implies an initial wrong answer, they may change what they have said when in fact they should have maintained it. And this indeed happens.

Under repeated questioning, four- to six-year-olds typically offer inconsistent answers to questions in conservation tasks when they are asked to make judgements about number and length. In a typical task, children may be shown twelve counters, at first aligned in two sets of six, and then with one line spread apart. After an initial judgement that the two lines of six are the same, children are asked about the second arrangement to see whether they conserve number when the physical spacing is changed. The question here is the one that is generally repeated to make sure the child *can* conserve. When Siegal, Waters, and Dinwiddy (1988) gave children a number-conservation task, they asked just one question on the test

---

[1] For children from some cultural groups entering mainstream school systems in the United States, learning to deal with such questions may present a major hurdle to coping at all in the classroom (see Dumont 1972; Philips 1972, 1976).

trial instead of the usual two. They found considerable consistency across trials for all the children (even four-year-olds), who appeared able to conserve. They then showed children videotapes where puppets doing conservation tasks responded to two successive questions on a trial and changed their answers. The children, asked to account for these changes, typically claimed that the puppet wanted to please the questioner and therefore changed the original (correct) answer. This suggests that four- to six-year-olds construe the pragmatic intention behind a repeated question as demanding a change in answer. But changes in answers with tasks like this have then been interpreted as showing that children cannot yet conserve. Siegal and his colleagues argued that, for children, repeating a question signals a wrong answer (see further Siegal 1997).

In summary, sorting out differences between everyday conversation and classroom interactions can be a source of confusion for children over the course of several years (Willes 1981). Learning when to stick by an answer because it is correct can depend as much on the social dynamics as on cognitive ability.

Established patterns of interaction also play a role in how teachers manage group problem-solving sessions with older students. The status of one student versus another can readily lead to the contribution of an appropriate solution being either ignored or dismissed as impractical. Where the proposer of a solution has low status, for instance, acceptance would cause higher-status students in the group to lose face. They therefore find ways to dismiss it or to elicit alternatives from others with higher social status. The social dynamics of a classroom and of the subgroups established there can counter the learning that may come from problem-solving activities of small groups. The local social history of who has status in which groups, and how they exert their influence, can override the collaborative learning that might otherwise take place in small-group discussions (O'Connor 1996; see also Eckert 2000).

Children may also have to master a different dialect because their home language differs from the standard dialect used in school: They will need to become bidialectal and learn when and where to use each dialect. Or they may have to master an entirely different language upon entry to school and become bilingual, with a home language and school language that have no overlap at all. I take up some of what is involved for these children in Chapter 14.

## Telling stories

Another skill that emerges only gradually is telling stories. Speakers must keep track of the setting, pertinent events, characters, mood, motives, goals, and the final outcome. To tell a good story, they need to mark suspense, keep track of subthemes alongside the main story line, point to the climax, and entertain their listeners. All this takes memory and detailed planning to present characters and events, choosing the right linguistic options for each kind of information. While children pick up some rhetorical devices early, for instance, "Once upon a time …," they take years to master an appropriate repertoire for the telling of a story.

Storytelling has been studied in some detail for children and adults in languages ranging from English and Spanish to Hebrew and Turkish. Berman and Slobin (1994a) were interested in how the options in a language affected children's development of storytelling skills and, in particular, their choices of what to put in to a story and what to omit. For instance, languages like Polish distinguish whether an event is completed or not, iterated or not, or is still ongoing, while others, like Hebrew, have no grammatical system to mark aspect, so the information about events encoded by inflections in Polish either goes unmentioned or is partially encoded through verbs like *finish* or *begin* and adverbs or phrases like *completely* or *over and over again*. To make comparisons across languages, one has to start from the identical story content. This has been done by using a story told through a sequence of pictures, without words, as the pages are turned. The story used in Berman and Slobin's research was *Frog, where are you?* (Mayer 1969), the story of a small boy's search for his missing pet frog.

To tell a story with even minimal skill, speakers need to do three things. They need to know enough about the *structural* options in a language – the morphological and syntactic forms available. They need to know something about the *rhetorical* options for storytelling – the range of devices used in the construction of texts. And they need to know enough about *discursive* alternatives so they can select the language or register best suited to the narrative. They must also be able to integrate their knowledge of these resources with their cognitive ability to maintain an *updated representation* of what the addressee knows (and doesn't yet know) at each moment in the narrative. Storytelling probably demands more elaborate planning than most conversation.

Consider two versions of the frog story in which a little boy and his dog search for an escaped pet frog. Both stories were told after the child had looked through the book once and then turned the pages along with providing the narration. The first, in (34), was told by a child aged 3;4, who picked out details or actions that are incoherent without the pictures as accompaniment; the second, in (35), was told by a child aged 5;11 and tells a coherent story that can stand fairly well on its own[2].

(34)    CHILD (3;4): *they're looking at it and there's a frog. he's looking at the jar.* (whispers): *cause his frog's not there. getting out.* (turns several pages fast, looks at boy climbing tree) *climbing up the tree. running away.* (of the dog running from a swarm of bees) *fell off the tree.* (said of the boy) *and the boy's falling.* (of boy falling from deer's antlers) *he falled into the water. and there's frogs. they in the water.*

(35)    CHILD (5;11): *when the boy and the dog were as– asleep. the frog jumped out of the jar. and then the boy and the dog woke up. the frog was gone. then the boy got dressed, and the dog stuck his head in the jar. and then the boy opened up his window, and*

---

[2]  Both stories are adapted slightly from the transcribed versions in the CHILDES Archive (see Slobin 03b; Slobin 05k).

*called out for his frog. and the dog still had the jar on his
head. then the dog fell, the boy was was scared. and then the
boy was mad at the dog. and picked him up. and then he
called for his frog again. he called in a hole. and the dog
called in the beehive. and the dog got some bees out of the
hive. then the dog made the beehive fall. and the beehive–
all the bees came out of the beehive. and the boy looked in
the tree. and then the boy fell out. and the owl was flying.
and the bees were flying after the dog. and the boy got up on
some rocks. and the owl flew away. and the boy was calling
for his frog on the rocks. (moved and a moose–) the boy got
caught on the moose's– antlers. and then the moose carried
him over to a cliff and threw him. and the boy– and the boy
and the dog fell. and they splashed in some water. and they
looked. they saw a log. and the boy said shh to the dog. and
they looked over the log. and they saw the frog and some
baby frogs too. (moved and they–) and the boy said goodbye
to the frogs, and brought a baby frog home.*

What do children learn about telling a story as they get older? The most striking difference between the stories in (34) and (35) is the increase in content and coherence with age. The older child tells the story of the wordless picture book; but the younger one does little more than comment on a few pictures. What do children have to learn here?

To express a specific event in a story, speakers need to do two things – *filter* the experience to be represented and *package* it appropriately in the language. "The world does not present 'events' to be encoded in language. Rather experiences are filtered – (a) through choice of perspective and (b) through the set of options provided by the particular language – into verbalized events" (Berman & Slobin 1994b:611). Filtering and packaging are differentially shaped by each language, depending on the grammatical, lexical, and syntactic options available (Slobin 1996; Hickmann & Hendriks 1999; Wigglesworth 1997). As Boas and Sapir pointed out: (a) "[I]n each language only a part of the complete concept that we have in mind is expressed, and … each language has a peculiar tendency to select this or that aspect of the mental image that is conveyed by the expression of that thought" (Boas 1911/1966:38–39), and (b) "[The forms of each language] establish a definite relational feeling or attitude towards all possible contents of expression and, through them, towards all possible contents of experience, in so far, of course, as experience is capable of expression in linguistic terms" (Sapir 1924:152).

Young children know less about the structures of their language than older children, and this has an impact on storytelling. Late acquisitions that emerge only around age nine in narration include (a) uses of past perfect verb forms (e.g., *The boy who had climbed the tree*); (b) nonfinite forms (e.g., participles, as in *There's a deer hiding up there*, *The dog was shaking the tree with a beehive hanging from it*); and (c) multiple marking of aspectual information in a single verb phrase (e.g., *He's still calling frog*, *He kept on calling frog*). Adults use greater lexical diversity.

They produce many more distinct expressions for time-relations, more locative prepositions, and more temporal conjunctions. Adults also make use of much more complex syntactic packaging both within and across episodes in their stories.

Forms and functions, then, interact as children master storytelling. Take the use of present versus past tense. All the three-year-olds could already use present and past in the five sample languages studied (English, German, Hebrew, Spanish, and Turkish). But they used them only to talk about single events, described in single clauses. As the children got older, they would choose a dominant narrative tense and use it for all the main events in the story. This dominant tense was established by age four in English, Hebrew, and Spanish, and by five in German and Turkish. That is, in all the languages, children shifted from a perceptually based criterion for using past tense to a discourse-based one, where the narrator now used the same tense to mark each successive episode that advanced the plot. Younger children instead used the present for observable (pictured) events and the past for events that had to be inferred. Older ones used the past tense even for pictured events when those advanced the story. Over time, tense forms for verbs acquired additional functions in the narrative context.

Functions themselves also acquire forms. As they got older, children acquired forms that were more specific for a particular function and used those instead of the ones they had started out with. Consider the temporal relations in a story. There is the plot line from start to finish – the linear sequence; there are also occasions when two events overlap or occur simultaneously; and there are flashbacks, where the narrator refers to an earlier event in the story. To manage these temporal dimensions, children may begin with one form but, as they get older, use another more specialized form for the same function.

Take flashbacks. In referring to the jar the pet frog had been kept in, a three- or four-year-old was likely to use a simple possessive form to identify the jar and hence the earlier event, as in *The dog got stuck in the frog's jar*. By age six or seven, children instead alluded to this jar with a relative clause to convey the connection between now and then, as in *The dog got stuck in the jar that the frog had been kept in*. These children opted for a relative clause in place of the possessive; they also indicated the frog's earlier relation to the jar by using a pluperfect tense (*had been kept in*).

As children get older, they also shift from order of occurrence in talking about a sequence of events (talk about the first event first, the second event next, and so on) to a more complex account that interweaves sequence, simultaneity, and retrospection. They manage this by using temporal conjunctions like *before*, *while*, and *after* that allow them to talk about events out of order and by contrasting simple past with pluperfect (e.g., *he fell* vs. *he had fallen*), modals (to mark inferred events alongside ones that were witnessed, say, in Turkish), and present perfect forms to signal contrasting perspectives on an event.

Another change in their narratives comes from the use of cohesive devices like pronouns. Three- and four-year-olds typically use a full noun phrase like *the little boy* or *the dog* in the frog story. Older children replace the initial noun phrase with pronouns (*he*, *it*) for subsequent mentions. As Hickmann (1991:181) noted, "it is not until after seven years that children stop reintroducing referents across utterances as they go from picture to picture" (see also Bamberg 1987; Jisa 2000).

Children start to add referential cohesion with pronouns around age five, when they are learning to coordinate perspectives on the train of events and to track what the addressee knows. This is also when they add cohesion to their uses of tense across events and impose more global organization on their stories (Bamberg 1987). Although languages differ, children seem to add cohesion to their stories with pronouns and contrasting tenses at much the same age (Baumgartner & Devescovi 1996; Berman & Slobin 1994b; Hickmann & Hendriks 1999).

Learning to tell a story requires knowledge of both language structures and rhetorical devices. It also requires the ability to coordinate perspectives, track what the addressee knows, and hold the addressee's attention. It requires complicated planning too, to track and present each protagonist, the motives for their behavior, the background settings, and the main events. Learning how to do this leads children further still along the path to becoming skilled speakers of their language.

## Summary

Acquiring a language demands much more than knowledge of its sound system, grammatical distinctions, lexical choices, and constructions. It also requires knowledge of how to talk to different addressees on different occasions, in different settings. This includes conventions on how to talk in different roles and which register to choose when; how to mark social dimensions like power, status, age, and gender; and how to be polite in different settings and cultures. It includes mastery of everyday genres, such as how to be persuasive, how to resolve conflicts, how to give stage directions for play, how to talk in school, and how to tell stories. These represent only a sample of the uses to which people put language every day in all kinds of transactions, from buying toothpaste to explaining how to mend a bicycle tire, from teaching a new fingering technique for a piece by Debussy to giving directions on how to find a particular gallery in San Francisco. Children must learn how to use language to achieve a growing range of goals.

# 14    Two languages at a time

When children talk, like adults, they make use of the language of the community they are growing up in. But many communities make use of more than one language or more than one dialect. In these communities, children have to choose which language to speak whenever they talk. Their choices can depend on the family role, gender, status, power, and age of the interlocutor, as well as on the topic. It also depends on such factors as social class, since that in turn may affect decisions about when to use each language, and who to, in specific settings.

Choosing a language, just like choosing a speech style, reflects in part what the speaker shares as common ground with the addressee. How, then, does learning two languages – or two dialects – differ from learning just one? Growing up in a multilingual community results in the learning of not just one language, but two or more, either at the same time or within a few years of each other. What effect does exposure to more than one language have on the process and general course of acquisition? Are there differences in the road followed by bilingual versus monolingual children? In this chapter, the focus is on the social factors that affect choices of language and dialect. I first consider bilingualism in general, and then look at some of the social and cognitive issues for children learning two (or more) languages as they advance from babbling to words to constructions. I then consider children learning two dialects, a situation rather similar to that of two languages, and end with discussion of how each choice of language affects how one represents and talks about events.

## Bilingualism

Much more of the world is bilingual or multilingual than monolingual. Most people grow up speaking two or more languages (Grosjean 1982). And those not exposed to two languages from birth frequently start learning their second language when they enter school, with other languages coming later during the school years (Bialystok 2001; Bialystok & Hakuta 1994; McLaughlin 1984). Even in the United States, where the emphasis tends to be on English, with the assumption of a monolingual population, the census statistics for 2000 show that there were some 47 million speakers over age five reported as speaking a language other than English at home. This is an increase from the 32 million in 1990

(Bialystok & Hakuta 1994). And 26.5 million of these people (55%) reported speaking English "very well" (Census 2000 Brief).[1]

Official bilingualism or multilingualism is found in many countries, though one or two languages often have a more favored status as the official language or languages. In 2005, the *Ethnologue* website counted some 6,912 documented languages spoken in about 150 countries. Many speakers of the main languages live outside the source-group or country where that language originated. Consider the estimated numbers for speakers of the top ten languages in the world: Chinese comes first, with 1,205 million speakers (Chinese actually consists of a group of languages, but a large subset of people speak Mandarin and at least one other variety of Chinese); Spanish follows, with 322.5 million speakers; English, with 309.4 million; Arabic, with 206 million; Hindi, with 180.8 million; Portuguese, with 177.5 million; Bengali, with 171 million; Russian, with 145 million; Japanese, with 122.4 million; and German, with 95.4 million (Gordon 2005).

Use of these languages is typically the result of historical migration, conquest, and colonization. Many second languages are spoken by smaller groups for the same reasons. Examples of the latter include Afrikaans, in South Africa, and the Batak languages in Sumatra, Indonesia, each with some 6 million speakers, as well as Aymara, spoken in Bolivia and Peru, with over 2 million. The size of the country and the number of inhabitants is typically unrelated to how many languages are spoken. That number depends more on a combination of past history and current politics. Luxembourg, one of the smallest countries in Western Europe, has three official languages (French, German, and Luxembourgian). India has 200 "registered" languages (i.e., languages with some official status, either locally or nationally); and Papua New Guinea has some 800 distinct languages in its population of just 3.5 million.

### Defining bilingualism

Discussions of bilingualism have usually focussed on an ideal – the perfectly balanced bilingual – where the speaker's knowledge about and control of each language is regarded as equivalent to that displayed by a monolingual. Under this view, bilingual speakers would effectively be two speakers in one, with exactly equivalent skills in both languages. While much research began from this ideal, it is very likely the wrong starting point to choose. Many, perhaps all, bilingual speakers tend to use one language in some settings and the other

---

[1] Among the larger language groups represented in 2000 were Spanish (28.1 million), Chinese (2,022,143), French (1,643,838), German (1,383,442), Tagalog (1,224,241), Vietnamese (1,009,621), Italian (1,008,370), Korean (894,063), Russian (706,242), Polish (667,414), Portuguese (564,630), Japanese (477,997), Arabic (614,582), Greek (365,436), and Yiddish (178,945). In addition, there were speakers of Native American languages; Scandinavian, West Germanic, and Slavic languages; other Indo-European and Indic languages; Hungarian and Mon-Kmer; as well as 1 million speakers of other languages (Census 2000 Brief, Oct. 2003; also www.census.gov/population/www/socdemo/lang_use).

language in others. While they may have fairly balanced skills in both languages, these speakers typically have specialized vocabularies for many domains, and so would have difficulty talking about some aspects of their jobs or home lives, for example, in their "other" language (Grosjean 1982). So, when called on to translate from one language to the other, for example, bilinguals are not always able to do so because they lack the relevant vocabulary. They have never had occasion to learn it. So does one ever find perfectly balanced bilinguals? Probably not. In learning a language, as in using it later, one designs one's utterances for a particular addressee, occasion, and topic, in the appropriate register or speech style (Chapter 12). Choosing which language to use as well adds a further social layer to the mix.

Researchers have also commonly distinguished bilinguals from second-language learners. The bilingual generally starts to learn a second language between birth and age three, say, and every language tackled after that point is viewed as a case of second-language learning (McLaughlin 1984). Some researchers have opted for a far stricter criterion: They count as bilinguals only those exposed to both languages from birth (De Houwer 1995). Others, like Grosjean (1982), have argued for a broader definition that counts as bilingual any speakers who habitually use one language in setting A and another in setting B. As Malherbe (1969:50) put it: "The only practical line of approach … is to assess bilingualism *in terms of certain social and occupational demands of a practical nature* in a particular society … *Purpose and function* are the main determinants."

In effect, the entire setting for bilingual acquisition, one where different languages are in daily contact, differs from that of monolinguals (Weinreich 1953; Fishman 1971). There are typically differences not only in the level of knowledge about each language in the bilingual child's caretakers and interlocutors, but in their conversational skill too (Yip & Matthews 2007). This is particularly common in multicultural settings where one language is dominant, as in California, or in countries like Belgium or Switzerland where one language is dominant in specific geographic areas. The social circumstances that surround bilingualism, then, differ from those for monolinguals. Part of this difference stems from language contact between different languages, part of it from the relative status of each language. Consider Italian–German bilinguals growing up in Italy (Taeschner 1983), Hungarian–Serbian bilinguals in Serbia (Mikes 1967), or English–Spanish bilinguals in the UK (Deuchar & Quay 2000). Compared to monolinguals, whatever the patterns of language use in adult speech, young bilinguals necessarily receive less input for each of their languages. In addition, when the language of the surrounding community is dominant, the asymmetries in use affect people's attitudes towards each language, with both majority- and minority-language speakers generally attributing greater prestige to the dominant language (e.g., Metraux 1965; Lambert & Tucker 1972).

Within adult bilingual populations, there is now quite extensive research showing that speakers use two distinct systems in language processing. For example, eye-tracking data in studies of Russian–English bilinguals suggest there is parallel activation of words within and between languages. Follow-up studies show parallel activation in both languages, even when bilinguals hear words from only one language (Marian & Spivey 2003; Marian, Spivey, & Hirsch 2003). Marian and her colleagues (2003) argued that this activation of both languages represents a very early stage in language processing, perhaps for phonetic information only, with lexical and semantic information coming into play only later (see also Rodriguez-Fornells *et al.* 2002). This would be consistent with differential patterns of brain activity during language processing (see also Grosjean 1989). More generally, studies of brain representations of two languages show both lexicons are stored together, but with some differences in the storage of grammatical information, depending on whether the second language is acquired after age seven (Fabbro 2001). In addition, studies of Italian–English bilinguals showed differences in density in some areas of the brain for speakers who learnt a second language before age six, compared to after age twenty. Researchers found greater density of grey matter in the left hemisphere for bilinguals compared to monolinguals, and for more proficient bilinguals over less proficient ones (Mechelli *et al.* 2004).

Other studies of how distinct the two languages are in bilinguals have focussed on differences in naming patterns. Given that languages map words onto referents in different ways, bilinguals could either learn two distinct mappings for various areas of the lexicon (maintaining one mapping for each language), or else merge their two systems, in which case bilinguals might not resemble monolinguals from either language. In studies of Dutch and French monolinguals compared to Dutch/ French bilinguals, the labeling patterns for common household objects in the bilinguals tend to converge on a common naming pattern. Ameel and her colleagues (2005) argued that the mutual influence of the two languages in the bilingual case leads speakers to shift their category-boundaries so they no longer fully match the boundaries maintained by monolinguals. This suggests that bilinguals may differ at certain points from their monolingual counterparts for a specific language (see also Helmsley, Holm, & Dodd 2006).

Just how and whether bilinguals' processing of language as a whole differs from that of monolinguals requires further exploration. But the sources of any differences are likely to have their start in early acquisition of the languages involved.

## Two languages in childhood

Many children grow up with two languages. They have to learn two sound systems, two morphological systems, two lexicons, two syntactic systems, and two sets of systems for use. Researchers have long been interested in the acquisition of two languages in childhood. One of the earliest reports was by Ronjat (1913), who followed his son Louis' simultaneous learning of French and German. Louis appeared to distinguish the two languages early on and, for

instance, would try out any new word with both German and French pronunciations for as much as a week until he decided which "box" it belonged in (*le
casier mama* 'mama's box' or *le casier papa* 'papa's box'). Although he at first
favored German (his mother's language), he soon began to treat the two
languages evenly and, on learning a new word, would request its equivalent
in the other language. His parents had adopted a one person/one language
approach in talking to him, and the child treated his languages accordingly.
Once he had established which language a new person spoke, he would use
only that language to that person. If either parent slipped up in language choice,
Louis would reply in the language expected from that parent. This pattern of use
in development has been widely observed since (see also Pavlovitch 1920;
Arnberg 1981; Taeschner l983; McLaughlin 1984; Fantini 1985; Döpke 1992;
Zentella 1997).

### Early perception and babbling

Do children exposed to two languages begin with one system for each
from the very start, or do they only later come to realize that there are two sound
systems, two vocabularies, two languages? Researchers have focussed on two
kinds of data in tackling this question: (a) young children's perception and
production of sounds, and (b) their early production of words.

Infants appear to discriminate the rhythmical patterning that differentiates some
languages, for instance, stress-timing in English versus syllable-timing in French,
from as early as a few months old (Mehler *et al.* 1988; Moon, Cooper, & Fifer
1993; Nazzi, Bertoncini, & Mehler 1998). This ability may be particularly useful
for infants exposed to two languages. Indeed, by around five months, both
monolingual and bilingual infants can also distinguish between languages in the
same rhythmical group (Nazzi, Jusczyk, & Johnson 2000; Bosch & Sebastián-
Gallés 2001). So from very early on, bilingual infants attend to the sound systems
of both the languages they are hearing, and appear not to follow quite the same
route as monolingual infants.

Monolingual children typically show sensitivity to the legal sound sequences
of the ambient language by around eleven months of age, and so do bilingual
infants, who show it for word shapes from both their languages (Vihman *et al.*
2007). At the same time, young bilinguals may take time to perceive specific
differences among vowels that distinguish legal sound sequences of Catalan
from those of Spanish, say (e.g., Sebastián-Gallés, Echeverría, & Bosch 2005;
also Sebastián-Gallés & Bosch 2002; Bosch & Sebastián-Gallés 2001). When
English–French and English-only infants were tested on their ability to discriminate the relevant voice-onset times for stop consonants, by ten–twelve
months the monolingual English group attended only to the English onset
boundary, while the bilingual group continued to discriminate the two.
Researchers have argued that such findings show that infants exposed to
two languages can process both as native languages, so the development of

phonetic representations is not adversely affected by learning more than one language at a time (Burns *et al.* 2007).

To what extent can one detect the presence of two languages in infant babbling? The evidence appears mixed and may depend on how close the phonetic inventories of the two languages are. In one study of English–French bilingual thirteen-month-olds (Poulin-Dubois & Goodz 2001), researchers analyzed the articulation of consonants produced in sessions with each parent (the parents each spoke only one language to their children), but found no differences for either place or manner of articulation in the two language settings. So when do infants exposed to two languages display features specific to just one or other language in their babbling and early words? Poulin-Dubois and Goodz looked at a segmental distinction, but perhaps differences show up first in syllabic structure and prosody given that these properties tend to emerge earlier than segmental features. Maneva and Genesee (2002) examined the babbling produced by an English–French bilingual infant recorded at ten, eleven, twelve, thirteen, and fifteen months with his mother (English) and father (French). The child produced more consonant–vowel (CV) syllables in English than French, consistent with the relative proportions in the two languages and with the data on monolingual babbling in English and in French (Levitt & Utman 1992; see also Blake & Boysson-Bardies 1992). His CV sequences in English were more likely to contain stops, while those in French were more likely to contain approximants like /w/, /j/, or liquids like /l/ and /r/, again reflecting differences in distribution for the two languages. He also produced more monosyllabic and bisyllabic sequences in English, and more polysyllabic ones in French (which also resulted in longer babbled "utterances" in French). In short, this child's babbling followed the language of the relevant parent, and so prefigured some of the properties pertinent to the production of words in each language (see Elbers 1982).

## Lexical structure

Children exposed to just one language offer clear evidence of setting up representations for the words they hear based on the adult's system. These representations play a critical role both in their recognition and production of words and in their reliance on such target representations as models when they try to repair their own early productions (see Chapters 3 and 5). What does this predict for bilingual children? First, they should represent terms and phrases from both languages in memory. Second, they should take account of two phonological inventories and sets of constraints on syllable- and word-structures. Such representations for comprehension could provide them with an early basis for distinguishing their two languages. Yet assessing the role of such representations is difficult because researchers have traditionally focussed only on what young children produce. Even there, identifying the intended target word and language can often be difficult (see Paradis 1996; Vogel 1975).

One approach has been to look in detail at how individual children produce target words from each of their languages. For example, comparisons of word shapes in a two-year-old exposed to Hungarian and English showed that forms with Hungarian targets were consistently longer than forms with English targets (Bunta, Davidovich, & Ingram 2006). Surface differences in the words this child produced offered evidence for two systems even though his actual syllable shapes were the same for both languages. He was building up two systems from the same units, but he used the elements differentially in his Hungarian versus English words, to arrive, in the end, at different-sounding surface forms in the two languages.

Children also distinguish which word forms to use for which meanings early on. Here bilingual children also have to work out which terms in one of their languages are equivalent to which in their other language, as in the pair *chien* and *dog* in French and English, or *fles* and *biberon* in Dutch and French. (Note that *fles* is a doublet of both *biberon* 'baby's bottle' and *bouteille* 'bottle'.) Volterra and Taeschner (1978) suggested that the absence of doublets (translation equivalents) in bilingual children's early vocabulary would be evidence for a single system. However, the absence of doublets could stem from a variety of causes: Children might have no need for such equivalents early on, given their patterns of language use. With very small vocabularies, this absence is generally accidental: Children have simply not yet been exposed to the relevant words in both languages. It is, of course, possible that they might actively reject equivalent terms, in effect apply the principle of contrast across both their languages as if they formed a single system. But if they did, would this reflect their rejection of a new word for an already labeled referent (as mutual exclusivity would predict) or rejection of a different conceptual perspective on the same referent? Analysis of children's spontaneous rejections strongly suggests that perspective choice, and not the presence of two terms for the same referent, is what is critical for young children (Clark 1993, 1997). In fact, the existence of doublets is always inconsistent with mutual exclusivity because it is equivalent to allowing more than one label for the same referent. Finally, if children are already working on two systems, there would be no basis for them to apply contrast to both languages combined. Rather, given that they recognize there are two languages, they would apply contrast within each language, and take language choice as an additional dimension of contrast.

One way to distinguish whether children rely on one system or two at first is to examine the range of doublets or translation equivalents they produce in their earliest vocabularies, when they produce twelve words or fewer in each language, and look at how many doublets they produce as their vocabularies grow to the 500-word level. If children have a single system, the principle of contrast predicts no doublets (a doublet would count as a case of synonymy); but if they have two systems, contrast predicts that they should accumulate doublets freely as they acquire more vocabulary.

## 14A  Some translation equivalents or doublets in French and Dutch

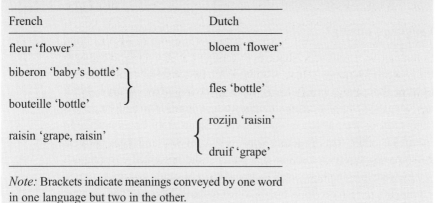

| French | Dutch |
|---|---|
| fleur 'flower' | bloem 'flower' |
| biberon 'baby's bottle' ⎫ | |
| ⎬ | fles 'bottle' |
| bouteille 'bottle' ⎭ | |
| | ⎧ rozijn 'raisin' |
| raisin 'grape, raisin' ⎨ | |
| | ⎩ druif 'grape' |

*Note:* Brackets indicate meanings conveyed by one word
in one language but two in the other.
Based on De Houwer, Bornstein, & De Coster 2006

What are the findings? In a study of twenty-seven Spanish/English bilinguals recorded between the ages of eight months and two-and-a-half years,
Zurer Pearson, Fernández, and Oller (1995) found that children produced
doublets or translation equivalents for 30% of the terms in their two vocabularies. Other researchers have also found that bilingual children, from their first
words on, produce some doublets (see Holowka, Brosseau-Lapré, & Petitto
2002 for English–French; Quay 1995 for English–Spanish; Schelletter 2002
for English–German; see also Junker & Stockman 2002; Bosch *et al.* 2005).
In production, then, bilingual children give evidence of developing two lexicons –
two independent systems – rather than a single, merged system, from very
early on. And since comprehension is typically ahead of production, we would
expect even more doublets to show up in comprehension than in production
during the second year.

Evidence that this is the case comes from a study of thirty-one young
children learning both French and Dutch in Belgium (De Houwer, Bornstein, &
De Coster 2006). When these children were assessed for comprehension against a
checklist for each of their languages at thirteen months of age, on average they
understood 18% of the doublets checked, but the children differed considerably in
how many doublets they each understood, from a low of less than 1% for one child
(3/361 of the doublets checked) up to a high of 61% in another (221/361 doublets).
When the words that any one child knew in only one of the two languages
(singlets) were examined, the fewer the meanings that child was judged to understand overall, the smaller that child's comprehension vocabulary was. Overall, the
higher the children's comprehension scores, the more likely they were to know the
pertinent meanings in *both* languages. This is strong evidence against bilingual
children's applying the principle of contrast *across* their languages (as if they had
just one system), rather than simply *within* each language. The comprehension of
doublets, then, provides further evidence that children set up two systems – two

languages – from the start. And then language per se, of course, offers a further dimension of contrast (Clark 1990, 1993).

### Language mixing?

A number of researchers have reported mixing of the child's languages during the earlier stages of acquisition (e.g., Burling 1959; Leopold 1939–1949; Oksaar 1970; Redlinger & Park 1980; Smith 1935; Tabouret-Keller 1964; Vihman 1982; Volterra & Taeschner 1978). In such cases, children produce words from both languages in the same utterance, or they attach morphological endings from one language to word-stems from the other. This apparent confusion between languages early in acquisition led some researchers to assume that children did not initially distinguish the languages they were learning but treated them instead as a single system.

But does mixing per se really support the view that children have just one system? Bilingual adults in many communities also mix their languages: Code-switching, as it is commonly called, is frequent and quite systematic as speakers consistently shift from one language to the other.[2] Within an utterance, speakers may code-switch on words, phrases, or whole sentences. One difference, of course, is that adults can also stay in just one language, especially when speaking to someone who knows just one of the languages in question. Another difference is that children between the ages of one and three, let's say, know much less of their languages than adult speakers do. Mixing of lexical items in a single utterance could therefore reflect the absence of appropriate words in one or other language. To remedy this, children could simply borrow a term from the other language when they need to fill a gap and already know a word that will do from the "wrong" language. This would be analogous to children's stretching words by overextending them in contexts where they lack a more appropriate term (see Chapter 4). As bilingual children acquire more vocabulary in both languages, this type of mixing should gradually vanish. With age, children would become more likely to know the appropriate terms in both languages. But some mixing could be retained to capture specific aspects of experience, from a desire to emphasize the point, or to express affect (Genesee 2006).

---

### 14B  Instances of language-mixing

(1)    CHILD (2;6): … laisse mes barrettes, touche pas papa.
       'leave my barrettes alone, don't touch daddy'
       Me's gonna put them back in the bag so no one's ganna took them!

(2)    ADULT: Mais je te gage par exemple … excuse my English, mais les odds
             sont là.
       'but I bet you for example … excuse my English but the odds are there'

Based on Genesee 2006

---

[2] For discussion of conditions on code-switching, see Grosjean 1982; Gumperz 1982; Morimoto 1999; Myers-Scotton 1993a, 1993b; Poplack 1980; and Sridhar & Sridhar 1980.

Children sometimes add inflections from one language to stems from the other. This may reflect differences in complexity for the inflectional systems in the two languages. Vihman (1985), for example, suggested that her son produced English function words in his otherwise Estonian utterances because the English elements were simpler and more salient[3] than the inflections marking the same meanings in Estonian (see also Tabouret-Keller 1964). Similar arguments have been made about syntactic mixing, where children may have mastered a specific construction-type in one language but not yet done so in the other because of its greater complexity. This would be consistent with the view that languages differ in which parts of the system are more complex and which simpler to acquire (Slobin 1973, 1985b).

Finally, mixing may reflect the fact that many children growing up bilingual hear mixing in the speech of the adults who talk to them. In many bilingual communities, code-switching is commonplace, but it has seldom been scrutinized in child-directed speech. But, as Lanza (1997) showed, the social setting plays a major role in children's choices of which language to use when in an exchange. She found that children tend to mix or code-switch in the same proportions as the adult speaker they are talking to. In effect, children become sensitive very early to who speaks which language(s) among the people they come in contact with, and they typically choose the appropriate one for each person (see De Houwer 1990; Fantini 1985; Meisel 1990; Nicoladis & Genesee 1996; Yip & Matthews 2007). This sensitivity extends to whether or not their interlocutors code-switch. If they do, children will do so too. And they do so in much the same proportions as the adult (Lanza 1997). This appears to be yet another instance where children track frequency of use in adult speech.

In summary, current research suggests that the kinds of mixing children use reflect the normal processes of acquisition (stretch the resources you have as far as you can when needed) as well as the models offered by the speakers around them. So a combination of cognitive and social factors could account for the mixing observed in some young bilingual speakers. Such findings therefore provide little support for the view that children are mixing their two languages because they cannot distinguish between them.

## More evidence for two systems

If children exposed to two languages early on start out with two systems, they must construct two sets of representations, one for each language. Additional evidence that they do so comes from children's choices of language in addressing specific adult speakers. In one study of Canadian French/English bilinguals (aged 1;10–2;2), Genesee, Nicoladis, and Paradis (1995) observed

---

[3] By more salient, Vihman seems to have meant that English inflections were more easily distinguished from the stems they were attached to and so more readily segmented and identified than their counterparts in Estonian.

Table 14.1 *Two bilingual children's uses of French and English by addressee*

| Addressee | French only (%) | English only (%) | Other (%) |
|---|---|---|---|
| William (3;0.6) | | | |
| To Eng.-stranger | 30 | 63 | 7 |
| To Eng.-parent | 21 | 66 | 13 |
| To Fr.-parent | 84 | 11 | 5 |
| Gene (2;8.9) | | | |
| To Eng.-stranger | 12 | 59 | 29 |
| To Eng.-parent | 15 | 72 | 13 |
| To Fr.-parent | 75 | 15 | 10 |

*Source*: Genesee, Nicoladis, & Paradis 1995:623. Used with permission from Cambridge University Press.

five children talking to each parent separately to see whether they usually chose the appropriate language for each parent. They also observed them talking to both parents together. When they analyzed the proportions of child utterances in the three settings – talk to mother, talk to father, talk to both parents together – four of the children clearly differentiated their two languages. They used more English to the English-speaking parent and more French to the French-speaking one. When both parents were present, the children showed the same effect in the proportions of utterances in each language addressed to each parent. In short, these children differentiated between their languages by addressee.

Two of the children were also recorded talking to an unfamiliar monolingual English speaker, as well as to each parent again, several months later. Both used the same proportion of English utterances to the stranger as to the English-speaking parent, but they used a much higher proportion of French (the community language) to the French-speaking parent, as shown in Table 14.1 (see also Genesee, Boivin, & Nicoladis 1996; Lanza 1992, 1997; Meisel 1990). Both children also failed on occasion to use the right language (the "Other" column of Table 14.1) and at times resorted to gestures, as in the exchanges in (1) and (2):

(1)     Stranger and William (3;0.6) looking at pictures:
        STRANGER: wow! he's riding his bicycle.
        WILLIAM: *vélo*. 'bicycle'
        STRANGER: it's a what?
        WILLIAM: (pause) (points to bicycle)

(2)     A train passes outside the house and Gene (2;8.9) goes to the window to look:
        GENE: *choo-choo train! he parti*. 'gone'
        STRANGER: I'm sorry, I didn't understand. It's a what?
        GENE: *parti*. 'gone'
        STRANGER: you can't see it?
        GENE: *this is a choo-choo*. (points at a picture of a train)

In short, children chose the "right" language for each parent, and also for strangers (see also Fantini 1985; Lanza 1997).

### Language dominance

For bilinguals, one language may be dominant in one period of their lives, and another at another period. Shifts in dominance often result from moving to another location where the community favors a different language. For example, in Switzerland, the community (dominant) language in Lausanne is French, while in Berne it is German. French–German bilinguals moving from one part of the country to the other typically shift from one language to the other at work and in the schools. For many children growing up bilingual, the dominance of one language may also be set by who the major caretaker is initially, so which language is dominant can shift from one year to the next, as well as when children begin to attend school. Family contacts and the presence of relatives from one or other side of the family can also shift language dominance from one language to the other and back again over time (see Fantini 1985; Yip & Matthews 2007).

Language dominance may affect the course of acquisition not only in the dominant language but also in the child's weaker language, through transfer. Yip and Matthews proposed that the stronger language may influence the form of the weaker one whenever there are measurable differences such as mean length of utterance (MLU) between the two. Furthermore, with any developmental asynchrony, such that a specific property *p-1* develops first in language-a, that property (*p-1*) may then be transferred by the bilingual child to language-b (Yip & Matthews 2007; Verhoeven 2007). One issue, then, is how children get rid of such transfers: At what point do they add the equivalent property (*p2*) to language-b and so "replace" earlier erroneous uses of *p-1* in language-b? For example, a child learning Hebrew and English might develop the Hebrew plural before the English one, and then use the Hebrew inflections on English words, as in *boy-im* [boy + PL MASC] for 'boys'. Since this is the same problem as getting rid of over regularizations within a language, it is presumably solved in the same way. As children hear more of the nondominant language, they will hear both general positive evidence (conventional usage from the speakers around them) and indirect negative evidence when adults check up on just what they mean (Chouinard & Clark 2003). Both sources of evidence offer conventional forms in place of child errors, and should eventually replace them.

Dominance has been measured by differences in amount of use, e.g., the number of utterances and their length in each language. Another indication of dominance is when bilingual children go through phases of speaking only one of their languages, while maintaining comprehension in both. Yet another is when they show asymmetries in mixing, adding French words to English, say, but not the reverse (e.g., Hulk & Müller 2000). It's important to point out here that such transfers from the dominant language do not support the proposal that the nondominant language is actually more like a (later) second language. Rather, development in the nondominant language is simply delayed (Meisel 2007).

Table 14.2 *Percentages of finite utterances produced in English versus French*

| Language | Interval 1 (~2;0) | Interval 2 (~2;6) | Interval 3 (~3;0) |
|---|---|---|---|
| English | 10 | 24 | 44 |
| French | 51 | 74 | 85 |

*Source*: Paradis & Genesee 1996:13. Used with permission from Cambridge University Press.

## Grammatical structure

Another source of evidence relevant to the one- versus two-system controversy is the bilingual development of grammatical structures. Studies here have tended to focus on the early acquisition of grammatical morphemes (free or inflectional) and on negation. The argument goes as follows: If children were acquiring a single system first, this should also be apparent in their acquisition of structure. But if the earliest constructions in their two languages diverge, this would be evidence for two distinct systems from the start.

Again, the evidence suggests that children are sensitive to structural differences between their two languages from the start. Paradis and Genesee (1996), for example, looked at the development of finite verb inflections and agreement, and at sentential negation, in three French/English bilinguals. They recorded them at six-month intervals from age two to three and found the two languages differed in the numbers of finite utterances produced (Table 14.2), with more finite verbs in French (where all finite verbs carry some inflection) than in English. The children were also much more likely to use a pronominal subject with a finite verb in French (e.g., *j'vais* 'I-go') than in English (*go*, with 'I' understood in context). They never used clitic subject pronouns with nonfinite, infinitive forms of the verb in French (e.g., with *donner* 'to-give', *aller* 'to-go', *prendre* 'to-take', etc.). In their English, the children used subject pronouns with finite and nonfinite verbs 24% and 21% of the time respectively. This suggests that they were treating subject pronouns in French and English as belonging to two different systems (see also Meisel 1994).

Negatives in the same children's speech also revealed a difference between their English and their French. In English, they consistently placed the negative *not* before the verb, but in French, they just as consistently placed the negative *pas* after the finite verb, as in (3):

(3) a.   WILLIAM (2;10): *People là, va pas là.* 'there', 'don't go there'
    b.   GENE (2;7): *Je veux pas dire quoi.* 'I don't want to say what'
    c.   OLIVIER (2;6): *Je veux pas parler à papa.* 'I don't want to talk to daddy'

They produced no English utterances with *not* placed after the verb, although they did produce a few negatives in utterance-initial position (see Chapter 9).

In summary, these children's early word combinations suggested they were treating the structures in their two languages differently from the start. They were attentive to differences in the marking of finiteness, the use of clitic and nonclitic subject pronouns, and the placement of sentential negatives (see also Paradis & Genesee 1997).

The evidence, then, favors the view that bilingual children set up separate systems from the start and build up their skill in each language fairly independently. At the same time, the course they follow, as bilinguals, is modified by their individual patterns of experience and exposure to each language. Indeed, exposure to two languages in childhood does not lead invariably to bilingualism. Studies have estimated that as many as 25% of children growing up in bilingual settings do not become bilingual. While quantity of input for each language appears to be the most critical factor, language status and attitudes about language also play a role. Children in effect may fail to learn the minority, low status language, for which they receive relatively less input. But if parents are positive about the minority language, value it, and use it daily with their children, then they learn it (Zurer Pearson 2007; see also White & Genesee 1996; Wong Fillmore 1979; Hakuta & D'Andrea 1992). These findings are reinforced by an extensive survey of 1,899 families where at least one parent spoke a language other than the majority language (De Houwer 2007). All the children in these families spoke the majority language, but they did not all speak the minority language. For children to speak the minority language, the amount of parental input was critical, with children much more likely to learn it if both parents used it, and if only one parent usually used the majority language. The amount children hear of each language, and the people they hear it from, are as critical to bilingual acquisition as to monolingual acquisition (Chapter 2).

## Acquiring two dialects

Children often acquire different dialects early on. By dialect, I mean the specific variety of a language spoken in a community or area. Some dialects are regarded as standard (they are still dialects, of course), and others as non-standard. These may be recognized as regional or social, depending on the culture, the language, and the country (e.g., Macaulay 1997; Milroy & Milroy 1991). Acquiring two dialects is both similar to and different from acquiring two languages. The process involved is similar in that children need to master two systems, but it is different in so far as there is extensive mutual intelligibility. While this helps children communicate from the start when they move to a new dialect area, it may also allow them to "get by" most of the time without mastering all the details of the second dialect.

As in the case of children exposed to two languages, where the amount of exposure is important in how much they learn and which language dominates, children exposed to two dialects show similar effects. Youssef (1991a, 1991b), for example, followed three children exposed to both the English-lexicon Trinidadian Creole (TC) and Standard English (SE). She found that the extent to which the children differentiated the two dialects in their uses of verb forms to mark the past, for example, as well as in their auxiliary verb form use, depended on both the degree and the contexts of exposure. In choosing which forms to use, children were sensitive primarily to who the addressee was (a TC or SE speaker). They were also sensitive to the setting (e.g., school vs. home, storytelling vs. casual conversation) and to emotional tone. Similar findings were reported by Kovac and Adamson (1981) in preschoolers' choices of Black English versus SE, and by Purcell (1984) in slightly older Hawaiian children with Hawaiian-English Creole versus SE. While their addressees largely determined which dialect was used, children's dialect choice was also often linked to specific topics and settings (e.g., school vs. home). Notice that addressee, setting, and topic are also the major factors in choices of language for children growing up bilingual.

In acquisition, local dialects are typically contrasted with whatever variety of SE is spoken in the school system, so the major contrast is school versus elsewhere (home, street, shops, playgrounds). But while children could start with a simple linkage to specific places or addressees, they must also learn which forms are judged to be appropriate when. The same speaker may favor SE in school settings yet use Hawaiian-English Creole even there on occasion to change the emotional tone, to express solidarity, or to indicate a shift away from the school setting when telling a story or presenting an anecdote. So learning the society's norms is an important part of mastering two (or more) dialects (Youssef 1993), just as in mastering two or more languages.

When children have to learn a second dialect, just as when they have to learn a second language, they are faced with learning a new phonology, morphology, lexicon, syntax, and conventions of usage. Like learners of a second language, children display different degrees of skill in this task and may take a long time to master the details. When children move to different dialect areas, the younger they are, the more likely they are to master the new phonological system (Payne 1980). But once past age ten or eleven, they may never acquire the more complex phonological rules of the new dialect (Chambers 1992).

## 14C  Principles of dialect acquisition

1. Children acquire new words faster than new pronunciations.
2. Children master new words rapidly at first and then slow down.
3. Children master simple phonological rules faster than complex ones.
4. Young children are more likely to master complex rules and new sounds in a new dialect than older children are.
5. In the early stages, there are individual differences in how well children master both categorical and variable rules of pronunciation.
6. Children first use new pronunciations as variants of old ones.
7. Children eliminate old rules faster than they acquire new ones.
8. Children acquire orthographically distinct variants of words faster than orthographically obscure ones.

Based on Chambers 1992

What generalizations can be made about the process of acquiring a new dialect? Chambers (1992) proposed eight principles of dialect acquisition, each supported by data from a range of studies. Just as in monolingual and bilingual acquisition, children are attentive to new words, but they take time to learn subtle differences between two forms representing the same meaning but different dialects. In phonology, they master simpler contrasts first (see Chapter 5). And the younger they are when they first encounter a second dialect, the more successful they tend to be in mastering it.

Chambers' generalizations point up differences between learning a second dialect and learning a second language in childhood. The second dialect is typically closer to the first than is a second language. This adds difficulty because it is often unclear which dialect children are "in." Where the phonology is the same, it may be harder to keep track of what they should be doing in the next phrase, where the phonologies of the two dialects diverge. In the cases Chambers considered, children moved to a new dialect area and were engaged in acquiring the new local speech. What is unclear is whether they discarded their previous dialect, or maintained it along the new one, and simply shifted from one to the other depending on who they were talking to. (The latter situation would be closer to bilingualism.) There is also considerably more overlap in lexicon and syntax between two dialects than between two languages. But there has been little or no investigation of how this affects acquisition. Most current work on dialect acquisition has focussed more on the acquisition of features of within-dialect variation (e.g., Roberts & Labov 1995; Roberts 1997; Smith, Durham, & Fortune 2007), where this is socially conditioned, than on the acquisition of two dialects at once.

The politics of using one or other dialect has tended to stifle research (Hakuta 1986; also Sledd 1988). In the 1970s, there were several attempts to teach children who spoke a nonstandard dialect of English to read first by using their nonstandard dialect. But this drew extensive protest from parents who saw schools and reading instruction as the way to learn the standard dialect (see Baratz 1969, 1970, 1971; also Sledd 1988). Parents therefore rejected any use of nonstandard dialects in classroom teaching.

The general expectation is that children will learn a standard dialect at school, and then use that dialect whenever it seems to be called for. This indeed happens in many countries, but how well this expectation is met for every child varies with social class and membership in other social groups, as well as the school systems involved.

## Social dimensions of language choice

When it comes to choosing a language or a dialect, speakers take a wide range of factors into account. They do this from a young age (Fantini 1985; Lanza 1997; Taeschner 1983; Zentella 1997). The choice of language may depend on whether the language options have equal status in the community or whether one is spoken by the majority and the other by a minority. It may also depend on whether the child is growing up in a family with a one parent/one language approach (Döpke 1992) or whether both languages are used by both parents to the child. Language choice also depends on topic. Speakers may prefer one language for one topic, and the other for another. Similar considerations apply when speakers choose dialects. Lastly, speakers make choices that depend on the social networks they belong to and the community norms for when and how to speak within each segment of their social network. Interestingly, middle-school and high-school children readily adopt phonological features that mark them as members of specific groups within school communities (Eckert 2000; Robertson & Murachver 2003). But the extent to which such features might be considered a distinct dialect remains unclear. Another factor that might be at work here is what sociolinguistics have called accommodation, where speakers adjust their pronunciation, intonation, and timing temporarily, to match that of their addressees (see Giles, Coupland, & Coupland 1991).

All the choices involved here are strongly influenced by the addressees. These may be family members, close friends, peers, relatives, acquaintances, or people who are unfamiliar to the child. Many addressees, of course, have a history of interactions with the (child-)speaker. Altogether, these factors contribute to what speakers think their addressees already know. Finally, the addressees' languages or dialects also influence both language choice and code-switching (see Genesee *et al.* 1996; Lanza 1997; Youssef 1991a, 1991b, 1993).

## Thinking for speaking

Whatever one's language, one has to plan as one goes from initial intention to producing the appropriate utterances. For bilinguals, long accustomed to using both their languages, the choices attendant on the language chosen seem to be a matter of routine, just as for a monolingual speaker. For speakers growing up speaking Russian, where verbs always mark when actions are complete, there is nothing special about describing an event as completed or not. Equally, for speakers growing up with Turkish, where verbs signal the evidential status of each event, it is an everyday matter to indicate whether each event is known directly by observation or only by hearsay. Since languages differ in the grammatical details required, speakers become accustomed to thinking for speaking *in that language* (Slobin 1996). They take for granted the distinctions they must think about every time they talk, yet they don't necessarily depend on the same distinctions in nonlinguistic tasks. People everywhere may have similar conceptual representations for objects and events, but they diverge by language when it comes to *talking* about those objects and events.

For many speakers, knowledge of a language is equated with knowledge of the culture of that community. Learning a language is often so closely tied to learning how to behave within a group that it is hard to disentangle the roots of a culture from the language (or languages) its members use (Berko Gleason 1988). Equally, losing a first language may be equated with losing the culture it exemplifies.[4] For many immigrants to a country like the United States, this loss may involve a loss of the ability to communicate even with close family members. When schools urge parents to use only English to their children (as happens in many parts of the United States), this may result in a breakdown in family life. Grandparents and parents with only limited proficiency in English have limited access to their children's and grandchildren's lives. The children grow up unable to talk to parents or other close relatives about what preoccupies them at school or at work (Wong Fillmore 1991, 1996). Yet where bilingualism is the norm, as in many parts of the world, it brings with it important social skills. For instance, bilingual children are more adept, at an earlier age, than monolinguals at conveying appropriate information in communication tasks (e.g., Genesee, Tucker, & Lambert 1976; see also Bialystok 2007).

Choosing a language, choosing a dialect, and choosing the words to use involve many social factors. These choices reflect attitudes in the larger community, decisions about solidarity, and the desire to mark membership in a particular group, as well as decisions based on one's history with each addressee on each topic. Bilingual speakers make these decisions every day with great skill and move with ease from one language to another, or from one dialect to another, depending on the addressee, setting, topic, and mutual history. The range of choices and skills required, though, makes clear why children take time to perfect their social repertoires in language use. Becoming a speaker of a language is not just a matter of mastering a grammar and a vocabulary; it is also learning *how* to speak in each social setting. And speakers learning more than one system must establish this in order to use each of their languages or dialects.

---

[4] Writers like Eva Hoffman (1989) have graphically described their sense of loss upon moving into a new culture where they "lost" their first language. See also Grosjean (1982) for discussion of how language is often the first target in a nation's attempt to eradicate minority cultures (e.g., Breton, Basque, Scots Gaelic).

# PART IV

## Process in acquisition

*[E]very child processes the speech to which he is exposed so as to induce from it a latent structure. This latent structure is so general that a child can spin out its implications all his life long. It is both semantic and syntactic. The discovery of latent structure is the greatest of the processes involved in language acquisition, and the most difficult to understand.*

Roger Brown & Ursula Bellugi 1964

The next two chapters take another look at the nature/nurture debate for language acquisition and consider some of the biological evidence for specialization for language. The first takes up what happens to language acquisition after brain damage and in certain special populations where acquisition cannot follow a normal course, as well as what happens when the normal social settings are not available to children. The second chapter focusses on general processing capacities, the role these play in acquisition, and the kinds of mechanisms that might account for some common patterns observable in the acquisition of different languages. It also considers the multiple representations needed for language and the general learning mechanisms children might rely on as they change their language into something closer to the language of their speech community.

# 15    Specialization for language

What are the biological underpinnings of language? To what extent are we, as humans, specialized for language? And just what do we mean by specialization here: Existing capacities in the service of language? Capacities unique to language? Specialized organs for language? Specific areas of the brain for the processing of linguistic information? Answering these questions turns out to be complicated. There are extensive behavioral observations of language use and acquisition, but much less firm data available on the neurological underpinnings of language. And still less is known about just how the behavioral data map onto areas of the brain.

The first issue, then, is whether there is *specialization* of the brain for language. Are there language skills assigned to specific areas of the brain – and if so, which areas and which skills? Such specialization could be present from birth, or the relevant areas might become assigned in the course of development. In either case, exposure to a language would appear essential for learning, but whether we store multiple languages in the same area of the brain or whether the area assigned depends on when during development that language is acquired remains unclear. All of language could be stored in a single area, or different languages or different aspects of a language could be distributed across different areas.

Second, are there *sensitive periods* during development for the acquisition of a language? Children may need to be exposed to a language before a particular age or stage of development in order to be able to learn it. But things can go awry, so if children are not exposed to language at the right time, do they fail to learn language? Finding out what disrupts normal acquisition and how certain disruptions affect language learning could add to what we know about specialization for language.

Some researchers have appealed to an *innate language capacity* – innate linguistic categories plus a specialized built-in "language acquisition device." The assumption is that such a device must exist to account for the speed and universality of acquisition in normal children. Two assumptions – that children acquire all the major syntactic structures of their language very early (by age four in most accounts) and that all (normal) children acquire language – are common to variations of this position.

This chapter is organized around three issues: specialization of the brain for language, sensitive periods for language learning, and potential innate learning mechanisms dedicated to language alone.

## Activity in the brain

In the past, data on the effects of brain injury came from two sources: (a) behavioral data after injury or stroke, and (b) inspection of brain tissue at autopsy. Identifying the site of a lesion from stroke or injury used to be possible only after death. Nowadays, it is possible to identify the site of an injury while the patient is still alive. One way is to measure electrical activity or blood flow in the functioning brain. This in turn has allowed researchers to link behavioral data to those areas of the brain that appear to be dedicated for particular kinds of processing – visual, auditory, motoric, and so on. These methods allow one to study specific areas in the intact as well as in the injured brain – hence, normal as well as disrupted processing of information.

In studies of language, researchers have looked at brain activity during processing of linguistic material. This activity can be measured while people read or listen to sets of words or sentences with ERPs (Event-Related Potentials), PET (Positron Emission Tomography) scans, and fMRI (functional Magnetic Resonance Imaging) scans. The ERP technique measures electrical activity picked up from a net of small electrodes placed over the skull. This method indicates where in the brain neurons have been activated by the current task. ERPs have fairly good temporal resolution for activity but fairly poor resolution for spatial location. PET scans offer better spatial information for brain activity. These monitor changes in blood flow in the brain, and the assumption is that increased brain activity requires more oxygen and hence greater blood flow to any areas that are currently active. PET scans have helped researchers identify the visual areas that respond to seeing color or motion, and those that become active during the recognition of written words. But the poor resolution of this technique still doesn't allow for enough detail either for interpreting the findings or for identifying interactions among different (sub)systems that deal with language or vision, or both. As Barinaga (1995:803) pointed out:

> A PET study that localizes a certain visual function, such as word recognition, to a particular fold in the cerebral cortex is a bit like a spy-satellite photo that reveals a missile base on a hill. Without a detailed map that shows the hill's location relative to national borders, you still don't know who owns the missile base.

The problem is that one square millimeter of brain activity may involve millions of brain cells. The coarse spatial resolution here is improved on by fMRI scans. These also track blood flow but in finer detail than in PET studies. Researchers have also designed ways to enhance fMRI data so they can examine each cortical area in a more fine-grained way with 3-D computer modeling (see, e.g., Courtney & Ungerleider 1997 and Engel *et al.* 1994 on the visual cortex).

PET and fMRI focus mainly on *where* the activity in the brain is occurring. They offer more or less detailed spatial information, with fMRI offering the most detail. None of these methods offer fully satisfactory temporal information. They can't follow the details of the precise millisecond-by-millisecond *time course* for processing information as someone listens to an utterance, understands a joke, presents the addressee with a question, or produces an atrocious pun. The problem is that the measures don't track the neural transmission of information directly. Rather, they detect only concomitants to neural activity, namely electrical activity or increased blood flow, that result from increased brain activation. At best, they can tell us about the site of storage or retrieval operations needed in language processing. They can't yet tell us much about the time course of operations used, for example, in interpreting an utterance, versus identifying an implicature in context, versus planning the reply to a question.

## Is there specialization for language?

Is there evidence for specialization in the brain specific to language? One of the first people to find such evidence was Paul Broca, a French surgeon. In 1861, he published a report on a patient who had had great difficulty producing speech. At autopsy, Broca found that he had damage in the lower edge of the left frontal lobe, in an area now called "Broca's area." Four years later, Broca published a further report where he showed that damage to areas in the left hemisphere produced aphasia, while damage to the corresponding areas in the right hemisphere did not (Broca 1856, 1861). In 1874, a German doctor, Carl Wernicke, followed up this research in a monograph where he described patients with deficits in language comprehension, deficits associated with lesions or injury in the left hemisphere but outside Broca's area.

Since the studies by Broca and Wernicke, it has been clear that damage to certain areas of the brain affects language without impairing vision or other capacities. Autopsy findings suggested that the left hemisphere was the primary site. These early studies led researchers to identify several areas, normally in the left hemisphere, where injury appeared to impair language in comprehension (Wernicke's area), in production (Broca's area), or in both. These areas are indicated in Figure 15.1.

When people are listening to speech, the auditory signals received through the ears travel first to an area on each side of the brain called Herschl's area, part of the auditory cortex. Information from the right ear goes directly to the left hemisphere of the brain, and from the left ear goes to the right hemisphere. Then there appears to be a division of labor, with the words of a message going mainly to the left hemisphere, and properties such as intonation, rate of speech, pitch, rhythm, and stress going mainly to the right hemisphere. While these two kinds of information may be stored separately, they are connected by fibers that link the two hemispheres, the corpus callosum.

Comprehension appears to take place largely in Wernicke's area (see Figure 15.1). The angular gyrus and the supramarginal gyrus allow linguistic information to be integrated with information from other modalities (visual, auditory, and tactile, for example). When these areas suffer damage, people may become unable to connect

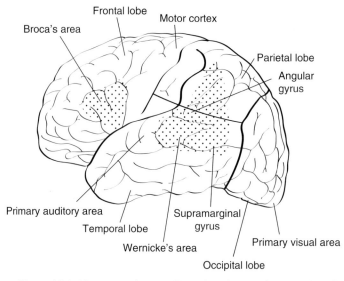

Figure 15.1 *Major speech areas (Broca's and Wernicke's areas) in the brain*

written and spoken language because they can no longer integrate visual information with auditory signals. These two gyri are also involved in remembering words (the angular gyrus) and processing syntactic constructions (the supramarginal gyrus). In general, words and their meanings seem to be stored throughout the temporal lobe, while conceptual information is distributed throughout the cortex (Geschwind & Levitsky 1968; Thatcher & John 1977).

Speakers make use of areas in and around Wernicke's area and depend on Broca's area (see Figure 15.1). Broca's area appears to be involved in organizing linear sequences of linguistic elements and setting up detailed articulatory programs for speaking once a speaker has formulated a message. Once the articulatory program is ready, it is passed on to those parts of the motor cortex that deal with movements of the tongue, lips, velum, and glottis, control of air volume and loudness, control of breathing, and so on. Damage to any of these areas can interfere with the production of speech, and often with its comprehension as well. Briefly, damage in Wernicke's area appears to have the most drastic effects, since this can disturb both comprehension and production. Damage in Broca's area can result in great difficulty in producing speech, while comprehension of both spoken and written language may be relatively unimpaired.

Overall, evidence of specialization in the brain for language has traditionally been drawn from three main sources: hemispheric dominance, effects of trauma or injury, and the effects on language of hemispherectomy (Lenneberg 1967).

***Hemispheric dominance***. Almost everyone shows left hemisphere dominance. When people listen to words played simultaneously into each ear through headphones, they tend to hear words played to the right ear and not those played to the left ear. Words into the right ear go directly to the left or contralateral hemisphere for processing (e.g., recognition, identification, etc.), while those going into the left ear go first to the right hemisphere. Information enters faster through the right ear – a right ear advantage[1] – because it goes directly to the left hemisphere.

*Hemispheric damage*. When someone has a stroke or receives a brain injury, only injuries to the left hemisphere affect language. In particular, only left hemisphere injuries in or near Wernicke's and Broca's areas are consistently associated with language loss or disturbance. Injuries to the right hemisphere are rarely linked to such a disturbance. In short, injuries to the brain are asymmetric in their effects on language, further evidence for the specialization of the left hemisphere.

*Hemispherectomies*. When there has been extensive trauma to the brain, it is sometimes necessary to remove one or other hemisphere entirely. Whether the removal is partial or complete, the two hemispheres again show that they are not symmetrical. Removal of the left hemisphere typically results in loss of language, whereas removal of the right hemisphere leaves language unaffected (Dennis & Whitaker 1975).

In summary, all three sources of evidence identify the left hemisphere as specialized for language, although it is not the only site where language is stored. Researchers have also looked at how specialization for language emerges during development. (The brain does not arrive fully partitioned with areas already assigned for specific types of processing.) Much of this evidence comes from comparisons of hearing speakers versus deaf signers, and from changes in children between the ages of one and two.

## Hearing versus deaf

Researchers have used fMRI to examine sentence-processing carried out by native English speakers with normal hearing and by native signers of American Sign Language. The signers were either hearing (and hence bilingual in ASL and English) or congenitally deaf. The areas of the brain activated in the two populations were the classical language areas in the left hemisphere (Bavelier *et al.* 1998). That is, language is processed in the left hemisphere regardless of the modality of language perception – auditory for spoken languages, visual for ASL. Native ASL signers also made use of areas in the right hemisphere, regardless of whether they were deaf or hearing. Since the right hemisphere processes most visual information, the requirements of a visual language like ASL also help determine organization of language systems in the brain.[2]

---

[1] This right ear advantage holds for right-handers in the population and for many left-handers. For a few (true) left-handers, though, language is located in the right rather than the left hemisphere, and they show a left ear advantage instead.

[2] Presumably, the reading of written forms of language should involve the right hemisphere, since the input is visual even though it can usually be said to represent spoken forms of a language (left hemisphere).

In another study of the deaf, researchers looked at the ERPs elicited by anomalies in either signed or spoken sentences. They compared four groups of adults: (a) deaf adults, born of deaf parents, who had learnt ASL at a young age; (b) hearing adults, also born of deaf parents, who had likewise learnt ASL young as a first language; (c) hearing adults, born of hearing parents, who learnt ASL after age seventeen; and, finally, (d) hearing adults with no experience of ASL at all. The left hemisphere showed extensive activity for all four groups.[3] But the right hemisphere was also involved in language processing for the deaf adult children of deaf parents, and, to a lesser extent, the hearing adult children of deaf parents. People in both these groups had learnt ASL, a language wholly dependent on the visual rather than the auditory mode, very early. So acquisition of ASL as a first language appears to involve the right hemisphere and the parietal cortex for both hearing and deaf signers. It also involves the posterior temporal and occipital areas but only in the deaf early first-language signers. This may be attributable to auditory deprivation. Since these signers have no auditory input to take up this part of the brain, they use it for visual processing instead (Courtney *et al.* 1997; Jiang *et al.* 2000; Ungerleider 1995).

In summary, the left hemisphere is the main site for language, but the modality of the language (spoken versus signed) and the age at which a signed language is acquired (whether by congenitally deaf or hearing signers) affect how much of the right hemisphere is also recruited for language.

### Changes during infancy

Six-month-old and thirteen-month-old infants attend more to infant-directed speech than to adult-directed speech, as evidenced by neural activity. The younger infants showed more activity to familiar words only, while the older ones responded to both familiar and unfamiliar words. This suggests that infant-directed speech serves as an indicator of potentially meaningful material (words or phrases, say) and so triggers brain activity (Zangl & Mills 2007). But at what point do infants show evidence of hemispheric specialization for language? One proposal is that brain organization depends on the infant's exposure to language, so one should not see much evidence of hemispheric specialization before the start of language learning. Mills, Coffey-Corina, and Neville (1997) therefore looked for changes in the localization associated with early comprehension in infants (aged 1;1 to 1;8). They recorded ERPs as the small children listened to familiar words (words they understood), unfamiliar words (not understood), and words played backwards. In the younger one-year-olds, aged 1;1 to 1;5, there was activity in both left and right hemispheres for both familiar and unfamiliar words, and it was broadly distributed over anterior and posterior regions of the brain. But by 1;8, these effects were limited to the left hemisphere and to the

---

[3] There was also evidence for some differential specialization of anterior and posterior cortical regions for various aspects of semantic and grammatical processing (Neville *et al.* 1997).

temporal and parietal regions. In short, there is a shift with age in where the first-language processing takes place – to the temporal and parietal areas of the left hemisphere (Bates *et al*. 2002; Mills, Coffey-Corina, & Neville 1993).

Another factor here is familiarity. Do the infants recognize the words they hear? In an ERP study of eleven-month-olds, researchers found that infants this age shifted their attention within 250 ms to familiar words, but not to unfamiliar ones (Thierry *et al*. 2003). Moreover, as infants are exposed to and learn more words, they become more efficient in processing them and show greater left-hemisphere specialization (Mills *et al*. 2005; see also Friedrich & Friederici 2005). In other studies using ERPs with eleven-month-olds, researchers found that infants respond with differential neural activity to native vs. foreign sounds (Rivera-Gaxiola *et al*. 2005). This is consistent with behavioral measures of discrimination at the same age (see Chapter 3), and offers a partial explanation of familiarity effects. The words tagged as familiar must contain familiar sounds and be ones the child has heard on other occasions.

## A sensitive period for language acquisition?

Sensitive periods in development have long intrigued biologists. In many species, there are periods when learning of certain kinds can take place more effectively than later in development. Sometimes the sensitive period is critical in that, once it is past, that learning can no longer occur, as in imprinting in chicks, or the acquisition of the pertinent songs in young songbirds.[4] There are sensitive periods for other phenomena too, where age of exposure to the relevant stimuli is critical (e.g., Hubel & Wiesel 1970 on critical period effects in vision).

In 1967, Eric Lenneberg marshaled an impressive array of evidence for a critical period for the learning of language. He drew on evidence from brain injuries and the resultant aphasias in children, from feral children and children who had been isolated and neglected, and from second-language learning. Provided the injury or isolation occurred early enough, children under three or four could relearn the language they had lost (see also Basser 1962), recovering what they had learnt prior to the injury, and then continue apparently normally. If the trauma or injury to the left hemisphere occurred after puberty, though, children typically failed to recover their language, just as adults may fail to recover from injury-induced aphasias.

Lenneberg argued that the reason language couldn't be recovered after puberty was that lateralization (specialization of the left hemisphere for language) was by

---

[4] But the second brood of hatchlings in a year can defer song-learning to the following spring, so that they will have more than two months in which to master the species-specific songs (Kroodsma & Pickert 1980). This suggests that the sensitive period in birds is fairly malleable and can vary in length with how late in the season a brood is raised.

then complete. And any areas of the right hemisphere that could deal with language were also assigned. After lateralization of both hemispheres, then, it is no longer possible to allocate language functions to other areas of the brain; and if areas already assigned for language become damaged, there is now nowhere else to "put" language. This argument suggested that full assignment of language to areas of the brain was complete around puberty. Language learning could only take place in the appropriate hemisphere between about age two and thirteen.

These arguments for a critical period have been challenged by later work. Several studies have shown that lateralization for language is essentially complete earlier than Lenneberg proposed, around age five (e.g., Witelson & Pallie 1973). This in turn raises questions about whether the notion of a critical period for language is correlated with the completion of lateralization. If children found it easier to learn a language prior to lateralization, age five to six ought to mark a point at which all this changes. But children appear highly successful in learning additional languages up to age twelve and even later. Lateralization may therefore offer a less than compelling explanation of difficulties in later learning.

### Brain injury and asymmetry

Children with early brain injury appear to attain normal (or near-normal) language despite damage to areas critical for language in adults. Their language capacities appear to be fairly resilient. But sometimes children may have to have an entire hemisphere removed – for instance, to arrest seizures associated with Sturge-Weber-Dimitri syndrome. Their subsequent language abilities depend on which hemisphere was removed. Language is more affected by loss of the left hemisphere, and visual processing more by loss of the right hemisphere. Dennis and her colleagues, for example, followed three children after hemispherectomy. Two had had their left hemispheres removed and one the right hemisphere. At age ten, when given a variety of psychological and psycholinguistic tests, they appeared quite comparable in IQ. But when given commands varying in amount of information and in complexity of syntax, only the child with the intact left hemisphere did well. The other two had difficulty dealing with syntactically complex forms (see Dennis, Lovett, & Wiegel-Crump 1981; Newman, Lovett, & Dennis 1986).

In earlier research, Kohn and Dennis (1974) tested a larger sample with only one hemisphere (they ranged in age from fourteen to twenty-eight) on visual–spatial abilities versus language abilities. Whether they had had the left or right hemisphere removed, they performed equally well on tests of visual–spatial relations, sense of direction and orientation, and route-finding skills, provided the tests didn't exceed the level of skill attained by normal ten-year-olds. But on tests of later spatial abilities, those lacking the right hemisphere were severely impaired. After removal of the right hemisphere, then, there are continuing deficits in spatial analysis where this is now controlled only by the left hemisphere. The converse asymmetry appeared in language skills. Four right hemisphere and five left hemisphere decorticates (aged eight to twenty-eight years, matched for verbal IQ) were asked to discriminate the meanings of statements differing in syntactic form (Dennis & Kohn 1975). Although some syntactic forms were processed equally well by all patients, those with only a left hemisphere did better on others than those with only a right hemisphere (see also Dennis 1980).

The interpretation of such findings, of course, should take into account how development itself interacts with injuries that temporarily disrupt it. Many researchers have assumed that disruptions during development parallel disruptions to the adult brain, but in adults, all the functions are already in place. The child brain may not have developed some functions yet and so is necessarily in a different state. After injury, the child brain may well follow a different developmental course from that already established by the normal adult brain (see further Dennis 1988, 2000).

Overall, loss of the left hemisphere in children is more problematic for language skills, and loss of the right for visual skills. For both, the severity depends on the age of hemispherectomy. The earlier this occurs, the greater the recovery. In short, the brain appears highly plastic in its reassignment of functions. But if an area is already "taken," it cannot be *re*-assigned to deal with language or with visual processing, for example. So the earlier the hemispherectomy, the more likely the child is to show general recovery: Not as much of the brain has been assigned already, so there is some space, so to speak, that can take up needed functions and make up in part for the areas lost.

## Feral and isolated children

In the last 300 years, there have been several reports of children found in the wild, who apparently survived on their own or were brought up by wild animals (Singh & Zingg 1939). These feral children were regarded as critical evidence for nature – what is built into the genes – or nurture – what is learnt from socialization – in determining human behavior. The argument from nature runs as follows: If the capacity to learn language is the characteristic that distinguishes humans from other animals, then feral children removed from the wild should be able to learn language. From nurture, the position is a little different: It is unsurprising that feral children have no language because they have had no exposure to human society and so no opportunity to learn. Once in society, they would of course learn language.

All these children lacked language, and, even with intensive attention and training, they were unable to acquire normal language. But one difficulty in assessing feral children has been a lack of information about their early life. At what age were they abandoned, and why? Were they abandoned because their parents were unable to care for them, or because they were mentally retarded or deformed? Did they run away or were they driven out after some years of normal social life? Among feral children, one whose development was recorded in particular detail was Victor. He was about twelve years old when found, and the

French physician Itard tried for five years to teach him to talk and to read. Although he learnt to understand many words and phrases, he never learnt to talk himself (Itard 1801; Lane 1976). Another feral child, Kamala, found together with an eighteen-month-old in a wolf's litter in the 1850s in India, was about eight years old, and she eventually learnt to speak a little (Singh & Zingg 1939). However, most accounts of feral children report that they do not learn any language, even if they become somewhat responsive to their caretakers.

While the feral children who have been studied failed to learn language, children who have been deliberately isolated (to hide social shame over illegitimacy, for example), but not maltreated, have typically recovered once placed in more normal social settings. One child called Isabelle, found in Ohio in the late 1930s, had lived with her deaf mute mother in a darkened room away from the rest of the family until she was around six-and-a-half. When released from this confinement, she had no speech. After care and treatment, including intensive speech training, she learnt language with great rapidity and also learnt to read. Over the next two years, she caught up to her peers and became hard to distinguish from them, with an IQ now in the normal range (Davis 1947; see also Mason 1942).

Isabelle, who did learn language, was unlike two other children. Anna, aged six, found in Illinois tied to a chair in an attic, had received minimal care and attention from birth. Once removed and cared for, she learned to walk, to dress, and produce a few utterances, but she was probably suffering from congenital retardation, so this, together with the trauma from her isolation, probably accounts for why her language did not develop normally (Davis 1940). Genie, another child confined by her parents, with minimal caretaker contact from around age two until about twelve, also showed little recovery. While she responded to care, she made only limited progress in her acquisition of language (Curtiss 1977). Once she was institutionalized some years later, the progress she had made lapsed markedly. Again, her limitations may be as much or more attributable to the emotional trauma she had suffered for years, plus some general retardation, than to her having passed a sensitive period for language acquisition.

Can these observations tell us more about a sensitive period for language acquisition? The answer may well be no. These children had most likely been abandoned either because the parents were unable to care for them or because the children appeared retarded. Even when people tried later to socialize them and teach them language, they appeared quite unable to learn. Lenneberg (1967) argued that this was because they were, in many cases, beyond the sensitive period for acquisition.

However, the emotional trauma produced by extreme social isolation can interfere with learning. So can retardation. What such studies do suggest is that children require exposure to language in normal social settings (Chapter 2). Isolation and mistreatment, resulting in emotional and social deprivation, have highly adverse effects on general development, even for children who might otherwise have developed normally.

### Second-language learning

If there is a critical period for language learning, it has been argued, people who learn a second language after the critical period should be unable to attain native skill. Some researchers, using this logic, have argued *for* a critical period on the basis of differences between first- and second-language speakers' skill in judging whether sentences are grammatical or not. In one ERP study, researchers looked at Chinese speakers exposed to English as a second language at different ages (Weber-Fox & Neville 1996). These speakers were asked to read and judge sentences containing semantic anomalies (e.g., *the event of the theorem* instead of *the proof of the theorem*) and syntactic violations (e.g., *of proof the theorem* instead of *the proof of the theorem*). Grammaticality judgements were affected in speakers exposed to English after age three, while judgements of semantic anomalies were affected in speakers exposed to English after age sixteen. (Before age sixteen, semantic judgements were closer to those of native speakers.) And there was a difference in ERP measures for speakers exposed to English before versus after age ten. So the later the exposure to a language, the greater the effect on language proficiency and on cerebral organization for language processing. Also, the subsystems responsible for processing semantic anomaly versus syntactic violation appeared to have different sensitive periods. However, since one goes on learning vocabulary throughout school and beyond, it is rather unclear what these differences in ERP (especially the N400 response) mean if they distinguish children exposed to a second language before, versus after, age ten, as in Weber-Fox and Neville's (1996) study.

Grammaticality judgements were also the focus of studies by Johnson and Newport (1989, 1991). In their first study, they asked Chinese and Korean second-language learners of English to listen to recordings of 246 sentences and offer a grammaticality judgement (okay vs. not okay) for each one. The sentences exemplified twelve basic rule-types of English (e.g., past tense and plural inflections, determiners, particles, auxiliary verbs, and basic word order). From their findings, Johnson and Newport argued for a critical period ending around age twelve to fourteen.

In another study, they focussed on the syntactic principle of subjacency. This specifies the conditions under which a *wh-* question can be extracted from an embedded clause (Johnson & Newport 1991). English allows the extraction of a *wh-* word for a question over only one node (underlined) in an embedded, subordinate, clause. Compare the assertions and associated questions in (1) and (2):

(1)    My mother heard that *Tam is buying a computer.*
       QUESTION: *What* did my mother hear that *Tam is buying?*
(2)    My mother heard the news that *Tam is buying a computer.*
       **What* did my mother hear the news that *Tam is buying?*

Johnson and Newport tested adult native speakers of Chinese who had arrived in the United States between age four and thirty-eight, and had spent at least five years in the US. Since there is no movement in Chinese *wh-* questions, there is no subjacency to violate in that language. If mechanisms for language acquisition are accessible only during a critical period, then anyone learning a language like English after the critical period should not be able to achieve native-speaker levels of skill. This position also assumes uniformity in how skilled every language learner becomes, which may also be a little problematic.

These speakers showed non-native performance no matter what age they arrived. But the younger their age of arrival, the more native-like their linguistic judgements about English. After age fifteen, though, their performance dropped to near-chance levels. These second language speakers did not distinguish between the one-node subjacency forms, as in (1) (grammatical), and those with more than one node, as in (2) (ungrammatical). Johnson and Newport concluded that older learners no longer have access to the same learning mechanisms as young learners.

But what if one takes into account both age of arrival and number of years of exposure? In a reanalysis of these data, Bialystok and Hakuta (1999) looked at age of immigration rather than age of initial acquisition of the second language. The children who immigrated between age three and seven looked most like native speakers of English. They were learning the new language as if it were a first language (see Chapter 14). Bialystok and Hakuta argued that the major change in grammaticality judgements came at age twenty rather than around fifteen. When they divided the second-language speakers into two groups (below vs. above age twenty at age of arrival), they found significant correlations between age of arrival and amount of experience with the language for both groups. Age of acquisition *and* amount of exposure over the years play a role here, but this undermines the claim that the same learning mechanisms are no longer available for older language learners.

The jury is still out on whether there is a sensitive period for some aspects of language at around puberty. If intensive exposure can result in effective acquisition (with better acquisition from more exposure), this suggests that the mechanisms and strategies for first language acquisition can be recruited for each new language. Children may not be *better* at learning a (second) language than adults, but they spend more *time* doing so – much more time. If experience and practice play a role (as they do in the acquisition of other complex skills, from reading to playing the flute to riding a unicycle), then children may be no better at learning a new language than adults. This in fact appears to be the case. In a study of highly proficient language users (all second-language learners of English), the younger learners were more likely to attain near-native proficiency, but, in accuracy of judgements, nearly all were indistinguishable from native speakers, regardless of age (White & Genesee 1996). Lastly, in another study, researchers followed English-speaking families who moved to the Netherlands. They tested family members three times in the course of their first year to assess their acquisition of Dutch. What they found was that the adolescents (aged twelve to fifteen) and adults were better learners than children aged three to five

(Snow & Hoefnagel-Hohle 1978). Young children don't always have the advantage over adolescents and adults when it comes to learning another language.

## Is there an innate language acquisition device?

Many researchers have proposed that people have an innate capacity for language acquisition, a capacity that distinguishes humans from other species. The question is, just what is innate? Are there special areas of the brain dedicated to language? Here, as we have seen, the answer appears to be yes, but the specialization in these areas develops with exposure to language. And lateralization for language, then, only begins during the second year of life. Could there be built-in categories, universal in human languages, such as "noun" and "verb"? Are there any built-in structures? How might built-in categories and structures affect the process of acquisition? Or, instead of this, could humans be endowed with learning mechanisms specialized just for language? These questions have elicited considerable debate. Here we look at some of the proposals that have been made.

In the 1960s, Chomsky proposed that the human capacity for language was innate. The assumptions here are that: (a) natural-language syntax is too complex for children to learn from what they hear around them, because (b) adults offer such a distorted and imperfect source of data. And (c) children learn their first language so fast that they must rely on some innate capacity, specifically for syntactic categories and syntactic structure. As Chomsky put it, "The grammar has to be discovered by the child on the basis of the data available to him, through the use of the innate capacities with which he is endowed" (1972:183).

Over the years, at least two of these assumptions have been shown to be empirically incorrect. First, adults actually offer highly grammatical speech to children (see Chapter 2), and second, children take considerably longer to acquire syntactic structure in their first language than originally estimated (see Chapters 7–10). This leaves open the question of whether the syntactic categories and constructions of natural languages are in fact too complex to learn from available child-directed speech combined with any overheard speech that they attend to as they get older. If it can be demonstrated that some syntactic structures are too complex to learn, then one could make a case for there being certain language-relevant structures that are innate. But this remains an empirical question.[5]

---

[5] In the mid-1960s, several studies of how people learnt small artificial language systems suggested that certain rule-types found in natural languages were not learnable (e.g., Miller 1967). However, further research showed that, if such miniature artificial language types were presented as expressing systematic *meanings* in the syntax, this strongly affected the learning of that syntax. For instance, Moeser and Bregman (1972) showed that, once syntactic structures were systematically associated with a semantics, adults could learn even complex artificial languages quite readily. But without a semantics, adults were unable to learn them.

Current positions on the status of innate categories and structures tend to espouse one of two main views: the *continuity* view and the *maturational* view (see O'Grady 1997). Both focus on syntax, which is treated as autonomous, independent of phonology and the lexicon. Morphology is sometimes included with syntax, because it too can be viewed as rule-based and because it marks syntactic distinctions such as "subject of" and "predicate," as well as parts of speech (by distinguishing nouns from verbs from adjectives, for instance). The continuity view assumes that children use the same notions and relations throughout development; they are present from birth. These researchers generally subscribe to an innate Universal Grammar (UG) common to speakers at every stage of development (e.g., Pinker 1984). The strong version of this approach assumes that children just beginning to speak have the same mental representations for linguistic constructions as adults (e.g., Lust 1994). A weaker version assumes that, although children come with all the categories and operations, they don't make use of them all immediately. They first have to learn how to instantiate such elements as relativizers (*that, who, which*), complementizers (*to, for, whether*), or *wh-* forms for questions (*what, where, why*). One result is that the focus in most studies has been limited to the learning of grammatical elements.

But languages differ, and researchers have to take that into account. One version of UG that has been invoked contains parameters that allows for variation across languages. Some languages, for example, have complement constructions that are head-initial – the term introducing a complement comes first, followed by the complement, as in English (e.g., *They said **that** he came in at five*). Others are head-final and place the head after the complement, as in Japanese. In UG, this difference is captured by a *word-order parameter* with two values: head-initial and head-final. Upon exposure to a language, children "discover" the value of this parameter and set it accordingly. Languages also differ in whether finite verbs appear with an overt subject in the form of a nominal or pronoun, as in French (e.g., ***je** veux partir* 'I want to-go'), or whether they can omit these, as in Italian (e.g., *voglio partire* 'I-want to-go'). This variation is captured by the parameter called *subject-drop*, which is either permitted or not. Both these parameters are assumed to be present from the start in acquisition, but they can only be set after experience with a language.

Children also need to acquire relevant words with which to display their syntactic knowledge. Until they use nouns and verbs, there is no way to tell what underlying grammatical categories or structures they might know. Take two-year-olds who haven't yet learnt *I* or *me* in self-reference and usually use a verb alone for their own actions (e.g., *Throw ball*), or three-year-olds who don't yet use complementizers like *whether* or *that* (e.g., *Rod said Nico coming*). Have these children set the appropriate parameters yet? The values on some parameters are associated directly with specific lexical items, such as *him* versus *himself*, which determine the domain for the antecedent of the pronoun, as in *Ken washed him* (i.e., someone else) versus *Ken washed himself*. This parameter either sets the domain as the smallest clause containing the pronoun or as the sentence containing the pronoun. In English, both *him* and *himself* are associated with the first setting (the smallest clause), but in other languages, the pronoun *him* may be associated with the first setting and the reflexive *himself* with the second, as in Japanese.

The continuity view offers a potentially simple and elegant account of acquisition for syntax (Macnamara 1982; Pinker 1984). If UG in its entirety is present from the start, then children have only to set a certain number of parameters and learn any lexical items with syntactic consequences. There is no need to track changes in learning mechanisms since they remain unchanged, as do children's representations of linguistic categories and structures.

The maturational view of what is innate differs from the continuity view on the role of experience. In the maturational account, children make progress in syntactic acquisition without much regard to experience. Development is driven instead by a biological timetable. As a result, groups with different kinds of experience adhere to the same timetable. For example, Gleitman (1981) argued that children with normal hearing, children who are blind, and children who are deaf (and not exposed to a sign language) follow much the same timing. All, for instance, produce their first one-word forms around age one; two- and three-word expressions by age two; and some simple grammatical sequences by age three. But notice that all three groups require normal intelligence and normal input to arrive at these milestones.

Proponents of UG often prefer maturation over continuity because biological maturation can be relatively independent of experience. As Felix (1988:371) put it, "The mechanism that 'pushes' the child through the sequence of developmental stages is therefore the maturational schedule." What is innate, then, is UG combined with a biologically based schedule for the emergence of each parameter setting.[6] To take one example, Borer and Wexler (1987) proposed that subject-drop as a parameter in UG is just not available until a particular point in acquisition (also Hyams 1986, but see Ingham 1992). Before this point, exposure to any relevant information in child-directed speech can have no effect. This allows researchers to ignore what happens in acquisition prior to the setting of each parameter. There is no need, in the maturational view, to account for early errors, since they are assumed to play no role in the later emergence of the target construction. Borer and Wexler also proposed that the passive construction (as in *The cat was chased by the boy*) "matures" only at around age five, thus accounting for its relatively late emergence in English. Here, however, the maturational account runs into distinct difficulty. First, Demuth (1989) showed that, for speakers of Sesotho (a Bantu language), the passive is well established in young children before age three, and, second, several researchers have shown that the passive in English is also acquired considerably before age five

---

[6] The claims about just what is innate are sometimes even stronger. Felix (1988) proposed that early word combinations are the way they are for young children because they are not yet old enough for specific version of syntax (X-bar ) to have emerged as part of the general maturation of UG.

(e.g., Clark & Carpenter 1989a; Pinker *et al.* 1987). They have also shown that emergence of the passive depends heavily on the precise verbs used (e.g., Maratsos *et al.* 1985).

Another maturational account was put forward by Radford (1990). He proposed that young children go through three stages. The first is *pre-grammatical* in that any terms used have yet to be categorized as nouns or verbs, say. Next (at around 1;8) comes the *lexical* stage. This is marked by an increase in vocabulary size, especially for nouns, verbs, prepositions, and adjectives, and by the appearance of word combinations like *X* + Complement (e.g., *open box*, *in bag*), Modifier + *X* (e.g., *nice book*, *back in*, *very good*), and Possessor + *X* (e.g., *baby cup*, *daddy gone*, *doggy down*, *hand cold*). Absent from this lexical stage, according to Radford, are all "functional categories," such as determiners (*a*, *the*, *this*, *that*, etc.) and complementizers (*whether*, *that*), as well as inflections, such as tense suffixes (*wants*, *jumped*), modal auxiliaries (*can*, *must*), and the infinitival marker *to*. These emerge only in the third, *functional*, stage.

Functional categories emerge when they do, according to Radford (1990:274), because they "are genetically programmed to come into operation at different biologically determined stages of maturation." But in other languages, a variety of functional categories emerge much earlier (e.g., determiners in Sesotho: Demuth 1992), and even in English, some members of a specific functional set emerge many months before others (Fletcher 1985; Ingham 1998). These data raise serious questions about the status of a functional stage per se.

An alternative to Radford's maturational account is that functional categories come in later than some instances of lexical categories because they are semantically more complex and so require more structural knowledge. They are also often pragmatically complex as well. This account is consistent with the data on Korean determiners, a *lexical* category that emerges relatively late, near age three (O'Grady 1993), and also with the rather long period of acquisition (three years or more) for functional categories in English (e.g., Brown 1973). A major determinant of acquisition there is relative semantic complexity, with less complex meanings mastered before more complex ones (see Chapter 8). If so, complexity of meaning may offer a more general explanation, cross-linguistically, than the stages proposed by Radford.

To return to the continuity and maturational views: Both are linked to specific theories of syntax. This is both a strength and a weakness. On the one hand, both approaches can derive precise predictions. On the other, this leads both views to ignore data not directly pertinent to the syntactic account in question. Both approaches also depend on strong assumptions that, up to now, have little or no empirical support.

There are also many unspecified details. Just what belongs in UG? How many parameters are there? How much exposure to a language and what kind of evidence do children need to set each parameter in the continuity account? Is it reasonable to assume that syntax is quite distinct in learning from the rest of language – the lexicon, phonology, morphology, and all the pragmatic conditions on usage? Notice that all of these are involved in acquisition from the start. It is also hard to separate language from affect, from perception, and from cognition – all broad domains that play major roles in child development as well as in every-day adult functioning. Neither view here takes account of all the nonlinguistic factors implicated in language acquisition.

What these approaches share is a common emphasis on the innateness of grammatical categories like noun and verb, as well as other syntactic structures. Because they postulate that everything is built-in and just needs triggering to emerge, they pay no attention to learning. Yet even if all syntactic notions were innate, children would still need to connect them to the relevant words, phrases, and constructions of their language. But the continuity and maturational accounts have little to say about how innate categories become linked to actual linguistic forms,[7] although that clearly requires some learning. For example, some children must learn *put* as a verb and *cat* as a noun, where others must instead learn *prendre* as a verb and *jardin* as a noun. As speakers, we master very large vocabularies. We learn early on how to identify and produce the sounds of our language community. And, over the years, we learn the local conventions of use.

Perhaps, then, the question of what is innate is rather a question of whether we make use of innate learning mechanisms unique to language, and if so, what form these might take. The real debate here should be over the specificity or generality of the learning mechanisms themselves, not the categories or structures to be learnt. As Lenneberg (1967:394) put it:

> [N]o features that are characteristics of only certain natural languages, either particulars of syntax, or phonology, or semantics, are assumed … to be innate. However, there are many reasons to believe that the processes by which the realized, outer structure of a natural language comes about are deep-rooted, species-specific, innate properties of man's biological nature.

What is innate in this view is the manner in which humans *process* information. For example, the mammalian auditory system is finely tuned, and even small babies can distinguish fine gradations among speech sounds (Chapter 3). Humans produce sounds through the larynx, sounds modulated by a myriad of fine motor adjustments along the vocal tract, from glottis and pharynx to velum, tongue, teeth, and lips. While the adjustments for a particular sound must be learnt, children are born with a vocal tract and must then learn how to use it (Chapter 5), just as they learn to use their hearing. Within the brain, humans devote considerable space to auditory and visual information, two domains that must be linked to each other as well as to memory in general; both are also essential for a communication system of any complexity. Humans can store large amounts of information in memory. They have to learn how to adopt appropriate

---

[7] Pinker (1984), who proposed that children make the linkage between innate grammatical categories and actual terms in a language through semantic bootstrapping via child-directed speech, is a clear exception (see further Chapters 2 and 16).

strategies for chunking, storing, and retrieving information effectively in their uses of language. And very similar abilities are known to play a role in general cognitive functioning and in the processing of nonlinguistic information.

The basic question, then, is whether there are innate learning mechanisms dedicated just to syntax, insulated from other learning mechanisms, and from any possible interaction with other domains of knowledge (see Scholz & Pullum 2006). What evidence is there for the existence of a language acquisition device, a module prewired solely for the learning of syntax? One justification for assuming such a device has been the supposed uniformity and speed of language acquisition in normal children. But although children appear to go through similar stages, there is little evidence for strict uniformity. Speed is also in question: There is growing evidence that children learn syntactic constructions slowly and conservatively (see Chapters 7–10). Some are not mastered until the early teen years, even though they may appear in primitive form as young as age three. Although children start to produce embedded clauses, for instance, during their third year, they take several years to perfect their forms and learn their uses. In short, there is no good measure of speed here for syntactic acquisitions.

## A learning mechanism, just for syntax?

Some researchers have argued that there is a module in the brain for the rule-governed portion of language. Humans are unique in having developed language; there is strong evidence for specialization of the left hemisphere for language, and part of this specialization consists in a module devoted to the syntactic (rule-based) component of language. As a result, they have argued, whatever mechanisms are used for language acquisition must be specialized and quite distinct from any used for other cognitive acquisitions. In short, language is distinct from cognition, and mechanisms for acquisition can be used only for language.

What it the evidence for this position? First, language is unique to people and is not found in other species. Second, some language disorders show selective impairment of the rule-governed aspects of language (specifically, syntactic rules and regular morphological paradigms).[8] This has been viewed as evidence that language is encapsulated and hence distinct from other capacities (Curtiss 1988). For instance, studies of children with Williams Syndrome initially suggested that WS children's language was normal but their nonverbal skills were not (e.g., Mervis 1999; Morris & Mervis 1999). This population therefore offered strong evidence for a dissociation between linguistic skills and general cognitive skills. Children's cognition could be seriously impaired, in short, but their language remained intact. Yet, as researchers looked more closely at the Williams Syndrome child, that picture became much cloudier.

---

[8] Irregular morphology is excluded because it requires one-by-one learning for each irregular form in a paradigm.

Some researchers claim that data from WS provide evidence for a discrete or encapsulated capacity for syntax, for the rule-governed aspects of language. One study of four Williams Syndrome adolescents' mastery of the syntactic rules governing morphology, for instance, showed that, despite low IQs, the children appeared to do well on tasks that tested syntax and regular inflections (but not irregular ones). WS children, Clahsen and Almazan (1988) argued, were intact in their ability to make use of rules (syntax and regular morphology), even though they were impaired in their ability to access irregular forms (presumably stored in memory). By comparison, children with specific language impairment (SLI) did poorly on both syntactic and morphological tasks (Bishop 1997; Leonard 1998).

Other researchers question whether WS children and adolescents really exhibit fully normal syntactic ability (e.g., Karmiloff-Smith *et al.* 1998; Stevens & Karmiloff-Smith 1997; Tyler *et al.* 1997). In testing for several kinds of syntactic knowledge in people with Williams Syndrome, they found a number of places where development did not look normal. Karmiloff-Smith and her colleagues concluded that WS syntax is not intact, as had been claimed. In further studies of morphology, Karmiloff-Smith and her colleagues (1997) looked at individuals with WS who spoke either English or French. They tested the English speakers on inflections for regular and irregular forms, and on subject–verb agreement, and the French speakers on gender assignment (e.g., agreement for article, noun, adjective, and pronoun). WS adults had difficulty even with regular morphology, a part of language acquired early by normal children. The French speakers, for instance, had difficulty assigning gender across several elements, and, in both languages, speakers had difficulty understanding embedded clauses. These findings also challenge the view that regular, rule-governed morphology is intact in Williams Syndrome.

Karmiloff-Smith and her colleagues have also made a more fundamental theoretical point about development: Because syndromes like Williams are present from the onset of language development, the path such children will follow is necessarily different all along from the normal path of acquisition. This in turn questions whether non-normal development can ever illuminate normal development, as well as whether data from Williams Syndrome, for example, show that the processes central to cognitive development and language development are in fact dissociated from each other (see Thomas *et al.* 2001; Thomas & Karmiloff-Smith 2003). This argument necessarily applies to all neurological impairments that in any way affect language development (see also Lewis & Elman 2008).

WS children and adolescents have also been flagged as having extensive vocabularies. But do they rely on the same processes in acquisition as normal children? Stevens and Karmiloff-Smith (1997) compared the learning of new words in WS and normal children, and found that the former did not observe the same constraints on new words and so were not computing appropriate inferences about meanings. (This is consistent with Johnson and Carey's [1998] finding that Williams Syndrome children also fail to develop folk-biological theories beyond the level found in normally developing six-year-olds.) Yet in semantic-priming tasks, WS individuals appear to display the same taxonomic category and thematic-functional priming effects as normal controls (Tyler *et al.* 1997). Tyler and her colleagues suggested that, although semantic memory and access to information for individual words appears normal, WS individuals have difficulty integrating semantic information across utterances. This would account for why their ability to understand sentences often appears quite abnormal, and their conversational interactions often go awry.

The findings across tasks and languages show that WS individuals do not after all present evidence for an encapsulated language capacity. The initially rosy picture of their syntactic abilities was exaggerated. Children with Williams Syndrome do not follow the normal course of acquisition for syntax, morphology, or the lexicon. Their syntax and morphology do not, after all, represent a unified, neatly modular syntactic or computational skill, distinct from other linguistic and communicative abilities.

In summary, humans exploit various physiological and neurological factors in their use of language. They rely on the vocal tract to make speech sounds and on the auditory system to recognize them, or else on the hands and face for signed languages, along with the visual system for recognition and analysis. The left hemisphere is specialized for language but does not confine language just to the main language areas (Broca's and Wernicke's areas). Rather, language is stored in a distributed manner. Remember that language is just one part, albeit a major one, in the overall system of human communication and representation. As a result, it tends to be closely integrated with gesture, facial expression, affective expression, conceptual structure, memory, and attention. In communication, all these systems are seamlessly coordinated, so it might not be surprising to find that language is acquired via many of the same mechanisms used in cognitive and perceptual development as well as in later functioning.

All of this makes it difficult to ask what might be innate with respect *only* to language and, more specifically than that, *only* to the syntactic, rule-governed, part of language. Indeed, it may not make sense to ask such a question before we understand how people *use* language as part of an extensive, general, coordinated system of communication.

## Summary

We began with three questions: Is there specialization for language in the brain? Are there sensitive periods for language learning? And is there some built-in language acquisition device? The answer to the first two is a qualified yes. There is strong evidence for specialization for language, mainly in the left hemisphere. There is also evidence for sensitive periods during which it is easier to learn certain aspects of language. But there does not appear to be a clear cut-off, as there would be for a critical period, after which language learning would become impossible. Rather, acquisition becomes more difficult in the teen years, but it is still unclear why. One factor may well be the sheer amount of time young children can spend on language compared to adults. Three-year-olds devote as much as seventy hours a week to using a new language. By comparison, adults learning a second (or third or fourth) language may spend only four or five hours a week. It's hardly surprising that they fail to learn as much as a child tackling a first language. At the same time, older children are more efficient learners of language than very young children, probably because they already know one language and are better at deploying learning strategies based on what they know.

The answer to the third question is much less clear. Some of the evidence for a language acquisition device (mechanisms and built-in structures specific only to language) has relied on assumptions about speed and universality that we now know to be incorrect. Other evidence has been drawn from children with defective language where, at first glance, the syntactic component of what was being learned seemed to be intact, while lexical and pragmatic aspects of language appeared disrupted. This seemed to support a learning mechanism specific to at least one component of language, namely syntax. But is that component of language really as distinct as claimed from the lexicon, say, which does not require language-specific learning mechanisms for acquisition? The answer here will most likely depend on the identification of learning mechanisms and how they apply to language *and* to cognitive and social acquisitions.

# 16   Acquisition and change

Children follow an extraordinary trajectory as they learn their first language. They start in on the speech stream within months, weeks, or even days of birth and break it into manageable pieces. By age one, they have started to associate groups of sounds with meanings and to use them to express their own intentions. In the next several years, they analyze many expressions, assign meanings to the parts, and start making use of a larger range of constructions to express their intentions. Another three to four years later, they have attained a vocabulary of close to 14,000 words and are becoming increasingly skillful in how they use language in a range of settings. They have by now mostly mastered the conventional forms for expressing common meanings used in the speech community.

Within acquisition, researchers need to account for both *continuity* and *change* in what children know about their first language. This in turn requires us to decide what counts in assessing continuity as well as change. And while most changes move children closer to the conventional patterns of the speech community, it may be harder to identify the developmental links between forms and functions produced at one-and-a-half and at four without scrutiny of the paths children follow. Another factor is general cognitive development, which affects or interacts with their growing skill with language. Finally, we need to specify the general mechanisms children rely on as they acquire language.

Children do not progress in a single bound from identifying the sequence of sounds in *bottle* to making a request of the form *I want my bottle* or *Can I have some more milk now?* To achieve this progression, they apply a variety of procedures. In this chapter, I review some of the ingredients most likely to be required in learning a language and assess the empirical support for them. Critical to this account are the sheer amount that has to be learnt and how much is known about possible learning mechanisms.

## Continuity in development

Many systems unfold with development, such that the roots of later forms can be traced to earlier ones. In their capacity to learn, children change enormously between six months and six years. This suggests there could be complex interactions between the learning mechanisms infants start out with and the stages of knowledge those mechanisms are applied to. At the same time, it is important to track continuities in how infants communicate. For example, there is evidence for continuity in the speech acts used to express child-speakers' intentions, whether they are making assertions or requests. But can we attribute to children the same intention at age one-and-a-half as at age four, when their grasp of linguistic forms has changed so radically? Whatever the answer, there is a good case for continuity in language use as children move from one stage to the next.

When we look at the same syntactic constructions at different ages, it becomes clear that continuity resides more in the functions than in the forms. Take relative clauses. The most primitive versions of these involve a simple adjunction, with the relative clause juxtaposed to the end of the main clause, for example, D (2;0.1, picking up his doll): *Here* [ə] *doll | Shelli give Damon*. Only later do children add in relativizers like *that* or *who*, and produce relative clauses attached to nonfinal noun phrases (see Chapter 10). Yet even the earliest relative clauses appear to have a function similar to that of later ones: They modify noun phrases so as to better identify the referent the speaker has in mind.

Continuity is more discernible in phonology, in the relations between babbled sequences and the sound structure of early words (Chapter 5). There, it appears to stem from the articulatory patterns practiced so far, not necessarily from the sound structures per se. Also, in phonology, there are no meaning connections between babble-sequences and later words. The continuity here is a continuity of form, not meaning. In the lexicon, children often come up with substitutes for adult expressions in the earlier stages. But there is local continuity, typically, with no evidence of abrupt shifts, for example, in how children use referring expressions.

Despite many lines of continuity, one cannot fully infer the starting point or the developmental course children are most likely to follow by looking only at the end point (Karmiloff-Smith 1999). There can be multiple routes to adultlike use of language. And adult speakers differ greatly in the skill with which they use language, in the size of their vocabularies, and in the range of constructions they use. Speakers in each community share a good deal of common ground, make use of a similar sound system, and share many conventions on how to use language. But even within such a community, speakers at every age also exhibit large individual differences. They differ on how well they tell jokes or stories, how clearly they can give instructions, how persuasive they can be, how good they are at crossword puzzles, and in how much (and what) they read. In short, in development, there are many paths to the same end point, many differences in linguistic skill, and as much individual variation along all those paths as there are individual differences everywhere else.

## Getting started

When adults hear speech in their own language, they automatically segment it into clauses, phrases, words, stems, and affixes, all on the basis of what they know about that language. But infants start knowing nothing. They must discover all these units. How can they get started? They can't take up ready-made chunks given in continuous speech by markers like pauses or lexical stress or even the distributions of sound segments in initial versus final position. To make use of any word-boundary markers like these presupposes that one knows where the boundaries are. This is one of the many things infants have to discover.

How might infants start on this? One approach is to consider a mechanism that allows recognition of similarity (Hayes & Clark 1970). One could then start to perceive sequences or chunks in a speech stream, not because specific markers delimit their boundaries, but because one has recognized a pattern of sounds that recurs. That pattern could constitute a "word" or some other unit. If infants achieved segmentation through such a recognition mechanism, they could learn recurring patterns from exposure to the target language. What mechanisms might one need for such pattern recognition? Hayes and Clark identified three types: (a) *bracketing* mechanisms – to identify sequences in terms of preceding and following markers; (b) *reference* mechanisms – to identify patterns of sound segments (**d-o-g**) strongly correlated with some external reference object (a dog) or event; and (c) *clustering* mechanisms – to detect recurrent patterns as units, without the aid of either markers or meanings. Clustering mechanisms would look for units that had strong correlations among sound segments (within-unit correlations), versus weaker correlations across unit-boundaries. Strongly clustered sequences of adjacent segments (Harris 1955) would be candidate units (let's say words) to attend to further. Reliance on a clustering mechanism would allow infants to detect regular patterns in the speech addressed to them, prior to any acquisition of meaning or form. Hayes and Clark showed that such clustering was possible for adults who listened to an artificial language composed of a continuous stream of computer-generated tones that made up recurring "words" of different lengths. Afterwards, these adults recognized sequences that made up the "words" and failed to recognize sequences that crossed word-boundaries.

Could infants be using a clustering mechanism to break up the speech stream? Saffran and her colleagues (Saffran *et al.* 1996; Aslin et al. 1998, 1999) showed that eight-month-olds could segment out "words" solely on the basis of the statistical patterns among sounds (Chapter 3). Young infants, then, appear to make use of clustering, a powerful learning mechanism. Saffran and her colleagues also looked further at the statistical computation required, namely conditional probabilities, and found that infants can segment continuous speech into recurrent patterns (words) on the basis of transitional probabilities of constituent syllable pairs.

Clustering appears to be a general learning mechanism, available to both infants and adults. Both seven-year-olds and adults are able to make use of clustering for both linguistic stimuli – a stream of syllables – and nonlinguistic stimuli – a stream of tones (Aslin *et al.* 1999; Saffran *et al.* 1999). In other studies with adults, Saffran and her colleagues compared adults' ability to use transitional probabilities to identify recurring patterns with their ability to make use of an added prosodic cue, vowel-lengthening (Saffran *et al.* 1996). They found that performance on word-identification with prosodic cues was enhanced. Effectively, when clustering is supplemented by bracketing (the prosodic cues), people do better in the identification of "words" than with just clustering alone. This suggests that, once infants have identified their first recurrent patterns, they can use additional mechanisms to boost their initial learning. Such added mechanisms may include bracketing (using additional cues to word-boundaries), and also reference mechanisms as they assign their first meanings to words (see Chapters 3, 4, 6).

At the start, infants may rely heavily on a clustering mechanism to break up the stream of speech. But clustering can only work if one has some measure of *similarity* for deciding whether this pattern matches another one heard earlier. To identify recurrent patterns, one must use a mechanism that detects similarity (see Tversky 1977). Once one has picked out several recurring patterns with clustering, one can use bracketing mechanisms to extract further chunks (words or phrases) from the speech stream. Sequences isolated this way then become candidates for association with objects and events in the immediate context, using reference mechanisms.

## Starting small

Children learn language at a stage when they themselves are developing rapidly. One issue is how these developmental changes themselves affect the ability to learn complex material. In a series of simulations using connectionist models, Elman (1993) showed that training of such linguistic structures as number agreement, verb-argument structure, and relative clauses only succeeded when the models began with a limited working memory and gradually "matured" to an adultlike state. When they started out fully formed with an adult memory capacity, they failed to learn the same material. Elman concluded that developmental restrictions on resources like working memory may actually be a prerequisite for learning complex domains. This limitation itself enables learning.

This general finding is consistent with many studies of acquisition. In research on American Sign Language (ASL), Newport (1988) found that the younger children are when first exposed to ASL, the more likely they are to acquire complex details of its inflectional system. Like Elman, Newport argued that her findings were due not solely to differences in age but also to differences in how the young children processed the ASL they were seeing. By starting small and attending only to some of the language they hear (or see), children will arrive ultimately at a more detailed analysis (Newport 1990).

Starting small may be critical also to children's discovery of word-classes – their discovery that certain groups of words act alike. Mintz and his colleagues (2002) analyzed transcripts of speech directed to children under two-and-a-half[1] for any information it could offer about patterns of use for word-types – the distributions of nouns and definite articles, or verbs and auxiliary verbs, for

---

[1] They chose this age cut-off because, by 2;6, most children have begun to produce a variety of word combinations and have started to use a number of inflections appropriately, both of which indicate that any categorization of word-classes must precede that stage.

example – and for the circumstances under which this distributional information might help identify word-classes (see also Manning & Schütze 1999). To do this, they compared four analyses of child-directed speech. In the first, they selected a target word (a noun, say), then looked at the term to its left and the term to its right. In the next three analyses, they varied the context for each target, for example, by increasing the number of terms counted to the left and to the right; by increasing the number of terms but stopping at a phrase-structure boundary; and finally by reducing the amount of detail they took note of (whether a term was a definite article or not, or just whether it was a determiner of some kind). The analysis sensitive to phrase-structure boundaries was the best at finding nouns and verbs. This analysis also required the fewest computational resources.

These data show two things: First, it is possible for children to deduce word-classes from their distributional characteristics in child-directed speech, and second, starting small is an effective approach. The findings are consistent with a natural progression from the use of clustering alone to clustering augmented by reference with what children already know – any meanings they have already attached to words – and by bracketing, with any boundaries they have identified. Early limits on processing capacities appear to facilitate learning by restricting the number of factors young children need attend to (Newport 1991).

Further evidence that children start small comes from studies by Santelmann and Jusczyk (1998). They noted that, by eighteen months, infants seem to attend to grammatical morphemes (e.g., Gerken, Landau, & Remez 1990; Gerken & McIntosh 1993; Shipley, Smith, & Gleitman 1969). If they have begun to track the occurrence of such morphemes and attend to their co-occurrence with each other (e.g., *is* and *-ing*), they should be able to distinguish legitimate co-occurrences (as in *He is jumping*) from illegitimate ones (as in *He can jumping*): They can and do. In addition, sixteen-month-olds, but not fourteen- or fifteen-month-olds, are attentive to the order and distribution of grammatical morphemes like *the* and *was*, and prefer sequences like *the kitten was hiding* to ones like *was kitten the hiding* (Shady & Gerken 1999).

Santelmann and Jusczyk followed up on these observations, first to establish that eighteen-month-olds were attentive to discontinuous grammatical morphemes (*is* V-*ing*), and then to find out how big a window learners this age apply to incoming language. Infants aged fifteen and eighteen months listened to passages containing either the target dependency, for example, *is* + *walking*, or an unnatural one like *can* + *walking*. Santelmann and Jusczyk then measured how long the infants looked towards the voice producing each one. At eighteen months (but not earlier), infants looked significantly longer towards the voices uttering natural passages. In further studies, they focussed on the size of the child's processing span. They varied the number of syllables between the auxiliary verb (*is*) and the main verb (*walking*) by inserting two, three, or four added syllables, again pairing natural and unnatural versions of each passage. These variants tested whether eighteen-month-olds could track the target dependency. When there were three intervening syllables (as in *everybody is often baking bread*), infants looked for significantly longer overall towards the voice producing natural passages. But

Table 16.1 *Looking times (secs) for infants who do and don't combine words*

|  | Infants who combine words | | Infants who don't combine words | |
|---|---|---|---|---|
| Separation | Natural | Unnatural | Natural | Unnatural |
| 1-syllable | 10.59 | 6.54 | 9.62 | 8.97 |
| 3-syllable | 10.51 | 6.41 | 9.30 | 7.97 |
| 4-syllable | 7.55 | 6.80 | 5.8 | 6.47 |
| 5-syllable | 8.08 | 8.52 | 8.20 | 9.21 |

*Source*: Santelmann & Jusczyk 1998:126. Reprinted from *Cognition* 69, Lynn M. Santelmann & Peter W. Jusczyk, Sensitivity to discontinuous dependencies in language learners: Evidence for limitations in processing space, 105–134, copyright 1998, with permission from Elsevier Science.

with four or five intervening syllables, infants no longer showed any preference. Those eighteen-month-olds who produced word combinations were more likely to look longer with natural than unnatural passages, as shown in Table 16.1.

In summary, eighteen-month-olds can track dependencies between linguistic units provided that the relevant elements occur within their processing span. They can manage three syllables between *is* and *-ing*, but not four or five syllables. Once again, children start small. Adults can track dependencies like these over much longer distances (Bock & Miller 1991).

With age, children make increasing use of meanings they already have for words. They also use more information about boundaries – whether between words, phrases, or clauses. Although they produce few grammatical morphemes before age two, children use them in comprehension. They consistently treat novel terms introduced with articles (*the dax*) as common nouns and those without as proper names (*Dax*) (Gelman & Taylor 1984; Katz, Baker, & Macnamara 1974). Children who produce word combinations (*Fall block*, *That car*) also show better comprehension of utterances with grammatical morphemes (*Can you throw the ball?*) than utterances where they have been omitted or are used inappropriately (*Throw ball* or *Throw ball the*) (Gerken & McIntosh 1993; Petretic & Tweney 1977; Shipley *et al.* 1969). So children this age are attentive to distributional and morphological properties of language, even though they don't yet produce the pertinent forms. The more children know, the more easily they can isolate and analyze any elements they don't know. This will always facilitate the next step in acquisition.

## Keeping a tally

Children must keep track of which forms occur where, and how often, if they are to discover words and their meanings. They must also track the contexts where adults use words and sequences of words. This will allow them to track frequency for both tokens and types. The token-frequency of each element is important in establishing mental representations in memory for the form of each word or expression, as well as in making inferences about possible meanings as children check out their hypotheses in context (Clark 2002a). Type-frequency is important for any generalizations children make about nouns versus verbs, say, or about particular groups of nouns (e.g., all nouns in *-er*, all nouns in *-ment*, etc.), about transitive versus intransitive verbs, and so on. Information about type-frequency plays an important role in children's generalizations about patterns observable in the language they are learning (see Chapter 8).

Tracking both tokens and types is critical for building up paradigms and identifying the productivity of morphemes (e.g., Clark & Berman 1984; MacWhinney 1978, 1985; Maratsos & Chalkley 1980). In early acquisition, children give priority to type-frequency over token-frequency. They track how widespread an inflection is by how many types it occurs with. They choose type over token in deciding how to inflect a new noun- or verb-stem (Chapter 8). They also prefer more productive over less productive morphemes in the formation of new words (Chapter 11). This is all evidence that they tally frequency during acquisition.

What form do their tallies take? And what mechanism do children use for keeping such tallies? To start with, they must be able to identify instances of words, morphemes, even phrases, as "the same" or not. For this, they must store representations of the stems and affixes they encounter. They need not have analyzed all stem–affix combinations (*pick + ed*) and they may store many unanalyzed wholes (e.g., Peters 1983, 1985; Wong Fillmore 1979). As soon as some representation has been stored, though, it becomes available for comparison with others and so provides a means of tracking frequency. Comparisons presumably focus first on form, not meaning, since linguistic forms provide communicative stability: They instantiate the conventions speakers rely on.

Linguistic forms can be analyzed at several levels – individual sounds or syllables, stems and affixes, phrases, clauses. Children may start from phrases or even clauses, from words, and, later still, from stems and affixes inside words. The comparisons children make in identifying a sequence as familiar need not be specific to language. They also compare and elaborate visual dimensions in pattern recognition and color matching, as well as in tracking instances of conceptual categories. In each domain, the initial comparison could be quite simple (again, starting small) but become more complex as it is fine-tuned to the material being analyzed.

If children keep a tally for each form, this could include co-occurring elements and so track distributional facts. While they may start with forms alone, they soon attach meaning to them. This is essential for using words and checking hypotheses about meaning. The main source of information about the frequencies of words and constructions is child-directed speech (Chapter 2). This may be supplemented by what adults read to children, by speech overheard from others, and, once in day care or nursery school, by conversations among peers. Representations for comprehension also allow children to access the right forms for production when they need them (Clark 1982, 1993).

In summary, keeping track of linguistic units is central to analyzing each new form children encounter. They must establish that a form *f* heard on occasion *o* is the same as one heard on previous occasions. If they already have some meaning for that form, that serves as an additional basis for deciding whether it is the same word. Keeping track of form–meaning pairs also allows children to conclude that *f1* and *f2* are variants of the same stem, for instance, differing only in its inflections (*dog* vs. *doggie, jump* vs. *jumping*). Children can also compare their representations of inflections across different forms. These comparisons all depend on children's representations and the uses they are able to make of them at each stage in acquisition.

## Representing language: Comprehension versus production

Comprehension precedes production. This asymmetry is critical to the process of acquisition. It holds for adults too. For example, speakers of American English can understand most Irish English speakers but are quite unable to produce Irish English. Modern-day speakers find earlier states of the language comprehensible and can readily understand sixteenth- or seventeenth-century varieties of English, yet cannot produce them. People may know a language from comprehension alone, with no production (e.g., Fourcin 1975). This may also be the case when they acquire reading knowledge of a second language (comprehension), for instance, without being able to speak or write it. Comprehension is not only ahead of production but may outstrip it by far – people can understand rare words (e.g., *boustrophedon, anechoic*) and rare constructions (e.g., *Had he not done X, …*) that they never produce. This asymmetry is widespread in acquisition (e.g., Clark & Berman 1984; Clark & Hecht 1982; Harris *et al.* 1995).

What role might this asymmetry play in the process of acquisition? Children use it in monitoring and repairing any mismatches between what they intended and what they produced. The general idea is this: Speakers monitor what they say and how they say it (Levelt 1989). They monitor themselves as they express their intentions and may reject their initial formulation even before it gets uttered, or after it's been begun. They monitor for whether the forms they produce could confuse or mislead the addressee; if so, they can add to the original utterance, for instance, by filling in the referent of a pronoun with a noun phrase. They monitor what they say for social appropriateness – the level of formality, for example; and they monitor for appropriate syntactic constructions, morphology, lexical choice, pronunciation, fluency, speed, and volume. In children, this monitoring is particularly important during the early stages of acquisition because they still make many errors.

Do people monitor everything they say? Probably not. The evidence suggests that people don't always notice their errors. Monitoring is often context-sensitive. People are more careful in some settings than in others, and the attention they pay to their own speech can fluctuate during an utterance (Levelt 1989). Children appear to monitor pronunciation more closely in the early stages, when their primary goal is to get the addressee to recognize the words they say. Once they achieve reasonable accuracy here, they turn the spotlight onto inflections, gender and gender agreement, definiteness, or any of the myriad other subsystems they are learning. The spotlight results in clusters of repairs around specific error-types. And once each subsystem is mastered, the spotlight moves on (e.g., Clark 1982; Clark & Bowerman 1986).

In monitoring their utterances, children rely on their own internal representations, set up for understanding others. They use these representations to recognize the same phrase or word on other occasions. This requires that they set up form–meaning "entries" in their mental lexicon, entries they can adjust as they fine-tune the sound system as well as subtle details of meanings and meaning differences. These representations have a dual role: They enable comprehension when children hear others, and they provide the adult targets against which children can measure their own production. When they detect a mismatch with a target, the target representation itself provides an immediate model for any repair. What children repair when depends on what they are currently acquiring and on the extent to which they are monitoring what they say. This may differ somewhat for children much as it does for adults. For example, children tend to pronounce words more clearly and carefully (which suggests more monitoring) when talking to nonfamily members than to family members (e.g., Tomasello *et al.* 1984). The latter, of course, are more used to any idiosyncrasies in how their children produce specific words. What is important is that children monitor what they say and make repairs. They make these repairs in response to requests for clarification, but they also make many spontaneous, self-initiated repairs from as young as age one to one-and-a-half (Käsermann & Foppa 1981; Scollon 1976). For both self- and other-initiated repairs, they make use of the targets offered by their representations for comprehension.

### Changes over time

As children are exposed to more language, they gain more experience of how to understand and produce it. A four-year-old knows more about language and how to use it than a one- or two-year-old. This change is obvious in the utterances they produce. Compare *Throw ball?* with *Can I throw the ball now?* What changes in children's representations as they progress from the two-word combination to the more elaborate, polite request? One way to examine these changes is to consider the representations children set up at each age and stage for understanding the language they hear.

If children set up a representation for each new term or phrase they notice in the speech they hear, attach some meaning to it, and then adjust that representation in the light of further analyses, they can use it to access that meaning when they next encounter that form. As they hear more language, they will add to their store of such representations (Clark 1993). These representations for comprehension (C-representations) consist first of an acoustic template, to which children will then add information about meaning, syntax, and use.

These C-representations are not the only representations children need. They must also represent the information needed for *producing* each expression. For this, they need specifications for articulating the sounds in the target word or phrase. Their representations for production (P-representations), then, necessarily differ from C-representations. Their first P-representations also differ from the adult's, since children rarely achieve the appropriate pronunciations for their targets in the early stages of production (Chapter 5). In fact, they work hard to change their P-representations in their first three or four years, to the point where they are readily understood. This takes time and practice. How do children achieve the changes needed as they go from *ga* to *squirrel*, *no* to *snow*, or *mumik* to *monkey*? It is implausible that adults supply "models" of the words children have in mind just before they produce them. Yet children do change their erroneous pronunciations in the direction of the adult versions. One way they can do this is by using their C-representations.

How would this work? Suppose a child is trying to produce the word *snow*. If children can access their C-representation for *snow*, they can compare their own production with that C-representation, and if they detect any mismatch, they can then repair their own utterance. The C-representation is a model of what the word should sound like so others can recognize it. Under this view, C-representations provide model targets for what children produce. They also provide targets that the products of P-representations must match. So as children adjust their P-representations to match what they hear from others, they will align them more and more closely with their C-representations. This gradual alignment is reflected in changes in children's own productions of words and phrases.

In summary, I propose that C-representations have two functions for children during acquisition. They are needed for the *recognition* of words and phrases heard from others, and they provide *targets* for production. In this way, they enable children to align their P-representations with their C-representations and so adjust their own production until it matches the speech around them (see also Levelt 1989; Postma 2000). Children continually update their C-representations, adding details about form and meaning. They also add new C-representations whenever they hear new words and expressions. The disparity between comprehension and production is what allows children to change their language over time with the steady addition of more C-representations, more P-representations, more details added to each, and the gradual alignment of the two (Clark 1993).

## Multiple representations

Speakers may need multiple representations in both comprehension and production. They can access linguistic units by form (words that rhyme), by meaning (words from the same semantic domain, from related domains; words for particular objects or events, and so on), and by collocation (special phrases, idioms, or expressions with a limited set of variants). They store forms and meanings according to language, and since many people in the world are bilingual or multilingual, they may need to store elements for several languages in memory.

Most languages are spoken, so this will be reflected in people's primary representations for comprehension and production. But many languages are also written, so with literacy, people must add representations for reading and writing as well. Just as people learn to deal with different dialects within a language, so too they learn different fonts in printing and different forms of handwriting. And they learn to write, by hand or on a keyboard. In addition, readers may have to interpret more than one alphabet (e.g., Roman, Cyrillic, Hebrew, Devanagari) or more than one writing system (e.g., alphabetic versus syllabic), where writing systems may represent vowels and consonants, consonants only, or syllables rather than segments. The direction of writing and reading may be left to right, right to left, boustrophedonic, or top to bottom (see further Daniels & Bright 1996; Nunberg 1996; Sampson 1987; Watt 1994). The number of possibilities and the range of representations people will need increase with the languages they speak and read.

## Time and practice

Children spend a lot more time learning a language than adults do. At a conservative estimate, they are attentive to what people are saying at least ten hours a day, seventy hours a week. Contrast this with adults who spend a mere five hours a week in a language class, with an added hour or so in the language laboratory, for a total of five or six hours – less than a tenth of the time children spend. Small children have little else to occupy themselves with and are less self-conscious than adults about how they appear to others. Adults are used to presenting themselves through language, so their incomplete mastery may also inhibit them socially and further impede their language learning.

Children practice what they learn. Casual observation suggests they often do this in play, with no addressee. This may take the form of an extended monologue-as-commentary on whatever the child is doing. Younger children practice too, especially in bedtime monologues before they fall asleep (see Chapter 5). In their monologues, they comment on words they can't say properly; they practice sets of related sounds in words that sound alike; they try out sequences that build in complexity and break down other sequences into small units; they give question–answer sequences and miniature language-lab pattern-drills; and they rehearse the events of the day (Weir 1962; see also Kuczaj 1983; Nelson 1989).

Children learning a second language also rely on practice, but their practice is often covert. For example, in a second language classroom, although they observe everything intently and communicate with gesture, they talk to others hardly at all during their first three or four months. They do, however, talk softly to themselves, in "private speech." They repeat what others have said (single words or whole phrases), rehearse possible utterances before they try them out loud, recall words and phrases heard earlier, experiment with sound sequences in the new language, and play with substitution patterns in the form of mini-language drills (Saville-Troike 1988; Wong Fillmore 1979). At the end of that period, they talk to other children using routines, a rapidly growing vocabulary, and a good grasp of the sound system. They also use private speech, again in the second language, when carrying out tasks that demand concentration (e.g., Amodeo & Cárdenas 1983). The greater the use of private speech in early second-language learning, the greater their subsequent skill in the new language.

Practice with words, inflections, and constructions all help children increase their fluency in what they say. It should also help them in accessing and retrieving the terms they need. Overall, then, it will help them become more skilled as speakers, whether in a first or a second language.

## Operating principles

As children analyze what they hear, they rely on strategies for segmenting the stream of speech into phrases, words, and morphemes. In the early stages of acquisition, they appear to rely on some basic strategies or operating principles, regardless of language. If children's earliest utterances, cross-linguistically, mirror what they first attend to, one can identify the properties of words and phrases that are most salient.

In 1973, Dan Slobin looked at the available data from several languages and made an initial analysis of early processing, where he identified several general operating principles. He characterized them as general instructions like "Look for systematic modifications in the forms of words" or "Avoid interruption or rearrangement of linguistic units." Some of them were about the semantic coherence of the expression children were analyzing; others were about properties of the surface forms they were trying to understand or produce. Later, when more cross-linguistic data became available, Slobin proposed a more elaborate battery of operating principles (Slobin 1985b). He argued that children come equipped with universal assumptions about the distinctions language can encode. In doing this, he worked back from the data to identify "systems of knowledge and information processing that seem to be prerequisite for the sorts of data we encounter cross-linguistically" (1985b:1158). These systems represent a universal first grammar, the general starting point for language acquisition, so their identification would represent a first pass at identifying "the mechanisms of the L[anguage] M[aking] C[apacity] that may be responsible for children's PREFERENCES to construct language in particular ways, knowing full well that such abstracted and generalized preferences cannot account in detail for the acquisition patterns of particular, individual children" (Slobin 1985b:1162).[2] This universal "Basic Child Grammar," he proposed, is later modified as children become attentive to specific features of the language they are acquiring. If children begin from a universal Basic Child Grammar, some structures should be acquired readily because they "match" initial schemas for mapping language. Structures

---

[2] At the same time, it remains unclear how specific such procedures are to language alone (as against being common to other cognitive systems too) or the degree to which the starting-point procedures might be specified from birth, before any exposure to the world around and before any interaction with other aspects of cognition.

Table 16.2 *Some strategies for grammatical organization of stored information*

---

*OP(UNITS): Word Forms.* If you discover more than one form of a word or word-stem in storage, or if monitoring reveals a mismatch between your word form and that in the input, try to find a phonological or semantic basis for distinguishing the forms:

(a) Phonologically attempt to change your word form in the given environment, following a hierarchy of possible adjustments of word forms. At first try to maintain the consonant frame and syllable structure (number of syllables, stress placement).
(b) Try to find distinct meanings for words or word-stems that occur in varying forms, checking for relevant Notions.
(c) If you cannot find a principled basis for differentiating the forms of a word or word-stem, pick one form as basic and use it in all environments.

*OP(UNITS): Morphological Paradigms.* If you find more than one functor expressing a given notion relative to a particular word class, and choice of functor cannot be determined by phonological conditioning:

(a) Try to find semantic grounds for subdividing the notion expressed by the functors, and map each new notion onto one of the functors.
(b) If you cannot find semantic grounds for choice of functor, check the citation forms of the associated words or stems and try to differentiate them on systematic phonological grounds. If you succeed, set up a paradigm in which choice of functor is conditioned by the phonological shape of the citation form.
(c) If you do not succeed in setting up a paradigm based on the phonology of the citation form, and if your procedural capacities allow you to check the immediate environments of citation forms, try to differentiate the functors on the basis of elements that systematically co-occur with the citation forms, and set up a paradigm in which choice of functor is conditioned by factors that regularly co-occur with the citation form.
(d) If you fail, use only the most salient and applicable functor to express the given notion in the given position.

---

*Source*: Slobin 1985b:1252–1253. Used with permission from Lawrence Erlbaum Associates.

that do *not* map into the initial universal schemas should take longer to acquire. Most of these may be structures specific to one language, so children must tune in to that typology in order to acquire those structures.

Slobin derived the operating principles from data on many languages. He focussed on forms that children acquire early, with little effort, regardless of language, and on forms that were more difficult, consistently elicited errors, and took longer to master. The latter, he suggested, require children to develop special procedures over and above their initial operating principles to deal with constructions specific to each language. Two operating principles, Word Forms and Morphological Paradigms, are shown in Table 16.2. Both capture common patterns of use in early acquisition. How children apply each principle depends on the language being acquired. As they learn more about a language, they either elaborate their initial principles to fit its specific properties or set up new procedures tailored to the language in question.

The general approach here is to pull apart various dimensions of acquisition data on word- and morpheme-order, inflectional paradigms, and the marking of grammatical roles, for instance, to identify common strategies for dealing with the relevant structures. Where some languages rely solely on word order to mark grammatical relations, others rely on inflection and agreement, and still others use a mixed system with both word order and agreement. Slobin proposed that one can look at how children first deal with such dimensions – what they notice and what they ignore, and the extent to which attention to a factor like "natural order" (where the order of linguistic elements mirrors order in the event itself: Haiman 1985) underlies early attempts to talk about canonical causative events with an agent, action, and object affected (see also Slobin 1981). What is most accessible early on, it is assumed, is universal and simple to acquire.

Slobin's proposals offer an account of the kind of learning system children could rely on during their first years of acquisition. Children all start with the same basic conceptual preferences for identifying, storing, and using linguistic forms even though they are exposed to different languages with different grammatical structures.

Further evidence for a general conceptual base comes from emergent categories during acquisition (Clark 2001). Children sometimes try to express meaning distinctions that have no conventional expression in the language being acquired. For instance, they may give consistent expression to a notion like "source" and, in English, mark not only place and time with the preposition *from* (e.g., *from San Francisco*) but also agents (*I was chased from you*), causes (*I cried a bit from you go get him*), possessors (*a hand from the man*), and standards of comparison (*big from me*) (Clark & Carpenter 1989a, 1989b; also Chapter 9). Or they use contrasting forms of first-person pronouns (*I* vs. *me*) to express degree of control, as in *I throw* (wishing to obtain the ball) versus *Me throw* (holding the ball and planning to throw) (Budwig 1989), and only later learn that *I* marks the grammatical subject and *me* the grammatical object. These categories emerge and then vanish again, often within weeks. But the fact that they do emerge testifies to their conceptual robustness and generality. They are represented in many languages, but not all. These categories, combined with other categories children grasp early on, offer evidence for a universal set of basic grammatical distinctions (Clark 2001).

Slobin's Basic Child Grammar represents the preferences children appear to come with – their learning mechanisms for analyzing, storing, understanding, and producing language. But even if these represent children's entry point into language, they are soon modified to deal with differences among languages as well. Children find out, for each language, which grammatical distinctions are obligatory (Slobin 1996, 2001a). So the initial operating principles are modified and elaborated as they take more data into account. The move to the procedures adults use could simply require elaboration of their initial procedures. It could also require adding some procedures and dropping others, depending on the typology of the language.[3] The number of operating principles is fairly large, and they are assumed to interact both with each other and with what children already know. The effects of these interactions have yet to be assessed.

## Attending to typology

Children show some evidence of being sensitive to typological properties of language from the very start. And some researchers have argued from this against a Basic Child Grammar. Could children's experience with language account for the phenomena that operating principles are designed to explain? As Bowerman (1985b:1271) put it, we need to look first at "explanations that focus on children's experience with the structural properties of the language being learned." She argued (1985b:1284) that

> [c]hildren are prepared from the beginning to accept linguistic guidance as to which distinctions – from among the set of distinctions that are salient to them – they should rely on in organizing particular domains of meaning. In consequence, there is no single, universally shared "Basic Child Grammar." Children begin with grammars that are slanted towards the semantic structure of the input language, even if not yet in perfect accordance with it.

Children are attentive to what they hear in child-directed speech. Adults offer them words for objects and actions, relations and properties, and they offer information about how these words are linked to other words as well (Clark 2002b; Clark & Wong 2002). In their talk about events, adults display the ways in which their language encodes grammatical distinctions (e.g., number, case, gender; tense, aspect, person) and also how it represents objects and actions within events. In languages like Tzeltal, speakers distinguish many actions like *walk*, *crawl*, *stagger*, *roll*, *lie*, *sit*, but have no general-purpose verbs like *do* or *go* (unlike English). Children exposed to languages like this should come to expect a new verb each time they encounter an unfamiliar action, and, it appears, they do (Brown 1998). In other languages, speakers encode motion and location with prepositions or with case endings for the relation between an object and its location, as in English (prepositions) or Hungarian (case endings). In others still, they use verbs for all such relations, as in Korean. Children learning these languages show evidence of picking up on how spatial relations are encoded from as young as eighteen months (e.g., Brown 1998; Bowerman 1985b; Choi & Bowerman 1991; Clark 1973b; Pléh 1998). Under this view, children pick up on the typology of their language from the very beginning.

While this would argue against the Basic Child Grammar that Slobin (1985b) proposed, it leaves open the question of why some linguistic distinctions are particularly salient. In the Basic Child Grammar view, these distinctions are

---

[3] This is where work on adult processing may offer some valuable insights (e.g., Hawkins 1988; Greenberg 1963, 1966; Tanenhaus 1988).

linguistic universals built on conceptual structures. And if they are conceptually salient, they could show up, temporarily, even in languages that lack conventional expressions for them (Clark 2001). Rather than starting from a universal conceptual basis and later adapting to a particular language, children could start instead by focussing on the semantic structures of a language. Their attention to semantics, it is argued, shapes their patterns of acquisition (Bowerman 1985b; Slobin 2001b). They build directly on this primary information about which grammatical distinctions to attend to and how semantic structures encode experience.

### Using evidence about language

Children use what adults say to them in two ways. First, they use it as evidence about how to express intentions. Adult utterances reveal the conventions of the language they are learning. This is the primary information children receive about how to express meanings. Second, they use it as evidence that the way they have said something *doesn't* conform to the conventions. When children make mistakes, adults often reformulate what the children said, in conventional form, to check up on what they had intended (Chouinard & Clark 2003). These reformulations of erroneous child utterances often take the form of side-sequences in conversation, as in the exchange in (1) (Kuczaj, CHILDES Archive data, Abe 12:6). Abe's utterance is reformulated by his father at the start of the side sequence (the first indented line).

(1)        ABE (2;6.4): *milk. milk.*
                FATHER: you want milk?
                    ABE: *uh-huh.*
                FATHER: ok. just a second and I'll get you some.

Reformulations that fill in missing terms (here, "you want") and that correct erroneous forms provide children with the conventional way to say what they intend. In checking up on the child's meaning, adults simultaneously highlight differences between adjacent child and adult utterances. Because their reformulations repeat the same content, they imply that what the child said had something wrong with it, so children should pay attention when they encounter another way of expressing the selfsame meaning (see Chouinard & Clark 2003; Walker 1996; see also Saxton 1997; Saxton *et al.* 1998).

The immediate contrast between the child and adult forms for the same meaning in these exchanges indicates to children that only one of the forms should be used. Since speakers rely on established, conventional forms, the conventional forms take priority over any other (erroneous) ones for the same meaning: The verb *scale* yields to conventional *weigh*, the nouns *sleepers* and *climber* to *pyjamas* and *ladder* (Clark 1993). For children, the comparison between their own forms and the adult forms for the same meanings is what is critical for their eventual corrections of errors. And children show evidence of attending to adult reformulations: They take up some of them directly and correct their own utterances in their next turn, as in (2); they reject others that don't capture their intent, as in (3); and they acknowledge others with a *yeah* or *uh-huh* before going on, as in (3) and (4).

(2)        ABE (2;5.10): *I want butter mine.*
           FATHER:        ok give it here and I'll put butter on it.
           ABE:             I need butter **on it**.
(3)        ABE (2;5.7): the plant didn't cried.
           FATHER:        the plant cried?
           ABE:             ***no***.
           FATHER:        oh. the plant didn't cry.
           ABE:             ***uh-huh***.
(4)        ABE (2;6.4): *milk. milk.*
           FATHER:        you want milk?
           ABE:             ***uh-huh***.

Or they tacitly accept the reformulation by just going on with the exchange, as in (5).

(5)        ABE (2;4.24): *he falled. he falled again.*
           FATHER:        ok he fell but no he's at the boat now. put him in front of the car.
           ABE:             *I do that!*

In summary, when adults talk to children, they offer positive evidence of the conventional way to say something. But such evidence has the potential of providing corrections of child errors as well. It can take on this role whenever adults produce reformulations of children's errors in expressing particular meanings. An utterance that counts as positive on one occasion may serve to correct an error on another. What makes adult speech count as positive or negative evidence, then, is the nature of the exchange. So what is critical for children making use of the speech they hear is that some utterances are clearly intended to express the same intention that they have just uttered but make use of a different form. The juxtaposition of the two highlights negative evidence. It doesn't, of course, make for instantaneous changes in children's systems. They may correct some errors shortly after taking notice of the discrepancies between their own form and the adult's, or they make take several weeks (and many examples) before they learn that part of the system. We know very little still about the time course of change in children's language.

## Poverty of the stimulus?

Some researchers have argued that children cannot learn certain structures because they are never exposed to them or because they are not exposed to them in a form that allows the analysis necessary for acquisition. The strong claim here is that "[p]eople attain knowledge of the structure of their language for which *no* evidence is available in the data to which they are exposed as children" (Hornstein & Lightfoot 1981:9). This position, known as "the argument from poverty of the stimulus," is a foundation stone for the innateness of syntax (see Chapter 15). It assumes that *only* positive evidence is available and that that evidence is full of errors and generally inadequate for the learning of any grammar that underlies it. This position is in direct opposition to the view that children learn their language on the basis of general learning mechanisms applied to the exposure they receive from the people around them. The argument from poverty of the stimulus makes an empirical claim – that some structures are never presented to the child and so are unavailable for learning. But its proponents have made no effort to test it against adult-to-child speech. And, as it turns out, there appears to be no empirical support so far for this claim (Pullum 1996; Pullum & Scholz 2002).

The most commonly cited case for the poverty of the stimulus position involves subject–auxiliary verb inversion in questions. The position of the inverted auxiliary verb depends on the structure of the sentence being used. Compare the sentence containing a relative clause in (6) with the one containing a conditional clause in (7), where the dash marks the site where the auxiliary would appear in the indicative version of each sentence:

(6)    <u>Could</u> the girl who lost her ticket – come to the desk?
(7)    If you don't need this, <u>can</u> I – have it?

In (6), the auxiliary verb, *could*, has been repositioned from seventh word in its indicative counterpart to first word in the question, but in (7), the auxiliary verb *can* is repositioned from seventh word only to sixth. The poverty-of-the-stimulus view argues that children never hear enough examples of such inversions, so they could never receive adequate information from which to learn that auxiliary inversion is *structure dependent*.

As one test of this view, Pullum (1996) examined the claim about rarity in 23,886 interrogatives in the 1987 *Wall Street Journal* (*WSJ*) corpus. The fifteenth question in the corpus offered evidence of structure dependence, as did several other examples in the first 500 interrogatives. Since such forms do occur, both there and in other types of text, they are probably available to children as well.[4] The most convincing test will be to examine child-directed speech. But, as Pullum (1996:508) pointed out, "the best and most often-repeated claim in support of the empirical premise of linguists' central argument for innate priming is false." Several other putative cases of poverty of the stimulus suffer the same fate (see further Pullum & Scholz 2002). They do appear in everyday speech and are nowhere near as rare as some linguists have claimed. Adults produce linguistic evidence for structure dependence, so children could therefore learn those constructions from child-directed speech.

In summary, child-directed speech and other sources of language – overheard speech, stories read aloud, speakers heard on radio or TV, for instance – provide

---

[4] Even in the *WSJ* corpus, the text often quotes people's utterances from interviews, so this is not simply a matter of written form.

such rich input that children should eventually learn enough of their language for all their needs. But if they can learn language, we need to specify what they learn, when, and how. Thorough analyses of child-directed speech, of learning mechanisms, and of viable routes for the discovery of word-classes and word meanings all contribute to this goal.

## Modeling language acquisition

Another approach to assessing theories about language acquisition is to use computer modeling to see how close a simulation comes to what children actually do as they acquire certain aspects of language. Some of the first simulations looked at data on the acquisition of regular versus irregular past tense verb forms in English (Rumelhart & McClelland 1986; Pinker *et al.* 2002). Rumelhart and McClelland used a connectionist network to simulate the growth patterns observed in children's early uses (and misuses) of past tense forms. Such networks consist of input layers, various hidden layers (where each pass through the network adds small changes to the strength of any connections), then an output layer. The simulation here was designed to link up the present tense verb forms to their appropriate past tense counterparts, and to track any errors made en route. This would allow researchers to see whether acquisition was in principle possible without relying on (innate) rules for producing past tense forms. So it tested a dual-access theory – that children use rules to produce regular past tense forms, but use associations to retrieve irregular pasts one by one, drawn "ready-made" from memory (e.g., Pinker 1999). The connectionist simulation was very successful in reproducing the patterns of use observed in acquisition both for overregularization and for subregularizations observable for small groups of irregular verbs (see also Plunkett & Marchman 1993; Bybee & Slobin 1982).

Researchers have since argued from such results that there is no need to postulate the existence of two processing systems, one based on rules for regular forms and one based on associations for irregular forms; rather, there may be just one retrieval system to deal with both regular and irregular forms. However, the debate over how to interpret both the data and such models is still ongoing. Ultimately, the resolution may require consideration of more complex cases of irregularity, in the French verb, for instance, where regular and irregular depend on tense, person, and conjugation in specific verbs, or in the Arabic noun, where the choice among many plural forms depends on certain features of the noun-type (see Plunkett & Nakisa 1997).

Researchers have also modeled the segmentation of continuous text into words with Bayesian segmentation routines comparing unigram and bigram dependencies between words; bigrams do better at segmentation (Goldwater, Griffiths, & Johnson 2006). This result may ultimately cast more light on how infants go about their initial segmentation of the speech stream (Saffran *et al.* 1996). Still other Bayesian models have been applied to how children might assign meanings to words given certain priors – background knowledge of particular kinds such as reliance on an expert (adult) speaker (Xu & Tenenbaum 2007a, 2007b).

Other uses of connectionist modeling have focussed on larger domains, and examined, for example, how network models might simulate the acquisition of complex sentences with relative clauses, number agreement, and various verb-argument arrays (Elman 1993). Training with these models succeeded only when the networks began with a limited working memory that gradually matured to an adultlike state. Here again, the small incremental changes over time within the network successfully linked the initial inputs (fragments akin to children's two-word utterances, for example) to increasingly complex syntactic forms (see also Hare & Elman 1995).

Other models have been designed to simulate use of statistical information about language to see whether this would allow for the extraction of linguistically useful units like nouns and verbs (Schütze 1993). Further research here has looked at how children might use information about distribution and co-occurrence in "frequent frames" from adult speech to discover word-classes (Mintz 2002, 2003). In short, such models reinforce the point that the language children hear offers multiple clues (and multiple routes) for discovering the syntactic building blocks used in utterances. Children have ready access to additional information as well, if we take into account their reliance on joint attention and the physical co-presence of whatever object or event is being talked about (Chapters 4 and 6).

Other research with modeling, focussed on how languages themselves might have evolved to become systems of communication for specific groups, has pointed to the importance of convention, and the establishing of conventions as fundamental to systems of communication (e.g., Galantucci 2005; Steels 2006; Griffiths & Kalish 2007). The communication systems devised in games of coordination, for example, suggest that, even though people start out with signs from different sources, they converge with each other's choices quite rapidly; that systems of signs observe contrast and are therefore parsimonious; and that such systems all share certain characteristics: They are distinctive, easy to produce, and tolerate variation. These properties are central to human languages, given their reliance on convention and on coordination. They are also central to recently constructed sign languages (e.g., Senghas & Coppola 2001; Senghas, Kita, & Özyürek 2004; Aronoff, Meir, & Sandler 2005; Sandler *et al.* 2005).

In summary, modeling can offer insight into how systems develop and interact, where the system here is a first language. While the models themselves do not necessarily capture the process whereby children arrive at the stages they do, with the errors characteristic of specific steps in development, they can show us how one might arrive at generalizations that go beyond the input, for example, and offer clues to how one could avoid making generalizations that are too broad.

## Learning so far

Once past the first stages of acquisition, children must build on more elaborate patterns in language, construct paradigms for inflections and word-formation, and build a repertoire of construction-types. But children are apparently conservative learners. They link inflections and constructions alike first to particular lexical items and only later generalize to other items (e.g., Bloom *et al.* 1984; Gathercole *et al.* 1999; Lieven *et al.* 1997).

If they learn one word at a time, do they rely on rote memory for each word? Do they use analogies to other forms already known and so use familiar items as models? Do they set up rules to capture generalizations for adding affixes to stems? Or do they use lexical schemas or templates based on the "shape" that the target form must have, regardless of the stem? Researchers have considered all these possibilities in accounts of how children arrive at generalizations about inflectional endings and why they overregularize irregular forms before they sort out regular from irregular along the same lines as adults.

If children rely only on rote memory, they should not make any errors of the kinds they do when they regularize irregular forms (e.g., *man/mans*, *foot/foots*). If they rely only on analogy, it is hard to account for how they get started: To use analogy, one needs a repertoire of models for inflecting more recently acquired items. So it seems reasonable to propose that children begin with rote memorization and then extend what they have learnt through analogy or rule use. Rule use assumes that children can identify stems and affixes, assign meanings to them, and then attach each affix to the relevant stem. Rules are *source oriented*: They begin from the stem and add an affix to it. They capture regularities in morphology but don't offer an account of irregular forms. This is why Marcus and his colleagues (1992) proposed the dual-processing model, where regular forms are associated with rule use and irregular ones with the storage of fixed forms in memory (Chapter 8). Children can then access regular stems and apply the pertinent rule (e.g., for past tense: *walk* + past → *walked*), but for irregular forms like *eat* or *child*, they are assumed to access the inflected form directly (e.g., *ate* for [*eat* + past]; *children* for [*child* + plural]). One question here is how and when children decide that a form is regular or irregular. At what point do they assign some forms to be stored as units in memory but represent other stems and affixes as ingredients to rules? Compare *tooth/teeth*, *foot/feet*, *goose/geese* (but *root/roots*, *roof/roofs*, *hoof/hoofs*) with *cat/cats*, *dog/dogs*, *spoon/spoons*, *cup/cups*, *chair/chairs*, even *hornbill/hornbills*.

Another way of asking this question is to ask how many forms need to be analyzed as "the same" for speakers to come up with a rule. What would lead children to label a form as irregular? Take a language where verbs can be regular in four tenses but irregular in one (or regular in two and irregular in all others). Some paradigms are regular and some irregular for the same verb: French *aller* 'to go' is regular in the past and imperfect (*je suis allé* 'I went', *j'allais* 'I was going'), and with a different stem in the future and conditional (*j'irai* 'I will go', *j'irais* 'I would go') (see also Orsolini *et al.* 1998). But *aller* is irregular in the present. Is this a regular verb or an irregular one? What evidence might children use in deciding that a stem is regular or irregular? Might they initially treat all forms as ones to memorize and then switch to a rule-based system? And what if they store stems, affixes, and whole forms for words (e.g., *jump*, *-ed*, and *jumped*)? The answers here have yet to be found.

In contrast to rules, lexical schemas or templates are *product oriented*. They specify what the word should look like once an affix has been added to a stem. If children are attentive to what the resultant word should be (once it is inflected), lexical schemas offer a solution where rules, source-oriented, produce the wrong forms, for example, overregularizations like *eated* and *goed* compared to the actual *ate* and *went*, which both "fit" the schema for past tense in that they end in an alveolar stop (**t**) (see further Bybee 1995). Lexical schemas also appear consistent with the lexically specific learning that underlies early syntax (Chapters 7 and 9) and call for one processing mechanism rather than two, unlike a dual-processing model.

Frequency is important in a schema-based approach since schemas also emphasize the role of type-frequency. This factor is generally ignored in rule-based approaches. In acquisition, forms with high *type*-frequency offer models for overregularization even when their *token*-frequency is low. And irregular forms with high token-frequency are less likely to be regularized than irregulars with low token-frequency (Chapter 8). In fact, early acquisition of a large number of regular verbs may encourage children to analyze regular past tense forms in English earlier and to start producing them before any irregular pasts (Maratsos 2000). In rule-based accounts, the rules are assumed to apply regardless of frequency (of type or token). But frequency affects processing, acquisition, and diachronic change (see Croft 2000; Ravid 1995). High token-frequency helps maintain an irregular form but does not make a paradigm productive. Type-frequency, on the other hand, helps children identify paradigms that are productive, even when the token-frequency of each contributing member is low (Bybee 1995, 1998).

Connectionist accounts of acquisition, like rule-based ones, have not paid much attention to productivity in their instantiations. But in their models of language learning, they build critically on the number of exposures to a form with the notion of a threshold for learning. They assume that one needs a criterial mass of information about a morphological form, for instance, before one accepts it (e.g., Marchman & Bates 1994). Children might need to hear *went* where they anticipate hearing *goed* a number of times before they will accept *went* as the established form for the meaning 'go + past'. However, most connectionist accounts don't include information about meaning for the forms being learnt. But this is information children must discover as they learn an irregular verb like *go*. At the same time, connectionist models offer important demonstrations of how starting small allows one to build up to more complex structures (see Elman 1993; Elman *et al.* 1996; Plunkett & Marchman 1993). This suggests that starting small is how children learn as complex a system as language.

What learning mechanisms do children start with? What comes with the newborn child? At this stage, we know little about possible innate mechanisms that might get learning off the ground. At the same time, identifying and comparing linguistic forms depend on a mechanism for capturing similarity. If children can detect similarity from the start, they will have a mechanism they can use to leverage whatever they know to a more complex level. This will then allow them to identify additional, more complex relations.

Children may rely on similarity detection as a mechanism for getting started and for adding complexity. Added complexity might include grasping relations, functions, and properties that are not always directly observable (cf. Carey 1985; Gentner & Medina 1998). So as children learn more about each conceptual or linguistic domain, they can make more complex judgements of similarity. Many of these judgements may involve analogy. Gentner and Medina (1998), for example, argued that the move from simple comparisons of surface similarity to comparisons based on nonobvious, more abstract properties offers a route for children to move from simple categorization to more complex comparisons. In language, as elsewhere, this could be the basis for abstractions from more complicated sources. Yet these more elaborate comparisons will require the same kinds of processing and analysis as those for a rule-based system designed to capture similar generalizations.

What we will need is a processing model that can account for (a) change during language acquisition, (b) asymmetries between comprehension and production, and (c) individual differences along the way. While we do not have such a model of acquisition yet, research on the many facets of acquisition is bringing us closer to understanding just what is required for the learning of a first language.

# Glossary

**adjacency pair** A pair of utterances initiated by one speaker and completed by another, as in "Where's the sail-cover?" – "Here it is", or at the end of a telephone conversation, "Goodbye" – "Goodbye."

**affix** Any morpheme added to a stem, including prefixes, suffixes, and internal modifications (infixes).

**affricate** A speech sound made up of a stop and a fricative, like the [dʒ] in *jay*.

**agentive** A case relation that names the role of instigator (the agent) for the action named by the verb.

**agreement** The correspondence of one word to another in gender, number, case, person, and so on, as in *He + goes* (singular) versus *They + go* (plural).

**allomorph** Variant of a morpheme, for instance the variants of the plural morpheme in English /-s/ (*cats*), /-z/ (*dogs*), and /-ɪz/ (*horses*). See **morpheme**.

**alveolar** Sound pronounced with constriction of the tip or blade of the tongue against the alveolar ridge, as in the [d] in *day*.

**anaphoric pronoun** Pronoun that refers back to an antecedent noun phrase identifying the person, object, or event in question.

**argument** A noun-phrase type that must appear with a particular verb, for instance the *agentive argument* required by break, as in ***John*** broke the vase. See also **benefactive, objective, locative**.

**article, definite and indefinite** In English the articles *the* (definite) and *a* (indefinite) indicate for the addressee whether the speaker considers a piece of information as "given" or known (*the gingko tree*) or as "new" (*a gingko tree*).

**ASL** American Sign Language of the Deaf.

**aspect** The inflectional system that signals whether an event is completed or not, ongoing, iterated, etc.

**auxiliary verb** Auxiliary verbs generally carry information about aspect, tense, person, and number in certain tenses (e.g., *he has arrived*; *they are coming soon*). See also **light verb, modal verb**.

**basic-level term** A term that refers to a basic-level category, one at a level of abstraction that is neither too general nor too specific, but optimal under certain criteria.

**benefactive** The argument identifying the beneficiary of the action denoted by the verb.

**bootstrapping, semantic and syntactic** Method of using semantic or syntactic information to advance learning.

**case relations or roles** The roles that noun phrases play with respect to the state, action, or process named by the verb. See **agentive, experiencer, locative**, and **objective** cases.

**cognitive complexity** The complexity of the ideas expressed in language. Compare **formal complexity**.

**commissive** A speech act that commits the speaker to a future course of action.

**common ground** Information shared by speaker and addressee.

**complement, complementation** A proposition in a noun-phrase slot of another proposition, as in *That he won was impressive*.

**compounding** Formation of (new) words from combinations of two or more word roots, e.g., *sun-dial*, *race-horse*. See **word-formation**.

**conditional** A sentence where one state of affairs is asserted to be contingent on another, as in most sentences containing *if*.

**content word** Word for an object, action, event, or property. Compare **function word**.

**conjunction, coordinating** *And, or, but*, and their relatives that conjoin two expressions by coordination, as in *Duncan and Helen*.

**conjunction, subordinating** A term that introduces an adverbial subordinate clause, e.g., *when, because, before, if*.

**consonant** A speech sound characterized by constriction in some part of the mouth, associated with audible friction, voicing, or temporary cessation of sound.

**constituent** A unit of language that has a single coherent function and is generally replaceable by a single word.

**contrast, principle of** The pragmatic principle whereby speakers assume any difference in form signals a difference in meaning.

**contrastive stress** Stress on a syllable or word to mark it as being in contrast with another, as in *ROD found the squirrel, not KATE*.

**conventionality, principle of** The pragmatic principle whereby speakers agree on the meaning of a form (a word or expression) for communicative consistency over time.

**Cooperative Principle** The assumption that people make that speakers and addressees try to be informative, truthful, relevant, and clear in conversation.

**coordination** A way of combining two clauses on a par with each other by use of a coordinating conjunction such as *and* or *but*.

**declaration** A speech act that brings about a new state of affairs by the mere uttering of the words.

**deictic term** A word that "points" at places, times, or participants in a conversation, e.g., *I, you, this, there, yesterday*.

**derivation** Formation of (new) words through addition of one or more affixes to a stem or root; e.g., *flower-y, watch-er, un-tidy, non-sens-ic-al*. See **word-formation**.

**determiner** The cover term for articles (*a, the*), possessives (*my, his*), demonstratives (*this, those*), and other words that precede attributes in noun phrases.

**direct object** The entity affected by the action of the verb.

**directive** A speech act that attempts to get the addressee to do something.

**discourse** Any extended stretch of language beyond a single utterance.

**ellipsis** The omission of words that are otherwise predictable from the linguistic or nonlinguistic context.

**embedded correction** A correction offered by the next speaker's substituting a different form for one used by the preceding speaker, and otherwise simply continuing with the conversation.

**experiencer** A case role that describes a being affected (the experiencer) by the psychological state or action named by the verb.

**expressive** A speech act that conveys the speaker's psychological state about something.

**formal complexity** The complexity of the linguistic form used to express ideas. Compare **cognitive complexity**.

**fricative** A speech sound produced with near closure of part of the mouth, producing turbulent air flow, as in the [z] in *zoo*.

**function word** A word, usually unstressed, that expresses a grammatical relationship, e.g., prepositions, conjunctions, articles, pronouns, and auxiliary verbs.

**fundamental frequency ($F_0$)** The lowest and primary pitch of the voice when speaking.

**given and new information** The information the speaker believes is already known to the addressee (given) and information the speaker thinks the addressee doesn't yet know (new).

**grammatical relation** The cover term for subject, (direct) object, oblique (indirect) object, predicate – all grammatical relations within a clause.

**idiom** An expression whose interpretation can't be determined from the meanings of its parts, e.g., *kick the bucket* meaning 'die'.

**indirect speech act** A speech act expressed by a sentence not primarily designed to convey that speech act, e.g., a request conveyed by an assertion. See **speech act**.

**inflection** An ending on a word-stem that adds grammatical information, e.g., plural -*s*, past tense -*ed*.

**joint attention** Locus of attention shared by speaker and addressee; basic in establishing and accumulating **common ground**.

**lateralization** The specialization of the left or right hemisphere of the brain for different functions. Speech is generally lateralized in the left hemisphere.

**light verb** A verb with bleached semantic content, typically used as an auxiliary, e.g., the future uses of *to go* in English (*he's going to bicycle home*).

**linguistic universal** A property of language claimed to be common to all languages.

**liquid** A cover term for the speech sounds [r] and [l] in English.

**locative** The case relation that denotes the location or orientation for the action or state named by the verb.

**locatum** Term for the object located in a particular place. Compare **locative**.

**main verb** The verb in each clause that denotes the primary action, process, or state being described.

**modal verb** In English, an auxiliary verb that expresses likelihood, possibility, predictability, or obligatoriness of the event named in the main verb, e.g., *must, will, could*.

**morpheme** A minimal unit of speech that is recurrent and carries meaning, e.g., the word-stem *gentle*, the suffix -*ly*, or the prefix *un-*. A free morpheme can stand alone as a word (e.g., *gentle, in, the*), while a bound morpheme is attached to a stem (e.g., -*ly* or plural -*s*).

**morphology** The study and analysis of the elements that make up the words of a language.

**nasal** Sound pronounced with the soft palate lowered so air can go out through the nose, as in the [m] in *may*.

**noun phrase** A constituent that expresses an argument of a proposition, e.g., *that man, what Jane said, him, the old one*.

**objective** The case relation whose role in the state or action named by a verb depends most closely on the meaning of the verb. See also **direct object**.

**overextension** The use of a word by children for a category of objects larger than the conventional adult category named by that word, as when a child uses *doggie* for both dogs and horses. See **underextension**.

**overregularization** The inclusion of irregular forms in regular paradigms; e.g., *go/goed* in lieu of *go/went*. See **paradigm**.

**paradigm** A complete set of inflected forms for a single word-stem, e.g., *jump*, *jumps*, *jumping*, *jumped*.

**parse** Break the sequence of words in a sentence into the sentence's constituent parts (noun phrase, verb phrase; article, noun, etc.).

**phonetics** The study, analysis, and classification of speech sounds, especially their pronunciation and acoustic properties.

**phonology** The study and analysis of the systems of sound patterns in a language.

**predicate** The part of a sentence that follows the subject, e.g., ***climbed onto the log*** in *The child climbed onto the log*.

**prefix** A morpheme added to the beginning of a word or stem, e.g., *un-, re-, dis-*.

**pronoun** A nominal form that takes the place of a noun phrase, e.g., *he, she, your, one*. An **anaphoric pronoun** refers back to an earlier lexical noun phrase, e.g., *...the man ... he*.

**prototype** The hypothetical instance in a category that represents the most typical conceivable member of that category.

**quantifier** A word that modifies another word and denotes quantity, e.g., *much, every, seven*.

**reference** The set of real-world entities, states, or events that an expression can pick out.

**referent** The entity in the real world that the speaker's expression is intended to pick out.

**relative clause** A clause introduced by a word like *who, that, which*, as in *The child who is climbing on the sofa*.

**relative pronoun** A word like *who, that*, or *which* that introduces a relative clause.

**segmentation** The division of sentences into words, morphemes, or sounds.

**semantics** The study and analysis of meaning.

**side sequence** A clarification question where the speaker echoes with rising intonation (and sometimes with corrective changes) what the first speaker just said, so as to check up on the first speaker's intention.

**spectogram** A graph that plots the intensity of the voice at various frequencies over time.

**speech act** The production of an utterance in order to express an intention the speaker wants the addressee to recognize.

**stem** A morpheme to which prefixes, suffixes, and inflections can be added, e.g., *common* and *sense* in *commonsensical*.

**stop consonant** A speech sound pronounced with complete closure of some part of the vocal tract, as in the [p] in *pod*.

**subject** The element in a sentence that governs number (singular or plural) in the verb, e.g., *Herons*, a plural subject requiring a plural verb, as in *Herons **eat** frogs*.

**suffix** A morpheme added to the end of a word-stem, e.g., *-ly, -ing, -s* in English.

**suppletion** A term filling a particular meaning-slot in a paradigm with a form that is unrelated, as in *went* as the past tense form of the verb *go* (*go, going, goes*).

**syllable** A unit of speech containing a vowel or diphthong preceded or followed by one or more consonants; it is produced and perceived as a unit.

**syntax** The study and analysis of how words combine to form sentences.

**tense** The inflectional system that signals when the process, event, or state denoted by a verb happened – present, past, or future.

**underextension** The use of a word by children for a category smaller than the adult one, as when a child restricts *doggie* to one specific dog. See **overextension**.

**velar** A sound pronounced with constriction of the back of the tongue against the velum or soft palate in the back of the mouth, as in the [g] in *tug*.

**verb phrase** A phrase that contains the verb, its auxiliaries, and any associated noun phrases, except for the subject noun phrase.

**voicing** A feature of consonants produced by vibration of the vocal cords, as in the initial segment of *zip* versus the voiceless [s] in *sip*.

**vowel** A speech sound produced by an unobstructed passage of air through the mouth; vowels are usually voiced.

***wh-* question** A sentence, generally introduced by a *wh-* word, such as *who*, *where*, *what*, or *how*, that requests the piece of information signaled by the *wh-* word.

**word-formation** The study and analysis of the internal structure of (complex) words. See also **compounding**; **derivation**.

***yes/no* question** A sentence, in English canonically signaled by inversion of the subject and auxiliary verb, that requests confirmation or denial of a proposition, as in *Is this the end?*

# References

Abbot-Smith, Kirsten, & Behrens, Heike. 2006. How known constructions influence the acquisition of other constructions: The German passive and future constructions. *Cognitive Science* 30, 995–1026.

Acredolo, Linda, & Goodwyn, Susan. 1988. Symbolic gesturing in normal infants. *Child Development* 59, 450–466.

Adams, Valerie. 1973. *An introduction to modern English word formation.* London: Longman.

Adone, Dany. 1994. *The acquisition of Mauritian creole.* Amsterdam: John Benjamins.

Aimard, Paule. 1975. *Les jeux de mots de l'enfant.* Villeurbanne: Simép Editions.

Akhtar, Nameera. 2005. The robustness of learning through overhearing. *Developmental Science* 8, 199–209.

Akhtar, Nameera; Carpenter, Malinda; & Tomasello, Michael. 1996. The role of discourse novelty in word learning. *Child Development* 67, 635–645.

Akhtar, Nameera; Jipson, Jennifer; & Callanan, Maureen. 2001. Learning words through overhearing. *Child Development* 72, 416–430.

Akhtar, Nameera, & Tomasello, Michael. 1997. Young children's productivity with word order and verb morphology. *Developmental Psychology* 33, 952–965.

Aksu-Koç, Ayhan. 1988. *The acquisition of tense and modality: The case of past reference in Turkish.* Cambridge: Cambridge University Press.

Aksu-Koç, Ayhan, & Alıcı, Didem M. 2000. Understanding sources of beliefs and marking of uncertainty: The child's theory of evidentiality. In E. V. Clark (ed.), *Proceedings of the thirtieth annual Child Language Research Forum 1999* (123–130). Stanford, CA: CSLI.

Aksu-Koç, Ayhan, & Slobin, Dan I. 1985. The acquisition of Turkish. In D. I. Slobin (ed.), *The crosslinguistic study of language acquisition*, vol. I (839–878). Hillsdale, NJ: Lawrence Erlbaum.

Albin, Drema D., & Echols, Catharine H. 1996. Stressed and word-final syllables in infant-directed speech. *Infant Behavior & Development* 19, 401–418.

Allen, Shanley E. M., & Schröder, Heike. 2003. Preferred argument structure in early Inuktitut spontaneous speech data. In J. W. Du Bois, L. E. Kumpf, & W. J. Ashby (eds.), *Preferred argument structure: Grammar as architecture for function* (301–338). Amsterdam: John Benjamins.

Ameel, Eef; Storms, Gert; Malt, Barbara C.; & Sloman, Steven A. 2005. How bilinguals solve the naming problem. *Journal of Memory & Language* 53, 60–80.

Ament, Wilhelm. 1899. *Die Entwicklung von Sprechen und Denken beim Kinde.* Leipzig: Ernst Wunderlich.

Ammon, Mary Sue. 1980. Development in the linguistic expression of causal relations: Comprehension of features of lexical and periphrastic causatives. PhD dissertation, University of California, Berkeley.

Ammon, Mary Sue. 1981. Semantic differentiation among expressions of causality by children and adults. *Papers & Reports on Child Language Development* [Stanford University] 20, 25–33.

Ammon, Mary Sue, & Slobin, Dan I. 1979. A cross-linguistic study of the processing of causative sentences. *Cognition* 7, 3–17.

Amodeo, Luiza B., & Cárdenas, Manuel. 1983. Private speech production during task performance by bilingual and monolingual children. In T. H. Escobedo (ed.), *Early childhood bilingual education: A Hispanic perspective* (50–62). New York: Teachers College Press.

Andersen, Elaine S. 1990. *Speaking with style: The sociolinguistic skills of children.* London: Routledge.

Anglin, Jeremy M. 1976. *Word, object, and conceptual development.* New York: Norton.

Anglin, Jeremy M. 1993. Vocabulary development: A morphological analysis. *Monographs of the Society for Research in Child Development* 58 (serial no. 238).

Anisfeld, Moshe; Rosenberg, Erica S.; Hoberman, Mara J.; & Gasparini, Don. 1998. Lexical acceleration coincides with the onset of combinatorial speech. *First Language* 18, 165–184.

Antinucci, Francesco, & Miller, Ruth. 1976. How children talk about what happened. *Journal of Child Language* 3, 167–189.

Antinucci, Francesco, & Volterra, Virginia. 1975. Lo sviluppo della negazione nel linguaggio infantile: Un studio pragmatico. *Lingua e Stile* 10, 231–260.

Archibald, John. 1995. The acquisition of stress. In J. Archibald (ed.), *Phonological acquisition and phonological theory* (81–109). Hillsdale, NJ: Lawrence Erlbaum.

Ardery, Gail. 1979. The development of coordinations in child language. *Journal of Verbal Learning & Verbal Behavior* 18, 745–756.

Ardery, Gail. 1980. On coordination in child language. *Journal of Child Language* 7, 305–320.

Arnberg, Lenore. 1981. *A longitudinal study of language development in four young children exposed to English and Swedish in their home.* Linköping Studies in Education Reports, no. 6. Linköping, Sweden: Department of Education, University of Linköping.

Aronoff, Mark; Meir, Irit; & Sandler, Wendy. 2005. The paradox of sign language morphology. *Language* 81, 301–344.

Arriaga, Rose I.; Fenson, Larry; Cronan, Terry; & Pethick, Stephen J. 1998. Scores on the MacArthur Communicative Development Inventory of children from low- and middle-income families. *Applied Psycholinguistics* 19, 209–223.

Aslin, Richard N. 2007. What's in a look? *Developmental Science* 10, 48–53.

Aslin, Richard N.; Saffran, Jenny R.; & Newport, Elissa L. 1998. Computation of conditional probabilities by 8-month-old infants. *Psychological Science* 9, 321–324.

Aslin, Richard N.; Saffran, Jenny R.; & Newport, Elissa L. 1999. Statistical learning in linguistic and nonlinguistic domains. In B. MacWhinney (ed.), *The emergence of language* (359–380). Mahwah, NJ: Lawrence Erlbaum.

Au, Terry K.-F.; Dapretto, Mirella; & Song, You-Kyung. 1994. Input vs. constraints: Early word acquisition in Korean and English. *Journal of Memory & Language* 33, 567–582.

Au, Terry K.-F., & Markman, Ellen M. 1987. Acquiring word meanings via linguistic contrast. *Cognitive Development* 2, 217–236.

Austin, John L. 1962. *How to do things with words.* Oxford: Oxford University Press.

Aviezer, Ora. 2003. Bedtime talk of three-year-olds: Collaborative repair of miscommunication. *First Language* 23, 117–139.

Axia, Giovanna. 1996. How to persuade mum to buy a toy. *First Language* 16, 301–317.

Axia, Giovanna, & Baroni, Maria R. 1985. Linguistic politeness at different ages. *Child Development* 56, 918–927.

Baayen, R. Harold. 1994. Productivity in language production. *Language & Cognitive Processes* 9, 447–469.

Baldwin, Dare A. 1989. Priorities in children's expectations about object-label reference: Form over color. *Child Development* 60, 1291–1306.

Baldwin, Dare A. 1991. Infants' contribution to the achievement of joint reference. *Child Development* 62, 875–890.

Baldwin, Dare A. 1993. Infants' ability to consult the speaker for clues to word reference. *Journal of Child Language* 20, 395–418.

Baldwin, Dare A.; Markman, Ellen M.; Bill, Brigitte; Desjardins, Renee; Irwin, Jane M.; & Tidball, Glynnis. 1996. Infants' reliance on a social criterion for establishing word-object relations. *Child Development* 67, 3135–3153.

Ballem, Kate D., & Plunkett, Kim. 2005. Phonological specificity in children at 1;2. *Journal of Child Language* 32, 159–173.

Bamberg, Michael G. W. 1987. *The acquisition of narratives: Learning to use language.* Berlin and New York: Mouton.

Baratz, Joan C. 1969. Teaching reading in an urban Negro school system. In J. C. Baratz & R. W. Shuy (eds.), *Teaching Black children to read* (92–116). Washington, DC: Center for Applied Linguistics.

Baratz, Joan C. 1970. Educational considerations for teaching Standard English to Negro children. In R. W. Fasold & R. W. Shuy (eds.), *Teaching Standard English in the Inner City* (20–40). Washington, DC: Center for Applied Linguistics.

Baratz, Joan C. 1971. Language and cognitive assessment of Negro children: Assumptions and research needs. In L. L. Barker & R. J. Kibler (eds.), *Speech communication behavior: Perspectives and principles* (133–143). Englewood Cliffs, NJ: Prentice-Hall.

Bard, Ellen G., & Anderson, Anne H. 1994. The unintelligibility of speech to children: Effects of referent availability. *Journal of Child Language* 21, 623–648.

Barinaga, Marcia. 1995. Researchers get a sharper image of the human brain. *Science* 268, 803–804.

Baroni, Maria R., & Axia, Giovanna. 1989. Children's meta-pragmatic abilities and the identification of polite and impolite requests. *First Language* 9, 285–297.

Barresi, John, & Moore, Chris. 1993. Sharing a perspective precedes understanding of that perspective. *Behavioral & Brain Sciences* 16, 513–514.

Barrett, Martyn D. 1978. Lexical development and overextension in child language. *Journal of Child Language* 5, 205–219.

Barrett, Martyn D. 1995. Early lexical development. In P. Fletcher & B. MacWhinney (eds.), *Handbook of child language* (362–392). Oxford: Blackwell.

Barton, David. 1978. The discrimination of minimally-different pairs of real words by children aged 2;3 to 2;11. In N. Waterson & C. Snow (eds.), *The development of communication* (255–261). New York: Wiley.

Barton, Michelle E., & Tomasello, Michael. 1991. Joint attention and conversation in mother-infant-sibling triads. *Child Development* 62, 517–529.

Barton, Michelle E., & Tomasello, Michael. 1994. The rest of the family: The role of fathers and siblings in early language development. In C. Gallaway & B. J. Richards (eds.), *Input and interaction in language acquisition* (109–134). Cambridge: Cambridge University Press.

Bassano, Dominique, & Eme, Pascale-Elsa. 2001. Development of noun determiner use in French children: Lexical and grammatical bases. In M. Almgren, A. Barreña, M.-J. Ezeizabarrena, I. Idiazabal, & B. MacWhinney (eds.), *Research on child language acquisition: Proceedings of the 8th Congress of the International Society for the Study of Child Language* (1207–1220). Boston, MA: Cascadilla Press.

Basser, L. S. 1962. Hemiplegia of early onset and the faculty of speech with special reference to the effects of hemispherectomy. *Brain* 85, 427–460.

Bates, Elizabeth. 1976. *Language and context: The acquisition of pragmatics*. New York: Academic Press.

Bates, Elizabeth; Camaioni, Luigia; & Volterra, Virginia. 1975. The acquisition of performatives prior to speech. *Merrill-Palmer Quarterly* 21, 205–226.

Bates, Elizabeth, & Silvern, Louise. 1977. Social adjustment and politeness in preschoolers. *Journal of Communication* 27, 104–111.

Bates, Elizabeth; Thal, Donna; Finlay, Barbara; & Clancy, Barbara. 2002. Early language development and its neural correlates. In F. Boller & J. Grafman (series eds.), S. J. Segalowitz & I. Rapin (vol. eds.), *Handbook of neuropsychology*, vol. VIII: *Child neurology* (2nd edn, 109–176) Amsterdam: Elsevier.

Baudouin de Courtenay, Jan. 1974. *Spostrzezenia nad jezykiem dziecka* [Observations on child language] (ed. M. Chmura-Klekotowa). Wroclaw: Polska Akademia Nauk, Komitet Jezykoznawstwa.

Bauer, Laurie. 1983. *English word-formation*. Cambridge: Cambridge University Press.

Baumgartner, Emma, & Devescovi, Antonella. 1996. *Come e perché nelle favole raccontate dai bambini*. Ripatransone: Edizioni Sestante.

Bavelier, Daphne; Corina, David; Jezzard, Peter; Clark, Vince; Karni, Avi; Lalwani, Anil; Rauschecker, Josef P.; Braun, Allen; Turner, Robert; & Neville, Helen J. 1998. Hemispheric specialization for English and ASL: Left invariance–right variability. *Neuroreport: An International Journal for the Rapid Communication of Research in Neuroscience* 9, 1537–1542.

Becker, Judith A. 1982. Children's strategic uses of requests to mark and manipulate social status. In S. A. Kuczaj II (ed.), *Language development*, vol. II (1–35). Hillsdale, NJ: Lawrence Erlbaum.

Becker, Judith A. 1994. "Sneak-shoes," "sworders," and "nose-beards": A case study of lexical innovation. *First Language* 14, 195–211.

Behne, Tanya; Carpenter, Malinda, & Tomasello, Michael. 2006. One-year-olds comprehend the communicative intentions behind gestures in a hiding game. *Developmental Science* 8, 492–499.

Behrend, Douglas A. 1990. Constraints and development: A reply to Nelson (1988). *Cognitive Development* 5, 313–330.

Behrend, Douglas A.; Harris, L. Lynn; & Cartwright, Kelly B. 1995. Morphological clues to verb meaning: Verb inflections and the initial mapping of verb meanings. *Journal of Child Language* 22, 89–106.

Behrens, Heike, & Gut, Ulrike. 2005. The relationship between prosodic and syntactic organization in early multiword speech. *Journal of Child Language* 31, 2–24.

Benoit, Pamela J. 1982. Formal coherence production in children's discourse. *First Language* 3, 161–179.

Benson, Nancy J., & Anglin, Jeremy M. 1987. The child's knowledge of English kin terms. *First Language* 7, 41–66.

Berko, Jean. 1958. The child's learning of English morphology. *Word* 14, 150–177.

Berko, Jean, & Brown, Roger. 1960. Psycholinguistic research methods. In P. H. Mussen (ed.), *Handbook of research methods in child development* (517–557). New York: Wiley.

Berko Gleason, Jean. 1977. Talking to children: Some notes on feedback. In C. E. Snow & C. A. Ferguson (eds.), *Talking to children: Language input and acquisition* (199–205). Cambridge: Cambridge University Press.

Berko Gleason, Jean. 1988. Language and socialization. In F. S. Kessel (ed.), *The development of language and language researchers* (269–280). Hillsdale, NJ: Lawrence Erlbaum.

Berko Gleason, Jean, & Greif, Esther B. 1983. Men's speech to young children. In B. Thorne, C. Kramarae, & N. Henley (eds.), *Language, gender, and society* (140–149). Rowley, MA: Newbury House.

Berko Gleason, Jean; Perlman, Rivka Y.; & Greif, Esther. 1984. What's the magic word: Learning language through politeness routines. *Discourse Processes* 7, 493–502.

Berlin, Brent; Breedlove, David E.; & Raven, Peter H. 1973. General principles of classification and nomenclature in folk biology. *American Anthropologist* 75, 214–242.

Berman, Ruth A. 1982. Verb-pattern alternation: The interface of morphology, syntax, and semantics in Hebrew child language. *Journal of Child Language* 9, 169–191.

Berman, Ruth A. 1985. The acquisition of Hebrew. In D. I. Slobin (ed.), *The crosslinguistic study of language acquisition*, vol. I (255–371). Hillsdale, NJ: Lawrence Erlbaum.

Berman, Ruth A. 1987. Productivity in the lexicon: New-word formation in modern Hebrew. *Folia Linguistica* 21, 425–461.

Berman, Ruth A., & Armon-Lotem, Sharon. 1997. How grammatical are early verbs? In *Actes du colloque international sur l'acquisition de la syntaxe en langue maternelle et en langue étrangère* (17–56). Nancy, France: Annales Littéraires de l'Université de Franche-Comté, no. 631.

Berman, Ruth A., & Clark, Eve V. 1989. Learning to use compounds for contrast: Data from Hebrew. *First Language* 9, 247–270.

Berman, Ruth A., & Slobin, Dan I. 1994a. *Relating events in narrative: A cross-linguistic developmental study.* Hillsdale, NJ: Lawrence Erlbaum.

Berman, Ruth A., & Slobin, Dan I. 1994b. Becoming a proficient speaker (Chapter Vʌ); Becoming a native speaker (Chapter Vʙ). In R. A. Berman & D. I. Slobin, *Relating events in narrative: A crosslinguistic developmental study* (597–610, 611–641). Hillsdale, NJ: Lawrence Erlbaum.

Bernicot, Josie, & Roux, Mireille. 1998. La structure et l'usage des énoncés: Comparaison d'enfants uniques et d'enfants seconds-nés. In J. Bernicot, H. Marcos, C. Day, M. Guidetti, V. Laval, J. Rabain-Jamin, & G. Babelot (eds.), *De l'usage des gestes et des mots chez l'enfant* (157–178). Paris: Colin.

Bernstein-Ratner, Nan, & Pye, Clifton. 1984. Higher pitch in BT is not universal: Acoustic evidence from Quiché Mayan. *Journal of Child Language* 11, 515–522.

Bertoncini, Josiane; Bijeljac-Babic, Ranka; Blumstein, Sheila E.; & Mehler, Jacques. 1987. Discrimination in neonates of very short CVs. *Journal of the Acoustical Society of America* 82, 31–37.

Bertoncini, Josiane, & Mehler, Jacques. 1981. Syllables as units in infants' speech perception. *Infant Behavior & Development* 4, 247–260.

Bialystok, Ellen. 2001. *Bilingualism in development: Language, literacy, and cognition.* Cambridge: Cambridge University Press.

Bialystok, Ellen. 2007. Language acquisition and bilingualism: Consequences for a multilingual society. *Applied Psycholingistics* 28, 393–397.

Bialystok, Ellen, & Hakuta, Kenji. 1994. *In other words: The science and psychology of second-language acquisition.* New York: Basic Books.

Bialystok, Ellen, & Hakuta, Kenji. 1999. Confounded age: Linguistics and cognitive factors in age differences for second language acquisition. In D. Birdsong (ed.), *Second language acquisition and the critical period* (161–181). Mahwah, NJ: Lawrence Erlbaum.

Bishop, Dorothy V. M. 1997. *Uncommon understanding: Development and disorders of language comprehension in children.* Hove, Sussex: Psychology Press.

Blake, Joanna, & Boysson-Bardies, Bénédicte. 1992. Patterns in babbling: A cross-linguistic study. *Journal of Child Language* 19, 51–74.

Blake, Joanna; Osborne, Patricia; Cabral, Marlene; & Gluck, Pamela. 2003. The development of communicative gestures in Japanese infants. *First Language* 23, 3–20.

Bloch, Oscar. 1924. La phrase dans le langage de l'enfant. *Journal de Psychologie* 21, 18–43.

Bloom, Lois. 1970. *Language development.* Cambridge, MA: MIT Press.

Bloom, Lois. 1973. *One word at a time.* The Hague: Mouton.

Bloom, Lois. 1991. *Language development from two to three.* Cambridge: Cambridge University Press.

Bloom, Lois. 1997. Intentionality is the basis for the social foundations of language development. Paper presented at the symposium on Social Foundations of Language Development: Theoretical Issues, Biennial Meeting of the Society for Research on Child Development, Washington, DC.

Bloom, Lois; Hood, Lois; & Lightbown, Patsy M. 1974. Imitation in language development: If, when, and why. *Cognitive Development* 6, 380–420.

Bloom, Lois; Lahey, Margaret; Hood, Lois; Lifter, Karen; & Fiess, Karen. 1980. Complex sentences: Acquisition of syntactic connectives and the meaning relations they encode. *Journal of Child Language* 7, 235–261.

Bloom, Lois; Lifter, Karen; & Hafitz, Jeremie. 1980. Semantics of verbs and the development of verb inflection in child language. *Language* 56, 386–412.

Bloom, Lois; Margulis, Cheryl; Tinker, Erin; & Fujita, Naomi. 1996. Early conversations and word learning: Contributions from child and adult. *Child Development* 67, 3154–3175.

Bloom, Lois; Miller, Patsy; & Hood, Lois. 1975. Variation and reduction as aspects of competence in language development. In A. Pick (ed.), *Minnesota symposia on child psychology*, vol. IX (3–55). Minneapolis: University of Minnesota Press.

Bloom, Lois; Rispoli, Matthew; Gartner, Barbara; & Hafitz, Jeremie. 1989. Acquisition of complementation. *Journal of Child Language* 16, 101–120.

Bloom, Lois; Tackeff, Jo; & Lahey, Margaret. 1984. Learning *to* in complement constructions. *Journal of Child Language* 11, 391–406.

Bloom, Lois; Tinker, Erin; & Margulis, Cheryl. 1993. The words children learn: Evidence against a noun bias in early vocabularies. *Cognitive Development* 8, 431–450.

Bloom, Paul. 2000. *How children learn the meanings of words*. Cambridge, MA: MIT Press.

Boas, Franz. 1911. Introduction, *Handbook of American Indian languages*. *Bulletin* 40, Part I, Bureau of American Ethnology. Washington, DC: Government Printing Office. (Reprinted in F. Boas, Introduction to handbook of American Indian languages. In J. W. Powell, *Indian linguistic families of America north of Mexico* [ed. P. Holder]. Lincoln: University of Nebraska Press, 1966.)

Bock, J. Kathryn, & Miller, Carol A. 1991. Broken agreement. *Cognitive Psychology* 23, 45–93.

Bohn, William E. 1914. First steps in verbal expression. *Pedagogical Seminary* 21, 578–595.

Bolinger, Dwight. 1972. *That's that*. The Hague: Mouton.

Bolinger, Dwight. 1975. *Aspects of language* (2nd edn). New York: Harcourt Brace Jovanovich.

Bolinger, Dwight. 1976. Meaning and memory. *Forum Linguisticum* 1, 1–14.

Bolinger, Dwight. 1977. Idioms have relations. *Forum Linguisticum* 2, 157–169.

Borer, Hagit, & Wexler, Ken. 1987. The maturation of syntax. In T. Roeper & E. Williams (eds.), *Parameter setting* (123–172). Dordrecht: Reidel.

Bosch, Laura; Ramón, Marta; Águila, Eva; & Pons, Ferrán. 2005. Efecto de la exposición bilingüe sobre el desarrollo léxico inicial. In E. Díez-Villoria, B. Zubiauz, & M. A. Mayor Cinca (eds.), *Estudio sobre la adquisición del lenguaje* (676–692). Salamanca, ES: Ediciones Universidad de Salamanca.

Bosch, Laura, & Sebastián-Gallés, Núria. 2001. Evidence of early language discrimination abilities in infants from bilingual environments. *Infancy* 2, 29–49.

Bouvier, Nadine, & Platone, Françoise. 1976. Etude génétique de la construction d'une détermination linguistique complexe: L'expression d'un même contenu par des enfants d'âges différents. *Etudes sur le développement du langage de l'enfant*, vol. I, 16A (25–165). Paris: Centre de Recherche de l'Education Spécialisée et de l'Adaptation Scolaire (Institut Pédagogique National).

Bowerman, Melissa. 1973a. *Early syntactic development: A cross-linguistic study with special reference to Finnish*. Cambridge: Cambridge University Press.

Bowerman, Melissa. 1973b. Structural relationships in children's utterances: Syntactic or semantic? In T. E. Moore (ed.), *Cognitive development and the acquisition of language* (197–213). New York: Academic Press.

Bowerman, Melissa. 1974. Learning the structure of causative verbs: A study in the relationship of cognitive, semantic, and syntactic development. *Papers & Reports on Child Language Development* [Stanford University] 8, 142–178.

Bowerman, Melissa. 1982a. Evaluating competing linguistic models with language acquisition data: Implications of developmental errors with causative verbs. *Quaderni di Semantica* 3, 5–66.

Bowerman, Melissa. 1982b. Reorganizational processes in lexical and syntactic development. In E. Wanner & L. R. Gleitman (eds.), *Language acquisition: The state of the art* (319–346). Cambridge: Cambridge University Press.

Bowerman, Melissa. 1985a. Beyond communicative adequacy: From piecemeal knowledge to an integrated system in the child's acquisition of language. In K. E. Nelson (ed.), *Children's language*, vol. V (369–398). Hillsdale, NJ: Lawrence Erlbaum.

Bowerman, Melissa. 1985b. What shapes children's grammars? In D. I. Slobin (ed.), *The crosslinguistic study of language acquisition*, vol. II (1257–1319). Hillsdale, NJ: Lawrence Erlbaum.

Bowerman, Melissa. 1986. First steps in acquiring conditionals. In E. C. Traugott, A. ter Meulen, J. S. Reilly, & C. A. Ferguson (eds.), *On conditionals* (285–307). Cambridge: Cambridge University Press.

Bowerman, Melissa. 1988. The "no negative evidence" problem: How do children avoid constructing an overly general grammar? In J. A. Hawkins (ed.), *Explaining language universals* (71–101). Oxford: Blackwell.

Bowerman, Melissa. 1990. Mapping thematic roles onto syntactic functions: Are children helped by innate linking rules? *Linguistics* 28, 1253–1289.

Bowerman, Melissa. 1996a. Argument structure and learnability: Is a solution in sight? In K. Johnson, M. L. Juge, & J. L. Moxley (eds.), *Proceedings of the 22nd annual meeting of the Berkeley Linguistics Society, Parasession on the role of learnability in grammatical theory* (454–468). Berkeley, CA: Berkeley Linguistics Society.

Bowerman, Melissa. 1996b. Learning how to structure space for language: A crosslinguistic perspective. In P. Bloom, M. A. Peterson, L. Nadel, & M. F. Garrett (eds.), *Language and space* (385–436). Cambridge, MA: MI.

Bowerman, Melissa. 2005. Why can't you "open" a nut or "break" a noodle? Learning covert object categories in action word meanings. In L. Gershkoff-Stowe & D. H. Rakison (eds.), *Building object categories in developmental time* (209–243). Mahwah, NJ: Lawrence Erlbaum.

Bowerman, Melissa, & Croft, William. 2008. The acquisition of the English causative. In M. Bowerman & P. Brown (eds.), *Crosslinguistic perspectives on argument structure: Implications for learnability* (279–308). New York: Erlbaum.

Boyle, Mary K., & Gerken, LouAnn. 1997. The influence of lexical familiarity on children's function morpheme omissions: A nonmetrical effect? *Journal of Memory & Language* 36, 117–128.

Braine, Martin D. S. 1963. On learning the grammatical order of words. *Psychological Review* 70, 323–348.

Braine, Martin D. S. 1971. The acquisition of language in infant and child. In C. Reed (ed.), *The learning of language* (7–95). New York: Appleton.

Braine, Martin D. S. 1976. Children's first word combinations. *Monographs of the Society for Research in Child Development* 41 (serial no. 164).

Braine, Martin D. S.; Brody, Ruth E.; Fisch, Shalom M.; & Weisberger, Mara J. 1990. Can children use a verb without exposure to its argument structure? *Journal of Child Language* 17, 313–342.

Brandone, Amanda C.; Pence, Khara L.; Golinkoff, Roberta M.; & Hirsh-Pasek, Kathy. 2007. Action speaks louder than words: Young children differentially weight perceptual, social, and linguistic cues to learn verbs. *Child Development* 78, 1322–1342.

Branigan, George. 1976. Syllabic structure and the acquisition of consonants: The great conspiracy in word formation. *Journal of Psycholinguistic Research* 5, 117–133.

Branigan, George. 1979. Some reasons why successive single word utterances are not. *Journal of Child Language* 6, 411–421.

Braunwald, Susan R. 1995. Differences in the acquisition of early verbs: Evidence from diary data from sisters. In M. Tomasello & W. E. Merriman (eds.), *Beyond names for things: Young children's acquisition of verbs* (81–111). Hillsdale, NJ: Lawrence Erlbaum.

Bréal, Michel. 1897. *Essai de sémantique*. Paris: Hachette.

Brent, Michael R., & Cartwright, Timothy A. 1996. Distributional regularity and phonotactic constraints are useful for segmentation. *Cognition* 61, 93–125.

Bresson, François. 1977. Semantics, syntax and utterance: Determining a referent. *International Journal of Psycholinguistics* 4, 31–41.

Bresson, François; Bouvier, Nadine; Dannequin, Claudine; Depreux, J.; Hardy, Marianne; & Platone, Françoise. 1970. *Quelques aspects du système des déterminants chez les enfants de l'école maternelle: Utilisation des articles défini et indéfini*. 2 (3–40). Paris: Centre de Recherche de l'Education Spécialisé et de l'Adaptation Scolaire (Institut Pédagogique National).

Bretherton, Inge. 1984. Representing the social world in symbolic play: Reality and fantasy. In I. Bretherton (ed.), *Symbolic play: The development of social understanding* (3–41). New York: Academic Press.

Brewer, William F., & Stone, J. Brandon. 1975. Acquisition of spatial antonym pairs. *Journal of Experimental Child Psychology* 19, 299–307.

Brinkmann, Ursula. 1995. The locative alternation: Its structure and acquisition. PhD dissertation, Katholieke Universiteit Nijmegen.

Broca, Paul. 1856. *Des aneurysmes et de leur traitement*. Paris: Labe.

Broca, Paul. 1861. Remarques sur le siège de la faculté du langage articulé, suivies d'une observation d'aphémie. *Bulletin de la Société d'Anatomie* 5, 33–357.

Broen, Patricia A. 1972. The verbal environment of the language-learning child. *Monograph of the American Speech & Hearing Association* 17.

Brooks, Patricia J.; Tomasello, Michael; Dodson, Kelly; & Lewis, Lawrence B. 1999. Young children's overgeneralizations with fixed transitivity verbs: The entrenchment hypothesis. *Child Development*, 70, 1325–1337.

Brown, H. Douglas. 1971. Children's comprehension of relativized English sentences. *Child Development* 42, 1923–1936.

Brown, Penelope. 1998. Children's first verbs in Tzeltal: Evidence for an early verb category. *Linguistics* 36, 713–753.

Brown, Penelope, & Levinson, Stephen C. 1987. *Politeness: Some universals in language usage*. Cambridge: Cambridge University Press.

Brown, Roger. 1957. Linguistic determinism and the part of speech. *Journal of Abnormal & Social Psychology* 55, 1–5.

Brown, Roger. 1958a. How shall a thing be called? *Psychological Review* 65, 14–21.

Brown, Roger. 1958b. *Words and things*. New York: Free Press.

Brown, Roger. 1968. The development of *wh* questions in child speech. *Journal of Verbal Learning & Verbal Behavior* 7, 279–290.

Brown, Roger. 1973. *A first language: The early stages*. Cambridge, MA: Harvard University Press.

Brown, Roger, & Bellugi, Ursula. 1964. Three processes in the child's acquisition of syntax. *Harvard Educational Review* 34, 133–151.

Brown, Roger, & Hanlon, Camille. 1970. Derivational complexity and order of acquisition in child speech. In J. R. Hayes (ed.), *Cognition and the development of language* (11–53). New York: Wiley.

Bruner, Jerome S. 1975. The ontogenesis of speech acts. *Journal of Child Language* 2, 1–20.

Bruner, Jerome S. 1983. *Child's talk: Learning to use language*. New York: Norton.

Budwig, Nancy. 1989. The linguistic marking of agentivity and control in child language. *Journal of Child Language* 16, 263–284.

Budwig, Nancy. 1990. The linguistic marking of nonprototypical agency: An exploration into children's use of passives. *Linguistics* 28, 1221–1252.

Budwig, Nancy. 1995. *A developmental-functionalist approach to child language.* Mahwah, NJ: Lawrence Erlbaum.

Bunta, Ferenc; Davidovich, Ingrid; & Ingram, David. 2006. The relationship between the phonological complexity of a bilingual child's words and those of the target languages. *International Journal of Bilingualism* 10, 71–88.

Buresh, Jennifer S., & Woodward, Amanda L. 2007. Infants track goals within and across agents. *Cognition* 104, 287–314.

Buresh, Jennifer S.; Woodward, Amanda; & Brune, Camille W. 2006. The roots of verbs in prelinguistic action knowledge. In K. Hirsh-Pasek & R. M. Golinkoff (eds.), *How children learn verbs* (208–277). Oxford: Oxford University Press.

Burling, Robbins. 1959. Language development of a Garo and English speaking child. *Word* 15, 45–68.

Burns, Tracey C.; Yoshida, Katherine A.; Hill, Karen; & Werker, Janet F. 2007. The development of phonetic representation in bilingual and monolingual infants. *Applied Psycholinguistics* 28, 455–474.

Butterworth, George, & Cochran, Edward. 1980. What minds have in common in space: A perceptual mechanism for joint reference in infancy. *International Journal of Behavioural Development* 3, 253–272.

Butterworth, George, & Jarrett, Nicholas. 1991. What minds have in common in space: Spatial mechanisms serving joint visual attention in infancy. *British Journal of Developmental Psychology* 9, 55–72.

Bybee, Joan L. 1985. *Morphology: A study of the relation between meaning and form.* Amsterdam: John Benjamins.

Bybee, Joan L. 1995. Regular morphology and the lexicon. *Language & Cognitive Processes* 10, 425–455.

Bybee, Joan L. 1998. The emergent lexicon. In M. C. Gruber, D. Higgins, K. S. Olson, & T. Wysocki (eds.), *Proceedings of the Chicago Linguistic Society* 34: *The Panels* (421–435). Chicago: Chicago Linguistic Society.

Bybee, Joan L., & Slobin, Dan I. 1982. Rules and schemas in the development and use of the English past tense. *Language* 58, 265–289.

Callanan, Maureen A. 1985. How parents label objects for young children: The role of input in the acquisition of category hierarchies. *Child Development* 56, 508–523.

Callanan, Maureen A. 1989. Maternal speech strategies and children's acquisition of hierarchical category labels. *Genetic Psychology* 17 (2), 3–12.

Callanan, Maureen A. 1990. Parents' descriptions of objects: Potential data for children's inferences about category principles. *Cognitive Development* 5, 101–122.

Callanan, Maureen, & Sabbagh, Mark A. 2004. Multiple labels for objects in conversations between young children: Parents' language and children's developing expectations about word meanings. *Developmental Psychology* 40, 746–763.

Campbell, Robin N. 2006. Prescientific studies of language development. In K. Brown (gen. ed.), *Encyclopedia of Language & Linguistics* (2nd edn), vol. VI (391–394). Oxford: Oxford University Press.

Capirci, Olga; Contaldo, Annarita; Caselli, M. Cristina; & Volterra, Virginia. 2005. From action to language through gesture. *Gesture* 5, 155–177.

Capirci, Olga; Iverson, Jana M.; Pizzuto, Elena; & Volterra, Virginia. 1996. Gestures and words during the transition to two-word speech. *Journal of Child Language* 23, 645–673.

Carey, Susan. 1985. *Conceptual change in childhood*. Cambridge, MA: MIT Press.

Carey, Susan, & Bartlett, Elsa. 1978. Acquiring a single new word. *Papers & Reports on Child Language Development* [Stanford University] 15, 17–29.

Carmichael, L.; Hogan, H. P.; & Walter, A. A. 1932. An experimental study of the effect of language on the reproduction of visually perceived forms. *Journal of Experimental Psychology* 15, 73–86.

Carter, Allyson, & Gerken, LouAnn. 2004. Do children's omissions leave traces? *Journal of Child Language* 31, 561–586.

Carter, Anne L. 1978. From sensori-motor vocalizations to words: A case study of the evolution of attention-directing communication in the second year. In A. Lock (ed.), *Action, gesture, and symbol: The emergence of language* (309–349). London: Academic Press.

Carter, Anne L. 1979. The disappearance schema: Case study of a second-year communicative behavior. In E. Ochs & B. B. Schieffelin (eds.), *Developmental pragmatics* (131–156). New York: Academic Press.

Cartmill, Erica A., & Byrne, Richard W. 2007. Orangutans modify their gestural signaling according to their audience's comprehension. *Current Biology* 17, 1345–1348.

Cartwright, Timothy A., & Brent, Michael R. 1997. Syntactic categorization in early language acquisition: Formalizing the role of distributional analysis. *Cognition* 63, 121–170.

Casadio, Paola, & Caselli, M. Cristina. 1989. Il primo vocabulario del bambino: Gesti e parole a 14 mesi. *Età Evolutiva* 33, 32–42.

Caselli, M. Cristina. 1983. Gesti comunicativi e primi parole. *Età Evolutiva* 16, 36–51.

Cazden, Courtney B. 1968. The acquisition of noun and verb inflections. *Child Development* 39, 433–448.

Cazden, Courtney B.; John, Vera P.; & Hymes, Dell (eds.). 1972. *Functions of language in the classroom*. Prospect Heights, IL: Waveland Press.

Chafe, Wallace. 1970. *Meaning and the structure of language*. Chicago: University of Chicago Press.

Chambers, James C., & Tavuchis, Nicholas. 1976. Kids and kin: Children's understanding of American kin terms. *Journal of Child Language* 3, 63–80.

Chambers, J. K. 1992. Dialect acquisition. *Language* 68, 673–705.

Chambers, J. K. 2003. *Sociolinguistic theory: Linguistic variation and social significance* (2nd edn). Oxford: Blackwell.

Cheung, Sik Lee. 1998. Causative verbs in child Cantonese. In E. V. Clark (ed.), *Proceedings of the 29th annual Child Language Research Forum 1997* (151–160). Stanford, CA: CSLI.

Chmura-Klekotowa, Maria. 1970. Odbicie tendencji slowotwórczych jezyka polskiego w neologizmach dzieci [Reflection of derivational trends of the Polish language in children's neologisms]. *Prace Filologiczne* (Warsaw) 20, 153–159.

Choi, Soonja. 1999. Early development of verb structures and caregiver input in Korean: Two case studies. *International Journal of Bilingualism* 3, 241–265.

Choi, Soonja. 2000. Caregiver input in English and Korean: Use of nouns and verbs in book-reading and toy-play contexts. *Journal of Child Language* 27, 69–96.

Choi, Soonja. 2006. Influence of language-specific input on spatial cognition: Categories of containment. *First Language* 26, 207–232.

Choi, Soonja, & Bowerman, Melissa. 1991. Learning to express motion events in English and Korean: The influence of language-specific lexicalization patterns. *Cognition* 41, 83–121.

Choi, Soonja, & Gopnik, Alison. 1995. Early acquisition of verbs in Korean: A cross-linguistic study. *Journal of Child Language* 22, 497–529.

Choi, Soonja; McDonough, Laraine; Bowerman, Melissa; & Mandler, Jean M. 1999. Early sensitivity to language-specific spatial categories in English and Korean. *Cognitive Development* 14, 241–268.

Chomsky, Carol S. 1969. *The acquisition of syntax in children from 5 to 10*. Cambridge, MA: MIT Press.

Chomsky, Noam. 1965. *Aspects of the theory of syntax*. Cambridge, MA: MIT Press.

Chomsky, Noam. 1972. *Language and mind* (enlarged edn). New York: Harcourt Brace Jovanovich.

Chouinard, Michelle M., & Clark, Eve V. 2003. Adult reformulations of child errors as negative evidence. *Journal of Child Language* 30, 637–669.

Christophe, Anne; Mehler, Jacques; & Sebastián-Gallés, Núria. 2001. Perception of prosodic boundary correlates by newborn infants. *Infancy* 2, 38–394.

Clahsen, Harald, & Almazan, Mayella. 1998. Syntax and morphology in Williams syndrome. *Cognition* 68, 167–198.

Clancy, Patricia M. 1985. The acquisition of Japanese. In D. I. Slobin (ed.), *The crosslinguistic study of language acquisition*, vol. I (373–524). Hillsdale, NJ: Lawrence Erlbaum.

Clancy, Patricia M. 1996. Referential strategies and the co-construction of argument structure in Korean acquisition. In B. Fox (ed.), *Studies in anaphora* (33–68). Amsterdam: John Benjamins.

Clancy, Patricia M. 2003. The lexicon in interaction: Developmental origins of preferred argument structure in Korean. In J. W. Du Bois, L. Kumpf, & W. Ashby (eds.), *Preferred argument structure: Grammar as architecture for function* (81–108) Amsterdam: John Benjamins.

Clark, Eve V. 1970. How young children describe events in time. In G. B. Flores d'Arcais & W. J. M. Levelt (eds.), *Advances in psycholinguistics* (275–293). Amsterdam: North-Holland Publishing.

Clark, Eve V. 1971. On the acquisition of *before* and *after*. *Journal of Verbal Learning & Verbal Behavior* 10, 266–275.

Clark, Eve V. 1972. On the child's acquisition of antonyms in two semantic fields. *Journal of Verbal Learning & Verbal Behavior* 11, 750–758.

Clark, Eve V. 1973a. What's in a word? On the child's acquisition of semantics in his first language. In T. E. Moore (ed.), *Cognitive development and the acquisition of language* (65–110). New York: Academic Press.

Clark, Eve V. 1973b. Nonlinguistic strategies and the acquisition of word meaning. *Cognition* 2, 161–182.

Clark, Eve V. 1973c. How children describe time and order. In C. A. Ferguson & D. I. Slobin (eds.), *Studies of child language development* (585–606). New York: Holt, Rinehart & Winston.

Clark, Eve V. 1977. Universal categories: On the semantics of classifiers and children's early word meanings. In A. Juilland (ed.), *Linguistic studies offered to Joseph Greenberg* (449–462). Saratoga, CA: Anma Libri.

Clark, Eve V. 1978a. Awareness of language: Some evidence from what children say and do. In A. Sinclair, R. Jarvella, & W. J. M. Levelt (eds.), *The child's conception of language* (17–43). New York: Springer-Verlag.

Clark, Eve V. 1978b. From gesture to word: On the natural history of deixis in language acquisition. In J. Bruner & A. Garton (eds.), *Human growth and development: Wolfson College lectures 1976* (95–120). Oxford: Oxford University Press.

Clark, Eve V. 1978c. Discovering what words can do. In D. Farkas, W. M. Jacobsen, & K. W. Todrys (eds.), *Papers from the parasession on the lexicon* (34–57). Chicago: Chicago Linguistic Society.

Clark, Eve V. 1979. Building a vocabulary: Words for objects, actions, and relations. In P. Fletcher & M. Garman (eds.), *Language acquisition* (149–160). Cambridge: Cambridge University Press.

Clark, Eve V. 1980. Here's the *top*: Nonlinguistic strategies in the acquisition of orientational terms. *Child Development* 51, 329–338.

Clark, Eve V. 1981. Negative verbs in children's speech. In W. Klein & W. J. M. Levelt (eds.), *Crossing the boundaries in linguistics* (253–264). Dordrecht: Reidel.

Clark, Eve V. 1982. Language change during language acquisition. In M. E. Lamb & A. L. Brown (eds.), *Advances in developmental psychology*, vol. II (173–197). Hillsdale, NJ: Lawrence Erlbaum.

Clark, Eve V. 1983. Meanings and concepts. In J. H. Flavell & E. M. Markman (eds.), *Handbook of child psychology*, vol. III: *Cognitive development* (787–840). New York: Wiley.

Clark, Eve V. 1984. Acquiring compounds. In G. Alvarez, B. Brodie, & T. McCoy (eds.), *Proceeedings of the Eastern States Conference on Linguistics 1984* (181–190). Columbus: Department of Linguistics, Ohio State University.

Clark, Eve V. 1987. The principle of contrast: A constraint on language acquisition. In B. MacWhinney (ed.), *Mechanisms of language acquisition* (1–33). Hillsdale, NJ: Lawrence Erlbaum.

Clark, Eve V. 1988. On the logic of contrast. *Journal of Child Language* 15, 317–335.

Clark, Eve V. 1990. The pragmatics of contrast. *Journal of Child Language* 17, 417–431.

Clark, Eve V. 1993. *The lexicon in acquisition*. Cambridge: Cambridge University Press.

Clark, Eve V. 1995. Later lexical development and word formation. In P. Fletcher & B. MacWhinney (eds.), *The handbook of child language* (393–412). Oxford: Blackwell.

Clark, Eve V. 1996. Early verbs, event types, and inflections. In C. E. Johnson & J. H. V. Gilbert (eds.), *Children's language*, vol. IX (61–73). Mahwah, NJ: Lawrence Erlbaum.

Clark, Eve V. 1997. Conceptual perspective and lexical choice in acquisition. *Cognition* 64, 1–37.

Clark, Eve V. 1998. Lexical structure and pragmatic directions in acquisition. In M. C. Gruber, D. Higgins, K. S. Olson, & T. Wysocki (eds.), *Papers from the 34th meeting of the Chicago Linguistic Society: The Panels* (437–446). Chicago: Chicago Linguistic Society.

Clark, Eve V. 1999. Acquisition in the course of conversation. *Studies in Linguistic Sciences* (Special Issue, Forum Lectures 1999, LSA Summer Institute) 29, 1–18.

Clark, Eve V. 2001. Emergent categories in first language acquisition. In M. Bowerman & S. C. Levinson (eds.), *Language acquisition and conceptual development* (379–405). Cambridge: Cambridge University Press.

Clark, Eve V. 2002a. Making use of pragmatic inferences in the acquisition of meaning. In D. Beaver, S. Kaufmann, B. Clark, & L. Casillas (eds.), *The construction of meaning* (45–58). Stanford, CA: CSLI.

Clark, Eve V. 2002b. Grounding and attention in language acquisition. In M. Andronis, C. Ball, H. Elston, & S. Neuvel (eds.), *Papers from the 37th meeting of the Chicago Linguistic Society*, vol. I (95–116). Chicago: Chicago Linguistic Society.

Clark, Eve V. 2006. Color, reference, and expertise in language acquisition. *Journal of Experimental Child Psychology* 94, 339–343.

Clark, Eve V. 2007. Young children's uptake of new words in conversation. *Language in Society* 36, 157–182.

Clark, Eve V. 2009. Adult offer, word-class, and child uptake in early lexical acquisition. *First Language* 00, in press.

Clark, Eve V., & Berman, Ruth A. 1984. Structure and use in the acquisition of word-formation. *Language* 60, 547–590.

Clark, Eve V., & Berman, Ruth A. 1987. Types of linguistic knowledge: Interpreting and producing compound nouns. *Journal of Child Language* 14, 547–567.

Clark, Eve V., & Bernicot, Josie. 2008. Repetition as ratification: How parents and children place information in common ground. *Journal of Child Language* 35, 349–371.

Clark, Eve V., & Bowerman, Melissa. 1986. On the acquisition of final voiced stops. In J. A. Fishman (ed.), *The Fergusonian impact, vol. I: From phonology to society* (51–68). Berlin and Amsterdam: Mouton/de Gruyter.

Clark, Eve V., & Carpenter, Kathie L. 1989a. The notion of source in language acquisition. *Language* 65, 1–30.

Clark, Eve V., & Carpenter, Kathie L. 1989b. On children's uses of *from*, *by*, and *with* in oblique noun phrases. *Journal of Child Language* 16, 349–364.

Clark, Eve V.; Carpenter, Kathie L.; & Deutsch, Werner. 1995. Reference states and reversals: Undoing actions with verbs. *Journal of Child Language* 22, 633–662.

Clark, Eve V., & Clark, Herbert H. 1979. When nouns surface as verbs. *Language* 55, 767–811.

Clark, Eve V., & Cohen, Sophia R. 1984. Productivity and memory for newly-formed words. *Journal of Child Language* 11, 611–625.

Clark, Eve V., & Garnica, Olga K. 1974. Is he coming or going? On the acquisition of deictic verbs. *Journal of Verbal Learning & Verbal Behavior* 13, 559–572.

Clark, Eve V.; Gelman, Susan A.; & Lane, Nancy M. 1985. Compound nouns and category structure in young children. *Child Development* 56, 84–94.

Clark, Eve V., & Grossman, James B. 1998. Pragmatic directions and children's word learning. *Journal of Child Language* 25, 1–18.

Clark, Eve V., & Hecht, Barbara F. 1982. Learning to coin agent and instrument nouns. *Cognition* 12, 1–24.

Clark, Eve V.; Hecht, Barbara F.; & Mulford, Randa C. 1986. Acquiring complex compounds: Affixes and word order in English. *Linguistics* 24, 7–29.

Clark, Eve V.; Neel-Gordon, Amy; & Johnson, Susan. 1993. Convention and contrast in the acquisition of verbs. Paper presented at the Sixth International Congress for the Study of Child Language, Trieste, Italy.

Clark, Eve V., & Nikitina, Tatiana. 2009. One vs. more than one: Antecedents to plurality in early language acquisition. *Linguistics* 47(1), in press.

Clark, Eve V., & Sengul, C. J. 1978. Strategies in the acquisition of deixis. *Journal of Child Language* 5, 457–475.

Clark, Eve V., & Svaib, Trisha A. 1997. Speaker perspective and reference in young children. *First Language* 17, 57–74.

Clark, Eve V., & Wong, Andrew D.-W. 2002. Pragmatic directions about language use: Words and word meanings. *Language in Society* 31, 181–212.

Clark, Herbert H. 1973. Space, time, semantics, and the child. In T. E. Moore (ed.), *Cognitive development and the acquisition of language* (27–63). New York: Academic Press.

Clark, Herbert H. 1996. *Using language*. Cambridge: Cambridge University Press.

Clark, Herbert H., & Marshall, Catherine R. 1981. Definite reference and mutual knowledge. In A. K. Joshi, B. L. Weber, & I. A. Sag (eds.), *Elements of discourse understanding* (10–63). Cambridge: Cambridge University Press.

Clark, Ruth A., & Delia, Jesse G. 1976. The development of functional persuasive skills in childhood and early adolescence. *Child Development* 47, 1008–1014.

Cohen-Bacri, Jean. 1978. Langage et processus cognitifs: Interprétation de phrases complexes avec proposition relative chez l'enfant. *La Linguistique* 14, 89–110.

Colas, Annie. 1999. Introducing infants to referential events: A developmental study of material ostensive marking in French. *Journal of Child Language* 26, 113–131.

Collis, Glyn M. 1977. Visual co-orientation and maternal speech. In H. R. Schaffer (ed.), *Studies in mother-infant interaction* (355–375). London: Academic Press.

Collis, Glyn M., & Schaffer, H. Rudolph. 1975. Synchronization of visual attention in mother-infant pairs. *Journal of Child Psychology & Psychiatry* 16, 315–320.

Compayré, Gabriel. 1896. *L'évolution intellectuelle et morale de l'enfant* (2nd edn). Paris: Hachette.

Cook-Gumperz, Jenny, & Corsaro, William A. 1977. Social-ecological constraints on children's communicative strategies. *Sociology* 11, 411–434.

Cook-Gumperz, Jenny, & Scales, Barbara. 1996. Girls, boys, and just people: The interactional accomplishment of gender in the discourse of the nursery school. In D. I. Slobin, J. Gerhardt, A. Kyratzis, & J. Guo (eds.), *Social interaction, social context, and language: Essays in honor of Susan Ervin-Tripp* (513–527). Mahwah, NJ: Lawrence Erlbaum.

Corsaro, William A. 1977. The clarification request as a feature of adult interactive styles with young children. *Language in Society* 6, 183–207.

Corsaro, William A., & Rizzo, Thomas A. 1990. Disputes in the peer culture of American and Italian nursery-school children. In A. D. Grimshaw (ed.), *Conflict talk: Sociolinguistic investigations of arguments in conversations* (21–66). Cambridge: Cambridge University Press.

Corson, David. 1995. *Using English words*. Boston: Kluwer Academic Press.

Courtney, Susan M., & Ungerleider, Leslie G. 1997. What fMRI has taught us about human vision. *Current Opinion in Neurobiology* 7, 554–561.

Courtney, Susan M.; Ungerleider, Leslie G.; Keil, Katrina; & Haxby, James V. 1997. Transient and sustained activity in a distributed neural system for human working memory. *Nature* 386, 608–611.

Croft, William. 1991. *Syntactic categories and grammatical relations*. Chicago: University of Chicago Press.

Croft, William. 2000. *Explaining language change: An evolutionary approach*. London: Longman.

Crutchley, Alison. 2004. 'If she had of shutted the cage, the rabbit wouldn't escape': Past counterfactuals elicited from 6- to 11-year-old children. *First Language* 24, 209–240.

Cruttenden, Alan. 1994. Phonetic and prosodic aspects of Baby Talk. In C. Gallaway & B. J. Richards (eds.), *Input and interaction in language acquisition* (135–152). Cambridge: Cambridge University Press.

Csibra, Gergely; Bíró, Szilvia; Koos, Orsolya; & Gergely, György. 2003. One-year-old infants use teleological representations of actions productively. *Cognitive Science* 27, 111–133.

Curtiss, Susan. 1977. *Genie: A psycholinguistic study of a modern-day "wild child."* New York: Academic Press.

Curtiss, Susan. 1988. Abnormal language acquisition and the modularity of language. In F. Newmeyer (ed.), *Linguistics: The Cambridge survey, vol. II: Linguistic Theory: Extensions and implications* (96–116). Cambridge: Cambridge University Press.

Cutting, James E., & Rosner, Burton S. 1974. Categories and boundaries in speech and music. *Perception & Psychophysics* 16, 564–570.

Dabrowska, Ewa. 2000. From formula to schema: The acquisition of English questions. *Cognitive Linguistics* 11, 83–102.

Daniels, Peter T., & Bright, William (eds.). 1996. *The world's writing systems*. Oxford: Oxford University Press.

Davis, K. 1940. Extreme social isolation of a child. *American Journal of Sociology* 45, 554–565.

Davis, K. 1947. Final note on a case of extreme social isolation. *American Journal of Sociology* 52, 432–437.

Deák, Gedeon O., & Maratsos, Michael P. 1998. On having complex representations of things: Preschoolers use multiple labels for objects and people. *Developmental Psychology* 34, 224–240.

de Boysson-Bardies, Benedicte, & Vihman, Marilyn M. 1991. Adaptation to language: Evidence from babbling and first words in four languages. *Language* 67, 297–318.

DeCasper, Anthony J., & Fifer, William P. 1980. Of human bonding: Newborns prefer their mothers' voices. *Science* 208, 1174–1176.

DeCasper, Anthony J., & Spence, Melanie J. 1986. Prenatal maternal speech influences newborns' perception of speech sounds. *Infant Behavior & Development* 9, 133–150.

Deffebach, Kim P., & Adamson, Lauren B. 1994. Teaching referential and social-regulative words to toddlers: Mothers' use of metalingual language. *First Language* 14, 249–261.

De Houwer, Annick. 1990. *The acquisition of two languages from birth: A case study*. Cambridge: Cambridge University Press.

De Houwer, Annick. 1995. Bilingual language acquisition. In P. Fletcher & B. MacWhinney (eds.), *The handbook of child language* (219–250). Oxford: Blackwell.

De Houwer, Annick. 2007. Parental language input patterns and children's bilingual use. *Applied Psycholinguistics* 28, 411–424.

De Houwer, Annick; Bornstein, Marc H.; & De Coster, Sandrine. 2006. Early understanding of two words for the same thing: A CDI study of lexical comprehension in infant bilinguals. *International Journal of Bilingualism* 10, 331–347.

de Lemos, Claudia. 1981. Interactional processes in the child's construction of language. In W. Deutsch (ed.), *The child's construction of language* (57–76). London: Academic Press.

de León, Lourdes. 1998. The emergent participant: Interactive patterns in the socialization of Tzotzil (Mayan) infants. *Journal of Linguistic Anthropology* 8 (2), 131–161.

Demuth, Katherine. 1986. Prompting routines in the language socialization of Basotho children. In B. B. Schieffelin & E. Ochs (eds.), *Language socialization across cultures* (51–79). Cambridge: Cambridge University Press.

Demuth, Katherine. 1989. Maturation and the acquisition of the Sesotho passive. *Language* 65, 56–80.

Demuth, Katherine. 1992. The acquisition of Sesotho. In D. I. Slobin (ed.), *The crosslinguistic study of language acquisition*, vol. III (557–638). Hillsdale, NJ: Lawrence Erlbaum.

Demuth, Katherine. 1994. On the underspecification of functional categories in early grammars. In B. Lust, M. Suñer, & J. Whitman (eds.), *Syntactic theory and first language acquisition: Crosslinguistic perspectives*, vol. I (119–134). Hillsdale, NJ: Lawrence Erlbaum.

Demuth, Katherine. 1996. The prosodic structure of early words. In J. Morgan & K. Demuth (eds.), *From signal to syntax: Bootstrapping from speech to grammar in early acquisition* (171–184). Hillsdale, NJ: Lawrence Erlbaum.

Dennis, Maureen. 1980. Capacity and strategy for syntactic comprehension after left or right hemidecortication. *Brain & Language* 10, 287–317.

Dennis, Maureen. 1988. Language and the young damaged brain. In T. Boll & B. K. Bryant (eds.), *Clinical neuropsychology and brain function: Research, measurement, and practice* (89–123). New York: Guilford Press.

Dennis, Maureen. 2000. Childhood medical disorders and cognitive impairment: Biological risk, time, development, and reserve. In K. O. Yeates & M. D. Ris (eds.), *Pediatric neuropsychology: Research, theory, and practice* (3–22). New York: Guilford Press.

Dennis, Maureen, & Kohn, Bruno. 1975. Comprehension of syntax in infantile hemiplegics after cerebral hemidecortication: Left-hemisphere superiority. *Brain & Language* 2, 472–482.

Dennis, Maureen; Lovett, Maureen; & Wiegel-Crump, Carole A. 1981. Written language acquisition after left or right hemidecortication in infancy. *Brain & Language* 12, 54–91.

Dennis, Maureen, & Whitaker, Harry. (1975). Language acquisition following hemidecortication: Linguistic superiority of left over the right hemisphere. *Brain & Language* 3, 404–433.

Deuchar, Margaret, & Quay, Suzanne. 2000. *Bilingual acquisition: Theoretical implications of a case study.* Oxford: Oxford University Press.

de Villiers, Jill G. 1985. Learning how to use verbs: Lexical coding and the influence of input. *Journal of Child Language* 12, 587–595.

de Villiers, Jill G., & de Villiers, Peter. 1973. A cross-sectional study of the acquisition of grammatical morphemes. *Journal of Psycholinguistic Research* 2, 267–278.

de Villiers, Peter A., & de Villiers, Jill G. 1979. Form and function in the development of sentence negation. *Papers & Reports on Child Language Development* [Stanford University] 17, 57–64.

Diesendruck, Gil, & Markson, Lori. 2001. Children's avoidance of lexical overlap: A pragmatic account. *Developmental Psychology* 27, 630–641.

Diessel, Holger, & Tomasello, Michael. 2000. Why complement clauses do not include a that-complementizer in early child language. In S. S. Chang, L. Liaw, & J. Ruppenhofer (eds.), *Proceedings of the 25th annual meeting of the Berkeley Linguistics Society* (86–97). Berkeley: Berkeley Linguistics Society.

Dockrell, Julie. 1981. The child's acquisition of unfamiliar words: An experimental study. PhD dissertation, University of Stirling, United Kingdom.

Dockrell, Julie, & Campbell, Robin N. 1986. Lexical acquisition strategies in the preschool child. In S. A. Kuczaj II & M. D. Barrett (eds.), *The development of word meaning: Progress in cognitive development research* (121–154). New York: Springer-Verlag.

Dockrell, Julie, & McShane, John. 1990. Young children's use of phrase structure and inflectional information in form-class assignments of novel nouns and verbs. *First Language* 10, 127–140.

Dockrell, Julie, & Ralli, Mina. 1996. Strategies in lexical acquisition: Constraint or context? Poster, Developmental Section, meeting of the British Psychological Society, Oxford.

Dodd, Barbara. 1975. Children's understanding of their own phonological forms. *Quarterly Journal of Experimental Psychology* 27, 165–172.

D'Odorico, Laura, & Carrubi, Stefania. 2003. Prosodic characteristics of early multi-word utterances in Italian children. *First Language* 23, 97–116.

Donaldson, Margaret, & Balfour, George. 1968. Less is more: A study of language comprehension in children. *British Journal of Psychology* 59, 461–471.

Donaldson, Margaret, & Wales, Roger J. 1970. On the acquisition of some relational terms. In J. R. Hayes (ed.), *Cognition and the development of language* (235–268). New York: Wiley.

Donaldson, Morag L. 1986. *Children's explanations*. Cambridge: Cambridge University Press.

Döpke, Susanne. 1992. *One parent one language: An interactional approach*. Amsterdam: John Benjamins.

Dor, Daniel. 1996. Representations, attitudes, and factivity evaluations. PhD dissertation, Stanford University.

Dowty, David. 1991. Thematic proto-roles and argument selection. *Language* 67, 547–619.

Dromi, Esther. 1987. *Early lexical development*. Cambridge: Cambridge University Press.

Drozd, Kenneth F. 1995. Child English pre-sentential negation as metalinguistic exclamatory sentence negation. *Journal of Child Language* 22, 583–610.

Du Bois, John W. 1987. The discourse basis of ergativity. *Language* 63, 805–855.

Dumont, Robert V. 1972. Learning English and how to be silent: Studies in Sioux and Cherokee classrooms. In C. Cazden, V. John, & D. Hymes (eds.), *Functions of language in the classroom* (344–369). New York: Teachers College Press.

Dunn, Judy, & Shatz, Marilyn. 1989. Becoming a conversationalist despite (or because of) having an older sibling. *Child Development* 60, 399–410.

Ebeling, Karen S., & Gelman, Susan A. 1994. Children's use of context in interpreting "big" and "little." *Child Development* 65, 1178–1192.

Ebeling, Karen S., & Gelman, Susan A. 1997. The influence of shape and representational status on children's naming. Paper presented at the biennial meeting of the Society for Research in Child Development, Washington, DC.

Echols, Catharine H. 1993. A perceptually-based model of children's earliest productions. *Cognition* 46, 245–296.

Echols, Catharine; Crowhurst, Megan J.; & Childers, Jane B. 1997. The perception of rhythmic units in speech by infants and adults. *Journal of Memory & Language* 36, 202–225.

Echols, Catharine H., & Newport, Elissa L. 1992. The role of stress and position in determining first words. *Language Acquisition* 2, 189–220.

Eckert, Penelope. 2000. *Linguistic variation as social practice*. Oxford: Blackwell.

Eckert, Penelope, & McConnell-Ginet, Sally. 1992. Think practically and look locally: Language and gender as community-based practice. *Annual Review of Anthropology* 21, 461–490.

Edwards, Derek, & Goodwin, Roger. 1986. Action words and pragmatic functions in early language. In S. A. Kuczaj II & M. D. Barrett (eds.), *The development of word meaning: Progress in cognitive development research* (257–273). New York: Springer-Verlag.

Edwards, Jon; Beckman, Mary E.; & Munson, Benjamin. 2004. The interaction between vocabulary size and phonotactic probability effects on children's production accuracy and fluency in nonword repetition. *Journal of Speech, Language, & Hearing Research* 47, 421–436.

Edwards, Mary Louise. 1974. Perception and production in child phonology: The testing of four hypotheses. *Journal of Child Language* 1, 205–219.

Egger, Emile. 1887. *Observations et réflexions sur le développement de l'intelligence et du langage chez les enfants*. Paris: Picard.

Eimas, Peter D. 1974. Auditory and linguistic processing of cues for place of articulation by infants. *Perception & Psychophysics* 16, 513–521.

Eimas, Peter D.; Siqueland, Einar R.; Jusczyk, Peter W.; & Vigorito, James. 1971. Speech perception in infants. *Science* 209, 1140–1141.

Eisenberg, Ann R., & Garvey, Catherine. 1981. Children's use of verbal strategies in resolving conflicts. *Discourse Processes* 4, 149–170.

Elbers, Loekie. 1982. Operating principles of repetitive babbling: A cognitive continuity approach. *Cognition* 12, 45–63.

Elbers, Loekie, & Ton, Josi. 1985. Play pen monologues: The interplay of words and babbles in the first words period. *Journal of Child Language* 12, 551–565.

Elbers, Loekie, & Wijnen, Frank. 1992. Effort, production skill, and language learning. In C. A. Ferguson, L. Menn, & C. Stoel-Gammon (eds.), *Phonological development: Models, research, implications* (337–368). Timonium, MD: York Press.

Elkonin, D. B. 1971. Development of speech. In A. V. Zaporozhets & D. B. Elkonin (eds.), *The psychology of pre-school children* (111–185). Cambridge, MA: MIT Press.

Elman, Jeffrey L. 1993. Learning and development in neural networks: The importance of starting small. *Cognition* 48, 71–99.

Elman, Jeffrey L.; Bates, Elizabeth A.; Johnson, Mark H.; Karmiloff-Smith, Annette; Parisi, Domenico; & Plunkett, Kim. 1996. *Rethinking innateness: A connectionist perspective on development*. Cambridge, MA: MIT Press.

Elsen, Hilke. 1994. Phonological constraints and overextensions. *First Language* 14, 305–315.

Elsen, Hilke. 1997. The acquisition of past participles: One or two mechanisms? In A. Tabri, A. Orfmann, & T. Paredi (eds.), *Models of inflection* (134–151). Tübingen: Niemeyer.

Engel, Stephen A.; Rumelhart, David E.; Wandell, Brian A.; Lee, Adrian T.; Glover, Gary H.; Chichilnisky, Eduardo-José; & Shadlen, Michael N. 1994. FMRI of human visual cortex. *Nature* 369, 525.

Erbaugh, Mary S. 1992. The acquisition of Mandarin. In D. I. Slobin (ed.), *The crosslinguistic study of language acquisition*, vol. III (373–455). Hillsdale, NJ: Lawrence Erlbaum.

Ervin, Susan. 1964. Imitation and structural change in children's language. In E. H. Lenneberg (ed.), *New directions in the study of language* (163–189). Cambridge, MA: MIT Press.

Ervin-Tripp, Susan. 1970. Discourse agreement: How children answer questions. In J. R. Hayes (ed.), *Cognition and the development of language* (79–107). New York: Wiley.

Ervin-Tripp, Susan. 1973. Some strategies for the first two years. In T. E. Moore (ed.), *Cognitive development and the acquisition of language* (261–286). New York: Academic Press.

Ervin-Tripp, Susan. 1974. The comprehension and production of requests by children. *Papers & Reports on Child Language Development* [Stanford University] 8, 188–195.

Ervin-Tripp, Susan. 1979. Children's verbal turn-taking. In E. Ochs & B. B. Schieffelin (eds.), *Developmental pragmatics* (391–414). New York: Academic Press.

Ervin-Tripp, Susan; Guo, Jiansheng; & Lampert, Martin. 1990. Politeness and persuasion in children's control acts. *Journal of Pragmatics* 14, 307–331.

Estes, Katharine G.; Evans, Julia L.; Alibabli, Martha W.; & Saffran, Jenny R. 2007. Can infants map meaning to newly segmented words? *Psychological Science* 18, 254–260.

Estigarribia, Bruno. 2007. Asking questions: Language variation and language acquisition. PhD dissertation, Stanford University.

Estigarribia, Bruno, & Clark, Eve V. 2007. Getting and maintaining attention in talk to young children. *Journal of Child Language* 34, 799–814.

Evans, Gary W.; Maxwell, Lorraine E.; & Hart, Betty. 1999. Parental language and verbal responsiveness to children in crowded homes. *Developmental Psychology* 35, 1020–1023.

Fabbro, Franco. 2001. The bilingual brain: Cerebral representation of languages. *Brain & Language* 79, 211–222.

Fantini, Alvino E. 1985. *Language acquisition of a bilingual child: A sociolinguistic perspective*. San Diego, CA: College-Hill Press.

Felix, Sascha. 1988. Universal Grammar in language acquisition. *Canadian Journal of Linguistics* 33, 367–393.

Fenson, Larry; Dale, Philip S.; Reznick, J. Steven; Bates, Elizabeth; Thal, Donna J.; & Pethick, Steven J. 1994. Variability in early communicative development. *Monographs of the Society for Research in Child Development* 59 (serial no. 242).

Ferguson, Charles A. 1977. Baby talk as a simplified register. In C. E. Snow & C. A. Ferguson (eds.), *Talking to children: Language input and acquisition* (209–235). Cambridge: Cambridge University Press.

Ferguson, Charles A. 1978. Learning to pronounce: The earliest stages of phonological development in the child. In F. D. Minifie & L. L. Lloyd (eds.), *Communicative and cognitive abilities: Early behavioral assessment* (273–297). Baltimore, MD: University Park Press.

Ferguson, Charles A. 1994. Dialect, register, and genre: Working assumptions about conventionalization. In D. Biber & E. Finegan (eds.), *Sociolinguistic perspectives on register* (15–30). Oxford: Oxford University Press.

Ferguson, Charles A., & Farwell, Carol B. 1975. Words and sounds in early language acquisition. *Language* 51, 419–439.

Ferguson, Charles A.; Peizer, David B.; & Weeks, Thelma E. 1973. Model-and-replica phonological grammar of a child's first words. *Lingua* 31, 35–65.

Ferguson, Charles A., & Slobin, Dan I. (eds.). 1973. *Studies of child language development*. New York: Holt Rinehart & Winston.

Fernald, Anne. 1985. Four-month-old infants prefer to listen to motherese. *Infant Behavior & Development* 8, 181–195.

Fernald, Anne. 1989. Intonation and communicative intent in mothers' speech to infants: Is the melody the message? *Child Development* 60, 1497–1510.

Fernald, Anne. 1992. Meaningful melodies in mothers' speech to infants. In H. Papousek, U. Jürgens, & M. Papousek (eds.), *Nonverbal communication: Comparative and developmental approaches* (262–282). Cambridge: Cambridge University Press.

Fernald, Anne, & Hurtado, Nereyda. 2006. Names in frames: infants interpret words in sentence frames faster than words in isolation. *Developmental Science* 9, F33–F40.

Fernald, Anne, & Kuhl, Patricia K. 1987. Acoustic determinants of infant preference for motherese speech. *Infant Behavior & Development* 10, 279–293.

Fernald, Anne, & Mazzie, Claudia. 1991. Prosody and focus in speech to infants and adults. *Developmental Psychology* 27, 209–221.

Fernald, Anne; Perfors, Amy; & Marchman, Virginia A. 2006. Picking up speed in understanding: Speech processing efficiency and vocabulary growth across the 2nd year. *Developmental Psychology* 42, 98–116.

Fernald, Anne, & Simon, Thomas. 1984. Expanded intonation contours in mothers' speech to newborns. *Developmental Psychology* 20, 104–113.

Fernald, Anne; Taeschner, Traute; Dunn, Judy; Papousek, Mechthild; de Boysson-Bardies, Benedicte; & Fukui, Ikuko. 1989. A cross-language study of prosodic modifications in mothers' and fathers' speech to preverbal infants. *Journal of Child Language* 16, 477–501.

Ferreiro, Emilia. 1971. *Les relations temporelles dans le langage de l'enfant*. Geneva: Droz.

Ferrier, Linda J. 1978. Some observations of error in context. In N. Waterson & C. Snow (eds.), *The development of communication* (301–309). New York: Wiley.

Figueira, Rosa Attié. 1984. On the development of the expression of causativity: A syntactic hypothesis. *Journal of Child Language* 11, 109–127.

Fikkert, Paula. 1994. *On the acquisition of prosodic structure*. Leiden: Holland Institute of Linguistics.

Fillmore, Charles J. 1968. The case for case. In E. Bach & R. T. Harms (eds.), *Universals of linguistic theory* (1–90). New York: Holt, Rinehart & Winston.

Fillmore, Charles J. 1979. On fluency. In C. J. Fillmore, D. Kempler, & W. S.-Y. Wang (eds.), *Individual differences in language ability and language behavior* (85–101). New York: Academic Press.

Fisher, Cynthia. 1996. Structural limits on verb mapping: The role of analogy in children's interpretations of sentences. *Cognitive Psychology* 31, 41–81.

Fisher, Cynthia; Klingler, Stacy L.; & Song, Hyun-joo. 2006. What does syntax say about space? 2-year-olds use sentence structure to learn new prepositions. *Cognition* 101, B19–B29.

Fisher, Cynthia, & Tokura, Hisayo. 1995. The given-new contract in speech to infants. *Journal of Memory & Language* 34, 287–310.

Fishman, Joshua A. 1971. Sociolinguistic perspective on the study of bilingualism. In J. A. Fishman, R. L. Cooper, & R. Ma (eds.), *Bilingualism in the barrio* (3–10). Bloomington: Indiana University Press.

Fletcher, Paul. 1985. *A child's learning of English*. Oxford: Blackwell.

Flynn, Valerie, & Masur, Elise F. 2007. Characteristics of maternal verbal style: Responsiveness and directiveness in two natural contexts. *Journal of Child Language* 34, 519–543.

Fonagy, Ivan. 1972. A propos de la génèse de la phrase enfantine. *Lingua* 30, 31–71.

Forrester, Michael A. 1988. Young children's polyadic conversation monitoring skills. *First Language* 7, 145–158.

Foulkes, Paul; Docherty, Gerry J.; & Watt, Dominic. 2005. Phonological variation in child-directed speech. *Language* 81, 177–206.

Fourcin, Adrian J. 1975. Speech perception in the absence of speech productive ability. In N. O'Connor (ed.), *Language, cognitive deficits, and retardation* (33–43). London: Butterworth.

Fowler, Carol A. 1988. Differential shortening of repeated content words produced in various communicative contexts. *Language & Speech* 31, 307–319.

Fowler, Carol A., & Housum, Jonathan. 1987. Talkers' signaling of "new" and "old" words in speech and listeners' perception and use of the distinction. *Journal of Memory & Language* 26, 489–504.

Franco, Fabia, & Butterworth, George. 1996. Pointing and social awareness: Declaring and requesting in the second year. *Journal of Child Language* 23, 307–336.

French, Lucia A., & Nelson, Katherine. 1981. Temporal knowledge expressed in preschoolers' descriptions of familiar activities. *Papers & Reports on Child Language Development* [Stanford University] 20, 61–69.

Friederici, Angelika D., & Wessels, Jeanine M. I. 1993. Phonotactic knowledge of word boundaries and its use in infant speech-perception. *Perception & Psychophysics* 54, 287–295.

Friedrich, Manuela, & Friederici, Angela D. 2005. Phonotactic knowledge and lexical–semantic processing in one-year-olds: Brain responses to words and nonsense words in picture contexts. *Journal of Cognitive Neuroscience* 17, 1785–1802.

Fromkin, Victoria. 1971. The non-anomalous nature of anomalous utterances. *Language* 47, 27–52.

Galantucci, Bruno. 2005. An experimental study of the emergence of human communication systems. *Cognitive Science* 29, 737–767.

Galati, Alexia, & Brennan, Susan E. (2006). Given-new attenuation effects in spoken discourse: For the speaker, or for the addressee? Abstracts of the Psychonomic Society, 47th annual meeting, Dallas, TX.

Gallagher, Tanya M. 1977. Revision behaviors in the speech of normal children developing language. *Journal of Speech & Hearing Research* 20, 303–318.

Ganea, Patricia A., & Saylor, Megan M. 2007. Infants' use of shared linguistic information to clarify ambiguous requests. *Child Development* 78, 493–502.

Garnica, Olga K. 1973. The development of phonemic speech perception. In T. E. Moore (ed.), *Cognitive development and the acquisition of language* (215–222). New York: Academic Press.

Garnica, Olga K. 1977. Some prosodic and paralinguistic features of speech to children. In C. E. Snow & C. A. Ferguson (eds.), *Talking to children: Language input and acquisition* (63–88). Cambridge: Cambridge University Press.

Garrett, Merrill F. 1975. The analysis of sentence production. In G. H. Bower (ed.), *The psychology of learning and motivation*, vol. IX (133–177). New York: Academic Press.

Garvey, Catherine. 1975. Requests and responses in children's speech. *Journal of Child Language* 2, 41–63.

Garvey, Catherine. 1977. Play with language. In B. Tizard & D. Harvey (eds.), *Biology of play* (74–99). London: Heinemann.

Garvey, Catherine. 1979. Contingent queries and their relations in discourse. In E. Ochs & B. B. Schiefflin (eds.), *Developmental pragmatics* (363–372). New York: Academic Press.

Garvey, Catherine. 1984. *Children's talk*. Cambridge, MA: Harvard University Press.

Gathercole, Virginia C. Mueller; Sebastián, Eugenia; & Soto, Pilar. 1999. The early acquisition of Spanish verbal morphology: Across-the-board or piecemeal knowledge? *International Journal of Bilingualism* 3, 133–182.

Gelman, Susan A., & Coley, John D. 1990. The importance of knowing a dodo is a bird: Categories and inferences in two-year-olds. *Developmental Psychology* 26, 796–804.

Gelman, Susan A.; Coley, John D.; Rosengren, Karl S.; Hartman, Erin; & Pappas, Athina. 1998a. Beyond labeling: The role of maternal input in the acquisition of richly structured categories. *Monographs of the Society for Research in Child Development* 63 (serial no. 253).

Gelman, Susan A.; Croft, William; Fu, Panfang; Clausner, Timothy C.; & Gottfried, Gail. 1998b. Why is a pomegranate an *apple?* The role of shape, taxonomic relatedness, and prior lexical knowledge in children's overextensions. *Journal of Child Language* 25, 267–291.

Gelman, Susan A., & Eveling, Karen S. 1998. Shape and representational status in children's early naming. *Cognition* 66, B35–B47.

Gelman, Susan A., & Tardif, Twila. 1998. Acquisition of nouns and verbs in Mandarin and English. In E. V. Clark (ed.), *Proceedings of the 29th annual Child Language Research Forum 1997* (27–36). Stanford, CA: CSLI.

Gelman, Susan A., & Taylor, Marjorie. 1984. How two-year-old children interpret proper and common names for unfamiliar objects. *Child Development* 55, 1535–1540.

Genesee, Fred. 1989. Early bilingual development: One language or two? *Journal of Child Language* 16, 161–179.

Genesee, Fred. 2006. Bilingual first language acquisition in perspective. In P. McCardle & E. Hoff (eds.), *Childhood bilingualism* (45–67). Clevedon, UK: Multilingual Matters.

Genesee, Fred; Boivin, Isabelle; & Nicoladis, Elena. 1996. Talking with strangers: A study of bilingual children's communicative competence. *Applied Psycholinguistics* 17, 427–442.

Genesee, Fred; Nicoladis, Elena; & Paradis, Johanne. 1995. Language differentiation in early bilingual development. *Journal of Child Language* 22, 611–631.

Genesee, Fred; Tucker, G. Richard; & Lambert, Wallace E. 1976. Communication skills of bilingual children. *Child Development* 46, 1010–1014.

Gentner, Dedre. 1982. Why nouns are learned before verbs: Linguistic relativity versus natural partitioning. In S. A. Kuczaj (ed.), *Language development,* vol. II: *Language, thought, and culture* (301–334). Hillsdale, NJ: Lawrence Erlbaum.

Gentner, Dedre, & Boroditsky, Lera. 2001. Individuation, relativity and early word learning. In M. Bowerman & S. C. Levinson (eds.), *Language acquisition and conceptual development* (215–256). Cambridge: Cambridge University Press.

Gentner, Dedre, & Medina, José. 1998. Similarity and the development of rules. *Cognition* 65, 263–297.

Gergely, György; Bekkering, Harold; & Király, Ildikó. 2002. Rational imitation in preverbal infants. *Nature* 415, 755 (14 February 2002).

Gergely, György, & Csibra, Gergely. 2003. Teleological reasoning in infancy: The naïve theory of rational action. *Trends in Cognitive Sciences* 7, 287–292.

Gerken, LouAnn. 1991. The metrical basis of children's subjectless sentences. *Journal of Memory & Language* 30, 431–451.

Gerken, LouAnn. 1994a. A metrical template account of children's weak syllable omissions from multisyllabic words. *Journal of Child Language* 21, 565–584.

Gerken, LouAnn. 1994b. Young children's representations of prosodic phonology: Evidence from English-speakers' weak syllable productions. *Journal of Memory & Language* 33, 19–38.

Gerken, LouAnn. 1996. Prosodic structure in young children's language production. *Language* 72, 683–712.

Gerken, LouAnn; Landau, Barbara; & Remez, Robert E. 1990. Function morphemes in young children's speech perception and production. *Developmental Psychology* 26, 204–216.

Gerken, LouAnn, & McIntosh, Bonnie J. 1993. The interplay of function morphemes and prosody in early language. *Developmental Psychology* 29, 448–457.

Geschwind, Norman, & Levitsky, Walter. 1968. Human brain: Left-right asymmetries in temporal speech region. *Science* 161, 186–187.

Gesell, Arnold, & Thompson, Helen. 1934. *Infant behavior: Its genesis and growth.* New York: McGraw-Hill.

Giles, Howard; Coupland, Nikolas; & Coupland, Justine (eds.). 1991. *Contexts of accommodation: Developments in applied sociolinguistics.* Cambridge: Cambridge University Press.

Givón, Talmy. 1979. *Understanding grammar.* New York: Academic Press.

Gleitman, Lila R. 1981. Maturational determinants of language growth. *Cognition* 10, 103–114.

Gleitman, Lila R. 1990. The structural sources of verb meanings. *Language Acquisition* 1, 3–55.

Goffman, Lisa; Schwartz, Richard G.; & Marton, Klara. 1996. Information level and young children's phonological accuracy. *Journal of Child Language* 23, 337–347.

Gogate, Lakshmi J.; Bahrick, Lorraine E.; & Watson, Jilayne D. 2000. A study of multimodal motherese: The role of temporal synchrony between verbal labels and gestures. *Child Development* 71, 878–894.

Goldberg, Adele E. 1995. *Constructions: A construction grammar approach to argument structure.* Chicago: University of Chicago Press.

Goldberg, Adele E. 1999. The emergence of the semantics of argument structure constructions. In B. MacWhinney (ed.), *The emergence of language* (197–212). Mahwah, NJ: Lawrence Erlbaum.

Goldfield, Beverly A., & Reznick, J. Steven. 1990. Early lexical acquisition: Rate, content, and the vocabulary spurt. *Journal of Child Language* 17, 171–183.

Goldfield, Beverly A., & Reznick, J. Steven. 1992. Rapid change in lexical development in comprehension and production. *Developmental Psychology* 28, 406–413.

Goldfield, Beverly A., & Reznick, J. Steven. 1996. Measuring the vocabulary spurt: A reply to Mervis & Bertrand. *Journal of Child Language* 23, 241–246.

Goldin-Meadow, Susan; Goodrich, Whitney; Sauer, Eve; & Iverson, Jana. 2007. Young children use their hands to tell their mothers what to say. *Developmental Science* 10, 778–785.

Goldin-Meadow, Susan; Seligman, Martin E. P.; & Gelman, Rochel. 1976. Language in the two-year-old. *Cognition* 4, 189–202.

Goldwater, Sharon; Griffiths, Thomas L.; & Johnson, Mark. 2006. Contextual dependencies in unsupervised word segmentation. *Proceedings of the 21st International Conference on Computational Linguistics and the 44th annual meeting of the Association for Computational Linguistics* (673–680), Sydney, Australia.

Golinkoff, Roberta M. 1983. The preverbal negotiation of failed messages: Insights into the transition period. In R. M. Golinkoff (ed.), *The transition from prelinguistic to linguistic communication* (57–78). Hillsdale, NJ: Lawrence Erlbaum.

Golinkoff, Roberta M. 1986. "I beg your pardon?": The preverbal negotiation of failed messages. *Journal of Child Language* 13, 455–476.

Golinkoff, Roberta M.; Mervis, Carolyn B.; & Hirsh-Pasek, Kathryn. 1994. Early object labels: A case for a developmental lexical principles framework. *Journal of Child Language* 21, 125–155.

Goodman, Judith C.; McDonough, Laraine; & Brown, Natasha B. 1998. The role of semantic context and memory in the acquisition of novel nouns. *Child Development* 69, 1330–1344.

Goodwin, Marjorie H. 1990. *He-said-she-said: Talk as social organization among black children*. Bloomington: Indiana University Press.

Goodwin, Marjorie H. 1993. Tactical uses of stories: Participation frameworks within boys' and girls' disputes. In D. Tannen (ed.), *Gender and conversational interaction* (110–143). Oxford: Oxford University Press.

Goodwyn, Susan W., & Acredolo, Linda P. 1993. Symbolic gesture vs. word: Is there a modality advantage for onset of symbol use? *Child Development* 55, 903–910.

Gordon, Raymond G. (ed.). 2005. *Ethnologue: Languages of the world* (15th edn). Dallas, TX: SIL International.

Grassmann, Susanne, & Tomasello, Michael. 2007. Two-year-olds use primary sentence accent to learn new words. *Journal of Child Language* 34, 677–687.

Greenberg, Joseph H. (ed.). 1963. *Universals of language*. Cambridge, MA: MIT Press.

Greenberg, Joseph H. 1966. *Language universals*. The Hague: Mouton.

Greenfield, Patricia M. 1979. Informativeness, presupposition, and semantic choice in single-word utterances. In E. Ochs & B. B. Schiefflin (eds.), *Developmental pragmatics* (159–166). New York: Academic Press.

Greenfield, Patricia M., & Smith, Joshua. 1976. *The structure of communication in early language development*. New York: Academic Press.

Grégoire, Antoine. 1939, 1947. *L'apprentissage du langage*, 2 vols. Liège: Librairie Droz.

Grevisse, Maurice. 1964. *Le bon usage: Grammaire française avec des remarques sur la langue française d'aujourd'hui* (8th edn). Paris: Hatier.

Grice, H. Paul. 1989. *Studies in the way of words*. Cambridge, MA: Harvard University Press.

Grieser, DiAnne L., & Kuhl, Patricia K. 1988. Maternal speech to infants in a tonal language: Support for universal prosodic features. *Developmental Psychology* 24, 14–20.

Grieve, Robert; Hoogenraad, Robert; & Murray, Diarmid. 1977. On the young child's use of lexis and syntax in understanding locative instructions. *Cognition* 5, 235–250.

Griffiths, Patrick D., & Atkinson, Martin. 1978. A 'door' to verbs. In N. Waterson & C. Snow (eds.), *The development of communication* (311–319). London: Wiley.

Griffiths, Thomas L., & Kalish, Michael L. 2007. Language evolution by iterated learning with Bayesian agents. *Cognitive Science* 31, 441–480.

Grimm, Hannelore. 1973. *Strukturanalytische Untersuchung der Kindersprache*. Bern: Verlag Huber.

Grimm, Hannelore. 1975. Analysis of short-term dialogues in 5–7 year olds: Encoding of intentions and modifications of speech acts as a function of negative feedback. Paper presented at the Third International Child Language Symposium, London.

Grimm, Hannelore, & Schöler, Hans. 1975. Erlauben–befehlen–lassen: Wie gut verstehen kleine Kindere kausativierende Beziehungen? In H. Grimm, H. Schöler, & M. Wintermentel, *Zur Entwicklung sprachlicher Strukturformen bein Kindern* (100–120). Weinheim: Beltz.

Grimshaw, Jane. 1981. Form, function, and the language acquisition device. In C. L. Baker & J. J. McCarthy (eds.), *The logical problem of language acquisition* (165–182). Cambridge, MA: MIT Press.

Gropen, Jess; Pinker, Steven; Hollander, Michelle; & Goldberg, Richard. 1991. Syntax and semantics in the acquisition of locative verbs. *Journal of Child Language* 18, 115–151.

Grosjean, François. 1982. *Life with two languages*. Cambridge, MA: Harvard University Press.

Grosjean, François. 1989. Neurolinguists, beware! The bilingual is not two monolinguals in one person. *Brain & Language* 36, 3–15.

Gross, Maurice. 1975. On the relations between syntax and semantics. In E. L. Keenan (ed.), *Formal semantics of natural language* (389–405). Cambridge: Cambridge University Press.

Gruber, Jeffrey S. 1973. Correlations between the syntactic constructions of the child and the adult. In C. A. Ferguson & D. I. Slobin (eds.), *Studies of child language development* (440–445). New York: Holt Rinehart & Winston.

Guerriero, A. M. Sonia; Oshima-Takane, Yuriko; & Kuriyama, Yoko. 2006. The development of referential choice in English and Japanese: A discourse-pragmatic perspective. *Journal of Child Language* 33, 823–857.

Guidetti, Michèle. 2002. The emergence of pragmatics: Forms and functions of conventional gestures in young French children. *First Language* 22, 265–285.

Guillaume, Paul. 1927. Le développement des éléments formels dans le langage de l'enfant. *Journal de Psychologie* 24, 203–229.

Gumperz, John J. 1982. *Discourse strategies*. Cambridge: Cambridge University Press.

Gvozdev, Alexandr N. 1961. *Voprosy izucheniya detskoy rechi* [The development of language in children]. Moscow: Akademii Pedagogicheskikh Nauk RSFSR.

Haiman, John (ed.). 1985. *Iconicity in syntax*. Amsterdam: John Benjamins.

Hakuta, Kenji. 1981. Grammatical description versus configurational arrangement in language acquisition – The case of relative clauses in Japanese. *Cognition* 9, 197–236.

Hakuta, Kenji. 1986. *Mirror of language: The debate on bilingualism*. New York: Basic Books.

Hakuta, Kenji, & D'Andrea, Daniel. 1992. Some properties of bilingual maintenance and loss in Mexican background high-school students. *Applied Psycholinguistics* 13, 72–99.

Hall, D. Geoffrey, & Graham, Susan A. 1999. Lexical form class information guides word-to-object mapping in preschoolers. *Child Development* 70, 78–91.

Hall, D. Geoffrey; Quantz, Darryl H.; & Persoage, Kelley A. 2000. Preschoolers' use of form class cues in word learning. *Developmental Psychology* 36, 449–462.

Halle, Tamara, & Shatz, Marilyn. 1994. Mothers' social regulatory language to young children in family settings. *First Language* 14, 83–104.

Halliday, Michael A. K. 1975. *Learning how to mean – Explorations in the development of language*. London: Edward Arnold.

Hare, Mary, & Elman, Jeffrey L. 1995. Learning and morphological change. *Cognition* 56, 61–98.

Harris, Catherine L., & Shirai, Yasuhiro. 1997. Selecting past-tense forms for new words: What's meaning got to do with it? In *Proceedings of the 19th annual conference of the Cognitive Science Society* (295–300). Mahwah, NJ: Lawrence Erlbaum.

Harris, Margaret; Barlow-Brown, Fiona; & Chasin, Joan. 1995. The emergence of referential understanding: Pointing and the comprehension of object names. *First Language* 15, 19–34.

Harris, Margaret; Jones, David; & Grant, Julia. 1984/1985. The social-interactional context of maternal speech to infants: An explanation for the event-bound nature of early word use? *First Language* 5, 89–100.

Harris, Margaret; Yeeles, Caroline; Chasin, Joan; & Oakley, Yvonne. 1995. Symmetries and asymmetries in early lexical comprehension and production. *Journal of Child Language* 22, 1–18.

Harris, Paul L.; German, Tim; & Mills, Patrick. 1996. Children's use of counterfactual thinking in causal reasoning. *Cognition* 61, 233–259.

Harris, Zellig S. 1955. From phoneme to morpheme. *Language* 31, 190–222.

Hart, Betty, & Risley, Todd R. 1992. American parenting of language-learning children: Persisting differences in family-child interactions observed in natural home environments. *Developmental Psychology* 28, 1096–1105.

Hart, Betty, & Risley, Todd R. 1995. *Meaningful differences in the everyday experience of young American children*. Baltimore, MD: H. Paul Brookes.

Haryu, Etsuko, & Imai, Mutsumi. 2002. Reorganizing the lexicon by learning a new word: Japanese children's interpretations of the meaning of a new word for a familiar artifact. *Child Development* 73, 1378–1391.

Haviland, Susan E., & Clark, Eve V. 1974. "This man's father is my father's son": A study of the acquisition of English kin terms. *Journal of Child Language* 1, 23–47.

Hawkins, John A. (ed.). 1988. *Explaining language universals*. Cambridge: Cambridge University Press.

Hayes, J. Richard, & Clark, Herbert H. 1970. Experiments on the segmentation of an artificial speech analogue. In J. R. Hayes (ed.), *Cognition and the development of language* (221–234). New York: Wiley.

Heath, Shirley Brice. 1983. *Ways with words*. Cambridge: Cambridge University Press.

Hecht, Barbara F. 1983. Situations and language: Children's use of plural allomorphs in familiar and unfamiliar settings. PhD dissertation, Stanford University.

Heibeck, Tracy H., & Markman, Ellen M. 1987. Word learning in children: An examination of fast mapping. *Child Development* 58, 1021–1034.

Hemsley, Gayle; Holm, Alison; & Dodd, Barbara. 2006. Diverse but not different: The lexical skills of two primary age bilingual groups in comparison to monolingual peers. *International Journal of Bilingualism* 10, 453–476.

Hickmann, Maya. 1991. The development of discourse cohesion: Some functional and cross-linguistic issues. In G. Piéraut-Le-Bonniec & M. Dolitsky (eds.), *Language bases, discourse bases: Some aspects of contemporary French-language psycholinguistics research* (157–185). Amsterdam: John Benjamins.

Hickmann, Maya, & Hendriks, Henriëtte. 1999. Cohesion and anaphora in children's narratives: A comparison of English, French, German, and Mandarin Chinese. *Journal of Child Language* 26, 419–452.

Hirsh-Pasek, Kathryn; Kemler Nelson, Deborah G.; Jusczyk, Peter W.; Cassidy, Kimberly W.; Druss, Benjamin; & Kennedy, Lori. 1987. Clauses are perceptual units for young infants. *Cognition* 26, 269–286.

Hirsh-Pasek, Kathryn; Treiman, Rebecca; & Schneiderman, Maita. 1984. Brown & Hanlon revisited: Mothers' sensitivity to ungrammatical forms. *Journal of Child Language* 11, 81–88.

Hochberg, Judith G. 1986. Children's judgments of transitivity errors. *Journal of Child Language* 13, 317–334.

Hoff, Erika. 2006. How social contexts support and shape language development. *Developmental Review* 26, 55–88.

Hoff-Ginsberg, Erika. 1991. Mother-child conversation in different social classes and communicative settings. *Child Development* 62, 782–796.

Hoff-Ginsberg, Erika. 1998. The relation of birth order and socioeconomic status to children's language experience and language development. *Applied Psycholinguistics* 19, 603–629.

Hoff-Ginsberg, Erika, & Tardif, Twila. 1995. Socioeconomic status and parenting. In M. H. Bornstein (ed.), *Handbook of parenting*, vol. II: *Ecology and biology of parenting* (161–188). Mahwah, NJ: Lawrence Erlbaum.

Hoffman, Eva. 1989. *Lost in translation: A life in a new language*. Harmondsworth, Middlesex: Penguin Books.

Hollich, George; Jusczyk, Peter W.; & Luce, Paul A. 2001. Lexical neighborhood effects on 17-month-old word learning. *Proceedings of the 26th annual Boston University Conference on Language Development* (314–323). Boston, MA: Cascadilla Press.

Hollos, Marida, & Beeman, William. 1978. The development of directives among Norwegian and Hungarian children: An example of communicative style in culture. *Language in Society* 7, 345–355.

Holowka, Siobhan; Brosseau-Lapré, Françoise; & Petitto, Laura. 2002. Semantic and conceptual knowledge underlying bilingual babies' first signs and words. *Language Learning* 52, 205–262.

Hood, Bruce M.; Willen, J. Douglas; & Driver, Jon. 1998. Adults' eyes trigger shifts of visual attention in human infants. *Psychological Science* 9, 131–134.

Hood, Lois, & Bloom, Lois. 1979. What, when, and how about why: A longitudinal study of early expressions of causality. *Monographs of the Society for Research in Child Development* 44 (serial no. 181).

Hopper, Paul J., & Thompson, Sandra A. 1980. Transitivity in grammar and discourse. *Language* 56, 251–299.

Horgan, Dianne. 1978. The development of the full passive. *Journal of Child Language* 5, 65–80.

Horn, Laurence R. 1988. Morphology, pragmatics, and the *un-* verb. In J. Powers & K. de Jong (eds.), *Proceedings of the 5th Eastern States Conference on Linguistics*. Columbus: Department of Linguistics, Ohio State University.

Hornby, Peter A. 1971. Surface structure and the topic-comment distinction: A developmental study. *Child Development* 42, 1975–1988.

Hornby, Peter A., & Hass, Wilbur A. 1970. Use of contrastive stress by preschool children. *Journal of Speech & Hearing Research* 13, 395–399.

Hornstein, Norbert, & Lightfoot, David. 1981. Introduction. In *Explanation in linguistics: The logical problem of language acquisition* (9–31). London: Longman.

Horowitz, Frances D. (ed.). 1974. Visual attention, auditory stimulation, and language discrimination in young infants. *Monographs of the Society for Research in Child Development* 39 (serial no. 158).

Hubel, David, & Wiesel, Torsten. 1970. The period of susceptibility to the physiological effects of unilateral eye closure in kittens. *Journal of Physiology* 206, 419–436.

Hulk, Aafke, & Müller, Natascha. 2000. Bilingual first language acquisition at the interface between syntax and pragmatics. *Bilingualism: Language & Cognition* 3, 227–244.

Huttenlocher, Janellen; Haight, Wendy; Bryk, Anthony; Seltzer, Michael; & Lyons, Thomas. 1991. Early vocabulary growth: Relation to language input and gender. *Developmental Psychology* 17, 236–248.

Huttenlocher, Janellen, & Smiley, Patricia. 1987. Early word meanings: The case of object names. *Cognitive Psychology* 19, 63–89.

Huttenlocher, Janellen; Smiley, Patricia; & Charney, Rosalind. 1983. Emergence of action categories in the child: Evidence from verb meanings. *Psychological Review* 90, 72–93.

Hyams, Nina. 1986. *Language acquisition and the theory of parameters*. Dordrecht: Reidel.

Imai, Mutsumi; Haryu, Etsuko; & Okada, Hiroyuki. 2005. Mapping novel nouns and verbs onto dynamic action events: Are verb meanings easier to learn than noun meanings for Japanese children? *Child Development* 76, 340–355.

Ingham, Richard. 1992. The optional subject phenomenon in young children's English: A case study. *Journal of Child Language* 19, 133–151.

Ingham, Richard. 1998. Tense without agreement in early clause structure. *Language Acquisition* 7, 51–81.

Ingram, David. 1971. Transitivity in child language. *Language* 47, 888–910.

Ingram, David. 1974. Phonological rules in young children. *Journal of Child Language* 1, 49–64.

Itard, Jean M. G. 1801. *De l'education d'un homme sauvage ou des premiers développements physiques et moraux du jeune sauvage d'Aveyron*. Paris: Gouyon.

(Translated into English: G. Humphrey & M. Humphrey. 1932. *The wild boy of Aveyron.* New York: Appleton-Century-Crofts.)

Iverson, Jana M. 1999. How to get to the cafeteria: Gesture and speech in blind and sighted children's spatial description. *Developmental Psychology* 35, 1132–1142.

Iverson, Jana M.; Capirci, Olga; & Caselli, M. Cristina. 1994. From communication to language in two modalities. *Cognitive Development* 9, 23–43.

Iverson, Jana M.; Capirci, Olga; Longobardi, Emiddia; & Caselli, M. Cristina. 1999. Gesturing in mother-child interactions. *Cognitive Development* 14, 57–75.

Iverson, Jana M., & Goldin-Meadow, Susan. 2005. Gesture paves the way for language development. *Psychological Science* 16, 368–371.

Jackendoff, Ray S. 1983. *Semantics and cognition.* Cambridge, MA: MIT Press.

Jakobson, Roman. 1968. *Child language, aphasia, and phonological universals.* The Hague: Mouton. (Originally published in German, 1941.)

James, Sharon L. 1978. Effect of listeners' age and situation on the politeness of children's directives. *Journal of Psycholinguistic Research* 4, 307–317.

Jaswal, Vikram K., & Malone, Lauren S. 2007. Turning believers into skeptics: 3-year-olds' sensitivity to cues to speaker credibility. *Journal of Cognition & Development* 8, 263–283.

Jefferson, Gail. 1982. On exposed and embedded correction in conversation. *Studium Linguisticum* 14, 58–68.

Jespersen, Otto. 1922. *Language: Its nature, development, and origin.* London: Allen & Unwin.

Jiang, Yang; Haxby, James V.; Martin, Alex; Ungerleider, Leslie G.; & Parasuraman, Raja. 2000. Complementary neural mechanisms for tracking items in human working memory. *Science* 287, 643–646.

Jisa, Harriet. 2000. Increasing cohesion in narratives: A developmental study of maintaining and reintroducing subjects in French. *Linguistics* 38, 591–620.

Johnson, Carolyn E. 1981. Children's questions and the discovery of interrogative syntax. PhD dissertation, Stanford University.

Johnson, Carolyn E. 1983. The development of children's interrogatives: From formulas to rules. *Papers & Reports on Child Language Development* [Stanford University] 22, 108–115.

Johnson, Carolyn E. 2000. What you see is what you get: The importance of transcription for interpreting children's morphosyntactic development. In L. Menn & N. Bernstein Ratner (eds.), *Methods for studying language production* (181–204). Mahwah, NJ: Lawrence Erlbaum.

Johnson, Helen L. 1975. The meaning of *before* and *after* for preschool children. *Journal of Experimental Child Psychology* 19, 88–99.

Johnson, Jacqueline S., & Newport, Elissa. 1989. Critical period effects in second language learning: The influence of maturational state on the acquisition of English as a second language. *Cognitive Psychology* 21, 60–99.

Johnson, Jacqueline S., & Newport, Elissa. 1991. Critical period effects on universal properties of language: The status of subjacency on the acquisition of a second language. *Cognition* 39, 215–258.

Johnson, Susan C., & Carey, Susan. 1998. Knowledge enrichment and conceptual change in folkbiology: Evidence from Williams syndrome. *Cognitive Psychology* 37, 156–200.

Johnston, Judith R., & Slobin, Dan I. 1979. The development of locative expressions in English, Italian, Serbo-Croatian and Turkish. *Journal of Child Language* 6, 529–545.

Jörg, Sabine, & Hörmann, Hans. 1978. The influence of general and specific verbal labels on the recognition of labeled and unlabeled parts of pictures. *Journal of Verbal Learning & Verbal Behavior* 17, 445–454.

Junker, Dörte A., & Stockman, Ida J. 2002. Expressive vocabulary of German-English bilingual toddlers. *American Journal of Speech-Language Pathology* 11, 381–394.

Jusczyk, Peter W. 1992. Developing phonological categories from the speech signal. In C. A. Ferguson, L. Menn, & C. Stoel-Gammon (eds.), *Phonological development: Models, research, implications* (17–64). Parkton, MD: York Press.

Jusczyk, Peter W. 1997. *The discovery of spoken language*. Cambridge, MA: MIT Press.

Jusczyk, Peter W., & Aslin, Richard N. 1995. Infants' detection of the sound patterns of words in fluent speech. *Cognitive Psychology* 29, 1–23.

Jusczyk, Peter W.; Cutler, Anne; & Redanz, Nancy J. 1993. Infants' preference for the predominant stress patterns of English words. *Child Development* 64, 675–687.

Jusczyk, Peter W.; Friederici, Angelika D.; Wessels, Jeanine M. I.; Svenkerud, Vigdis Y.; & Jusczyk, Ann M. 1993. Infants' sensitivity to segmental and prosodic characteristics of words in their native language. *Journal of Memory & Language* 32, 402–420.

Kaper, Willem. 1980. The use of the past tense in games of pretend. *Journal of Child Language* 7, 213–215.

Karmiloff-Smith, Annette. 1979. *A functional approach to child language: A study of determiners and reference*. Cambridge: Cambridge University Press.

Karmiloff-Smith, Annette. 1981. The grammatical marking of thematic structure in the development of language production. In W. Deutsch (ed.), *The child's construction of language* (121–147). New York and London: Academic Press.

Karmiloff-Smith, Annette. 1998. Is atypical development necessarily a window on the normal mind/brain? The case of Williams syndrome. *Developmental Science* 1, 273–277.

Karmiloff-Smith, Annette. 1999. Taking development seriously. *Human Development* 42, 325–327.

Karmiloff-Smith, Annette; Grant, Julia; Berthoud, Ioanna; Davies, Mark; Howlin, Patricia; & Udwin, Orlee. 1997. Language and Williams syndrome: How intact is "intact"? *Child Development* 68, 246–262.

Karmiloff-Smith, Annette; Tyler, Lorraine K.; Voice, J. Kate; Sims, Kerry; Udwin, Orlee; Howlin, Patricia; & Davies, Mark. 1998. Linguistic dissociations in Williams syndrome: Evaluating receptive syntax in on-line and off-line tasks. *Neuropsychologia* 36, 343–351.

Käsermann, Marie-Louise, & Foppa, Klaus. 1981. Some determinants of self-correction: An interactional study of Swiss-German. In W. Deutsch (ed.), *The child's construction of language* (77–104). London: Academic Press.

Katz, Nancy; Baker, Erica; & Macnamara, John. 1974. What's in a name? On the child's acquisition of proper and common names. *Child Development* 45, 269–273.

Kauschke, Christina; Lee, HaeWook; & Pae, Soyeong. 2007. Similarities and variation in noun and verb acquisition: A crosslinguistic study of children learning German, Korean, and Turkish. *Language & Cognitive Processes* 22, 1045–1072.

Keenan, Elinor O. 1974a. Norm-makers, norm-breakers: Uses of speech by men and women in a Malagasy community. In J. Baumann & J. Sherzer (eds.), *Explorations in the ethnography of speaking* (125–143). Cambridge: Cambridge University Press.

Keenan, Elinor O. 1974b. Conversational competence in children. *Journal of Child Language* 1, 163–183.

Keenan, Elinor O., & Klein, Ewan. 1975. Coherency in children's discourse. *Journal of Psycholinguistic Research* 4, 365–380.

Kehoe, Margaret, & Stoel-Gammon, Carol. 1997a. The acquisition of prosodic structure: An investigation of current accounts of children's prosodic development. *Language* 73, 113–144.

Kehoe, Margaret, & Stoel-Gammon, Carol. 1997b. Truncation patterns in English-speaking children's word productions. *Journal of Speech, Language, & Hearing Research* 40, 526–541.

Keller-Cohen, Deborah. 1987. Context and strategy in acquiring temporal connectives. *Journal of Psycholinguistic Research* 16, 165–183.

Kessel, Frank S. 1970. The role of syntax in children's comprehension from ages six to twelve. *Monographs of the Society for Research in Child Development* 35 (serial no. 139).

Ketrez, Fatma N., & Aksu-Koç, Ayhan. 2003. Acquisition of noun and verb categories in Turkish. In A. Sumru Özsoy, D. Akar, M. Nakipoglu-Demiralp, E. Erguvanlı Taylan, & A. Aksu-Koç (eds.), *Studies in Turkish linguistics* (239–246). Istanbul: Bogazici University Press.

Kim, John J.; Marcus, Gary F.; Pinker, Steven; Hollander, Michelle; & Coppola, Marie. 1994. Sensitivity of children's inflection to grammatical structure. *Journal of Child Language* 21, 173–209.

Kim, Mikyong; McGregor, Karla K.; & Thompson, Cynthia K. 2000. Early lexical development in English- and Korean-speaking children: Language-general and language-specific patterns. *Journal of Child Language* 27, 225–254.

Kiparsky, Paul, & Menn, Lise. 1977. On the acquisition of phonology. In J. Macnamara (ed.), *Language learning and thought* (47–78). New York: Academic Press.

Kirk, Cecilia, & Demuth, Katherine. 2005. Asymmetries in the acquisition of word-initial and word-final consonant clusters. *Journal of Child Language* 2, 709–734.

Kirk, Cecilia, & Demuth, Katherine. 2006. Accounting for variability in 2-year-olds' production of coda consonants. *Journal of Learning & Development* 2, 97–118.

Klatzky, Roberta L.; Clark, Eve V.; & Macken, Marlys M. 1973. Asymmetries in the acquisition of polar adjectives: Linguistic or conceptual? *Journal of Experimental Child Psychology* 16, 32–46.

Klibanoff, Raquel S., & Waxman, Sandra R. 1999. Syntactic cues to word meaning: Initial expectations and the development of flexibility. In A. Greenhill, H. Littlefield, & C. Tano (eds.), *Proceedings of the 23rd annual Boston University Conference on Language Development* (361–372). Somerville, MA: Cascadilla Press.

Klima, Edward S., & Bellugi, Ursula. 1966. Syntactic regularities in the speech of children. In J. Lyons & R. J. Wales (eds.), *Psycholinguistics papers* (183–208). Edinburgh: University of Edinburgh Press.

Kluender, Keith R.; Diehl, Randy L.; & Killeen, Peter R. 1987. Japanese quail can learn phonetic categories. *Science* 237, 1195–1197.

Koenig, Melissa A.; Clément, Fabrice; & Harris, Paul L. 2004. Trust in testimony: Children's use of true and false statements. *Psychological Science* 10, 694–698.

Koenig, Melissa A., & Echols, Catharine H. 2003. Infants' understanding of false labeling events: The referential roles of words and the speakers who use them. *Cognition* 87, 179–208.

Koenig, Melissa A., & Harris, Paul L. 2005. Preschoolers mistrust ignorant and inaccurate speakers. *Child Development* 76, 1261–1277.

Kohn, Bruno, & Dennis, Maureen. 1974. Selective impairments of visuo-spatial abilities in infantile hemiplegics after right cerebral hemidecortication. *Neuropsychologia* 12, 505–512.

Köpcke, Klaus-Michael. 1998. The acquisition of plural marking in English and German revisited: Schemata versus rules. *Journal of Child Language* 25, 293–319.

Kovac, Ceil, & Adamson, H. D. 1981. Variation theory and first language acquisition. In D. Sankoff & H. Cedergren (eds.), *Variation omnibus* (403–410). Edmonton, Alberta: Linguistic Research.

Kroodsma, Donald E., & Pickert, Roberta. 1980. Environmentally dependent sensitive periods for avian vocal learning. *Nature* 288, 477–479.

Krott, Andrea, & Nicoladis, Elena. 2005. Large constituent families help children parse compounds. *Journal of Child Language* 32, 139–158.

Kuczaj, Stan A., II. 1977. The acquisition of regular and irregular past tense forms. *Journal of Verbal Learning & Verbal Behavior* 16, 589–600.

Kuczaj, Stan A., II. 1978. Children's judgments of grammatical and ungrammatical irregular past tense verbs. *Child Development* 49, 319–326.

Kuczaj, Stan A., II. 1981. More on children's initial failures to relate specific acquisitions. *Journal of Child Language* 8, 485–487.

Kuczaj, Stan A., II. 1983. *Crib speech and language play.* Berlin: Springer-Verlag.

Kuczaj, Stan A., II, & Daly, Mary J. 1979. The development of hypothetical reference in the speech of young children. *Journal of Child Language* 6, 563–579.

Kuczaj, Stan A., II, & Maratsos, Michael P. 1975. On the acquisition of *front, back,* and *side. Child Development* 46, 202–210.

Kuczaj, Stan A., II, & Maratsos, Michael P. 1983. Initial verbs of yes-no questions: A different kind of grammatical category. *Developmental Psychology* 19, 440–444.

Kuhl, Patricia K. 1985. Methods in the study of infant speech perception. In G. Gottlieb & N. Krasnegor (eds.), *Measurement of audition and vision in the first year of postnatal life: A methodological overview* (223–251). Norwood, NJ: Ablex.

Kuhl, Patricia K.; Andruski, Jean E.; Chistovich, I. A.; Chistovich, L. A.; Kozhevnikova, E. V.; Ryskina, V. L.; Stolyarova, E. I.; Sundberg, Ulla; & Lacersa, Francisco. 1997. Cross-language analysis of phonetic units in language addressed to infants. *Science* 277, 684–686.

Kuhl, Patricia K., & Miller, James D. 1975. Speech perception in the chinchilla: Voiced-voiceless distinction in alveolar plosive consonants. *Science* 190, 69–72.

Kuhl, Patricia K., & Padden, Denise M. 1982. Enhanced discriminability at the phonetic boundaries for the voicing feature in macaques. *Perception & Psychophysics* 32, 542–550.

Küntay, Aylin C. 2002. Development of the expression of indefiniteness: Presenting new referents in Turkish picture-series stories. *Discourse Processes* 33, 77–101.

Küntay, Aylin, & Slobin, Dan I. 1996. Listening to a Turkish mother: Some puzzles for acquisition. In D. I. Slobin, J. Gerhardt, A. Kyratzis, & J. Guo (eds.), *Social interaction, social context, and language: Essays in honor of Susan Ervin-Tripp* (265–286). Mahwah, NJ: Lawrence Erlbaum.

Kyratzis, Amy. 1993. Pragmatic and discursive influences on the acquisition of subordination-coordination. In E. V. Clark (ed.), *Proceedings of the 25th annual Child Language Research Forum 1993* (324–332). Stanford, CA: CSLI.

Labov, William, & Labov, Teresa. 1978. The phonetics of *cat* and *mama*. *Language* 54, 816–852.

Laing, Emma; Butterworth, George; Ansari, Daniel; Gsödl, Marisa; Longli, Elena; Panagiotaki, Georgia; Paterson, Sarah; & Karmiloff-Smith, Annette. 2002. Atypical development of language and social communication in toddlers with Williams Syndrome. *Developmental Science* 5, 233–246.

Lambert, Wallace E., & Tucker, G. Richard. 1972. *Bilingual education of children: The St. Lambert experiment.* Rowley, MA: Newbury House.

Landau, Barbara; Smith, Linda; & Jones, Susan. 1998. Object shape, object function, and object name. *Journal of Memory & Language* 38, 1–27.

Lane, Harlan. 1976. *The wild boy of Aveyron.* Cambridge, MA: Harvard University Press.

Lanza, Elizabeth. 1992. Can bilingual two-year-olds code-switch? *Journal of Child Language* 19, 633–658.

Lanza, Elizabeth. 1997. *Language mixing in infant bilingualism: A sociolinguistic perspective.* Oxford: Oxford University Press.

Lawrence, Valerie W., & Shipley, Elizabeth F. 1996. Parental speech to middle- and working-class children from two racial groups in three settings. *Applied Psycholinguistics* 17, 233–255.

Lempers, Jacques; Flavell, Eleanor L.; & Flavell, John H. 1977. The development in very young children of tacit knowledge concerning visual perception. *Genetic Psychology Monographs* 95, 3–53.

Lenneberg, Eric. 1967. *Biological foundations of language.* New York: Wiley.

Leonard, Laurence B. 1998. *Children with specific language impairment.* Cambridge, MA: MIT Press.

Leopold, Werner F. 1939–1949. *Speech development of a bilingual child,* 4 vols. Evanston, IL: Northwestern University Press.

Leung, Eleanor H., & Rheingold, Harriet L. 1981. Development of pointing as social gesture. *Developmental Psychology* 17, 215–220.

Levelt, Clara C. 1994. *The acquisition of place.* Leiden: Holland Institute of Generative Linguistics Publications.

Levelt, Willem J. M. 1989. *Speaking: From intention to articulation.* Cambridge, MA: MIT Press.

Levin, Beth. 1993. *English verb classes and alternations.* Chicago: University of Chicago Press.

Levinson, Stephen C. 1983. *Pragmatics.* Cambridge: Cambridge University Press.

Levinson, Stephen C. 2000. *Presumptive meanings: The theory of generalized conversational implicature.* Cambridge, MA: MIT Press.

Levitt, Andrea G., & Utman, Jennifer G. A. 1992. From babbling towards the the the sound systems of English and French: A longitudinal two-case study. *Journal of Child Language* 19, 19–49.

Lewis, David K. 1969. *Convention: A philosophical study.* Cambridge, MA: Harvard University Press.

Lewis, John D., & Elman, Jeffrey L. 2008. Growth-related neural reorganization and the autism phenotype: A test of the hypothesis that altered brain growth leads to altered connectivity. *Developmental Science* 11, 135–155.

Li, Ping, & MacWhinney, Brian. 1996. Cryptotype, overgeneralization, and competition: A connectionist model of the learning of English reversive prefixes. *Connectionist Science* 8, 3–30.

Liberman, Alvin M.; Cooper, Frank S.; Shankweiler, Donald P.; & Studdert-Kennedy, Michael G. 1967. Perception of the speech code. *Psychological Review* 74, 431–461.

Lieven, Elena V. M. 1978. Turn-taking and pragmatics: Two issues in early child language. In R. N. Campbell & P. T. Smith (eds.), *Recent advances in the psychology of language* (215–236). London: Plenum.

Lieven, Elena V. M. 1997. Variation in a crosslinguistic context. In D. I. Slobin (ed.), *The crosslinguistic study of language acquisition*, vol. V (199–263). Mahwah, NJ: Lawrence Erlbaum.

Lieven, Elena; Behrens, Heike; Speares, Jennifer; & Tomasello, Michael. 2003. Early syntactic creativity: A usage-based approach. *Journal of Child Language* 30, 333–370.

Lieven, Elena V. M.; Pine, Julian M.; & Baldwin, Gillian. 1997. Lexically-based learning and early grammatical development. *Journal of Child Language* 24, 187–219.

Lindblom, Björn. 1992. Phonological units as adaptive emergents of lexical development. In C. A. Ferguson, L. Menn, & C. Stoel-Gammon (eds.), *Phonological development: Models, research, implications* (131–163). Parkton, MD: York Press.

Lindner, Gustav. 1898. *Aus dem Naturgarten der Kindersprache: Ein Beitrag zur kindlichen Sprach- und Geistentwicklung in den ersten vier Lebensjahren.* Leipzig: Grieben.

Liszkowski, Ulf; Carpenter, Malinda; Henning, Anne; Striano, Tricia; & Tomasello, Michael. 2004. Twelve-month-olds point to share attention and interest. *Developmental Science* 7, 297–307.

Liszkowski, Ulf; Carpenter, Malinda; Striano, Tricia; & Tomasello, Michael. 2006. 12- and 18-month-olds point to provide information for others. *Journal of Cognition & Development* 7, 173–187.

Locke, John L. 1993. *The child's path to spoken language.* Cambridge, MA: Harvard University Press.

Lodge, K. R. 1979. The use of the past tense in games of pretend. *Journal of Child Language* 6, 365–369.

Loftus, Elizabeth F. 1979. *Eye-witness testimony.* Cambridge, MA: Harvard University Press.

Lord, Catherine. 1979. "Don't you fall me down": Children's generalizations regarding cause and transitivity. *Papers & Reports on Child Language Development* [Stanford University] 17, 81–89.

Lust, Barbara. 1977. Conjunction reduction in child language. *Journal of Child Language* 4, 257–287.

Lust, Barbara. 1994. Functional projection of CP and phrase structure parametrization: An argument for the Strong Continuity Hypothesis. In B. Lust, M. Suñer, & J. Whitman (eds.), *Syntactic theory and first language acquisition,* vol. I: *Heads, projections, and learnability* (85–118). Hillsdale, NJ: Lawrence Erlbaum.

Macaulay, Ronald K. S. 1997. *Standards and variation in urban speech.* Philadelphia: John Benjamins Publishing.

McCabe, Ann E.; Evely, Susan; Abramovitch, Rona; Corter, Carl M.; & Pepler, Debra J. 1983. Conditional statements in young children's spontaneous speech. *Journal of Child Language* 10, 253–258.

Maccoby, Eleanor E., & Bee, Helen L. 1965. Some speculations concerning the lag between perceiving and performing. *Child Development* 36, 367–377.

McCune, Lorraine; Vihman, Marilyn M.; Roug-Hellichius, Liselotte; Delery, Diane B.; & Gogate, Lakshmi. 1996. Grunt communication in human infants (Homo sapiens). *Journal of Comparative Psychology* 110, 27–37.

McGregor, Karla K. 1994. Article use in the spontaneous samples of children with specific language impairment: The importance of considering syntactic contexts. *Clinical Linguistics & Phonetics* 8, 153–160.

McGregor, Karla K.; Sheng, Li; & Smith, Bruce. 2005. The precocious two-year-old: Status of the lexicon and links to the grammar. *Journal of Child Language* 32, 563–585.

Macken, Marlys A. 1980. The child's lexical representation: The "puzzle-puddle-pickle" evidence. *Journal of Linguistics* 16, 1–17.

McLaughlin, Barry. 1984. *Second language acquisition in childhood,* vol. I: *Preschool children* (2nd edn). Hillsdale, NJ: Lawrence Erlbaum.

McMurray, Bob. 2007. Defusing the childhood vocabulary explosion. *Science* 317, 631.

Maclay, Howard, & Osgood, Charles E. 1959. Hesitation phenomena in spontaneous English speech. *Word* 15, 19–44.

Macnamara, John. 1982. *Names for things: A study of human learning.* Cambridge, MA: MIT Press.

McShane, John. 1980. *Learning to talk.* Cambridge: Cambridge University Press.

McTear, Michael. 1978. Repetition in child language: Imitation or creation? In R. N. Campbell & P. T. Smith (eds.), *Recent advances in the psychology of language* (293–311). London: Plenum.

McTear, Michael. 1985. *Children's conversation.* Oxford: Blackwell.

MacWhinney, Brian. 1978. The acquisition of morphophonology. *Monographs of the Society for Research in Child Development* 43 (serial no. 174).

MacWhinney, Brian. 1985. Hungarian language acquisition as an exemplification of a general model of grammatical development. In D. I. Slobin (ed.), *The crosslinguistic study of language acquisition*, vol. II (1069–1155). Hillsdale, NJ: Lawrence Erlbaum.

MacWhinney, B., & Snow, Catherine. 1985. The Child Language Data Exchange System. *Journal of Child Language* 12, 271–296.

MacWhinney, B., & Snow, Catherine. 1990. The Child Language Data Exchange System: An update. *Journal of Child Language* 17, 457–472.

McWilliam, Donna, & Howe, Christine. 2004. Enhancing pre-schoolers' reasoning skills: An intervention to optimise the use of justificatory speech acts during peer interaction. *Language & Education* 18, 504–524.

Maekawa, Junko, & Storkel, Holly L. 2006. Individual differences in the influence of phonological characteristics on expressive vocabulary development by young children. *Journal of Child Language* 33, 439–459.

Major, D. R. 1906. *First steps in mental growth: A series of studies in the psychology of infancy.* New York: Macmillan.

Malherbe, E. G. 1969. Comments on "How and when do persons become bilingual?" In L. G. Kelly (ed.), *Description and measurement of bilingualism* (325–327). Toronto: University of Toronto Press.

Mandler, Jean M., & McDonough, Laraine. 1993. Concept formation in infancy. *Cognitive Development* 8, 291–318.

Maneva, Blagovesta, & Genesee, Fred. 2002. Bilingual babbling: Evidence for language differentiation in dual language acquisition. In B. Skarabela, S. Fish, & A. H.-J. Do (eds.), *Proceedings of the 26th Boston University Conference on Language Development* (383–392). Somerville, MA: Cascadilla Press.

Manning, Christopher D., & Schütze, Hinrich. 1999. *Foundations of statistical natural language processing*. Cambridge, MA: MIT Press.

Maratsos, Michael P. 1973. Nonegocentric communication abilities in preschool children. *Child Development* 44, 697–700.

Maratsos, Michael P. 1974. Preschool children's use of definite and indefinite articles. *Child Development* 45, 446–455.

Maratsos, Michael P. 1976. *The use of definite and indefinite reference in young children: An experimental study in semantic acquisition*. Cambridge: Cambridge University Press.

Maratsos, Michael P. 1993. Artifactual overregularizations? In E. V. Clark (ed.), *Proceedings of the 24th annual Child Language Research Forum* (139–148). Stanford, CA: CSLI.

Maratsos, Michael P. 2000. More overregularizations after all: New data and discussion on Marcus, Pinker, Ullman, Hollander, Rosen, & Xu. *Journal of Child Language* 27, 183–212.

Maratsos, Michael P., & Chalkley, Mary Anne. 1980. The internal language of children's syntax: The ontogenesis and representation of syntactic categories. In K. E. Nelson (ed.), *Children's language*, vol. II (127–214). New York: Gardner Press.

Maratsos, Michael P.; Fox, Dana E. C.; Becker, Judith A.; & Chalkley, Mary Anne. 1985. Semantic restrictions on children's passives. *Cognition* 19, 167–191.

Marchand, Hans. 1969. *English word-formation* (2nd rev. edn). Munich: C. H. Beck.

Marchman, Virginia, & Bates, Elizabeth. 1994. Continuity in lexical and morphological development: A test of the critical mass hypothesis. *Journal of Child Language* 21, 339–366.

Marcos, Haydée. 1991. Reformulating requests at 18 months: Gestures, vocalizations, and words. *First Language* 11, 361–375.

Marcos, Haydée, & Kornhaber-Le Chanu, Mila. 1992. Learning how to insist and clarify in the second year: Reformulation of requests in different contexts. *International Journal of Behavioral Development* 15, 359–376.

Marcos, Haydée; Ryckebusch, Céline; & Rabain-Jamin, Jacqueline. 2003. Adult responses to young children's communicative gestures: Joint achievement of speech acts. *First Language* 23, 213–237.

Marcus, Gary F. 1993. Negative evidence in language acquisition. *Cognition* 46, 53–85.

Marcus, Gary F.; Pinker, Steven; Ullman, Michael; Hollander, Michelle; Rosen, T. John; & Xu, Fei. 1992. Overregularization in language acquisition. *Monographs of the Society for Research in Child Development* 57 (serial no. 228).

Marian, Viorica, & Spivey, Michael. 2003. Competing activation in bilingual language processing: Within- and between-language competition. *Bilingualism: Language & Cognition* 6, 97–115.

Marian, Viorica; Spivey, Michael; & Hirsch, Joy. 2003. Shared and separate systems in bilingual language processing: Converging evidence from eye-tracking and brain-imaging. *Brain & Language* 86, 70–82.

Markman, Ellen M. 1987. How children constrain the possible meanings of words. In U. Neisser (ed.), *Concepts and conceptual development: Ecological and intellectual factors in categorization* (255–287). Cambridge: Cambridge University Press.

Markman, Ellen M. 1989. *Categorization and naming in children: Problems of induction.* Cambridge, MA: MIT Press.

Markman, Ellen M., & Hutchinson, Jean E. 1984. Children's sensitivity to constraints on word meaning: Taxonomic versus thematic relations. *Cognitive Psychology* 16, 1–27.

Markman, Ellen M., & Wachtel, Gwyn F. 1988. Children's use of mutual exclusivity to constrain the meanings of words. *Cognitive Psychology* 20, 121–157.

Martlew, Margaret; Connolly, Kevin; & McCleod, Christine. 1978. Language use, role and context in a five-year-old. *Journal of Child Language* 5, 81–99.

Mason, M. K. 1942. Learning to speak after six and one-half years. *Journal of Speech Disorders* 7, 295–304.

Masur, Elise F. 1997. Maternal labeling of novel and familiar objects: Implications for children's development of lexical constraints. *Journal of Child Language* 24, 427–439.

Matthews, Danielle; Lieven, Elena; Theakston, Anna; & Tomasello, Michael. 2006. The effect of perceptual availability and prior discourse on young children's use of referring expressions. *Applied Psycholinguistics* 27, 403–422.

Matthews, Danielle; Lieven, Elena; & Tomasello, Michael. 2007. How toddlers and preschoolers learn to uniquely identify referents for others: A training study. *Child Development* 78, 1744–1759.

Mattys, Sven L.; Jusczyk, Peter W.; Luce, Paul A.; & Morgan, James L. 1999. Phonotactic and prosodic effects on word segmentation in infants. *Cognitive Psychology* 38, 465–494.

Maye, Jessica; Werker, Janet F.; & Gerken, LouAnn. 2002. Infant sensitivity to distributional information can affect phonetic discrimination. *Cognition* 82, B101–B111.

Mayer, Mercer. 1969. *Frog, where are you?* New York: Dial Press.

Mechelli, Andrea; Crinion, Jennifer T.; Noppeney, Uta; O'Doherty, John; Ashburner, John; Frackowiak, Richard S.; & Price, Cathy J. 2004. Structural plasticity in the bilingual brain. *Nature* 143, 757.

Mehler, Jacques; Bertoncini, Josiane; Barrière, Michèle; & Jassik-Gerschenfeld, Dora. 1978. Infant recognition of mother's voice. *Perception* 7, 491–497.

Mehler, Jacques.; Jusczyk, Peter W.; Lambertz, Ghislaine; Halsted, Nilofar; Bertoncini, Josiane; & Amiel-Tison, Claudine. 1988. A precursor of language acquisition in young infants. *Cognition* 29, 143–178.

Meisel, Jürgen (ed.). 1990. *Two first languages: Early grammatical development in bilingual children.* Dordrecht: Foris.

Meisel, Jürgen. 1994. Code-switching in young bilingual children: The acquisition of grammatical constraints. *Studies in Second Language Acquisition* 16, 413–441.

Meisel, Jürgen M. 2007. The weaker language in early child bilingualism: Acquiring a first language as a second language? *Applied Psycholinguistics* 28, 495–514.

Menn, Lise. 1971. Phonotactic rules in beginning speech. *Lingua* 26, 225–241.

Merriman, William E., & Bowman, Laura L. 1989. The mutual exclusivity bias in children's word learning. *Monographs of the Society for Research in Child Development* 54 (serial no. 220).

Mervis, Carolyn B. 1987. Child-basic object categories and early lexical development. In U. Neisser (ed.), *Concepts and conceptual development: Ecological and intellectual factors in categorization* (201–233). Cambridge: Cambridge University Press.

Mervis, Carolyn B. 1999. Williams syndrome cognitive profile: Strengths, weaknesses, and interrelations among auditory short-term memory, language, and visuospatial constructive cognition. In E. Winograd & R. Fivush (eds.), *Ecological approaches to cognition: Essays in honor of Ulric Neisser* (193–227). Mahwah, NJ: Lawrence Erlbaum.

Mervis, Carolyn B., & Greco, Carolyn. 1984. Parts and early conceptual development: Comment on Tversky & Hemenway. *Journal of Experimental Psychology: General* 113, 194–197.

Mervis, Carolyn B., & Johnson, Kathy E. 1991. Acquisition of the plural morpheme: A case study. *Developmental Psychology* 27, 222–235.

Mervis, Carolyn B., & Long, Laurel M. 1987. Words refer to whole objects: Young children's interpretation of the referent of a novel word. Paper presented at the biennial meeting of the Society for Research in Child Development, Baltimore, MD.

Messer, David J. 1978. The integration of mothers' referential speech with joint play. *Child Development* 49, 781–787.

Messer, Stanley. 1967. Implicit phonology in children. *Journal of Verbal Learning & Verbal Behavior* 6, 609–613.

Metraux, R. W. 1965. Study of bilingualism among children of U.S.-French parents. *French Review* 38, 650–665.

Mikes, Melanie. 1967. Acquisition des catégories grammaticales dans le langage de l'enfant. *Enfance* 20, 289–298.

Miller, George A. 1967. Project grammarama. In *The psychology of communication* (125–187). New York: Basic Books.

Miller, James D.; Weir, C.; Pastore, L.; Kelly, W. J.; & Dooling, Robert J. 1976. Discrimination and labeling of noise-buzz sequences with varying noise-lead times: An example of categorical perception. *Journal of the Acoustical Society of America* 60, 410–417.

Miller, Peggy. 1982. *Amy, Wendy, and Beth: Learning language in South Baltimore.* Austin: University of Texas Press.

Miller, Peggy. 1986. Teasing as language socialization in a white working-class community. In B. B. Schieffelin & E. Ochs (eds.), *Language socialization across cultures* (199–212). Cambridge: Cambridge University Press.

Miller, Wick, & Ervin, Susan. 1964. The development of grammar in child language. In U. Bellugi & R. Brown (eds.), The acquisition of language (9–34). *Monographs of the Society for Research in Child Development* 29 (serial no. 92).

Mills, Debra L.; Coffey-Corina, Sharon; & Neville, Helen J. 1993. Language acquisition and cerebral specialization in 20-month-old infants. *Journal of Cognitive Neuroscience* 5, 317–334.

Mills, Debra L.; Coffey-Corina, Sharon; & Neville, Helen J. 1997. Language comprehension and cerebral specialization from 13 to 20 months. *Developmental Neuropsychology* 13, 397–445.

Mills, Debra L.; Plunkett, Kim; Prat, Chantal; & Schafer, Graham. 2005. Watching the infant brain learn words: Effects of vocabulary size and experience. *Cognitive Development* 20, 19–31.

Milroy, James, & Milroy, Lesley. 1991. *Authority in language: Investigating language standardization*. London: Routledge.

Milroy, Lesley. 1980. *Language and social networks*. Oxford: Blackwell.

Mintz, Toben H. 2002. Category induction from distributional cues in an artificial language. *Memory & Cognition* 30, 678–686.

Mintz, Toben H. 2003. Frequent frames as a cue for grammatical categories in child directed speech. *Cognition* 90, 91–117.

Mintz, Toben H.; Newport, Elissa L.; & Bever, Thomas G. 2002. The distributional structure of grammatical categories in speech to young children. *Cognitive Science* 26, 393–424.

Moerk, Ernst L. 1983. *The mother of Eve as a first language teacher*. Norwood, NJ: Ablex.

Moeser, Shannon D., & Bregman, Albert S. 1972. The role of reference in the acquisition of a miniature artificial language. *Journal of Verbal Learning & Verbal Behavior* 11, 759–769.

Moffitt, Alan R. 1971. Consonant cue perception by 20 and 24-week-old infants. *Child Development* 42, 717–731.

Moll, Henrike; Koring, Cornelia; Carpenter, Malinda; & Tomasello, Michael. 2006. Infants determine others' focus of attention by pragmatics and exclusion. *Journal of Cognition & Development* 7, 411–430.

Moon, Christine; Cooper, Robin P.; & Fifer, William P. 1993. Two-day-olds prefer their native language. *Infant Behavior & Development* 16, 495–500.

Moore, Chris, & Dunham, Philip J. (eds.), 1995. *Joint attention: Its origins and role in development*. Hillsdale, NJ: Lawrence Erlbaum.

Morgan, James L., & Saffran, Jenny R. 1995. Emerging integration of sequential and suprasegmental information in preverbal speech segmentation. *Child Development* 66, 911–936.

Morgan, James L., & Travis, Lisa L. 1989. Limits on negative information in language input. *Journal of Child Language* 16, 531–552.

Morikawa, Hiromi. 1991. Acquisition of causatives in Japanese. *Papers & Reports on Child Language Development* [Stanford University] 30, 80–87.

Morimoto, Yukiko. 1999. Making words in two languages: A prosodic account of Japanese-English language mixing. *International Journal of Bilingualism* 3, 23–44.

Morris, Colleen A., & Mervis, Carolyn B. 1999. Williams syndrome. In S. Goldstein & C. R. Reynolds (eds.), *Handbook of neurodevelopmental and genetic disorders in children* (555–590). New York: Guilford Press.

Morse, Philip A. 1972. The discrimination of speech and nonspeech stimuli in early infancy. *Journal of Experimental Child Psychology* 14, 477–492.

Morton, John, & Smith, Neilson V. 1974. Some ideas concerning the acquisition of phonology. In *Problèmes actuels de psycholinguistique/Current problems in psycholinguistics* (161–176). Paris: Editions du CNRS.

Mosier, Christine E., & Rogoff, Barbara. 1994. Infants' instrumental use of their mothers to achieve their goals. *Child Development* 65, 70–79.

Mowrer, O. Hobart. 1960. *Learning theory and symbolic processes*. New York: Wiley.

Muir, Darwin, & Hains, Sylvia. 1999. Young infants' perception of adult intentionality: Adult contingency and eye direction. In P. Rochat (ed.), *Early social cognition* (155–187). Mahwah, NJ: Erlbaum.

Mulford, Randa C. 1983. On the acquisition of derivational morphology in Icelandic: Learning about *-ari*. *Islenskt mál og almenn málfraeði* 5, 105–125.

Muller, Eric; Hollien, Harry; & Murry, Thomas. 1974. Perceptual responses to infant crying – identification of cry types. *Journal of Child Language* 1, 89–95.

Murphy, Catherine M., & Messer, David J. 1977. Mothers, infants, and pointing: A study of a gesture. In H. R. Schaffer (ed.), *Studies of mother-infant interaction* (325–354). London: Academic Press.

Myers-Scotton, Carol. 1993a. *Duelling languages: Grammatical structure in code-switching*. Oxford: Oxford University Press.

Myers-Scotton, Carol. 1993b. *Social motivations for code-switching: Evidence from Africa*. Oxford: Oxford University Press.

Nagy, William E., & Anderson, Richard C. 1984. How many words are there in printed school English? *Reading Research Quarterly* 19, 304–330.

Naigles, Letitia R., & Hoff-Ginsberg, Erika. 1995. Input to verb-learning: Evidence for the plausibility of syntactic bootstrapping. *Developmental Psychology* 31, 827–837.

Naigles, Letitia R., & Hoff-Ginsberg, Erika. 1998. Why are some verbs learned before other verbs? Effects of input frequency and structure on children's early verb use. *Journal of Child Language* 25, 95–120.

Naigles, Letitia R., & Mayeux, Lara. 2000. Television as an incidental teacher. In D. Singer & J. Singer (eds.), *Handbook of children and the media* (135–153). New York: Sage.

Nakamura, Keiko. 2001. The acquisition of polite language by Japanese children. In K. E. Nelson & A. Aksu-Koç (eds.), *Children's language*, vol. X (93–112). Mahwah, NJ: Lawrence Erlbaum.

Namy, Laura L., & Waxman, Sandra R. 1998. Words and gestures: Infants' interpretations of different forms of symbolic reference. *Child Development* 69, 295–308.

Namy, Laura L., & Waxman, Sandra R. 2000. Naming and exclaiming: Infants' sensitivity to naming contexts. *Journal of Cognition & Development* 1, 405–428.

Nayer, Samantha L., & Graham, Susan A. 2006. Children's communicative strategies in novel and familiar word situations. *First Language* 26, 403–420.

Nazzi, Thierry; Bertoncini, Josiane; & Mehler, Jacques. 1998. Language discrimination by newborns: Toward an understanding of the role of rhythm. *Journal of Experimental Psychology: Human Perceptioon & Performance* 24, 756–766.

Nazzi, Thierry; Jusczyk, Peter W.; & Johnson, Elizabeth K. 2000. Language discrimination by English-learning 5-month-olds: Effects of rhythm and familiarity. *Journal of Memory & Language* 43, 1–19.

Nelson, Katherine. 1973. Structure and strategy in learning to talk. *Monographs of the Society for Research in Child Development* 38 (serial no. 149).

Nelson, Katherine. 1975. The nominal shift in semantic-syntactic development. *Cognitive Psychology* 7, 461–479.

Nelson, Katherine. 1988. Constraints on word learning? *Cognitive Development* 3, 221–246.

Nelson, Katherine (ed.). 1989. *Narratives from the crib*. Cambridge, MA: Harvard University Press.

Nelson, Lauren, & Bauer, Harold R. 1991. Speech and language production at age 2: Evidence for tradeoffs between linguistic and phonetic processing. *Journal of Speech & Hearing Research* 34, 879–892.

Neville, Helen J.; Coffey, Sharon A.; Lawson, Donald S.; Fischer, Andrew; Emmorey, Karen; & Bellugi, Ursula. 1997. Neural systems mediating American Sign Language: Effects of sensory experience and age of acquisition. *Brain & Language* 57, 285–308.

Newcombe, Nora, & Zaslow, Martha. 1981. Do 2 1/2-year-olds hint? A study of directive forms in the speech of 2 1/2-year-old children to adults. *Discourse Processes* 4, 239–252.

Newman, Jean E.; Lovett, Maureen W.; & Dennis, Maureen. 1986. The use of discourse analysis in neurolinguistics: Some findings from the narratives of hemidecorticate adolescents. *Topics in Language Disorders* 7, 31–44.

Newport, Elissa L. 1988. Constraints on learning and their role in language acquisition: Studies of the acquisition of American Sign Language. *Language Sciences* 10, 147–172.

Newport, Elissa L. 1990. Maturational constraints on language learning. *Cognitive Science* 14, 11–28.

Newport, Elissa L. 1991. Contrasting conceptions of the critical period for language. In S. Carey & R. Gelman (eds.), *The epigenesis of mind: Essays on biology and cognition* (111–130). Hillsdale, NJ: Lawrence Erlbaum.

Newport, Elissa; Gleitman, Henry; & Gleitman, Lila R. 1977. "Mother, I'd rather do it myself": Some effects and non-effects of maternal speech style. In C. E. Snow & C. A. Ferguson (eds.), *Talking to children: Language input and acquisition* (109–149). Cambridge: Cambridge University Press.

Nicolaci-da-Costa, Ana, & Harris, Margaret. 1983. Redundancy of syntactic information: An aid to young children's comprehension of sentential number. *British Journal of Psychology* 74, 343–352.

Nicolaci-da-Costa, Ana, & Harris, Margaret. 1984/1985. Individual differences in the acquisition of number markers. *First Language* 5, 185–198.

Nicoladis, Elena, & Genesee, Fred. 1996. A longitudinal study of pragmatic differentiation in young bilingual children. *Language Learning* 46, 439–464.

Niemi, Jussi; Laine, Matti; & Tuominen, Juhani. 1994. Cognitive morphology in Finnish: Foundations of a new model. *Language & Cognitive Processes* 9, 423–446.

Ninio, Anat. 1999a. Pathbreaking verbs in syntactic development and the question of prototypical transitivity. *Journal of Child Language* 26, 619–653.

Ninio, Anat. 1999b. Model learning in syntax development. *International Journal of Bilingualism* 3, 111–131.

Noveck, Ira A. 2001. When children are more logical than adults: Experimental investigations of scalar implicature. *Cognition* 78, 165–188.

Nunberg, Geoffrey. 1996. Transfers of meaning. In J. Pustejovsky & B. Boguraev (eds.), *Lexical semantics: The problem of polysemy* (109–132). Oxford: Clarendon Press.

Ochs, Elinor. 1982. Talking to children in Western Samoa. *Language in Society* 11, 77–104.

Ochs, Elinor. 1992. Indexing gender. In A. Duranti & C. Goodwin (eds.), *Rethinking context* (335–358). Cambridge: Cambridge University Press.

Ochs, Elinor, & Schieffelin, Bambi B. 1984. Language acquisition and socialization: Three developmental stories. In R. Schweder & R. Levin (eds.), *Culture theory: Essays in mind, self and emotion* (276–320). Cambridge: Cambridge University Press.

Ochs, Elinor; Schieffelin, Bambi B.; & Platt, Martha L. 1979. Propositions across utterances and speakers. In E. Ochs & B. B. Schieffelin (eds.), *Developmental pragmatics* (251–268). New York: Academic Press.

Ochs, Elinor, & Taylor, Carolyn. 1995. The "father knows best" dynamic in dinnertime narratives. In K. Hall & M. Bucholtz (eds.), *Gender articulated: Language and the socially constructed self* (97–120). London: Routledge.

O'Connor, Mary Catherine. 1996. Managing the intermental: Classroom group discussion and the social context of learning. In D. I. Slobin, J. Gerhardt, A. Kyratzis, & J. Guo (eds.), *Social interaction, social context, and language: Esssays in honor of Susan Ervin-Tripp* (495–509). Mahwah, NJ: Lawrence Erlbaum.

O'Grady, William. 1993. Functional categories and maturation: Data from Korean. *Proceedings of the 5th Harvard International Symposium on Korean Linguistics* (96–112). Seoul: Hanshin.

O'Grady, William. 1997. *Syntactic development*. Chicago: University of Chicago Press.

Ogura, Tamiko; Dale, Philip S.; Yamashita, Yukie; Murase, Toshii; & Mahieu, Aki. 2006. The use of nouns and verbs by Japanese children and their caregivers in book-reading and toy-playing contexts. *Journal of Child Language* 33, 1–29.

Oksaar, Els. 1970. Zum Spracherwerb des Kindes in Zweisprachiger Umgebung. *Folia Linguistica* 4, 330–358.

Oller, D. Kimbrough; Wieman, Leslie A.; Doyle, William J.; & Ross, Carol. 1976. Infant babbling and speech. *Journal of Child Language* 3, 1–11.

Olmsted, D. L. 1971. *Out of the mouth of babes*. The Hague: Mouton.

Omar, Margaret K. 1973. *The acquisition of Egyptian Arabic as a native language*. The Hague: Mouton.

O'Neill, Daniela K. 1996. Two-year-olds' sensitivity to the parent's knowledge when making requests. *Child Development* 67, 659–677.

Orsolini, Margherita; Fanari, Rachele; & Bowles, Hugo. 1998. Acquiring regular and irregular inflection in a language with verb classes. *Language & Cognitive Processes* 13, 425–464.

Oviatt, Sharon L. 1980. The emerging ability to comprehend language: An experimental approach. *Child Development* 51, 97–106.

Oviatt, Sharon L.; Levow, Gina-Anne; Moreton, Elliot; & MacEachern, Margaret. 1998. Modeling global and focal hyperarticulation during human-computer error resolution. *Journal of the Acoustical Society of America* 104, 3080–3098.

Paley, Vivian G. 1984. *Boys and girls: Superheroes in the doll corner*. Chicago: University of Chicago Press.

Panneton Cooper, Robin, & Aslin, Richard. 1990. Preference for infant-directed speech in the first month after birth. *Child Development* 61, 1584–1595.

Papafragou, Anna, & Tantalou, Niki. 2004. The computation of implicatures by young children. *Language Acquisition* 12, 71–82.

Paradis, Johanne. 1996. Phonological differentiation in a bilingual child: Hildegard revisited. In A. Stringfellow, D. Cahana-Amitay, E. Hughes, & A. Zukowski (eds.), *Proceedings of the 20th annual Boston University Conference on Language Development* (528–539). Somerville, MA: Cascadilla Press.

Paradis, Johanne, & Genesee, Fred. 1996. Syntactic acquisition in bilingual children: Autonomous or independent? *Studies in Second Language Acquisition* 18, 1–25.

Paradis, Johanne, & Genesee, Fred. 1997. On continuity and the emergence of functional categories in bilingual first-language acquisition. *Language Acquisition* 6, 91–124.

Pasquini, Elisabeth S.; Corriveau, Kathleen H.; Koenig, Melissa A.; & Harris, Paul L. 2007. Preschoolers monitor the relative accuracy of informants. *Developmental Psychology* 43, 1216–1226.

Paul, Hermann. 1898. *Principien der Sprachgeschichte* (3rd edn). Halle: Max Niemeyer.

Pavlovitch, Milivoie. 1920. *Le langage enfantin: Acquisition du serbe et du français par un enfant serbe*. Paris: Champion.

Payne, Arvilla C. 1980. Factors controlling the acquisition of the Philadelphia dialect by out-of-state children. In W. Labov (ed.), *Locating language in time and space* (143–178). New York: Academic Press.

Peters, Ann M. 1983. *The units of language acquisition*. Cambridge: Cambridge University Press.

Peters, Ann M. 1985. Language segmentation: Operating principles for the perception and analysis of language. In D. I. Slobin (ed.), *The crosslinguistic study of language acquisition*, vol. II (1029–1067). Hillsdale, NJ: Lawrence Erlbaum.

Peters, Ann M., & Menn, Lise. 1993. False starts and filler syllables: Ways to learn grammatical morphemes. *Language* 69, 742–777.

Petretic, Patricia A., & Tweney, Ryan D. 1977. Does comprehension precede production? The development of children's responses to telegraphic sentences of varying grammatical adequacy. *Journal of Child Language* 4, 201–209.

Philips, Susan U. 1972. Participant structures and communicative competence: Warm Springs children in community and classroom. In C. Cazden, V. John, & D. Hymes (eds.), *Functions of language in the classroom* (370–394). New York: Teachers College Press.

Philips, Susan U. 1976. Some sources of cultural variability in the regulation of talk. *Language in Society* 5, 81–96.

Phillips, Juliet R. 1973. Syntax and vocabulary of mothers' speech to young children: Age and sex comparisons. *Child Development* 44, 182–185.

Piaget, Jean. 1952. *Play, dreams, and imitation in childhood* [La formation du symbole chez l'enfant]. (Translated by C. Gattegno & F. M. Hodgson.) New York: Norton.

Piché, Gene L.; Rubin, Donald L.; & Michlin, Michael L. 1978. Age and social class in children's use of persuasive communicative appeals. *Child Development* 49, 773–780.

Pine, Julian M., & Lieven, Elena V. M. 1993. Re-analysing rote-learned phrases: Individual differences in the transition to multi-word speech. *Journal of Child Language* 20, 551–571.

Pine, Julian M., & Lieven, Elena V. M. 1997. Slot and frame patterns and the development of the determiner category. *Applied Psycholinguistics* 18, 123–138.

Pine, Julian M.; Lieven, Elena V. M.; & Rowland, Caroline F. 1998. Comparing different models of the development of the English verb category. *Linguistics* 36, 807–830.

Pine, Julian M., & Martindale, Helen. 1996. Syntactic categories in the speech of young children: The case of the determiner. *Journal of Child Language* 23, 369–395.

Pinker, Steven. 1984. *Language learnability and language development*. Cambridge, MA: Harvard University Press.

Pinker, Steven. 1989. *Learnability and cognition: The acquisition of argument structure*. Cambridge, MA: MIT Press.

Pinker, Steven. 1999. *Words and rules*. New York: Basic Books.

Pinker, Steven; Lebeaux, David S.; & Frost, Loren A. 1987. Productivity and constraints in the acquisition of the passive. *Cognition* 26, 195–267.

Pinker, Steven; Ullman, Michael; McClelland, James L.; & Patterson, Karalyn. 2002. The past-tense debate. *Trends in Cognitive Sciences* 6, 456–474.

Pléh, Csaba. 1998. Early spatial case markers in Hungarian children. In E. V. Clark (ed.), *Proceedings of the 29th annual Child Language Research Forum 1997* (211–219). Stanford, CA: CSLI.

Plunkett, Kim. 1993. Lexical segmentation and vocabulary growth in early language acquisition. *Journal of Child Language* 20, 43–60.

Plunkett, Kim, & Marchman, Virginia. 1993. From rote learning to system building: Acquiring verb morphology in children and connectionist nets. *Cognition* 48, 21–69.

Plunkett, Kim, & Nakisa, Ramin C. 1997. A connectionist model of the Arabic plural system. *Language & Cognitive Processes* 12, 807–836.

Poplack, Shana. 1980. Sometimes I'll start a sentence in Spanish y termino en español: Toward a typology of code-switching. *Linguistics* 18, 581–618.

Postma, Albert. 2000. Detection of errors during speech production: A review of speech monitoring models. *Cognition* 77, 97–132.

Poulin-Dubois, Dianne, & Goodz, Naomi. 2001. Language differentiation in bilingual infants: Evidence form babbling. In J. Cenoz & F. Genesee (eds.), *Trends in bilingual acquisition* (95–106). Amsterdam: John Benjamins.

Poulin-Dubois, Diane; Graham, Susan A.; & Riddle, Andrea S. 1995. Salient object parts and infants' acquisition of novel object words. *First Language* 15, 301–316.

Povinelli, Daniel J.; Reaux, James E.; Bierschwale, Donna T.; Allain, Ashley D.; & Simon, Bridgett B. 1997. Exploitation of pointing as a referential gesture in young children, but not adolescent chimpanzees. *Cognitive Development* 12, 423–461.

Pratt, Michael W.; Kerig, Patricia; Cowan, Philip A.; & Pape Cowan, Carolyn. 1988. Mothers and fathers teaching 3-year-olds: Authoritative parenting and adult scaffolding of young children's learning. *Developmental Psychology* 24, 832–839.

Preissler, Melissa A., & Carey, Susan. 2004. Do both pictures and words function as symbols for 18- and 24-month-old children? *Journal of Cognition & Development* 5, 185–212.

Preyer, Wilhelm. 1882. *Die Seele des Kindes: Beobachtungen über die geistige Entwicklung des Menschen in den ersten Lebensjahren*. Leipzig: Schäfer.

Prince, Ellen. 1981. Toward a taxonomy of given-new information. In P. Cole (ed.), *Radical pragmatics* (223–255). New York: Academic Press.

Prudden, Shannnon M.; Hirsh-Pasek, Kathy; Golinkoff, Roberta M.; & Hennon, Elizabeth A. 2006. The birth of words: Ten-month-olds learn words through perceptual salience. *Child Development* 77, 266–280.

Pullum, Geoffrey K. 1996. Learnability, hyperlearning, and the poverty of the stimulus. In J. Johnson, M. L. Juge, & J. L. Moxley (eds.), *Proceedings of the 22nd annual meeting of the Berkeley Linguistics Society: Parasession on the role of learnability in grammatical theory* (498–513). Berkeley, CA: Berkeley Linguistics Society.

Pullum, Geoffrey K., & Scholz, Barbara C. 2002. Empirical assessment of stimulus poverty arguments. *The Linguistic Review* 19 (1–2).

Purcell, April K. 1984. Code shifting Hawaiian style: Children's accommodations along a decreolizing continuum. *International Journal of the Sociology of Language* 46, 71–86.

Pye, Clifton. 1986. Quiché Mayan speech to children. *Language* 59, 583–604.

Quay, Suzanne. 1995. The bilingual lexicon: Implications for studies of language choice. *Journal of Child Language* 22, 369–387.

Quine, Willard v. O. 1960. *Word and object*. Cambridge, MA: MIT Press.

Radford, Andrew. 1990. *Syntactic theory and the acquisition of English syntax*. Oxford: Blackwell.

Ramscar, Michael. 2002. The role of meaning in inflection: Why the past tense doesn't require a rule. *Cognitive Psychology* 45, 45–94.

Ravid, Dorit D. 1995. *Language change in child and adult Hebrew*. Oxford: Oxford University Press.

Read, Barbara K., & Cherry, Louise J. 1978. Preschool children's production of directive forms. *Discourse Processes* 1, 233–245.

Redford, Melissa A., & Miikkulainen, Risto. 2007. Effects of acquisition rate on emergent structure in phonological development. *Language* 83, 737–769.

Redlinger, Wendy E., & Park, Tschang-zin. 1980. Language mixing in young bilinguals. *Journal of Child Language* 7, 337–352.

Reeder, Kenneth. 1980. The emergence of illocutionary skills. *Journal of Child Language* 7, 13–28.

Réger, Zita. 1986. The functions of imitation in child language. *Applied Psycholinguistics* 7, 323–352.

Reilly, Judy S. 1982. The acquisition of conditionals in English. PhD dissertation, University of California, Los Angeles.

Reilly, Judy S. 1986. The acquisition of temporals and conditionals. In E. C. Traugott, A. ter Meulen, J. S. Reilly, & C. A. Ferguson (eds.), *On conditionals* (309–331). Cambridge: Cambridge University Press.

Rescorla, Leslie A. 1980. Overextension in early language development. *Journal of Child Language* 7, 321–335.

Rheingold, Harriet L.; Hay, Dale F.; & West, Meredith J. 1976. Sharing in the second year of life. *Child Development* 47, 1148–1158.

Rice, Mabel; Huston, Aletha; Truglio, Rosemarie; & Wright, John C. 1990. Words from "Sesame Street": Learning vocabulary while viewing. *Developmental Psychology* 26, 421–428.

Rivera-Gaxiola, Martitza; Klarman, Lindsay; Garcia-Sierra, Adrian; & Kuhl, Patricia K. 2005. Neural patterns to speech and vocabulary growth in American infants. *NeuroReport* 16, 495–498.

Rizzi, Luigi. 1994. Early null subjects and root null subjects. In B. Lust, G. Hermon, & J. Kornfilt (eds.), *Syntactic theory and first language acquisition: Cross-linguistic perspectives,* vol. II: *Binding dependencies* (249–272). Hillsdale, NJ: Lawrence Erlbaum.

Robb, Michael P.; Bauer, Harold R.; & Tyler, Ann A. 1994. A quantitative analysis of the single-word stage. *First Language* 14, 37–48.

Roberts, Joanne E.; Burchinal, Margaret; & Durham, Meghan. 1999. Parents' report of vocabulary and grammatical development of African American preschoolers: Child and environmental associations. *Child Development* 70, 92–106.

Roberts, Julie. 1997. Acquisition of variable rules: A study of (-t, -d) deletion in preschool children. *Journal of Child Language* 24, 351–372.

Roberts, Julie, & Labov, William. 1995. Learning to talk Philadelphian. *Language Variation & Change* 7, 101–112.

Robertson, Kirsten, & Murachver, Tamar. 2003. Children's accommodation to gendered language styles. *Journal of Language & Social Psychology* 22, 321–333.

Robinson, Byron F., & Mervis, Carolyn B. 1998. Disentangling early language development: Modeling lexical and grammatical acquisition using an extension of case-study methodology. *Developmental Psychology* 34, 363–375.

Rodrigo, Maria J.; González, Angela; de Vega, Manuel; Muñetón-Ayala, Mercedes; & Rodriguez, Guacimara. 2004. From gestural to verbal deixis: A longitudinal study with Spanish infants and toddlers. *First Language* 24, 71–90.

Rodriguez-Fornells, Antoni; Rotte, Michael; Heinze, Hans-Jochen; Nösselt, Tömme; & Münte, Thomas F. 2002. Brain potential and functional MRI evidence for how to handle two languages with one brain. *Nature* 415, 1026–1029.

Rogers, Don. 1978. Information about word-meaning in the speech of parents to young children. In R. N. Campbell & P. T. Smith (eds.), *Recent advances in the psychology of language* (187–198). London: Plenum.

Rome-Flanders, Tibie; Cronk, Carolyn; & Gourde, Christine. 1995. Maternal scaffolding in mother-infant games and its relationship to language development: A longitudinal study. *First Language* 15, 339–355.

Ronjat, Jules. 1913. *Le développement du langage observé chez un enfant bilingue*. Paris: Champion.

Rosch, Eleanor. 1973. On the internal structure of perceptual and semantic categories. In T. E. Moore (ed.), *Cognitive development and the acquisition of language* (111–144). New York: Academic Press.

Rousseau, Jean-Jacques. 1992. *Emile, ou de l'éducation* [1792]. Classiques Garnier. Paris: Bordas.

Rowe, Meredith L. 2000. Pointing and talk by low-income mothers and their 14-month-old children. *First Language* 20, 305–330.

Rowland, Caroline F., & Pine, Julian M. 2000. Subject-auxiliary inversion errors and wh-question acquisition: "What do children know?" *Journal of Child Language* 27, 157–181.

Rozendaal, Margot I., & Baker, Anne E. 2008. A cross-linguistic investigation of the acquisition of the pragmatics of indefinite and definite reference in two-year-olds. *Journal of Child Language* 35, 773–808.

Ruke-Dravina, Velta. 1973. On the emergence of inflection in child language: A contribution based on Latvian speech data. In C. A. Ferguson & D. I. Slobin (eds.), *Studies of child language development* (252–267). New York: Holt Rinehart & Winston.

Rumelhart, David E., & McClelland, Jay L. 1986. On learning the past tenses of English verbs. In D. E. Rumelhart & J. L. McClelland (eds.), *Parallel distributed processing: Exploration in the microstructure of cognition*, vol. II: *Psychological and biological models* (216–271). Cambridge, MA: MIT Press.

Sachs, Jacqueline. 1979. Topic selection in parent-child discourse. *Discourse Processes* 2, 145–153.

Sachs, Jacqueline; Bard, Barbara; & Johnson, Marie L. 1981. Language learning with restricted input: Case studies of two hearing children of deaf parents. *Applied Psycholinguistics* 1, 33–54.

Sachs, Jacqueline; Brown, Robert; & Salerno, Raffaela A. 1976. Adults' speech to children. In W. von Raffler-Engel & Y. LeBrun (eds.), *Baby talk and infant speech* (special issue). *Neurolinguistics* 5, 240–245.

Sachs, Jacqueline, & Devin, Judith. 1976. Young children's use of age-appropriate speech styles in social interaction and role playing. *Journal of Child Language* 3, 81–98.

Sachs, Jacqueline, & Johnson, Marie. 1976. Language development in a hearing child of deaf parents. In W. von Raffler-Engel & Y. LeBrun (eds.), *Baby talk and infant speech* (special issue). *Neurolinguistics* 5, 246–252.

Saffran, Jenny R.; Aslin, Richard N.; & Newport, Elissa L. 1996. Statistical learning by 8-month-old infants. *Science* 274, 1926–1928.

Saffran, Jenny R.; Johnson, Elizabeth K.; Aslin, Richard N.; & Newport, Elissa L. 1999. Statistical learning of tone sequences by human infants and adults. *Cognition* 70, 27–52.

Saffran, Jenny R.; Newport, Elissa L.; & Aslin, Richard N. 1996. Word segmentation: The role of distributional cues. *Journal of Memory & Language* 35, 606–621.

Salazar Orvig, Anne; Hassan, Rouba; Leber-Marin, Jocelyne; Marcos, Haydée; Morgenstern, Aliyah; & Pares, Jacques. 2006. Peut-on parler d'anaphore chez le jeune enfant? Le cas des pronoms de 3e. personne. *Langages* 163, 10–24.

Sampson, Geoffrey. 1987. *Writing systems* (2nd edn). London: Hutchinson.

Sandler, Wendy; Meir, Irit; Padden, Carol; & Aronoff, Mark. 2005. The emergence of grammar in a new sign language. *Proceedings of the National Academy of Sciences* 102(7), 2661–2665.

Sandra, Dominiek, & Taft, Marcus (eds.). 1994. Morphological structure, lexical representations, and lexical access. *Language & Cognitive Processes* 9, 225–472.

Santelmann, Lynn M., & Jusczyk, Peter W. 1998. Sensitivity to discontinuous dependencies in language learners: Evidence for limitations in processing space. *Cognition* 69, 105–134.

Sapir, Edward. 1924. The grammarian and his language. *American Mercury* 1, 149–155. (Reprinted in D. G. Mandelbaum (ed.), *Selected writings of Edward Sapir in language, culture, and personality*. Berkeley and Los Angeles: University of California Press, 1958.)

Savage, Susan L., & Au, Terry K.-F. 1996. What word learners do when input contradicts the mutual exclusivity assumption. *Child Development* 67, 3120–3134.

Saville-Troike, Muriel. 1988. Private speech: Evidence for second language learning strategies during the "silent" period. *Journal of Child Language* 15, 567–590.

Sawyer, R. Keith. 1997. *Pretend play as improvisation*. Mahwah, NJ: Lawrence Erlbaum.

Saxton, Matthew. 1997. The contrast theory of negative input. *Journal of Child Language* 24, 139–161.

Saxton, Matthew; Kulcsar, Bela; Marshall, Greer; & Rupra, Mandeep. 1998. Longer-term effects of corrective input: An experimental approach. *Journal of Child Language* 25, 701–721.

Saylor, Megan M.; Baird, Jodie A.; & Gallerani, Catherine. 2006. Telling others what's new: Preschoolers' adherence to the given-new contract. *Journal of Cognition & Development* 7, 341–379.

Saylor, Megan M., & Sabbagh, Mark A. 2004. Different kinds of information affect word learning in the preschool years: The case of part-term learning. *Child Development* 75, 395–408.

Saylor, Megan M.; Sabbagh, Mark A.; & Baldwin, Dare A. 2002. Children use whole-part juxtaposition as a pragmatic cue to word meaning. *Developmental Psychology* 38, 993–1003.

Schelletter, Christina. 2002. The effect of form similarity on bilingual children's lexical development. *Bilingualism: Language & Cognition* 5, 93–107.

Schieffelin, Bambi B. 1979. Getting it together: An ethnographic approach to the study of the development of communicative competence. In E. Ochs & B. B. Schieffelin (eds.), *Developmental pragmatics* (73–108). New York: Academic Press.

Schlesinger, Itzak M. 1974. Relational concepts underlying language. In R. L. Scheifelbusch & L. L. Lloyd (eds.), *Language perspectives – acquisition, retardation, and intervention* (129–151). Baltimore, MD: University Park Press.

Schlesinger, Itzak M. 1995. *Cognitive space and linguistic case: Semantic and syntactic categories in English*. Cambridge: Cambridge University Press.

Schmidt, Chris L. 1996. Scrutinizing reference: How gesture and speech are coordinated in mother-child interaction. *Journal of Child Language* 23, 279–305.

Scholz, Barbara C., & Pullum, Geoffrey K. 2006. Irrational nativist exuberance. In R. Stainton (ed.), *Contemporary debates in cognitive science* (59–80). Oxford: Blackwell.

Schütze, Hinrich. 1993. Part-of-speech induction from scratch. In *Proceedings of the 31st annual meeting of the Association for Computational Linguistics* (251–258). Morristown, NJ: Association of Computational Linguistics.

Schütze, Hinrich. 1994. A connectionist model of verb subcategorization. In *Proceedings of the 16th annual Conference of the Cognitive Science Society* (784–788).

Schwartz, Richard G., & Leonard, Laurence B. 1982. Do children pick and choose? *Journal of Child Language* 9, 319–336.

Schwartz, Richard G.; Leonard, Laurence B.; Loeb, Diane M. F.; & Swanson, Lori A. 1987. Attempted sounds are sometimes not: An expanded view of phonological selection and avoidance. *Journal of Child Language* 14, 411–418.

Scollon, Ronald. 1976. *Conversations with a one year old: A case study of the developmental foundation of syntax*. Honolulu: University of Hawaii Press.

Scollon, Ronald. 1979. A real early stage: An unzippered condensation of a dissertation on child language. In E. Ochs & B. B. Schieffelin (eds.), *Developmental pragmatics* (215–227). New York: Academic Press.

Searle, John R. 1975. A taxonomy of illocutionary acts. In K. Gunderson (ed.), *Minnesota studies in the philosophy of language* (344–369). Minneapolis: University of Minnesota Press.

Sebastián-Gallés, Núria, & Bosch, Laura. 2002. Building phonotactic knowledge in bilinguals: Role of early exposure. *Journal of Experimental Psychology: Human Perception & Performance* 28, 974–989.

Sebastián-Gallés, Núria; Echeverría, Sagrario; & Bosch, Laura. 2005. The influence of early exposure on lexical representation: Comparing early and simultaneous bilinguals. *Journal of Memory & Language* 52, 240–255.

Seidl, Amanda, & Johnson, Elizabeth K. 2006. Infant word segmentation revisited: Edge alignment facilitates target extraction. *Developmental Science* 9, 565–573.

Senghas, Ann, & Coppola, Marie. 2001. Children creating language: How Nicaraguan sign language acquired a spatial grammar. *Psychological Science* 12, 323–328.

Senghas, Ann; Kita, Sotaro; Özyürek, Aslı. 2004. Children creating core properties of language: Evidence from an emerging Sign Language in Nicaragua. *Science* 305, 1779–1782.

Serratrice, Ludovica. 2005. The role of discourse pragmatics in the acquisition of subjects in Italian. *Applied Psycholinguistics* 26, 437–462.

Shady, Michele, & Gerken, LouAnn. 1999. Grammatical and caregiver cues in early sentence comprehension. *Journal of Child Language* 26, 163–175.

Shatz, Marilyn. 1978a. Children's comprehension of their mothers' question-directions. *Journal of Child Language* 5, 39–56.

Shatz, Marilyn. 1978b. On the development of communicative understanding: An early strategy for interpreting and responding to messages. *Cognitive Psychology* 10, 271–301.

Shatz, Marilyn. 1983. Communication. In J. H. Flavell & E. M. Markman (eds.), *Handbook of child psychology*, vol. III: *Cognitive development* (4th edn) (841–889). New York: Wiley.

Shatz, Marilyn, & Gelman, Rochel. 1973. The development of communication skills: Modifications in the speech of young children as a function of listener. *Monographs of the Society for Research in Child Development* 38 (serial no. 152).

Shatz, Marilyn, & O'Reilly, Anne W. 1990. Conversation or communicative skill? A reassessment of two-year-olds' behavior in miscommunication episodes. *Journal of Child Language* 17, 131–146.

Sheldon, Amy. 1974. The role of parallel function in the acquisition of relative clauses in English. *Journal of Verbal Learning & Verbal Behavior* 13, 272–281.

Sheldon, Amy. 1990. Pickle fights: Gendered talk in preschool disputes. *Discourse Processes* 13, 3–31.

Sheldon, Amy, & Rohleder, Lisa. 1996. Sharing the same world, telling different stories: Gender differences in co-constructed pretend narratives. In D. I. Slobin, J. Gerhardt, A. Kyratzis, & J. Guo (eds.), *Social interaction, social context, and language: Essays in honor of Susan Ervin-Tripp* (613–632). Mahwah, NJ: Lawrence Erlbaum.

Sherzer, Joel. 1973. Nonverbal and verbal deixis: The pointed lip gesture among the San Blas Cuna. *Language in Society* 2, 117–131.

Shi, Rushen; Morgan, James L.; & Allopenna, Paul. 1998. Phonological and acoustic bases for earliest grammatical category assignment: A cross-linguistic perspective. *Journal of Child Language* 25, 169–201.

Shibatani, Masayoshi (ed.). 1976. *Syntax and semantics*, vol. VI: *The grammar of causative constructions*. New York: Academic Press.

Shipley, Elizabeth F., & Kuhn, Ivy F. 1983. A constraint on comparisons: Equally detailed alternatives. *Journal of Experimental Child Psychology* 35, 195–222.

Shipley, Elizabeth F.; Smith, Carlota S.; & Gleitman, Lila R. 1969. A study in the acquisition of language: Free responses to commands. *Language* 45, 322–342.

Shirai, Yasuhiro. 1997. Is regularization determined by semantics, or grammar, or both? Comments on Kim, Marcus, Pinker, Hollander, & Coppola 1994. *Journal of Child Language* 24, 494–501.

Shirai, Yasuhiro, & Andersen, Roger W. 1995. The acquisition of tense-aspect morphology: A prototype account. *Language* 71, 743–762.

Short-Meyerson, Katherine J., & Abbeduto, Leonard J. 1997. Preschoolers' communication during scripted interactions. *Journal of Child Language* 24, 469–493.

Shvachkin, N. Kh. 1973. The development of phonemic perception in early childhood. In C. A. Ferguson & D. I. Slobin (eds.), *Studies of child language development* (92–127). New York: Holt, Rinehart & Winston.

Shwe, Helen, & Markman, Ellen M. 1997. Young children's appreciation of the mental impact of their communicative signals. *Developmental Psychology* 33, 630–636.

Siegal, Michael. 1997. *Knowing children: Experiments in conversation and cognition* (2nd edn). Hove, Sussex: Psychology Press.

Siegal, Michael; Waters, Lorraine J.; & Dinwiddy, L. Simon. 1988. Misleading children: Causal attributions for inconsistency under repeated questioning. *Journal of Experimental Child Psychology* 45, 438–456.

Sinclair, John McH., & Coulthard, Robert M. 1975. *Towards an analysis of discourse.* Oxford: Oxford University Press.

Singh, Joseph A. L., & Zingg, Robert M. 1939. *Wolf-children and feral man.* New York: Harper.

Sledd, James. 1988. Product in process: From ambiguities of Standard English to issues that divide us. *College English* 50, 168–176.

Slobin, Dan I. 1970. Universals of grammatical development in children. In G. B. Flores d'Arcais & W. J. M. Levelt (eds.), *Advances in psycholinguistics* (174–186). Amsterdam: North-Holland Publishing.

Slobin, Dan I. 1973. Cognitive prerequisites for the development of grammar. In C. A. Ferguson & D. I. Slobin (eds.), *Studies of child language development* (175–208). New York: Holt Rinehart & Winston.

Slobin, Dan I. 1978. A case study of early language awareness. In A. Sinclair, R. J. Jarvella, & W. J. M. Levelt (eds.), *The child's conception of language* (45–54). New York: Springer Verlag.

Slobin, Dan I. 1979. The role of language in language acquisition. Invited Address, 50th Annual Meeting of the Eastern Psychological Association, Philadelphia.

Slobin, Dan I. 1981. The origins of grammatical encoding of events. In W. Deutsch (ed.), *The child's construction of language* (185–199). London and New York: Academic Press.

Slobin, Dan I. (ed.). 1985a. *The crosslinguistic study of language acquisition*, vols. I–II. Hillsdale, NJ: Lawrence Erlbaum.

Slobin, Dan I. 1985b. Crosslinguistic evidence for the Language-Making Capacity. In D. I. Slobin (ed.), *The crosslinguistic study of language acquisition*, vol. II (1157–1249). Hillsdale, NJ: Lawrence Erlbaum.

Slobin, Dan I. (ed.). 1992. *The crosslinguistic study of language acquisition*, vol. III. Hillsdale, NJ: Lawrence Erlbaum.

Slobin, Dan I. 1994. Passives and alternatives in children's narratives in English, Spanish, German, and Turkish. In B. Fox & P. J. Hopper (eds.), *Voice: Form and function* (341–364). Amsterdam and Philadelphia: John Benjamins.

Slobin, Dan I. 1996. From "thought and language" to "thinking for speaking." In J. J. Gumperz & S. C. Levinson (eds.), *Rethinking linguistic relativity* (70–96). Cambridge: Cambridge University Press.

Slobin, Dan I. (ed.). 1997. *The crosslinguistic study of language acquisition*, vols. IV–V. Hillsdale, NJ: Lawrence Erlbaum.

Slobin, Dan I. 2001a. Form/function relations: How do children find out what they are? In M. Bowerman & S. C. Levinson (eds.), *Language acquisition and conceptual development* (406–449). Cambridge: Cambridge University Press.

Slobin, Dan I. 2001b. The child learns to think for speaking: Puzzles of crosslinguistic diversity in form-meaning mappings. Master lecture, biennial meeting of the Society for Research in Child Development, Minneapolis, MN.

Slobin, Dan I., & Bever, Thomas G. 1982. Children use canonical sentence schemas: A crosslinguistic study of word order and inflections. *Cognition* 12, 229–265.

Slobin, Dan I., & Welsh, Charles. 1973. Elicited imitation as a research tool in developmental psycholinguistics. In C. A. Ferguson & D. I. Slobin (eds.), *Studies of child language development* (485–497). New York: Holt, Rinehart & Winston.

Smith, Bruce L.; McGregor, Karla K.; & Demille, Darcie. 2006. Phonological development in lexically precocious 2-year-olds. *Applied Psycholinguistics* 27, 355–375.

Smith, Jennifer; Durham, Mercedes; & Fortune, Liane. 2007. "Mam, my trousers is fa'in doon!": Community, caregiver, and child in the acquisition of variation in a Scottish dialect. *Language Variation & Change* 19, 63–99.

Smith, Madorah E. 1935. A study of the speech of eight bilingual children of the same family. *Child Development* 6, 19–25.

Smith, Neilson V. 1973. *The acquisition of phonology: A case study.* Cambridge: Cambridge University Press.

Smoczyńska, Magdalena. 1985. The acquisition of Polish. In D. I. Slobin (ed.), *The crosslinguistic study of language acquisition*, vol. I (595–686). Hillsdale, NJ: Lawrence Erlbaum.

Snow, Catherine. 1972. Mothers' speech to children learning language. *Child Development* 43, 549–565.

Snow, Catherine. 1977. The development of conversation between mothers and babies. *Journal of Child Language* 4, 1–22.

Snow, Catherine. 1978. The conversational context of language acquisition. In R. N. Campbell & P. T. Smith (eds.), *Recent advances in the psychology of language* (253–269). London: Plenum.

Snow, Catherine; Arlman-Rupp, A.; Hassing, Y.; Jobse, J.; Joosten, J.; & Vorster, J. 1976. Mothers' speech in three social classes. *Journal of Psycholinguistic Research* 5, 1–20.

Snow, Catherine, & Hoefnagel-Hohle, Marian. 1978. The critical period for language acquisition. *Child Development* 49, 1114–1128.

Snyder, Alice D. 1914. Notes on the talk of a two-and-a-half year old boy. *Pedagogical Seminary* 21, 412–424.

Song, Hyun-joo, & Fisher, Cynthia. 2005. Who's "she"? Discourse prominence influences preschoolers' comprehension of pronouns. *Journal of Memory & Language* 52, 29–57.

Sosa, Anna V., & Stoel-Gammon, Carol. 2006. Patterns of intra-word phonological variability during the second year of life. *Journal of Child Language* 33, 31–50.

Spelke, Elizabeth S.; Gutheil, Grant; & Van der Walle, Gretchen. 1995. The development of object perception. In S. M. Kosslyn & D. N. Osherson (eds.), *Visual cognition: An invitation to cognitive science*, vol. II (297–330). Cambridge, MA: MIT Press.

Spence, Melanie J., & DeCasper, Anthony J. 1987. Prenatal experience with low-frequency maternal-voice sounds influences neonatal perception of maternal voice samples. *Infant Behavior & Development* 10, 133–142.

Sridhar, Shikaripur N., & Sridhar, Kamal K. 1980. The syntax and psycholinguistics of bilingual code switching. *Canadian Journal of Psychology* 34, 407–426.

Steels, Luc. 2006. Experiments on the emergence of human communication. *Trends in Cognitive Sciences* 10, 347–349.

Stern, Clara, & Stern, William. 1928. *Die Kindersprache: Eine psychologische und sprachtheoretische Untersuchung* (4th rev. edn; 1st edn, 1907). Leipzig: Barth. (Reprinted Darmstadt: Wissenschaftliche Buchgesellschaft, 1965.)

Stern, Daniel N. 1977. *The first relationship: Mother and infant.* Cambridge, MA: Harvard University Press.

Stern, Daniel N. 1985. *The interpersonal world of the infant.* New York: Basic Books.

Stern, Daniel N.; Spieker, Susan; Barnett, R. K.; & MacKain, Kristine. 1983. The prosody of maternal speech: Infant age and context related changes. *Journal of Child Language* 10, 1–15.

Stevens, Tassos, & Karmiloff-Smith, Annette. 1997. Word learning in a special population: Do individuals with Williams syndrome obey lexical constraints? *Journal of Child Language* 24, 737–765.

Storkel, Holly L. 2002. Restructuring of similarity neighborhoods in the developing mental lexicon. *Journal of Child Language* 29, 251–274.

Strauss, Sidney (ed.). 1982. *U-shaped behavioral growth*. New York: Academic Press.

Strohner, Hans, & Nelson, Keith E. 1974. The young child's development of sentence comprehension: Influence of event probability, nonverbal context, syntactic form, and strategies. *Child Development* 45, 567–576.

Strömqvist, Sven. 1984. Make-believe through words: A linguistic study of children's play with a doll's house. PhD dissertation, University of Göteborg, Sweden.

Stromswold, Karin. 1989. How conservative are children? Evidence from auxiliary errors. *Papers & Reports on Child Language Development* [Stanford University] 28, 148–155.

Stubbs, Michael. 1976. *Language, schools, and classrooms*. London: Methuen.

Studdert-Kennedy, Michael. 1987. The phoneme as a perceptuomotor structure. In A. Allport, D. MacKay, W. Prinz, & E. Scheerer (eds.), *Language, perception and production* (67–84). New York: Academic Press.

Sully, James. 1896. *Studies of childhood*. New York: Appleton.

Svartvik, Jan. 1966. *On voice in the English verb*. The Hague: Mouton.

Swingley, Daniel. 2005. 11-month-olds' knowledge of how familiar words sound. *Developmental Science* 8, 432–443.

Swingley, Daniel, & Aslin, Richard N. 2000. Spoken word recognition and lexical representation in very young children. *Cognition* 76, 147–166.

Swingley, Daniel, & Aslin, Richard N. 2002. Lexical neighborhoods and the word-form representations of 14-month-olds. *Psychological Science* 13, 480–484.

Swingley, Daniel, & Fernald, Anne. 2002. Recognition of words referring to present and absent objects by 24-month-olds. *Journal of Memory & Language* 46, 39–56.

Swingley, Daniel; Pinto, John P.; & Fernald, Anne. 1999. Continuous processing in word recognition at 24 months. *Cognition* 71, 73–108.

Tabouret-Keller, Andrée. 1964. L'acquisition du langage parlé chez un petit enfant en milieu bilingue. In J. de Ajuriaguerra *et al.* (eds.), *Problèmes de psycholinguistique* (205–219). Paris: Presses Universitaires de France.

Taeschner, Traute. 1983. *The sun is feminine*. Berlin and New York: Springer-Verlag.

Tager-Flusberg, Helen. 1982. The development of relative clauses in child speech. *Papers & Reports on Child Language Development* [Stanford University] 21, 104–111.

Taine, Hippolyte. 1870. Note sur l'acquisition du langage chez les enfants et dans l'espèce humaine. In *De l'intelligence*. Paris: Hachette.

Talmy, Leonard. 1985. Lexicalization patterns: Semantic structure in lexical forms. In T. E. Shopen (ed.), *Language typology and syntactic description*, vol. III: *Grammatical categories and the lexicon* (57–149). Cambridge: Cambridge University Press.

Tanenhaus, Michael K. 1988. Psycholinguistics: An overview. In F. J. Newmeyer (ed.), *Linguistics: The Cambridge survey*, vol. III: *Language: Psychological and biological aspects* (1–37). Cambridge: Cambridge University Press.

Tardif, Twila. 1996. Nouns are not always learned before verbs: Evidence from Mandarin speakers' early vocabularies. *Developmental Psychology* 32, 492–504.

Tardif, Twila; Shatz, Marilyn; & Naigles, Letitia. 1997. Caregiver speech and children's use of nouns versus verbs: A comparison of English, Italian, and Mandarin. *Journal of Child Language* 24, 535–565.

Templin, Mildred C. 1957. Certain language skills in children: Their development and interrelationships. *Institute of Child Welfare Monographs* 26. Minneapolis: University of Minnesota Press.

Thatcher, Robert W., & John, E. Roy. 1977. *Functional neuroscience*, vol. I: *Foundations of cognitive processes*. Hillsdale, NJ: Lawrence Erlbaum.

Theakston, Anna L.; Lieven, Elena V. M.; Pine, Julian M.; & Rowland, Caroline F. 2001. The role of performance limitations in the acquisition of verb-argument structure: An alternative account. *Journal of Child Language* 28, 127–152.

Thelen, Esther, & Smith, Linda B. 1994. *A dynamic systems approach to the development of cognition and action*. Cambridge, MA: MIT Press.

Thierry, Guillaume; Vihman, Marilyn; & Roberts, Mark. 2003. Familiar words capture the attention of 11-month-olds in less than 250 ms. *NeuroReport* 14, 2307–2310.

Thoermer, Claudia, & Sodian, Beate. 2001. Preverbal infants' understanding of referential gestures. *First Language* 21, 245–264.

Thomas, Michael S. C.; Grant, Julia; Barham, Zita; Gsödl, Marisa; Laing, Emma; Lakusta, Laura; Tyler, Lorraine K.; Grice, Sarah; Paterson, Sarah; & Karmiloff-Smith, Annette. 2001. Past tense formation in Williams syndrome. *Language & Cognitive Processes* 16, 143–176.

Thomas, Michael S. C., & Johnson, Mark H. 2006. The computational modeling of sensitive periods. *Developmental Psychobiology* 48, 337–344.

Thomas, Michael S. C., & Karmiloff-Smith, Annette. 2003. Modeling language acquisition in atypical phenotypes. *Psychological Review* 110, 647–682.

Thompson, Sandra A. 2002. "Object" complements and conversation: Towards a realistic account. *Studies in Language* 26, 125–164.

Thomson, Jean R., & Chapman, Robin S. 1977. "Who is daddy?" revisited: The status of two-year-olds' over-extended words in use and comprehension. *Journal of Child Language* 4, 359–375.

Tomasello, Michael. 1992. *First verbs: A case study of early grammatical development*. Cambridge: Cambridge University Press.

Tomasello, Michael. 1995. Joint attention as social cognition. In C. Moore & P. J. Dunham (eds.), *Joint attention: Its origins and role in development* (103–130). Hillsdale, NJ: Lawrence Erlbaum.

Tomasello, Michael. 2000. Do young children have adult syntactic competence? *Cognition* 74, 209–253.

Tomasello, Michael, & Akhtar, Nameera. 1995. Two-year-olds use pragmatic cues to differentiate reference to objects and actions. *Cognitive Development* 10, 201–224.

Tomasello, Michael; Akhtar, Nameera; Dodson, Kelly; & Rekau, Laura. 1997. Differential productivity in young children's use of nouns and verbs. *Journal of Child Language* 24, 373–387.

Tomasello, Michael, & Barton, Michelle E. 1994. Learning words in nonostensive contexts. *Developmental Psychology* 30, 639–650.

Tomasello, Michael, & Brooks, Patricia J. 1999. Early syntactic development: A construction grammar approach. In M. Barrett (ed.), *The development of language* (161–189). Hove, Sussex: Psychology Press.

Tomasello, Michael; Call, Josep; & Gluckman, Andrea. 1997. Comprehension of novel communicative signs by apes and human children. *Child Development* 68, 1067–1080.

Tomasello, Michael; Farrar, Michael J.; & Dines, Jennifer. 1984. Children's speech revisions for a familiar and an unfamiliar adult. *Journal of Speech & Hearing Research* 27, 359–363.

Tomasello, Michael, & Kruger, Ann C. 1992. Joint attention on actions: Acquiring verbs in ostensive and non-ostensive contexts. *Journal of Child Language* 19, 311–334.

Tomasello, Michael; Strosberg, Randi; & Akhtar, Nameera. 1996. Eighteen-month-old children learn words in non-ostensive contexts. *Journal of Child Language* 23, 157–176.

Trehub, Sandra E. 1973. Infants' sensitivity to vowel and tonal contrasts. *Developmental Psychology* 9, 91–96.

Trevarthen, Colwyn. 1977. Descriptive analyses of infant communication behaviour. In H. R. Schaffer (ed.), *Studies in mother–infant interaction* (227–270). London: Academic Press.

Tversky, Amos. 1977. Features of similarity. *Psychological Review* 84, 327–352.

Tversky, Barbara G., & Hemenway, Katherine. 1984. Objects, parts, and categories. *Journal of Experimental Psychology: General* 113, 169–193.

Tyack, Dorothy L., & Ingram, David. 1977. Children's production and comprehension of questions. *Journal of Child Language* 4, 211–224.

Tyler, Lorraine K.; Karmiloff-Smith, Annette; Voice, J. Kate; Stevens, Tassos; Grant, Julia; Udwin, Orlee; Davies, Mark; & Howlin, Patricia. 1997. Do individuals with Williams syndrome have bizarre semantics? Evidence for lexical organization using an on-line task. *Cortex* 33, 515–527.

Ungerleider, Leslie G. 1995. Functional brain imaging studies of cortical mechanisms for memory. *Science* 270, 769–775.

U.S. Census 2000 Brief. 2003, October. *Language use and English-speaking ability: 2000.* U.S. Census Bureau, U.S. Department of Commerce.

Valian, Virginia. 1986. Syntactic categories in the speech of young children. *Developmental Psychology* 22, 562–579.

Valian, Virginia. 1991. Syntactic subjects in the early speech of American and Italian children. *Cognition* 40, 21–81.

Valian, Virginia, & Casey, Lyman. 2003. Young children's acquisition of wh-questions: The role of structured input. *Journal of Child Language* 30, 117–143.

Valian, Virginia; Hoeffner, James; & Aubry, Stephanie. 1996. Young children's imitation of sentence subjects: Evidence of processing limitations. *Developmental Psychology* 32, 153–164.

van der Wal, Sjoukje. 1996. Negative polarity items and negation: Tandem acquisition. Groningen: Dissertations in Linguistics 17, University of Groningen.

van Geert, Paul. 1991. A dynamic systems model of cognitive and language growth. *Psychological Review* 98, 3–53.

Velten, H. V. 1943. The growth of phonemic and lexical patterns in infant language. *Language* 19, 281–292.

Vendler, Zeno. 1967. *Linguistics in philosophy*. Ithaca, NY: Cornell University Press.

Veneziano, Edy. 1985. "Replying" to mothers' questions: A way to lexical acquisition. *Journal of Pragmatics* 9, 433–452.

Veneziano, Edy. 1988. Vocal-verbal interaction and the construction of early lexical knowledge. In M. D. Smith & J. L. Locke (eds.), *The emergent lexicon: The child's development of a linguistic vocabulary* (109–147). New York: Academic Press.

Veneziano, Edy, & Sinclair, Hermine. 2000. The changing status of "filler syllables" on the way to grammatical morphemes. *Journal of Child Language* 27, 461–500.

Veneziano, Edy; Sinclair, Hermine; & Berthoud, Ioanna. 1990. From one word to two words: Repetition patterns on the way to structured speech. *Journal of Child Language* 17, 633–650.

Verhoeven, Ludo. 2007. Early bilingualism, language transfer, and phonological awareness. *Applied Psycholinguistics* 28, 425–439.

Verkuyl, Henk J. 1993. *A theory of aspectuality: The interaction between temporal and atemporal structure*. Cambridge: Cambridge University Press.

Vihman, Marilyn M. 1980. Formulas in first and second language acquisition. *Papers & Reports on Child Language Development* [Stanford University] 18, 75–92.

Vihman, Marilyn M. 1982. The acquisition of morphology by a bilingual child: The whole-word approach. *Applied Psycholinguistics* 3, 141–160.

Vihman, Marilyn M. 1985. Language differentiation by the bilingual infant. *Journal of Child Language* 12, 297–324.

Vihman, Marilyn M. 1996. *Phonological development: The origins of language in the child*. Oxford: Blackwell.

Vihman, Marilyn M.; Thierry, Guillaume; Lum, Jarrad; Keren-Portnoy, Tamar; & Martin, Pam. 2007. Onset of word form recognition in English, Welsh, and English-Welsh bilingual infants. *Applied Psycholinguistics* 28, 475–493.

Vogel, Irene. 1975. One system or two? An analysis of a two-year-old Romanian-English bilingual's phonology. *Papers & Reports on Child Language Development* [Stanford University] 9, 43–62.

Volterra, Virginia. 1972. Il "no": Prime fasi dello sviluppo della negazione nel linguaggio infantile. *Archivio de Psicologia, Neurologia e Psichiatria* 33, 16–53.

Volterra, Virginia, & Taeschner, Traute. 1978. The acquisition and development of language by a bilingual child. *Journal of Child Language* 5, 311–326.

Walker, Dale; Greenwood, Charles; Hart, Betty; & Carta, Judith. 1994. Prediction of school outcomes based on early language production and socioeconomic factors. *Child Development* 65, 606–621.

Walker, Marilyn A. 1996. Inferring acceptance and rejection in dialog by default rules of inference. *Language & Speech* 39, 265–304.

Wannemacher, Jill T., & Ryan, Mary L. 1978. *Less* is not *more*: A study of children's comprehension of *less* in various task contexts. *Child Development* 49, 660–668.

Warden, David A. 1976. The influence of context on children's use of identifying expressions and references. *British Journal of Psychology* 67, 101–112.

Warden, David A. 1981. Learning to identify referents. *British Journal of Psychology* 72, 93–99.

Waterson, Natalie. 1971. Child phonology: A prosodic view. *Journal of Linguistics* 7, 179–211.

Watson-Gegeo, Karen A., & Gegeo, David W. 1986a. The social world of Kwara'ae children: Acquisition of language and values. In J. Cook-Gumperz, W. A. Corsaro, & J. Streeck (eds.), *Children's worlds and children's language* (107–127). Berlin: Mouton de Gruyter.

Watson-Gegeo, Karen A., & Gegeo, David W. 1986b. Calling-out and repeating routines in Kwara'ae children's language socialization. In B. B. Schieffelin & E. Ochs (eds.), *Language socialization across cultures* (17–50). Cambridge: Cambridge University Press.

Watt, W. C. (ed.). 1994. *Writing systems and cognition: Perspectives from psychology, physiology, linguistics, and semiotics.* Dordrecht: Kluwer.

Waxman, Sandra R., & Booth, Amy E. 2001. Seeing pink elephants: Fourteen-month-olds' interpretations of novel nouns and adjectives. *Cognitive Psychology* 43, 217–242.

Waxman, Sandra R., & Hatch, Thomas. 1992. Beyond the basics: Preschool children label objects flexibly at multiple hierarchical levels. *Journal of Child Language* 19, 153–166.

Waxman, Sandra R., & Senghas, Ann. 1992. Relations among word meanings in early lexical development. *Developmental Psychology* 28, 862–873.

Weber-Fox, Christine M., & Neville, Helen J. 1996. Maturational constraints on functional specializations for language processing: ERP and behavioral evidence in bilingual speakers. *Journal of Cognitive Neuroscience* 8, 231–256.

Weinreich, Uriel. 1953. *Languages in contact.* The Hague: Mouton.

Weir, Ruth. 1962. *Language in the crib.* The Hague: Mouton.

Weisenburger, Janet L. 1976. A choice of words: Two-year-old speech from a situational point of view. *Journal of Child Language* 3, 275–281.

Weiss, Deborah M., & Sachs, Jacqueline. 1991. Persuasive strategies used by preschool children. *Discourse Processes* 14, 55–72.

Weissenborn, Jürgen. 1986. Learning how to become an interlocutor: The verbal negotiation of common frames of reference and actions in dyads of 7–14 year old children. In J. Cook-Gumperz, W. A. Corsaro, & J. Streeck (eds.), *Children's worlds and children's language* (377–404). Berlin: Mouton de Gruyter.

Wellman, Henry M., & Lempers, Jacques D. 1977. The naturalistic communicative abilities of two-year-olds. *Child Development* 48, 1052–1057.

Wells, Gordon. 1985. *Language development in the pre-school years.* Cambridge: Cambridge University Press.

Wells, Gordon, & Mongomery, Martin. 1981. Adult-child interaction at home and at school. In P. French & M. Maclure (eds.), *Adult-child conversation* (210–243). London: Croom Helm.

Werker, Janet F., & Lalonde, Chris E. 1988. Cross-language speech perception: Initial capabilities and developmental change. *Developmental Psychology* 24, 672–683.

Werker, Janet F., & McLeod, Peter J. 1989. Infant preference for both male- and female-infant-directed talk: A developmental study of attentional and affective responsiveness. *Canadian Journal of Higher Education* 19, 29–41.

Werker, Janet F.; Pegg, Judith E.; & McLeod, Peter J. 1994. A cross-language investigation of infant preference for infant-directed communication. *Infant Behavior & Development* 17, 323–333.

Werker, Janet F., & Tees, Richard C. 1984. Cross-language speech perception: Evidence for perceptual reorganization during the first year of life. *Infant Behavior & Development* 7, 49–63.

Werner, Heinz, & Kaplan, Bernard. 1963. *Symbol formation: An organismic-developmental approach to language and the expression of thought.* New York: Wiley.

Wernicke, Carl. 1874. *Der aphasische Symptomencomplex: Eine psychologische Studie auf anatomischer Basis.* Breslan: Cohn & Weigert.

White, Lydia, & Genesee, Fred. 1996. How native is near-native? The issue of ultimate attainment in adult second language acquisition. *Second Language Research* 12, 238–265.

Wieman, Leslie A. 1976. Stress patterns of early child language. *Journal of Child Language* 3, 283–286.

Wigglesworth, Gillian. 1997. Children's individual approaches to the organization of narrative. *Journal of Child Language* 24, 279–309.

Wilcox, Stephen, & Palermo, David S. 1974/1975. "In," "on," and "under" revisited. *Cognition* 3, 245–254.

Wiley, Angela. 1997. Religious affiliation as a source of variation in child rearing values and parental regulation of young children. *Mind, Culture, & Activity* 4, 86–107.

Wilkins, David. 2003. Why pointing with the index finger is not a universal (in socio-cultural and semiotic terms). In S. Kita (ed.), *Pointing: Where language, culture, and cognition meet* (171–215). Mahwah, NJ: Lawrence Erlbaum.

Wilkinson, Louise C.; Calculator, Steven; & Dollaghan, Christine. 1982. Ya wanna trade – Just for awhile: Children's requests and responses to peers. *Discourse Processes* 5, 161–176.

Willes, Mary. 1981. Learning to take part in classroom interaction. In P. French & M. Maclure (eds.), *Adult-child conversation* (73–95). London: Croom Helm.

Winitz, Harris, & Irwin, Orvis C. 1958. Syllabic and phonetic structure of infants' early words. *Journal of Speech & Hearing Research* 1, 250–256.

Witelson, Sandra F., & Pallie, W. 1973. Left hemisphere specialization for language in the newborn. *Brain* 96, 641–646.

Wittek, Angelika, & Tomasello, Michael. 2005a. German-speaking children's productivity with syntactic constructions and case morphology: Local cues act locally. *First Language* 25, 103–125.

Wittek, Angelika, & Tomasello, Michael. 2005b. Young children's sensitivity to listener knowledge and perceptual context in choosing referring expressions. *Applied Psycholinguistics* 26, 541–558.

Wong Fillmore, Lily. 1979. Individual differences in second language acquisition. In C. J. Fillmore, D. Kempler, & W. S.-Y. Wang (eds.), *Individual differences in language ability and language behavior* (203–228). New York: Academic Press.

Wong Fillmore, Lily. 1991. When learning a second language means losing the first. *Early Childhood Research Quarterly* 6, 323–346.

Wong Fillmore, Lily. 1996. What happens when languages are lost? An essay on language assimilation and cultural identity. In D. I. Slobin, J. Gerhardt, A. Kyratzis, & J. Guo (eds.), *Social interaction, social context, and language: Essays in honor of Susan Ervin-Tripp* (435–446). Mahwah, NJ: Lawrence Erlbaum.

Woodward, Amanda L. 1992. The role of the whole object assumption in early word learning. PhD dissertation, Stanford University.

Woodward, Amanda L. 2003. Infants' developing understanding of the link between looker and object. *Developmental Science* 6, 297–311.

Woodward, Amanda L., & Guajardo, Jose J. 2002. Infants' understanding of the point gesture as an object-directed action. *Cognitive Development* 17, 1061–1084.

Woodward, Amanda L., & Markman, Ellen M. 1991. Constraints on learning as default assumptions: Comments on Merriman & Bowman's "The mutual exclusivity bias in children's word learning." *Developmental Review* 14, 57–77.

Xu, Fei, & Tenenbaum, Joshua B. 2007a. Word learning as Bayesian inference. *Psychological Review* 114, 245–272.

Xu, Fei, & Tenenbaum, Joshua B. 2007b. Sensitivity to sampling in Bayesian word learning. *Developmental Science* 10, 288–297.

Yip, Virginia, & Matthews, Stephen. 2007. *The bilingual child: Early development and language contact*. Cambridge: Cambridge University Press.

Youssef, Valerie. 1991a. The acquisition of varilingual competence. *English World-Wide* 12, 87–102.

Youssef, Valerie. 1991b. Variation as a feature of language acquisition in the Trinidad context. *Language Variation & Change* 3, 75–101.

Youssef, Valerie. 1993. Children's linguistic choices: Audience design and societal norms. *Language in Society* 22, 257–274.

Yumitani, Chutatip Chiraporn. 1998. The acquisition of the causative alternation in Thai. In E. V. Clark (ed.), *Proceedings of the 29th Child Language Research Forum 1997* (141–149). Stanford, CA: CSLI.

Zager, David. 1981. A real time process model of morphological change. PhD dissertation, State University of New York, Buffalo.

Zajonc, Robert B. 1976. Family configuration and intelligence. *Science* 192, 227–236.

Zajonc, Robert B., & Mullally, Patricia R. 1997. Birth order: Reconciling conflicting effects. *American Psychologist* (July), 685–699.

Zangl, Renate, & Mills, Debra L. 2007. Increased brain activity to infant-directed speech in 6- and 13-month-old infants. *Infancy* 11, 31–62.

Zentella, Ana Celia. 1997. *Growing up bilingual: Puerto Rican children in New York*. Oxford: Blackwell.

Zukow, Patricia G. 1986. The relationship between interaction with the caregiver and the emergence of play activities during the one-word period. *British Journal of Developmental Psychology* 4, 223–234.

Zukow-Goldring, Patricia, & Rader, Nancy de V. 2001. Perceiving referring actions. *Developmental Science* 4, 28–30.

Zurer Pearson, Barbara. 2007. Social factors in childhood bilingualism in the United States. *Applied Psycholinguistics* 28, 399–410.

Zurer Pearson, Barbara; Fernández, Silvia C.; & Oller, D. Kimbrough. 1995. Cross-language synonyms in the lexicons of bilingual infants: One language or two? *Journal of Child Language* 22, 345–368.

Zwitserlood, Pienie; Kellerman, Eric; Klein, Wolfgang; Liang, James; & Perdue, Clive. 2002. The first minutes of foreign-language exposure. Unpublished MS, Department of Psychology, University of Münster.

# Name index

# Subject index